EIGHTY DAYS ™

CAN LOVE
OUTFLY THE SHADOW
OF WAR?

Published by
ARCHAIA ™

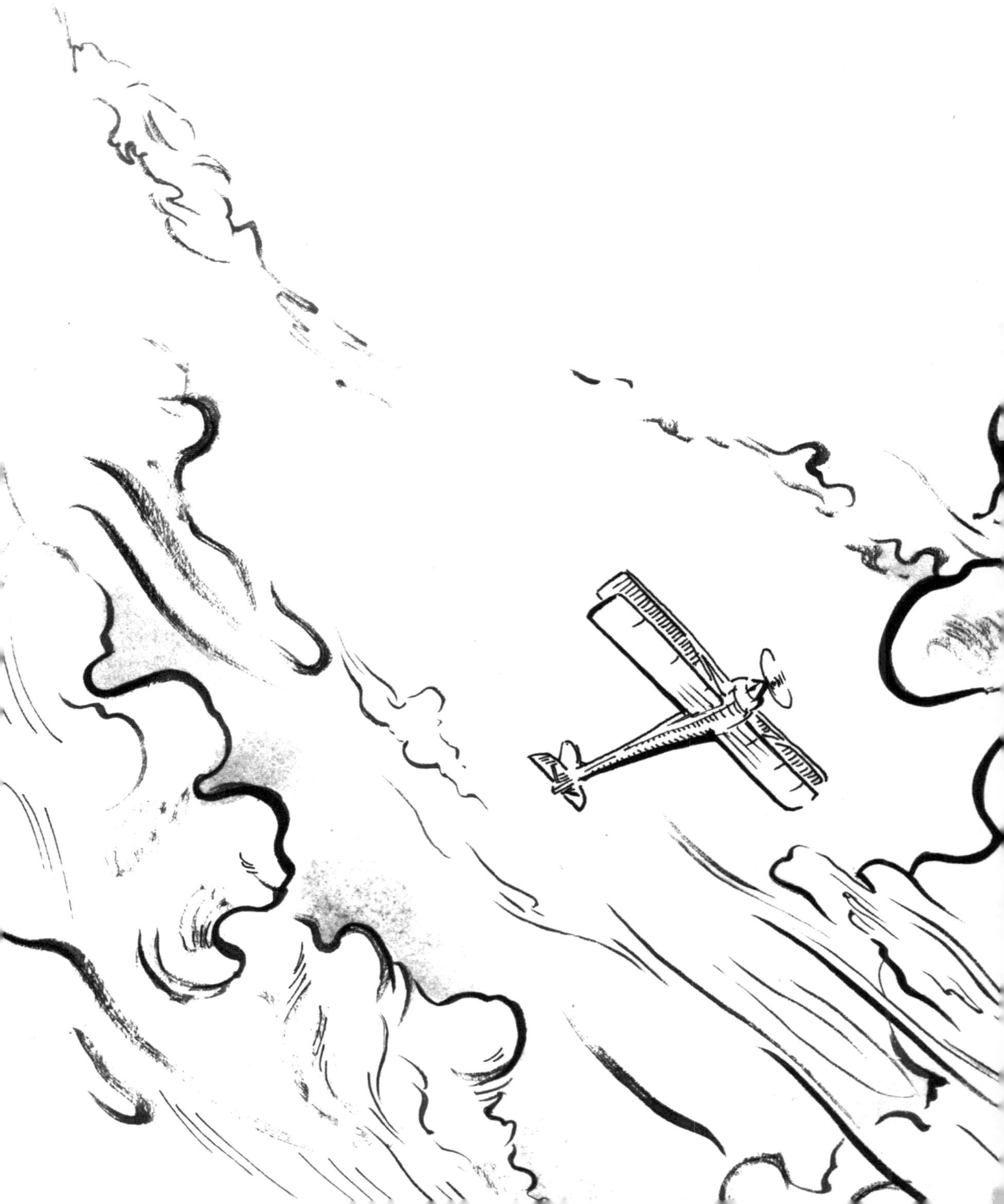

EIGHTY DAYS ™

A.C. ESGUERRA

ARCHAIA ™
Los Angeles, California

Cover by **A.C. Esguerra**

Designer **Scott Newman**
Assistant Editor **Allyson Gronowitz**
Editor **Sierra Hahn**

EIGHTY DAYS, September 2021. Published by Archaia, a division of Boom Entertainment, Inc. EIGHTY DAYS is ™ & © 2021 Amilia Catherine Louise Felizardo Esguerra. All rights reserved. Archaia™ and the Archaia logo are trademarks of Boom Entertainment, Inc., registered in various countries and categories. All characters, events, and institutions depicted herein are fictional. Any similarity between any of the names, characters, persons, events, and/or institutions in this publication to actual names, characters, and persons, whether living or dead, events, and/or institutions is unintended and purely coincidental.

BOOM! Studios, 5670 Wilshire Boulevard, Suite 400, Los Angeles, CA 90036-5679. Printed in China. First Printing.

ISBN: 978-1-68415-657-3, eISBN: 978-1-64668-142-6

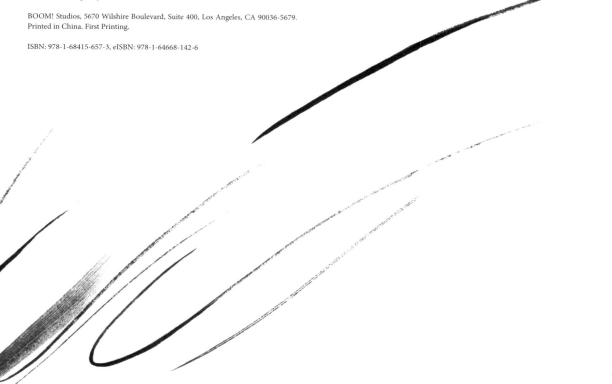

This book is dedicated,
in three parts with equal ardor,
to the following:

To my parents,
with thanks for the gift of story,

To my siblings,
by blood and in solidarity,

And to Emil,
co-pilot, always.

BOOK I
EIGHTY DAYS

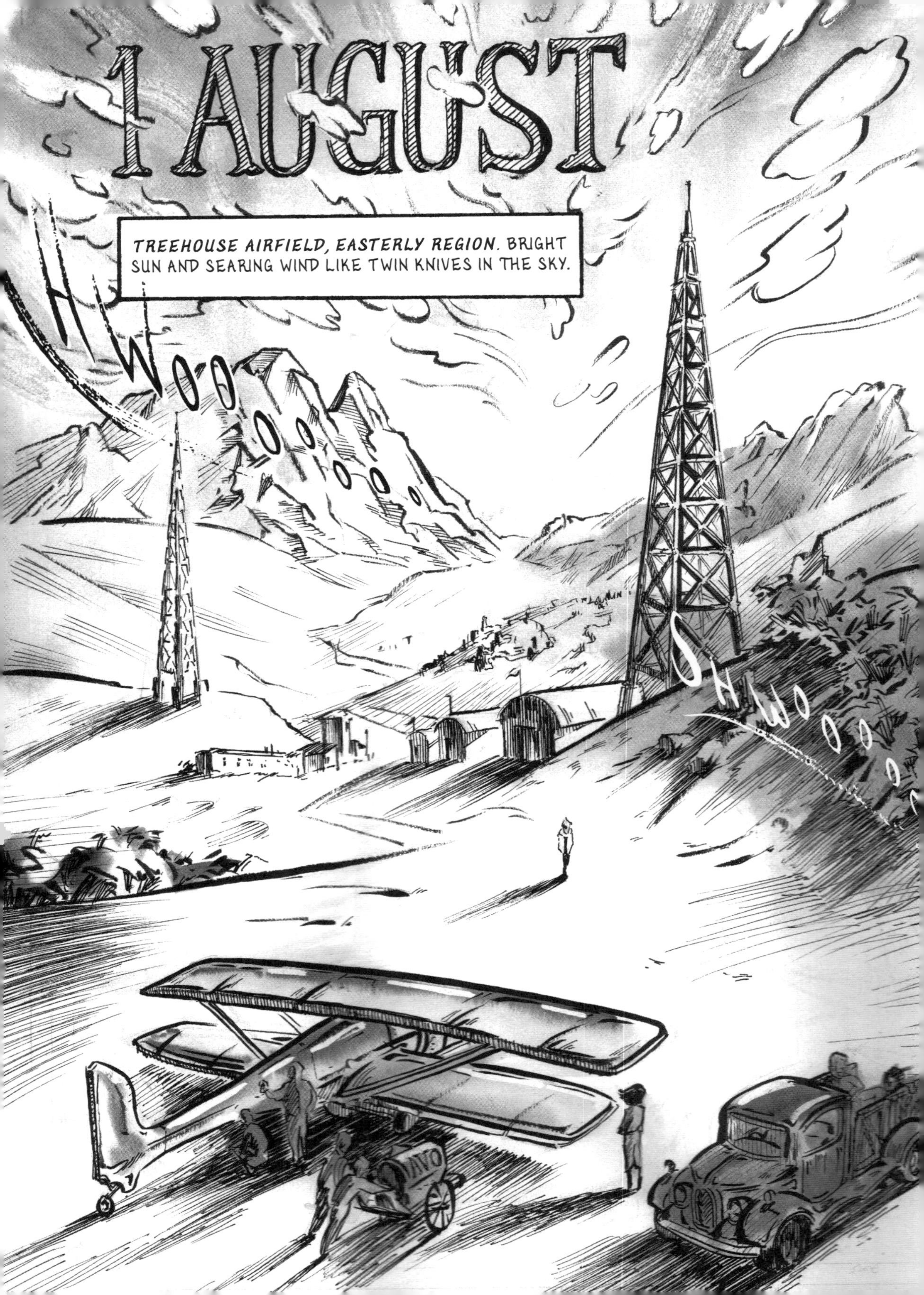
1 AUGUST
TREEHOUSE AIRFIELD, EASTERLY REGION. BRIGHT SUN AND SEARING WIND LIKE TWIN KNIVES IN THE SKY.
HWOOOOOOO
SHWOOOOO

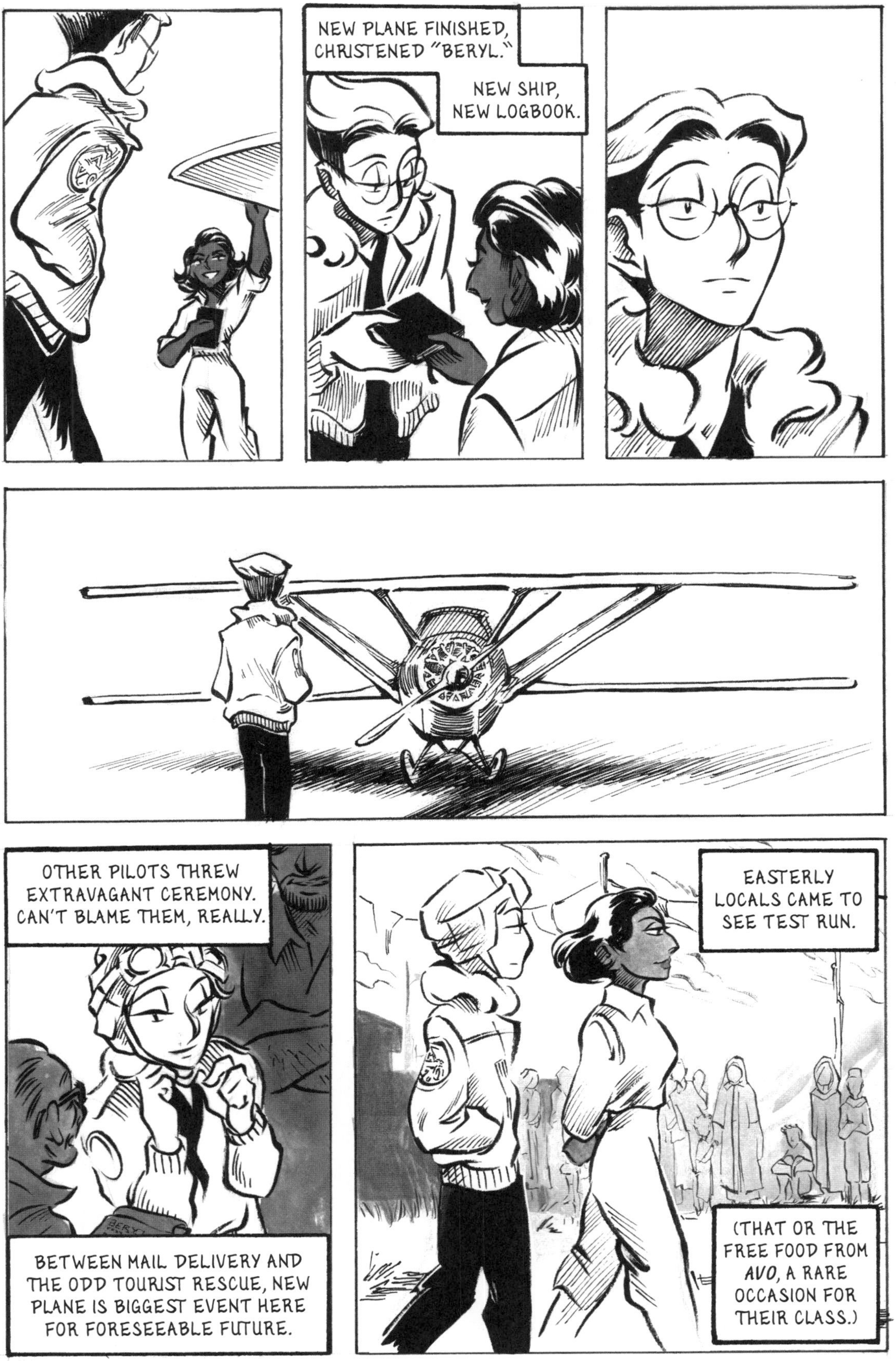
NEW PLANE FINISHED, CHRISTENED "BERYL."
NEW SHIP, NEW LOGBOOK.
OTHER PILOTS THREW EXTRAVAGANT CEREMONY. CAN'T BLAME THEM, REALLY.
BETWEEN MAIL DELIVERY AND THE ODD TOURIST RESCUE, NEW PLANE IS BIGGEST EVENT HERE FOR FORESEEABLE FUTURE.
EASTERLY LOCALS CAME TO SEE TEST RUN.
(THAT OR THE FREE FOOD FROM *AVO*, A RARE OCCASION FOR THEIR CLASS.)

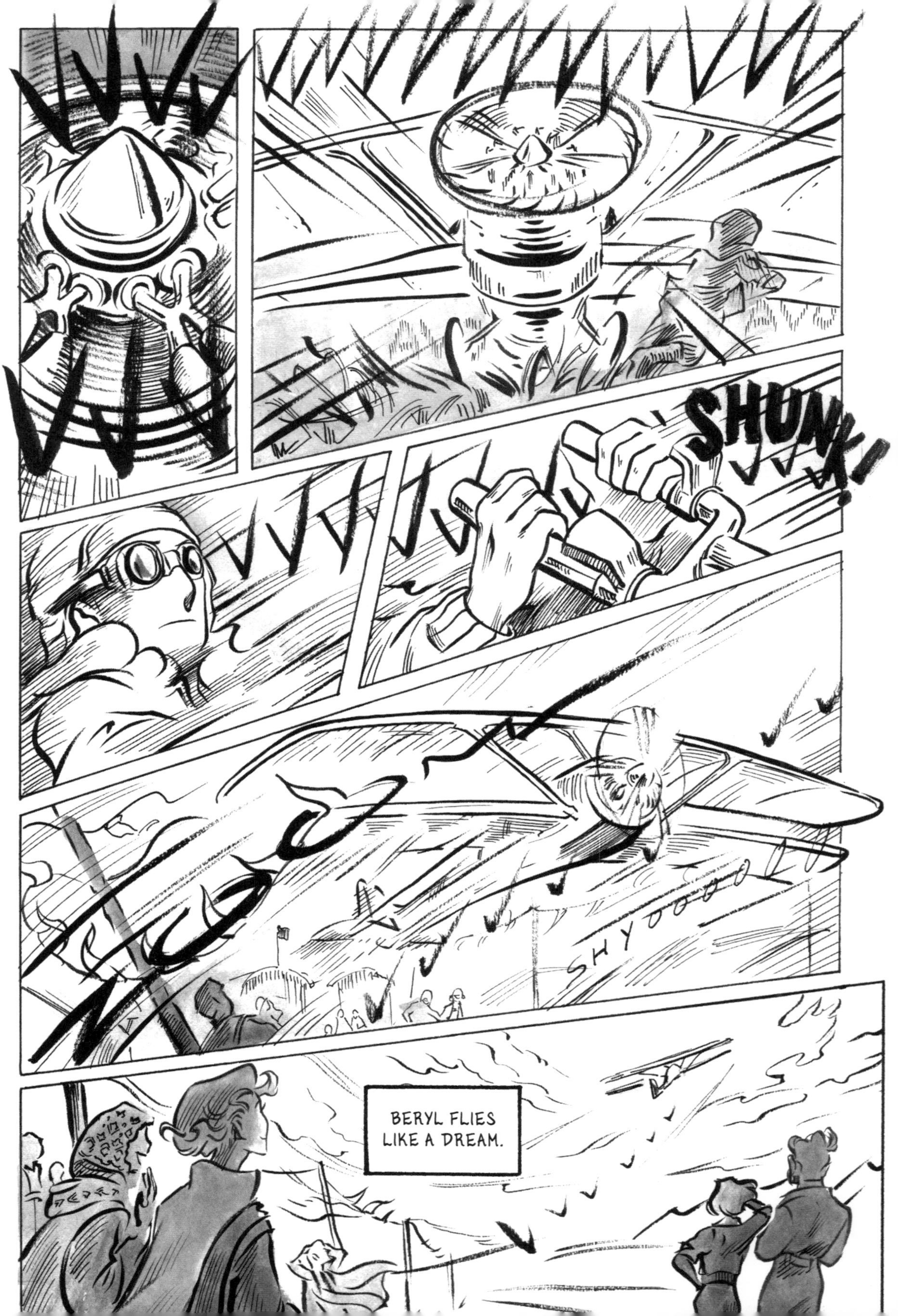
SHUNK!
SHYOOOOOO
BERYL FLIES LIKE A DREAM.

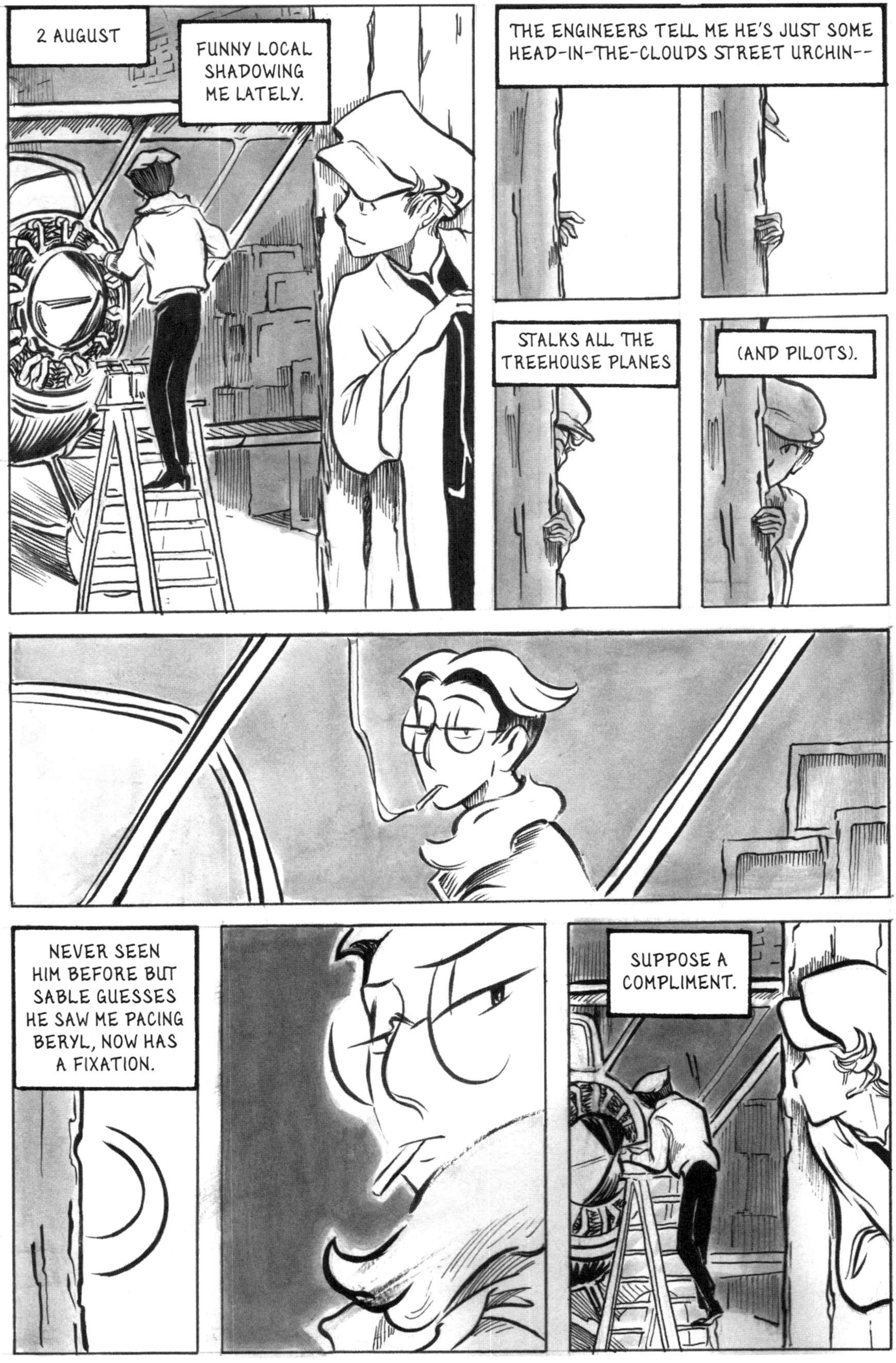
2 AUGUST
FUNNY LOCAL SHADOWING ME LATELY.
THE ENGINEERS TELL ME HE'S JUST SOME HEAD-IN-THE-CLOUDS STREET URCHIN--
STALKS ALL THE TREEHOUSE PLANES
(AND PILOTS).
NEVER SEEN HIM BEFORE BUT SABLE GUESSES HE SAW ME PACING BERYL, NOW HAS A FIXATION.
SUPPOSE A COMPLIMENT.

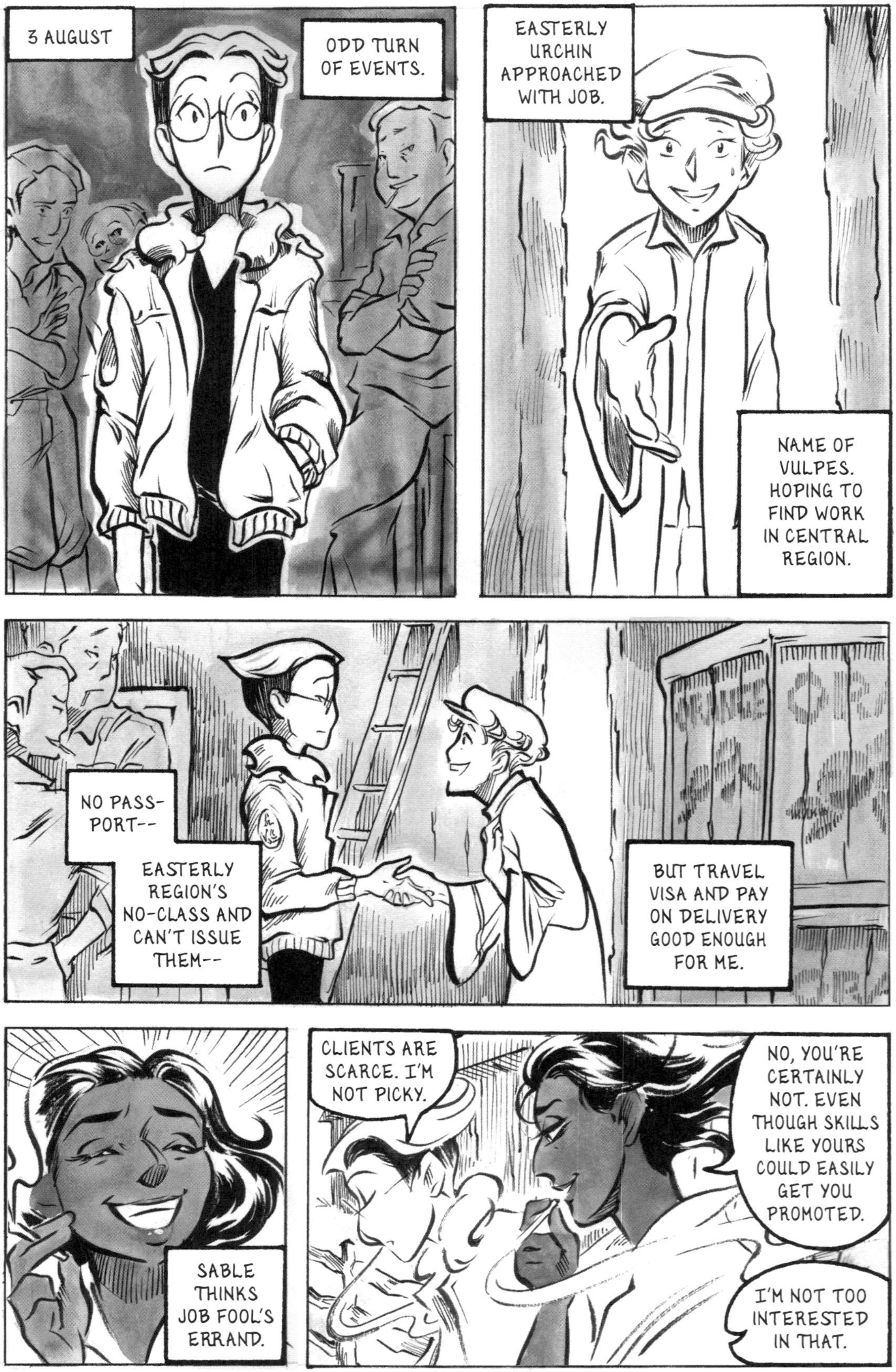
3 AUGUST
ODD TURN OF EVENTS.
EASTERLY URCHIN APPROACHED WITH JOB.
NAME OF VULPES. HOPING TO FIND WORK IN CENTRAL REGION.
NO PASSPORT--
EASTERLY REGION'S NO-CLASS AND CAN'T ISSUE THEM--
BUT TRAVEL VISA AND PAY ON DELIVERY GOOD ENOUGH FOR ME.
SABLE THINKS JOB FOOL'S ERRAND.
CLIENTS ARE SCARCE. I'M NOT PICKY.
NO, YOU'RE CERTAINLY NOT. EVEN THOUGH SKILLS LIKE YOURS COULD EASILY GET YOU PROMOTED.
I'M NOT TOO INTERESTED IN THAT.

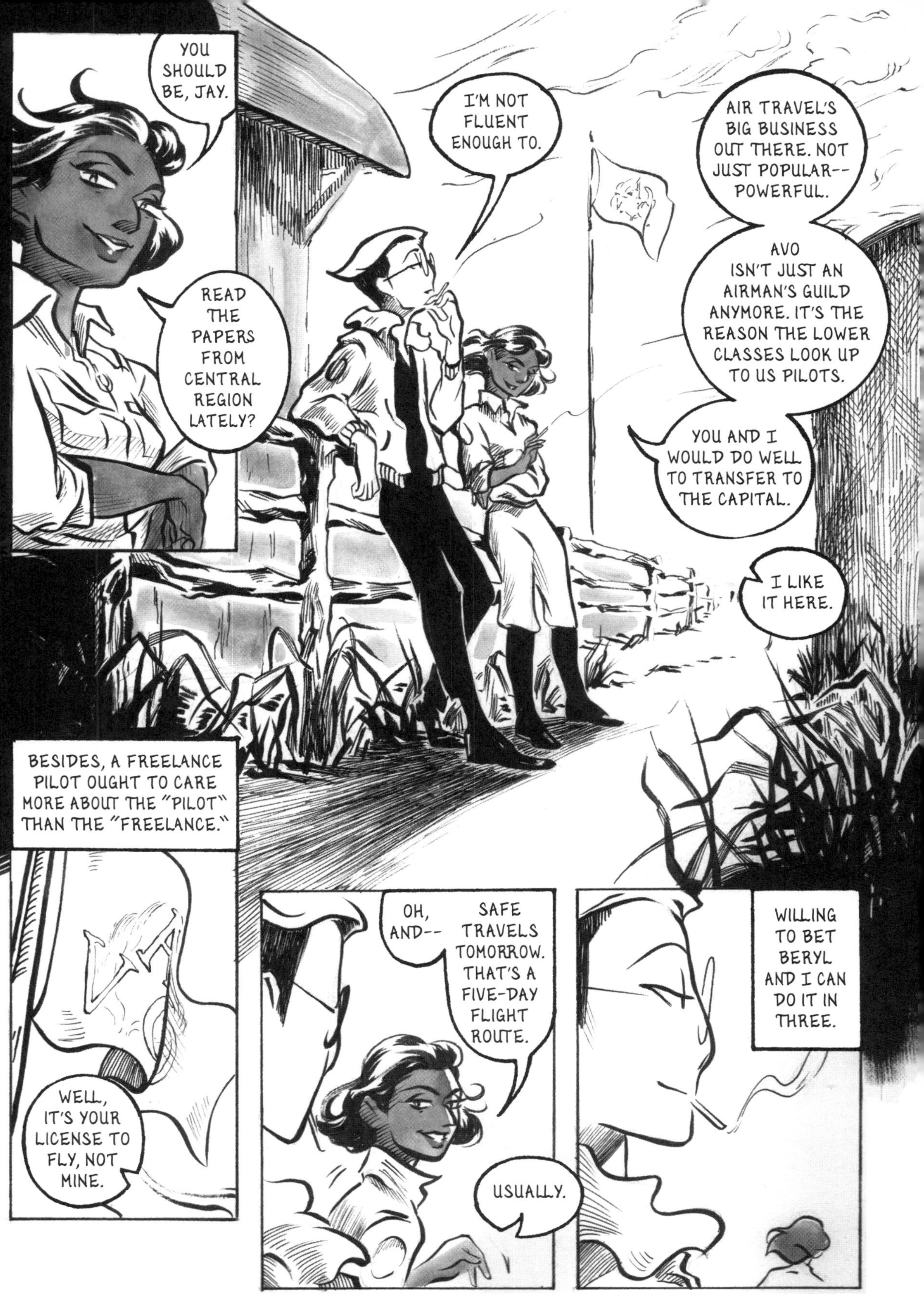
YOU SHOULD BE, JAY.
I'M NOT FLUENT ENOUGH TO.
READ THE PAPERS FROM CENTRAL REGION LATELY?
AIR TRAVEL'S BIG BUSINESS OUT THERE. NOT JUST POPULAR-- POWERFUL.
AVO ISN'T JUST AN AIRMAN'S GUILD ANYMORE. IT'S THE REASON THE LOWER CLASSES LOOK UP TO US PILOTS.
YOU AND I WOULD DO WELL TO TRANSFER TO THE CAPITAL.
I LIKE IT HERE.
BESIDES, A FREELANCE PILOT OUGHT TO CARE MORE ABOUT THE "PILOT" THAN THE "FREELANCE."
WELL, IT'S YOUR LICENSE TO FLY, NOT MINE.
OH, AND--
SAFE TRAVELS TOMORROW. THAT'S A FIVE-DAY FLIGHT ROUTE.
USUALLY.
WILLING TO BET BERYL AND I CAN DO IT IN THREE.

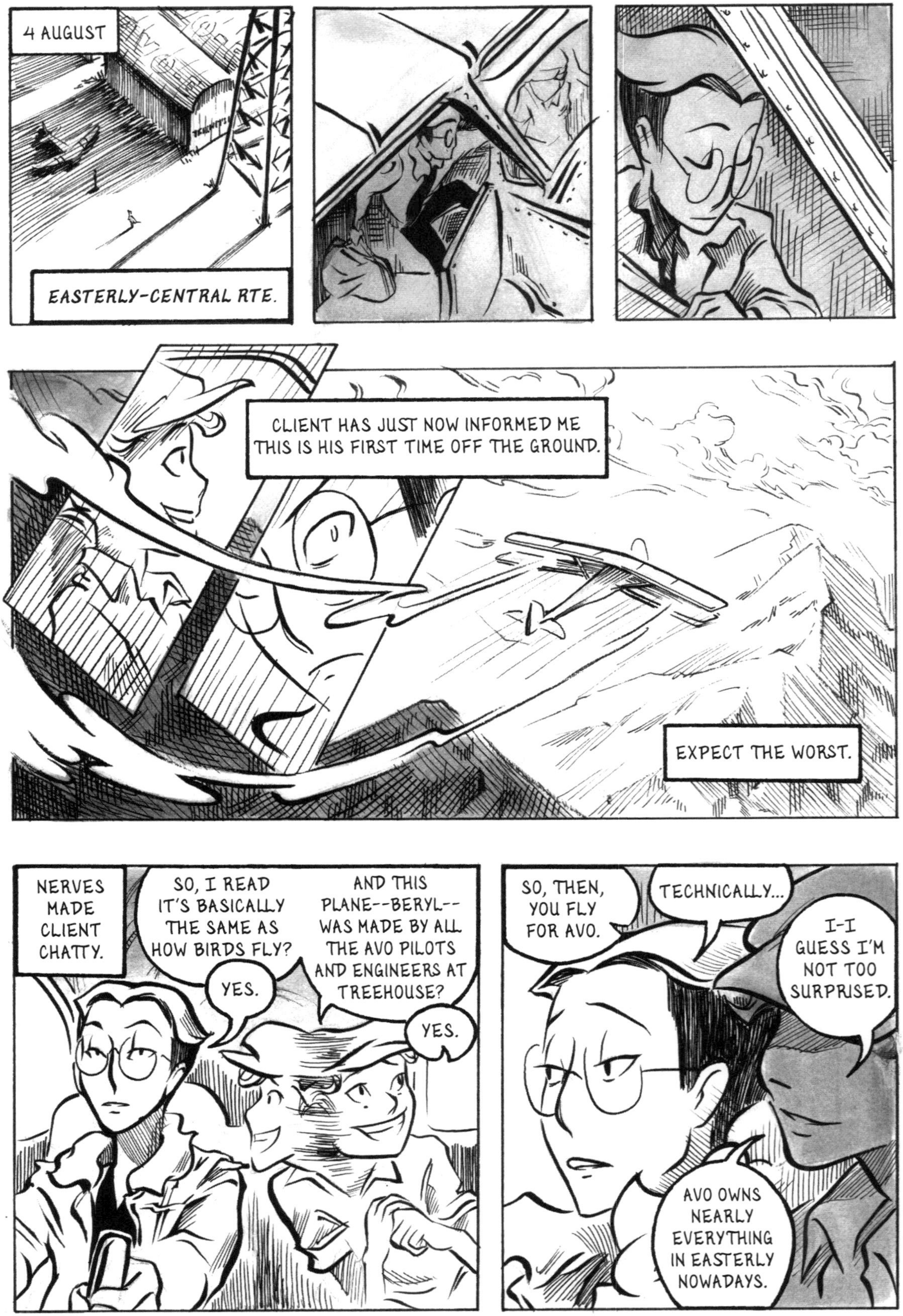

4 AUGUST
EASTERLY-CENTRAL RTE.
CLIENT HAS JUST NOW INFORMED ME THIS IS HIS FIRST TIME OFF THE GROUND.
EXPECT THE WORST.
NERVES MADE CLIENT CHATTY.
SO, I READ IT'S BASICALLY THE SAME AS HOW BIRDS FLY?
YES.
AND THIS PLANE--BERYL--WAS MADE BY ALL THE AVO PILOTS AND ENGINEERS AT TREEHOUSE?
YES.
SO, THEN, YOU FLY FOR AVO.
TECHNICALLY...
AVO OWNS NEARLY EVERYTHING IN EASTERLY NOWADAYS.
I-I GUESS I'M NOT TOO SURPRISED.

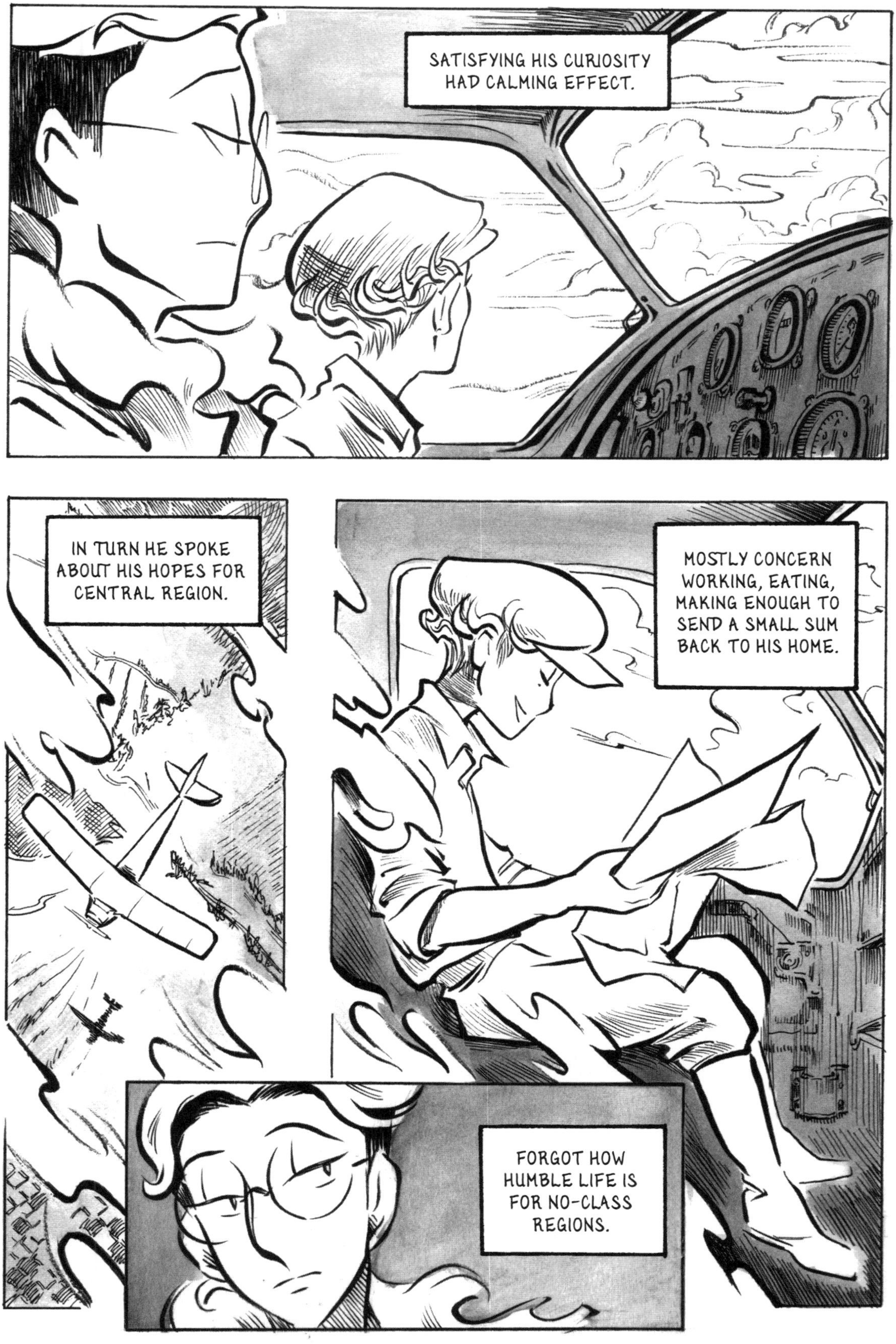
SATISFYING HIS CURIOSITY HAD CALMING EFFECT.
IN TURN HE SPOKE ABOUT HIS HOPES FOR CENTRAL REGION.
MOSTLY CONCERN WORKING, EATING, MAKING ENOUGH TO SEND A SMALL SUM BACK TO HIS HOME.
FORGOT HOW HUMBLE LIFE IS FOR NO-CLASS REGIONS.

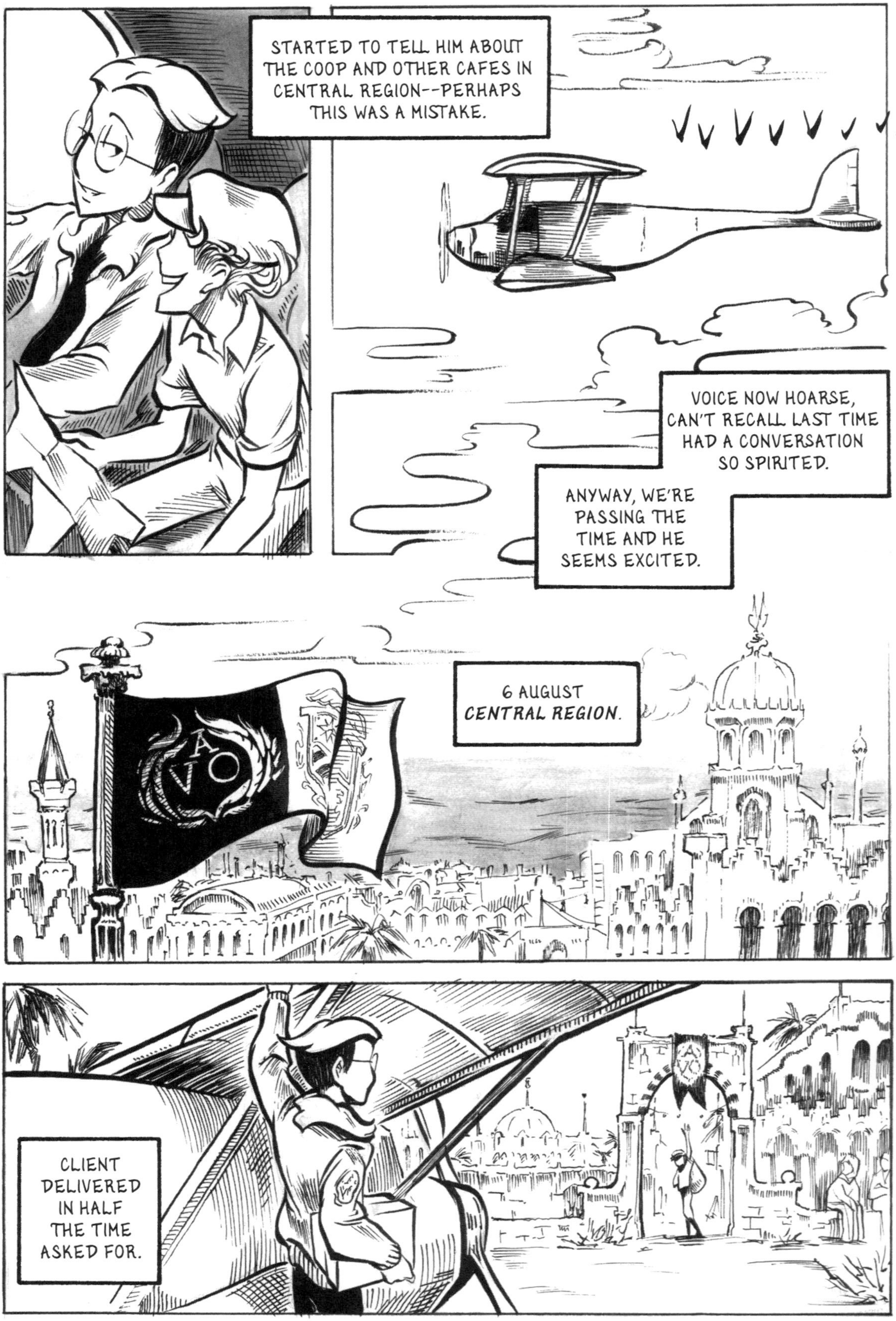
STARTED TO TELL HIM ABOUT THE COOP AND OTHER CAFES IN CENTRAL REGION--PERHAPS THIS WAS A MISTAKE.
VOICE NOW HOARSE, CAN'T RECALL LAST TIME HAD A CONVERSATION SO SPIRITED.
ANYWAY, WE'RE PASSING THE TIME AND HE SEEMS EXCITED.
6 AUGUST
CENTRAL REGION.
CLIENT DELIVERED IN HALF THE TIME ASKED FOR.

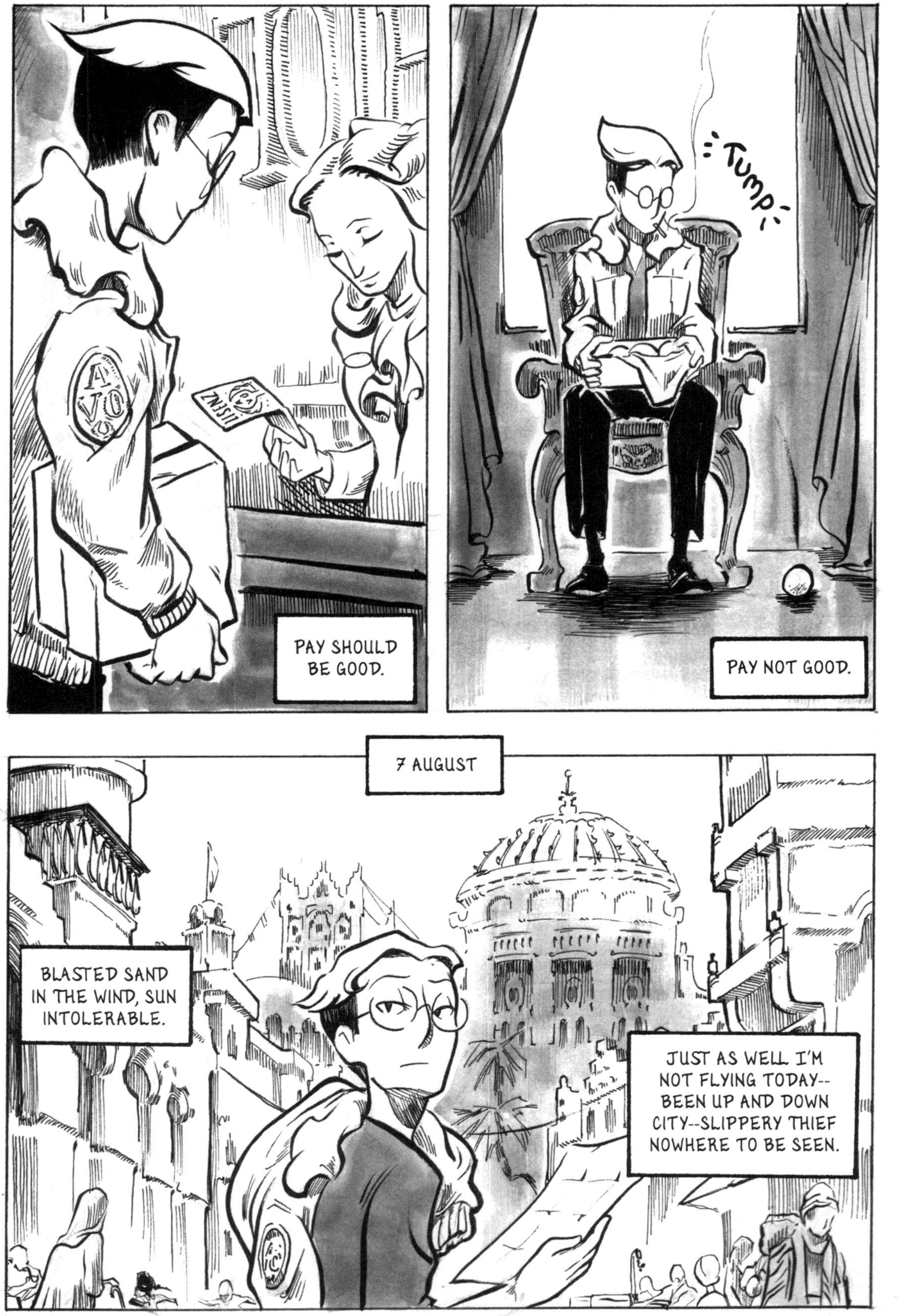
PAY SHOULD BE GOOD.
TUMP
PAY NOT GOOD.
7 AUGUST
BLASTED SAND IN THE WIND, SUN INTOLERABLE.
JUST AS WELL I'M NOT FLYING TODAY--BEEN UP AND DOWN CITY--SLIPPERY THIEF NOWHERE TO BE SEEN.

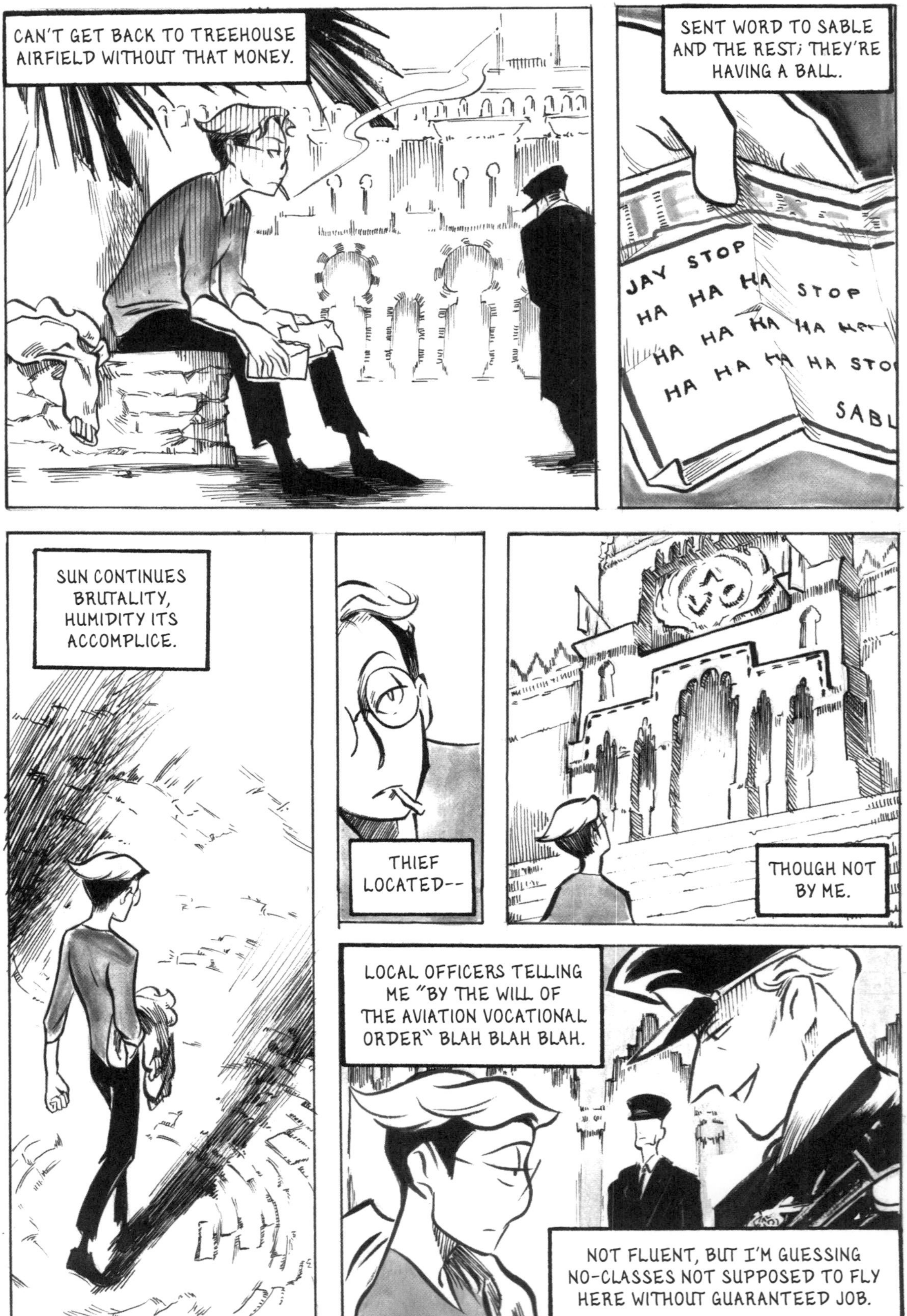
CAN'T GET BACK TO TREEHOUSE AIRFIELD WITHOUT THAT MONEY.
SENT WORD TO SABLE AND THE REST; THEY'RE HAVING A BALL.
JAY STOP
HA HA HA STOP
HA HA HA HA
HA HA HA HA
HA HA HA HA
SUN CONTINUES BRUTALITY, HUMIDITY ITS ACCOMPLICE.
THIEF LOCATED--
THOUGH NOT BY ME.
LOCAL OFFICERS TELLING ME "BY THE WILL OF THE AVIATION VOCATIONAL ORDER" BLAH BLAH BLAH.
NOT FLUENT, BUT I'M GUESSING NO-CLASSES NOT SUPPOSED TO FLY HERE WITHOUT GUARANTEED JOB.

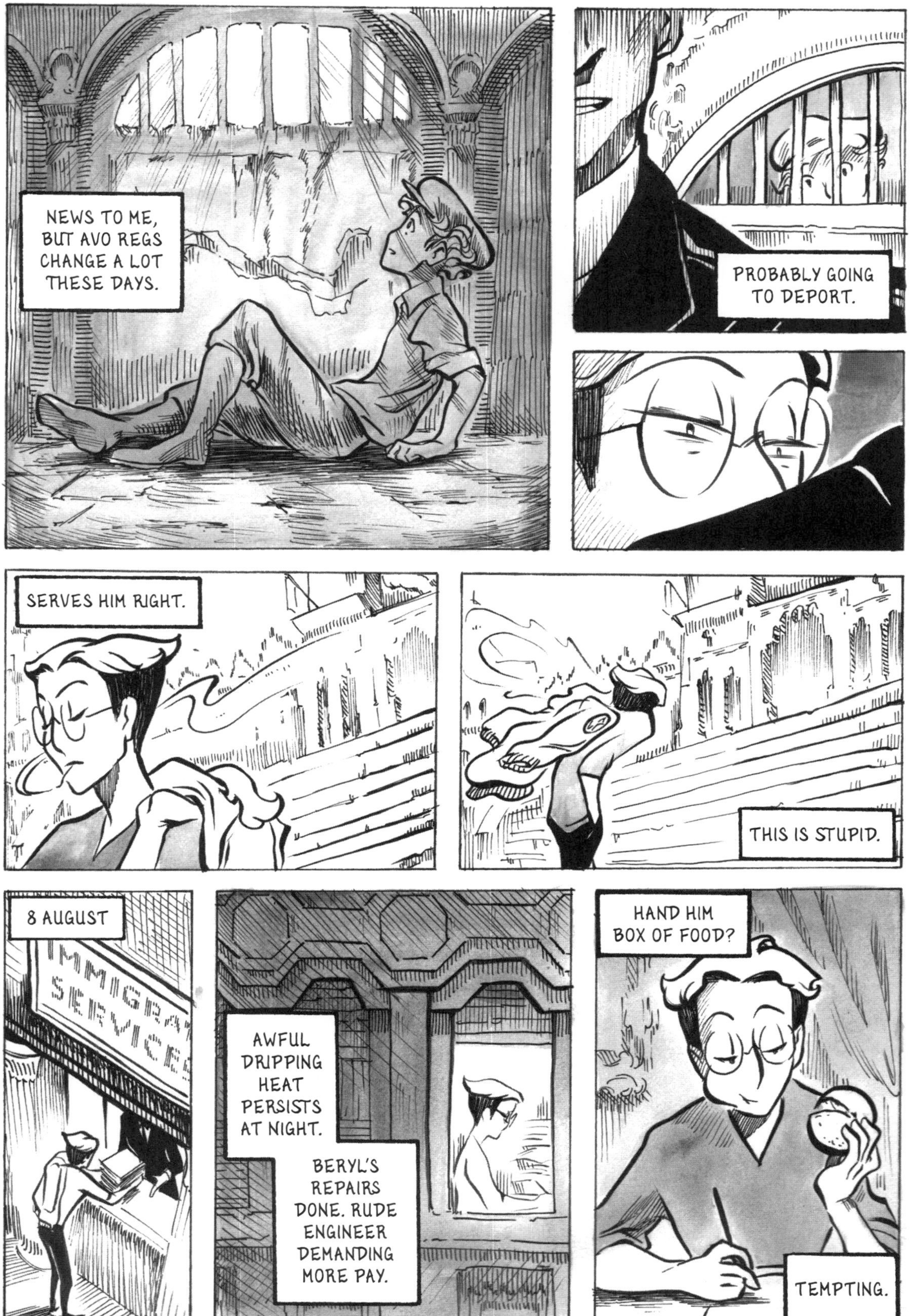
NEWS TO ME, BUT AVO REGS CHANGE A LOT THESE DAYS.
PROBABLY GOING TO DEPORT.
SERVES HIM RIGHT.
THIS IS STUPID.
8 AUGUST
IMMIGRA SERVICE
AWFUL DRIPPING HEAT PERSISTS AT NIGHT.
BERYL'S REPAIRS DONE. RUDE ENGINEER DEMANDING MORE PAY.
HAND HIM BOX OF FOOD?
TEMPTING.

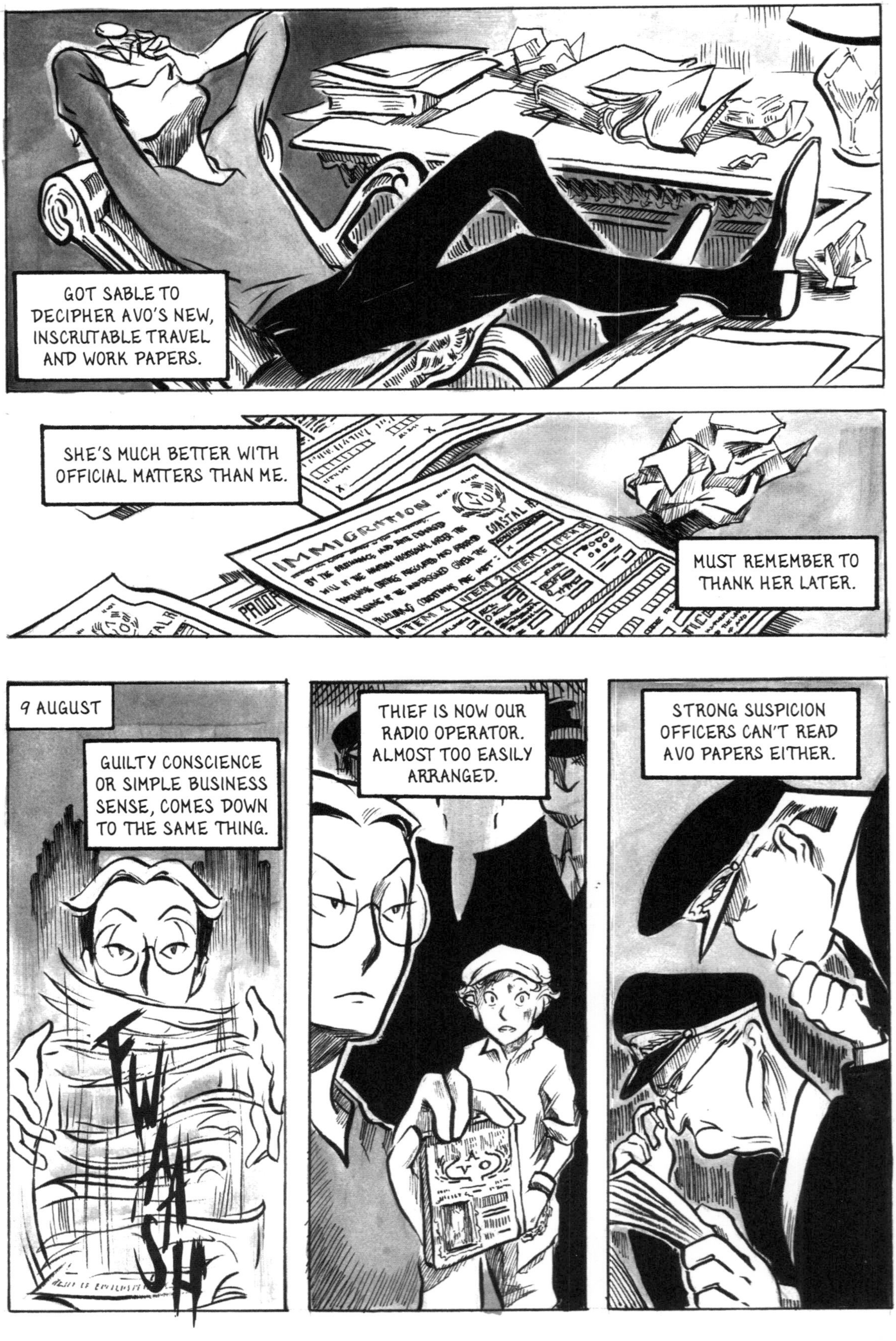
GOT SABLE TO DECIPHER AVO'S NEW, INSCRUTABLE TRAVEL AND WORK PAPERS.
SHE'S MUCH BETTER WITH OFFICIAL MATTERS THAN ME.
IMMIGRATION
MUST REMEMBER TO THANK HER LATER.
9 AUGUST
GUILTY CONSCIENCE OR SIMPLE BUSINESS SENSE, COMES DOWN TO THE SAME THING.
FWAASH
THIEF IS NOW OUR RADIO OPERATOR. ALMOST TOO EASILY ARRANGED.
STRONG SUSPICION OFFICERS CAN'T READ AVO PAPERS EITHER.

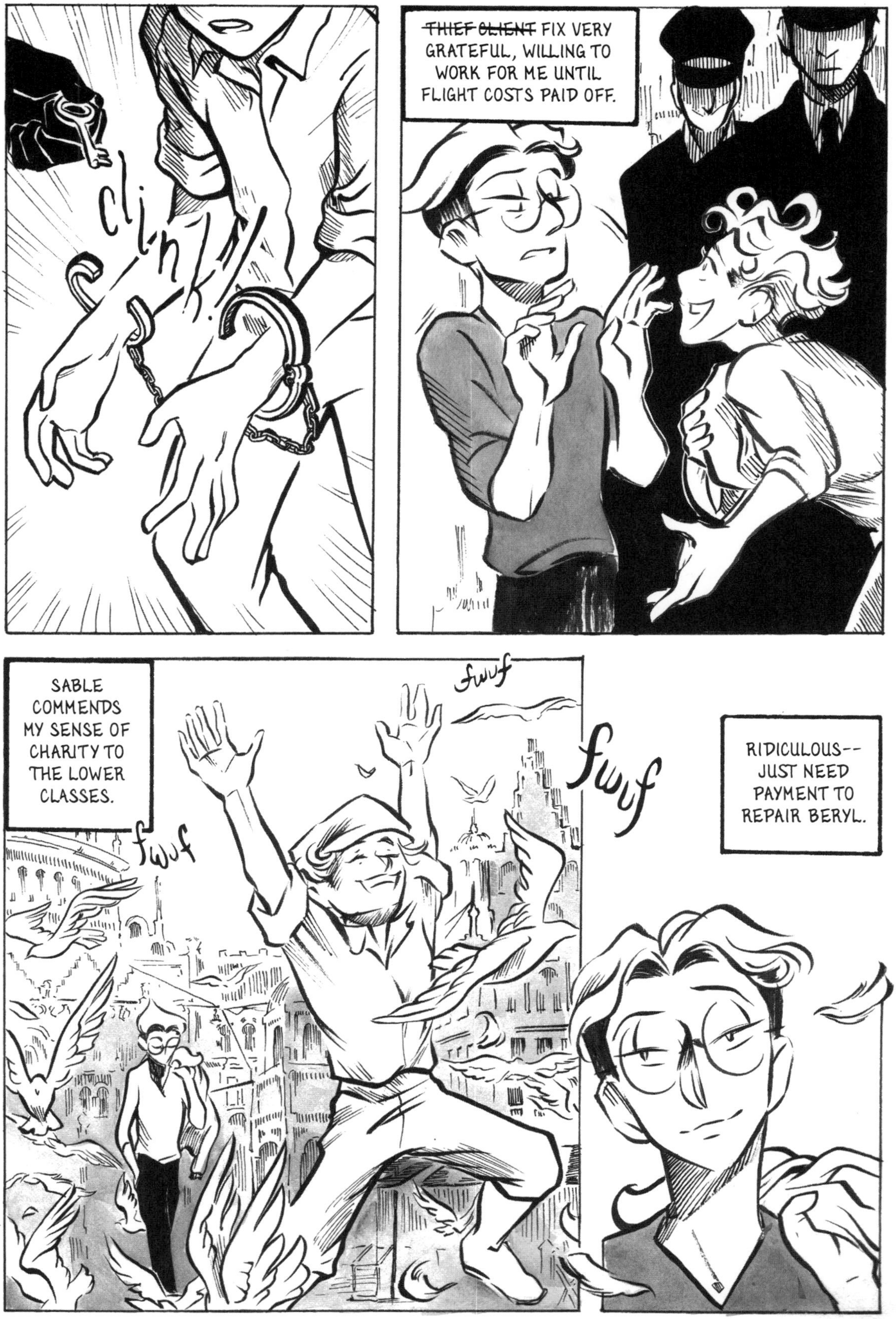
clink
~~THIEF~~ ~~CLIENT~~ FIX VERY GRATEFUL, WILLING TO WORK FOR ME UNTIL FLIGHT COSTS PAID OFF.
SABLE COMMENDS MY SENSE OF CHARITY TO THE LOWER CLASSES.
fwuf
fwuf
fwuf
RIDICULOUS-- JUST NEED PAYMENT TO REPAIR BERYL.

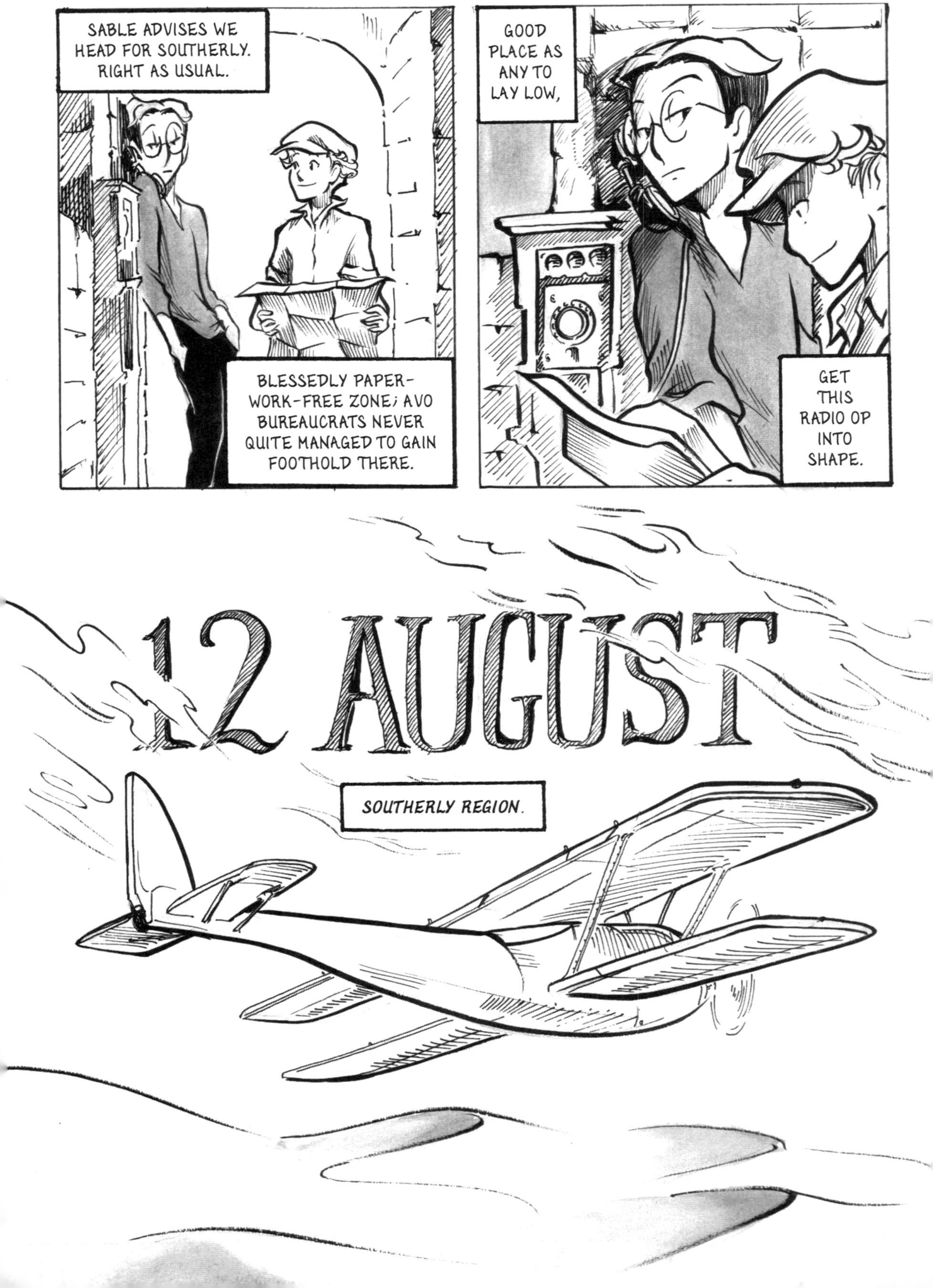

SABLE ADVISES WE HEAD FOR SOUTHERLY. RIGHT AS USUAL.
BLESSEDLY PAPER-WORK-FREE ZONE; AVO BUREAUCRATS NEVER QUITE MANAGED TO GAIN FOOTHOLD THERE.
GOOD PLACE AS ANY TO LAY LOW,
GET THIS RADIO OP INTO SHAPE.
12 AUGUST
SOUTHERLY REGION.

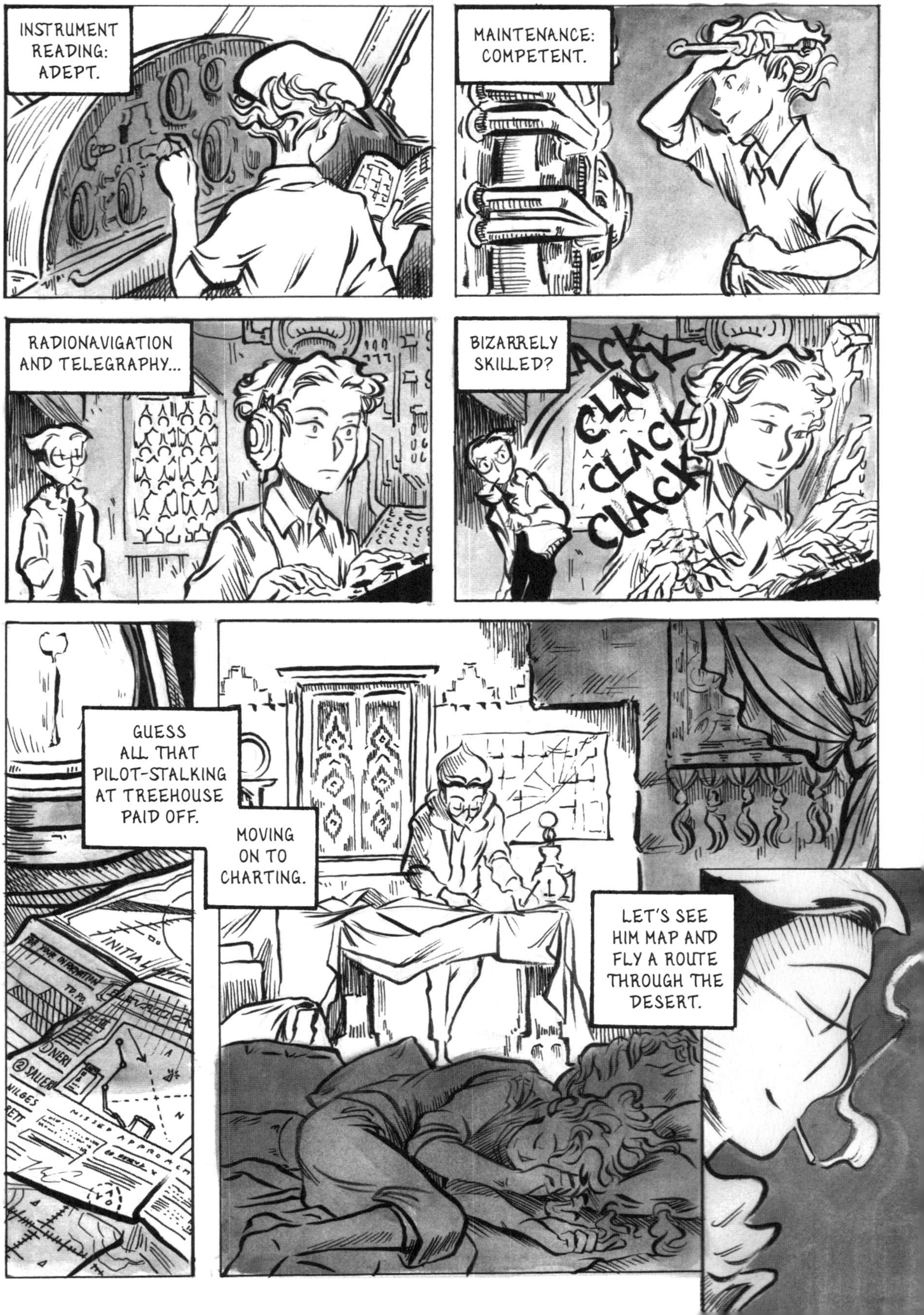
INSTRUMENT READING: ADEPT.
MAINTENANCE: COMPETENT.
RADIONAVIGATION AND TELEGRAPHY...
BIZARRELY SKILLED?
CLACK CLACK CLACK CLACK
GUESS ALL THAT PILOT-STALKING AT TREEHOUSE PAID OFF.
MOVING ON TO CHARTING.
LET'S SEE HIM MAP AND FLY A ROUTE THROUGH THE DESERT.
INITIAL
MISSED APPROACH

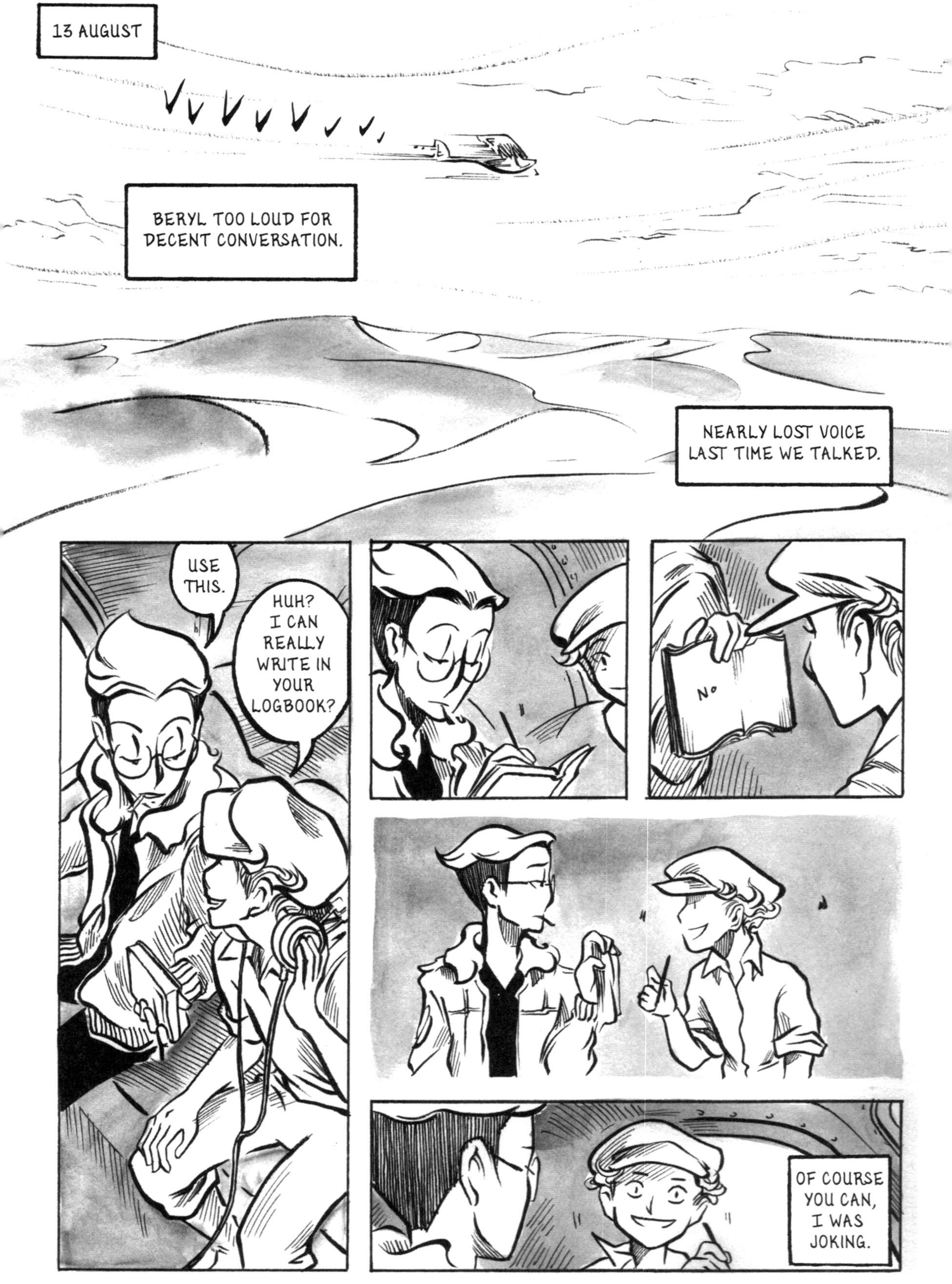
13 AUGUST
BERYL TOO LOUD FOR DECENT CONVERSATION.
NEARLY LOST VOICE LAST TIME WE TALKED.
USE THIS.
HUH? I CAN REALLY WRITE IN YOUR LOGBOOK?
No
OF COURSE YOU CAN, I WAS JOKING.

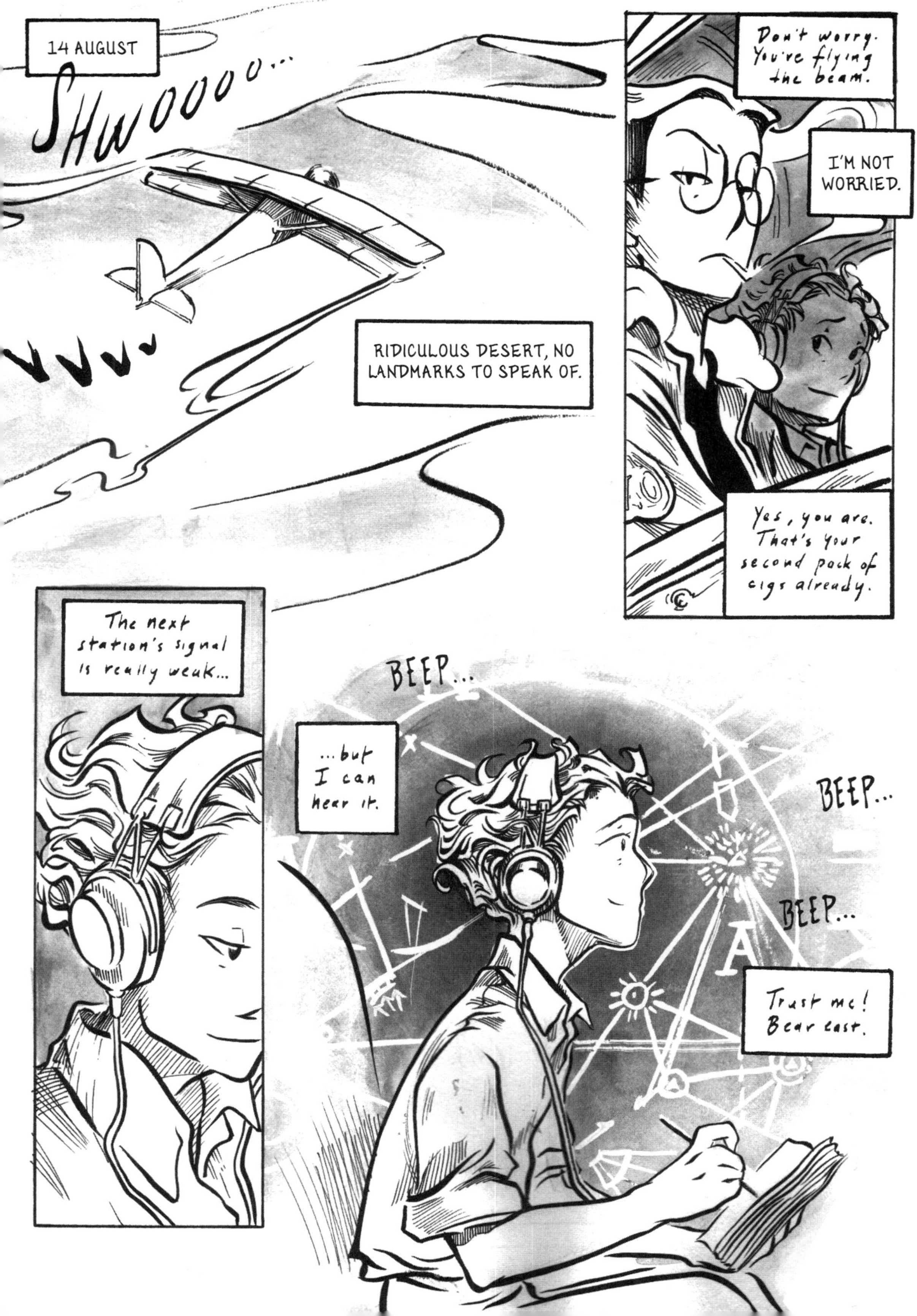

14 AUGUST
SHWOOOO...
VVVV
RIDICULOUS DESERT, NO LANDMARKS TO SPEAK OF.
Don't worry. You're flying the beam.
I'M NOT WORRIED.
Yes, you are. That's your second pack of cigs already.
The next station's signal is really weak...
...but I can hear it.
BEEP...
BEEP...
BEEP...
Trust me! Bear east.

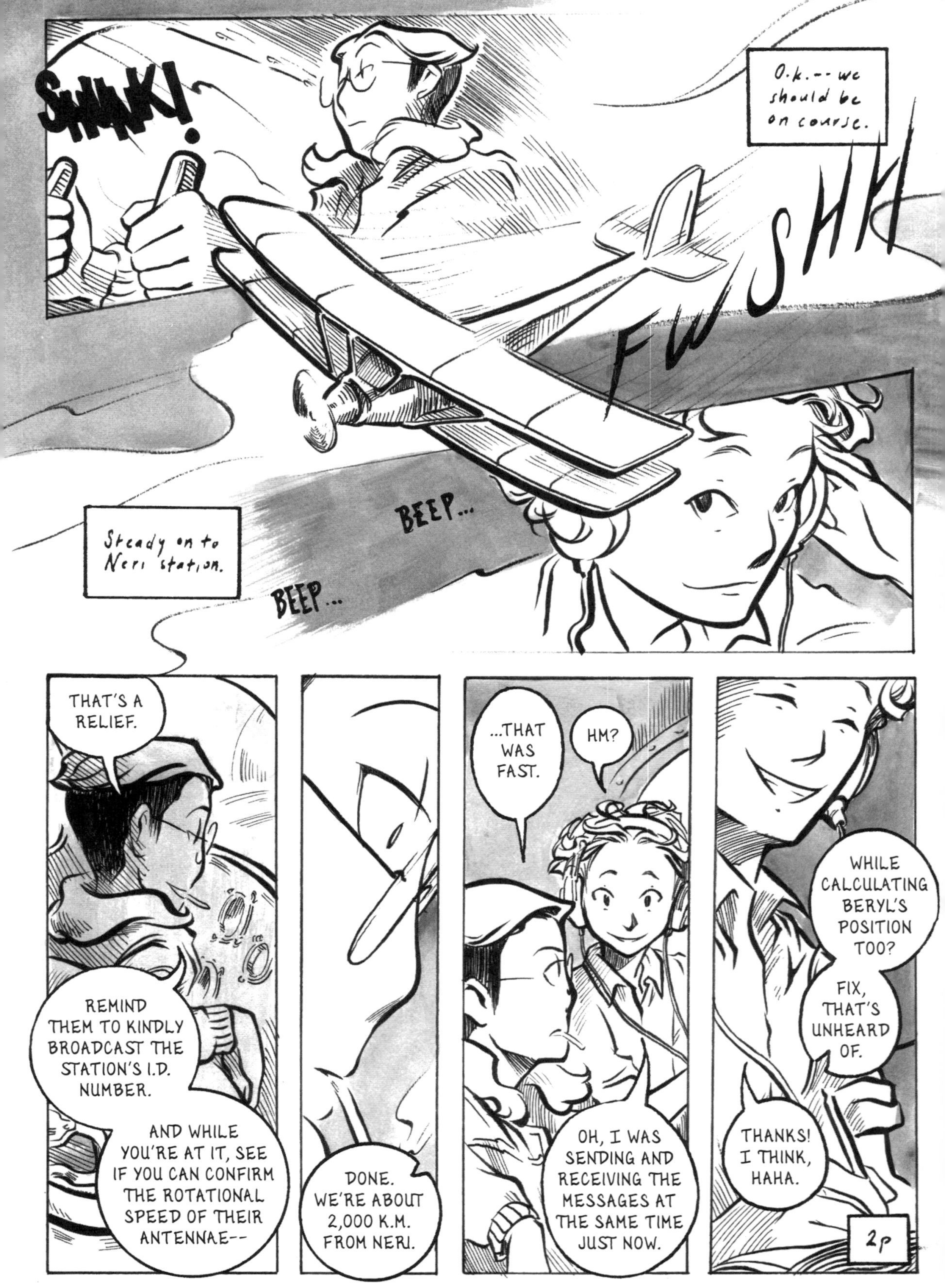
SHWAK!
O.k.-- we should be on course.
FWSHH
BEEP...
BEEP...
Steady on to Neri station.
THAT'S A RELIEF.
REMIND THEM TO KINDLY BROADCAST THE STATION'S I.D. NUMBER.
AND WHILE YOU'RE AT IT, SEE IF YOU CAN CONFIRM THE ROTATIONAL SPEED OF THEIR ANTENNAE--
DONE. WE'RE ABOUT 2,000 K.M. FROM NERI.
...THAT WAS FAST.
HM?
OH, I WAS SENDING AND RECEIVING THE MESSAGES AT THE SAME TIME JUST NOW.
WHILE CALCULATING BERYL'S POSITION TOO?
FIX, THAT'S UNHEARD OF.
THANKS! I THINK, HAHA.
2p

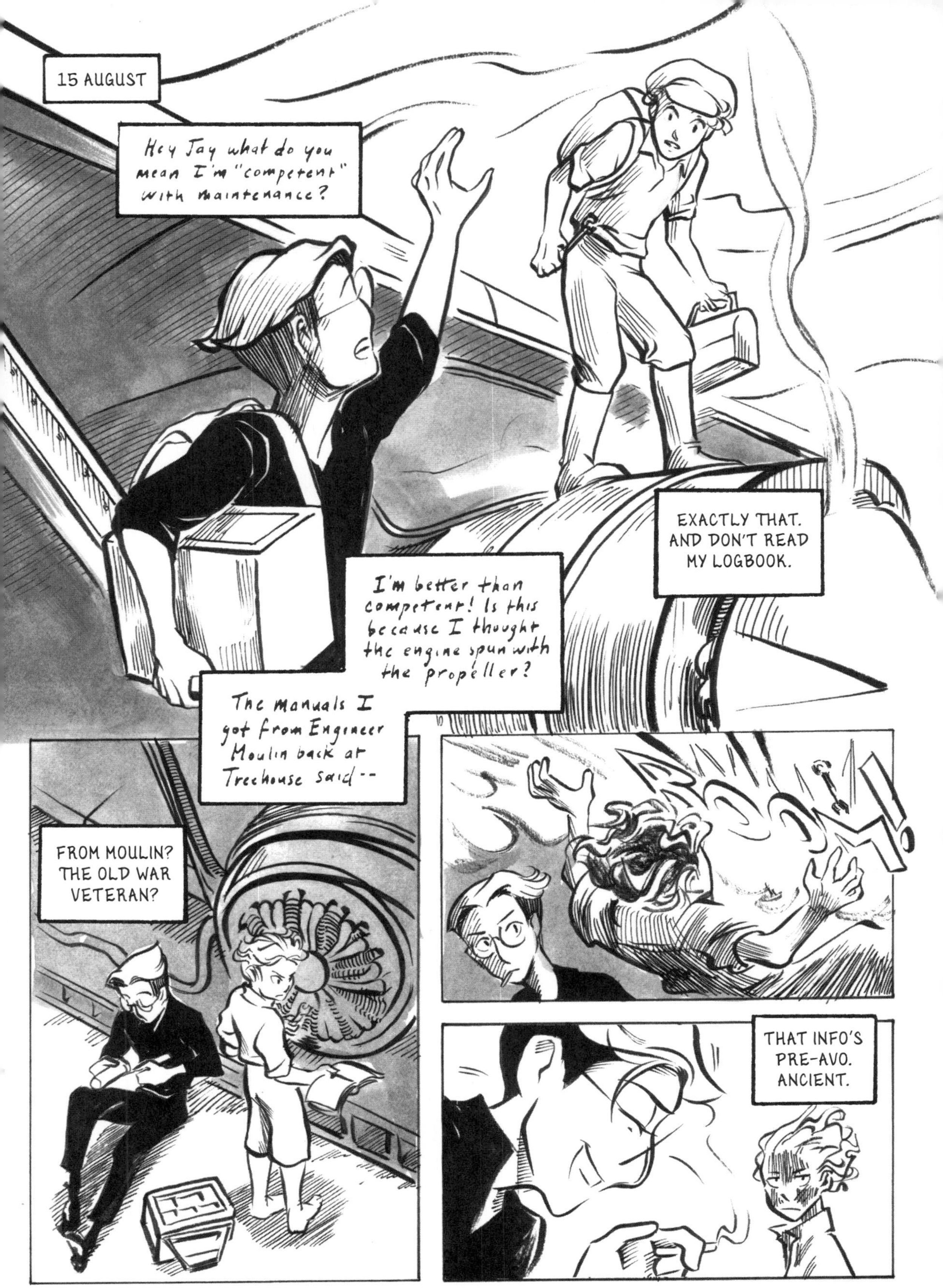
15 AUGUST
Hey Jay what do you mean I'm "competent" with maintenance?
EXACTLY THAT. AND DON'T READ MY LOGBOOK.
I'm better than competent! Is this because I thought the engine spun with the propeller?
The manuals I got from Engineer Moulin back at Treehouse said--
FROM MOULIN? THE OLD WAR VETERAN?
THAT INFO'S PRE-AVO. ANCIENT.

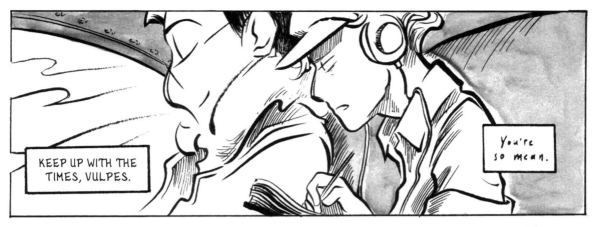

KEEP UP WITH THE TIMES, VULPES.

You're so mean.

No, I'm not giving you the pen.

Sorry, what?

What was that?

I can't hear you.

Beryl's fancy modern engine is just so loud, you know?

YOU'RE FIRED.

YES I'M JOKING.

2p

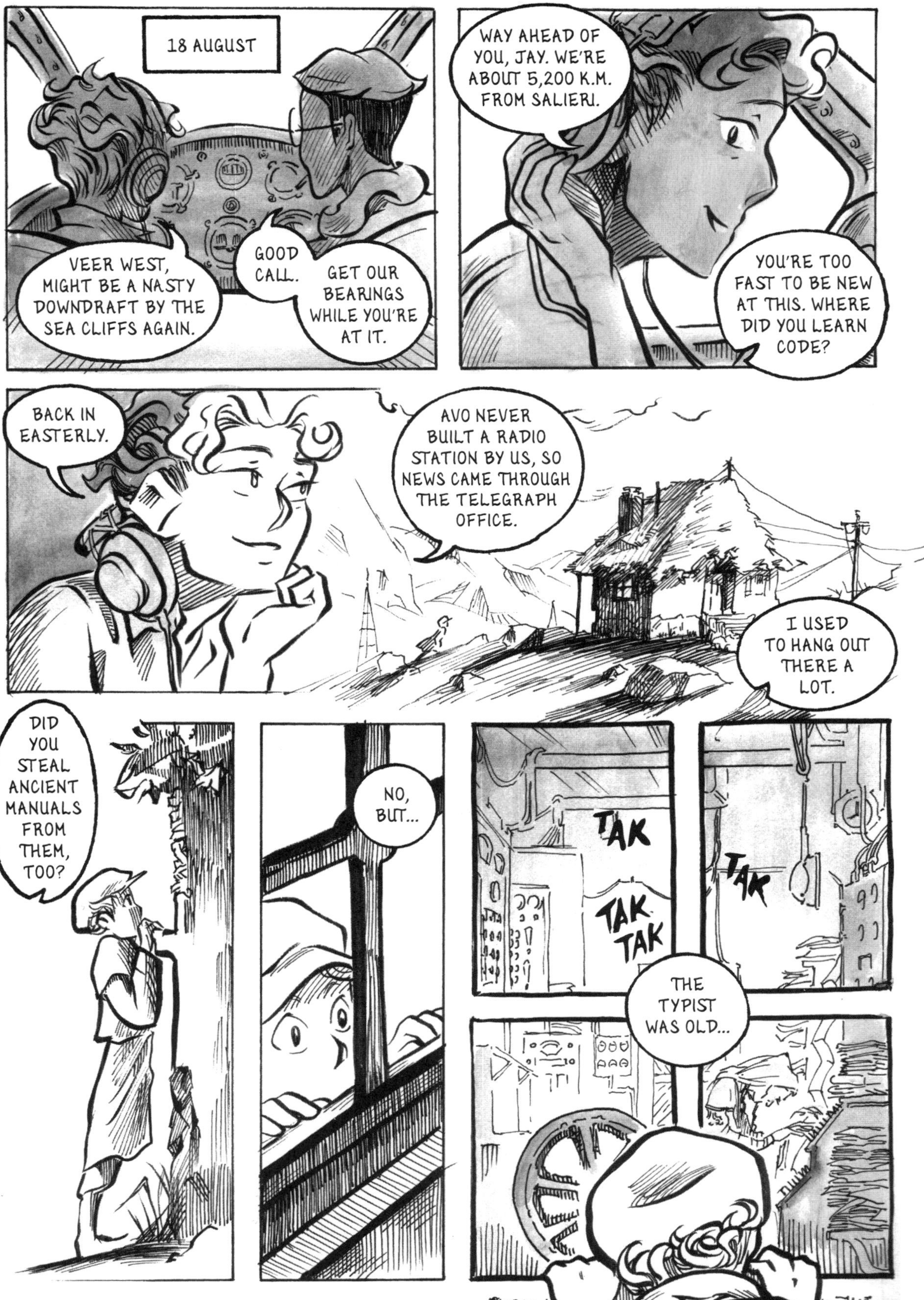
18 AUGUST
VEER WEST, MIGHT BE A NASTY DOWNDRAFT BY THE SEA CLIFFS AGAIN.
GOOD CALL.
GET OUR BEARINGS WHILE YOU'RE AT IT.
WAY AHEAD OF YOU, JAY. WE'RE ABOUT 5,200 K.M. FROM SALIERI.
YOU'RE TOO FAST TO BE NEW AT THIS. WHERE DID YOU LEARN CODE?
BACK IN EASTERLY.
AVO NEVER BUILT A RADIO STATION BY US, SO NEWS CAME THROUGH THE TELEGRAPH OFFICE.
I USED TO HANG OUT THERE A LOT.
DID YOU STEAL ANCIENT MANUALS FROM THEM, TOO?
NO, BUT...
TAK
TAK TAK
TAK
THE TYPIST WAS OLD...

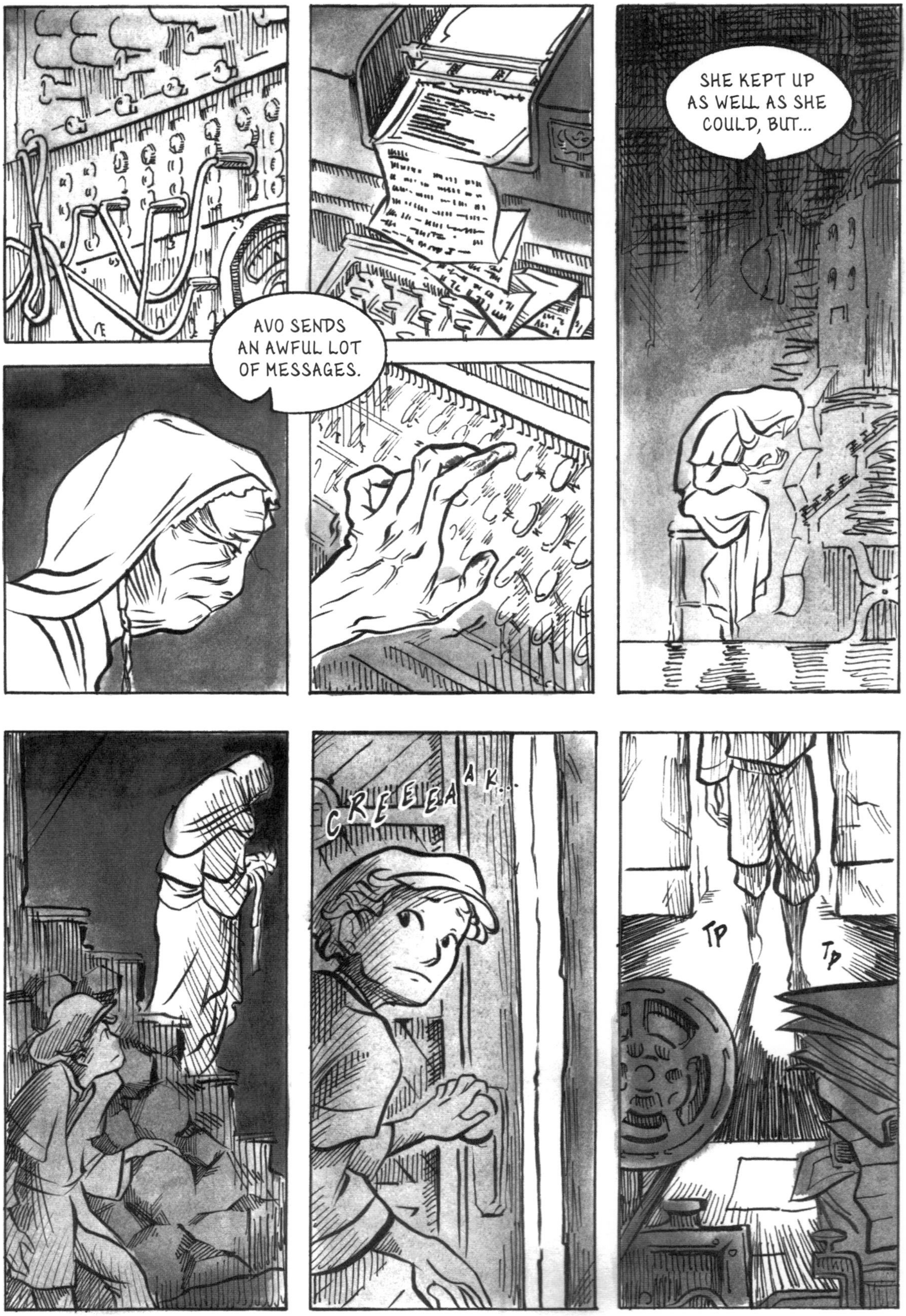
AVO SENDS AN AWFUL LOT OF MESSAGES.
SHE KEPT UP AS WELL AS SHE COULD, BUT...
CREEEAAK...
TP
TP

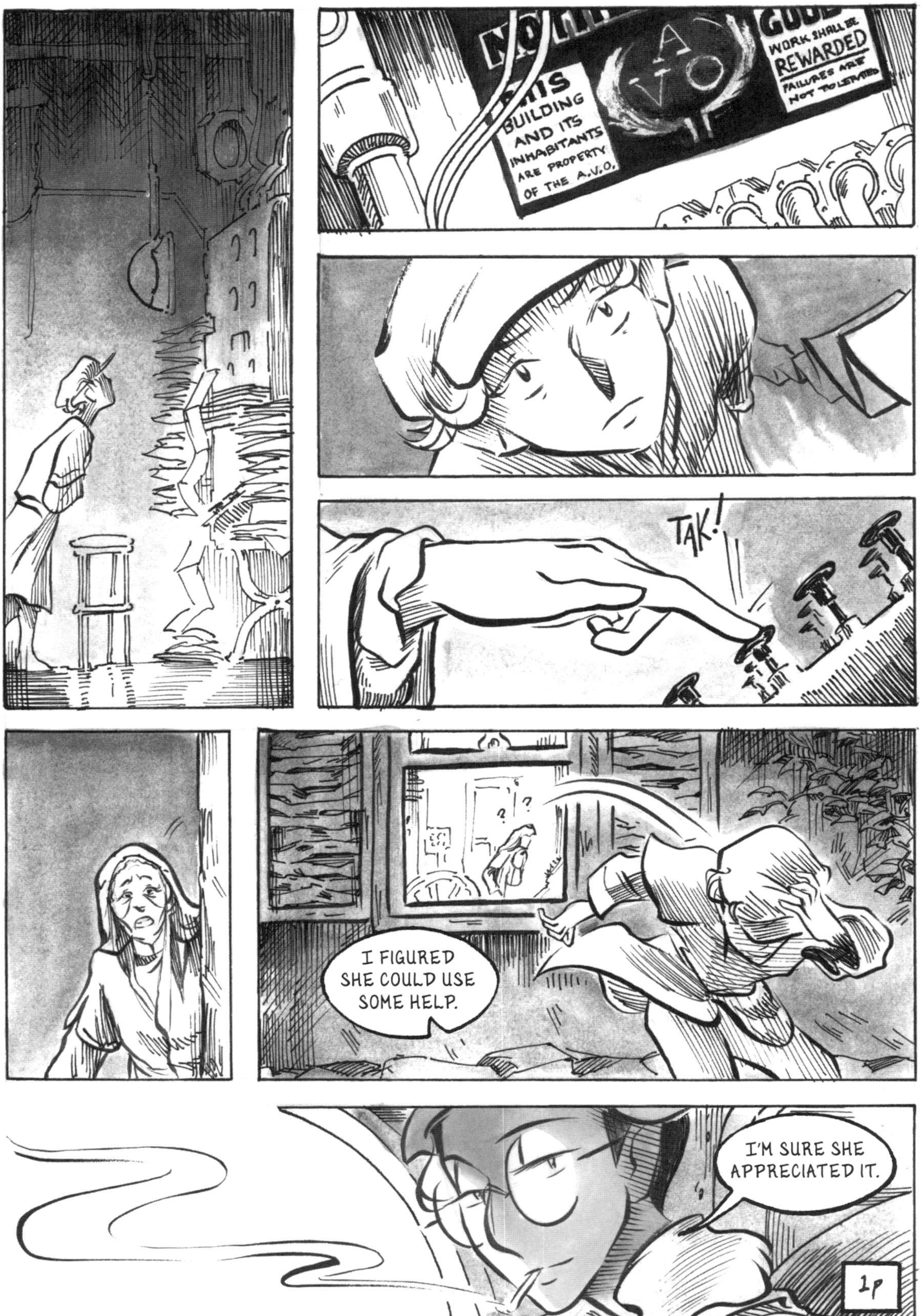
BUILDING AND ITS INHABITANTS ARE PROPERTY OF THE A.V.O.
WORK SHALL BE REWARDED
FAILURES ARE NOT TOLERATED
TAK!
I FIGURED SHE COULD USE SOME HELP.
I'M SURE SHE APPRECIATED IT.
1p

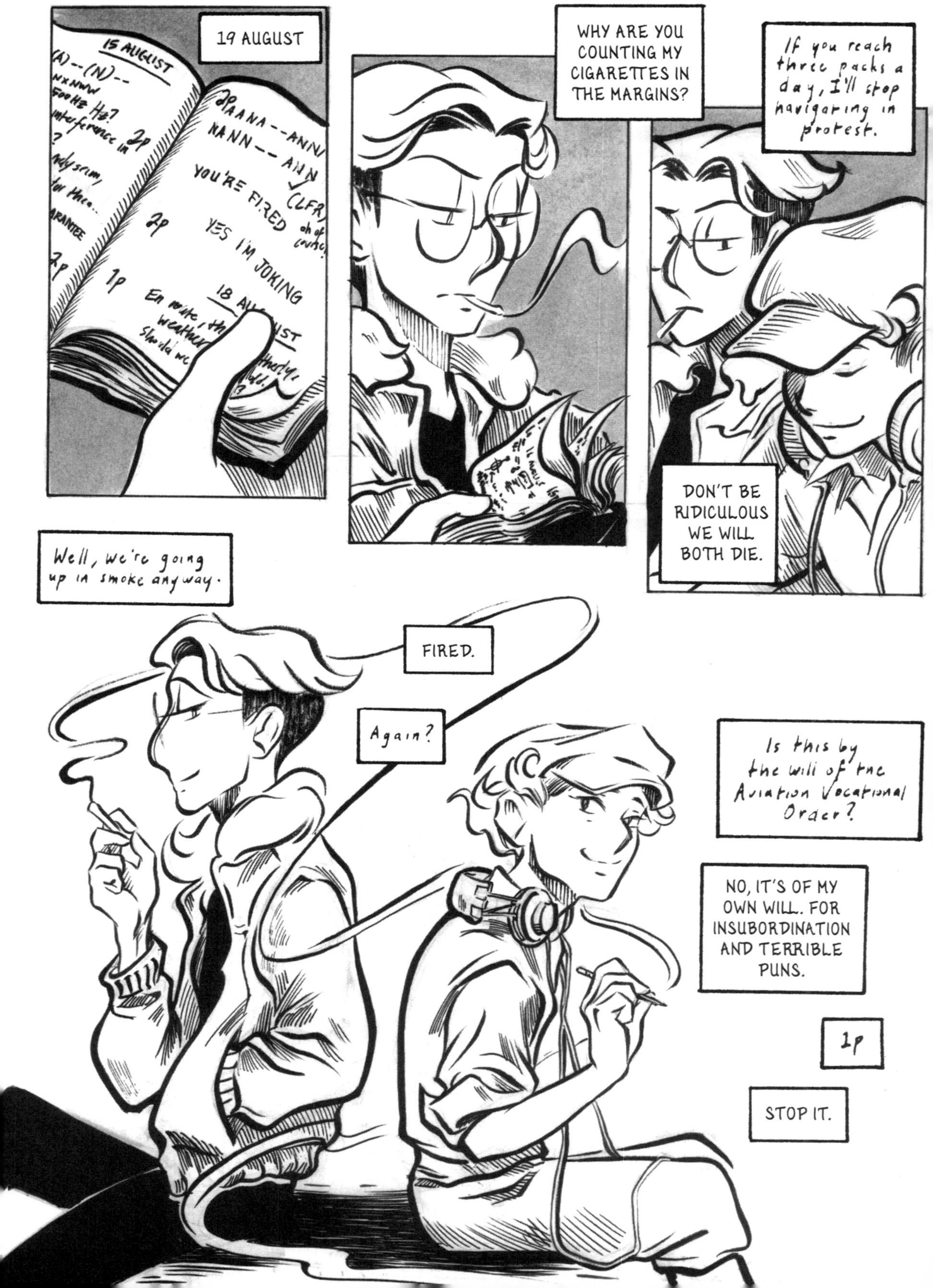
19 AUGUST
YOU'RE FIRED
YES I'M JOKING
WHY ARE YOU COUNTING MY CIGARETTES IN THE MARGINS?
If you reach three packs a day, I'll stop navigating in protest.
DON'T BE RIDICULOUS WE WILL BOTH DIE.
Well, we're going up in smoke anyway.
FIRED.
Again?
Is this by the will of the Aviation Vocational Order?
NO, IT'S OF MY OWN WILL.. FOR INSUBORDINATION AND TERRIBLE PUNS.
1p
STOP IT.

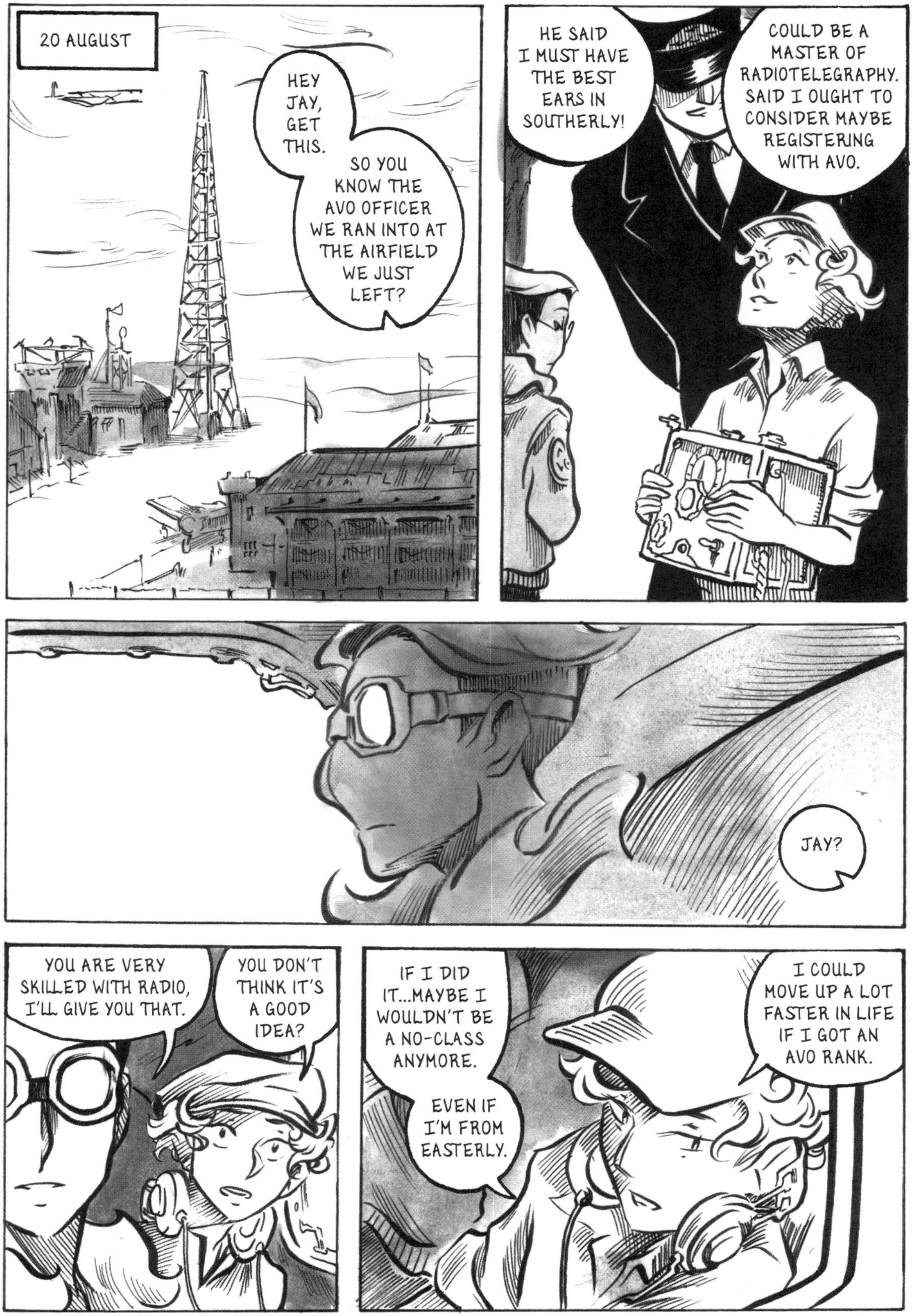
20 AUGUST
HEY JAY, GET THIS.
SO YOU KNOW THE AVO OFFICER WE RAN INTO AT THE AIRFIELD WE JUST LEFT?
HE SAID I MUST HAVE THE BEST EARS IN SOUTHERLY!
COULD BE A MASTER OF RADIOTELEGRAPHY. SAID I OUGHT TO CONSIDER MAYBE REGISTERING WITH AVO.
JAY?
YOU ARE VERY SKILLED WITH RADIO, I'LL GIVE YOU THAT.
YOU DON'T THINK IT'S A GOOD IDEA?
IF I DID IT...MAYBE I WOULDN'T BE A NO-CLASS ANYMORE.
EVEN IF I'M FROM EASTERLY.
I COULD MOVE UP A LOT FASTER IN LIFE IF I GOT AN AVO RANK.

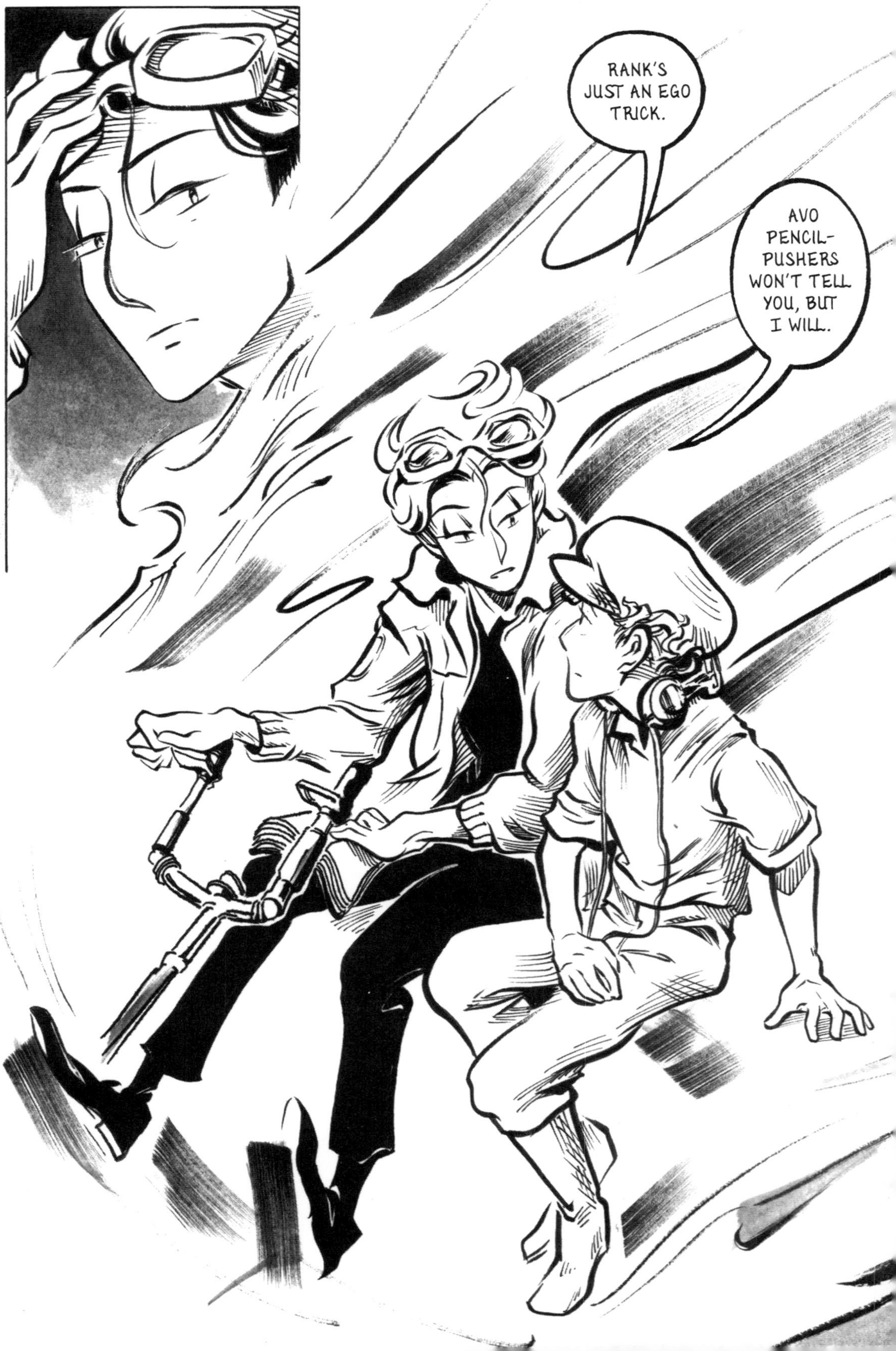
RANK'S JUST AN EGO TRICK.
AVO PENCIL-PUSHERS WON'T TELL YOU, BUT I WILL.

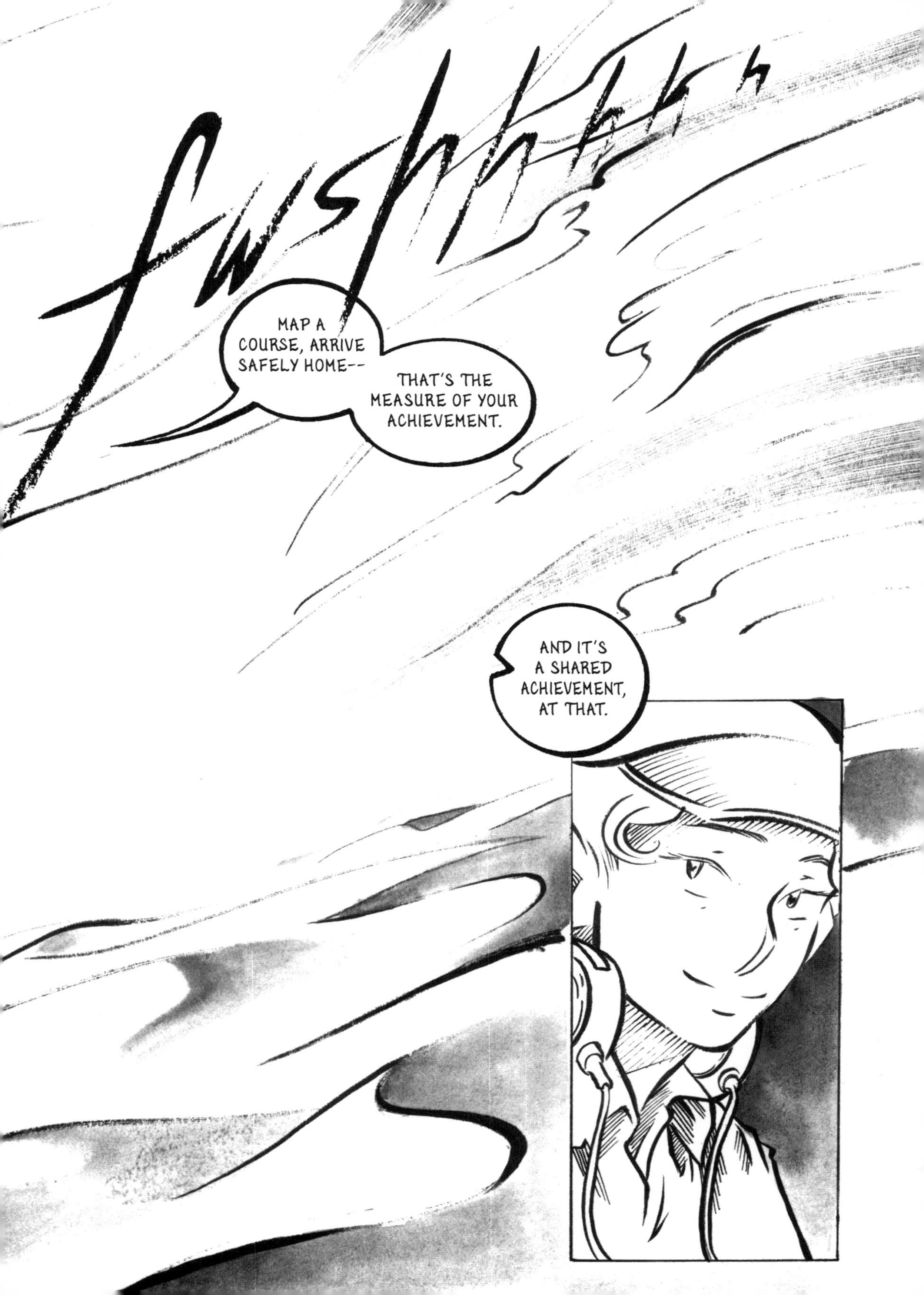
fwshhhh
MAP A COURSE, ARRIVE SAFELY HOME--
THAT'S THE MEASURE OF YOUR ACHIEVEMENT.
AND IT'S A SHARED ACHIEVEMENT, AT THAT.

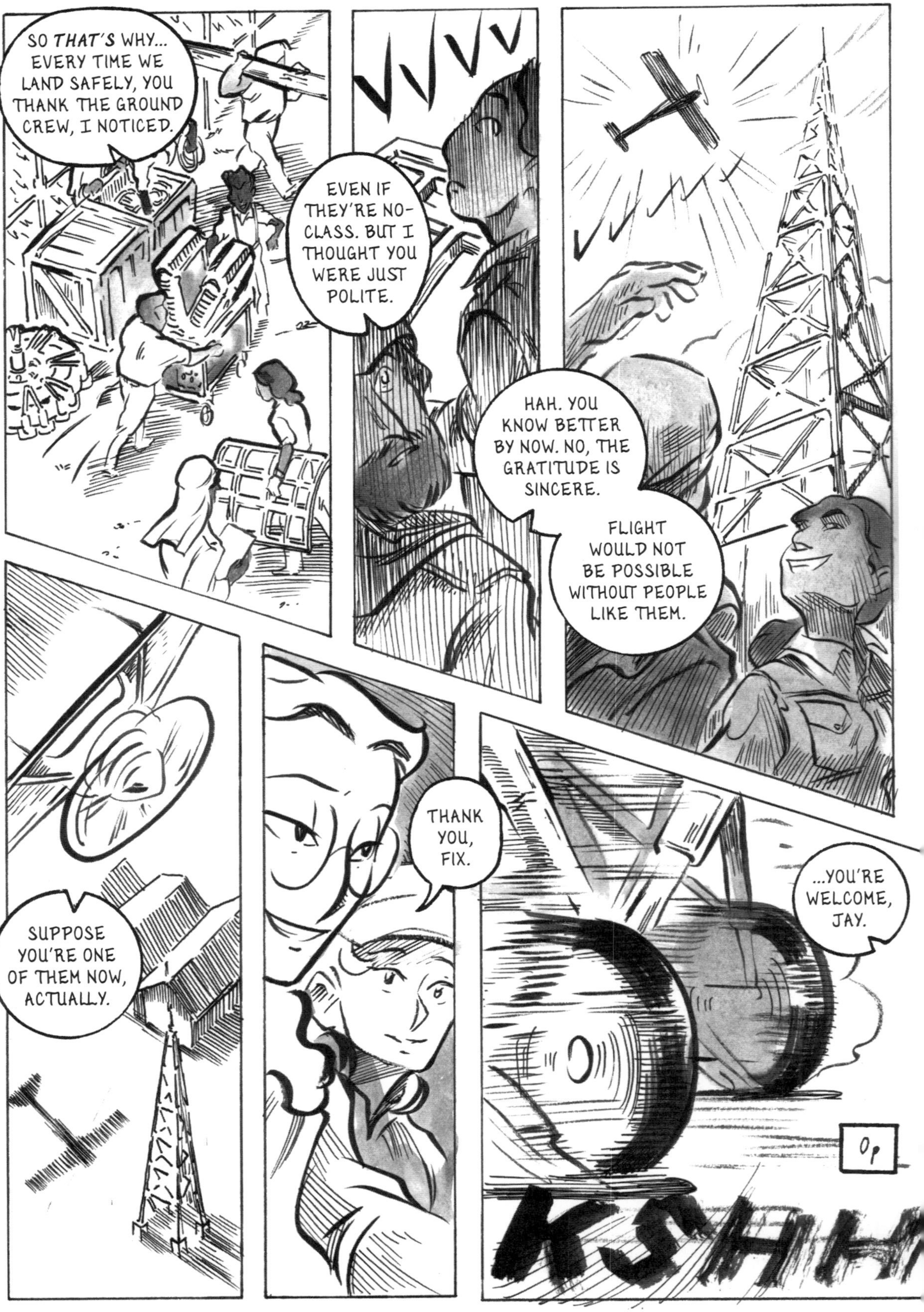
VVVV
SO *THAT'S* WHY... EVERY TIME WE LAND SAFELY, YOU THANK THE GROUND CREW, I NOTICED.
EVEN IF THEY'RE NO-CLASS. BUT I THOUGHT YOU WERE JUST POLITE.
HAH. YOU KNOW BETTER BY NOW. NO, THE GRATITUDE IS SINCERE.
FLIGHT WOULD NOT BE POSSIBLE WITHOUT PEOPLE LIKE THEM.
SUPPOSE YOU'RE ONE OF THEM NOW, ACTUALLY.
THANK YOU, FIX.
...YOU'RE WELCOME, JAY.
KSHH

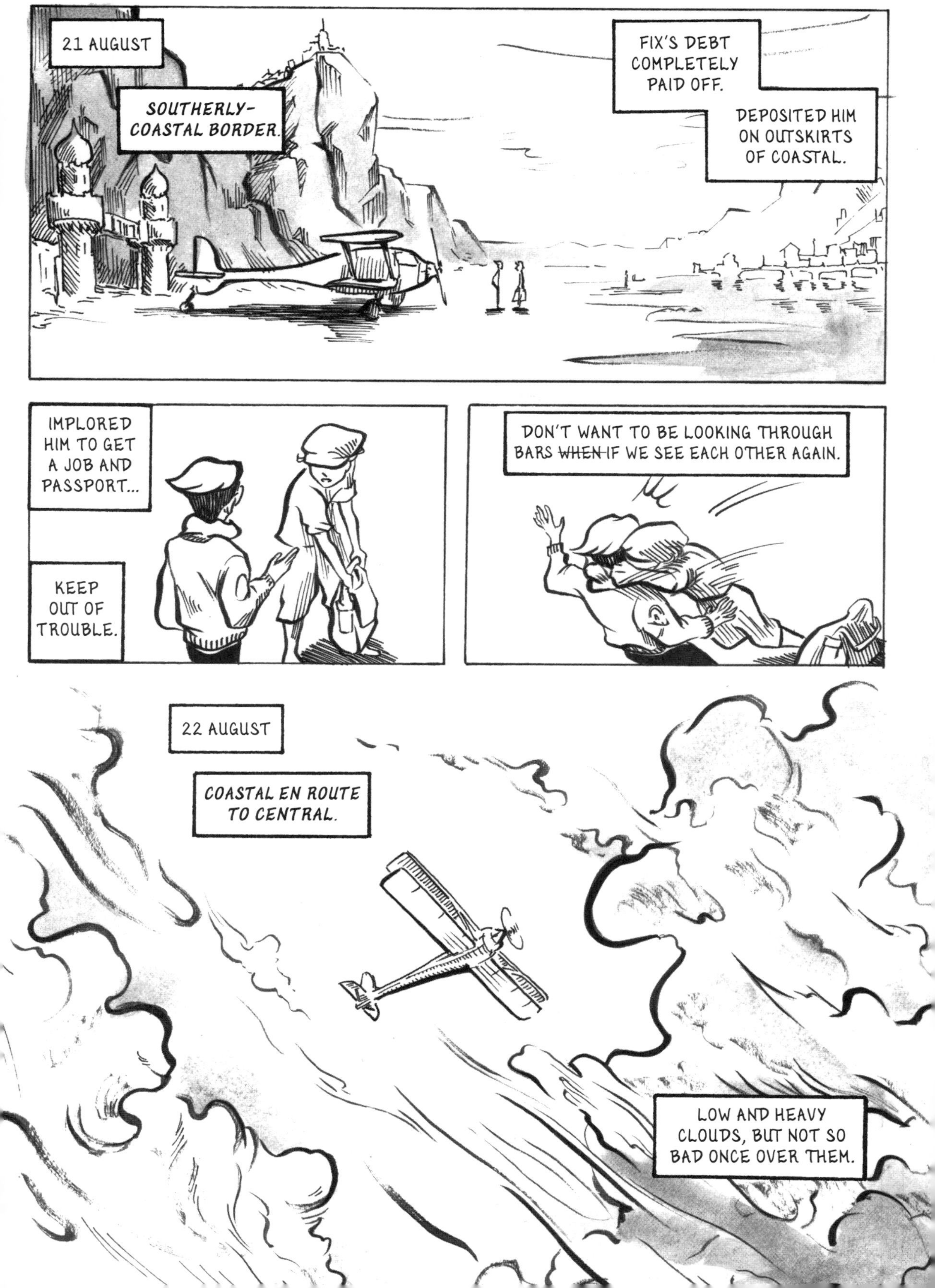

21 AUGUST
SOUTHERLY-COASTAL BORDER.
FIX'S DEBT COMPLETELY PAID OFF.
DEPOSITED HIM ON OUTSKIRTS OF COASTAL.
IMPLORED HIM TO GET A JOB AND PASSPORT...
KEEP OUT OF TROUBLE.
DON'T WANT TO BE LOOKING THROUGH BARS ~~WHEN~~ IF WE SEE EACH OTHER AGAIN.
22 AUGUST
COASTAL EN ROUTE TO CENTRAL.
LOW AND HEAVY CLOUDS, BUT NOT SO BAD ONCE OVER THEM.

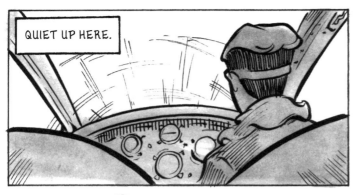

QUIET UP HERE.

WONDER WHERE HE IS NOW.

23 AUGUST

CENTRAL.

WIRE FROM SABLE.

AVO OFFICIALS ACTUALLY STOPPED BY TREEHOUSE FOR ONCE. MEDDLING, NO DOUBT.

PROOF ENCLOSED WITH LETTER. APPARENTLY AM NOW A "CAPTAIN."

LISENZ

NOTHING TO BE PUFFED ABOUT; EVERY SINGLE PILOT AT TREEHOUSE HAS BEEN MADE A "CAPTAIN."

NOBODY SURE WHAT IT MEANS.

SABLE HAPPY, HOPES THEY'LL UPGRADE HANGAR.

PERSONALLY WOULD PREFER AVO LEFT TREEHOUSE ALONE...

EVEN IF IT--WE--ARE TECHNICALLY THEIR PROPERTY.

TOOK LICENSE.

DECLINED PROMOTION.

12 SEPTEMBER

COASTAL.

CLOUD HOPPING OVER COASTAL, PICKED UP MESSAGE WITH BIZARRE SWING TO IT.

SEEMS THE SENDER RIGGED AN AVO RADIO CHANNEL TO BOOST SIGNAL.

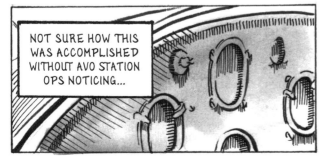

NOT SURE HOW THIS WAS ACCOMPLISHED WITHOUT AVO STATION OPS NOTICING...

BUT THAT'S GENIUS FOR YOU.

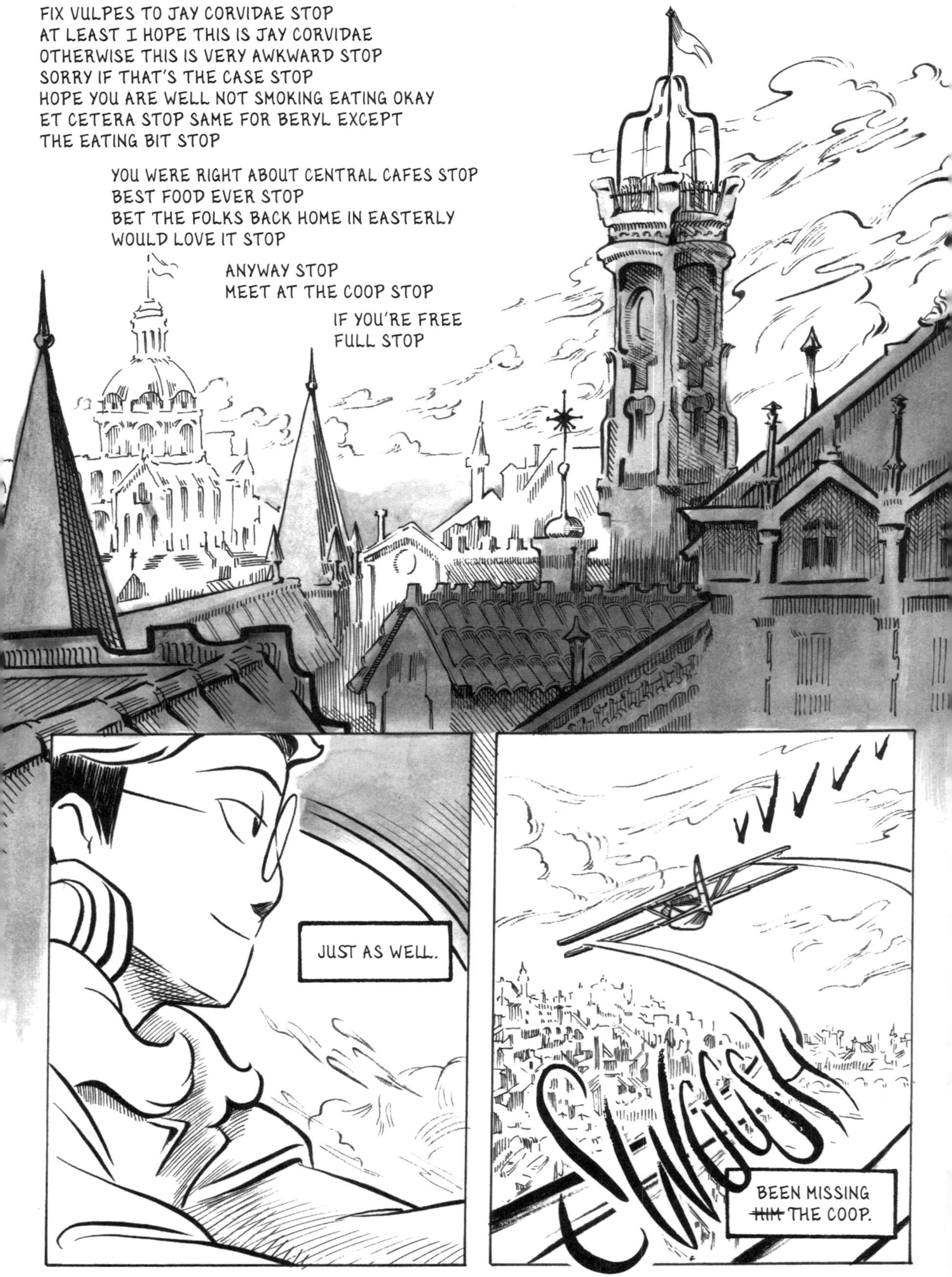
FIX VULPES TO JAY CORVIDAE STOP
AT LEAST I HOPE THIS IS JAY CORVIDAE
OTHERWISE THIS IS VERY AWKWARD STOP
SORRY IF THAT'S THE CASE STOP
HOPE YOU ARE WELL NOT SMOKING EATING OKAY
ET CETERA STOP SAME FOR BERYL EXCEPT
THE EATING BIT STOP
YOU WERE RIGHT ABOUT CENTRAL CAFES STOP
BEST FOOD EVER STOP
BET THE FOLKS BACK HOME IN EASTERLY
WOULD LOVE IT STOP
ANYWAY STOP
MEET AT THE COOP STOP
IF YOU'RE FREE
FULL STOP
JUST AS WELL.
BEEN MISSING ~~HIM~~ THE COOP.

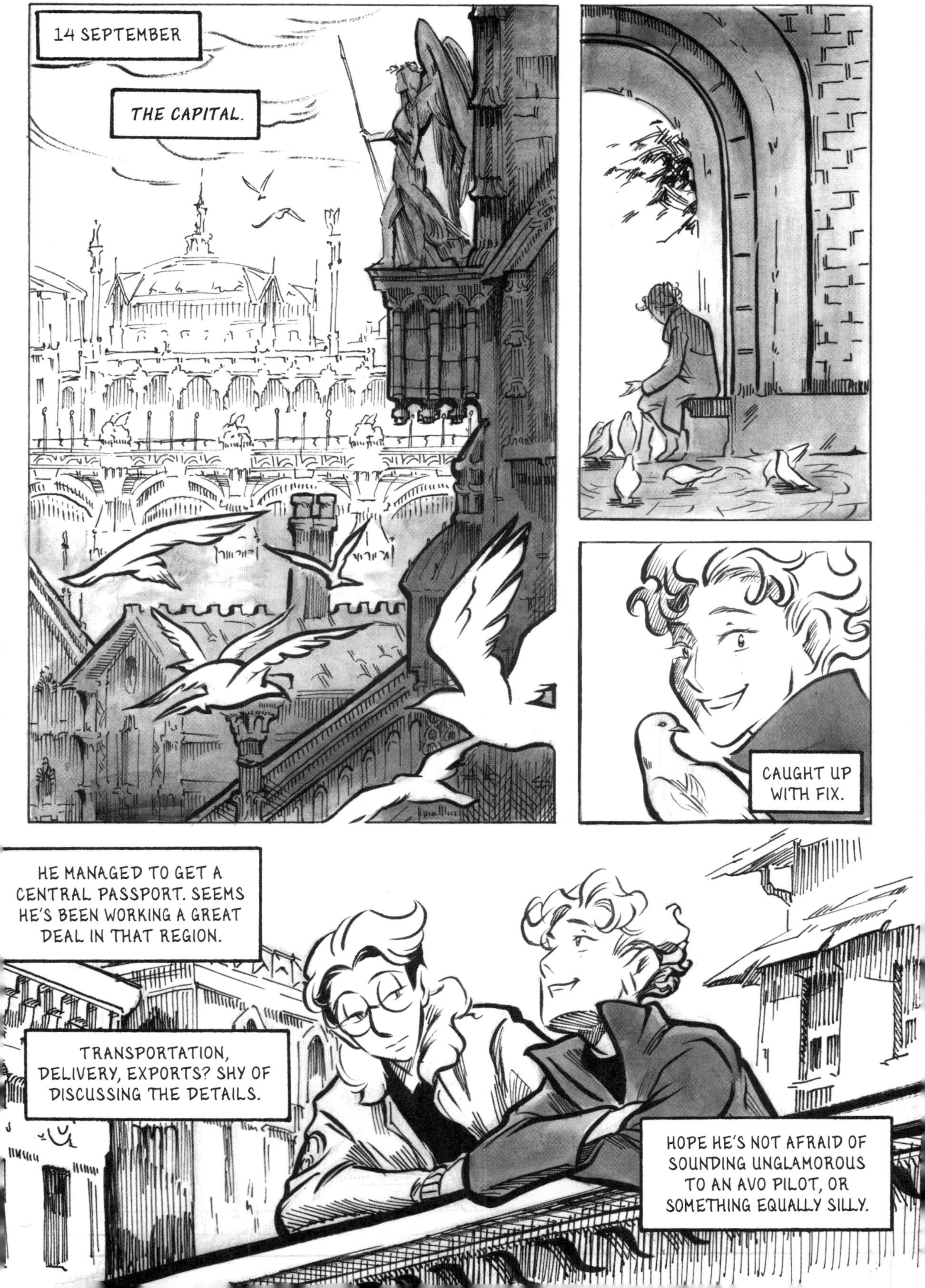
14 SEPTEMBER
THE CAPITAL.
CAUGHT UP WITH FIX.
HE MANAGED TO GET A CENTRAL PASSPORT. SEEMS HE'S BEEN WORKING A GREAT DEAL IN THAT REGION.
TRANSPORTATION, DELIVERY, EXPORTS? SHY OF DISCUSSING THE DETAILS.
HOPE HE'S NOT AFRAID OF SOUNDING UNGLAMOROUS TO AN AVO PILOT, OR SOMETHING EQUALLY SILLY.

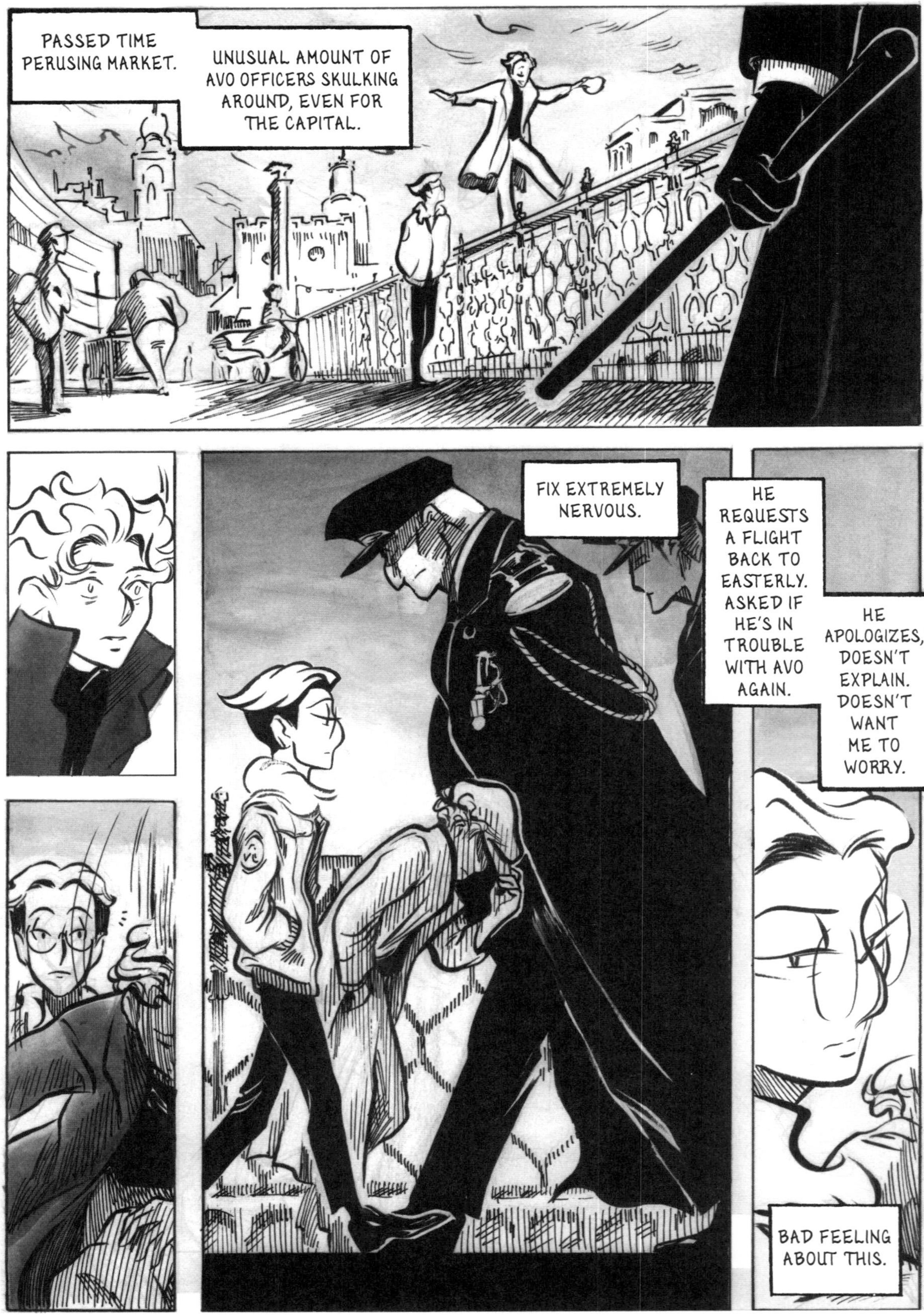
PASSED TIME PERUSING MARKET.
UNUSUAL AMOUNT OF AVO OFFICERS SKULKING AROUND, EVEN FOR THE CAPITAL.
FIX EXTREMELY NERVOUS.
HE REQUESTS A FLIGHT BACK TO EASTERLY. ASKED IF HE'S IN TROUBLE WITH AVO AGAIN.
HE APOLOGIZES, DOESN'T EXPLAIN. DOESN'T WANT ME TO WORRY.
BAD FEELING ABOUT THIS.

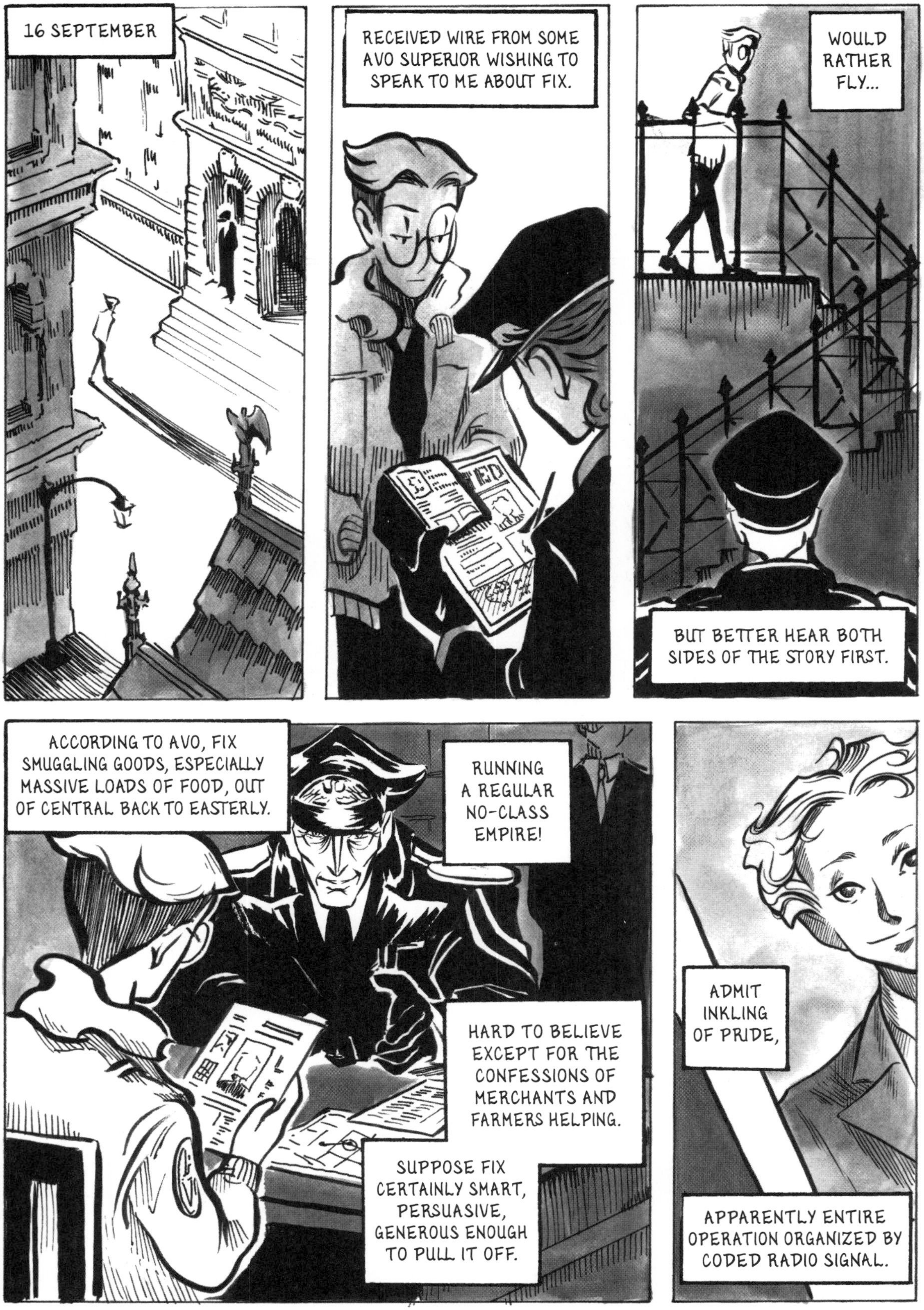
16 SEPTEMBER
RECEIVED WIRE FROM SOME AVO SUPERIOR WISHING TO SPEAK TO ME ABOUT FIX.
WOULD RATHER FLY...
BUT BETTER HEAR BOTH SIDES OF THE STORY FIRST.
ACCORDING TO AVO, FIX SMUGGLING GOODS, ESPECIALLY MASSIVE LOADS OF FOOD, OUT OF CENTRAL BACK TO EASTERLY.
RUNNING A REGULAR NO-CLASS EMPIRE!
HARD TO BELIEVE EXCEPT FOR THE CONFESSIONS OF MERCHANTS AND FARMERS HELPING.
SUPPOSE FIX CERTAINLY SMART, PERSUASIVE, GENEROUS ENOUGH TO PULL IT OFF.
ADMIT INKLING OF PRIDE,
APPARENTLY ENTIRE OPERATION ORGANIZED BY CODED RADIO SIGNAL.

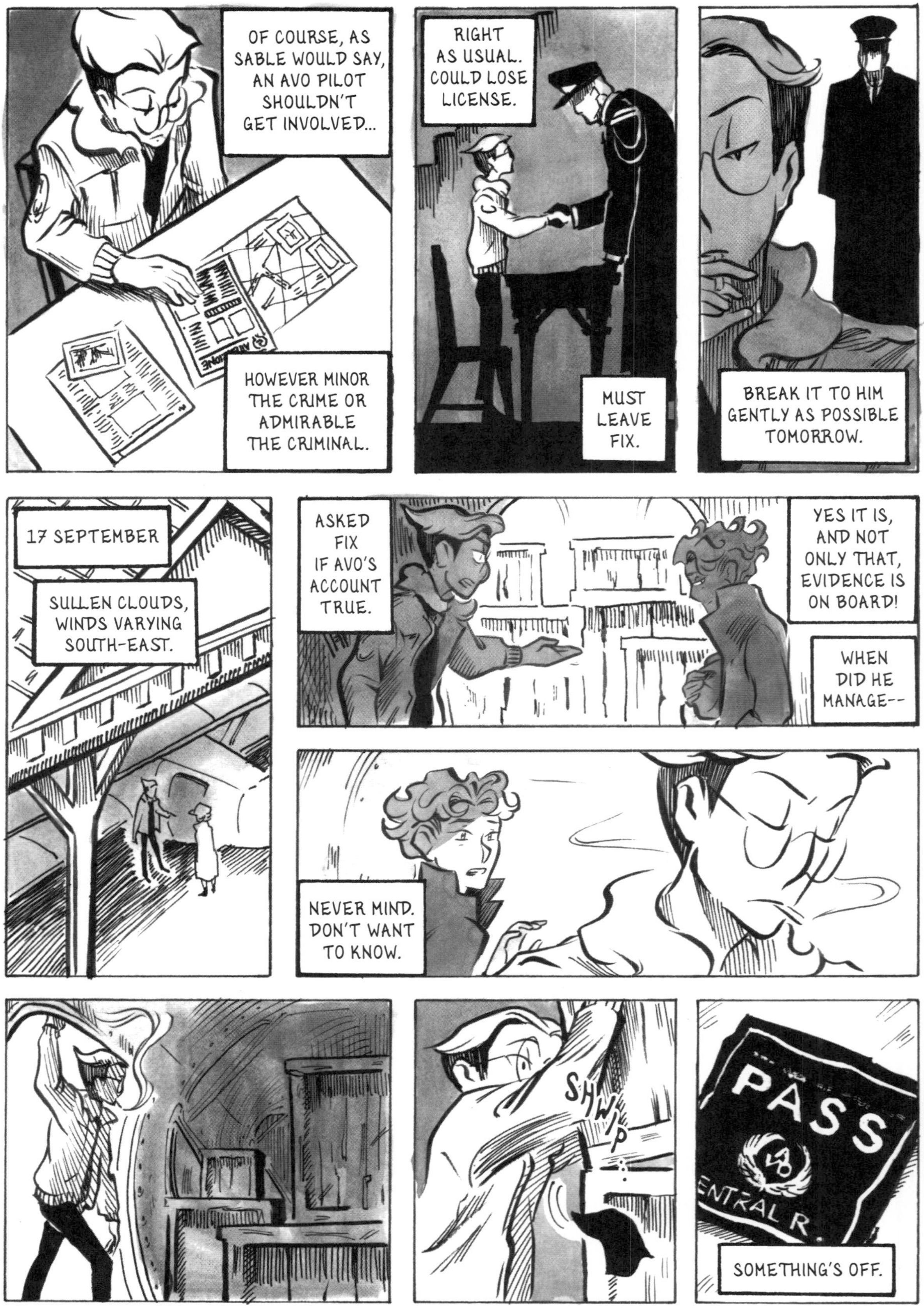
OF COURSE, AS SABLE WOULD SAY, AN AVO PILOT SHOULDN'T GET INVOLVED...
HOWEVER MINOR THE CRIME OR ADMIRABLE THE CRIMINAL.
RIGHT AS USUAL. COULD LOSE LICENSE.
MUST LEAVE FIX.
BREAK IT TO HIM GENTLY AS POSSIBLE TOMORROW.
17 SEPTEMBER
SULLEN CLOUDS, WINDS VARYING SOUTH-EAST.
ASKED FIX IF AVO'S ACCOUNT TRUE.
YES IT IS, AND NOT ONLY THAT, EVIDENCE IS ON BOARD!
WHEN DID HE MANAGE--
NEVER MIND. DON'T WANT TO KNOW.
SHWIP...
PASS
ENTRAL R.
SOMETHING'S OFF.

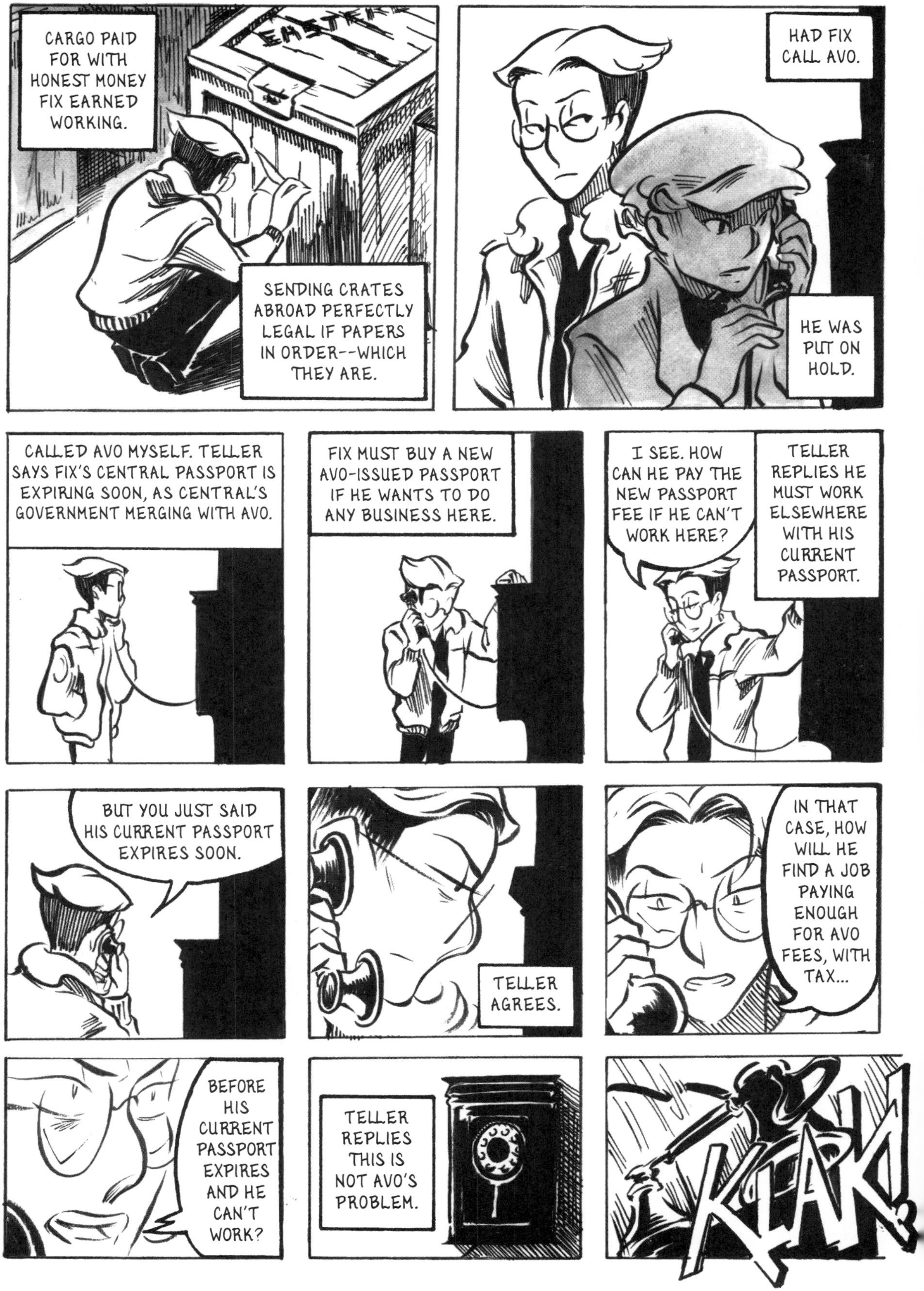
CARGO PAID FOR WITH HONEST MONEY FIX EARNED WORKING.
SENDING CRATES ABROAD PERFECTLY LEGAL IF PAPERS IN ORDER--WHICH THEY ARE.
HAD FIX CALL AVO.
HE WAS PUT ON HOLD.
CALLED AVO MYSELF. TELLER SAYS FIX'S CENTRAL PASSPORT IS EXPIRING SOON, AS CENTRAL'S GOVERNMENT MERGING WITH AVO.
FIX MUST BUY A NEW AVO-ISSUED PASSPORT IF HE WANTS TO DO ANY BUSINESS HERE.
I SEE. HOW CAN HE PAY THE NEW PASSPORT FEE IF HE CAN'T WORK HERE?
TELLER REPLIES HE MUST WORK ELSEWHERE WITH HIS CURRENT PASSPORT.
BUT YOU JUST SAID HIS CURRENT PASSPORT EXPIRES SOON.
TELLER AGREES.
IN THAT CASE, HOW WILL HE FIND A JOB PAYING ENOUGH FOR AVO FEES, WITH TAX...
BEFORE HIS CURRENT PASSPORT EXPIRES AND HE CAN'T WORK?
TELLER REPLIES THIS IS NOT AVO'S PROBLEM.
KLAK!

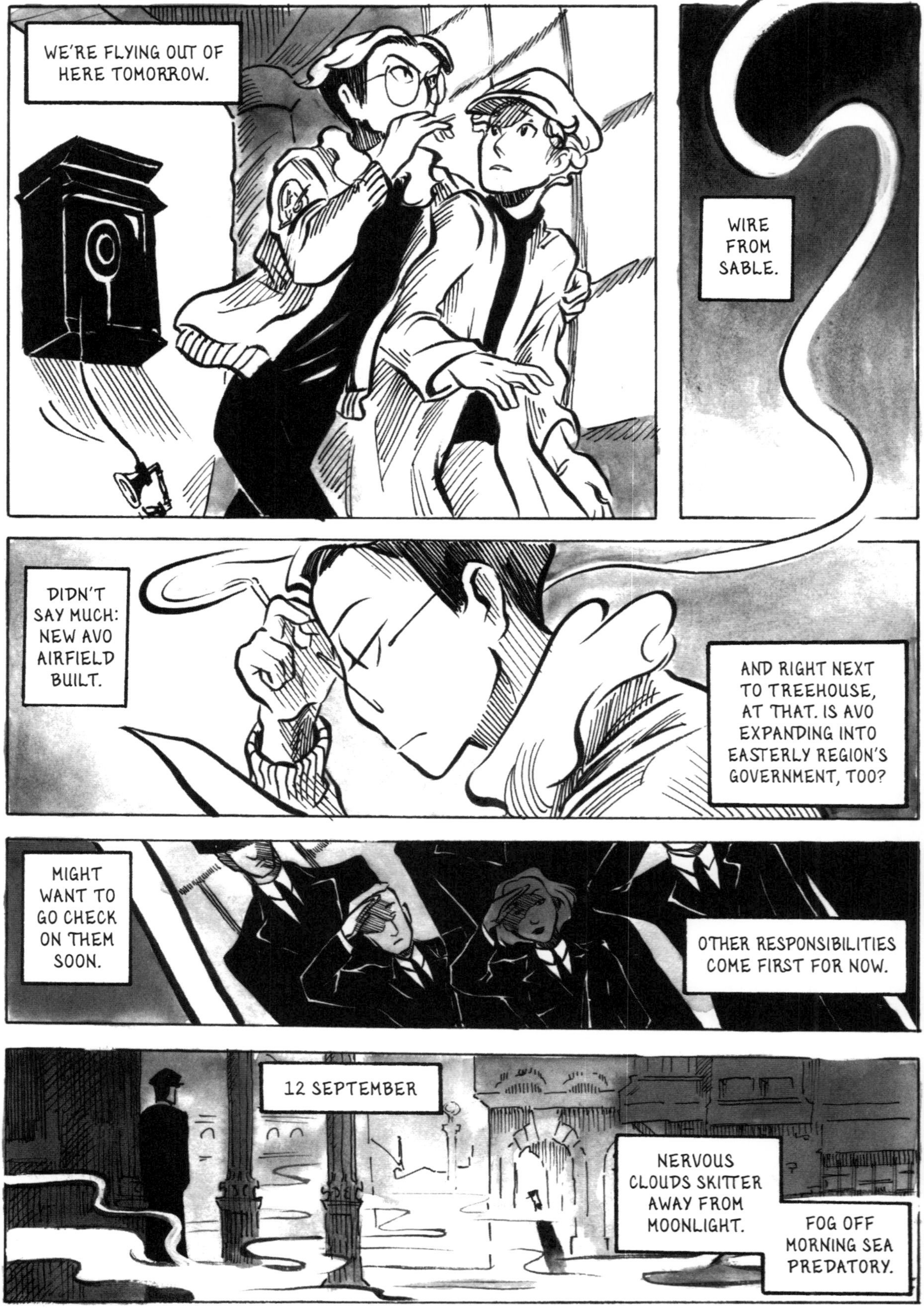
WE'RE FLYING OUT OF HERE TOMORROW.
WIRE FROM SABLE.
DIDN'T SAY MUCH: NEW AVO AIRFIELD BUILT.
AND RIGHT NEXT TO TREEHOUSE, AT THAT. IS AVO EXPANDING INTO EASTERLY REGION'S GOVERNMENT, TOO?
MIGHT WANT TO GO CHECK ON THEM SOON.
OTHER RESPONSIBILITIES COME FIRST FOR NOW.
12 SEPTEMBER
NERVOUS CLOUDS SKITTER AWAY FROM MOONLIGHT.
FOG OFF MORNING SEA PREDATORY.

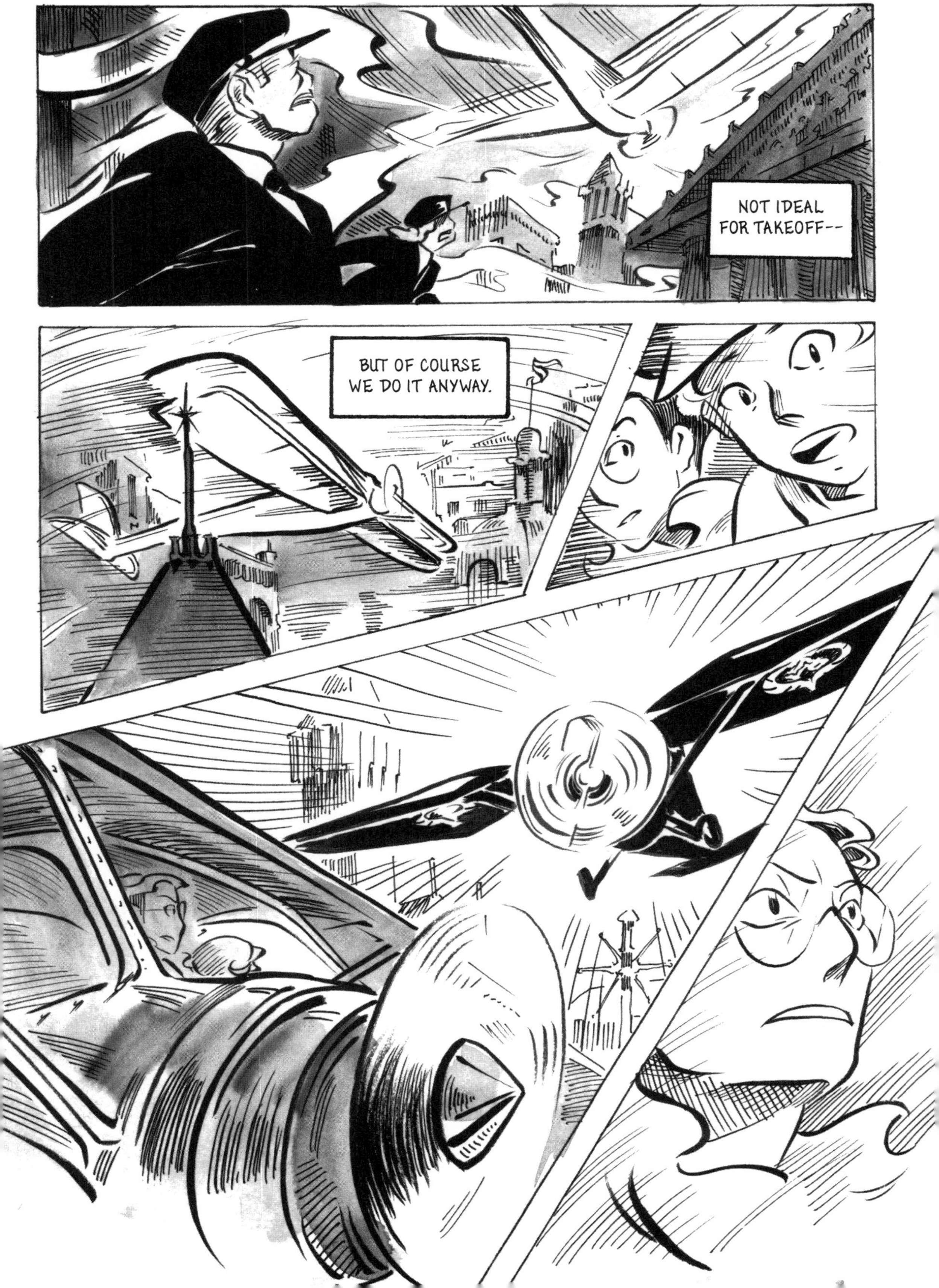
NOT IDEAL FOR TAKEOFF--
BUT OF COURSE WE DO IT ANYWAY.

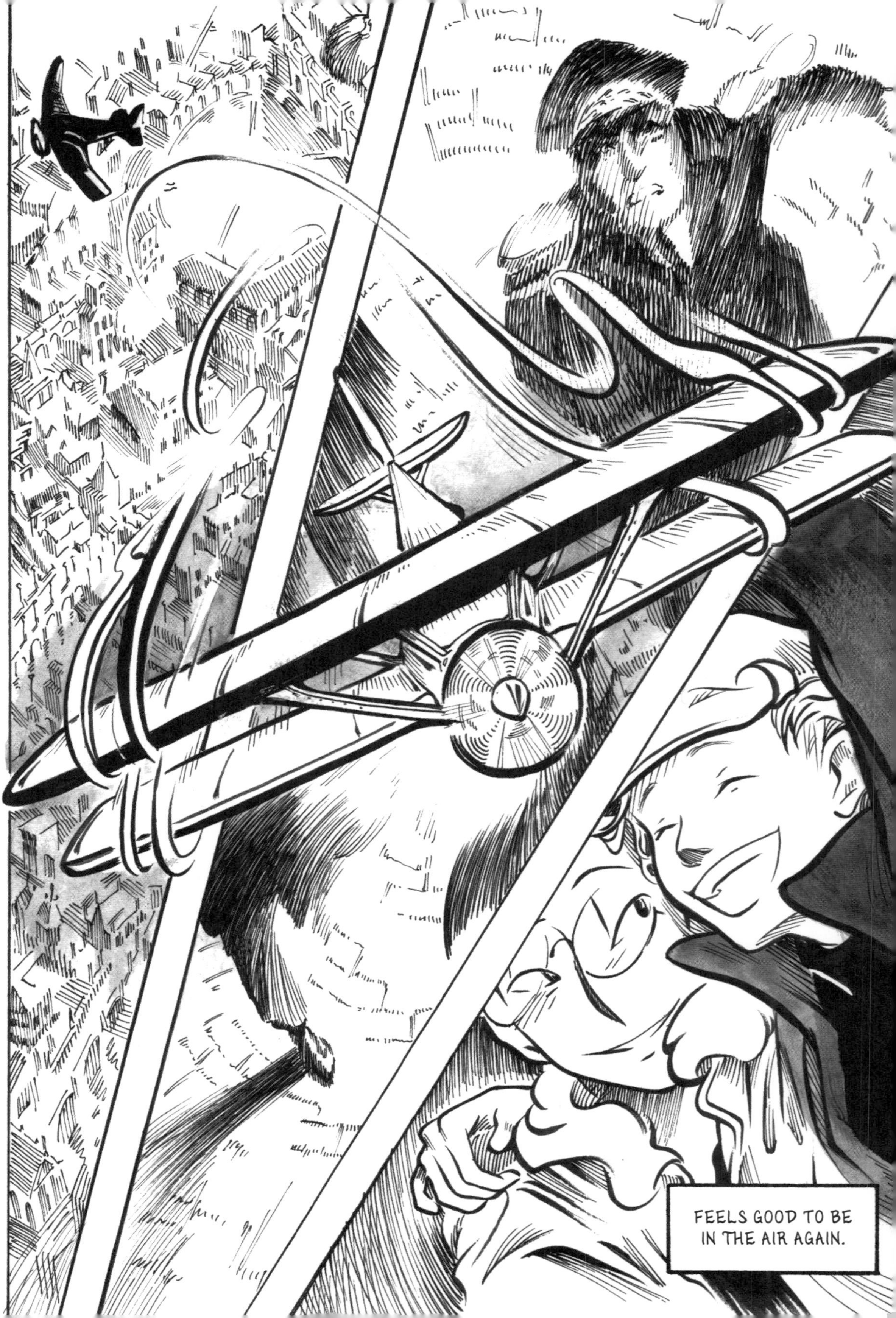
FEELS GOOD TO BE
IN THE AIR AGAIN.

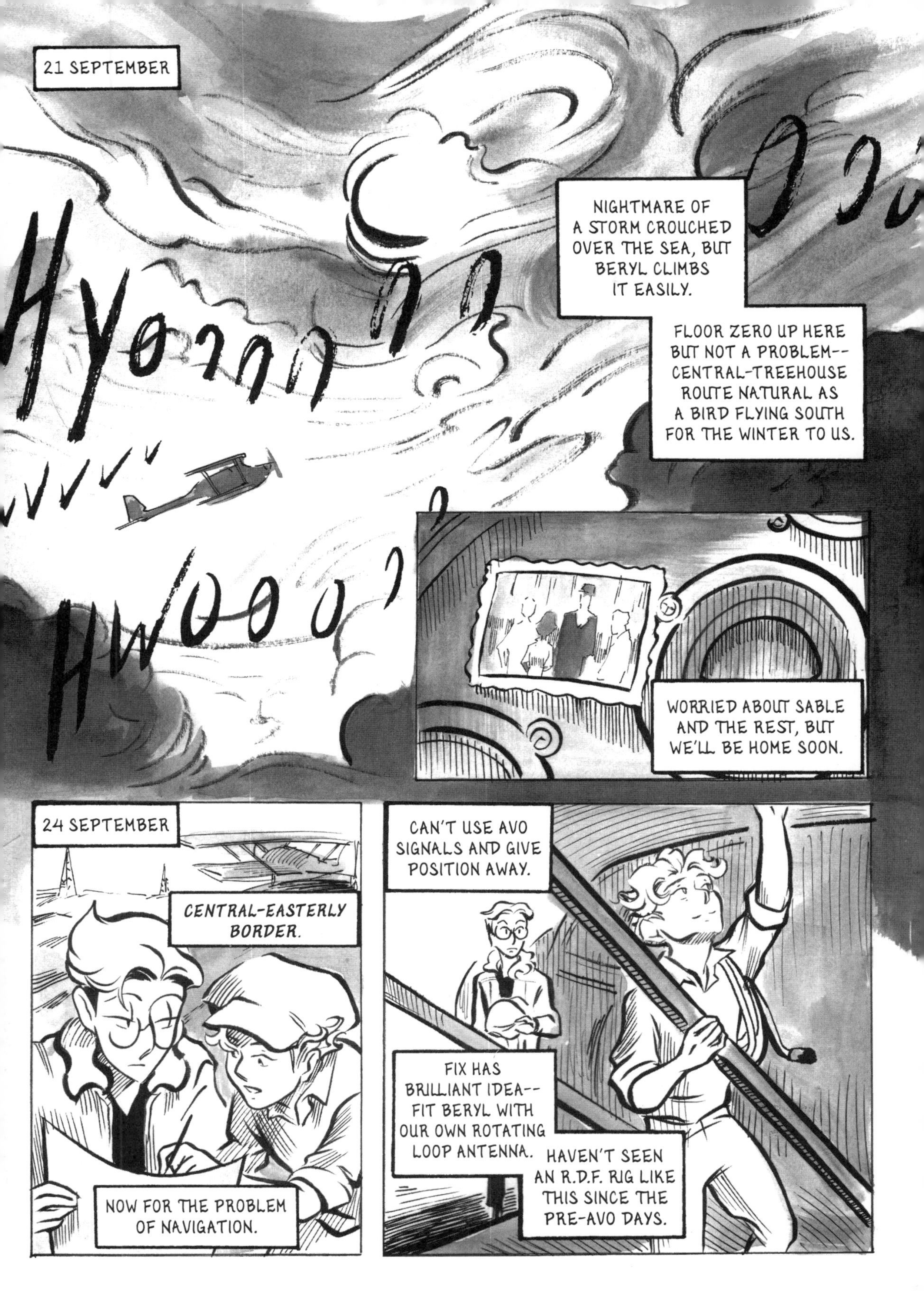
21 SEPTEMBER
Hyoooo
Hwooo
NIGHTMARE OF A STORM CROUCHED OVER THE SEA, BUT BERYL CLIMBS IT EASILY.
FLOOR ZERO UP HERE BUT NOT A PROBLEM--CENTRAL-TREEHOUSE ROUTE NATURAL AS A BIRD FLYING SOUTH FOR THE WINTER TO US.
WORRIED ABOUT SABLE AND THE REST, BUT WE'LL BE HOME SOON.
24 SEPTEMBER
CENTRAL-EASTERLY BORDER.
NOW FOR THE PROBLEM OF NAVIGATION.
CAN'T USE AVO SIGNALS AND GIVE POSITION AWAY.
FIX HAS BRILLIANT IDEA--FIT BERYL WITH OUR OWN ROTATING LOOP ANTENNA.
HAVEN'T SEEN AN R.D.F. RIG LIKE THIS SINCE THE PRE-AVO DAYS.

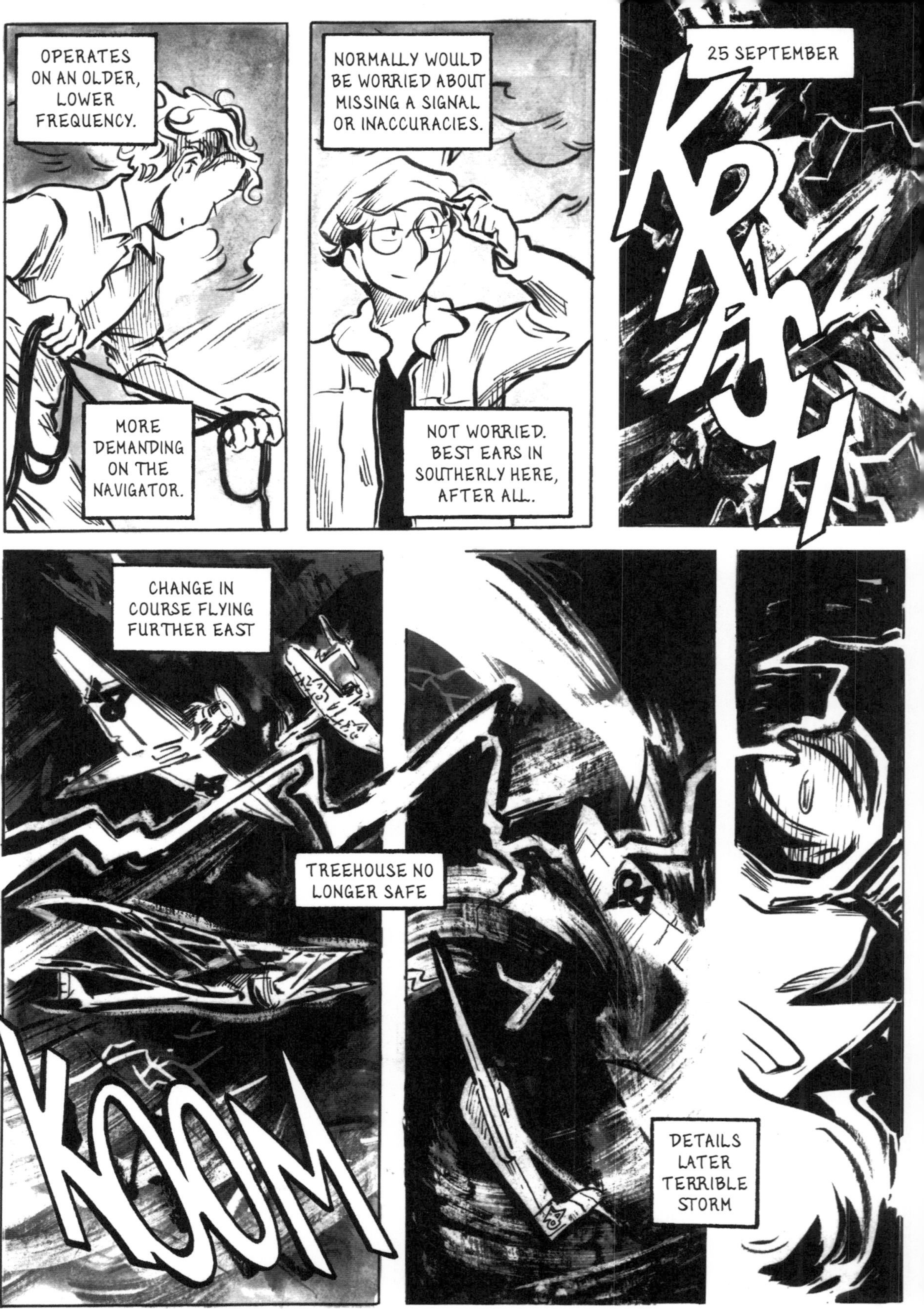

OPERATES ON AN OLDER, LOWER FREQUENCY.
MORE DEMANDING ON THE NAVIGATOR.
NORMALLY WOULD BE WORRIED ABOUT MISSING A SIGNAL OR INACCURACIES.
NOT WORRIED. BEST EARS IN SOUTHERLY HERE, AFTER ALL.
25 SEPTEMBER
KRAAASH
CHANGE IN COURSE FLYING FURTHER EAST
TREEHOUSE NO LONGER SAFE
KOOOM
DETAILS LATER TERRIBLE STORM

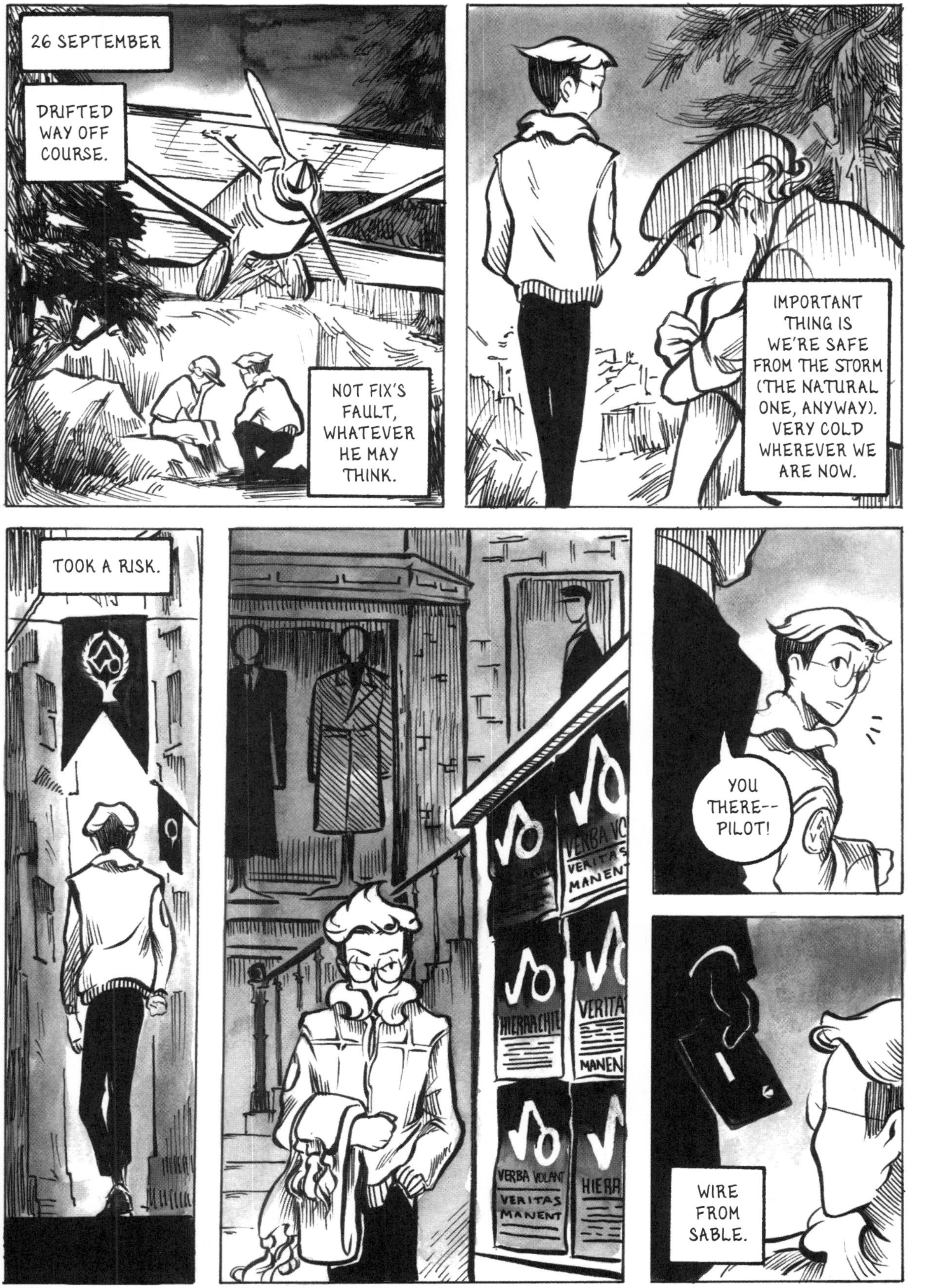
26 SEPTEMBER
DRIFTED WAY OFF COURSE.
NOT FIX'S FAULT, WHATEVER HE MAY THINK.
IMPORTANT THING IS WE'RE SAFE FROM THE STORM (THE NATURAL ONE, ANYWAY). VERY COLD WHEREVER WE ARE NOW.
TOOK A RISK.
VERITAS MANENT
VERBA VOLANT
VERITAS MANENT
YOU THERE-- PILOT!
WIRE FROM SABLE.

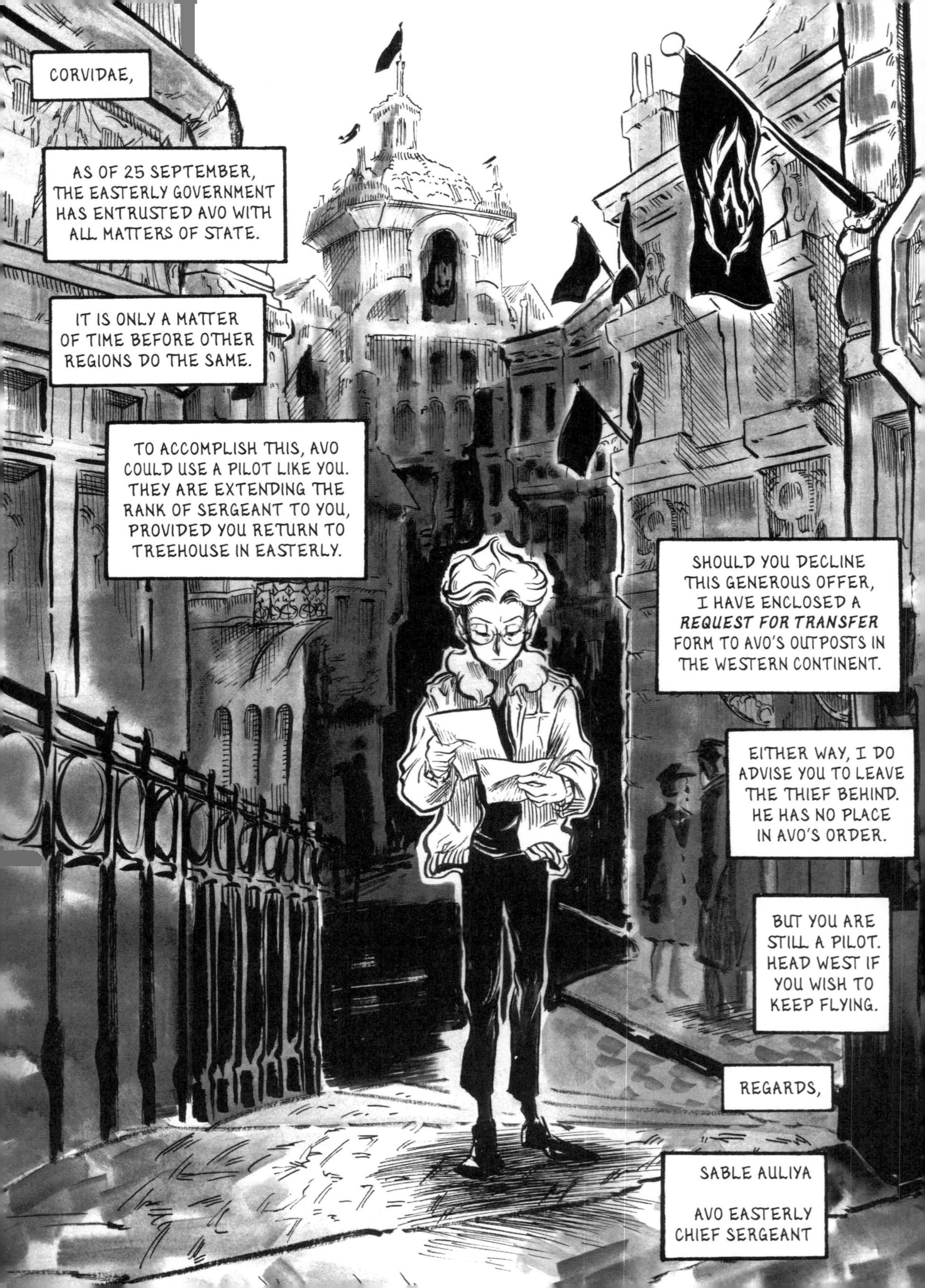
CORVIDAE,
AS OF 25 SEPTEMBER, THE EASTERLY GOVERNMENT HAS ENTRUSTED AVO WITH ALL MATTERS OF STATE.
IT IS ONLY A MATTER OF TIME BEFORE OTHER REGIONS DO THE SAME.
TO ACCOMPLISH THIS, AVO COULD USE A PILOT LIKE YOU. THEY ARE EXTENDING THE RANK OF SERGEANT TO YOU, PROVIDED YOU RETURN TO TREEHOUSE IN EASTERLY.
SHOULD YOU DECLINE THIS GENEROUS OFFER, I HAVE ENCLOSED A ***REQUEST FOR TRANSFER*** FORM TO AVO'S OUTPOSTS IN THE WESTERN CONTINENT.
EITHER WAY, I DO ADVISE YOU TO LEAVE THE THIEF BEHIND. HE HAS NO PLACE IN AVO'S ORDER.
BUT YOU ARE STILL A PILOT. HEAD WEST IF YOU WISH TO KEEP FLYING.
REGARDS,
SABLE AULIYA
AVO EASTERLY CHIEF SERGEANT

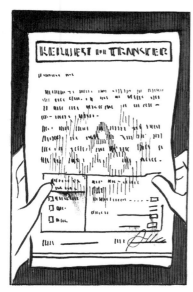

WIRED A REPLY:

NOT STRANDING FIX, NOT HEADING WEST.

I WANT TO FLY, BUT I'D RATHER STAY FREE.

THEY ARE NOT THE SAME THING ANYMORE.

3 OCTOBER

NORTHERN TERRITORIES.

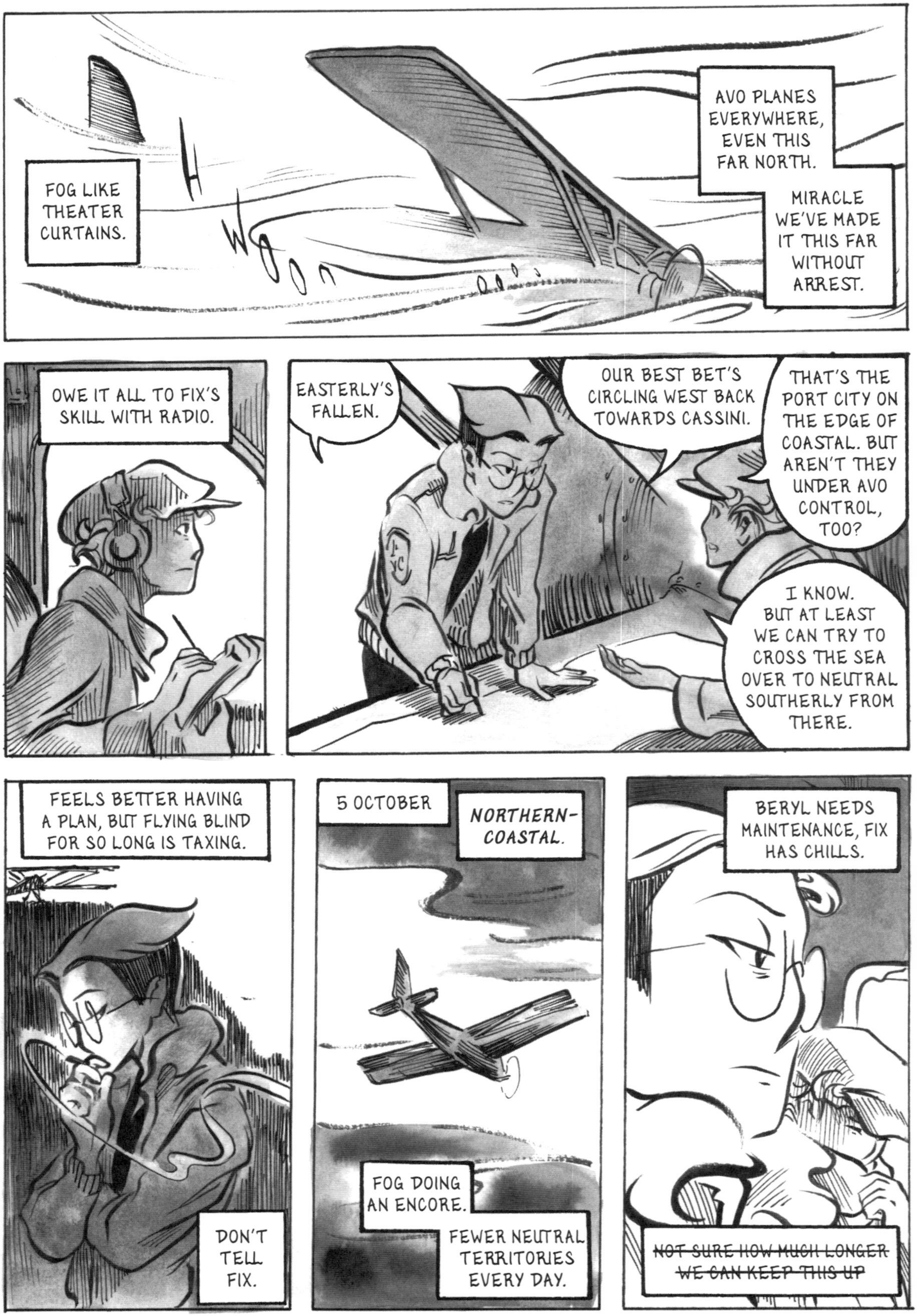

FOG LIKE THEATER CURTAINS.
AVO PLANES EVERYWHERE, EVEN THIS FAR NORTH.
MIRACLE WE'VE MADE IT THIS FAR WITHOUT ARREST.
OWE IT ALL TO FIX'S SKILL WITH RADIO.
EASTERLY'S FALLEN.
OUR BEST BET'S CIRCLING WEST BACK TOWARDS CASSINI.
THAT'S THE PORT CITY ON THE EDGE OF COASTAL. BUT AREN'T THEY UNDER AVO CONTROL, TOO?
I KNOW. BUT AT LEAST WE CAN TRY TO CROSS THE SEA OVER TO NEUTRAL SOUTHERLY FROM THERE.
FEELS BETTER HAVING A PLAN, BUT FLYING BLIND FOR SO LONG IS TAXING.
DON'T TELL FIX.
5 OCTOBER
NORTHERN-COASTAL.
FOG DOING AN ENCORE.
FEWER NEUTRAL TERRITORIES EVERY DAY.
BERYL NEEDS MAINTENANCE, FIX HAS CHILLS.
~~NOT SURE HOW MUCH LONGER WE CAN KEEP THIS UP~~

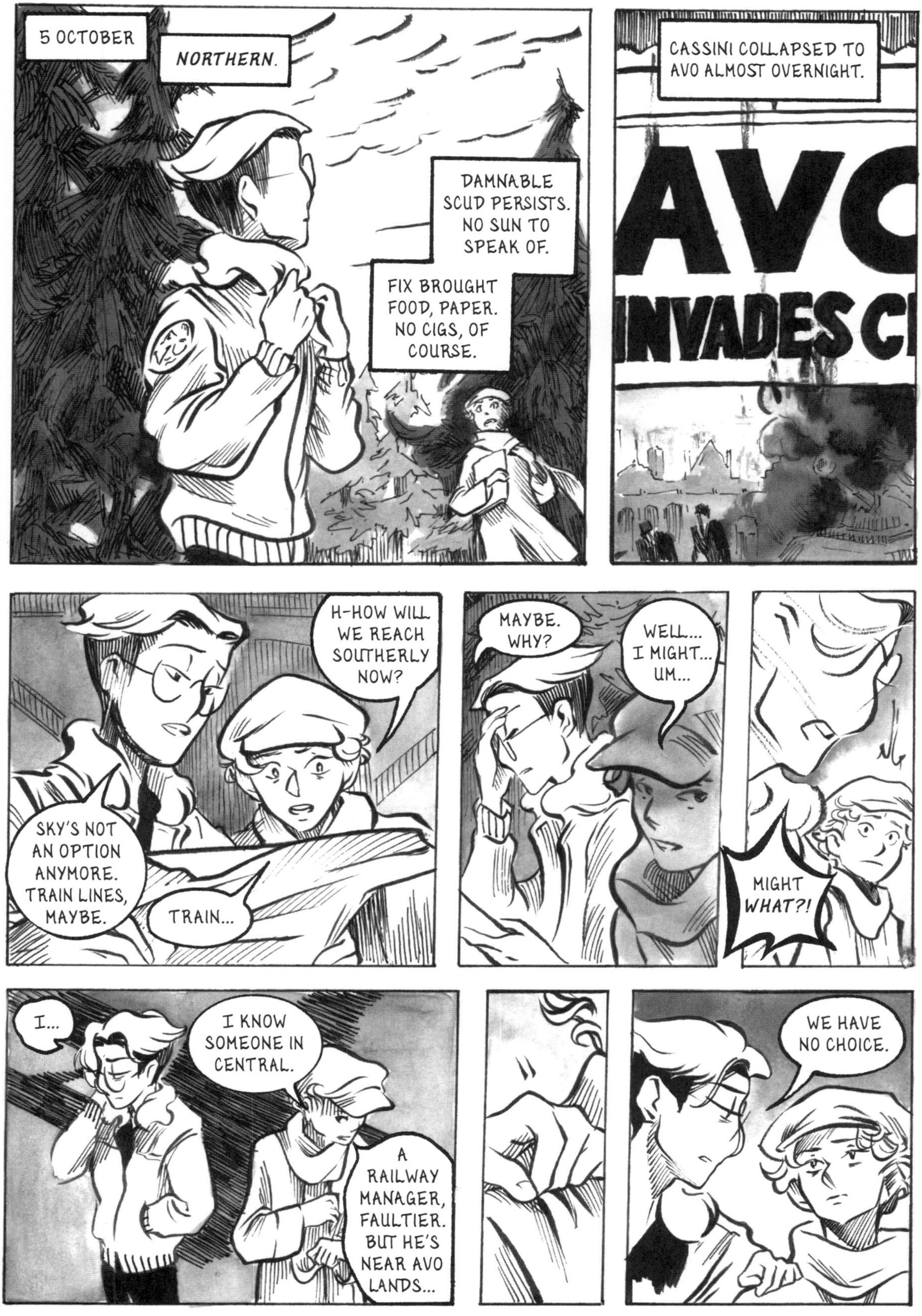
5 OCTOBER
NORTHERN.
DAMNABLE SCUD PERSISTS. NO SUN TO SPEAK OF.
FIX BROUGHT FOOD, PAPER. NO CIGS, OF COURSE.
CASSINI COLLAPSED TO AVO ALMOST OVERNIGHT.
AVO
INVADES C
H-HOW WILL WE REACH SOUTHERLY NOW?
SKY'S NOT AN OPTION ANYMORE. TRAIN LINES, MAYBE.
TRAIN...
MAYBE. WHY?
WELL... I MIGHT... UM...
MIGHT WHAT?!
I...
I KNOW SOMEONE IN CENTRAL.
A RAILWAY MANAGER, FAULTIER. BUT HE'S NEAR AVO LANDS...
WE HAVE NO CHOICE.

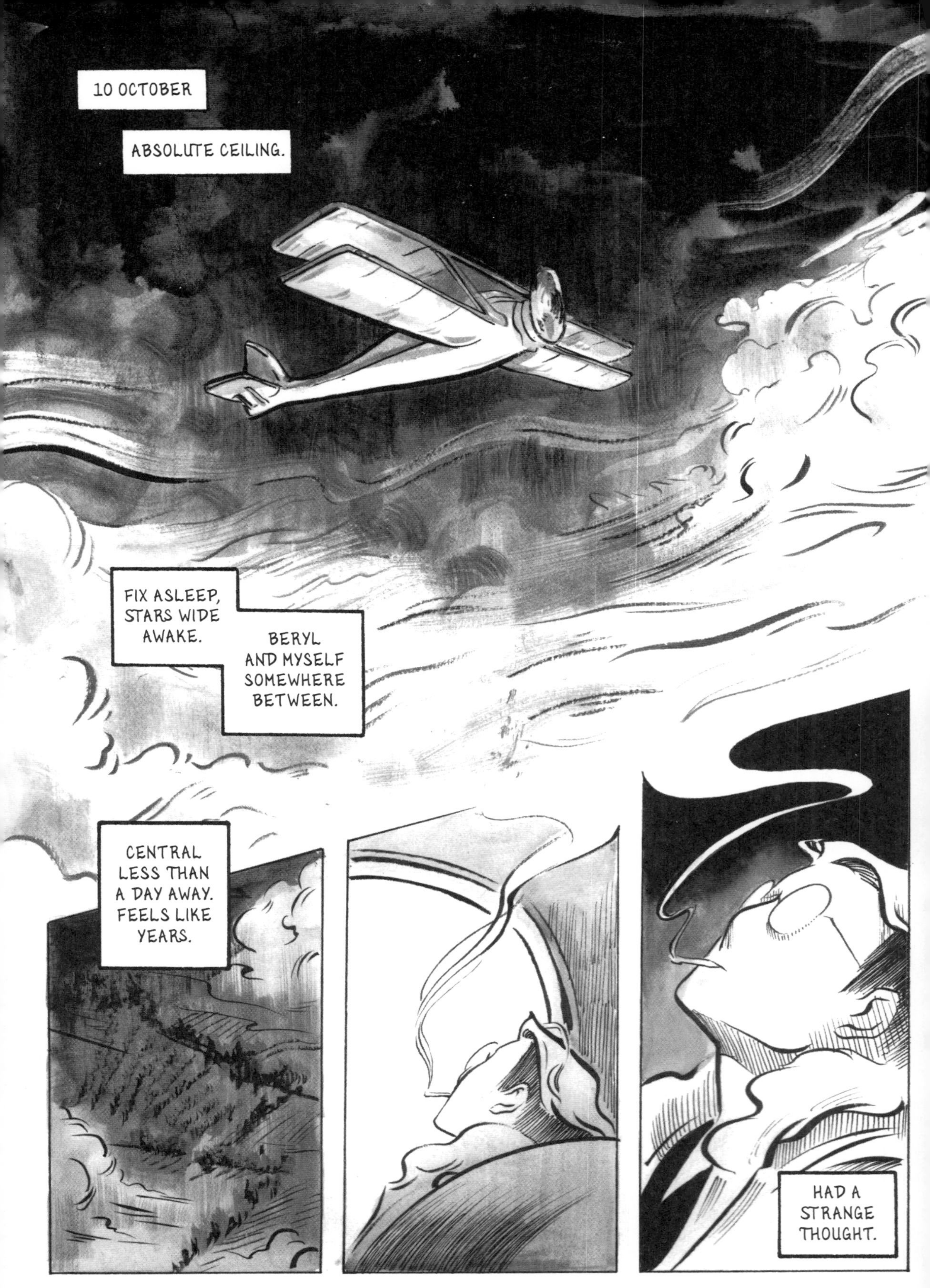
10 OCTOBER
ABSOLUTE CEILING.
FIX ASLEEP, STARS WIDE AWAKE.
BERYL AND MYSELF SOMEWHERE BETWEEN.
CENTRAL LESS THAN A DAY AWAY. FEELS LIKE YEARS.
HAD A STRANGE THOUGHT.

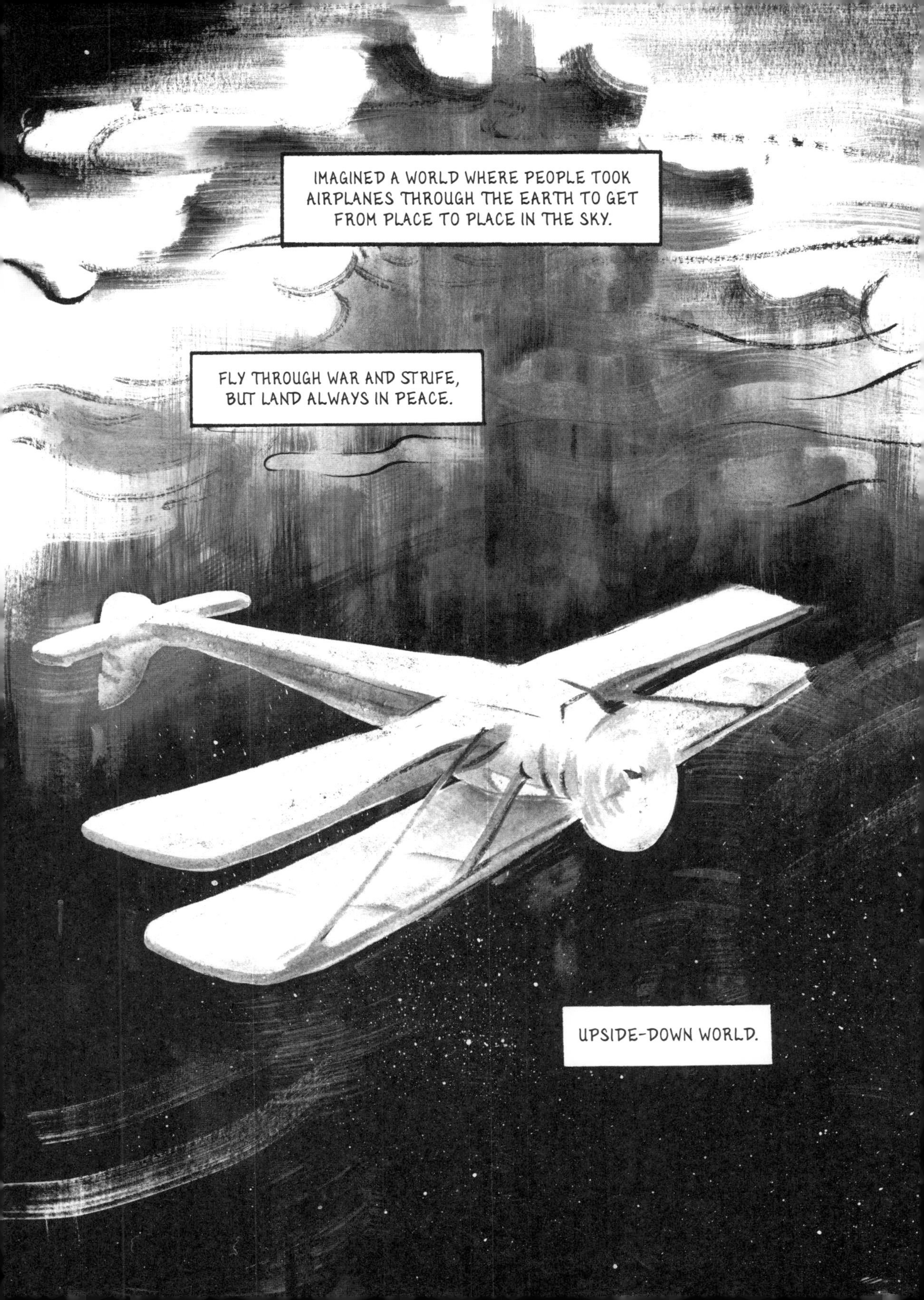

IMAGINED A WORLD WHERE PEOPLE TOOK AIRPLANES THROUGH THE EARTH TO GET FROM PLACE TO PLACE IN THE SKY.
FLY THROUGH WAR AND STRIFE, BUT LAND ALWAYS IN PEACE.
UPSIDE-DOWN WORLD.

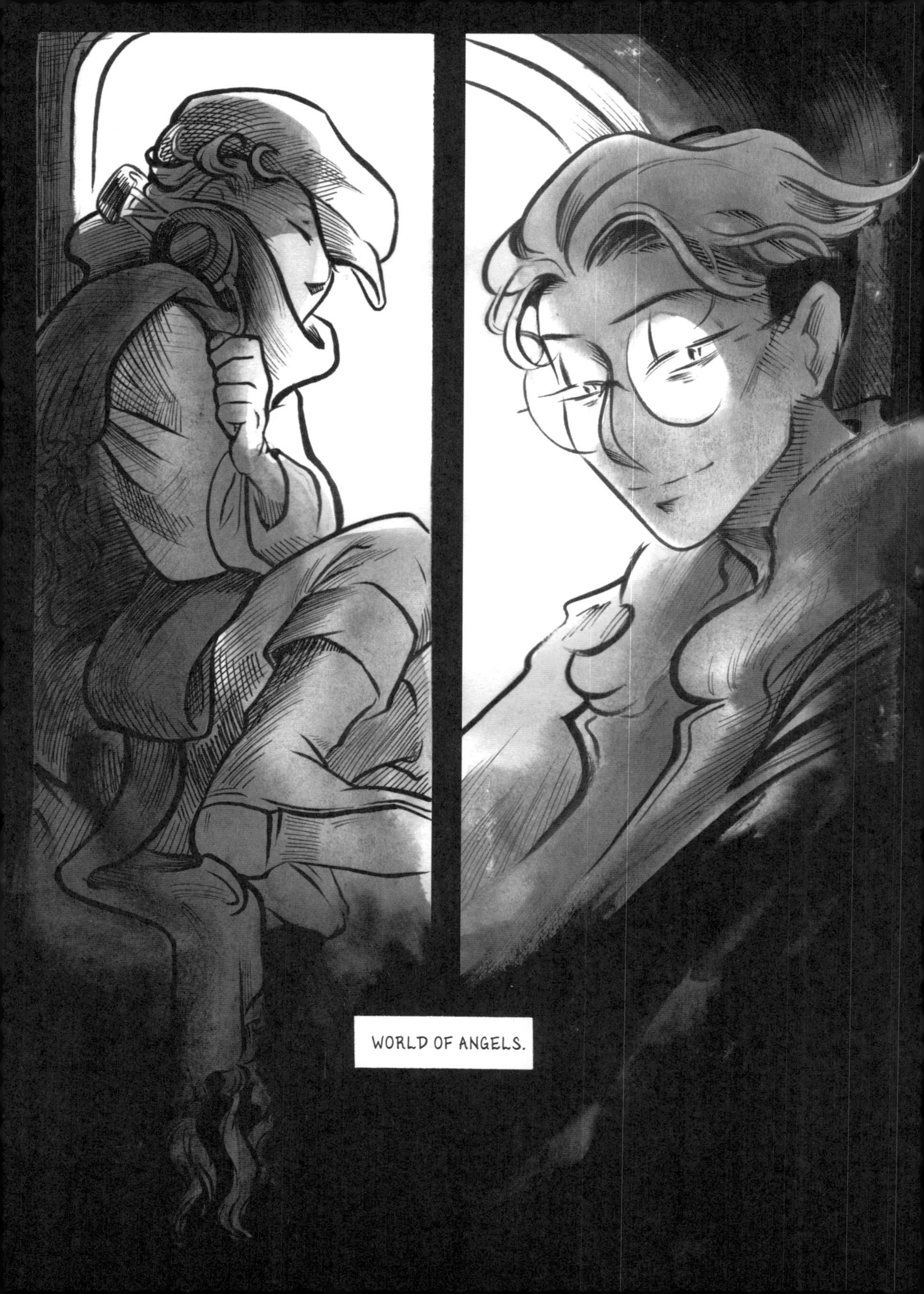
WORLD OF ANGELS.

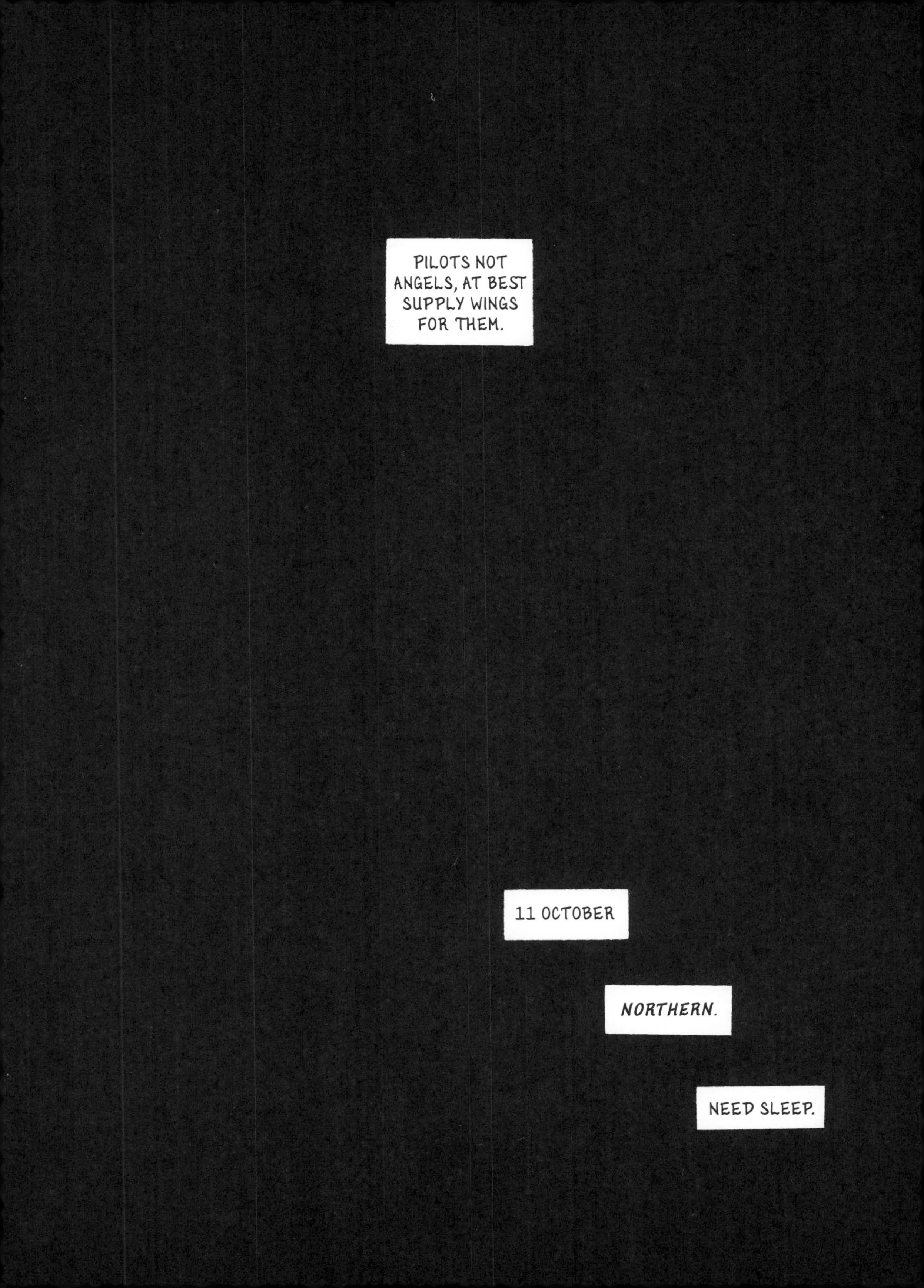
PILOTS NOT ANGELS, AT BEST SUPPLY WINGS FOR THEM.
11 OCTOBER
NORTHERN.
NEED SLEEP.

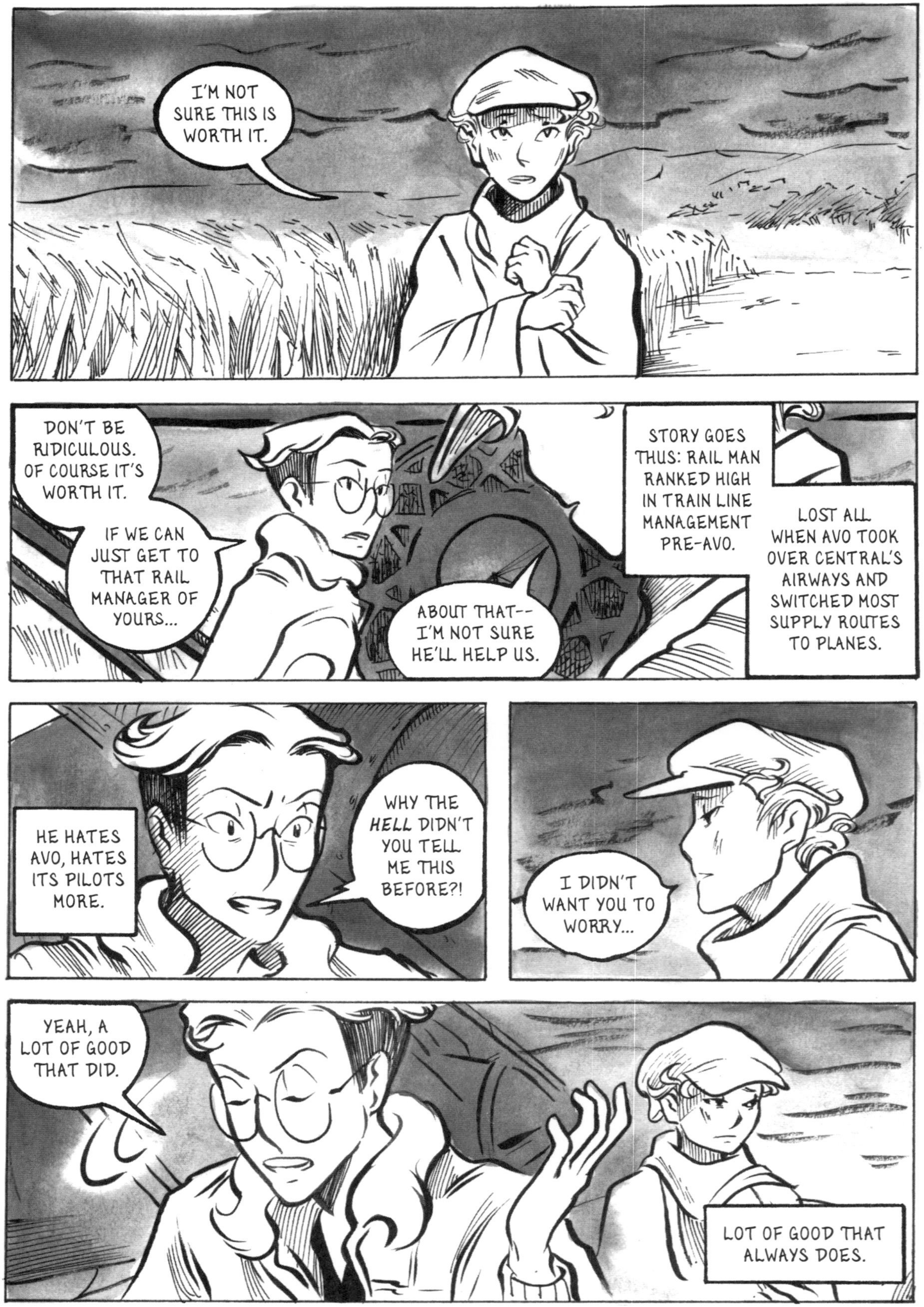
I'M NOT SURE THIS IS WORTH IT.
DON'T BE RIDICULOUS. OF COURSE IT'S WORTH IT.
IF WE CAN JUST GET TO THAT RAIL MANAGER OF YOURS...
ABOUT THAT-- I'M NOT SURE HE'LL HELP US.
STORY GOES THUS: RAIL MAN RANKED HIGH IN TRAIN LINE MANAGEMENT PRE-AVO.
LOST ALL WHEN AVO TOOK OVER CENTRAL'S AIRWAYS AND SWITCHED MOST SUPPLY ROUTES TO PLANES.
HE HATES AVO, HATES ITS PILOTS MORE.
WHY THE HELL DIDN'T YOU TELL ME THIS BEFORE?!
I DIDN'T WANT YOU TO WORRY...
YEAH, A LOT OF GOOD THAT DID.
LOT OF GOOD THAT ALWAYS DOES.

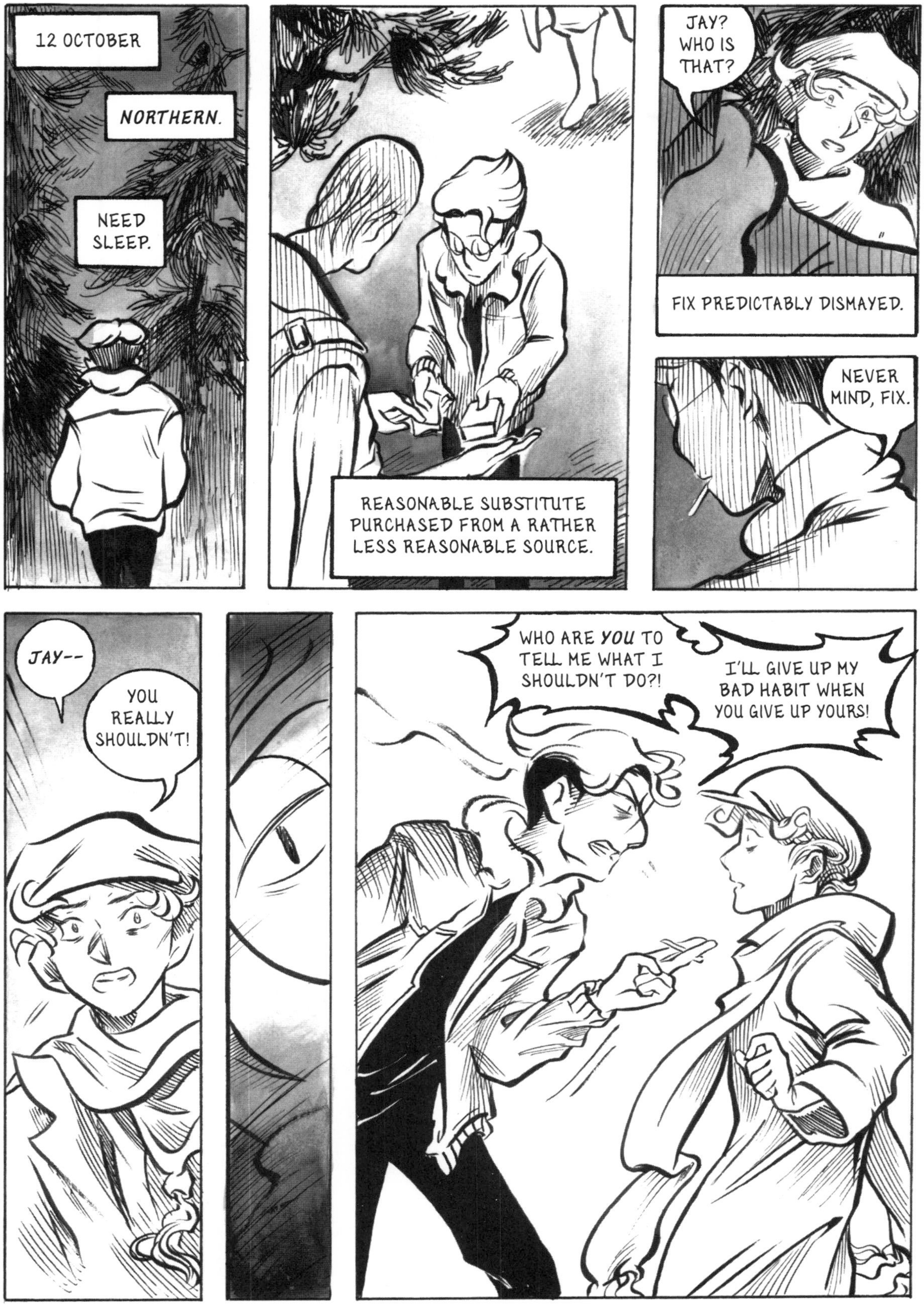
12 OCTOBER
NORTHERN.
NEED SLEEP.
REASONABLE SUBSTITUTE PURCHASED FROM A RATHER LESS REASONABLE SOURCE.
JAY? WHO IS THAT?
FIX PREDICTABLY DISMAYED.
NEVER MIND, FIX.
JAY--
YOU REALLY SHOULDN'T!
WHO ARE *YOU* TO TELL ME WHAT I SHOULDN'T DO?!
I'LL GIVE UP MY BAD HABIT WHEN YOU GIVE UP YOURS!

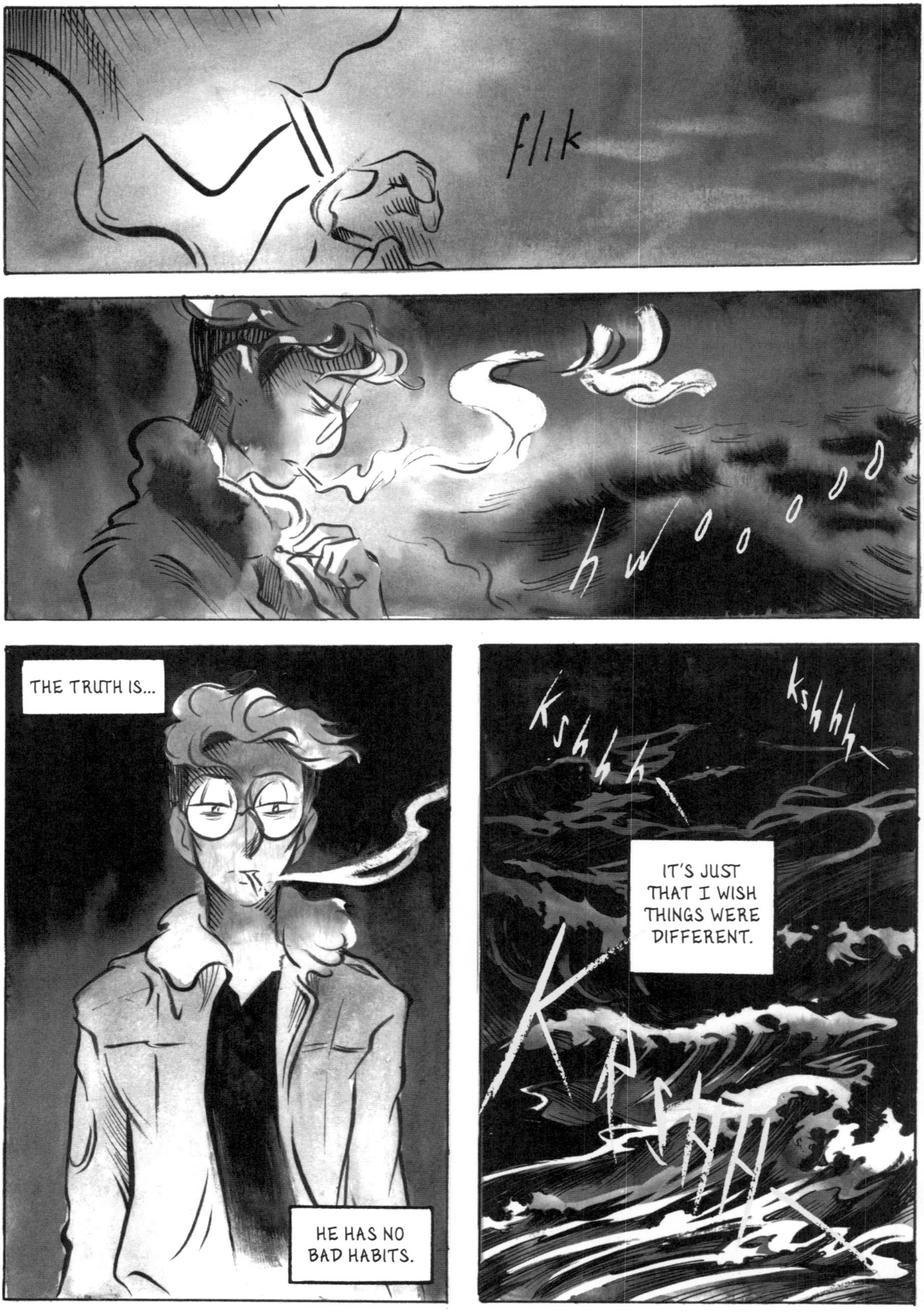
flik
hwooooo
THE TRUTH IS...
HE HAS NO BAD HABITS.
kshhh
kshhh
IT'S JUST THAT I WISH THINGS WERE DIFFERENT.
KRSHHH

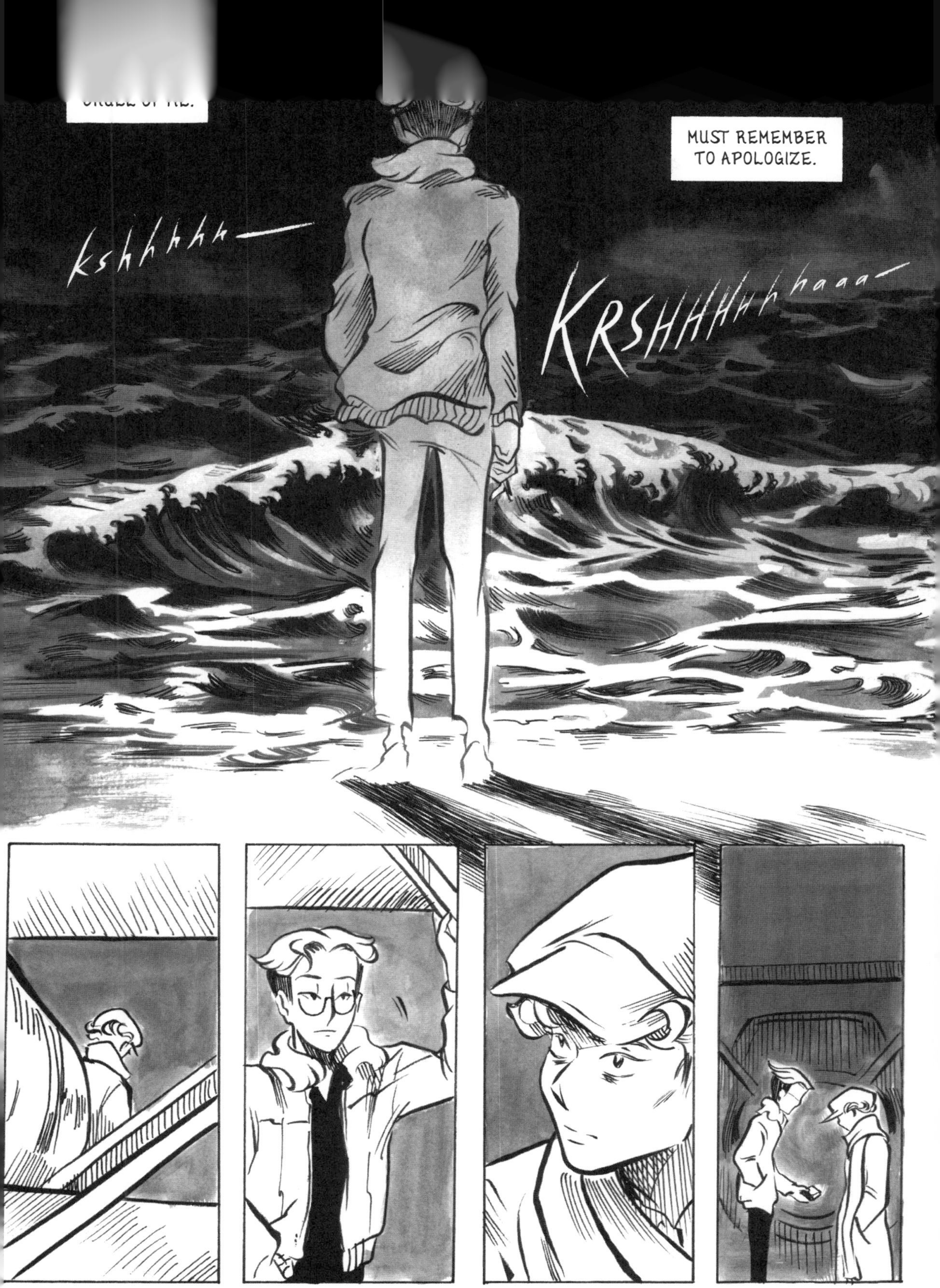
MUST REMEMBER TO APOLOGIZE.
kshhhhh—
KRSHHHhhhaaa—

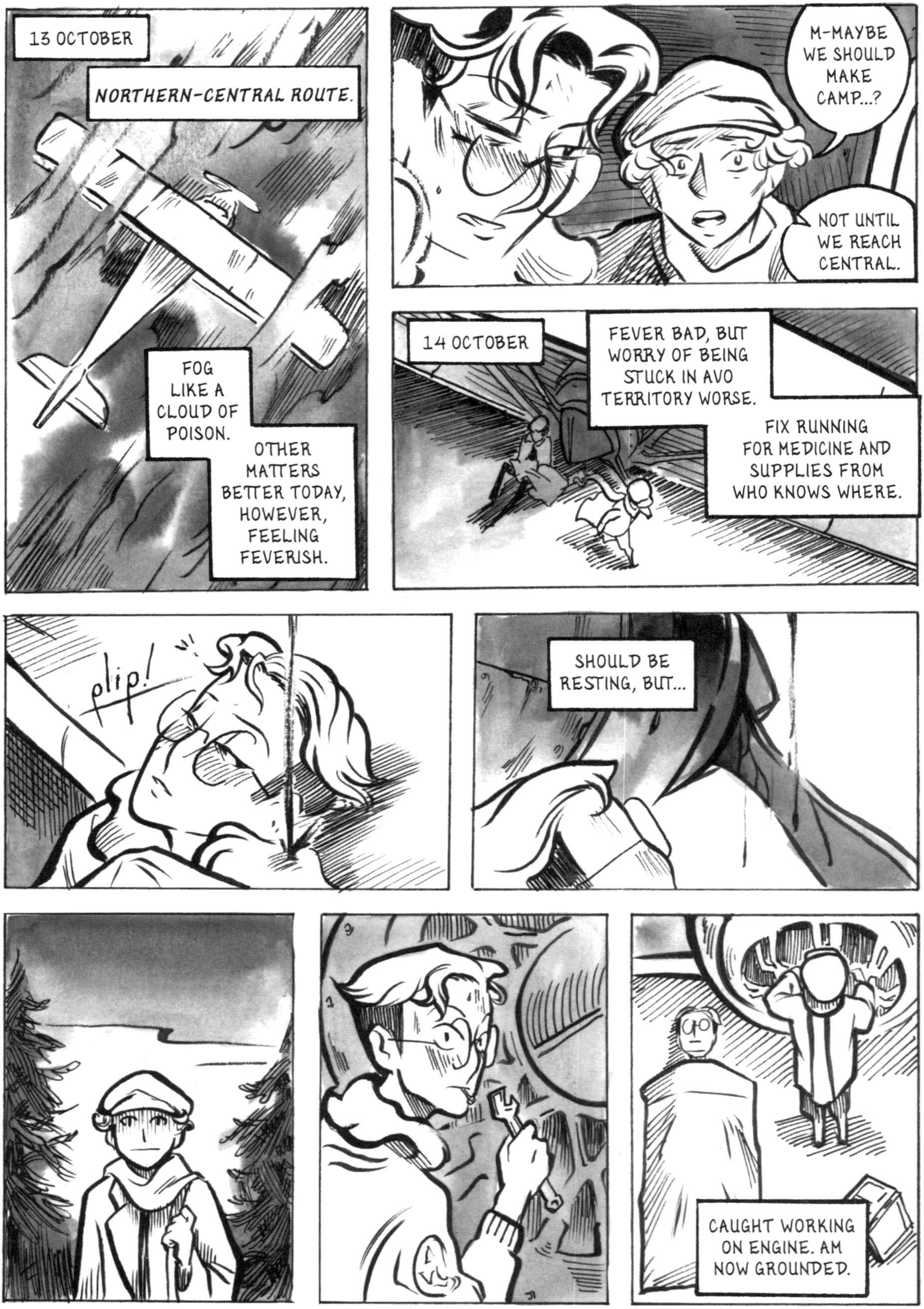
13 OCTOBER
NORTHERN-CENTRAL ROUTE.
FOG LIKE A CLOUD OF POISON.
OTHER MATTERS BETTER TODAY, HOWEVER, FEELING FEVERISH.
M-MAYBE WE SHOULD MAKE CAMP...?
NOT UNTIL WE REACH CENTRAL.
14 OCTOBER
FEVER BAD, BUT WORRY OF BEING STUCK IN AVO TERRITORY WORSE.
FIX RUNNING FOR MEDICINE AND SUPPLIES FROM WHO KNOWS WHERE.
plip!
SHOULD BE RESTING, BUT...
CAUGHT WORKING ON ENGINE. AM NOW GROUNDED.

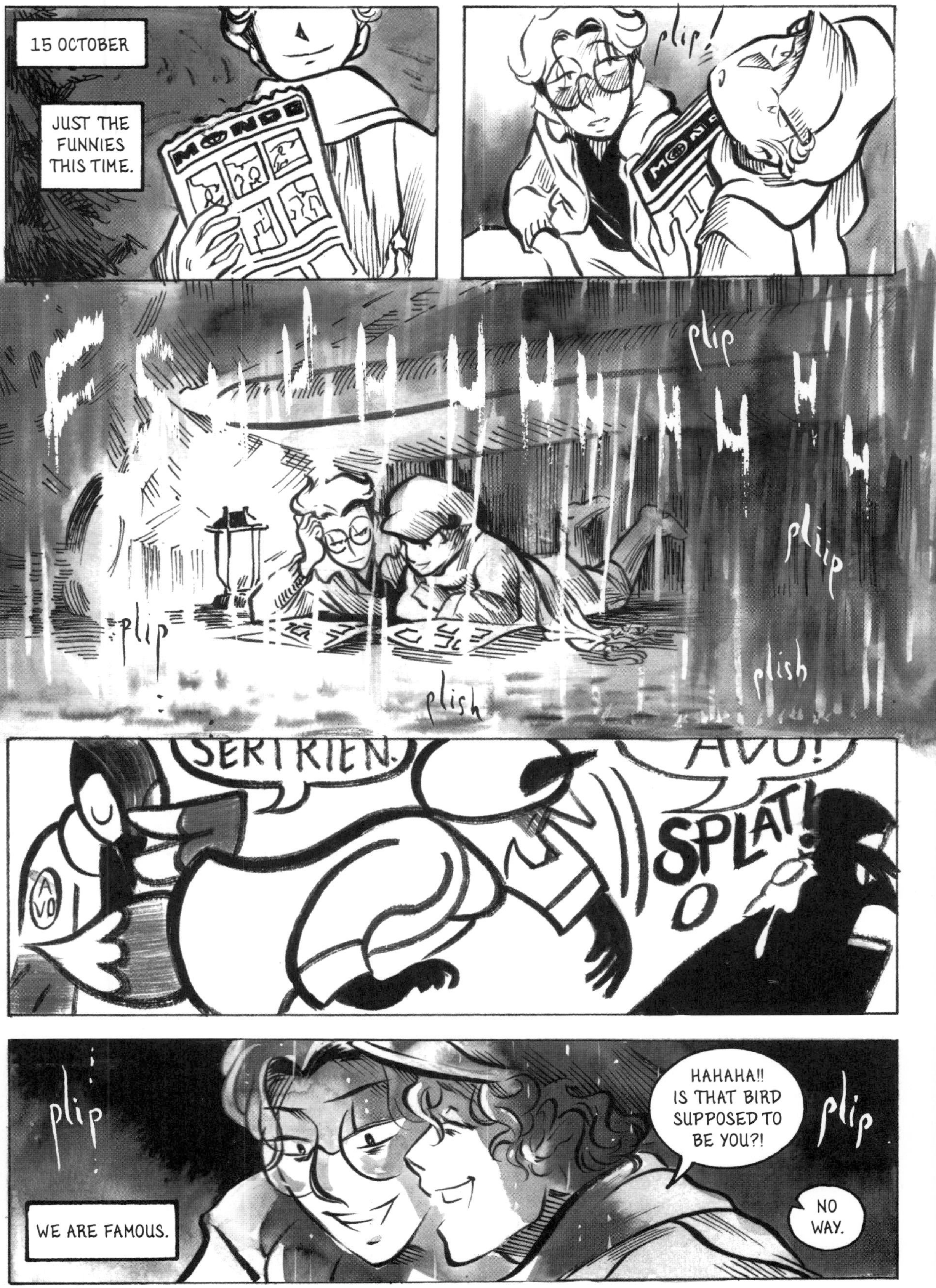
15 OCTOBER
JUST THE FUNNIES THIS TIME.
plip!
FSHHHHHHHHHHH
plip
pliip
plip
plish
plish
SERT RIEN.
AVO!
SPLAT!
AVO
plip
HAHAHA!! IS THAT BIRD SUPPOSED TO BE YOU?!
plip
WE ARE FAMOUS.
NO WAY.

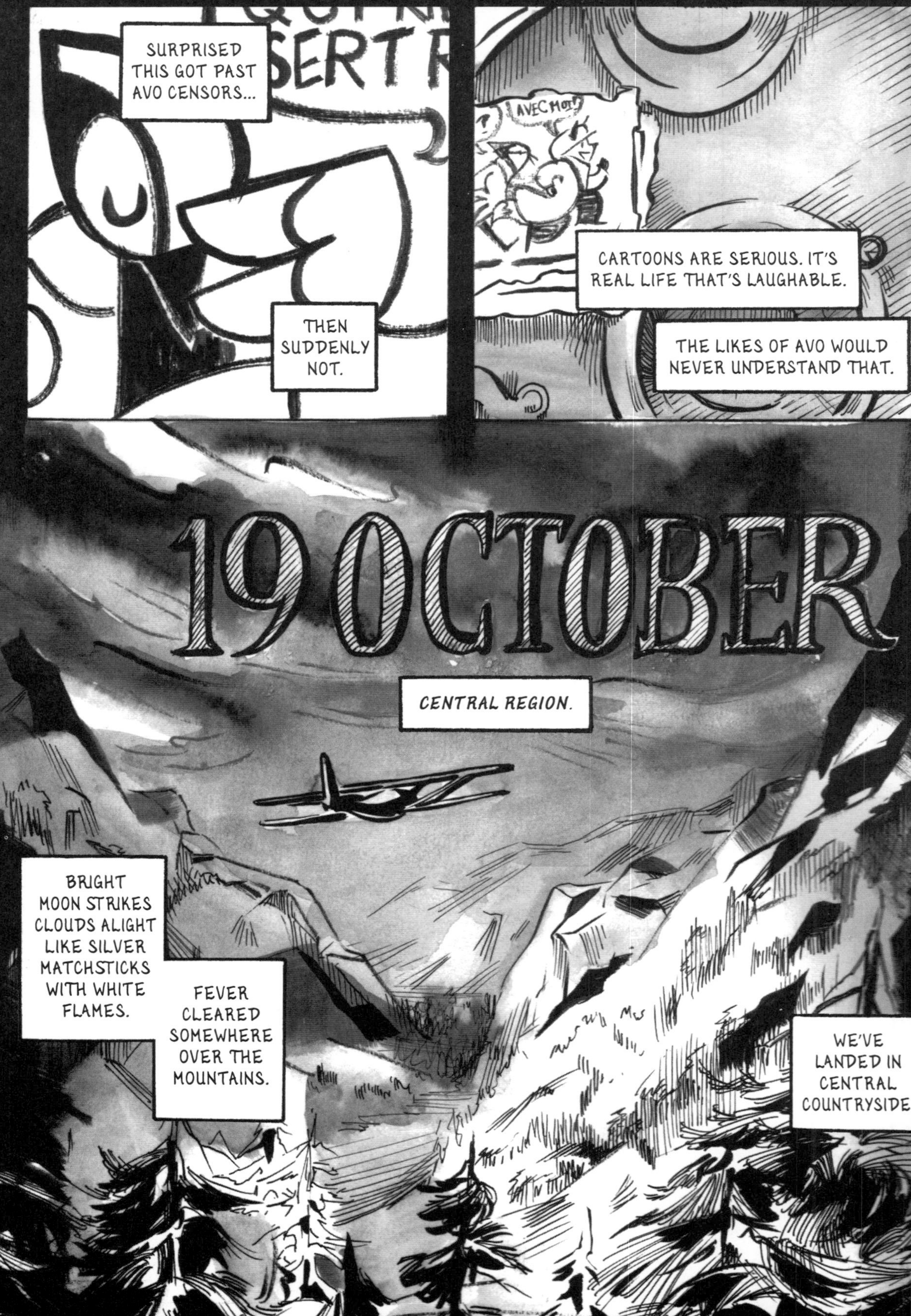
SURPRISED THIS GOT PAST AVO CENSORS...
THEN SUDDENLY NOT.
CARTOONS ARE SERIOUS. IT'S REAL LIFE THAT'S LAUGHABLE.
THE LIKES OF AVO WOULD NEVER UNDERSTAND THAT.
19 OCTOBER
CENTRAL REGION.
BRIGHT MOON STRIKES CLOUDS ALIGHT LIKE SILVER MATCHSTICKS WITH WHITE FLAMES.
FEVER CLEARED SOMEWHERE OVER THE MOUNTAINS.
WE'VE LANDED IN CENTRAL COUNTRYSIDE.

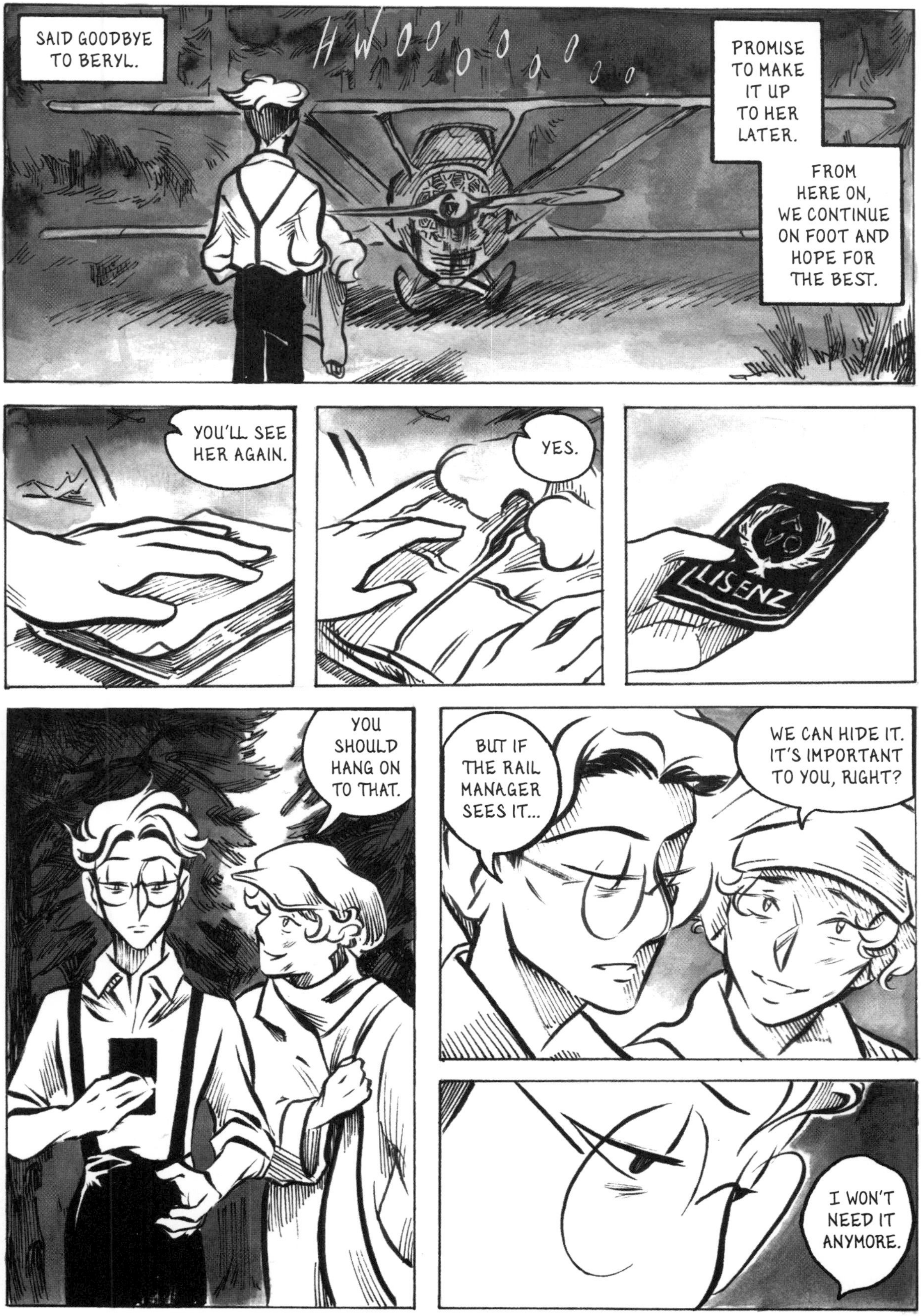
SAID GOODBYE TO BERYL.
HWOOOOOOOO
PROMISE TO MAKE IT UP TO HER LATER.
FROM HERE ON, WE CONTINUE ON FOOT AND HOPE FOR THE BEST.
YOU'LL SEE HER AGAIN.
YES.
LISENZ
YOU SHOULD HANG ON TO THAT.
BUT IF THE RAIL MANAGER SEES IT...
WE CAN HIDE IT. IT'S IMPORTANT TO YOU, RIGHT?
I WON'T NEED IT ANYMORE.

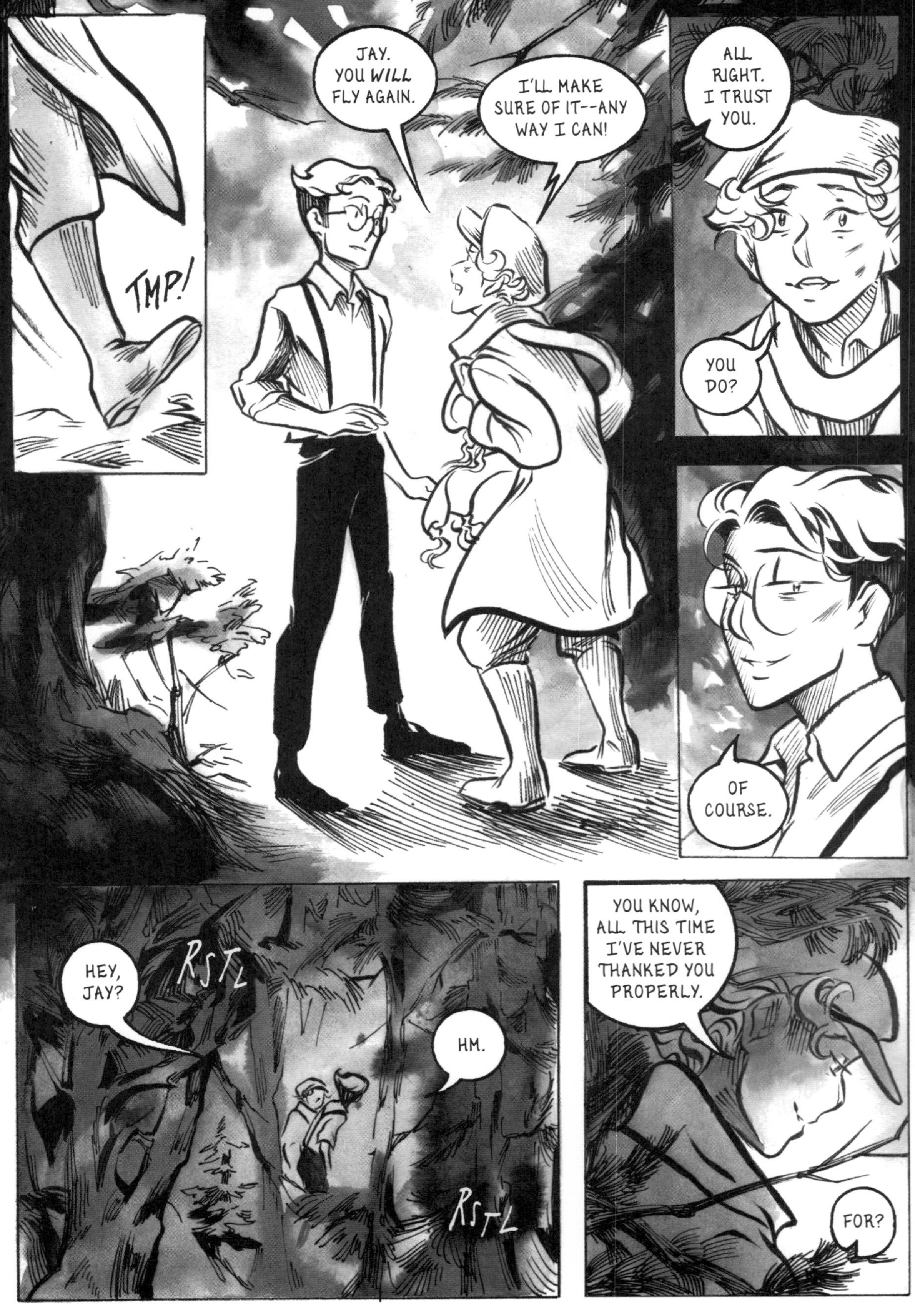
TMP!
JAY. YOU WILL FLY AGAIN.
I'LL MAKE SURE OF IT--ANY WAY I CAN!
ALL RIGHT. I TRUST YOU.
YOU DO?
OF COURSE.
HEY, JAY?
RSTL
HM.
RSTL
YOU KNOW, ALL THIS TIME I'VE NEVER THANKED YOU PROPERLY.
FOR?

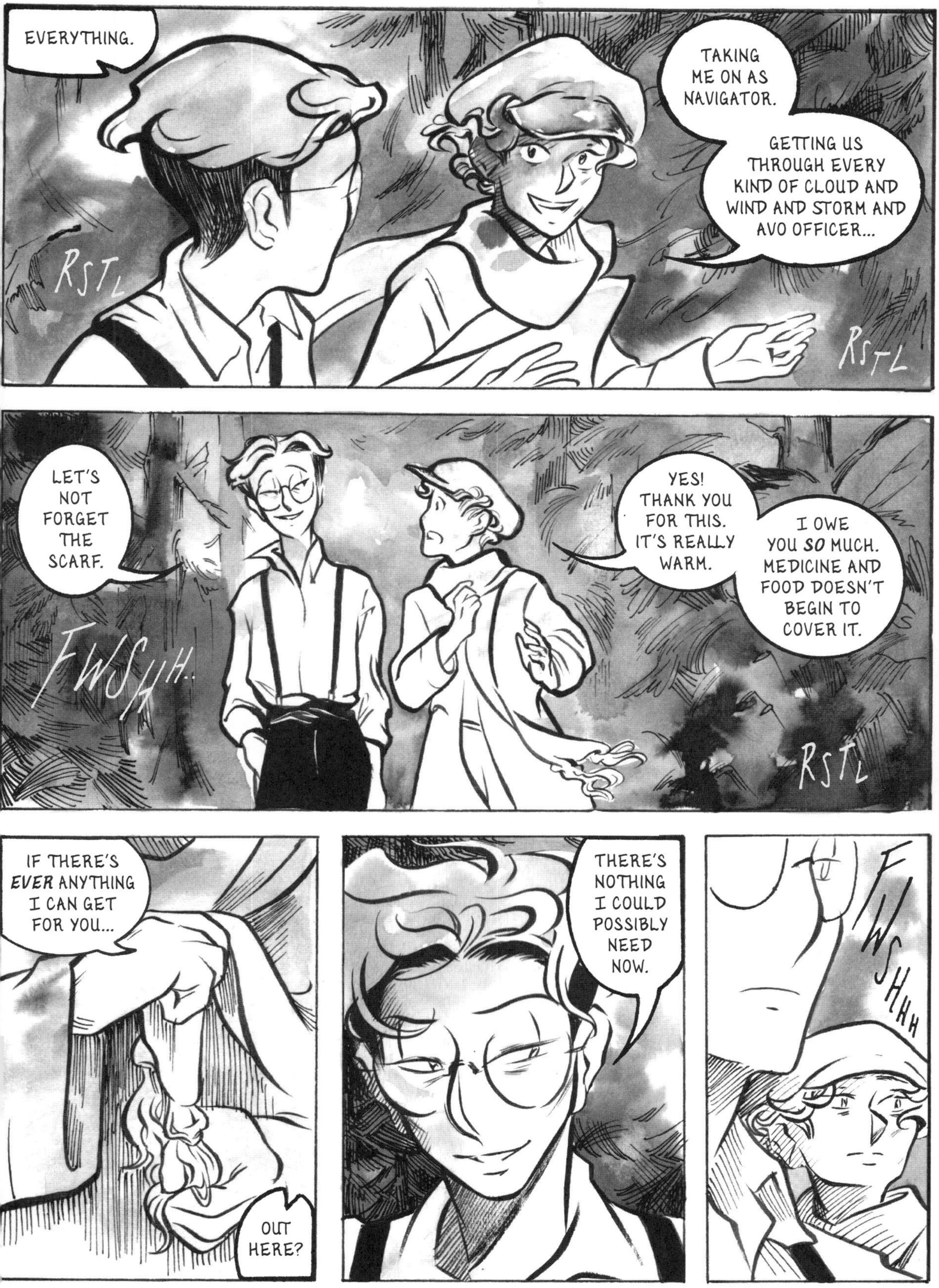
EVERYTHING.
TAKING ME ON AS NAVIGATOR.
GETTING US THROUGH EVERY KIND OF CLOUD AND WIND AND STORM AND AVO OFFICER...
RSTL
RSTL
LET'S NOT FORGET THE SCARF.
YES! THANK YOU FOR THIS. IT'S REALLY WARM.
I OWE YOU SO MUCH. MEDICINE AND FOOD DOESN'T BEGIN TO COVER IT.
FWSHH..
RSTL
IF THERE'S EVER ANYTHING I CAN GET FOR YOU...
OUT HERE?
THERE'S NOTHING I COULD POSSIBLY NEED NOW.
FWSHHH

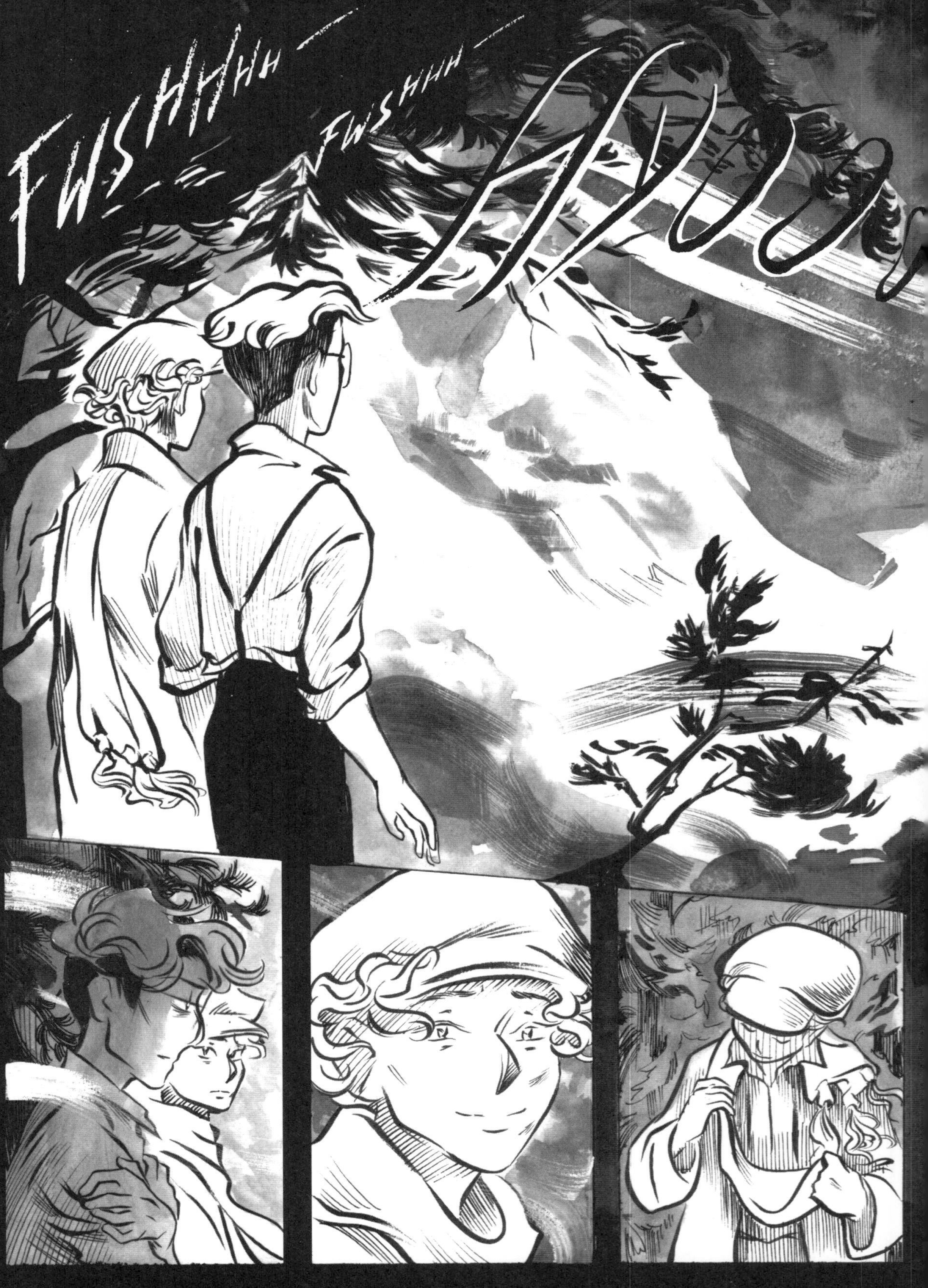
FWSHHHH—
FWSHHH—
HYUOO

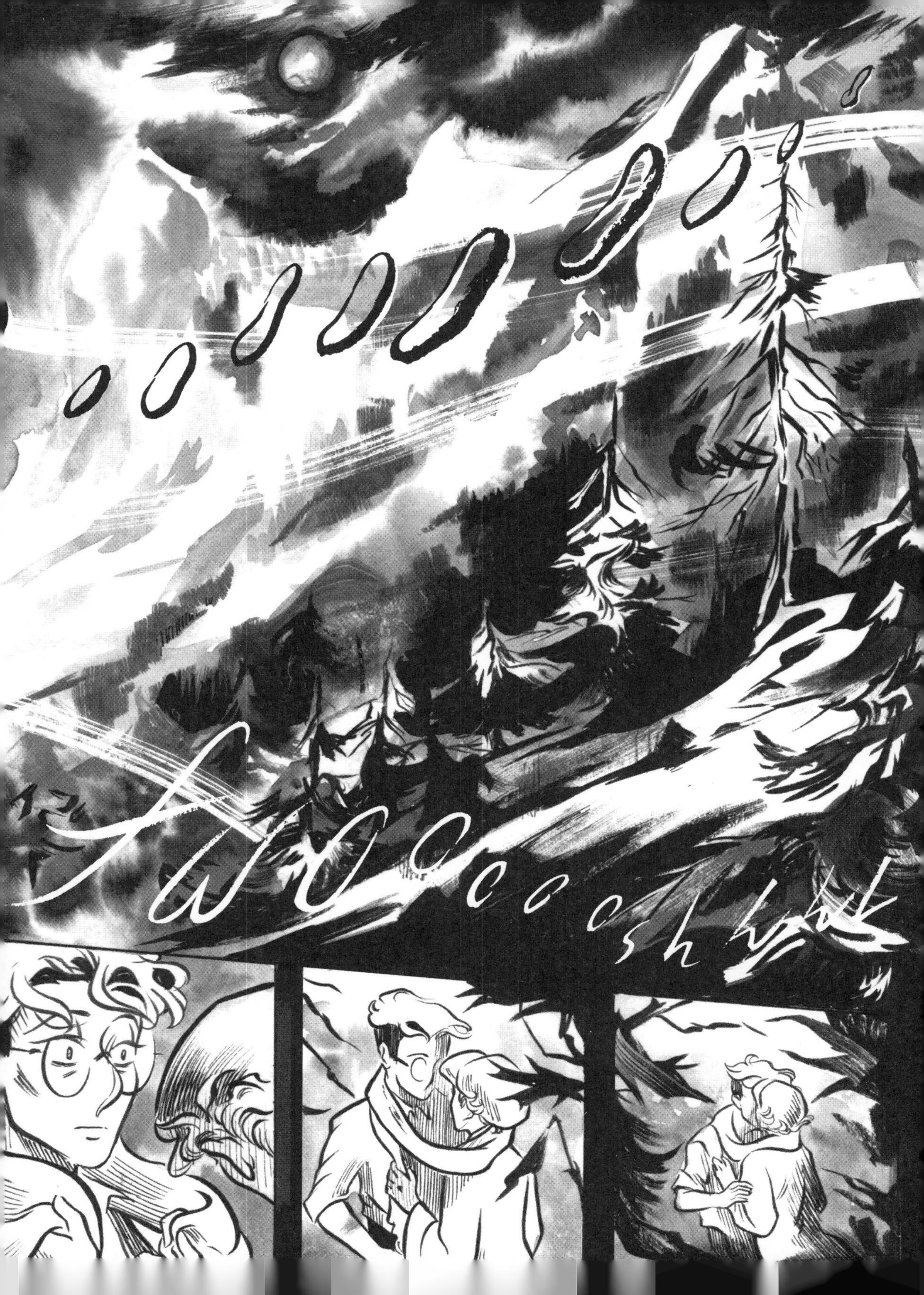
fwooooosh

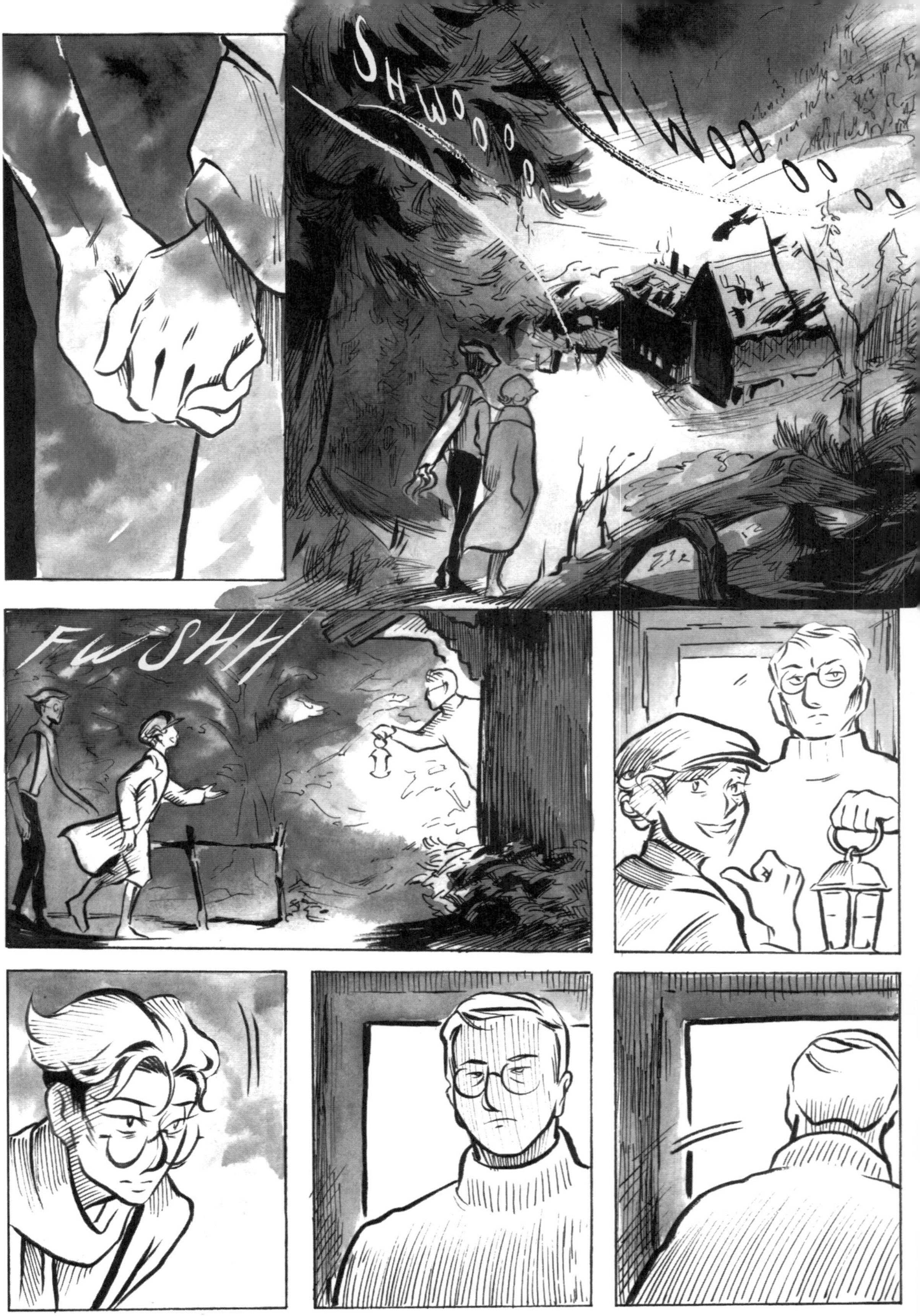
SHWOOOOO
HWOOOOOO
FWSHH

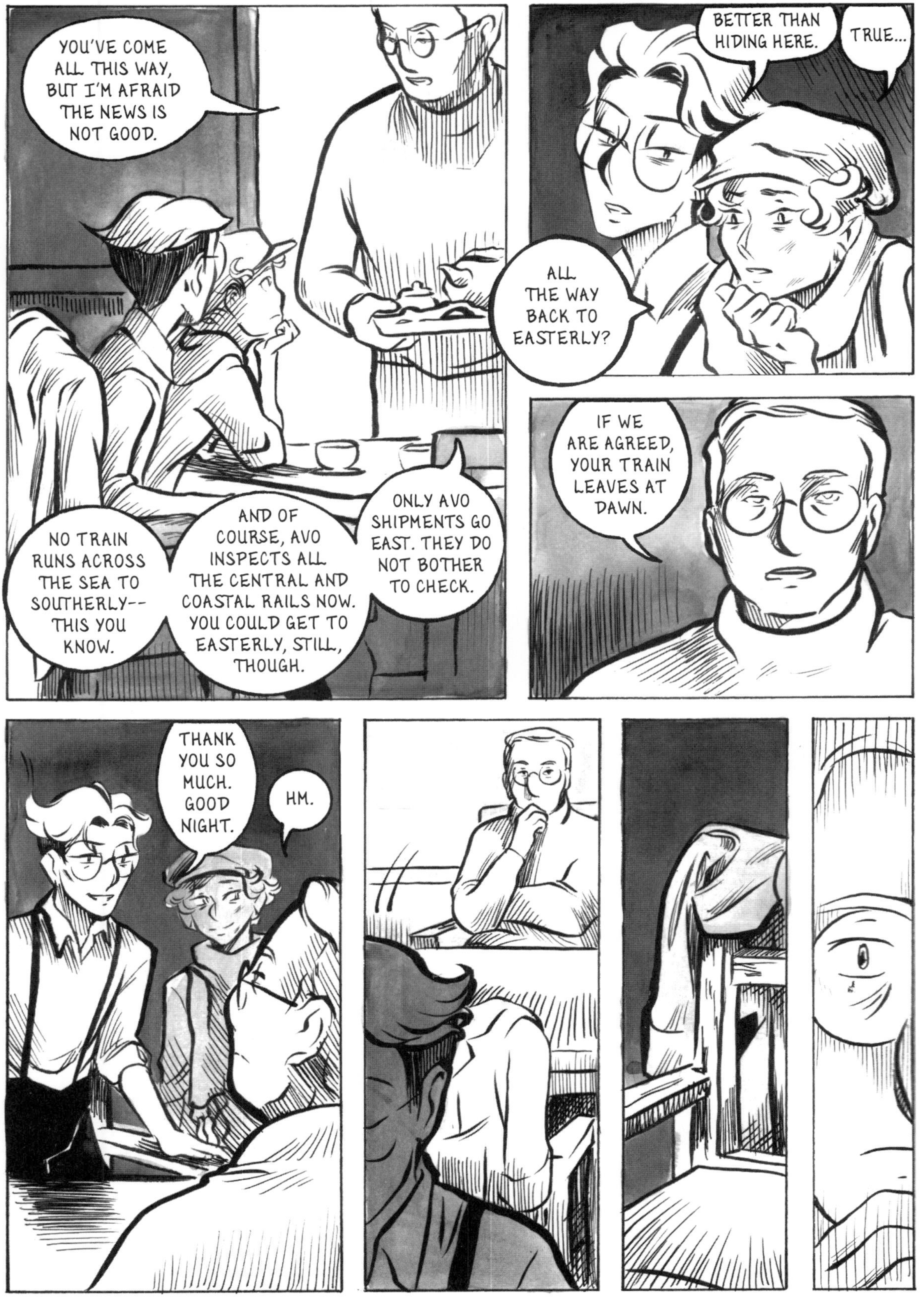
YOU'VE COME ALL THIS WAY, BUT I'M AFRAID THE NEWS IS NOT GOOD.
NO TRAIN RUNS ACROSS THE SEA TO SOUTHERLY-- THIS YOU KNOW.
AND OF COURSE, AVO INSPECTS ALL THE CENTRAL AND COASTAL RAILS NOW. YOU COULD GET TO EASTERLY, STILL, THOUGH.
ONLY AVO SHIPMENTS GO EAST. THEY DO NOT BOTHER TO CHECK.
ALL THE WAY BACK TO EASTERLY?
BETTER THAN HIDING HERE.
TRUE...
IF WE ARE AGREED, YOUR TRAIN LEAVES AT DAWN.
THANK YOU SO MUCH. GOOD NIGHT.
HM.

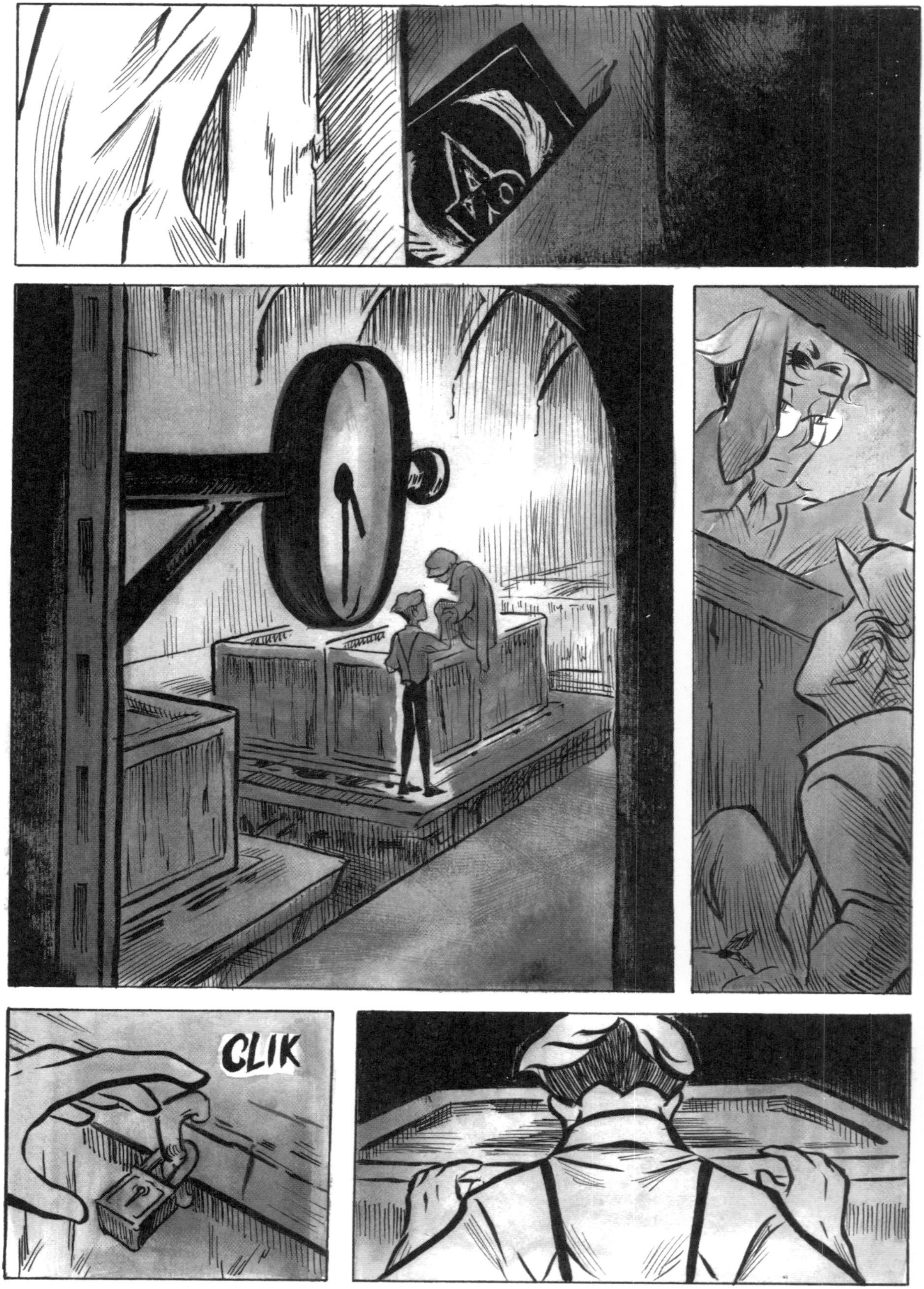
CLIK

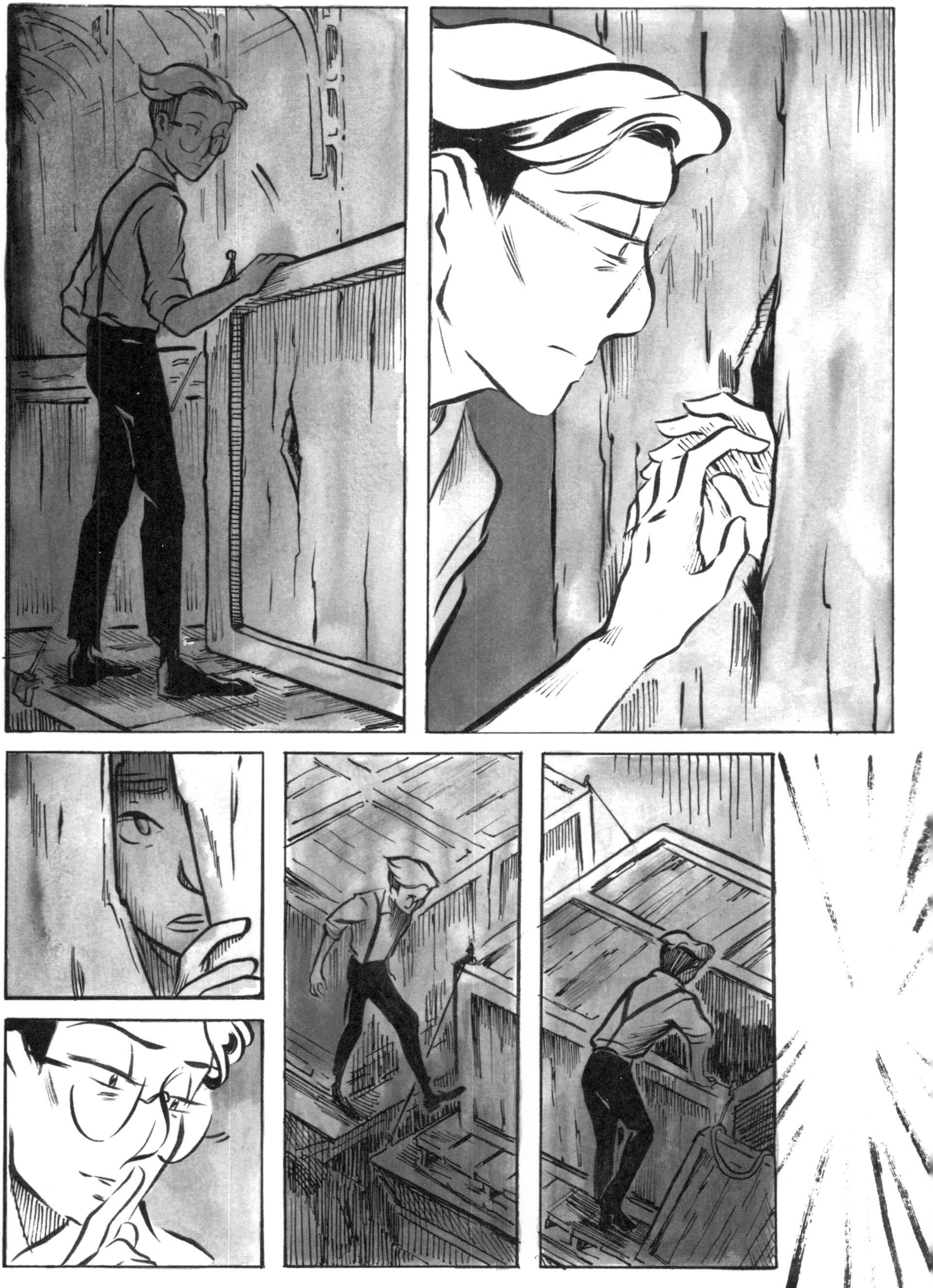

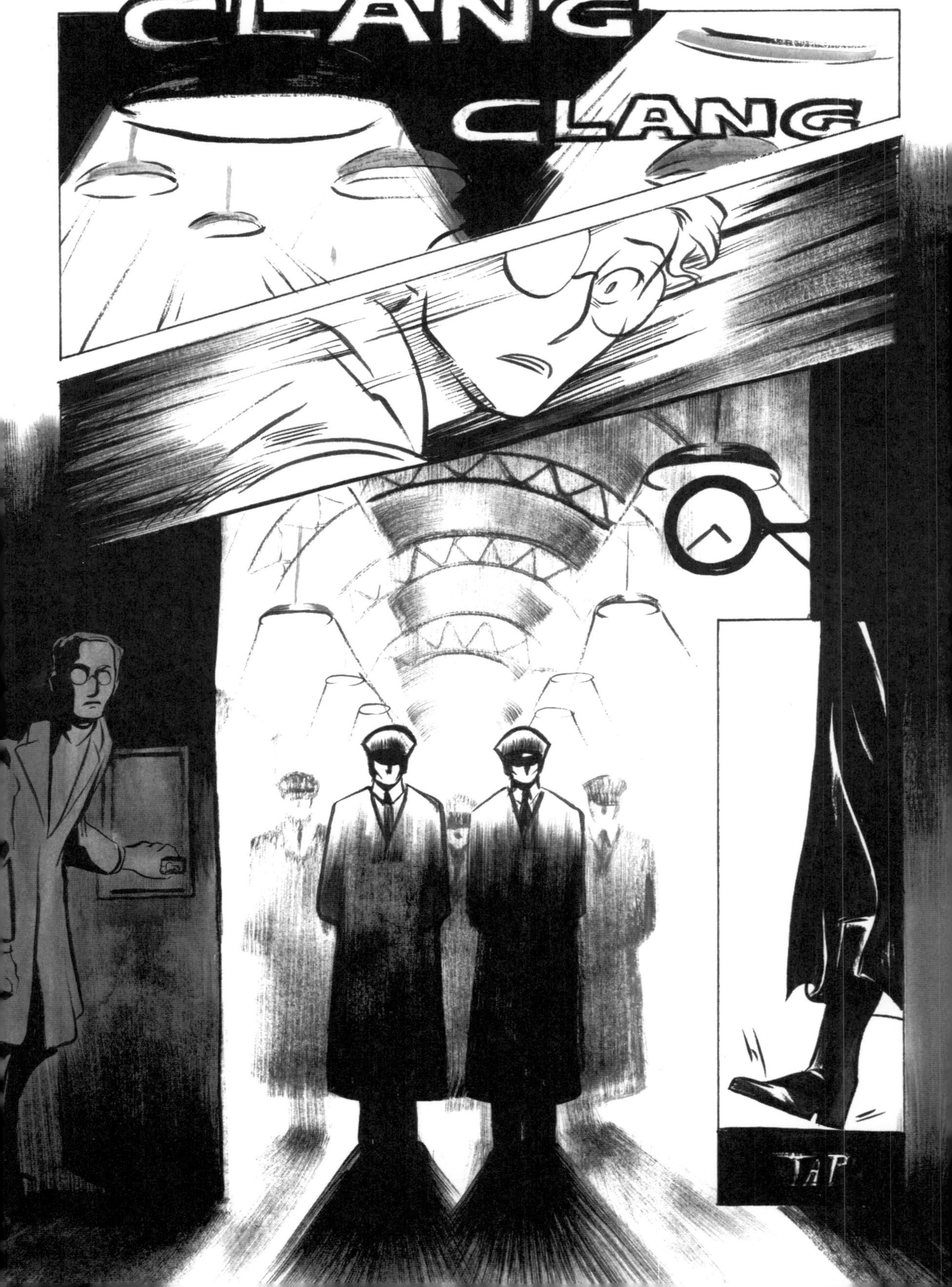
CLANG
CLANG
TAP

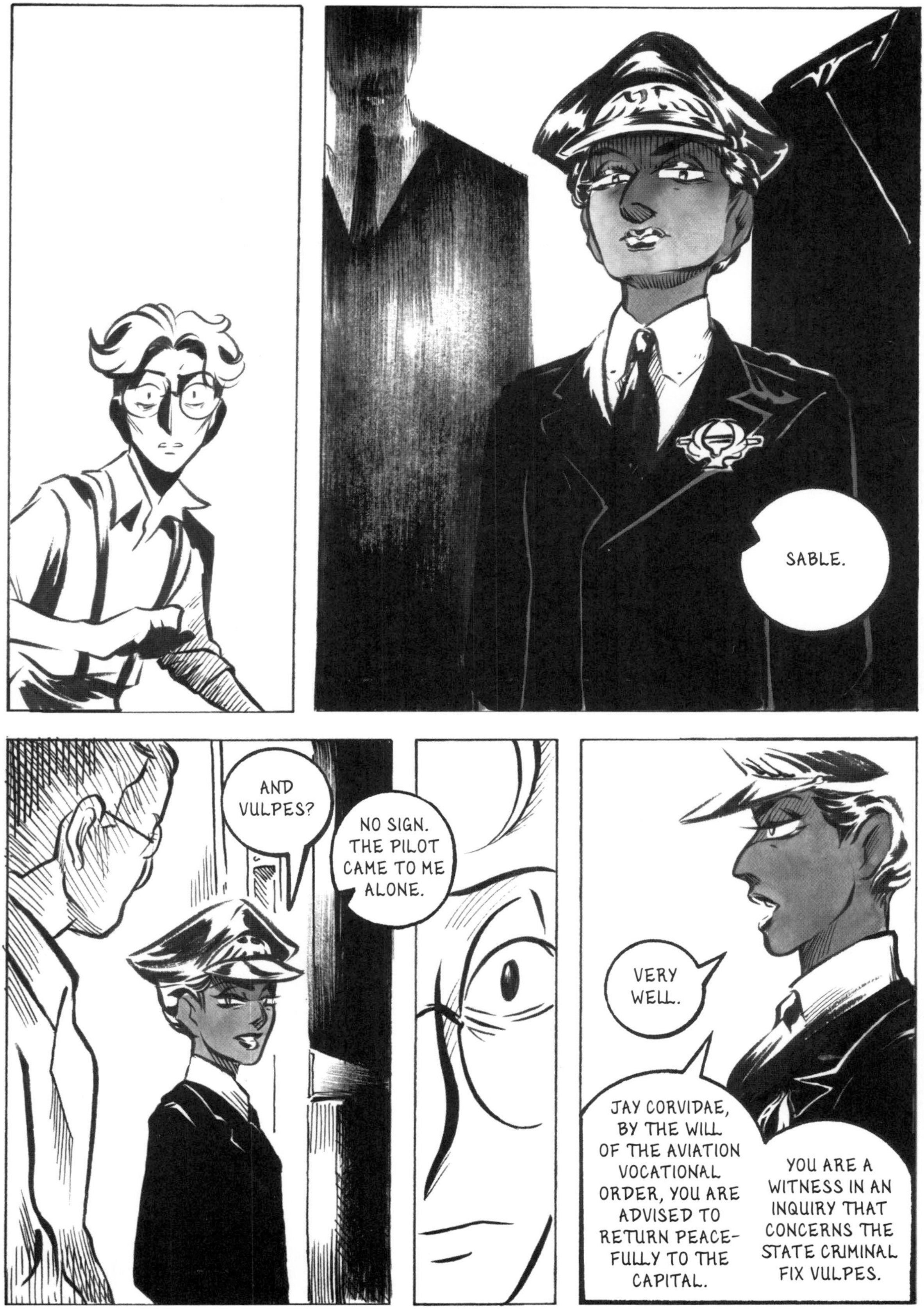
SABLE.
AND VULPES?
NO SIGN. THE PILOT CAME TO ME ALONE.
VERY WELL.
JAY CORVIDAE, BY THE WILL OF THE AVIATION VOCATIONAL ORDER, YOU ARE ADVISED TO RETURN PEACE-FULLY TO THE CAPITAL.
YOU ARE A WITNESS IN AN INQUIRY THAT CONCERNS THE STATE CRIMINAL FIX VULPES.

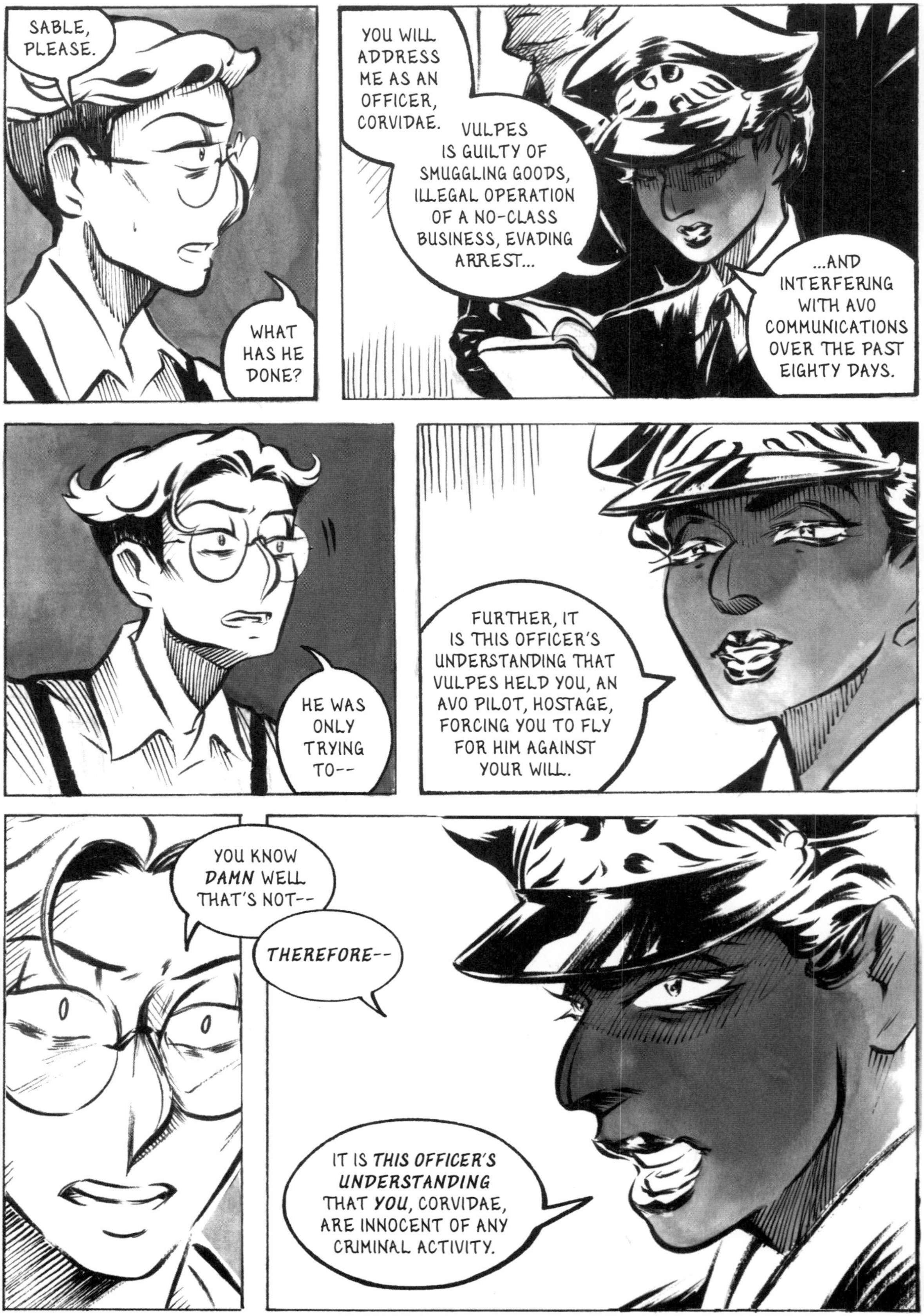
SABLE, PLEASE.
YOU WILL ADDRESS ME AS AN OFFICER, CORVIDAE.
VULPES IS GUILTY OF SMUGGLING GOODS, ILLEGAL OPERATION OF A NO-CLASS BUSINESS, EVADING ARREST...
WHAT HAS HE DONE?
...AND INTERFERING WITH AVO COMMUNICATIONS OVER THE PAST EIGHTY DAYS.
HE WAS ONLY TRYING TO--
FURTHER, IT IS THIS OFFICER'S UNDERSTANDING THAT VULPES HELD YOU, AN AVO PILOT, HOSTAGE, FORCING YOU TO FLY FOR HIM AGAINST YOUR WILL.
YOU KNOW *DAMN* WELL THAT'S NOT--
THEREFORE--
IT IS *THIS OFFICER'S UNDERSTANDING* THAT *YOU*, CORVIDAE, ARE INNOCENT OF ANY CRIMINAL ACTIVITY.

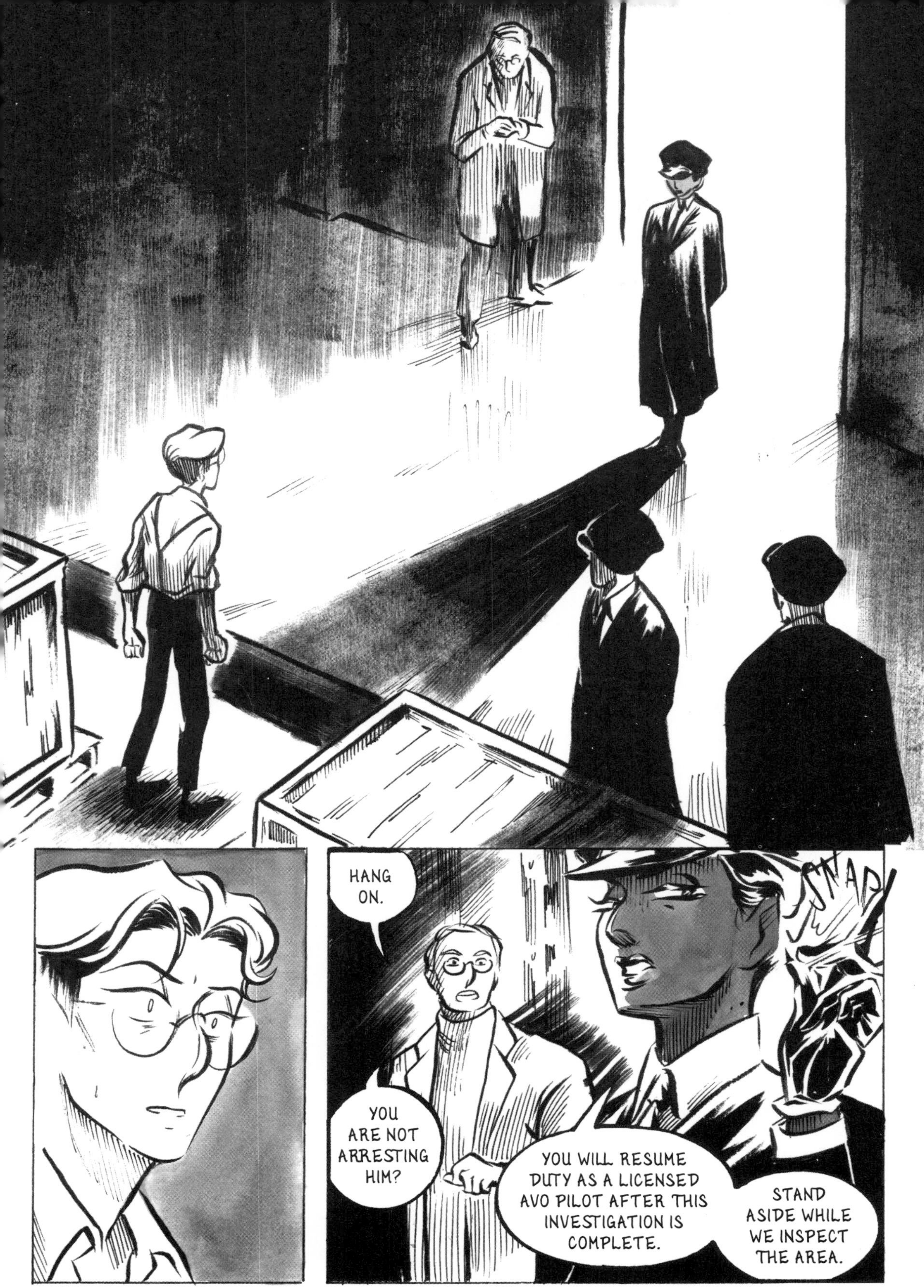
HANG ON.
YOU ARE NOT ARRESTING HIM?
SNAP
YOU WILL RESUME DUTY AS A LICENSED AVO PILOT AFTER THIS INVESTIGATION IS COMPLETE.
STAND ASIDE WHILE WE INSPECT THE AREA.

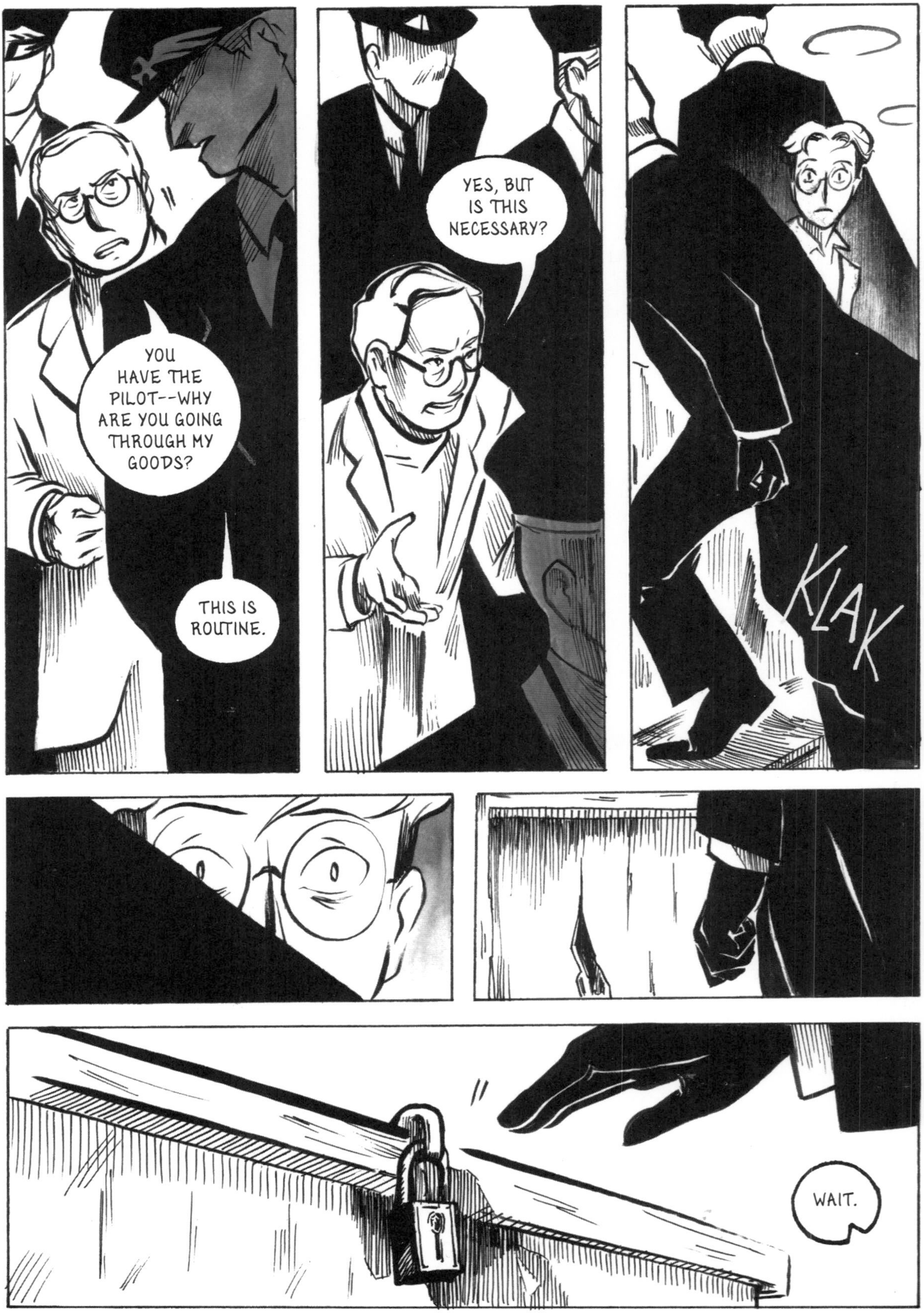
YOU HAVE THE PILOT--WHY ARE YOU GOING THROUGH MY GOODS?
THIS IS ROUTINE.
YES, BUT IS THIS NECESSARY?
KLAK
WAIT.

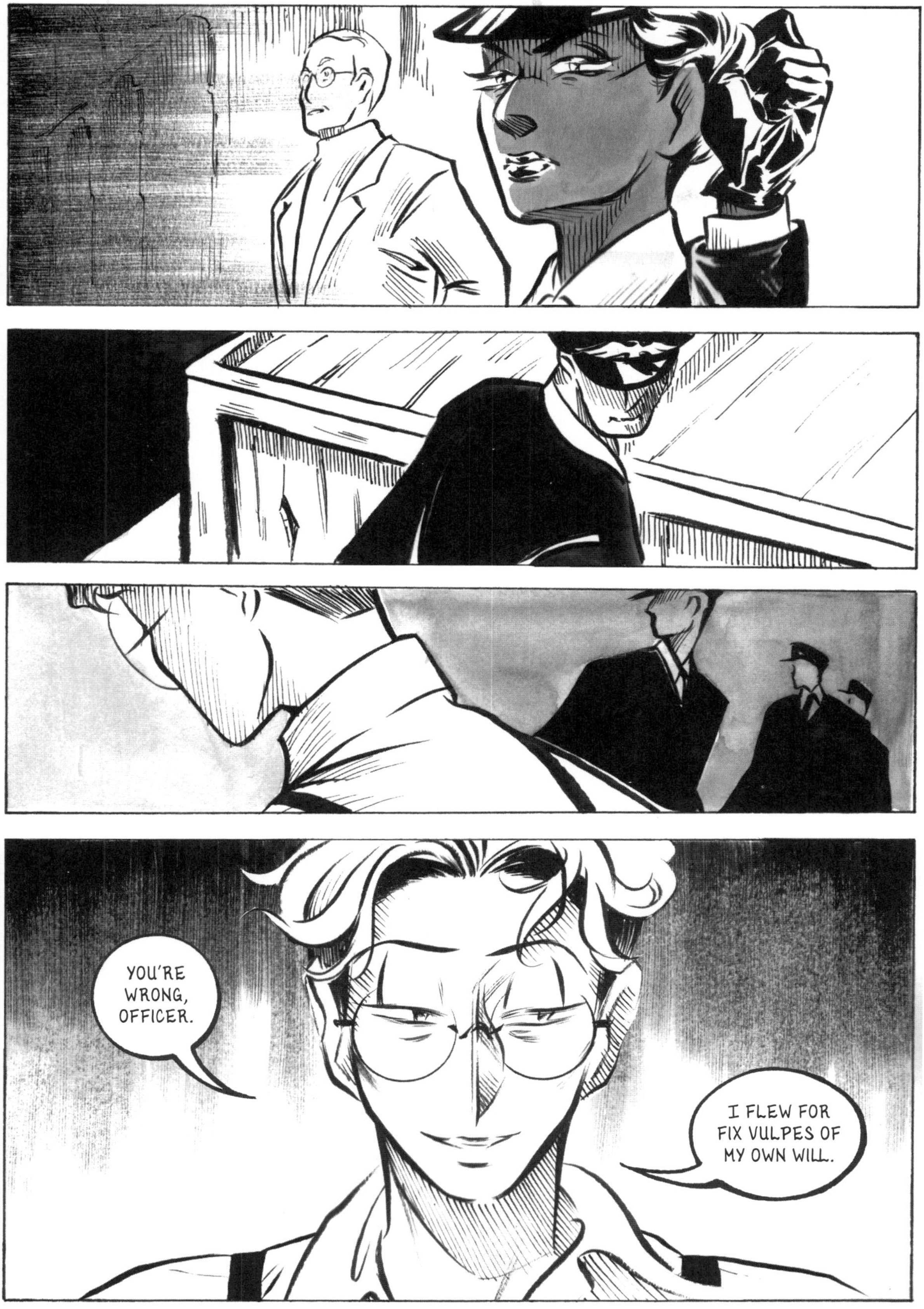
YOU'RE WRONG, OFFICER.
I FLEW FOR FIX VULPES OF MY OWN WILL.

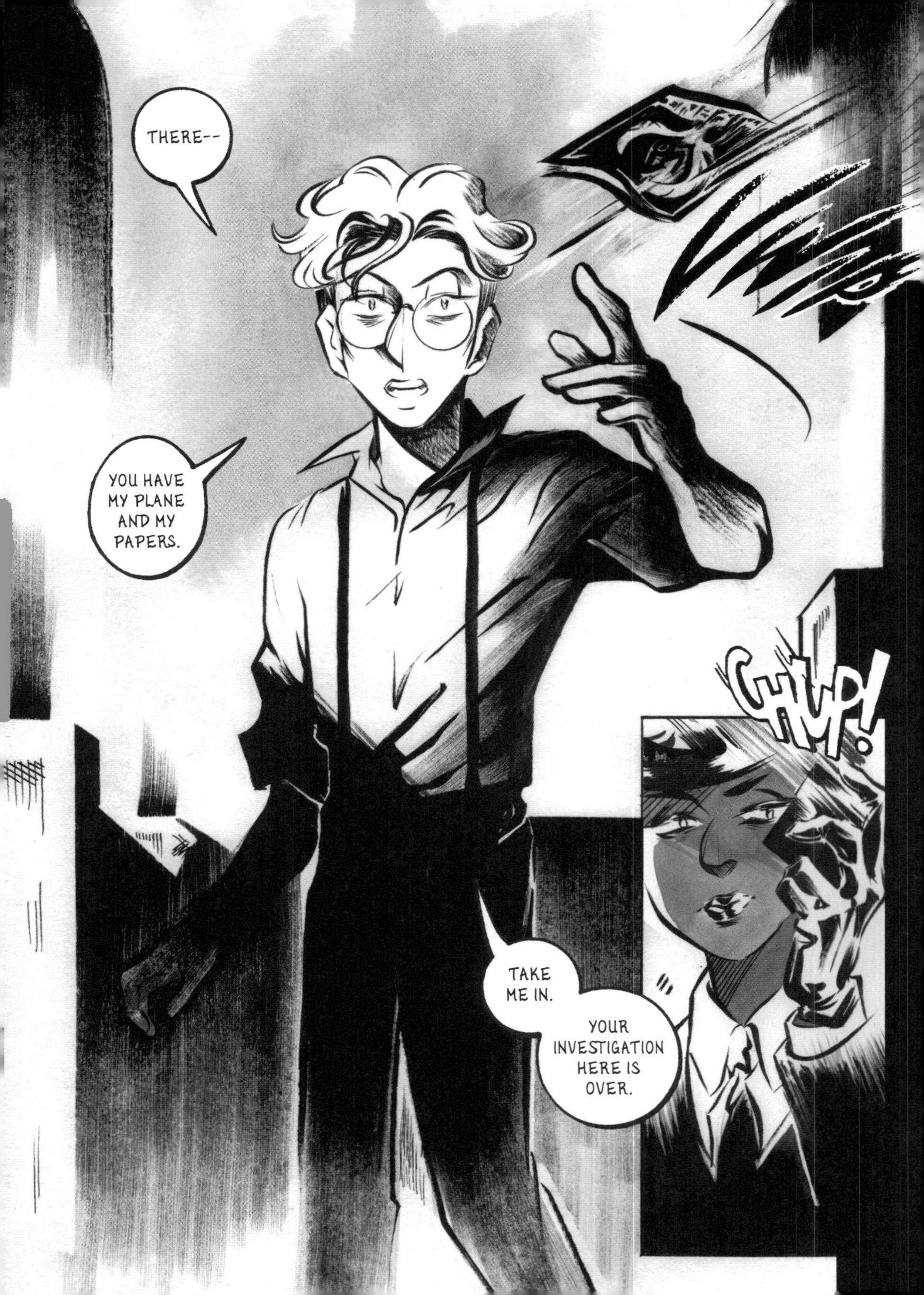
THERE--
WHIP
YOU HAVE MY PLANE AND MY PAPERS.
CHUP!
TAKE ME IN.
YOUR INVESTIGATION HERE IS OVER.

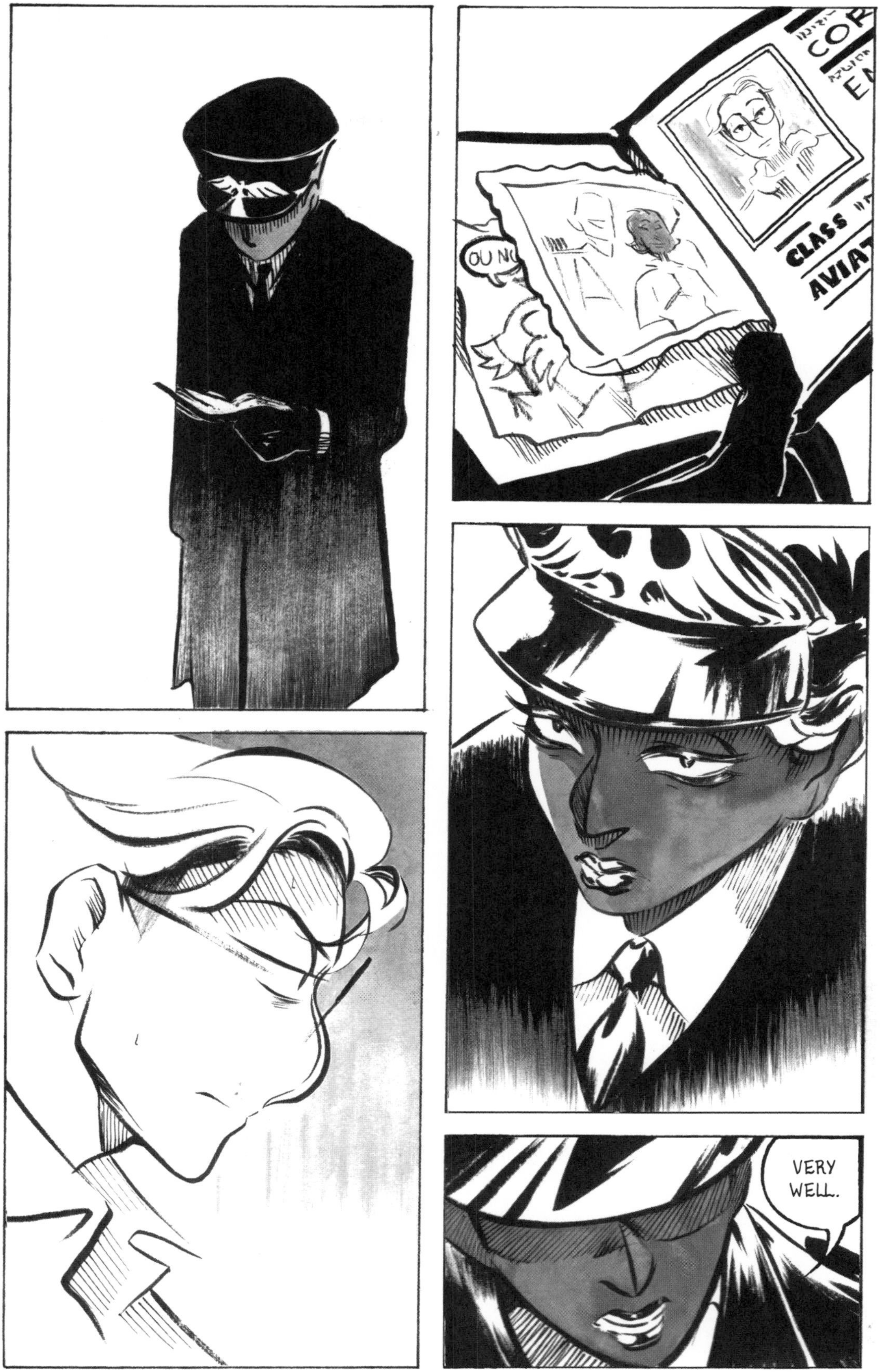
CLASS
VERY WELL.

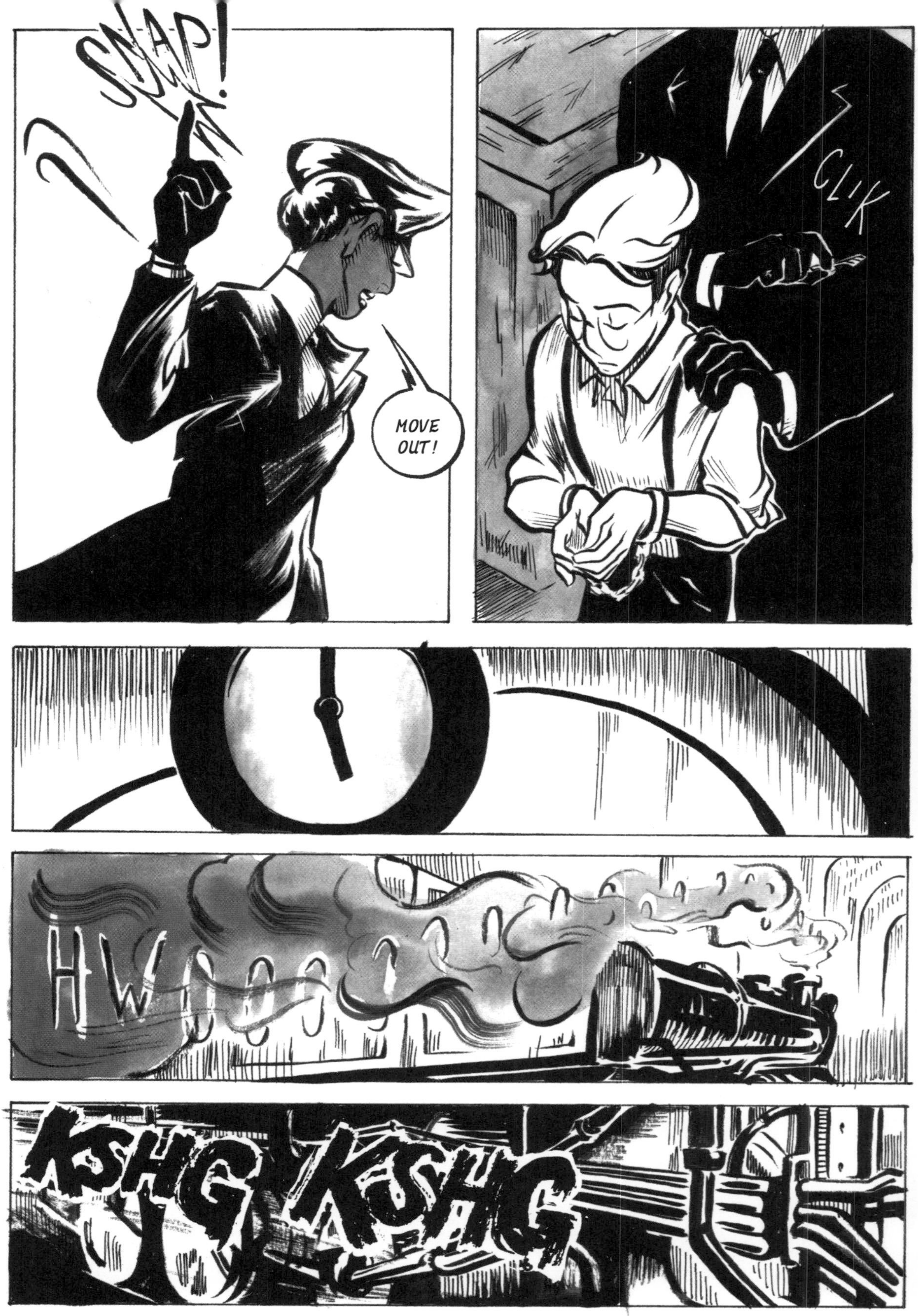
SNAP!
MOVE OUT!
CLIK
HWOOOO
KSHG KSHG

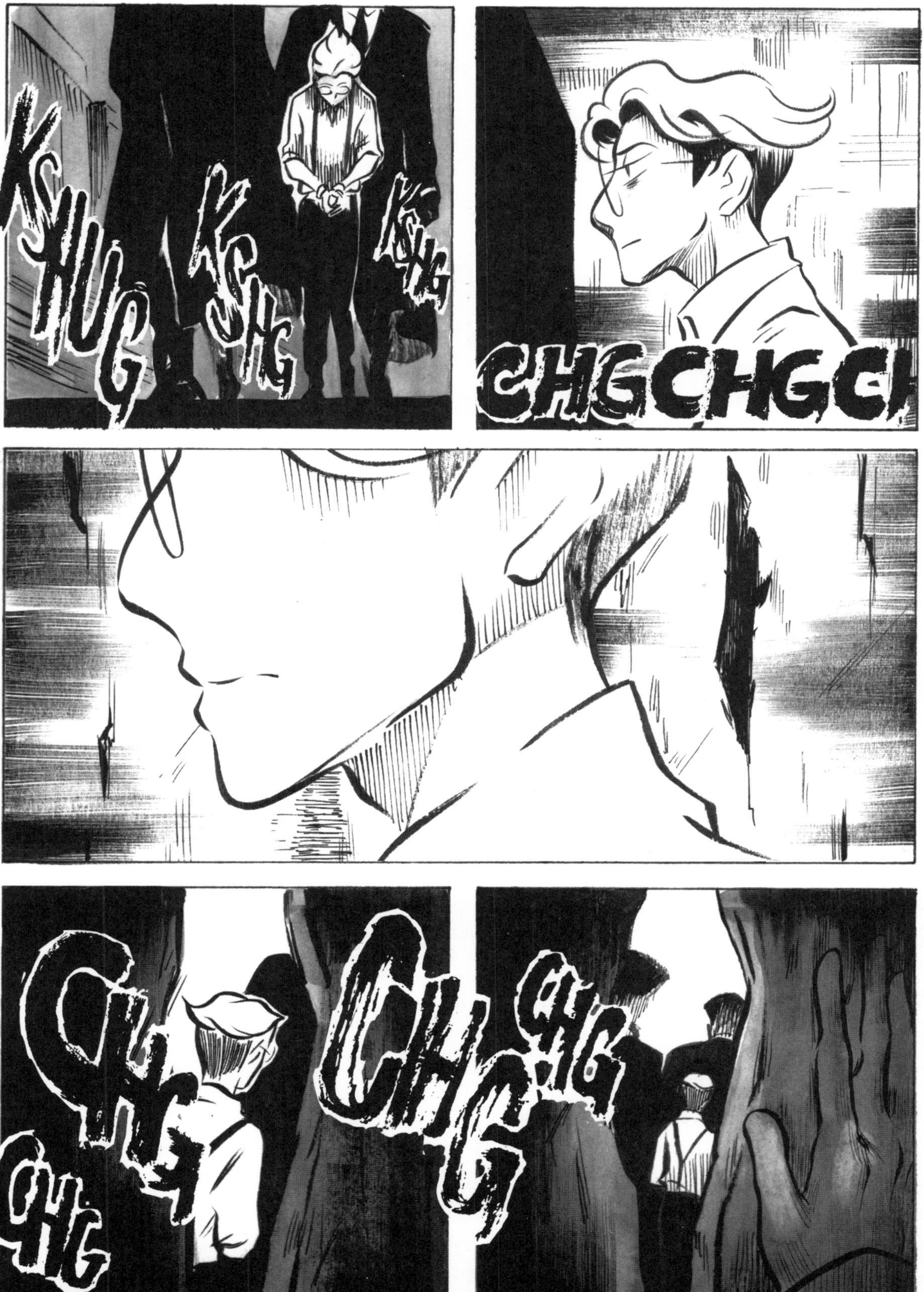
KSHUG
KSHG
KSHG
CHGCHGCH
CHG
CHG
CHG
CHG
CHG

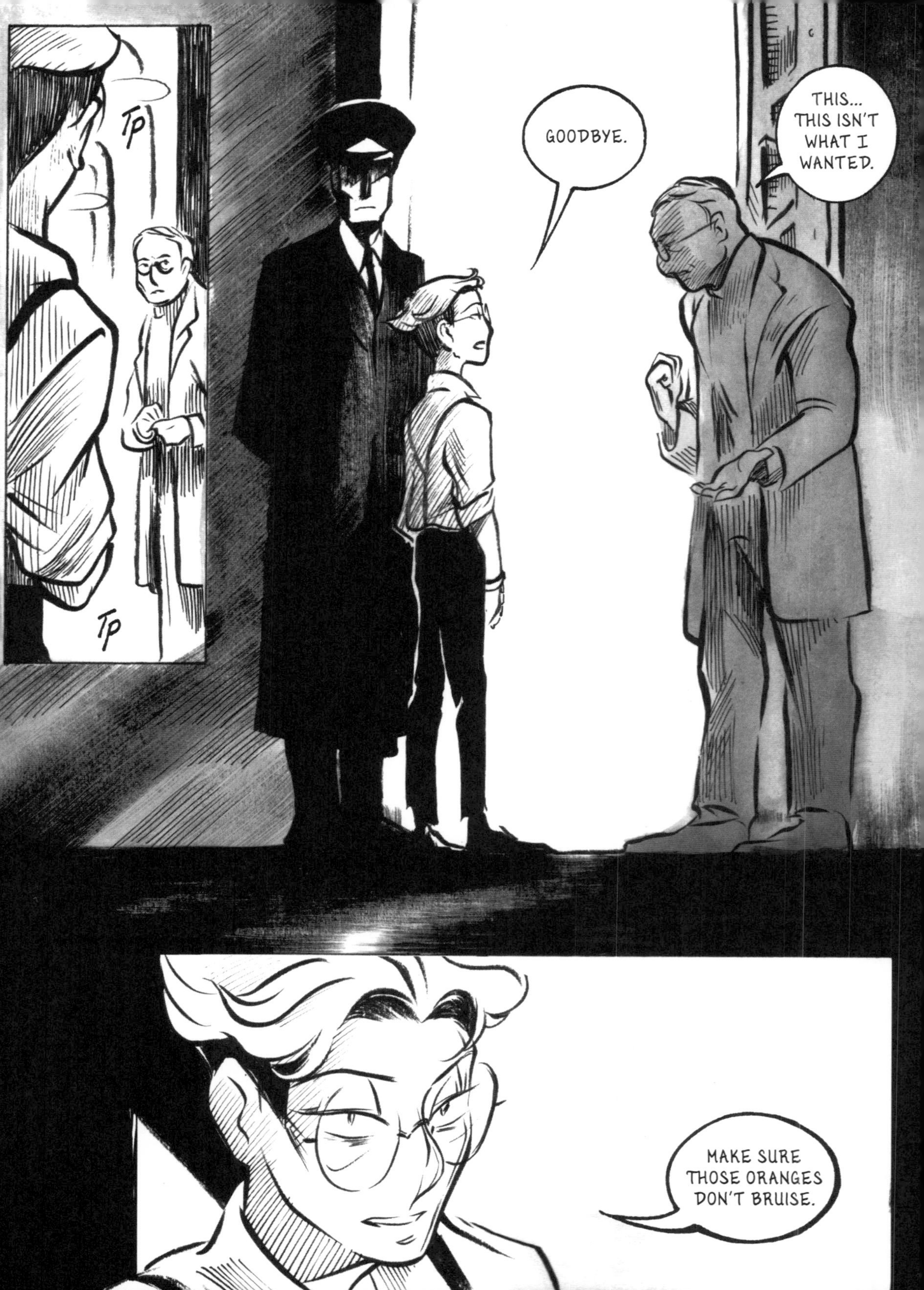
TP
TP
GOODBYE.
THIS...
THIS ISN'T
WHAT I
WANTED.
MAKE SURE
THOSE ORANGES
DON'T BRUISE.

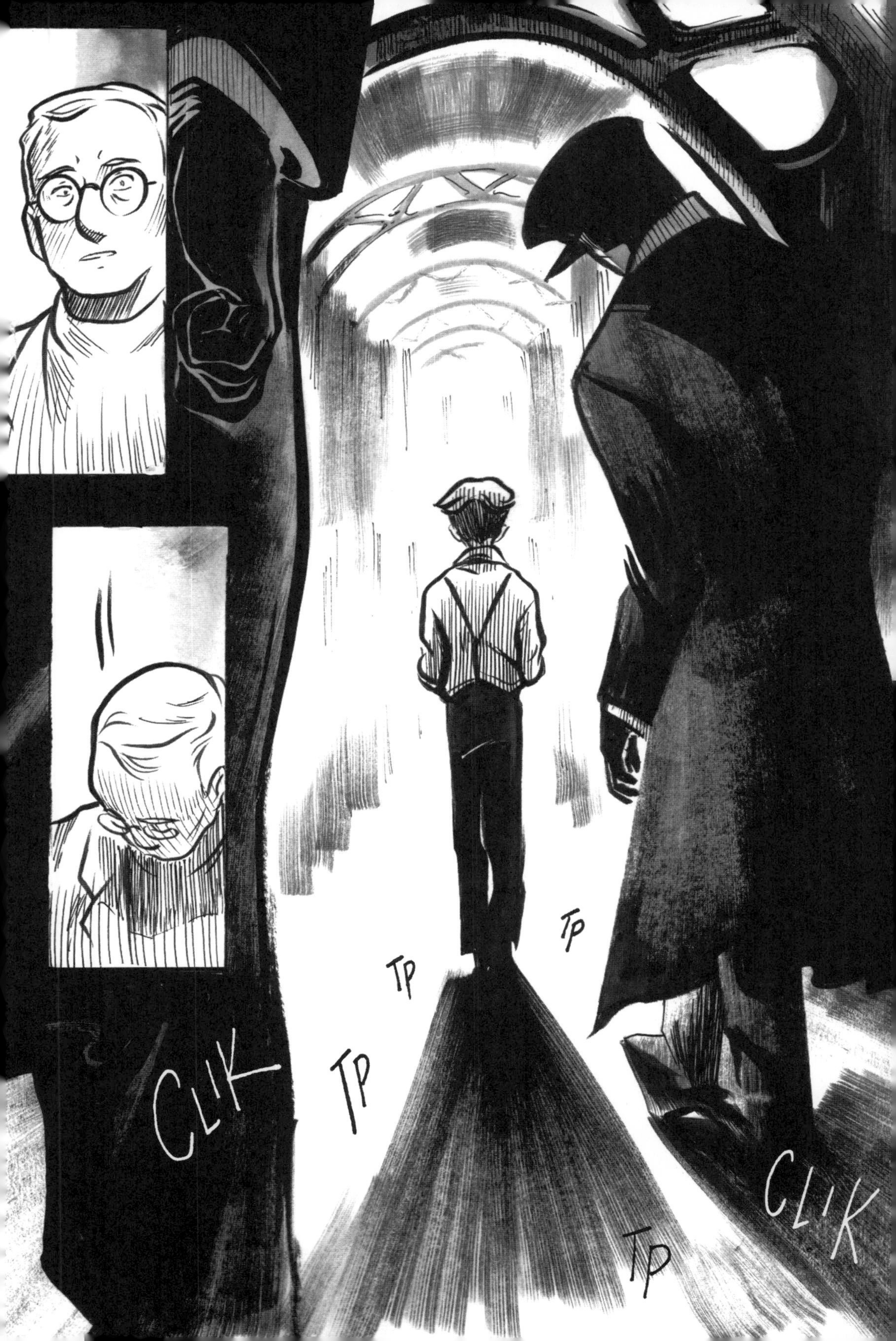
Tp
Tp
CLIK
Tp
Tp
CLIK

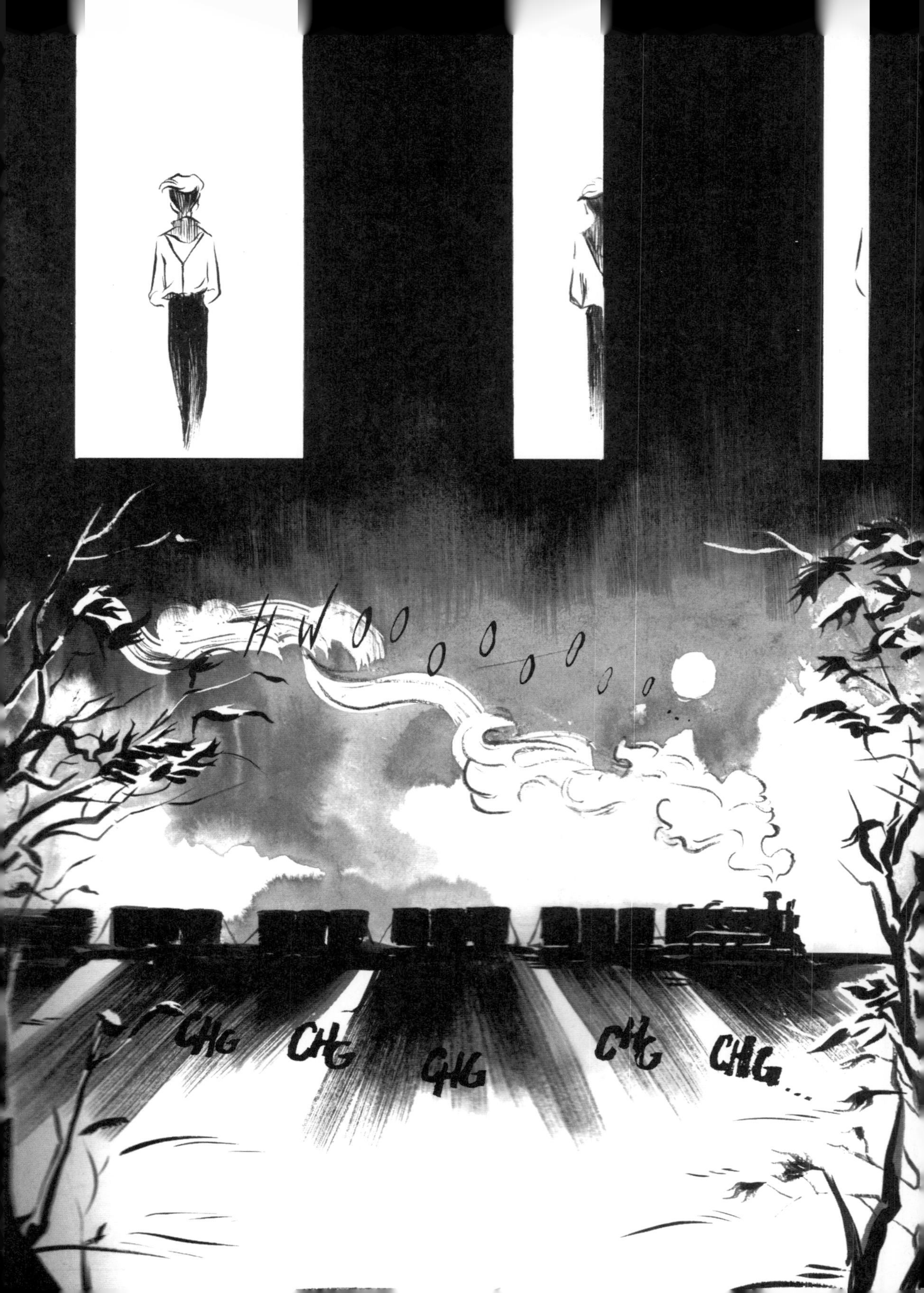
HWOOOOOOOOO
CHG CHG CHG CHG CHG...

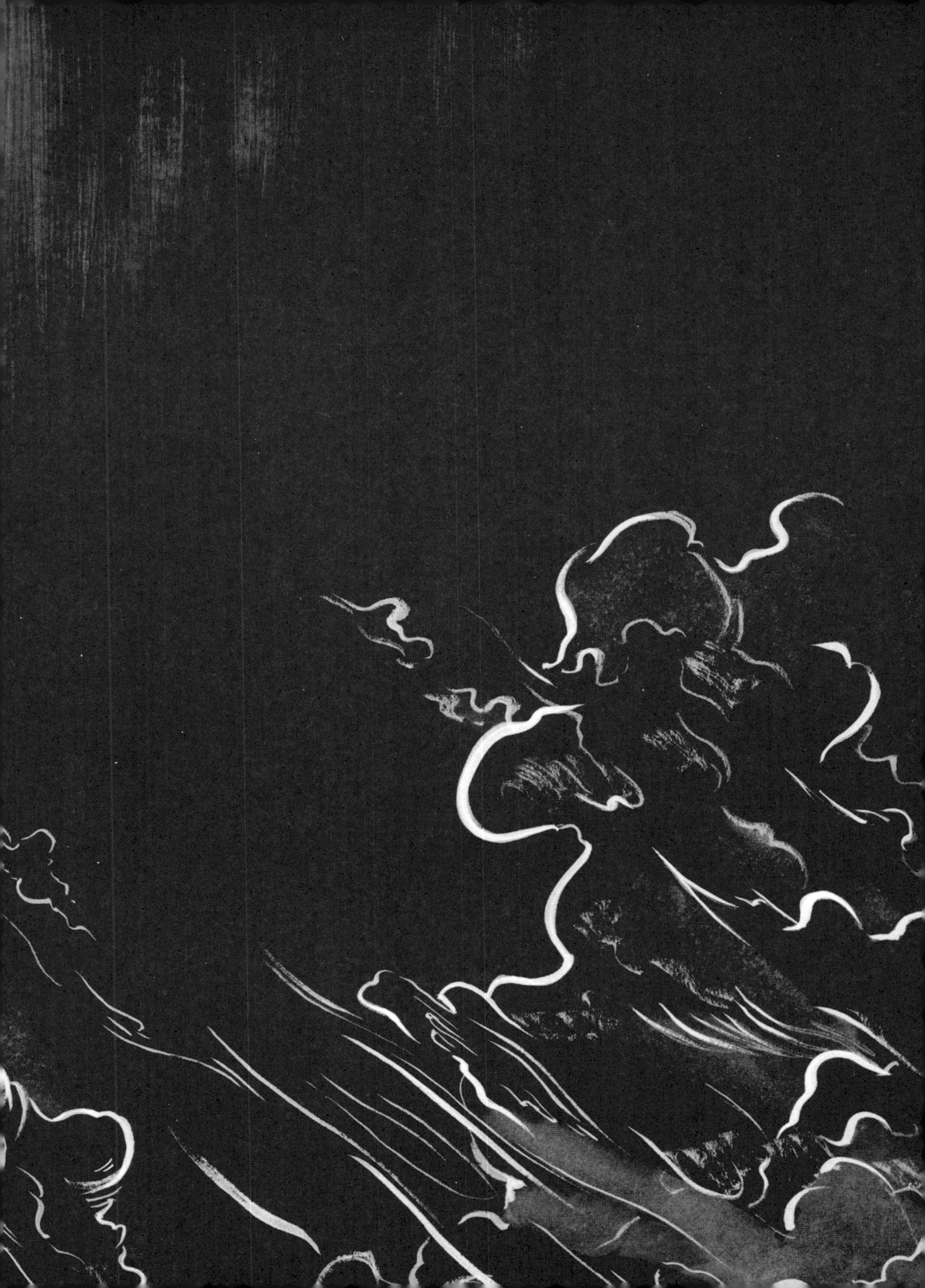

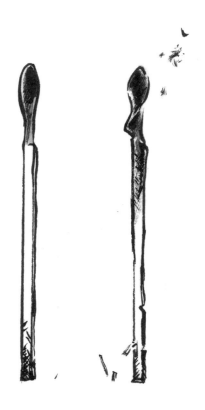

BOOK II
BLACK BOX

flik

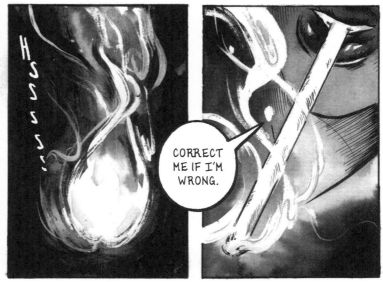

HSSSSS

CORRECT ME IF I'M WRONG.

THIS IS A TWO-WAY RADIOTELETYPE?

H.Q.'S VERY LATEST ARRAY. LONG-DISTANCE, NO CABLES NEEDED.

I'LL OPERATE IT, SO DON'T WORRY ABOUT THE DETAILS.

THE IMPORTANT THING IS, YOU CAN SPEAK FREELY WITH THE PRISONER FROM PRACTICALLY ANYWHERE.

SHALL WE TRY IT?

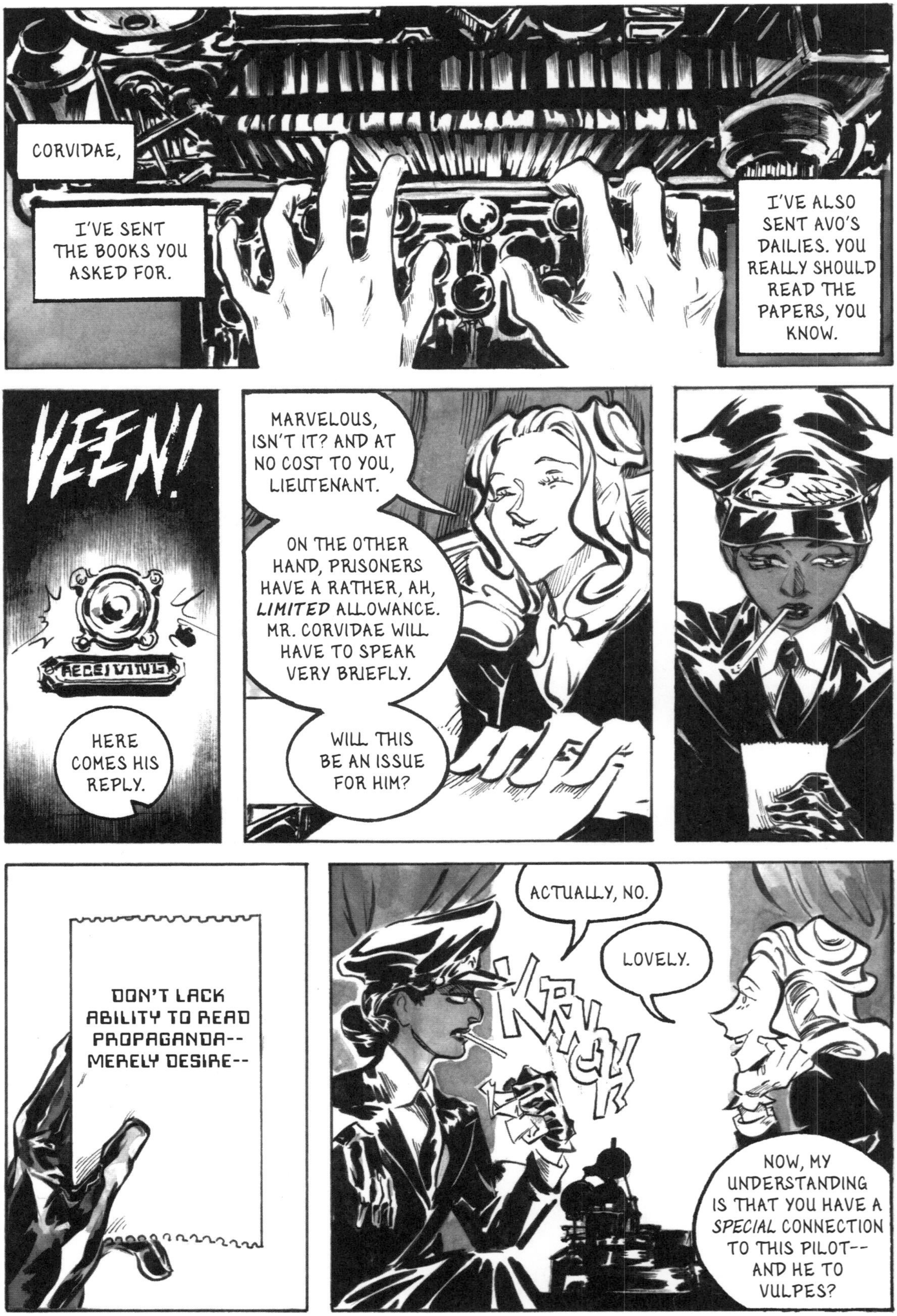
CORVIDAE,
I'VE SENT THE BOOKS YOU ASKED FOR.
I'VE ALSO SENT AVO'S DAILIES. YOU REALLY SHOULD READ THE PAPERS, YOU KNOW.
VEEN!
RECEIVING
HERE COMES HIS REPLY.
MARVELOUS, ISN'T IT? AND AT NO COST TO YOU, LIEUTENANT.
ON THE OTHER HAND, PRISONERS HAVE A RATHER, AH, *LIMITED* ALLOWANCE. MR. CORVIDAE WILL HAVE TO SPEAK VERY BRIEFLY.
WILL THIS BE AN ISSUE FOR HIM?
DON'T LACK ABILITY TO READ PROPAGANDA-- MERELY DESIRE--
ACTUALLY, NO.
KRUNCH
LOVELY.
NOW, MY UNDERSTANDING IS THAT YOU HAVE A *SPECIAL* CONNECTION TO THIS PILOT-- AND HE TO VULPES?

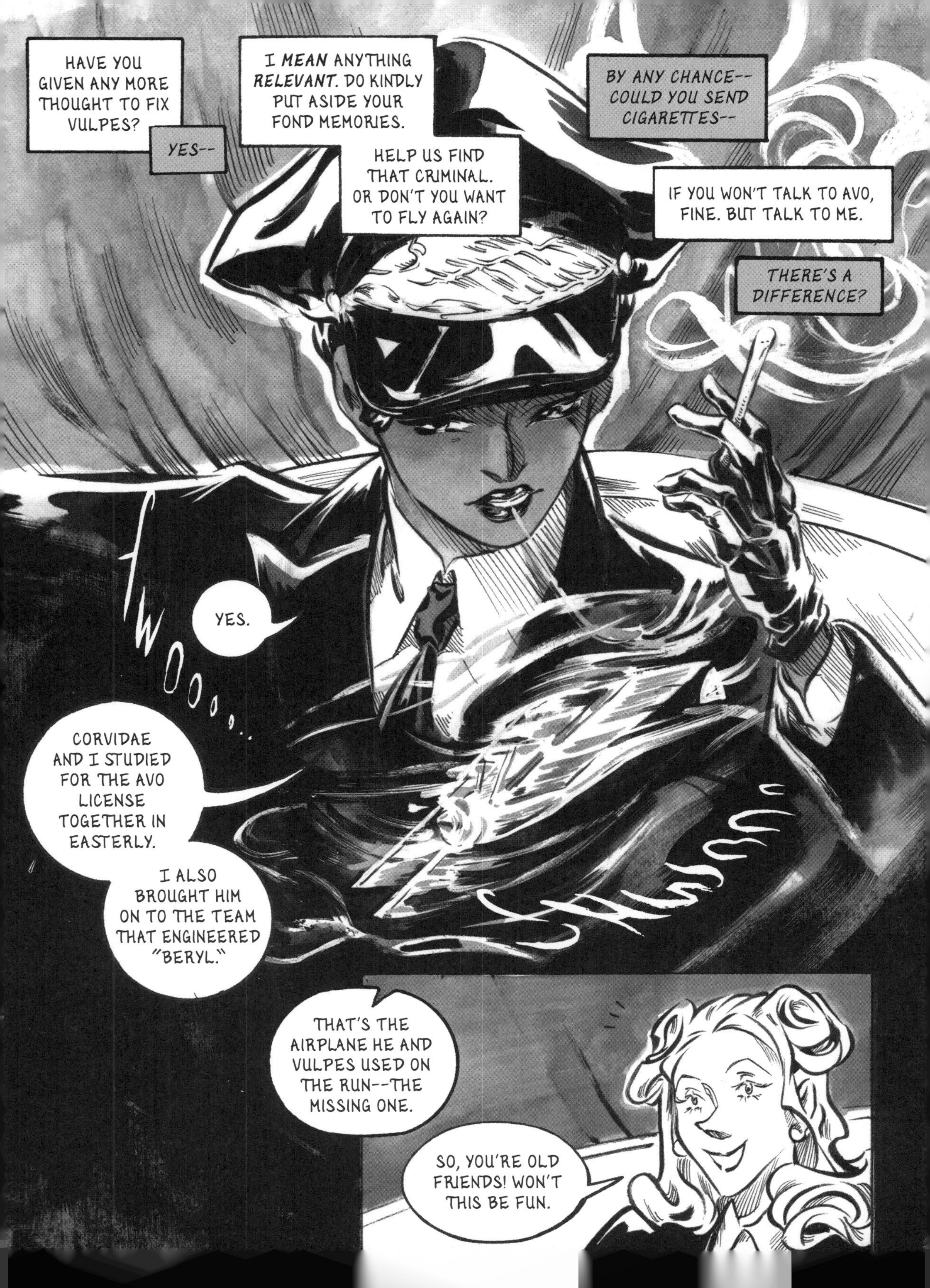
HAVE YOU GIVEN ANY MORE THOUGHT TO FIX VULPES?
YES--
I MEAN ANYTHING RELEVANT. DO KINDLY PUT ASIDE YOUR FOND MEMORIES.
HELP US FIND THAT CRIMINAL. OR DON'T YOU WANT TO FLY AGAIN?
BY ANY CHANCE-- COULD YOU SEND CIGARETTES--
IF YOU WON'T TALK TO AVO, FINE. BUT TALK TO ME.
THERE'S A DIFFERENCE?
FWOOoo...
YES.
CORVIDAE AND I STUDIED FOR THE AVO LICENSE TOGETHER IN EASTERLY.
I ALSO BROUGHT HIM ON TO THE TEAM THAT ENGINEERED "BERYL."
THAT'S THE AIRPLANE HE AND VULPES USED ON THE RUN--THE MISSING ONE.
SO, YOU'RE OLD FRIENDS! WON'T THIS BE FUN.

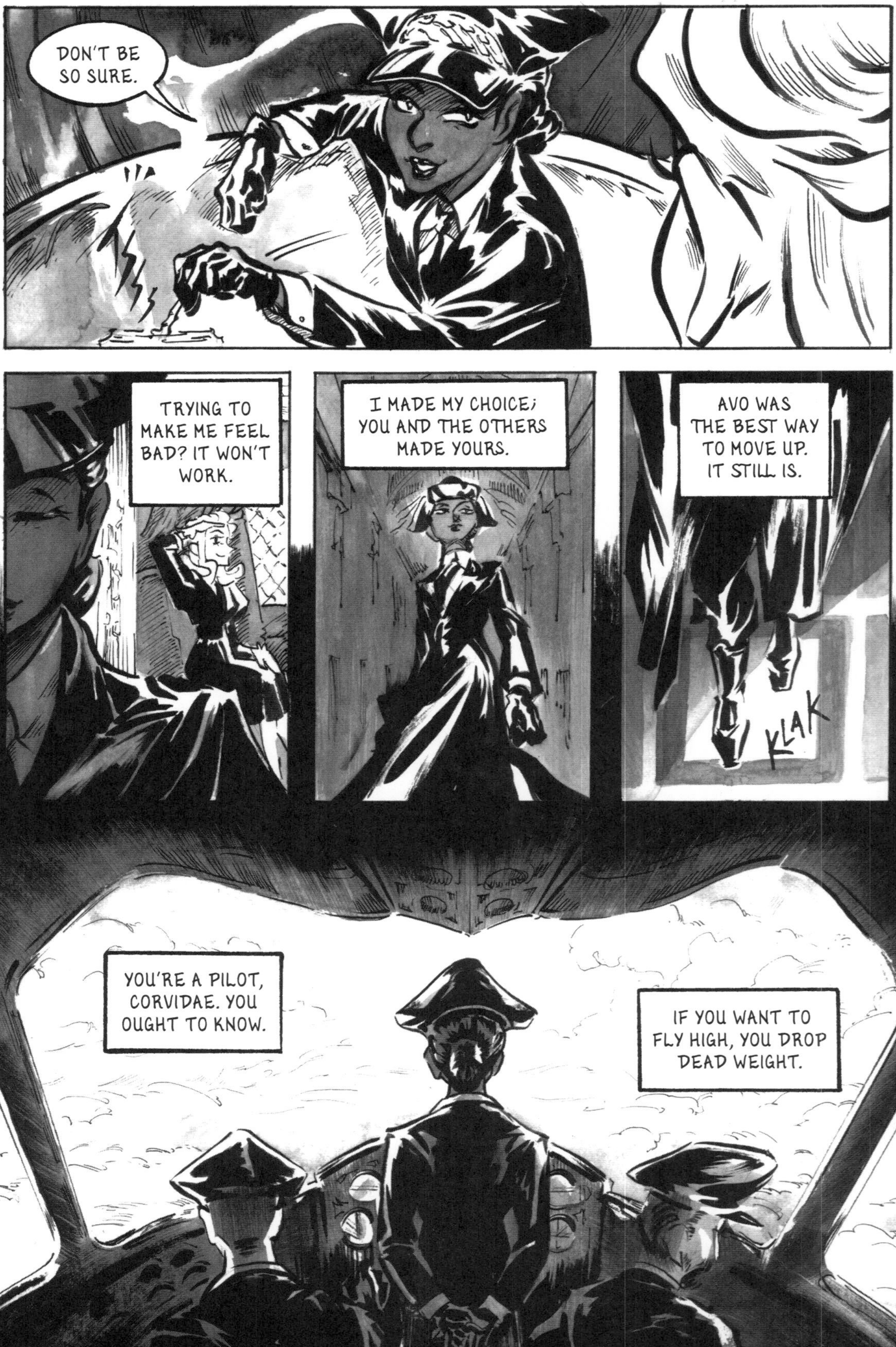
DON'T BE SO SURE.
TRYING TO MAKE ME FEEL BAD? IT WON'T WORK.
I MADE MY CHOICE; YOU AND THE OTHERS MADE YOURS.
AVO WAS THE BEST WAY TO MOVE UP. IT STILL IS.
KLAK
YOU'RE A PILOT, CORVIDAE. YOU OUGHT TO KNOW.
IF YOU WANT TO FLY HIGH, YOU DROP DEAD WEIGHT.

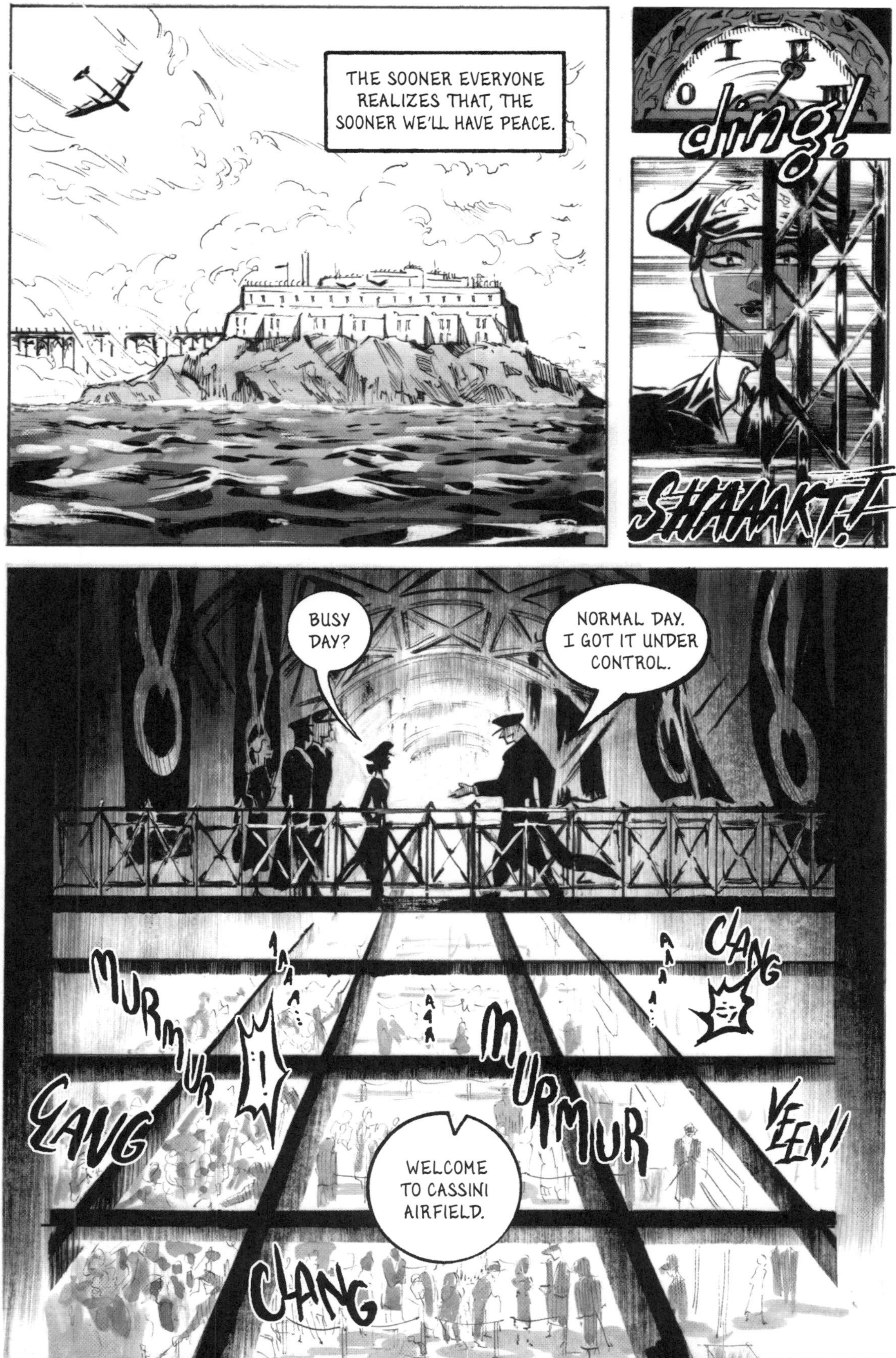
THE SOONER EVERYONE REALIZES THAT, THE SOONER WE'LL HAVE PEACE.
ding!
SHAAAKT!
BUSY DAY?
NORMAL DAY. I GOT IT UNDER CONTROL.
MURMUR
CLANG
MURMUR
CLANG
VEEN!
WELCOME TO CASSINI AIRFIELD.
CLANG

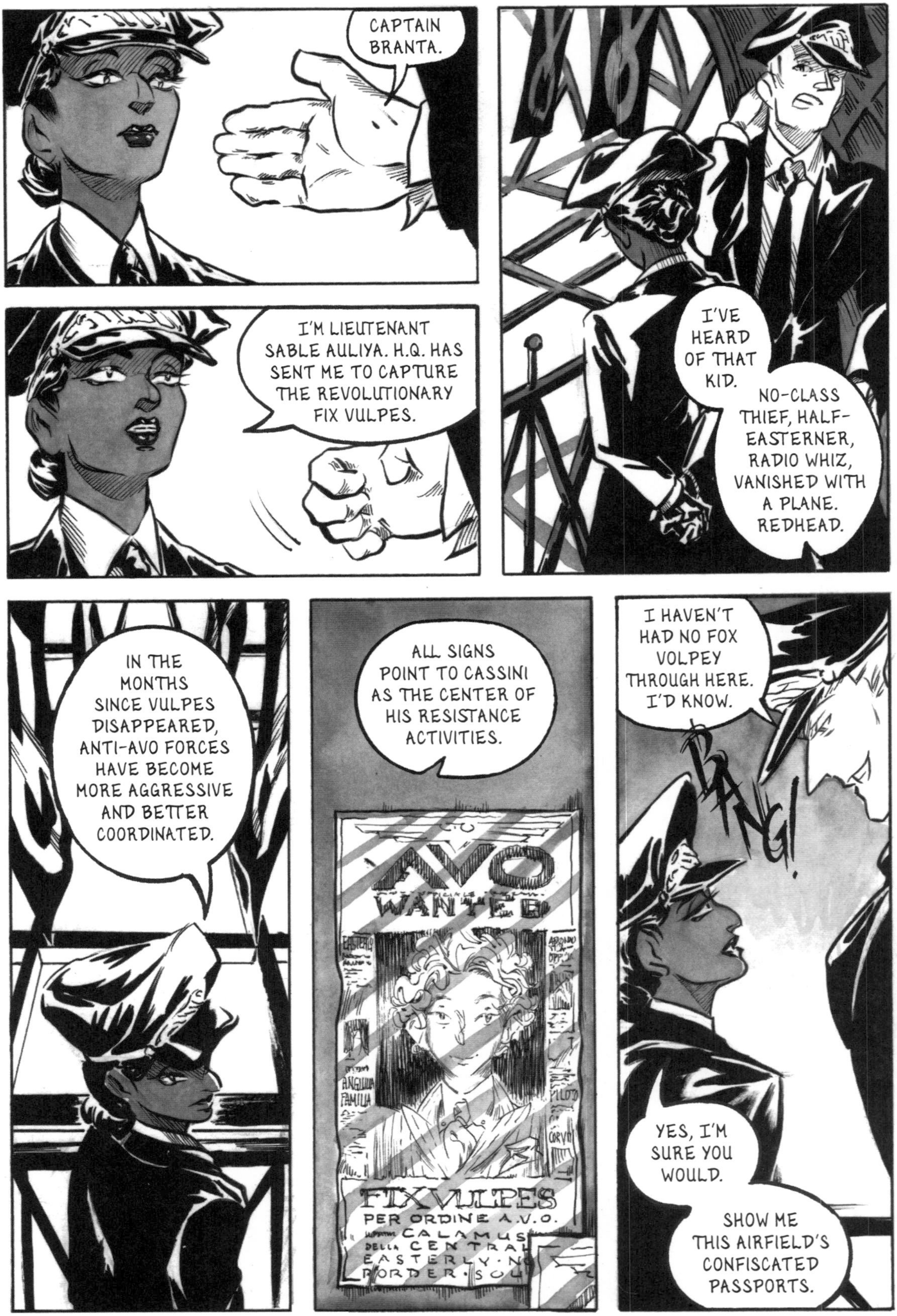
CAPTAIN BRANTA.
I'M LIEUTENANT SABLE AULIYA. H.Q. HAS SENT ME TO CAPTURE THE REVOLUTIONARY FIX VULPES.
I'VE HEARD OF THAT KID.
NO-CLASS THIEF, HALF-EASTERNER, RADIO WHIZ, VANISHED WITH A PLANE. REDHEAD.
IN THE MONTHS SINCE VULPES DISAPPEARED, ANTI-AVO FORCES HAVE BECOME MORE AGGRESSIVE AND BETTER COORDINATED.
ALL SIGNS POINT TO CASSINI AS THE CENTER OF HIS RESISTANCE ACTIVITIES.
AVO
FIX VULPES
PER ORDINE A.V.O.
I HAVEN'T HAD NO FOX VOLPEY THROUGH HERE. I'D KNOW.
BANG!
YES, I'M SURE YOU WOULD.
SHOW ME THIS AIRFIELD'S CONFISCATED PASSPORTS.

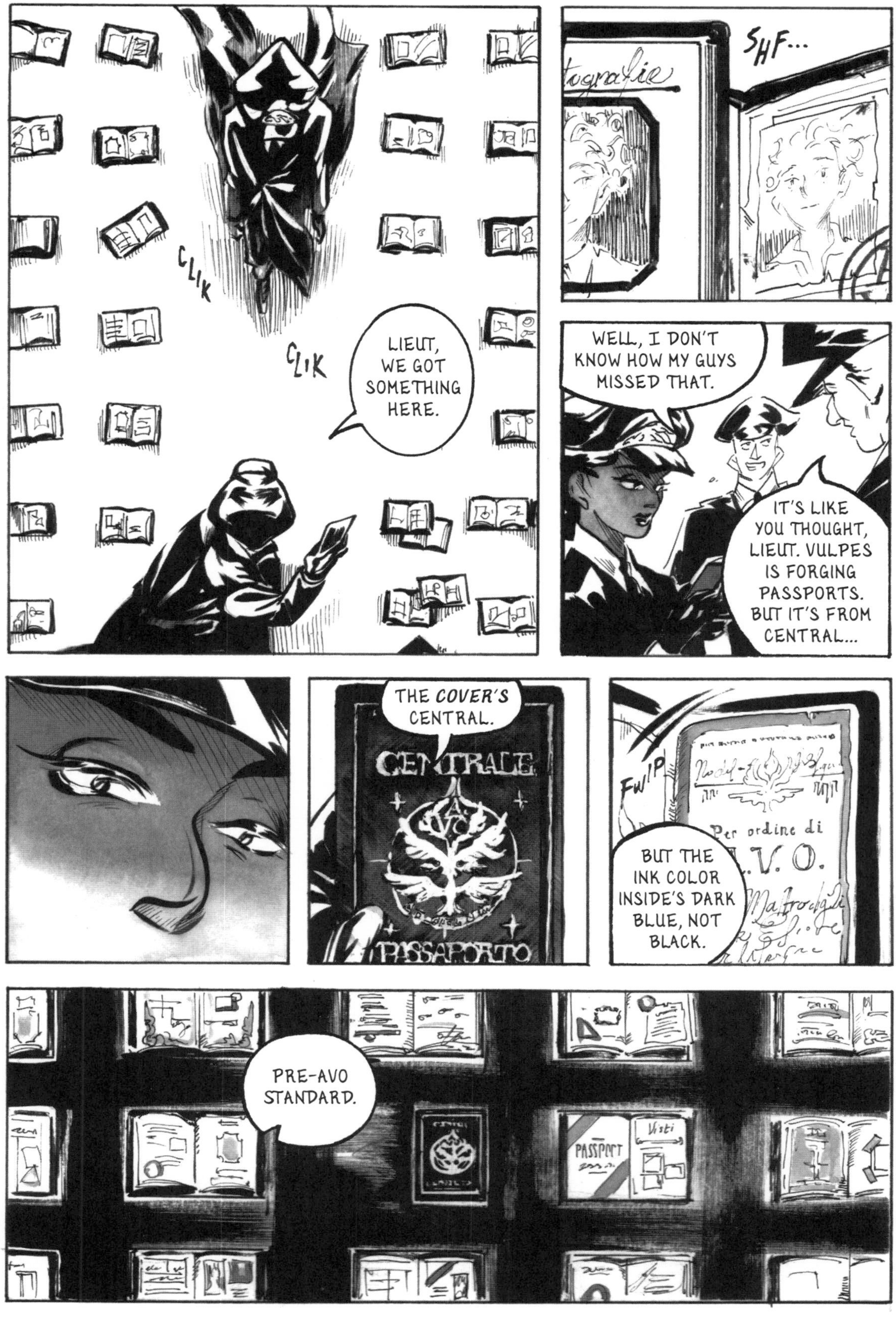
CLIK
CLIK
LIEUT, WE GOT SOMETHING HERE.
SHF...
tografie
WELL, I DON'T KNOW HOW MY GUYS MISSED THAT.
IT'S LIKE YOU THOUGHT, LIEUT. VULPES IS FORGING PASSPORTS. BUT IT'S FROM CENTRAL...
THE COVER'S CENTRAL.
CENTRALE
PASSAPORTO
FWIP
Per ordine di
BUT THE INK COLOR INSIDE'S DARK BLUE, NOT BLACK.
PRE-AVO STANDARD.
PASSPORT
Visti

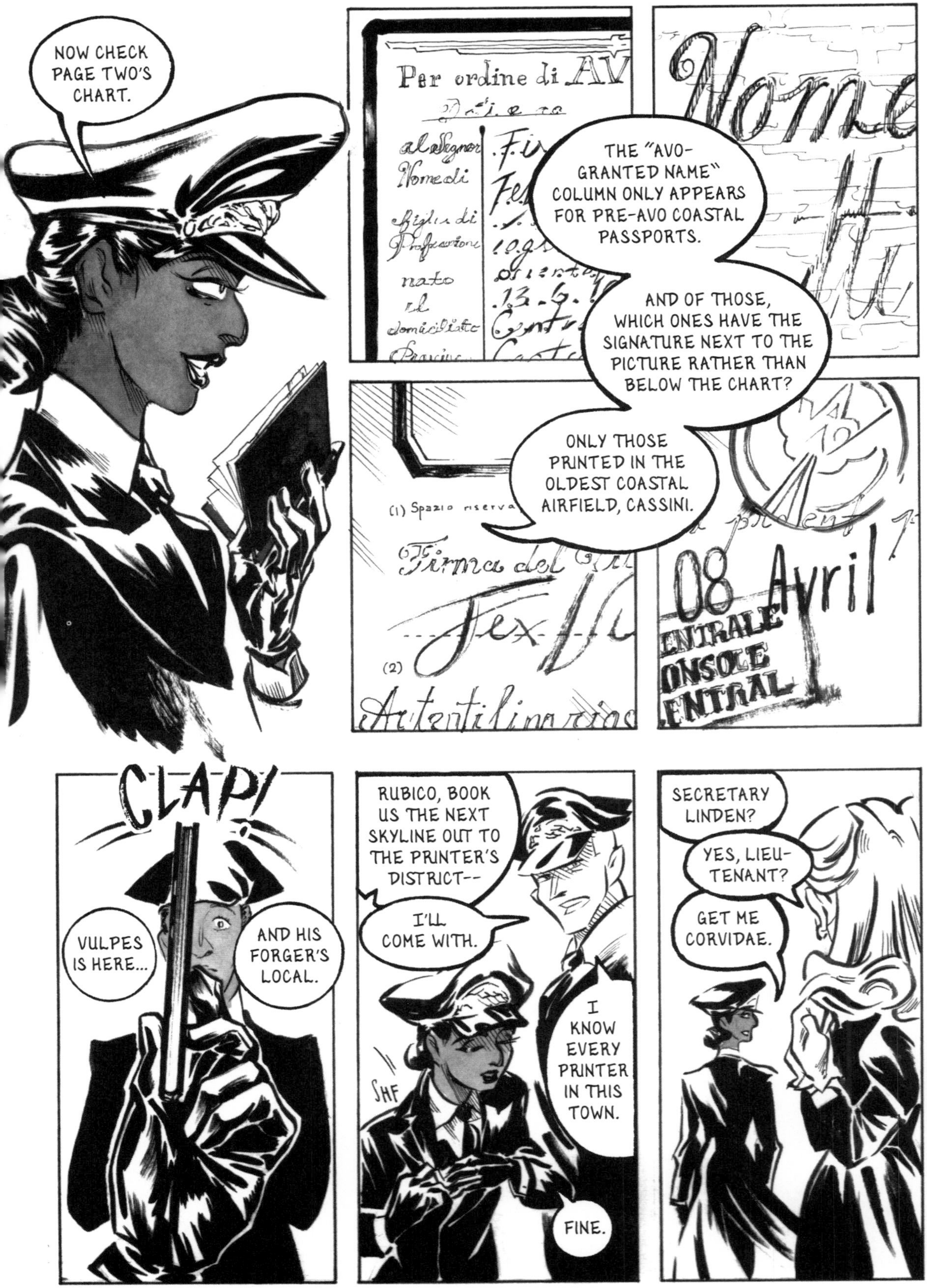
NOW CHECK PAGE TWO'S CHART.
Per ordine di AV
al Signor
Nome di
Figlio di
Professione
nato
il
domiciliato
THE "AVO-GRANTED NAME" COLUMN ONLY APPEARS FOR PRE-AVO COASTAL PASSPORTS.
AND OF THOSE, WHICH ONES HAVE THE SIGNATURE NEXT TO THE PICTURE RATHER THAN BELOW THE CHART?
ONLY THOSE PRINTED IN THE OLDEST COASTAL AIRFIELD, CASSINI.
(1) Spazio riserva
Firma del
(2)
08 Avril
ENTRALE
ONSOLE
ENTRAL
CLAP!
VULPES IS HERE...
AND HIS FORGER'S LOCAL.
RUBICO, BOOK US THE NEXT SKYLINE OUT TO THE PRINTER'S DISTRICT--
I'LL COME WITH.
I KNOW EVERY PRINTER IN THIS TOWN.
SHF
FINE.
SECRETARY LINDEN?
YES, LIEU-TENANT?
GET ME CORVIDAE.

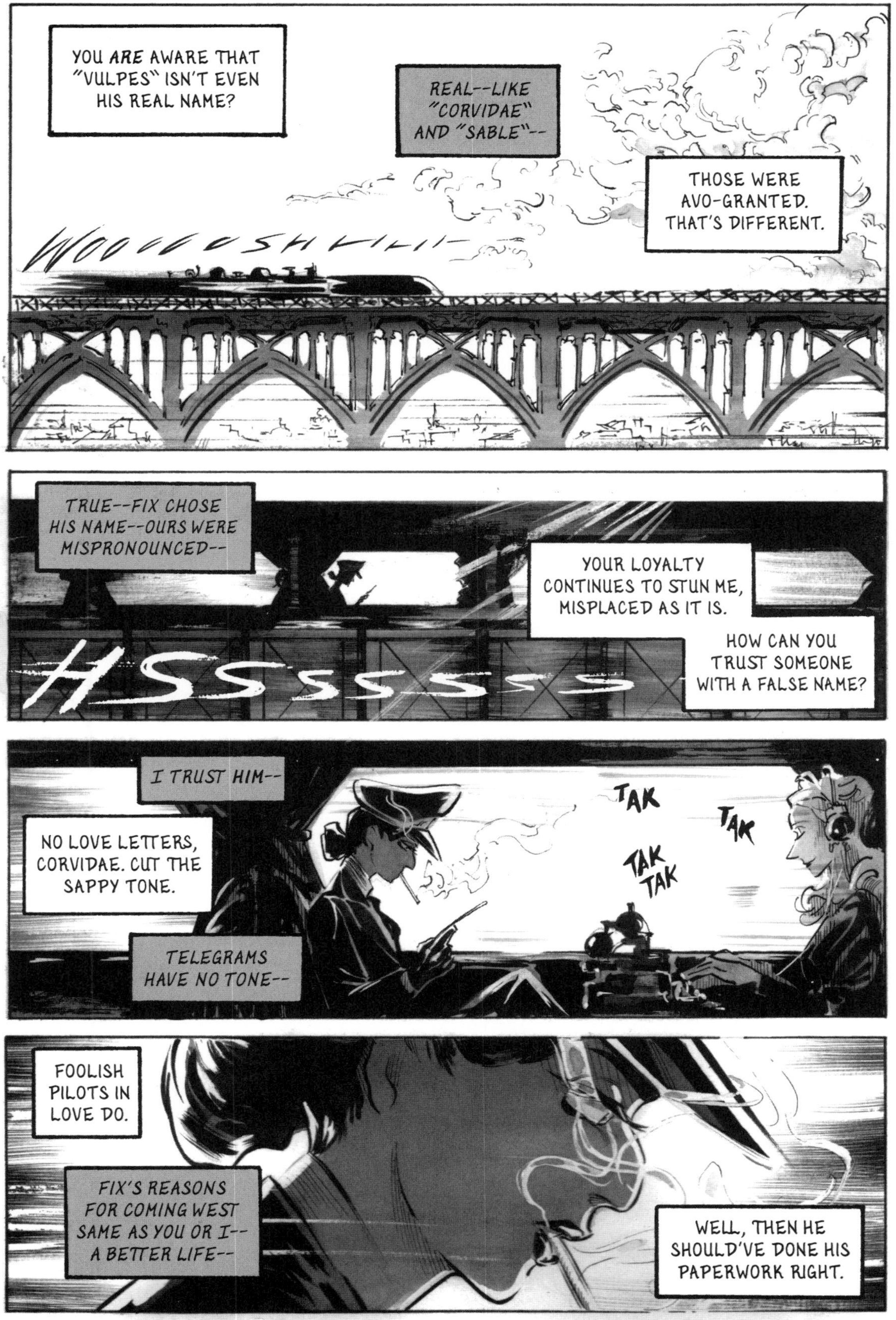
YOU ARE AWARE THAT "VULPES" ISN'T EVEN HIS REAL NAME?
REAL--LIKE "CORVIDAE" AND "SABLE"--
THOSE WERE AVO-GRANTED. THAT'S DIFFERENT.
WOOOOOSHHHH
TRUE--FIX CHOSE HIS NAME--OURS WERE MISPRONOUNCED--
YOUR LOYALTY CONTINUES TO STUN ME, MISPLACED AS IT IS.
HOW CAN YOU TRUST SOMEONE WITH A FALSE NAME?
HSSSSSS
I TRUST HIM--
NO LOVE LETTERS, CORVIDAE. CUT THE SAPPY TONE.
TAK
TAK
TAK TAK
TELEGRAMS HAVE NO TONE--
FOOLISH PILOTS IN LOVE DO.
FIX'S REASONS FOR COMING WEST SAME AS YOU OR I-- A BETTER LIFE--
WELL, THEN HE SHOULD'VE DONE HIS PAPERWORK RIGHT.

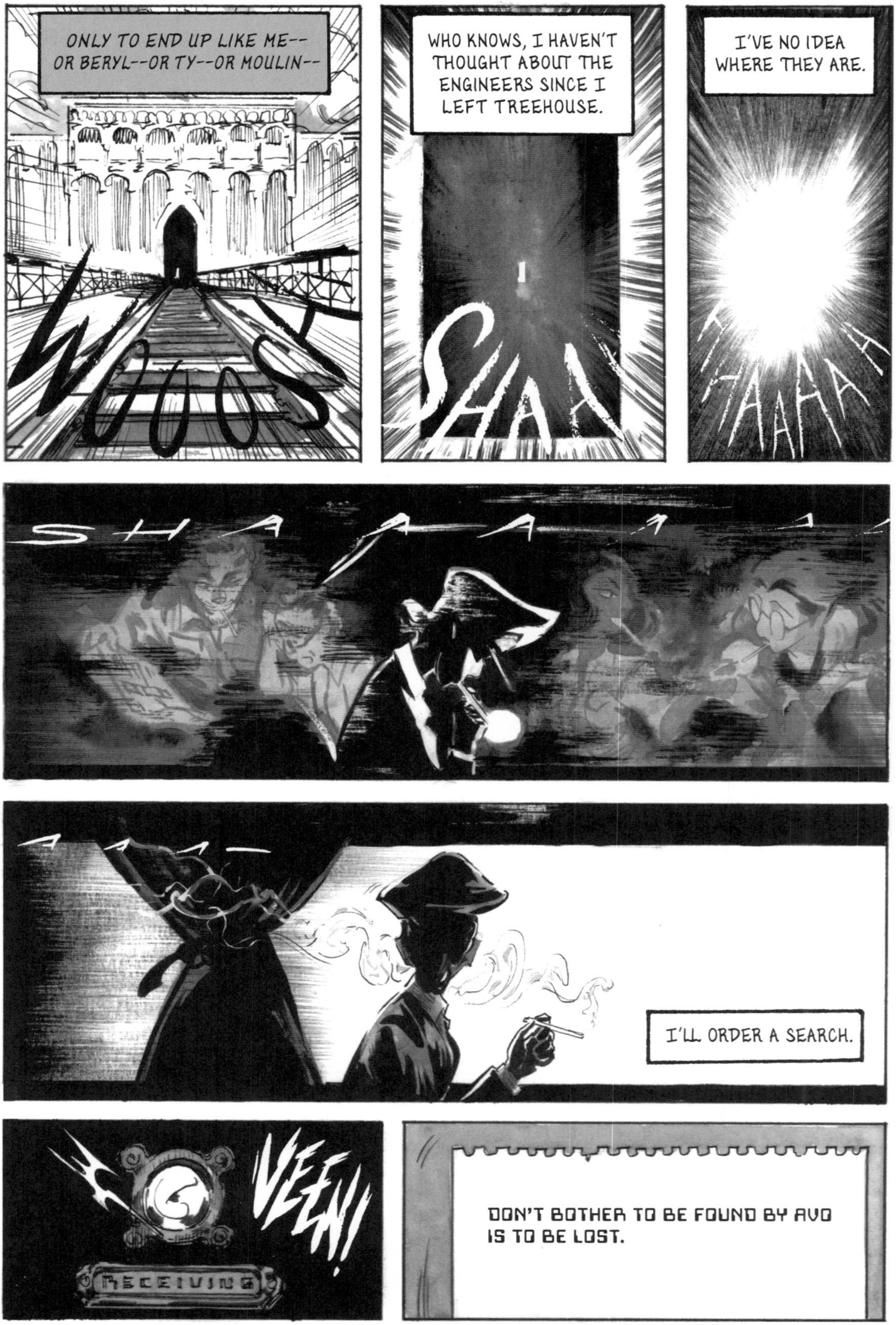
ONLY TO END UP LIKE ME--
OR BERYL--OR TY--OR MOULIN--
WHO KNOWS, I HAVEN'T THOUGHT ABOUT THE ENGINEERS SINCE I LEFT TREEHOUSE.
I'VE NO IDEA WHERE THEY ARE.
I'LL ORDER A SEARCH.
RECEIVING
DON'T BOTHER TO BE FOUND BY AVO IS TO BE LOST.

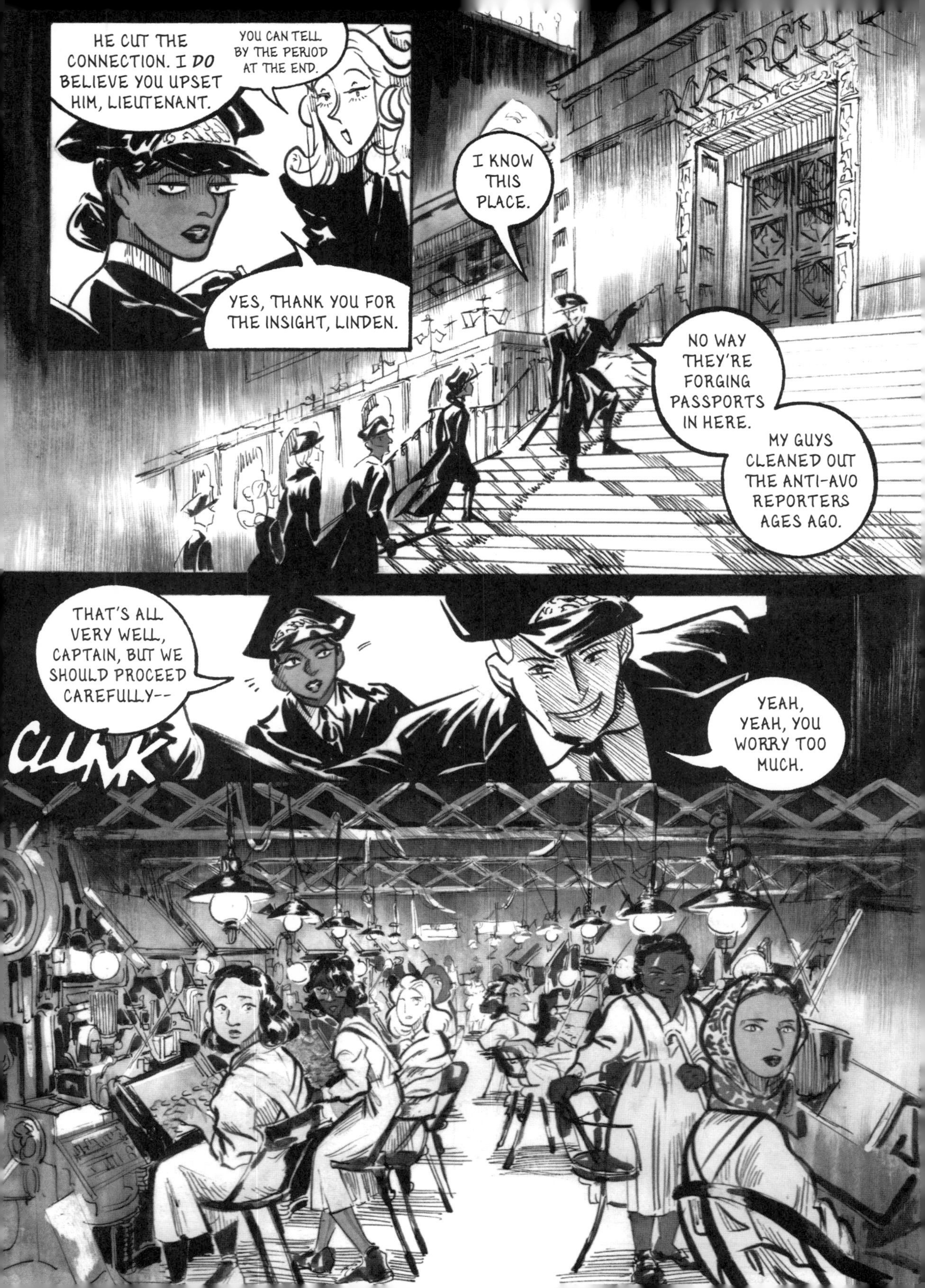
HE CUT THE CONNECTION. I *DO* BELIEVE YOU UPSET HIM, LIEUTENANT.
YOU CAN TELL BY THE PERIOD AT THE END.
YES, THANK YOU FOR THE INSIGHT, LINDEN.
I KNOW THIS PLACE.
NO WAY THEY'RE FORGING PASSPORTS IN HERE.
MY GUYS CLEANED OUT THE ANTI-AVO REPORTERS AGES AGO.
THAT'S ALL VERY WELL, CAPTAIN, BUT WE SHOULD PROCEED CAREFULLY--
YEAH, YEAH, YOU WORRY TOO MUCH.
CLUNK

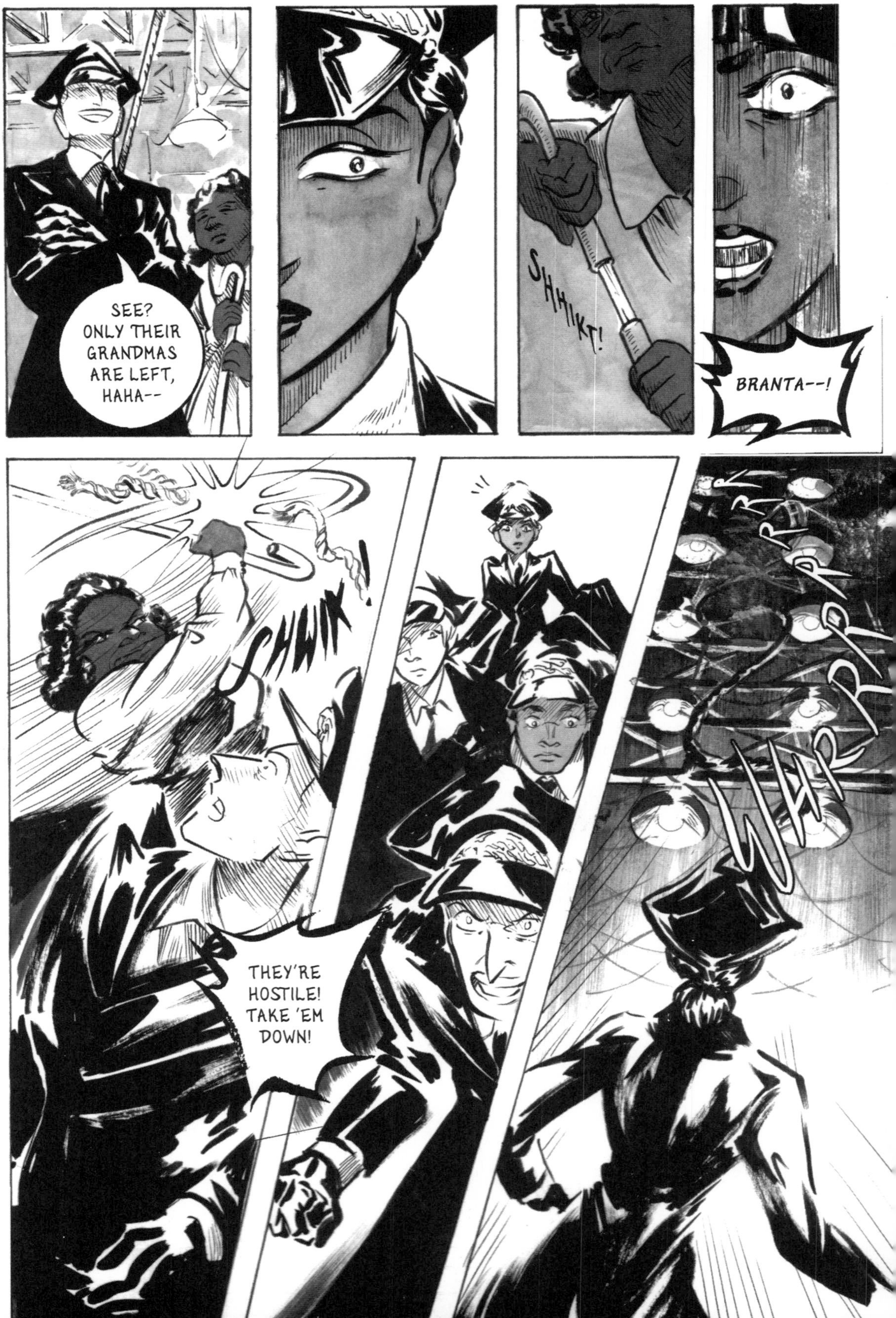
SEE? ONLY THEIR GRANDMAS ARE LEFT, HAHA--
SHHIKT!
BRANTA--!
SCHWIK!
THEY'RE HOSTILE! TAKE 'EM DOWN!
WHRRRRRR

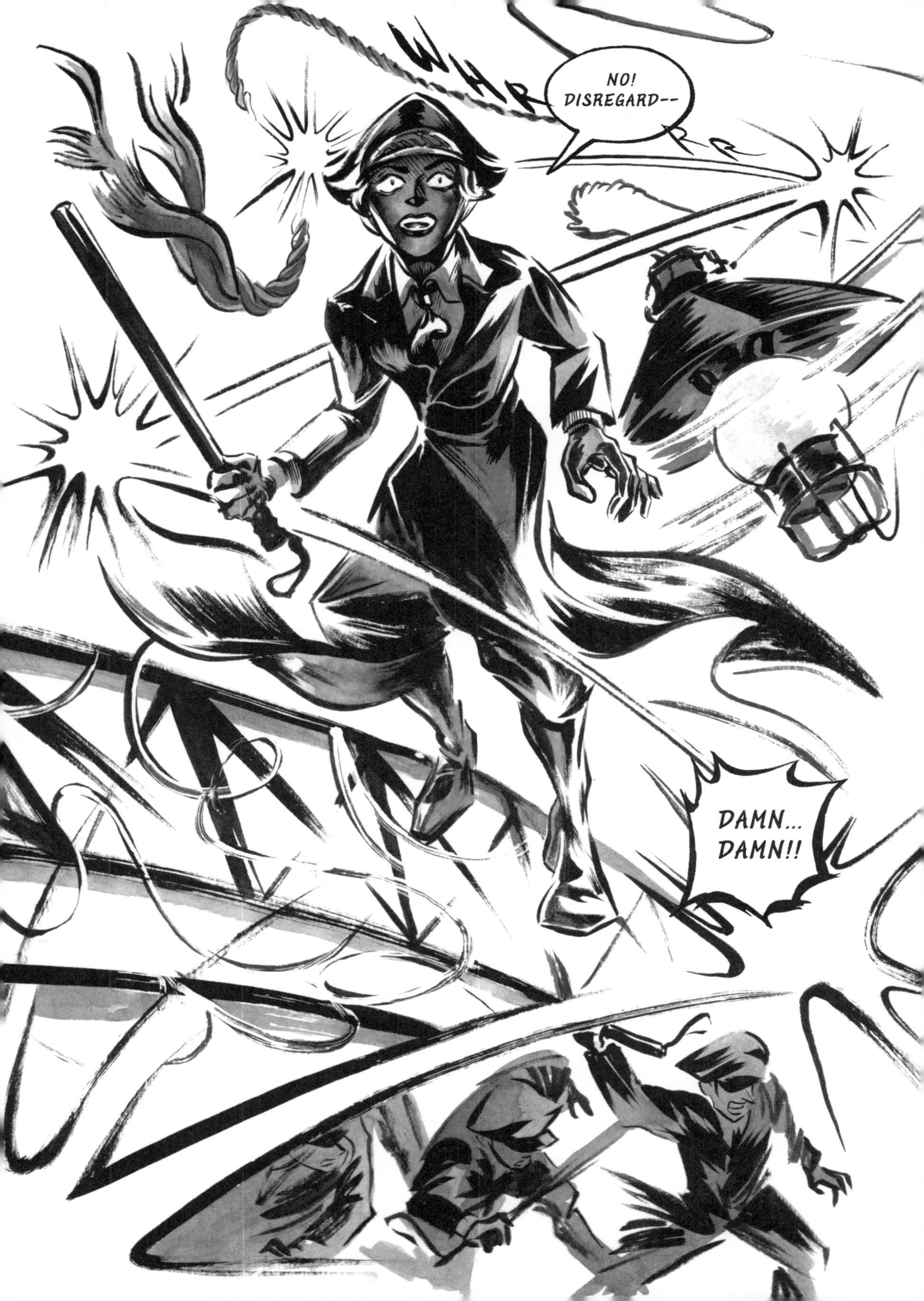
WHRRR
NO! DISREGARD--
DAMN... DAMN!!

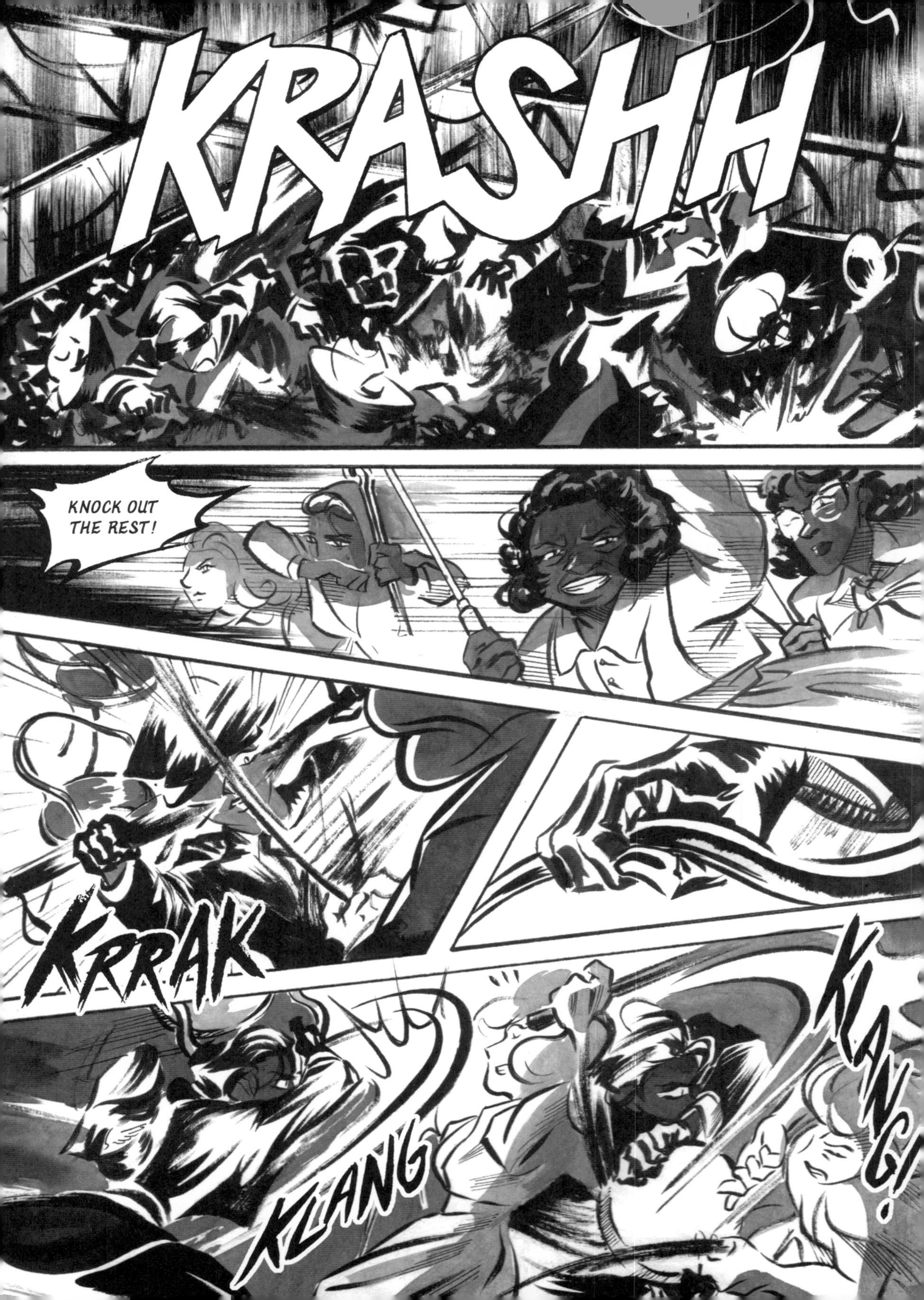
KRASHH
KNOCK OUT THE REST!
KRRAK
KLANG
KLANG!

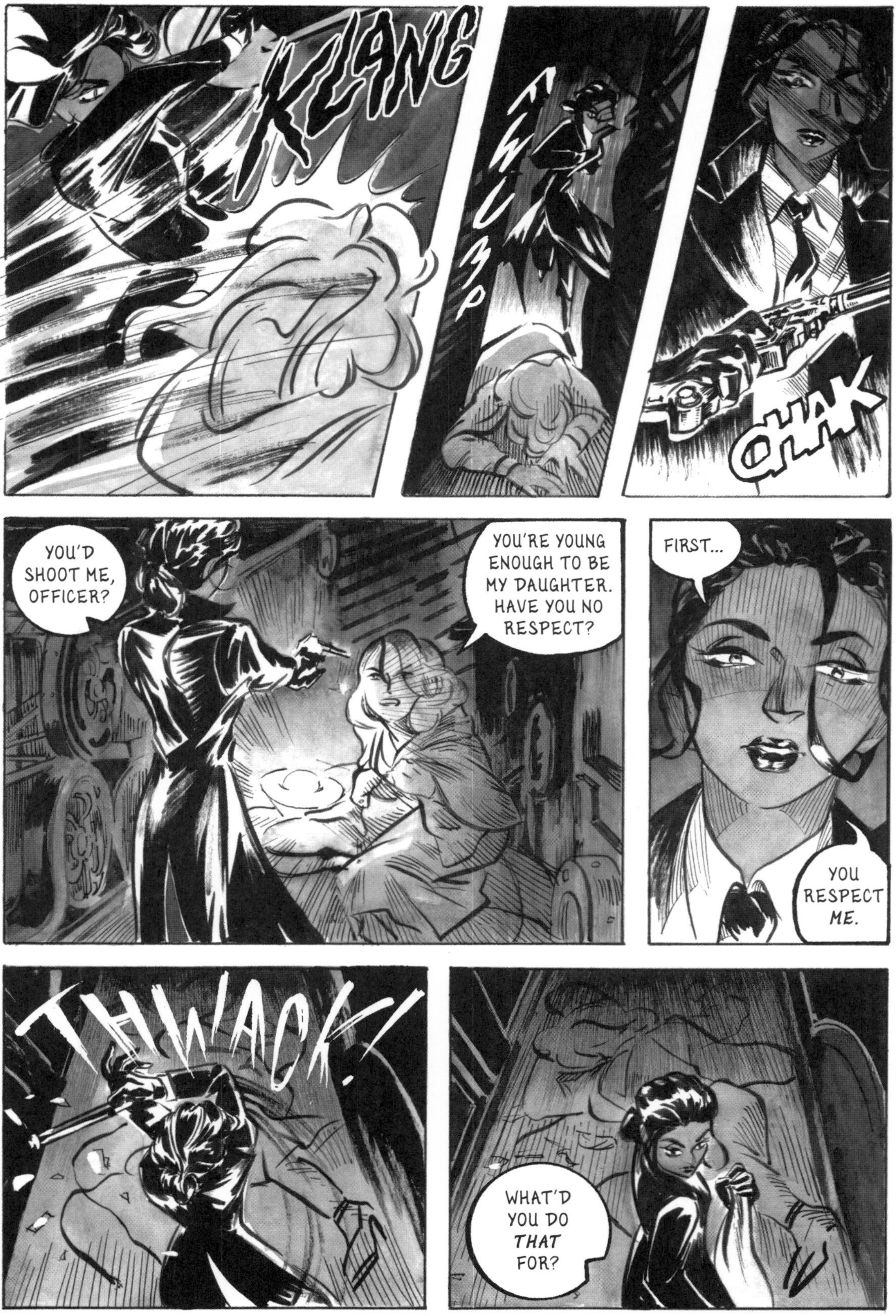
KLANG
FWUMP
CHAK
YOU'D SHOOT ME, OFFICER?
YOU'RE YOUNG ENOUGH TO BE MY DAUGHTER. HAVE YOU NO RESPECT?
FIRST...
YOU RESPECT *ME.*
THWACK!
WHAT'D YOU DO *THAT* FOR?

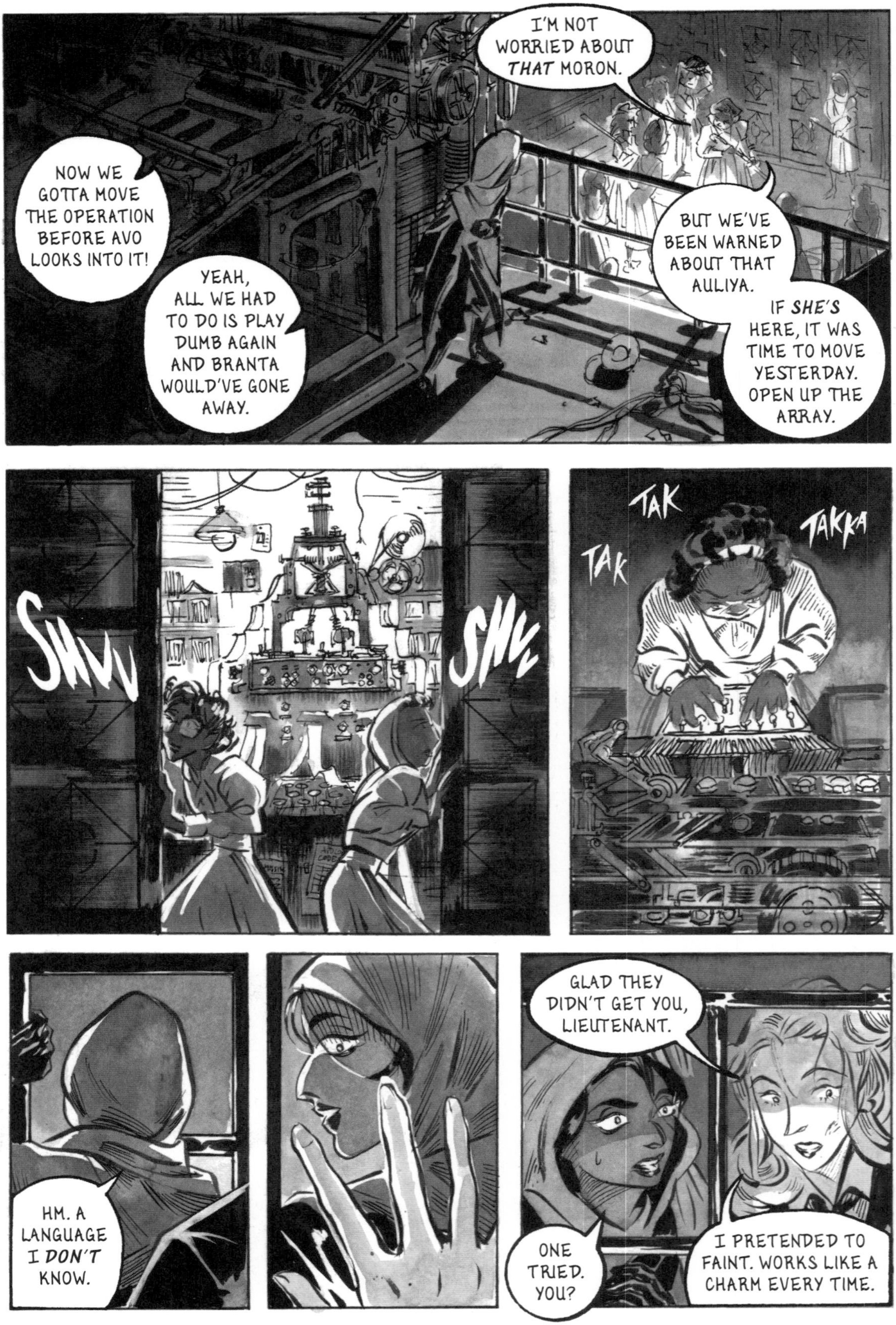
NOW WE GOTTA MOVE THE OPERATION BEFORE AVO LOOKS INTO IT!
YEAH, ALL WE HAD TO DO IS PLAY DUMB AGAIN AND BRANTA WOULD'VE GONE AWAY.
I'M NOT WORRIED ABOUT *THAT* MORON.
BUT WE'VE BEEN WARNED ABOUT THAT AULIYA.
IF *SHE'S* HERE, IT WAS TIME TO MOVE YESTERDAY. OPEN UP THE ARRAY.
SHVV
SHVV
TAK
TAK
TAKKA
HM. A LANGUAGE I *DON'T* KNOW.
GLAD THEY DIDN'T GET YOU, LIEUTENANT.
ONE TRIED. YOU?
I PRETENDED TO FAINT. WORKS LIKE A CHARM EVERY TIME.

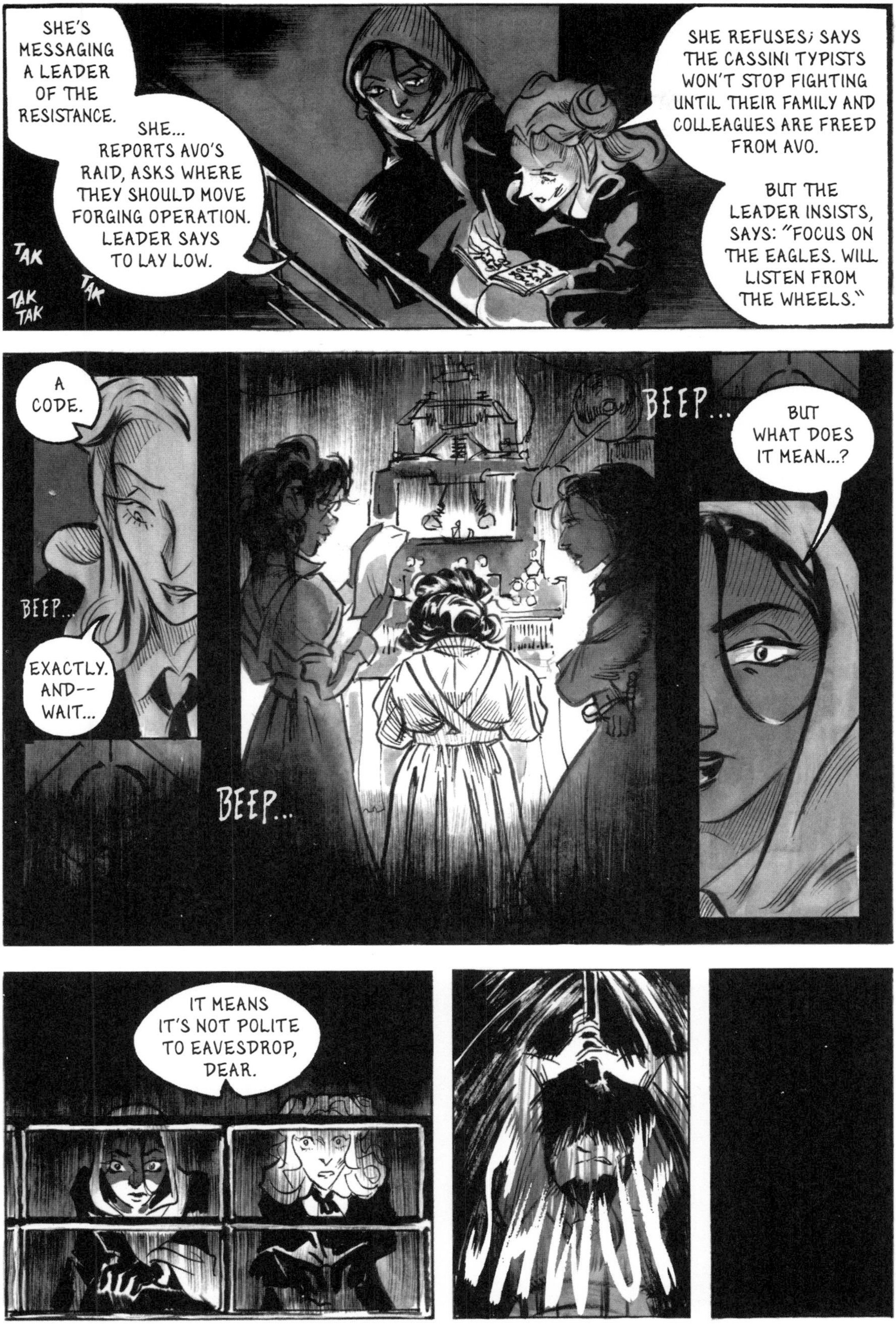
SHE'S MESSAGING A LEADER OF THE RESISTANCE.
SHE... REPORTS AVO'S RAID, ASKS WHERE THEY SHOULD MOVE FORGING OPERATION. LEADER SAYS TO LAY LOW.
TAK TAK TAK TAK
SHE REFUSES; SAYS THE CASSINI TYPISTS WON'T STOP FIGHTING UNTIL THEIR FAMILY AND COLLEAGUES ARE FREED FROM AVO.
BUT THE LEADER INSISTS, SAYS: "FOCUS ON THE EAGLES. WILL LISTEN FROM THE WHEELS."
A CODE.
BEEP...
BUT WHAT DOES IT MEAN...?
BEEP...
EXACTLY. AND-- WAIT...
BEEP...
IT MEANS IT'S NOT POLITE TO EAVESDROP, DEAR.

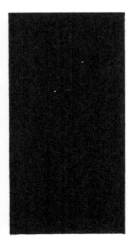

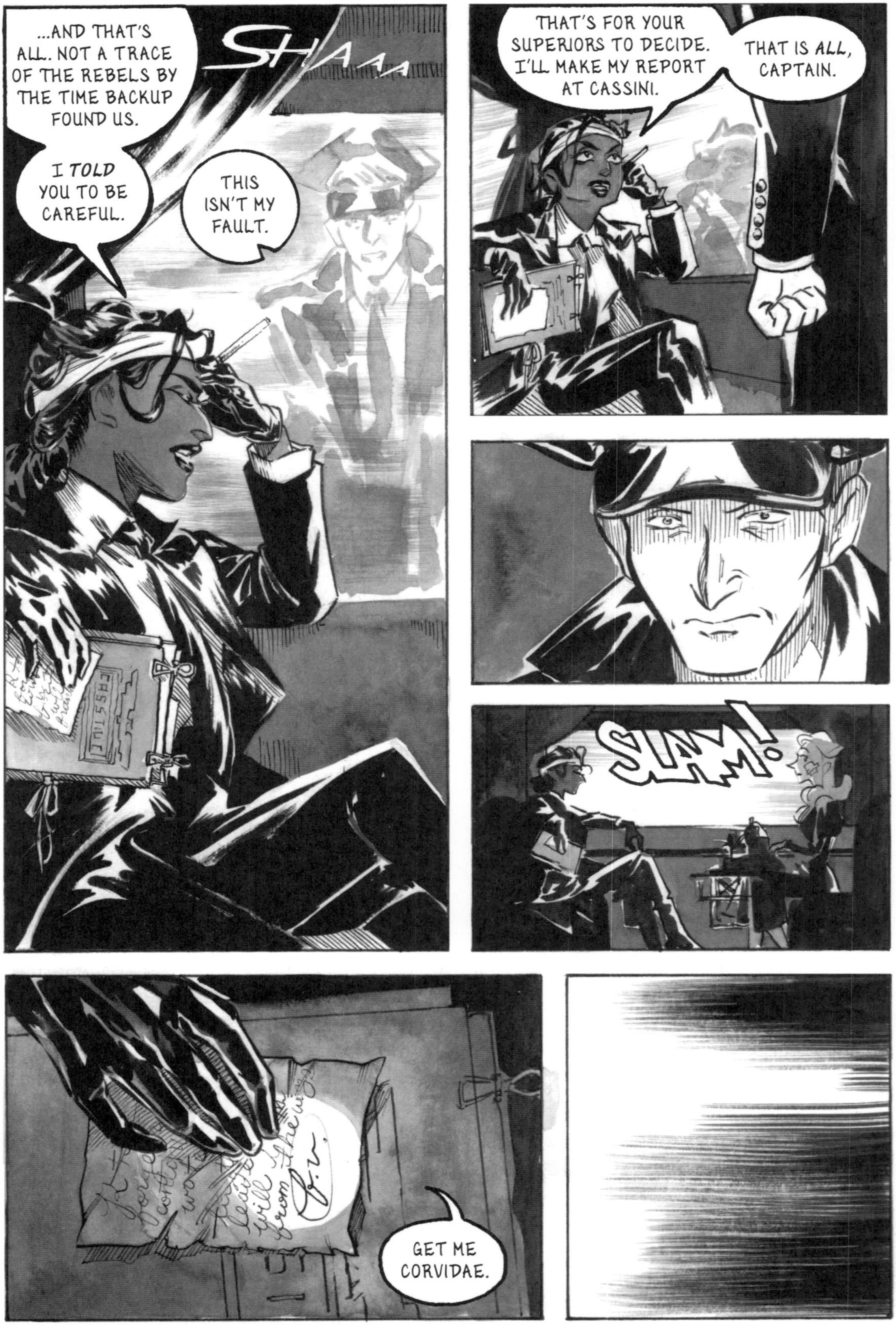
...AND THAT'S ALL.. NOT A TRACE OF THE REBELS BY THE TIME BACKUP FOUND US.
SHAAA
I TOLD YOU TO BE CAREFUL.
THIS ISN'T MY FAULT.
THAT'S FOR YOUR SUPERIORS TO DECIDE. I'LL MAKE MY REPORT AT CASSINI.
THAT IS ALL, CAPTAIN.
SLAM!
GET ME CORVIDAE.

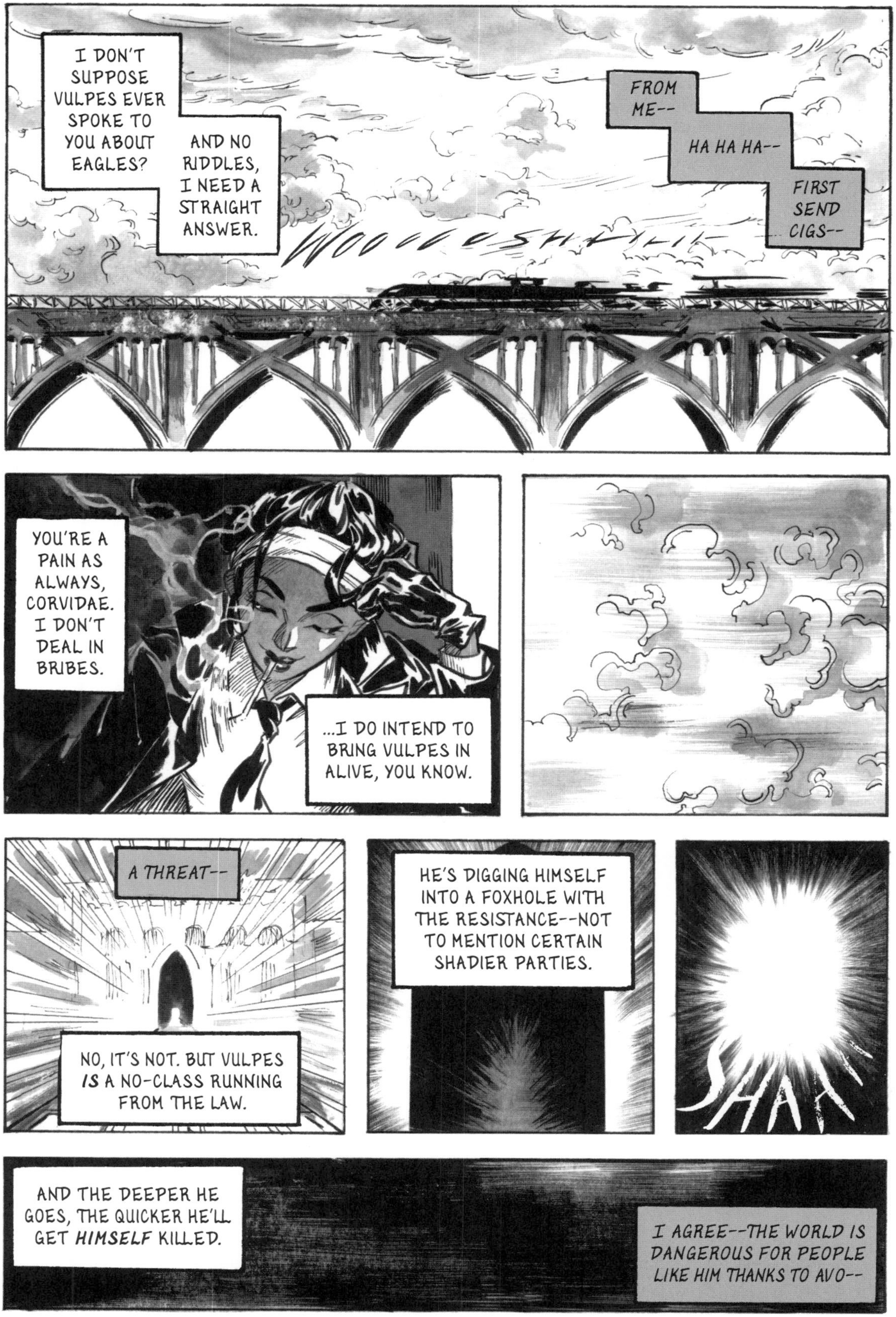

I DON'T SUPPOSE VULPES EVER SPOKE TO YOU ABOUT EAGLES?
AND NO RIDDLES, I NEED A STRAIGHT ANSWER.
FROM ME--
HA HA HA--
FIRST SEND CIGS--
WOOOOOOSHHHHHH
YOU'RE A PAIN AS ALWAYS, CORVIDAE. I DON'T DEAL IN BRIBES.
...I DO INTEND TO BRING VULPES IN ALIVE, YOU KNOW.
A THREAT--
NO, IT'S NOT. BUT VULPES *IS* A NO-CLASS RUNNING FROM THE LAW.
HE'S DIGGING HIMSELF INTO A FOXHOLE WITH THE RESISTANCE--NOT TO MENTION CERTAIN SHADIER PARTIES.
SHAH
AND THE DEEPER HE GOES, THE QUICKER HE'LL GET *HIMSELF* KILLED.
I AGREE--THE WORLD IS DANGEROUS FOR PEOPLE LIKE HIM THANKS TO AVO--

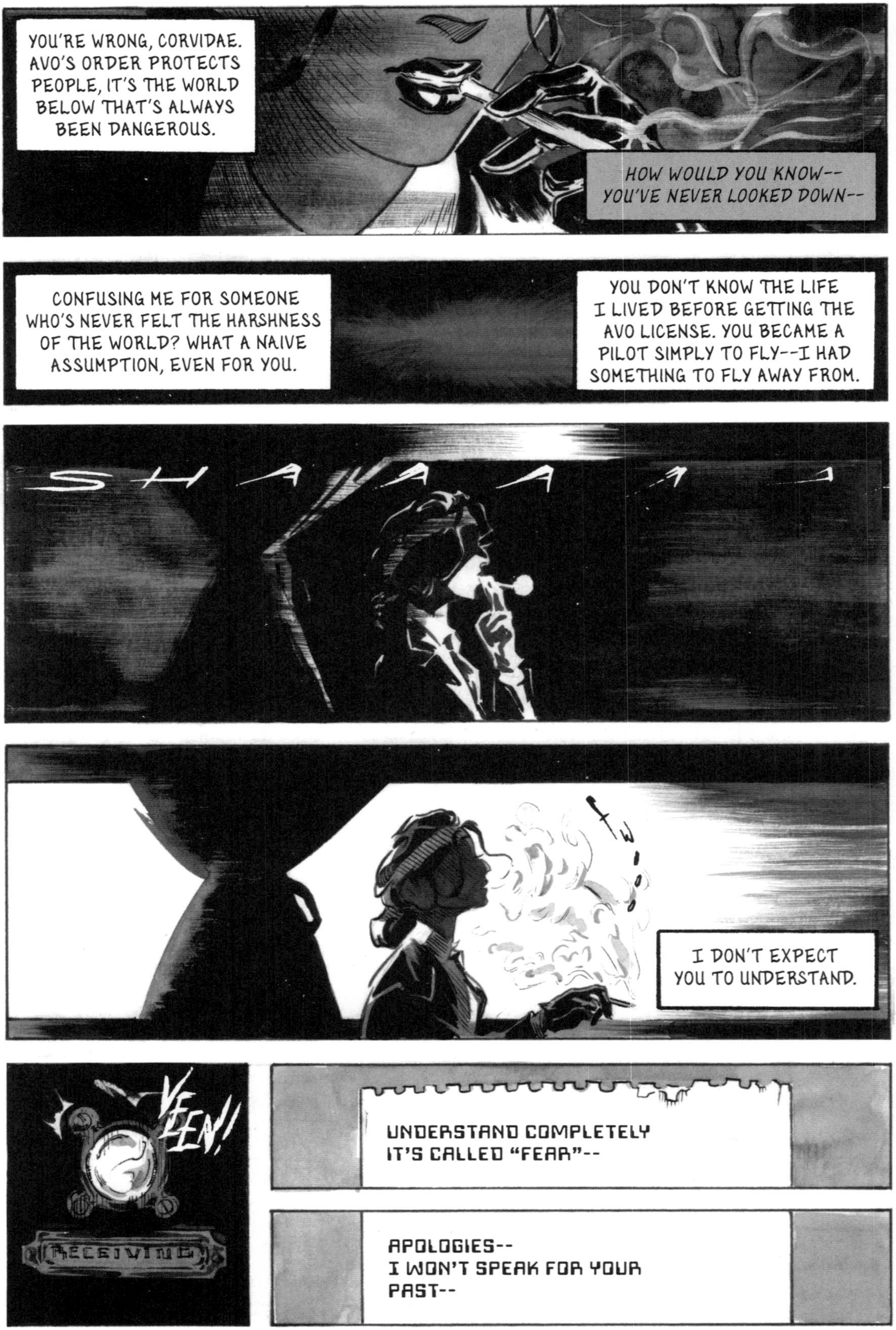
YOU'RE WRONG, CORVIDAE. AVO'S ORDER PROTECTS PEOPLE, IT'S THE WORLD BELOW THAT'S ALWAYS BEEN DANGEROUS.
HOW WOULD YOU KNOW-- YOU'VE NEVER LOOKED DOWN--
CONFUSING ME FOR SOMEONE WHO'S NEVER FELT THE HARSHNESS OF THE WORLD? WHAT A NAIVE ASSUMPTION, EVEN FOR YOU.
YOU DON'T KNOW THE LIFE I LIVED BEFORE GETTING THE AVO LICENSE. YOU BECAME A PILOT SIMPLY TO FLY--I HAD SOMETHING TO FLY AWAY FROM.
SHAAAA
I DON'T EXPECT YOU TO UNDERSTAND.
VEEN!
RECEIVING
UNDERSTAND COMPLETELY
IT'S CALLED "FEAR"--
APOLOGIES--
I WON'T SPEAK FOR YOUR
PAST--

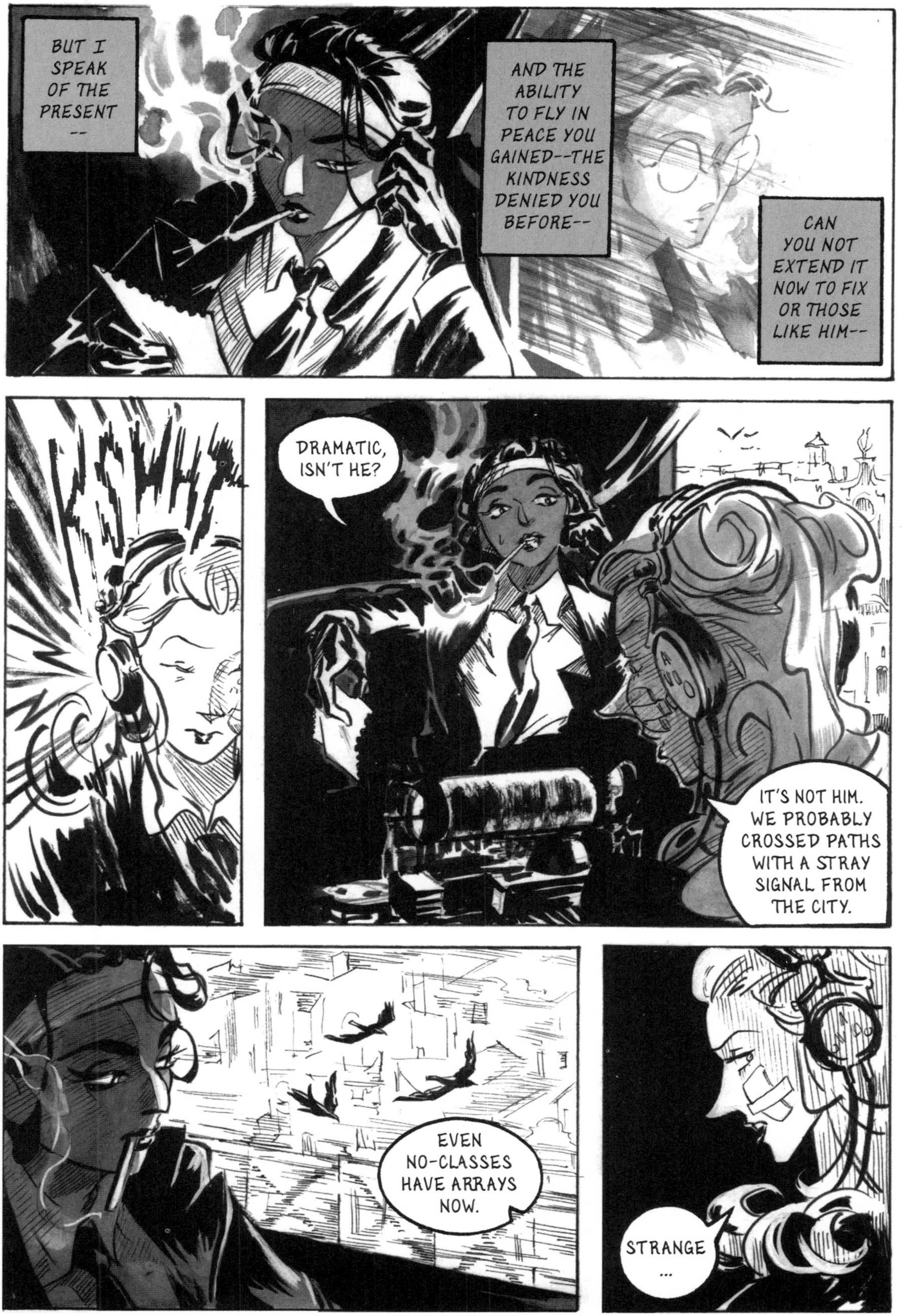
BUT I SPEAK OF THE PRESENT --
AND THE ABILITY TO FLY IN PEACE YOU GAINED--THE KINDNESS DENIED YOU BEFORE--
CAN YOU NOT EXTEND IT NOW TO FIX OR THOSE LIKE HIM--
KSHHZ
DRAMATIC, ISN'T HE?
IT'S NOT HIM. WE PROBABLY CROSSED PATHS WITH A STRAY SIGNAL FROM THE CITY.
EVEN NO-CLASSES HAVE ARRAYS NOW.
STRANGE ...

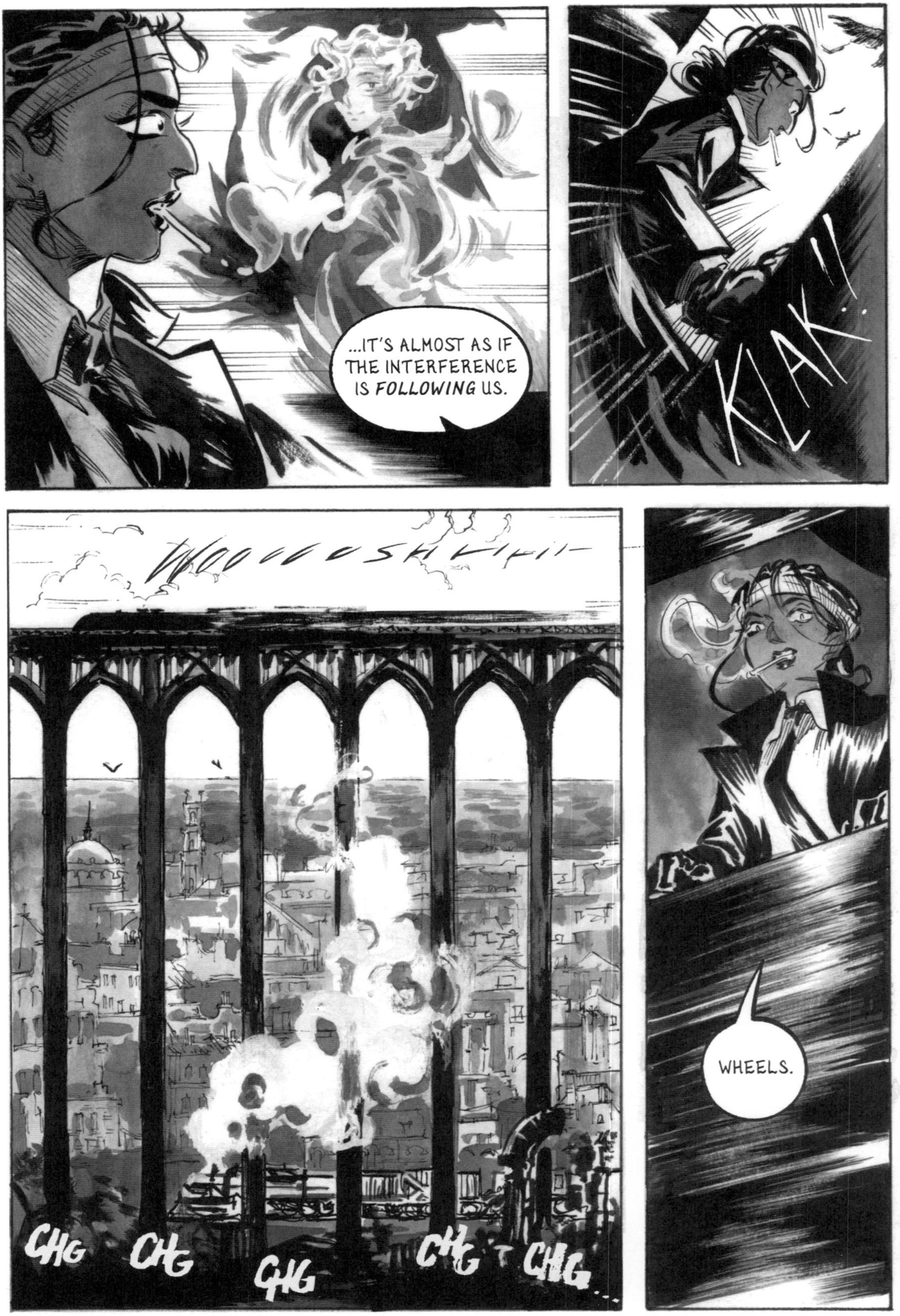
...IT'S ALMOST AS IF THE INTERFERENCE IS *FOLLOWING* US.
KLAK!!
WOOOOOOSHHHHH—
WHEELS.
CHG CHG CHG CHG CHG...

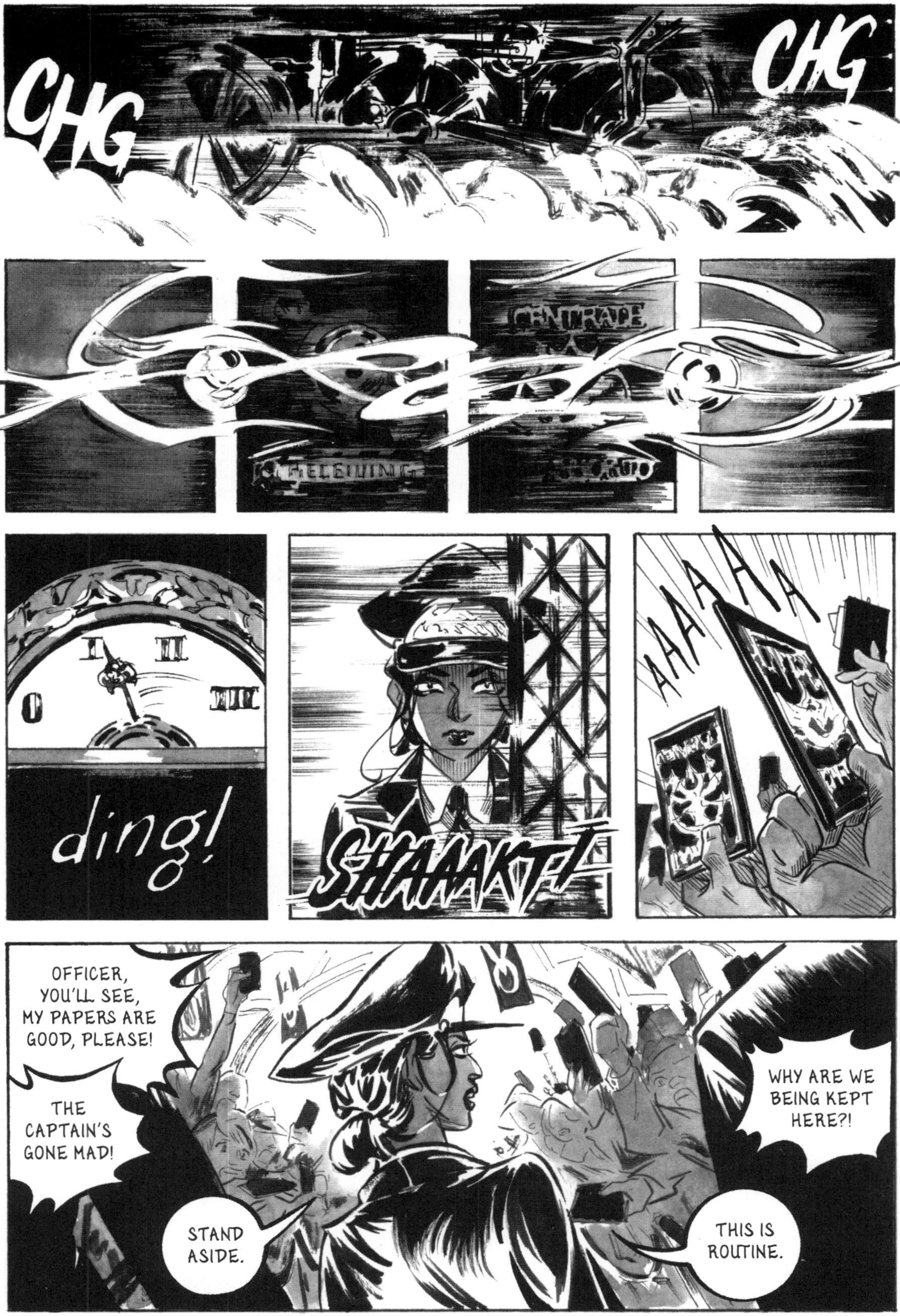
CHG
CHG
ding!
SHAAAKT!
AAAAAA
OFFICER, YOU'LL SEE, MY PAPERS ARE GOOD, PLEASE!
THE CAPTAIN'S GONE MAD!
WHY ARE WE BEING KEPT HERE?!
STAND ASIDE.
THIS IS ROUTINE.

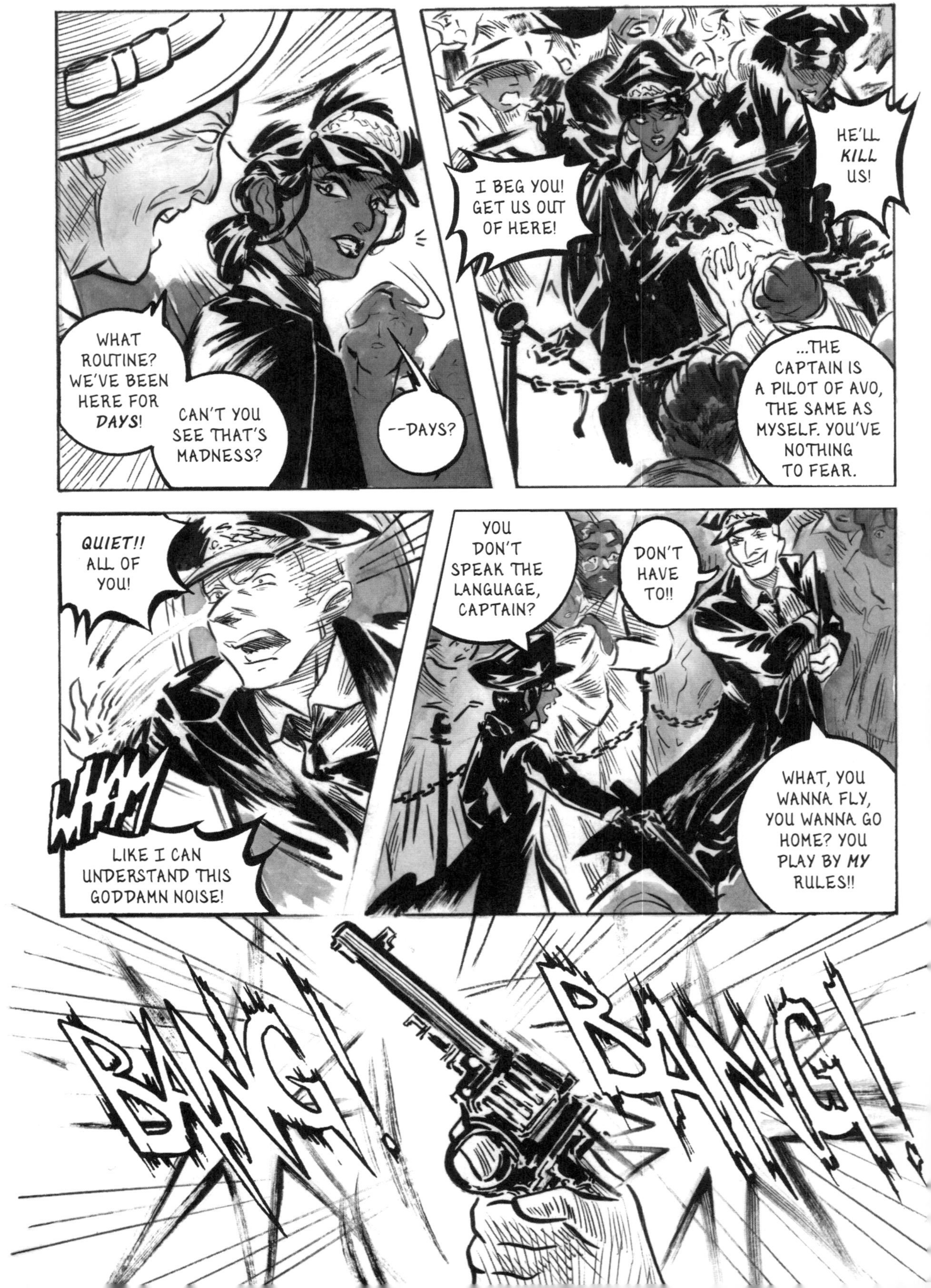
WHAT ROUTINE? WE'VE BEEN HERE FOR DAYS!
CAN'T YOU SEE THAT'S MADNESS?
--DAYS?
I BEG YOU! GET US OUT OF HERE!
HE'LL KILL US!
...THE CAPTAIN IS A PILOT OF AVO, THE SAME AS MYSELF. YOU'VE NOTHING TO FEAR.
QUIET!! ALL OF YOU!
WHAM
LIKE I CAN UNDERSTAND THIS GODDAMN NOISE!
YOU DON'T SPEAK THE LANGUAGE, CAPTAIN?
DON'T HAVE TO!!
WHAT, YOU WANNA FLY, YOU WANNA GO HOME? YOU PLAY BY MY RULES!!
BANG!
BANG!

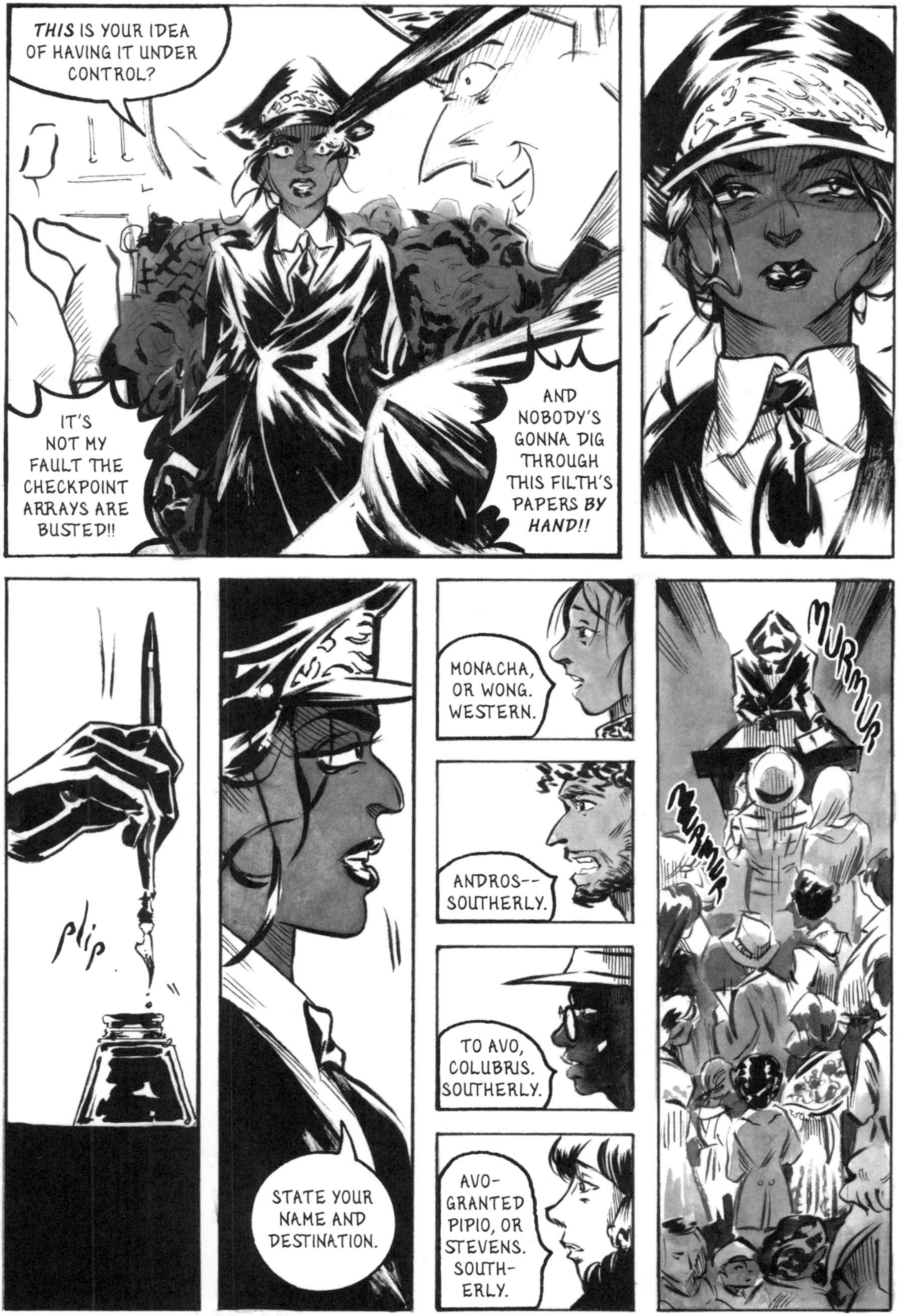
THIS IS YOUR IDEA OF HAVING IT UNDER CONTROL?
IT'S NOT MY FAULT THE CHECKPOINT ARRAYS ARE BUSTED!!
AND NOBODY'S GONNA DIG THROUGH THIS FILTH'S PAPERS BY HAND!!
plip
STATE YOUR NAME AND DESTINATION.
MONACHA, OR WONG. WESTERN.
ANDROS-- SOUTHERLY.
TO AVO, COLUBRIS. SOUTHERLY.
AVO-GRANTED PIPIO, OR STEVENS. SOUTH-ERLY.
MURMUR
MURMUR

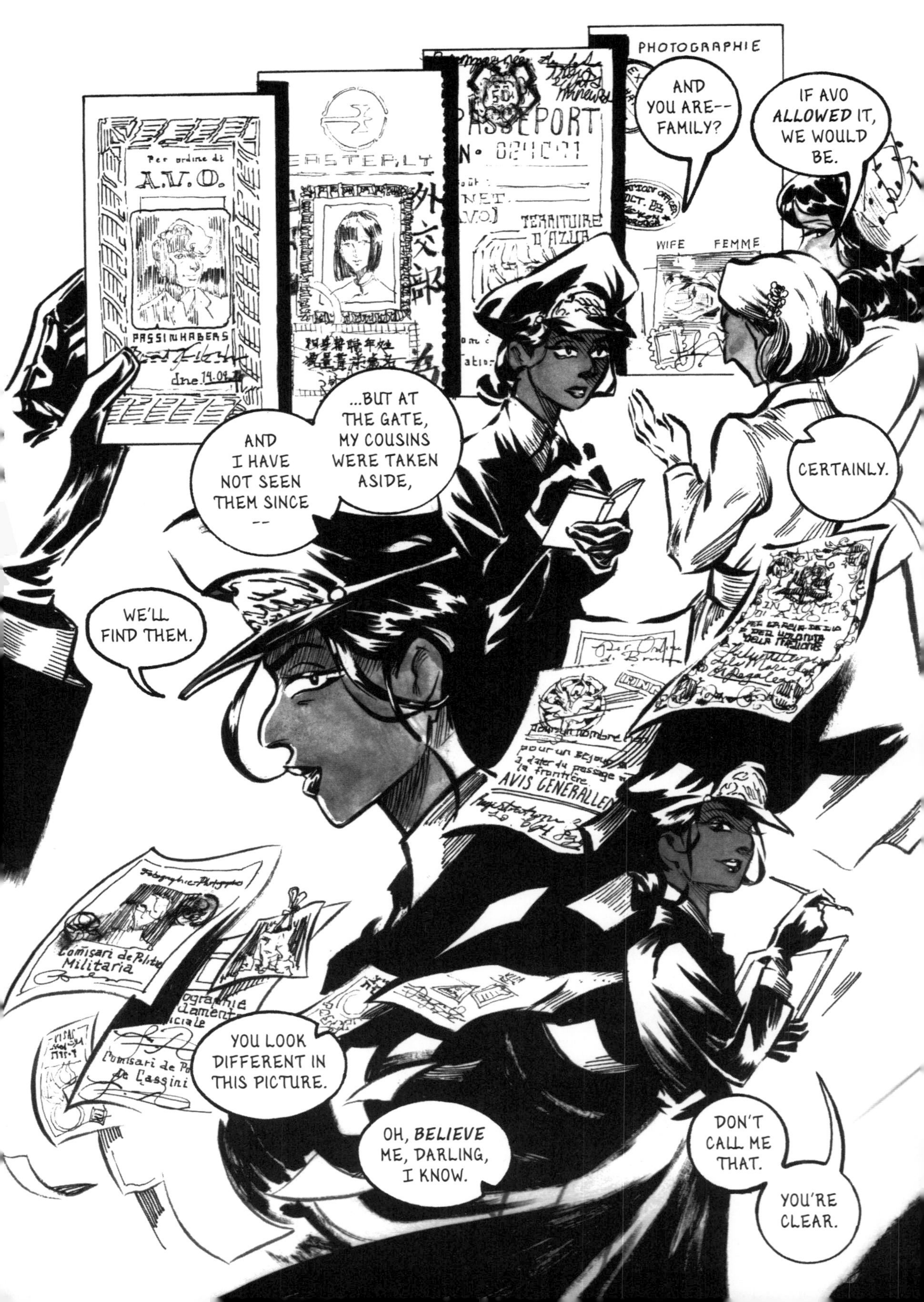
AND YOU ARE--FAMILY?
IF AVO ALLOWED IT, WE WOULD BE.
CERTAINLY.
AND I HAVE NOT SEEN THEM SINCE --
...BUT AT THE GATE, MY COUSINS WERE TAKEN ASIDE,
WE'LL FIND THEM.
YOU LOOK DIFFERENT IN THIS PICTURE.
OH, BELIEVE ME, DARLING, I KNOW.
DON'T CALL ME THAT.
YOU'RE CLEAR.
PASSEPORT
PHOTOGRAPHIE
WIFE FEMME
A.V.O.
AVIS GENERALLEN

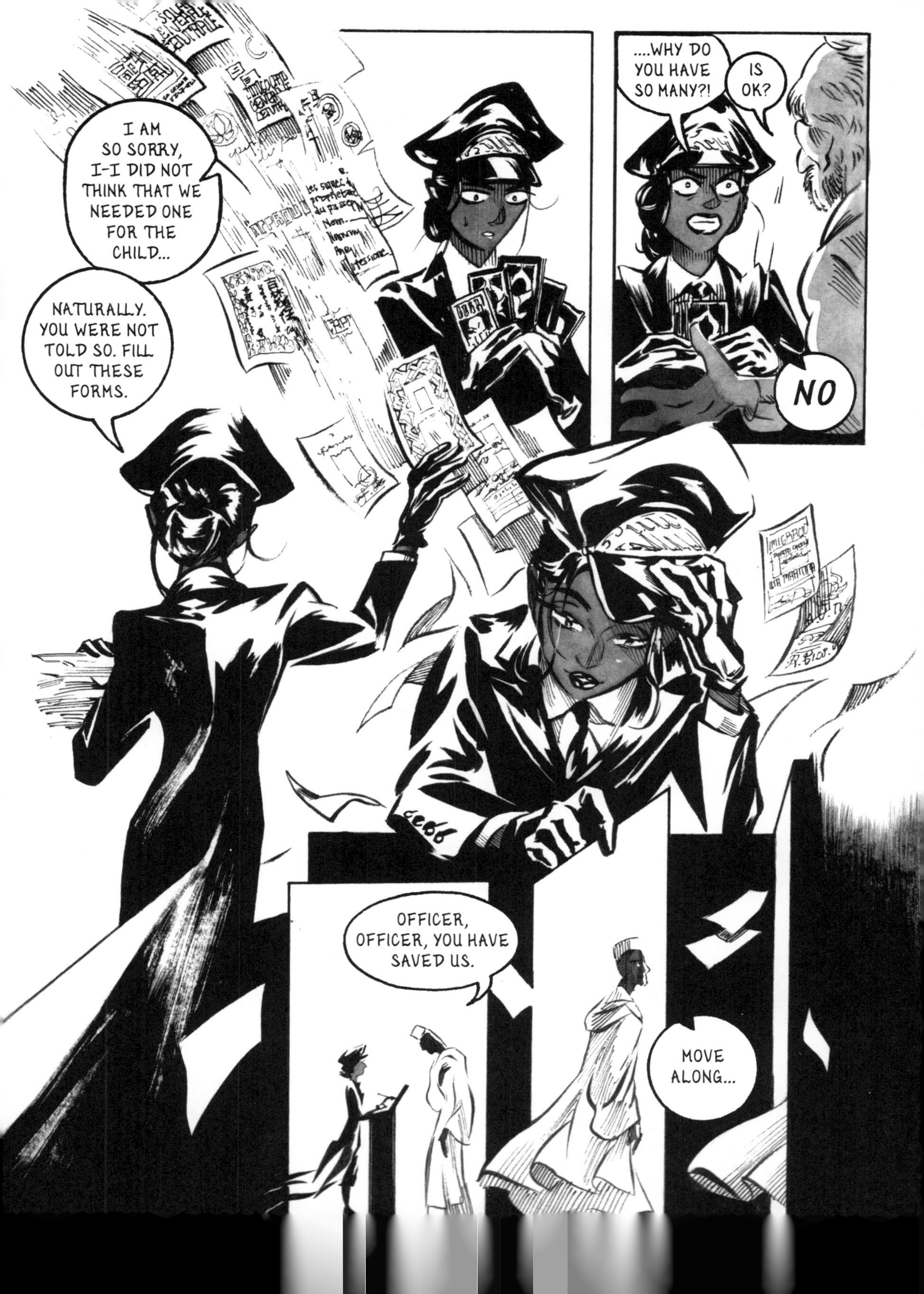

I AM SO SORRY, I-I DID NOT THINK THAT WE NEEDED ONE FOR THE CHILD...
NATURALLY. YOU WERE NOT TOLD SO. FILL OUT THESE FORMS.
....WHY DO YOU HAVE SO MANY?!
IS OK?
NO
OFFICER, OFFICER, YOU HAVE SAVED US.
MOVE ALONG...

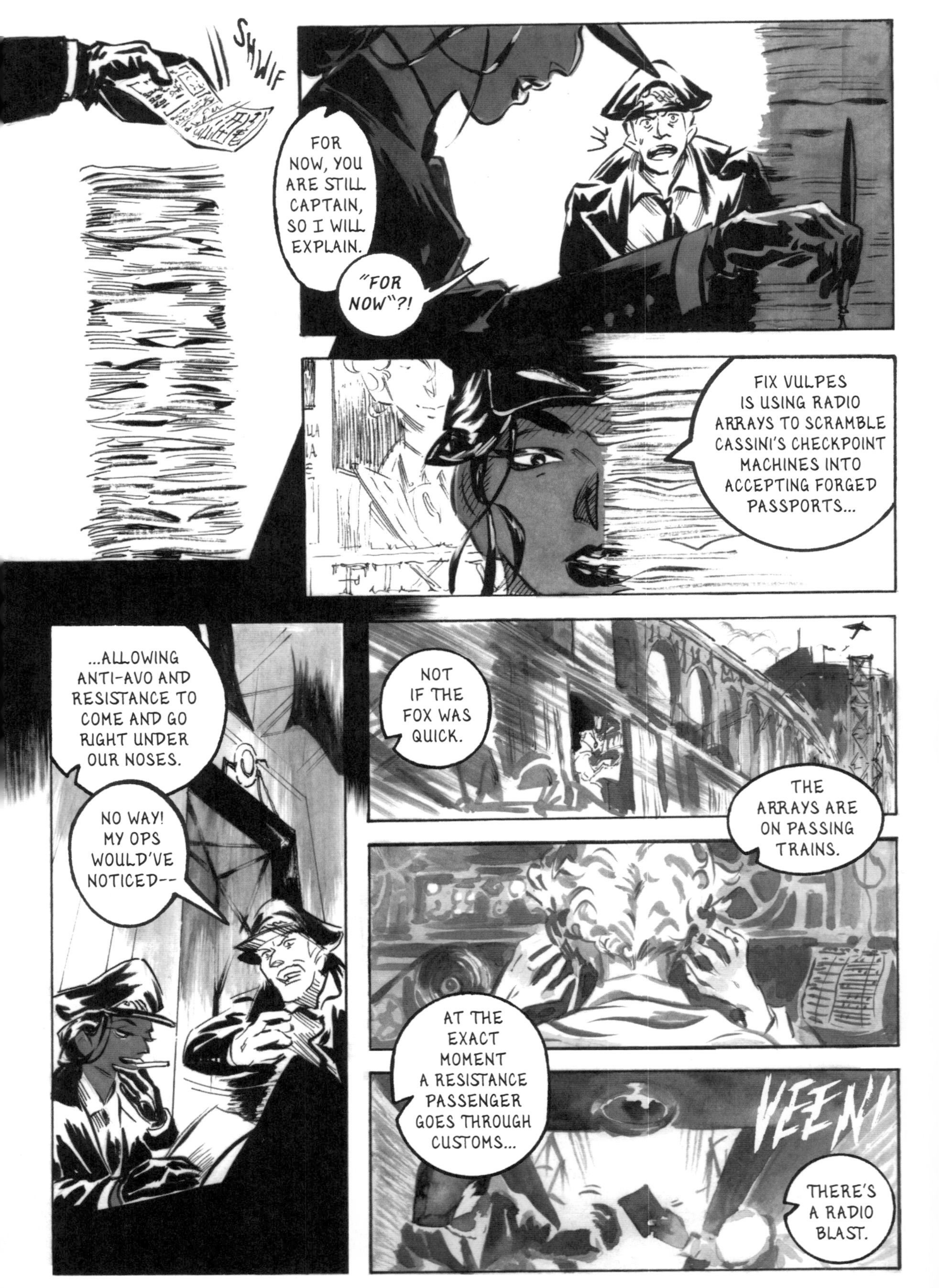
SHWIF
FOR NOW, YOU ARE STILL CAPTAIN, SO I WILL EXPLAIN.
"FOR NOW"?!
FIX VULPES IS USING RADIO ARRAYS TO SCRAMBLE CASSINI'S CHECKPOINT MACHINES INTO ACCEPTING FORGED PASSPORTS...
...ALLOWING ANTI-AVO AND RESISTANCE TO COME AND GO RIGHT UNDER OUR NOSES.
NO WAY! MY OPS WOULD'VE NOTICED--
NOT IF THE FOX WAS QUICK.
THE ARRAYS ARE ON PASSING TRAINS.
AT THE EXACT MOMENT A RESISTANCE PASSENGER GOES THROUGH CUSTOMS...
VEEN!
THERE'S A RADIO BLAST.

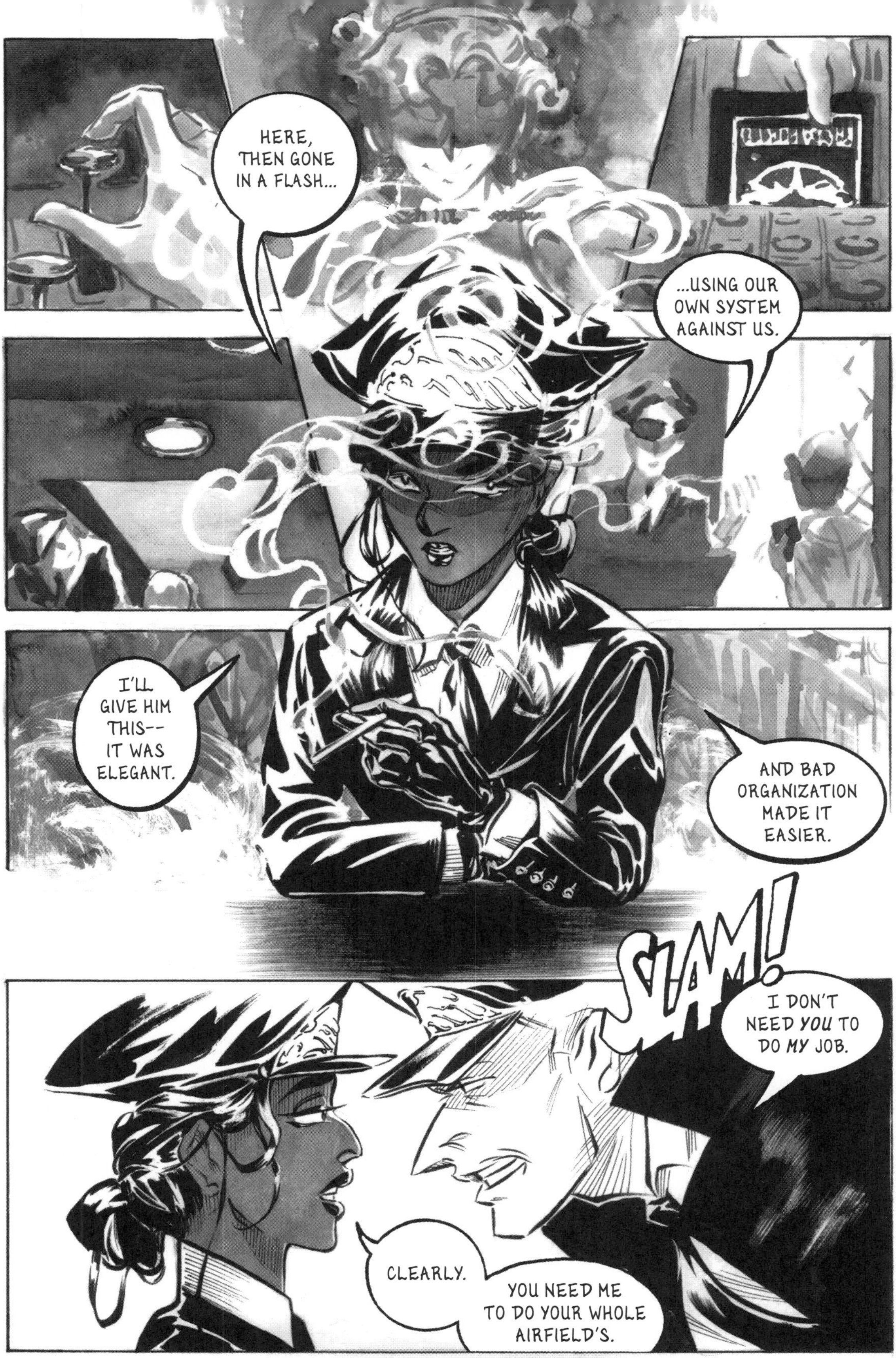
HERE, THEN GONE IN A FLASH...
...USING OUR OWN SYSTEM AGAINST US.
I'LL GIVE HIM THIS-- IT WAS ELEGANT.
AND BAD ORGANIZATION MADE IT EASIER.
SLAM!
I DON'T NEED *YOU* TO DO *MY* JOB.
CLEARLY.
YOU NEED ME TO DO YOUR WHOLE AIRFIELD'S.

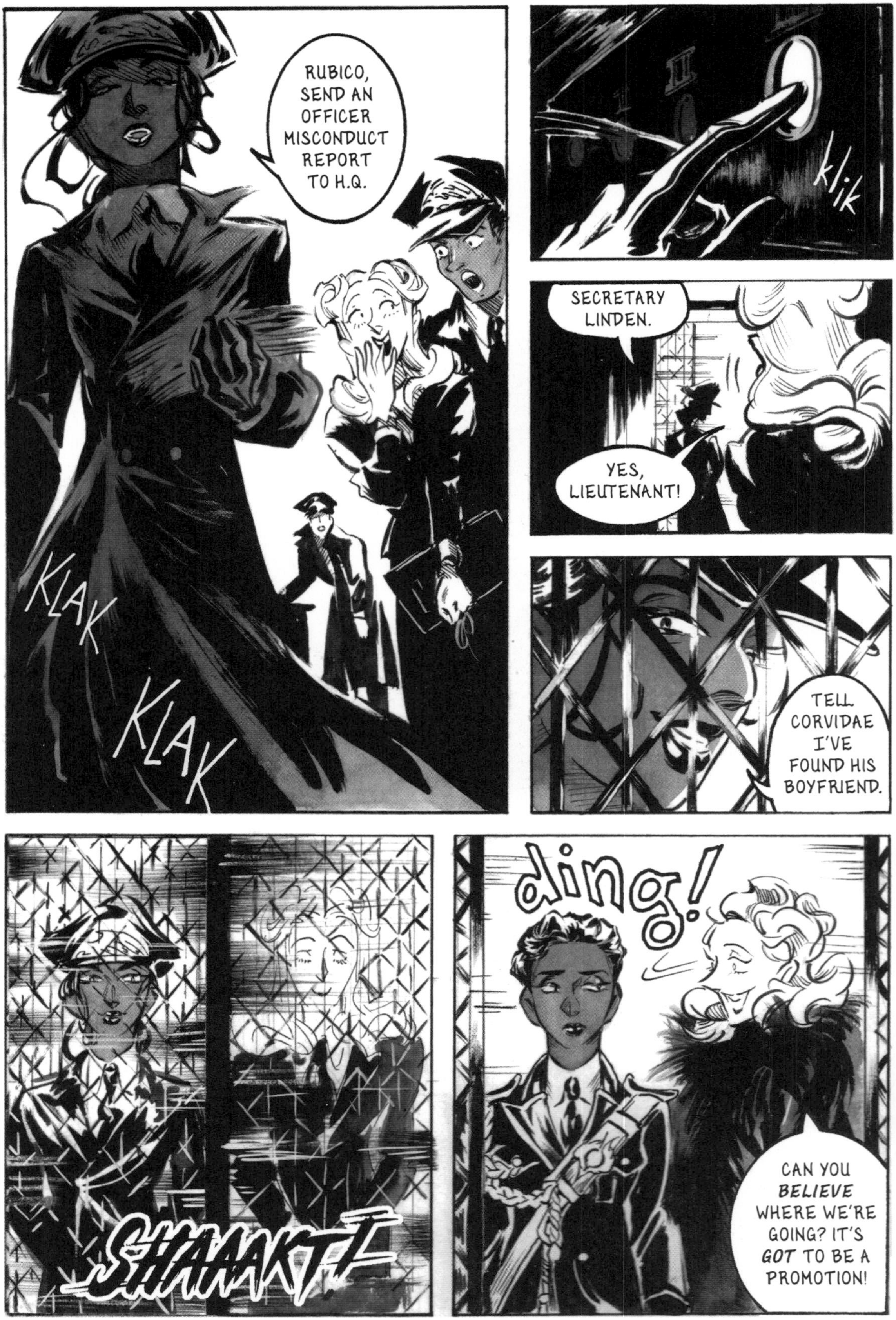
RUBICO, SEND AN OFFICER MISCONDUCT REPORT TO H.Q.
KLAK
KLAK
klik
SECRETARY LINDEN.
YES, LIEUTENANT!
TELL CORVIDAE I'VE FOUND HIS BOYFRIEND.
SHAAAKT!
ding!
CAN YOU BELIEVE WHERE WE'RE GOING? IT'S GOT TO BE A PROMOTION!

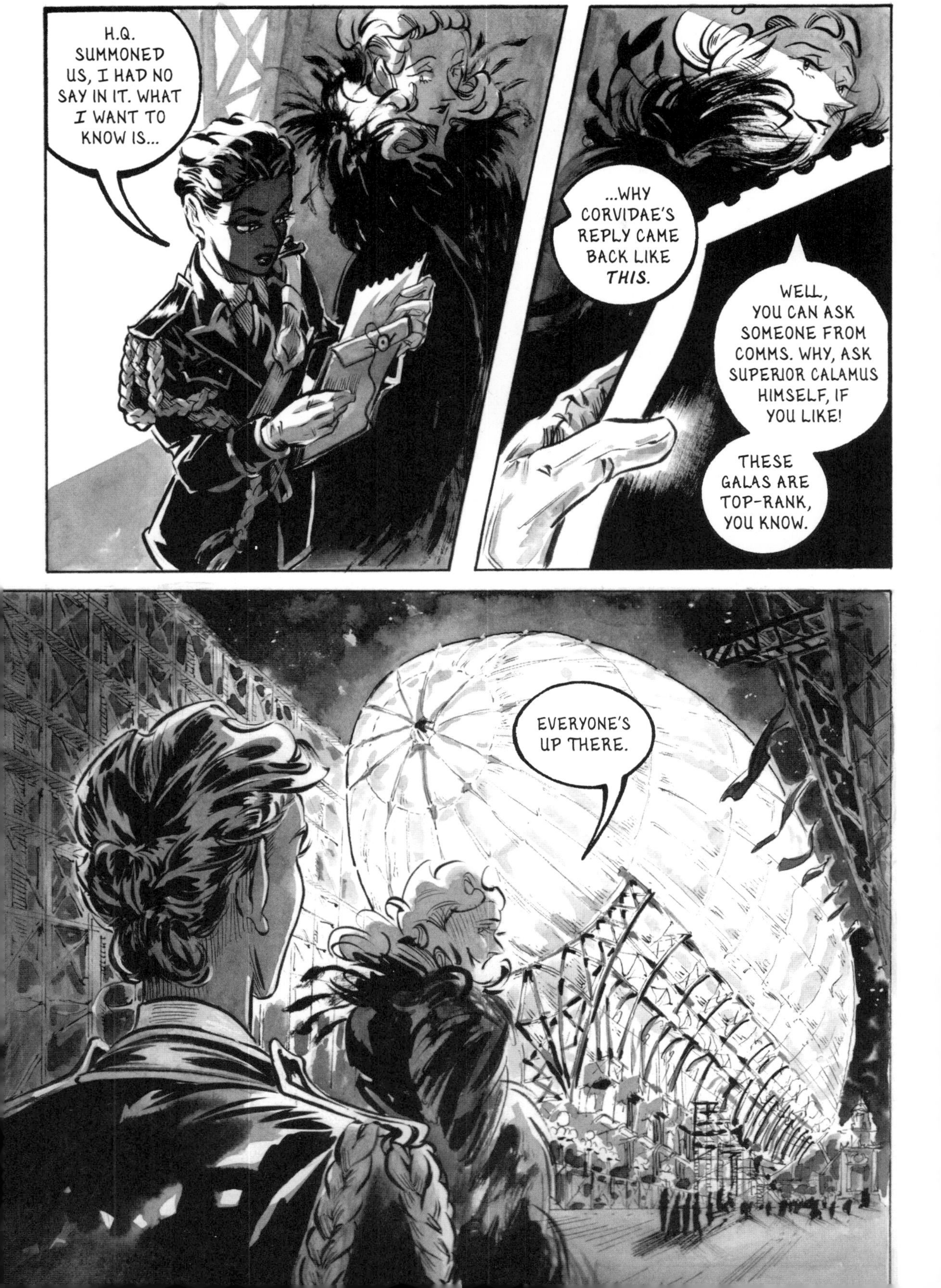
H.Q. SUMMONED US, I HAD NO SAY IN IT. WHAT *I* WANT TO KNOW IS...
...WHY CORVIDAE'S REPLY CAME BACK LIKE *THIS*.
WELL, YOU CAN ASK SOMEONE FROM COMMS. WHY, ASK SUPERIOR CALAMUS HIMSELF, IF YOU LIKE!
THESE GALAS ARE TOP-RANK, YOU KNOW.
EVERYONE'S UP THERE.

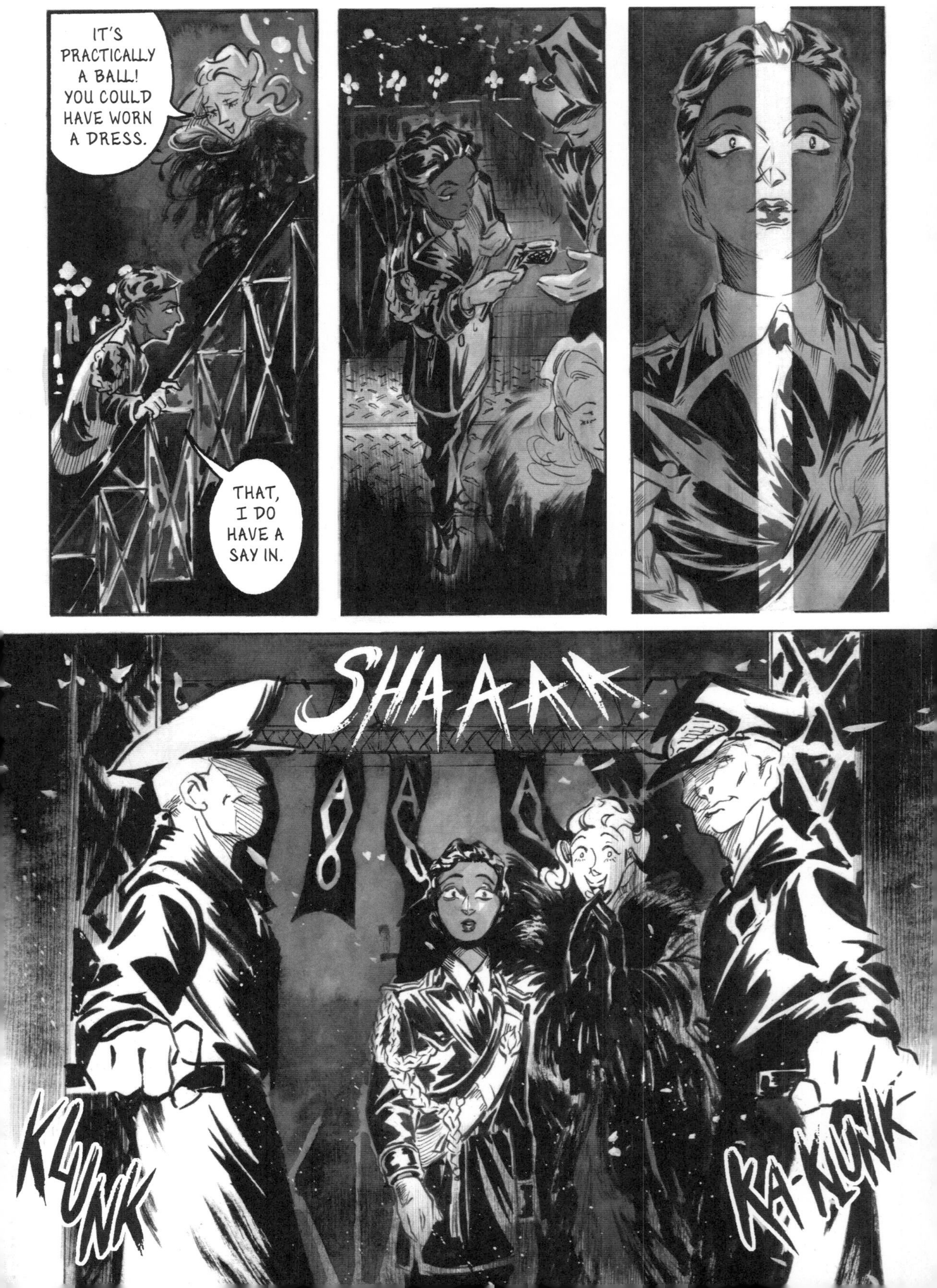
IT'S PRACTICALLY A BALL! YOU COULD HAVE WORN A DRESS.
THAT, I DO HAVE A SAY IN.
SHAAAK
KLUNK
KA-KLUNK

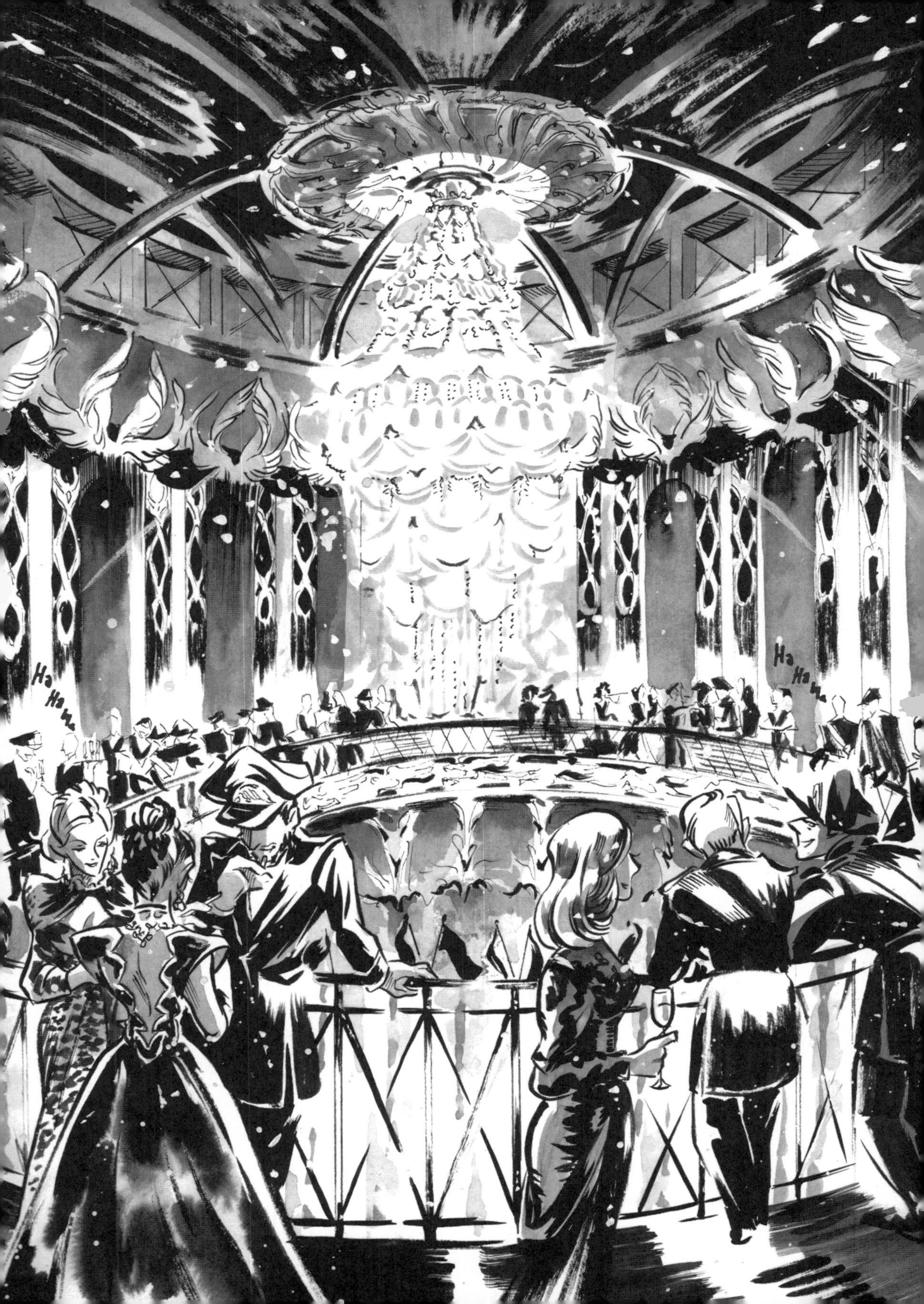
Ha Ha Ha
Ha Ha Ha

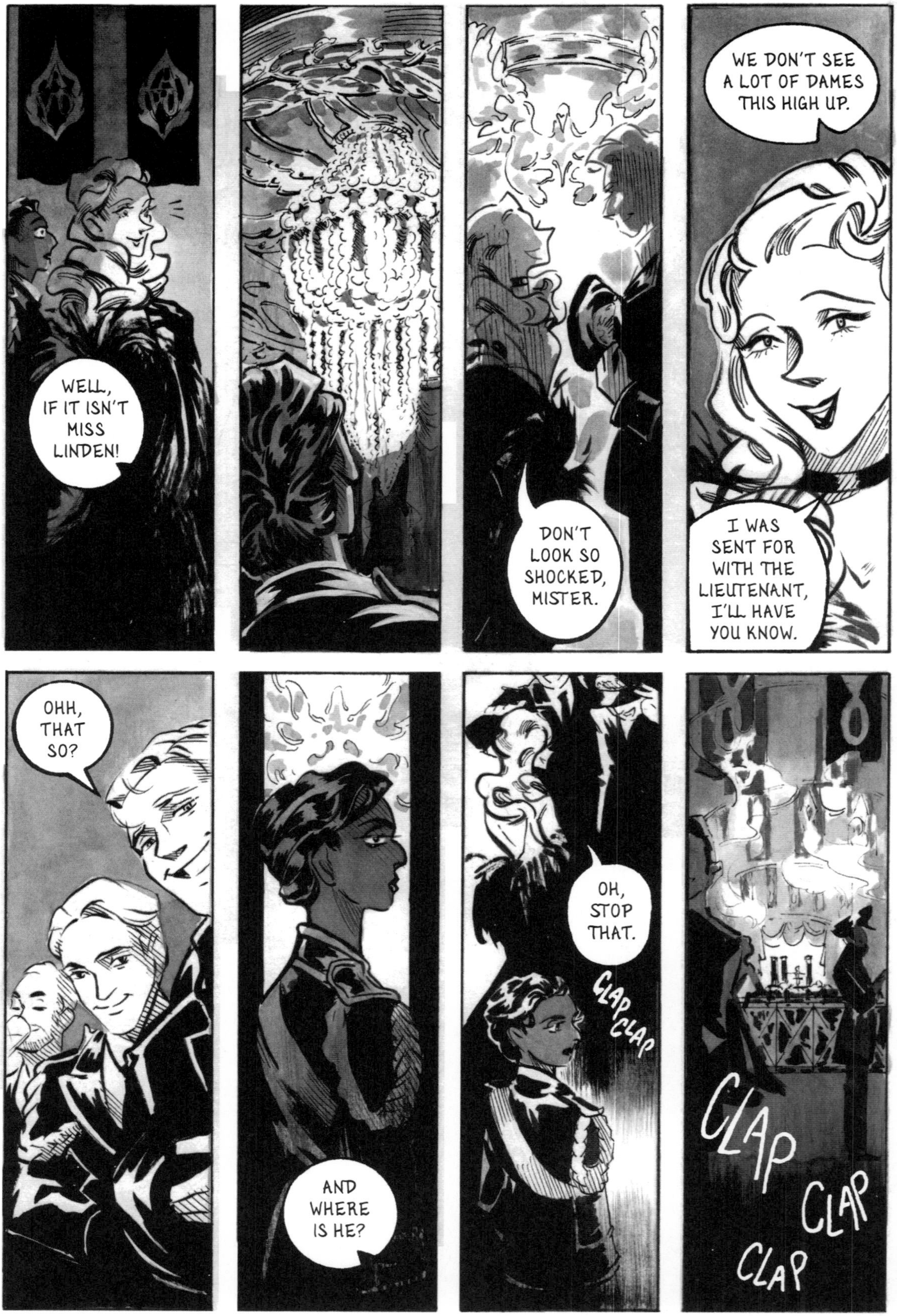
WELL, IF IT ISN'T MISS LINDEN!
DON'T LOOK SO SHOCKED, MISTER.
WE DON'T SEE A LOT OF DAMES THIS HIGH UP.
I WAS SENT FOR WITH THE LIEUTENANT, I'LL HAVE YOU KNOW.
OHH, THAT SO?
AND WHERE IS HE?
OH, STOP THAT.
CLAP CLAP
CLAP CLAP CLAP

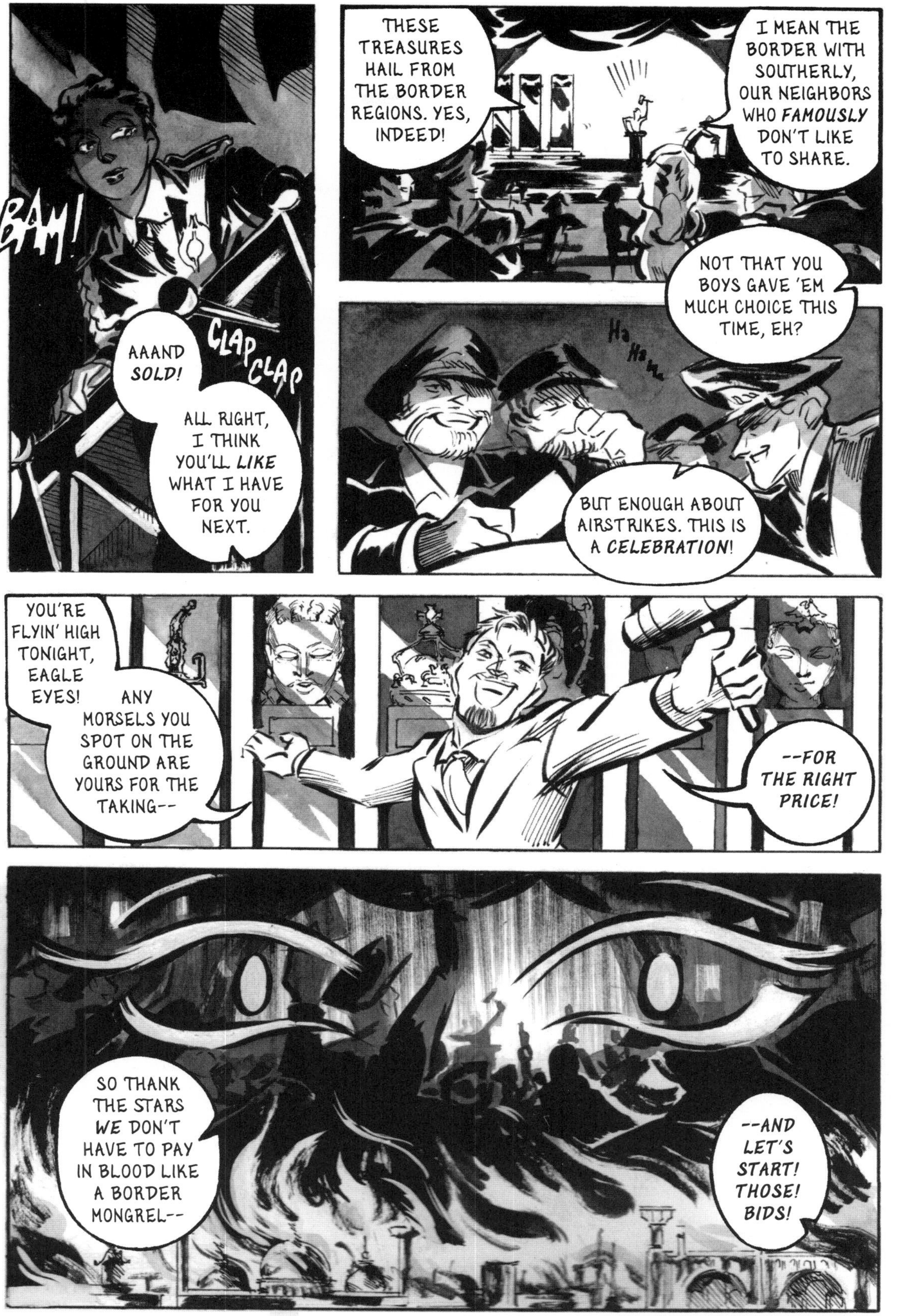
BAM!
CLAP CLAP
AAAND SOLD!
ALL RIGHT, I THINK YOU'LL LIKE WHAT I HAVE FOR YOU NEXT.
THESE TREASURES HAIL FROM THE BORDER REGIONS. YES, INDEED!
I MEAN THE BORDER WITH SOUTHERLY, OUR NEIGHBORS WHO FAMOUSLY DON'T LIKE TO SHARE.
NOT THAT YOU BOYS GAVE 'EM MUCH CHOICE THIS TIME, EH?
Ha Ha Ha
BUT ENOUGH ABOUT AIRSTRIKES. THIS IS A CELEBRATION!
YOU'RE FLYIN' HIGH TONIGHT, EAGLE EYES!
ANY MORSELS YOU SPOT ON THE GROUND ARE YOURS FOR THE TAKING--
--FOR THE RIGHT PRICE!
SO THANK THE STARS WE DON'T HAVE TO PAY IN BLOOD LIKE A BORDER MONGREL--
--AND LET'S START! THOSE! BIDS!

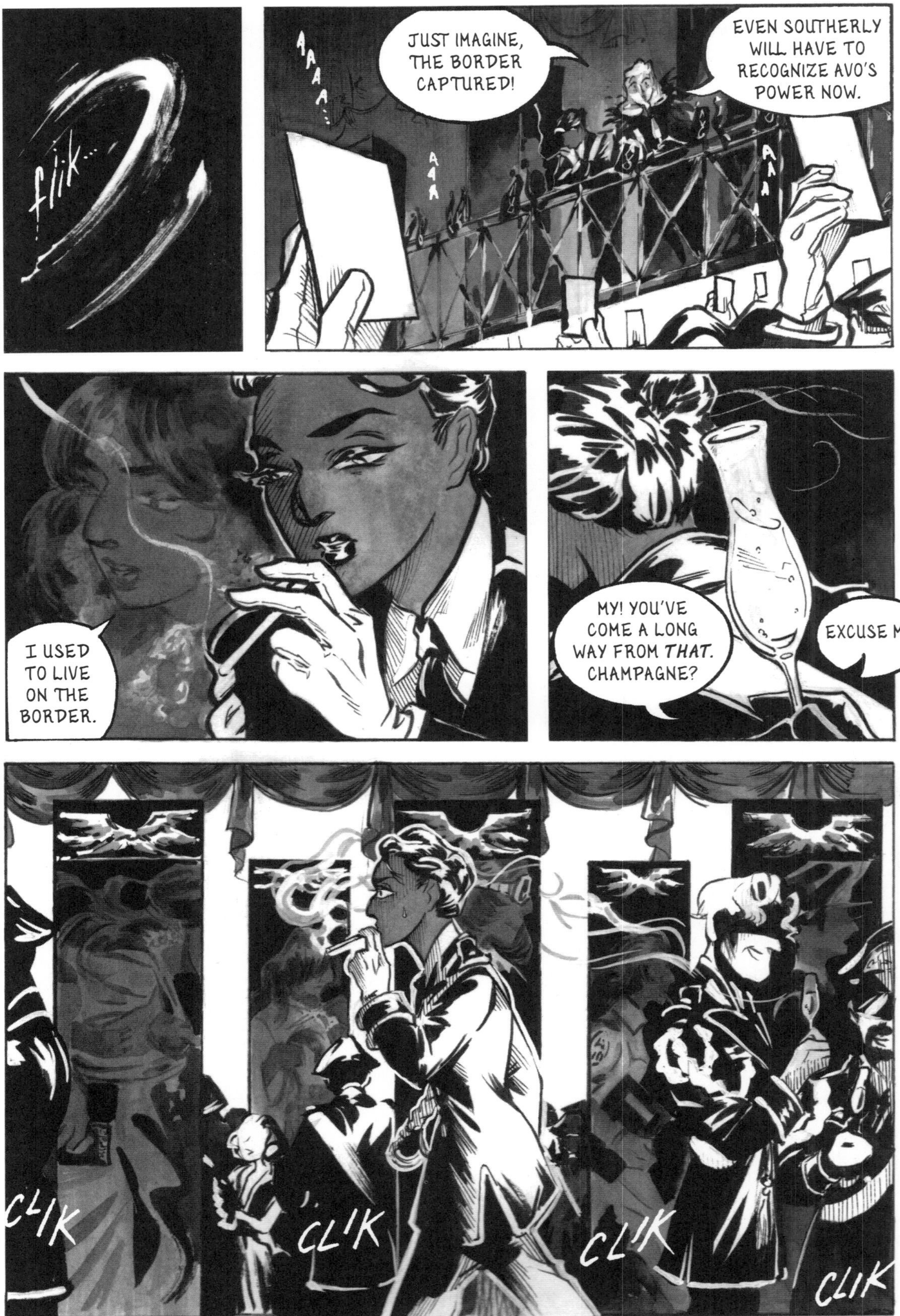
fliik...
AAAAA...
JUST IMAGINE, THE BORDER CAPTURED!
EVEN SOUTHERLY WILL HAVE TO RECOGNIZE AVO'S POWER NOW.
I USED TO LIVE ON THE BORDER.
MY! YOU'VE COME A LONG WAY FROM *THAT*. CHAMPAGNE?
EXCUSE ME.
CLIK
CLIK
CLIK
CLIK

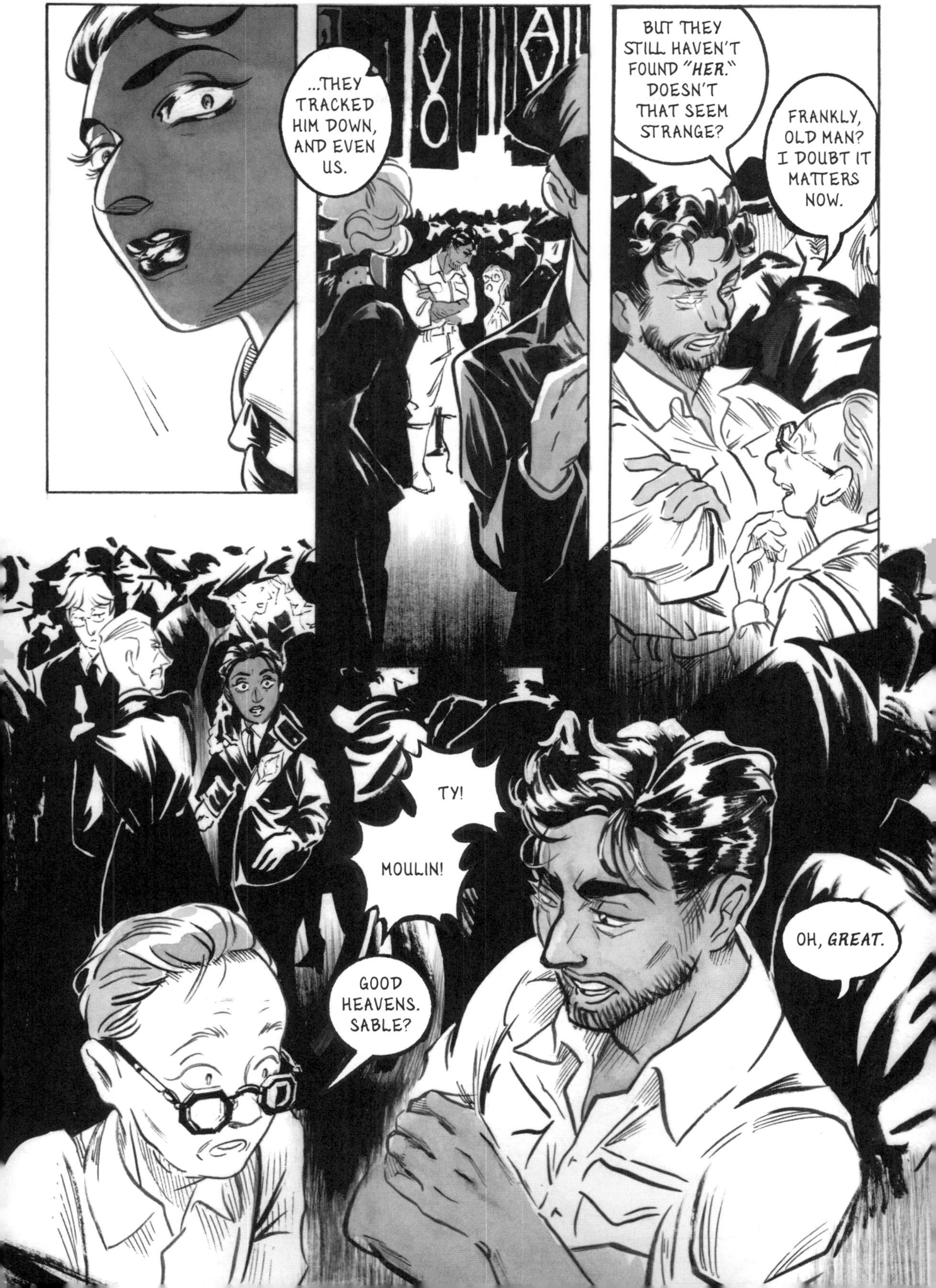
...THEY TRACKED HIM DOWN, AND EVEN US.
BUT THEY STILL HAVEN'T FOUND "HER." DOESN'T THAT SEEM STRANGE?
FRANKLY, OLD MAN? I DOUBT IT MATTERS NOW.
TY!
MOULIN!
GOOD HEAVENS. SABLE?
OH, GREAT.

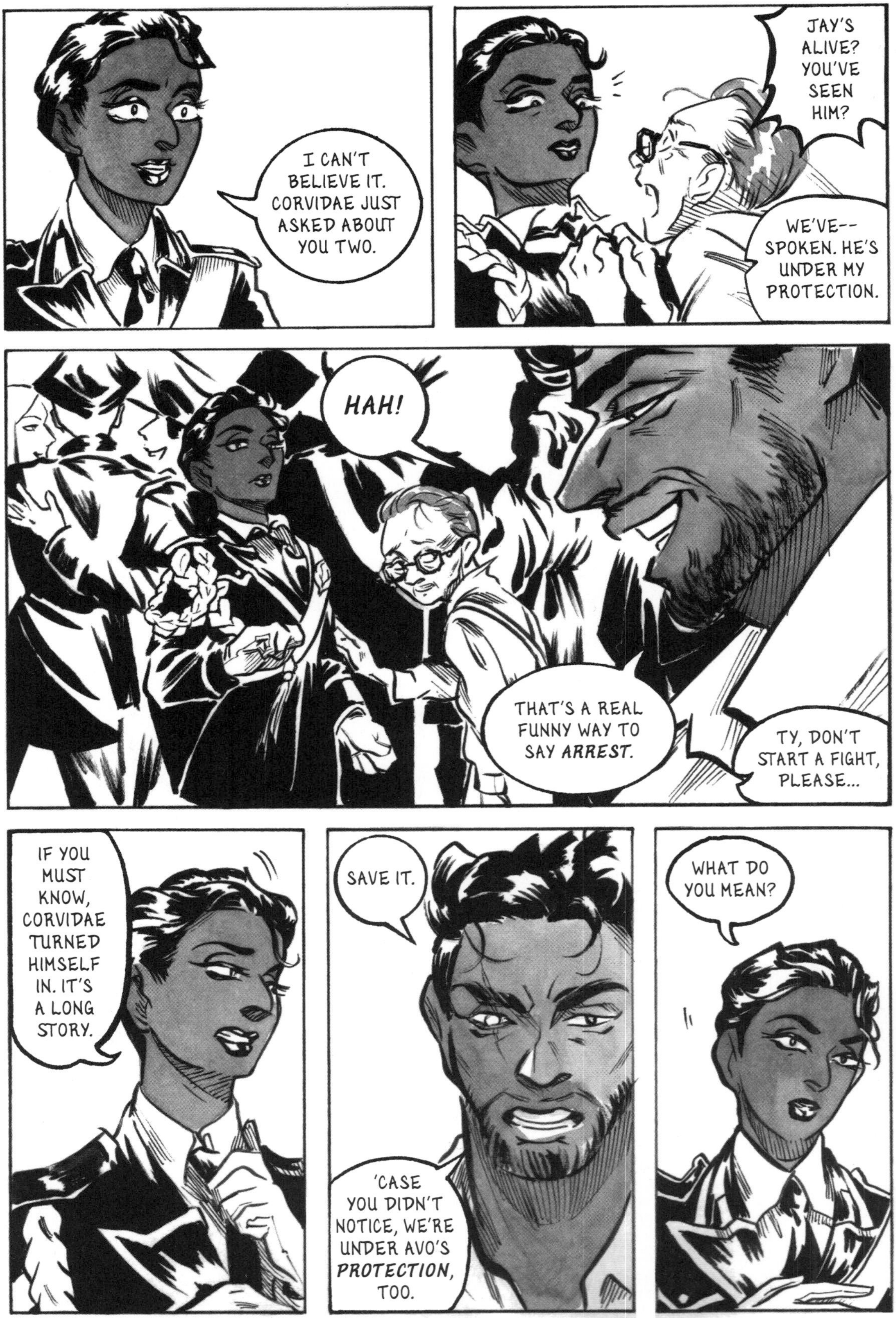
I CAN'T BELIEVE IT. CORVIDAE JUST ASKED ABOUT YOU TWO.
JAY'S ALIVE? YOU'VE SEEN HIM?
WE'VE-- SPOKEN. HE'S UNDER MY PROTECTION.
HAH!
THAT'S A REAL FUNNY WAY TO SAY *ARREST*.
TY, DON'T START A FIGHT, PLEASE...
IF YOU MUST KNOW, CORVIDAE TURNED HIMSELF IN. IT'S A LONG STORY.
SAVE IT.
'CASE YOU DIDN'T NOTICE, WE'RE UNDER AVO'S *PROTECTION*, TOO.
WHAT DO YOU MEAN?

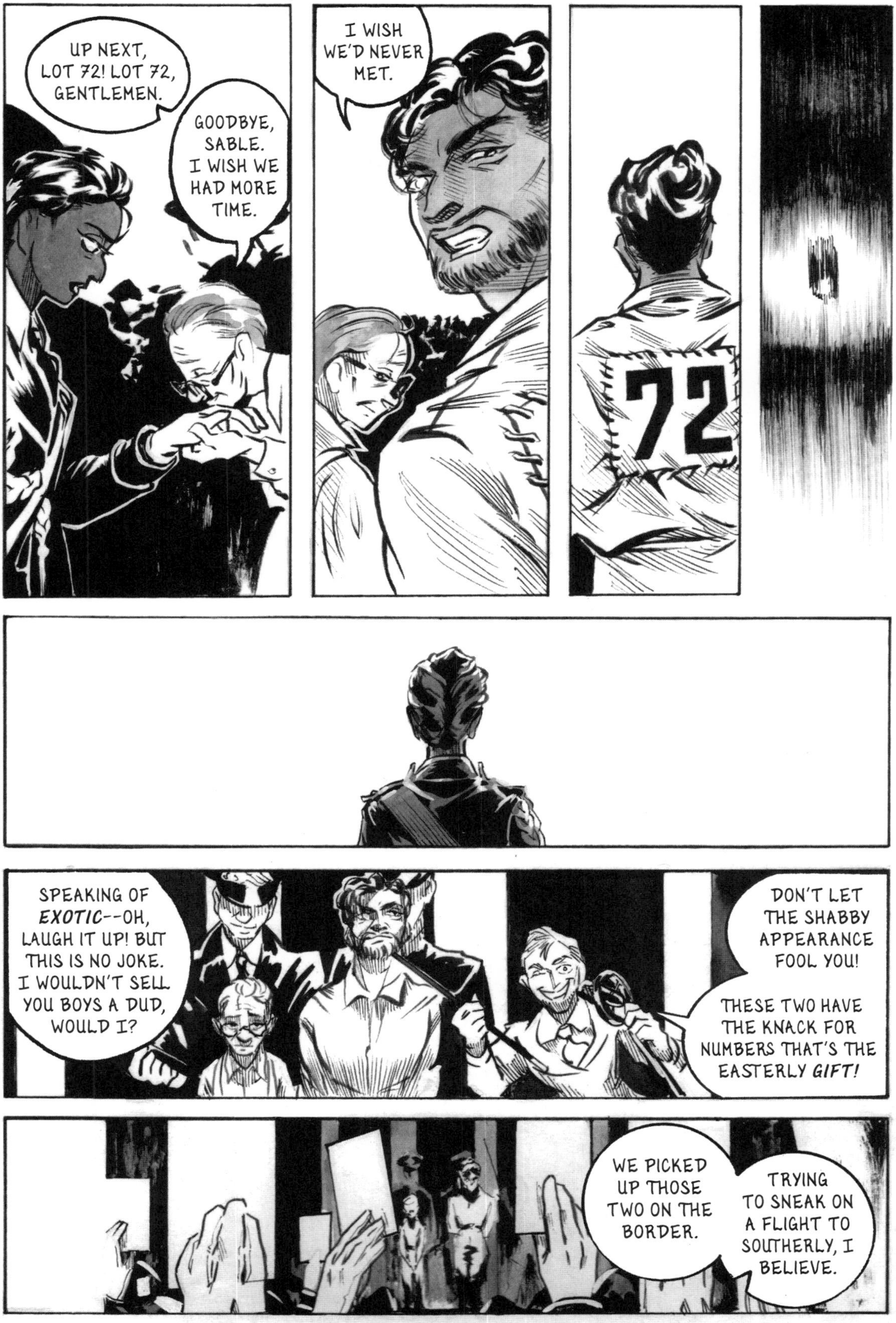
UP NEXT, LOT 72! LOT 72, GENTLEMEN.
GOODBYE, SABLE. I WISH WE HAD MORE TIME.
I WISH WE'D NEVER MET.
72
SPEAKING OF *EXOTIC*--OH, LAUGH IT UP! BUT THIS IS NO JOKE. I WOULDN'T SELL YOU BOYS A DUD, WOULD I?
DON'T LET THE SHABBY APPEARANCE FOOL YOU!
THESE TWO HAVE THE KNACK FOR NUMBERS THAT'S THE EASTERLY *GIFT!*
WE PICKED UP THOSE TWO ON THE BORDER.
TRYING TO SNEAK ON A FLIGHT TO SOUTHERLY, I BELIEVE.

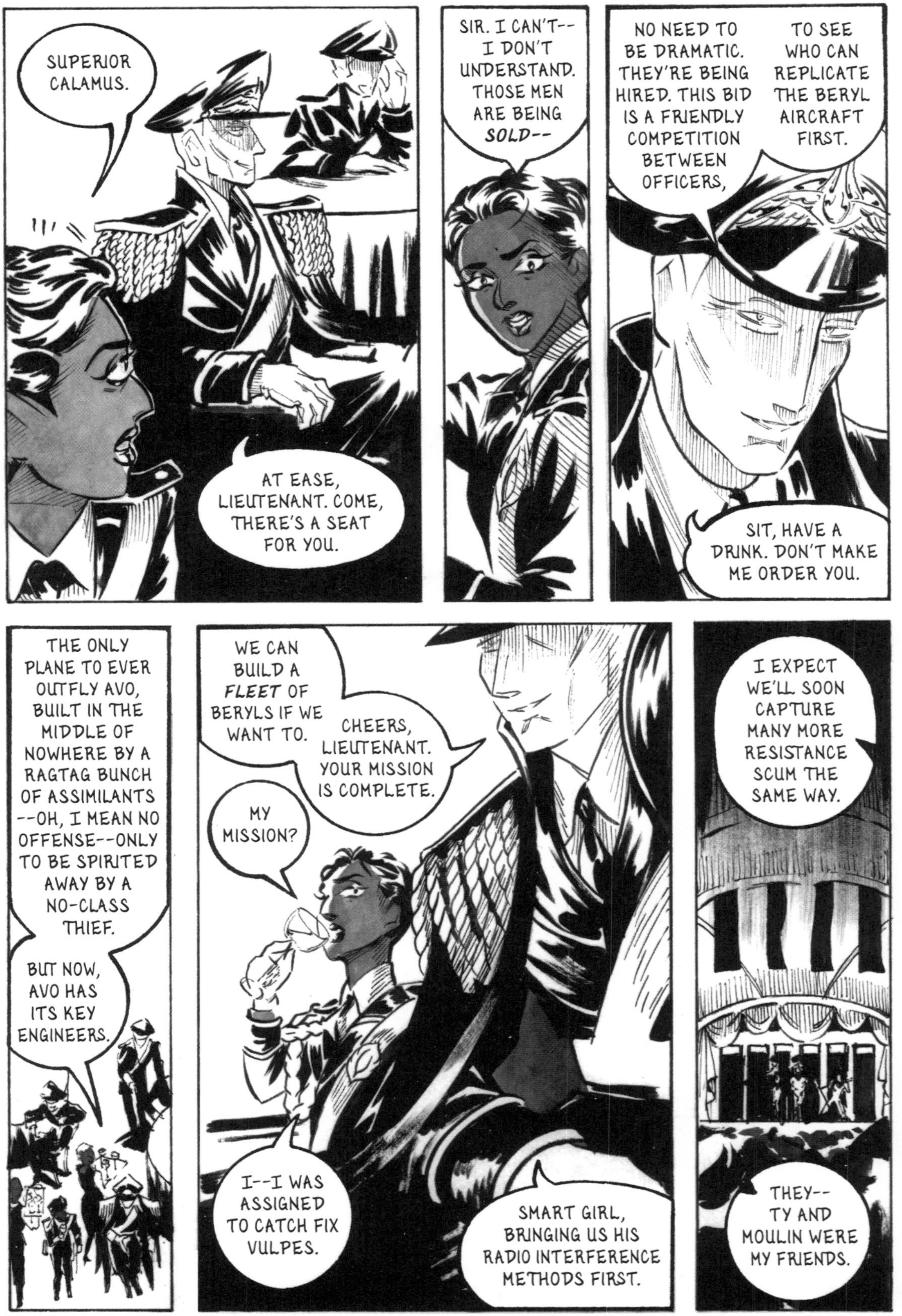
SUPERIOR CALAMUS.
AT EASE, LIEUTENANT. COME, THERE'S A SEAT FOR YOU.
SIR. I CAN'T-- I DON'T UNDERSTAND. THOSE MEN ARE BEING *SOLD*--
NO NEED TO BE DRAMATIC. THEY'RE BEING HIRED. THIS BID IS A FRIENDLY COMPETITION BETWEEN OFFICERS,
TO SEE WHO CAN REPLICATE THE BERYL AIRCRAFT FIRST.
SIT, HAVE A DRINK. DON'T MAKE ME ORDER YOU.
THE ONLY PLANE TO EVER OUTFLY AVO, BUILT IN THE MIDDLE OF NOWHERE BY A RAGTAG BUNCH OF ASSIMILANTS --OH, I MEAN NO OFFENSE--ONLY TO BE SPIRITED AWAY BY A NO-CLASS THIEF.
BUT NOW, AVO HAS ITS KEY ENGINEERS.
WE CAN BUILD A *FLEET* OF BERYLS IF WE WANT TO.
CHEERS, LIEUTENANT. YOUR MISSION IS COMPLETE.
MY MISSION?
I--I WAS ASSIGNED TO CATCH FIX VULPES.
SMART GIRL, BRINGING US HIS RADIO INTERFERENCE METHODS FIRST.
I EXPECT WE'LL SOON CAPTURE MANY MORE RESISTANCE SCUM THE SAME WAY.
THEY-- TY AND MOULIN WERE MY FRIENDS.

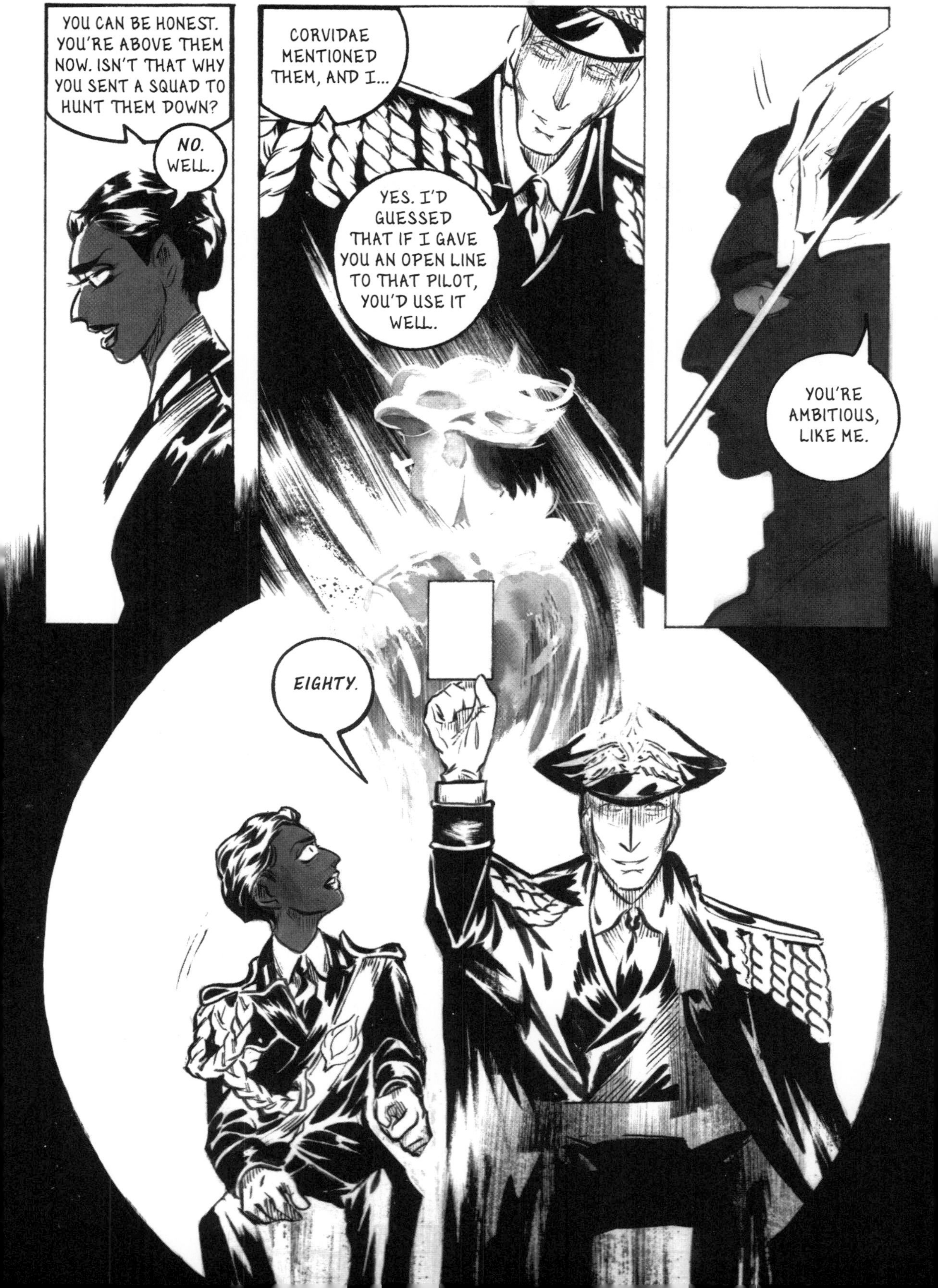
YOU CAN BE HONEST. YOU'RE ABOVE THEM NOW. ISN'T THAT WHY YOU SENT A SQUAD TO HUNT THEM DOWN?
NO. WELL..
CORVIDAE MENTIONED THEM, AND I...
YES. I'D GUESSED THAT IF I GAVE YOU AN OPEN LINE TO THAT PILOT, YOU'D USE IT WELL.
YOU'RE AMBITIOUS, LIKE ME.
EIGHTY.

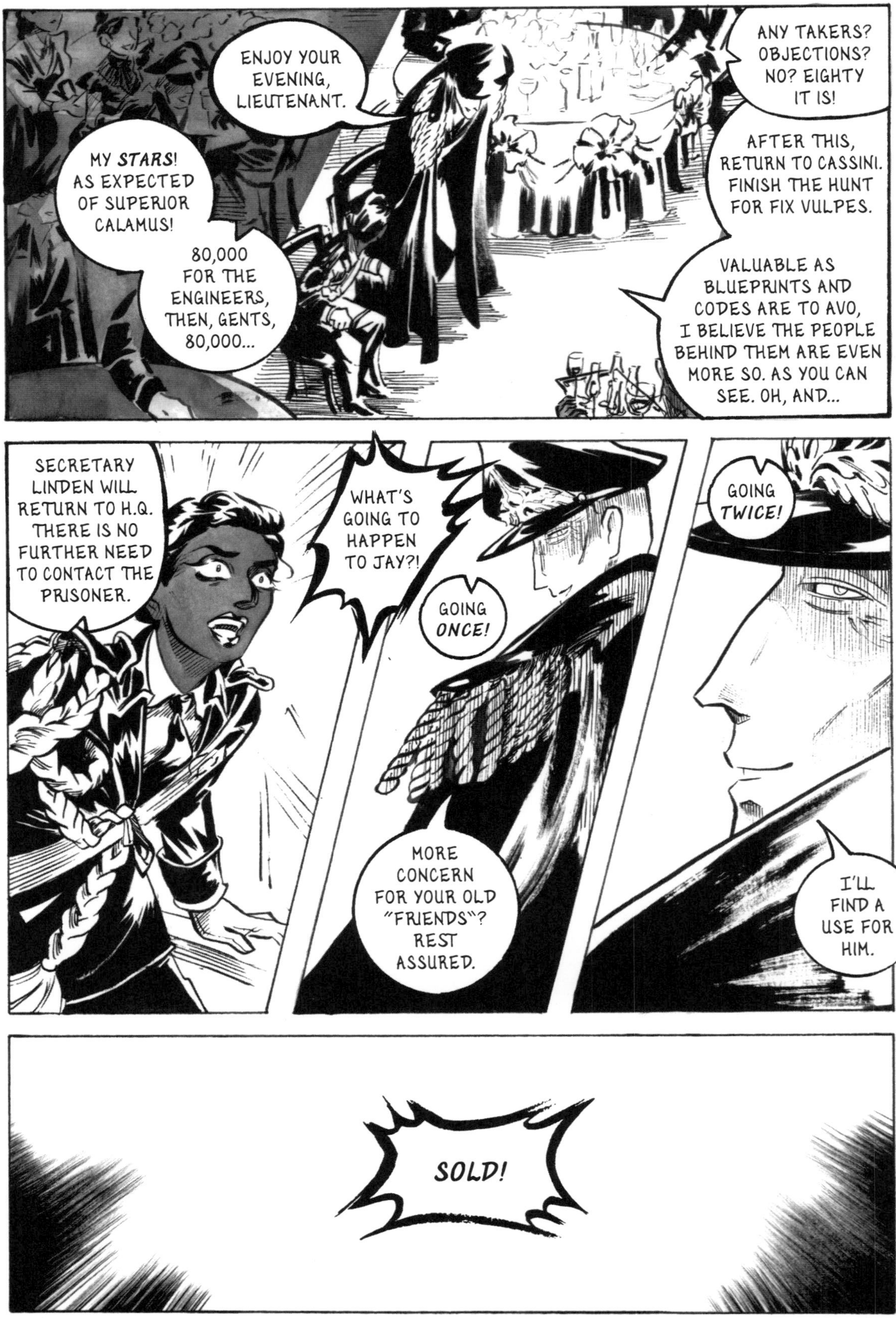
ENJOY YOUR EVENING, LIEUTENANT.
ANY TAKERS? OBJECTIONS? NO? EIGHTY IT IS!
MY *STARS*! AS EXPECTED OF SUPERIOR CALAMUS!
80,000 FOR THE ENGINEERS, THEN, GENTS, 80,000...
AFTER THIS, RETURN TO CASSINI. FINISH THE HUNT FOR FIX VULPES.
VALUABLE AS BLUEPRINTS AND CODES ARE TO AVO, I BELIEVE THE PEOPLE BEHIND THEM ARE EVEN MORE SO. AS YOU CAN SEE. OH, AND...
SECRETARY LINDEN WILL RETURN TO H.Q. THERE IS NO FURTHER NEED TO CONTACT THE PRISONER.
WHAT'S GOING TO HAPPEN TO JAY?!
GOING *ONCE*!
MORE CONCERN FOR YOUR OLD "FRIENDS"? REST ASSURED.
GOING *TWICE*!
I'LL FIND A USE FOR HIM.
SOLD!

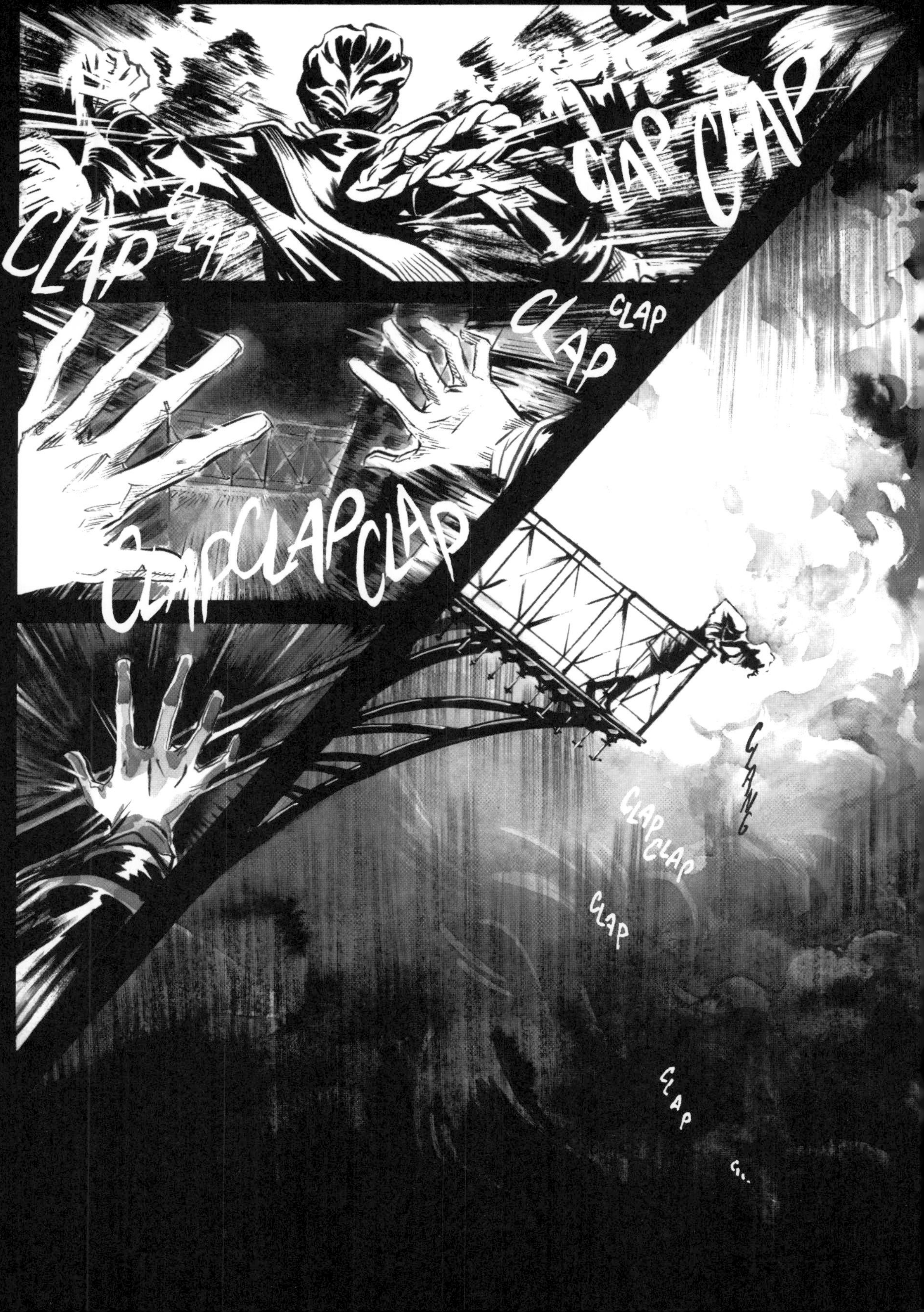
CLAP
CLAP
CLAP CLAP
CLAP
CLAP
CLAPCLAPCLAP
CLANG
CLAP
CLAP
CLAP
CLAP

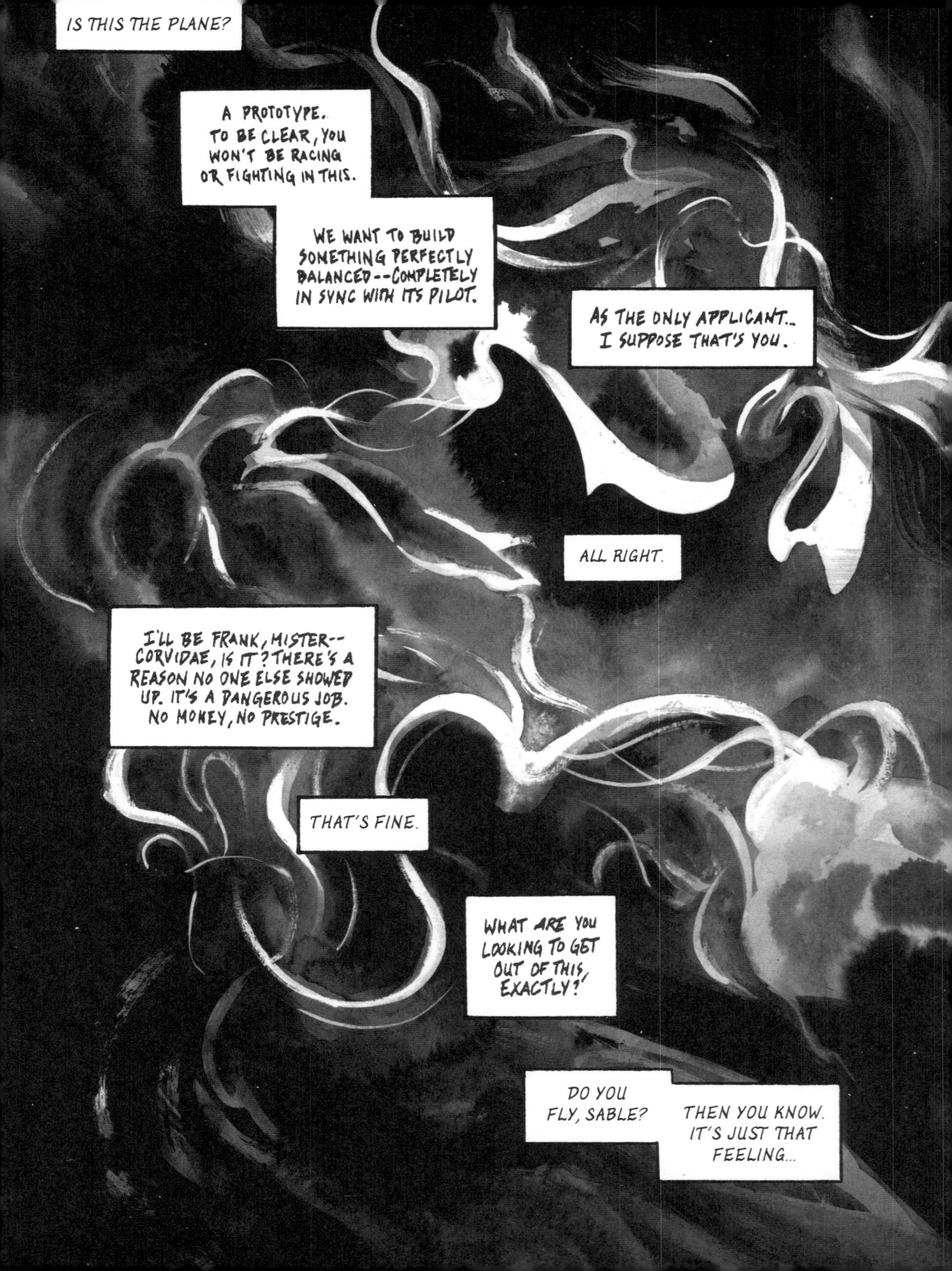
IS THIS THE PLANE?
A PROTOTYPE. TO BE CLEAR, YOU WON'T BE RACING OR FIGHTING IN THIS.
WE WANT TO BUILD SOMETHING PERFECTLY BALANCED--COMPLETELY IN SYNC WITH ITS PILOT.
AS THE ONLY APPLICANT... I SUPPOSE THAT'S YOU.
ALL RIGHT.
I'LL BE FRANK, MISTER--CORVIDAE, IS IT? THERE'S A REASON NO ONE ELSE SHOWED UP. IT'S A DANGEROUS JOB. NO MONEY, NO PRESTIGE.
THAT'S FINE.
WHAT ARE YOU LOOKING TO GET OUT OF THIS, EXACTLY?
DO YOU FLY, SABLE?
THEN YOU KNOW. IT'S JUST THAT FEELING...

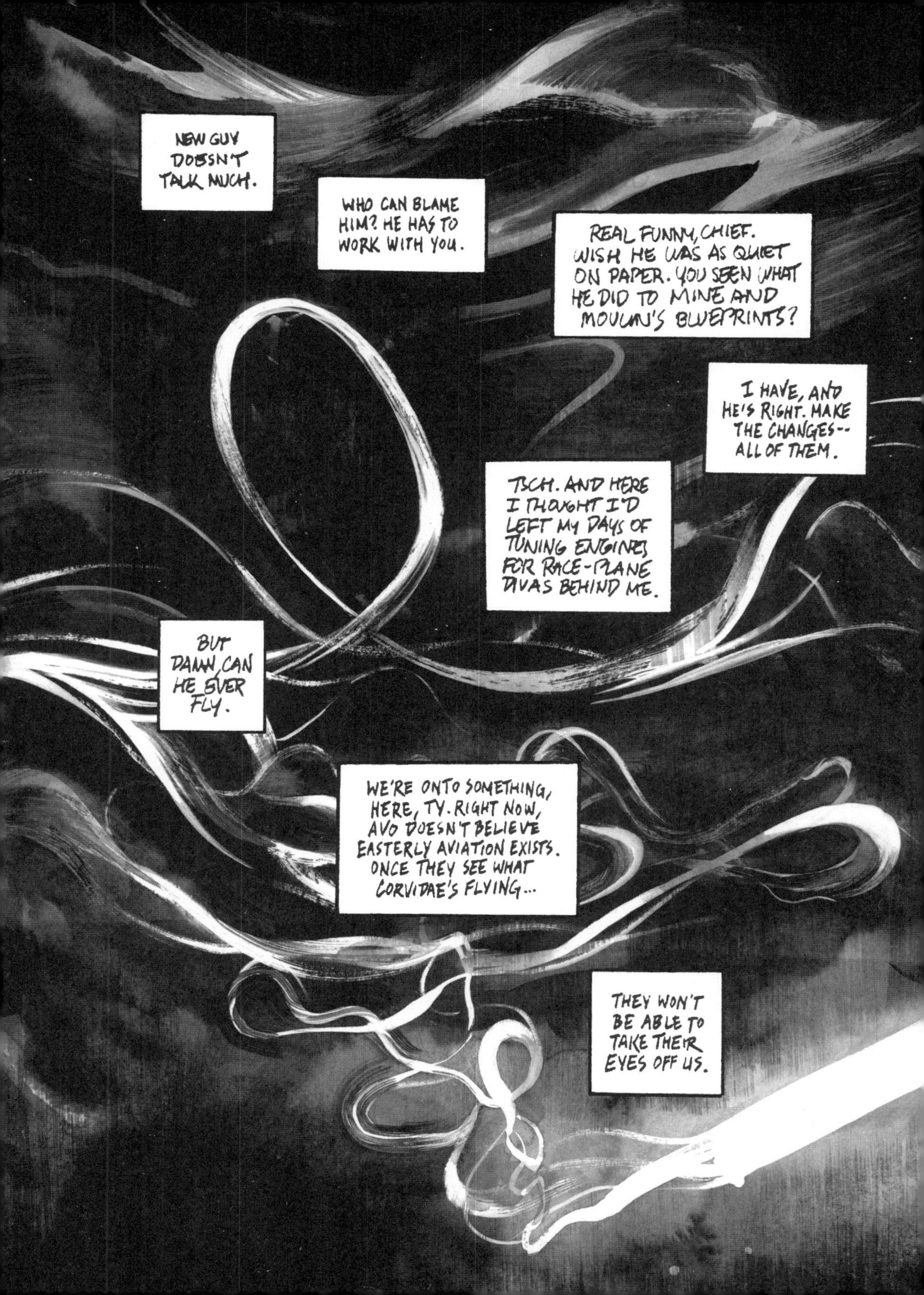
NEW GUY DOESN'T TALK MUCH.
WHO CAN BLAME HIM? HE HAS TO WORK WITH YOU.
REAL FUNNY, CHIEF. WISH HE WAS AS QUIET ON PAPER. YOU SEEN WHAT HE DID TO MINE AND MOULIN'S BLUEPRINTS?
I HAVE, AND HE'S RIGHT. MAKE THE CHANGES-- ALL OF THEM.
TSCH. AND HERE I THOUGHT I'D LEFT MY DAYS OF TUNING ENGINES FOR RACE-PLANE DIVAS BEHIND ME.
BUT DAMN CAN HE EVER FLY.
WE'RE ONTO SOMETHING, HERE, TY. RIGHT NOW, AVO DOESN'T BELIEVE EASTERLY AVIATION EXISTS. ONCE THEY SEE WHAT CORVIDAE'S FLYING...
THEY WON'T BE ABLE TO TAKE THEIR EYES OFF US.

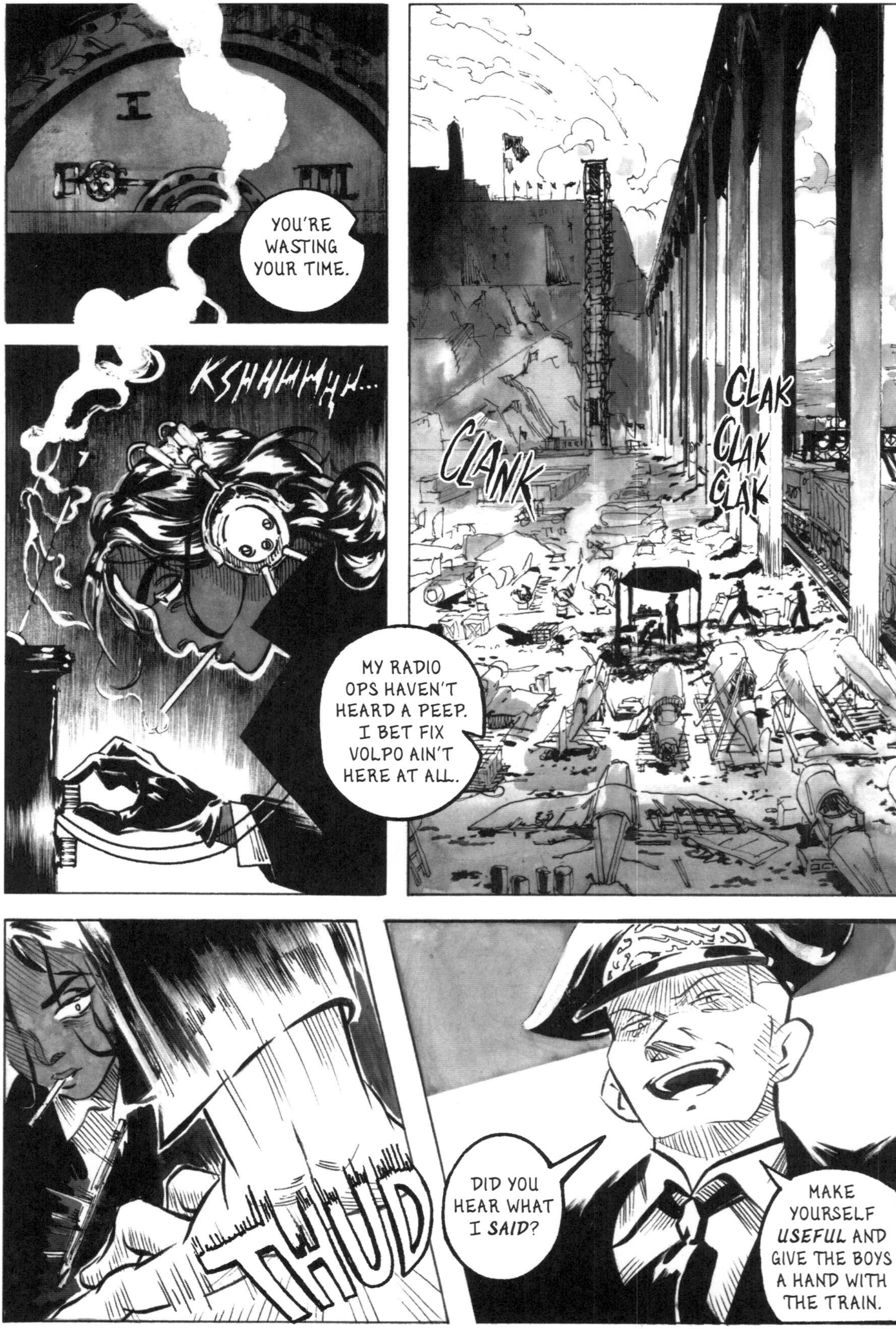
YOU'RE WASTING YOUR TIME.
KSHHHHHH...
MY RADIO OPS HAVEN'T HEARD A PEEP. I BET FIX VOLPO AIN'T HERE AT ALL.
CLANK
CLAK CLAK CLAK
THUD
DID YOU HEAR WHAT I *SAID*?
MAKE YOURSELF ***USEFUL*** AND GIVE THE BOYS A HAND WITH THE TRAIN.

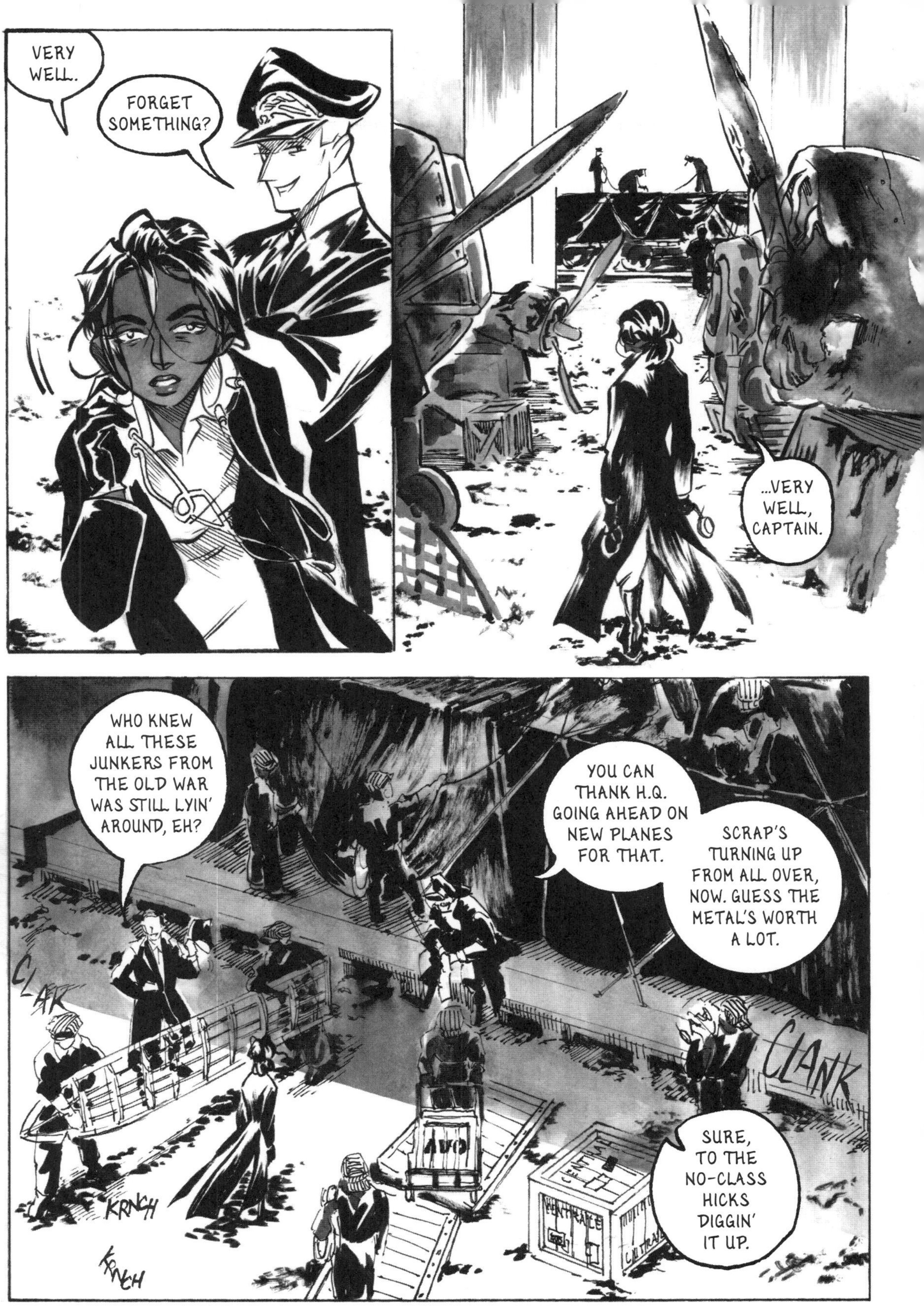
VERY WELL.
FORGET SOMETHING?
...VERY WELL, CAPTAIN.
WHO KNEW ALL THESE JUNKERS FROM THE OLD WAR WAS STILL LYIN' AROUND, EH?
YOU CAN THANK H.Q. GOING AHEAD ON NEW PLANES FOR THAT.
SCRAP'S TURNING UP FROM ALL OVER, NOW. GUESS THE METAL'S WORTH A LOT.
CLAK
CLANK
SURE, TO THE NO-CLASS HICKS DIGGIN' IT UP.
KRNCH
KRNCH

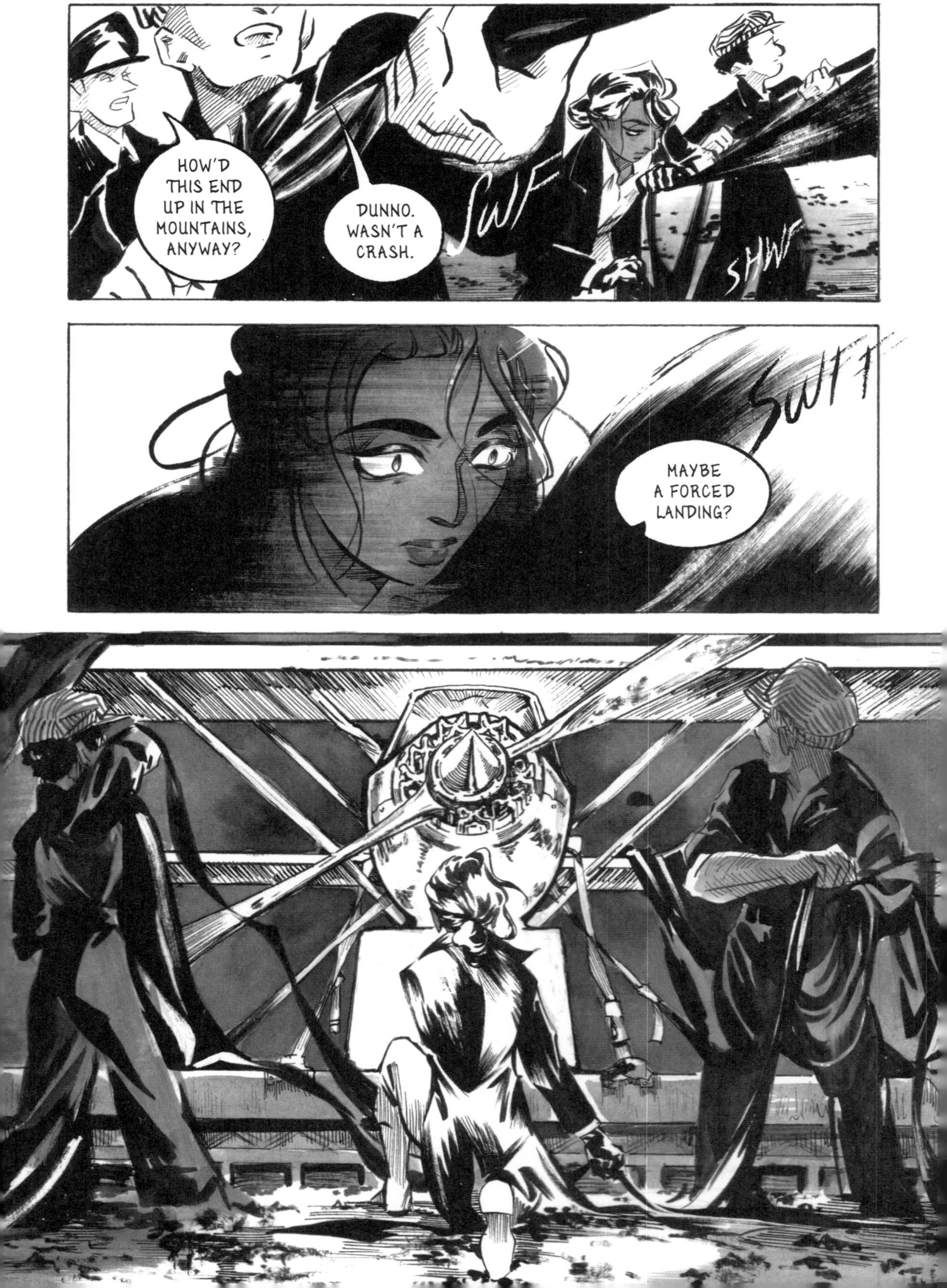
HOW'D THIS END UP IN THE MOUNTAINS, ANYWAY?
DUNNO. WASN'T A CRASH.
SWF
SHWF
SWFF
MAYBE A FORCED LANDING?

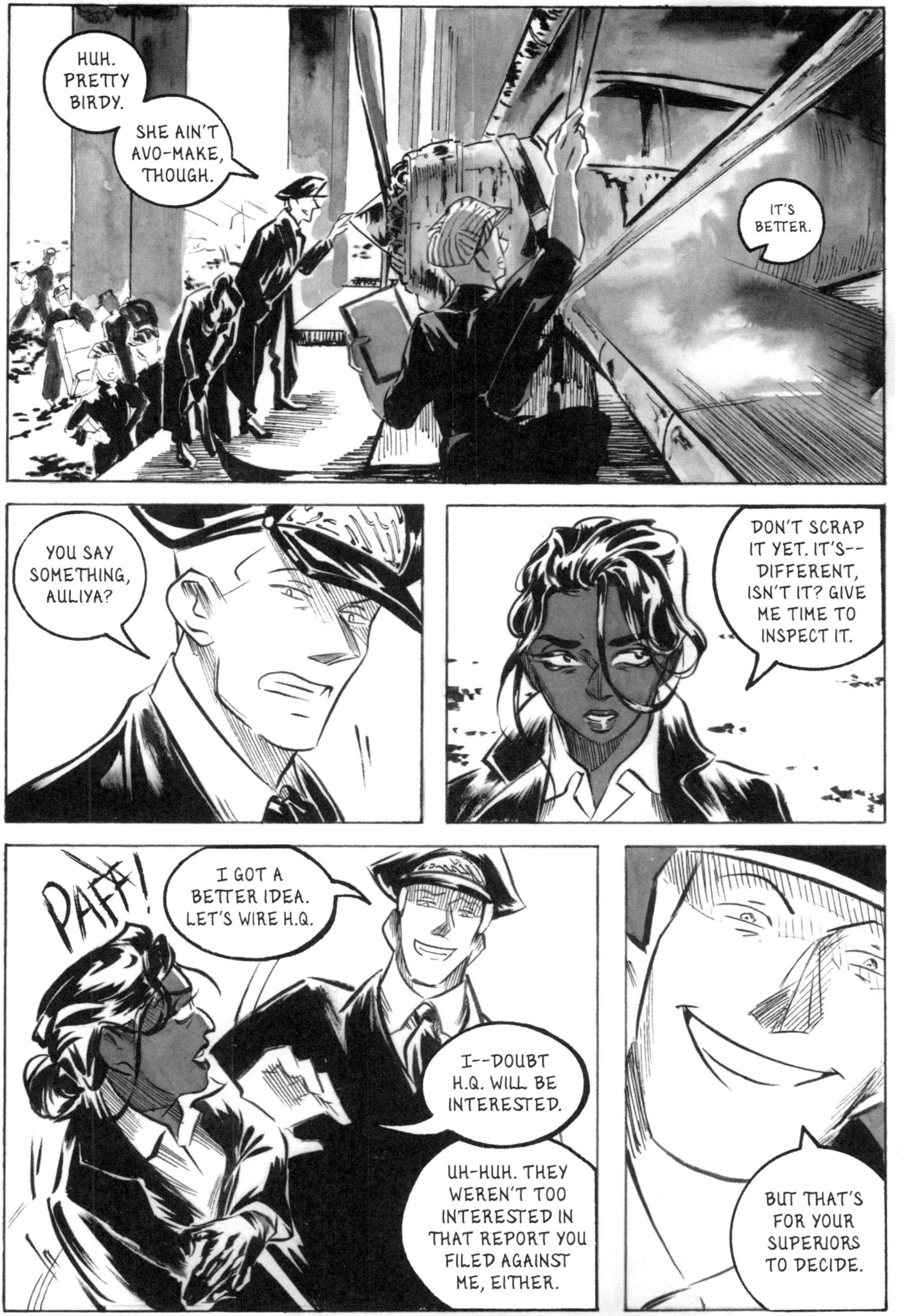
HUH. PRETTY BIRDY.
SHE AIN'T AVO-MAKE, THOUGH.
IT'S BETTER.
YOU SAY SOMETHING, AULIYA?
DON'T SCRAP IT YET. IT'S-- DIFFERENT, ISN'T IT? GIVE ME TIME TO INSPECT IT.
PAFF!
I GOT A BETTER IDEA. LET'S WIRE H.Q.
I--DOUBT H.Q. WILL BE INTERESTED.
UH-HUH. THEY WEREN'T TOO INTERESTED IN THAT REPORT YOU FILED AGAINST ME, EITHER.
BUT THAT'S FOR YOUR SUPERIORS TO DECIDE.

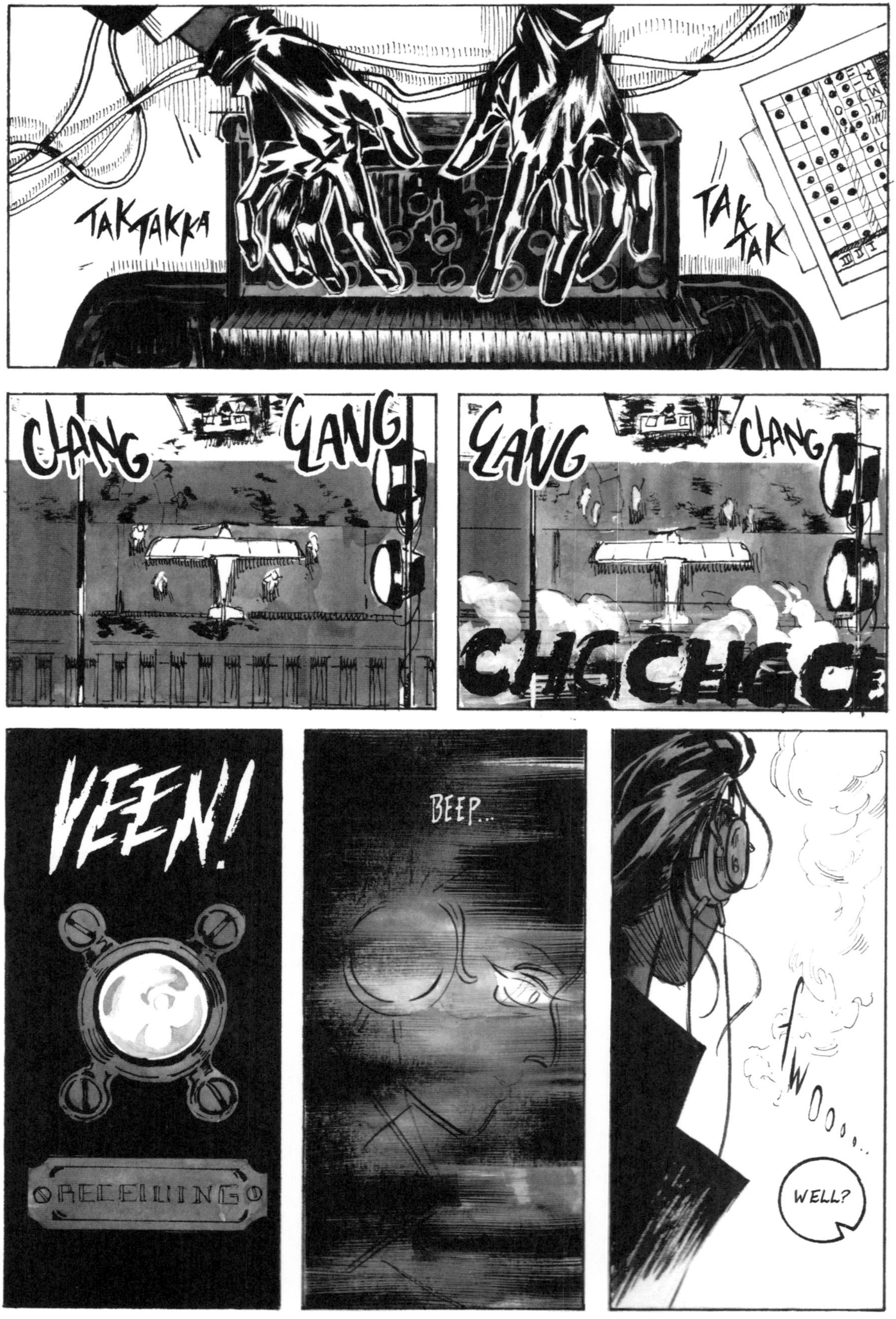
TAK TAKKA
TAK TAK TAK
CLANG
CLANG
CLANG
CLANG
CHGCHGCE
VEEN!
RECEIVING
BEEP...
FWOOOO...
WELL?

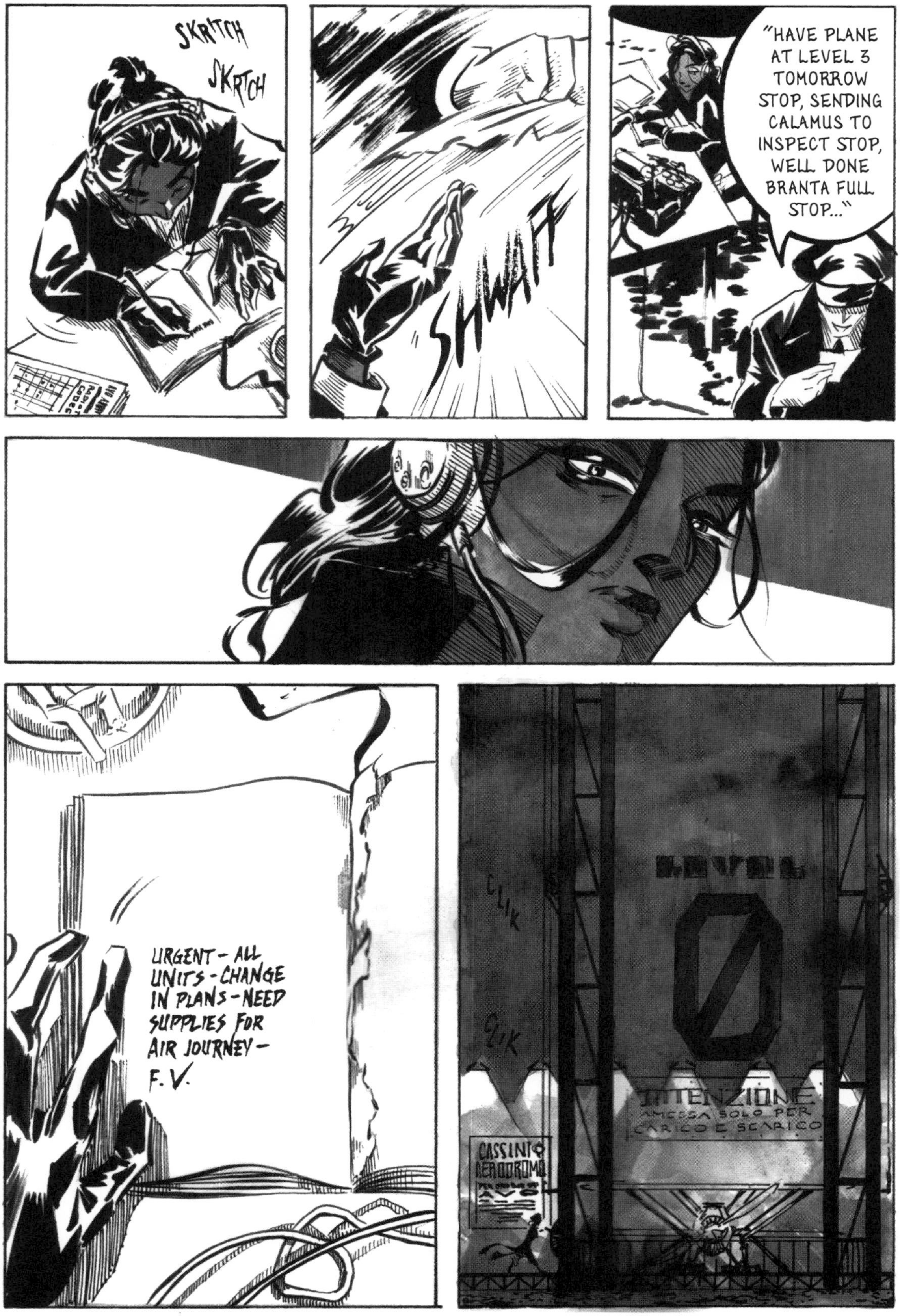
SKRITCH
SKRITCH
SHWAFF
"HAVE PLANE AT LEVEL 3 TOMORROW STOP, SENDING CALAMUS TO INSPECT STOP, WELL DONE BRANTA FULL STOP..."
URGENT - ALL UNITS - CHANGE IN PLANS - NEED SUPPLIES FOR AIR JOURNEY - F. V.
CLIK
CLIK
LEVEL 0
ATTENZIONE
AMESSA SOLO PER CARICO E SCARICO
CASSINI AERODROMO

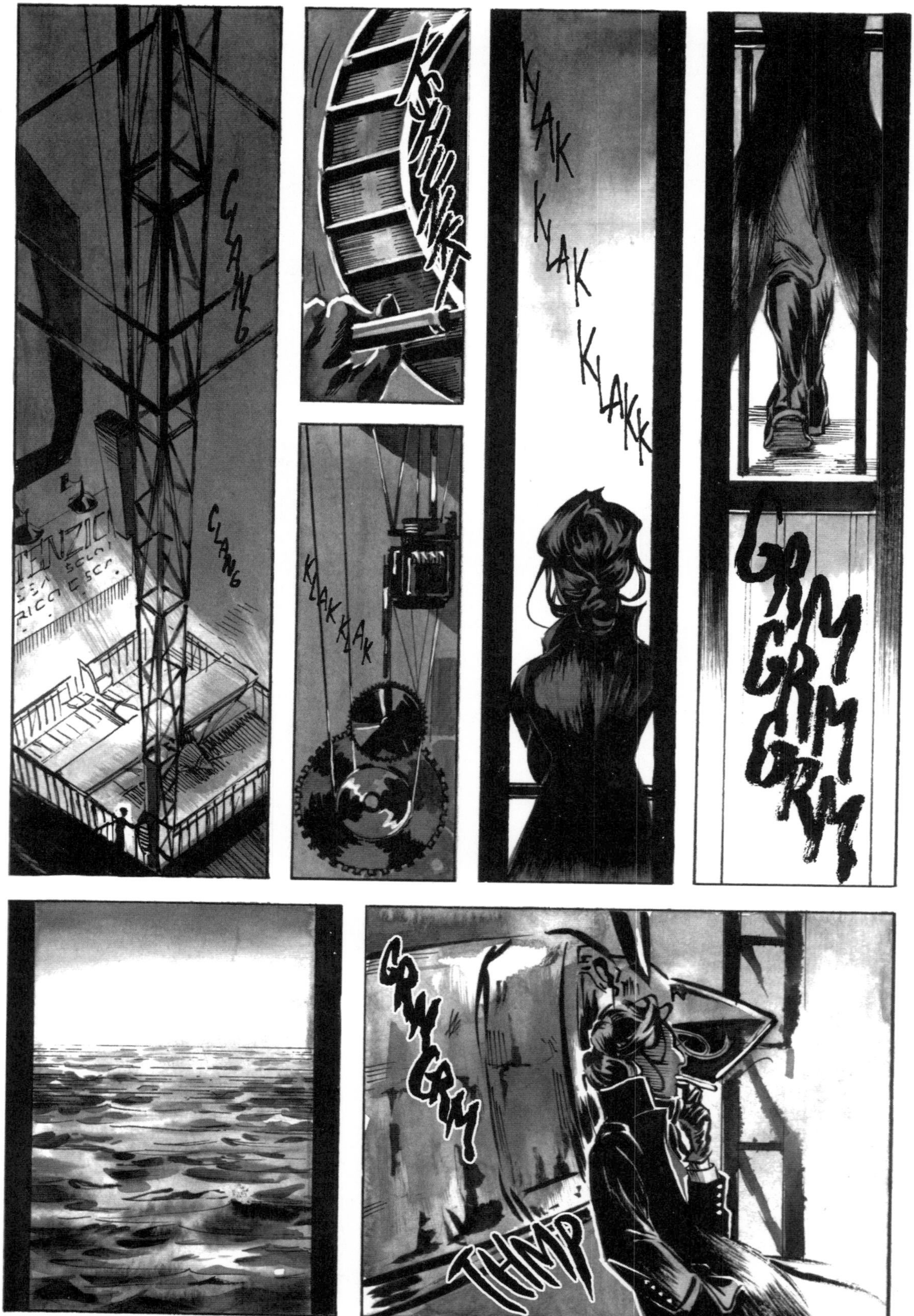
CLANG
CLANG
KSHUNKT
KLAK KLAK
KLAK KLAK KLAKKK
GRM GRM GRM GRM
GRM GRM
THMP

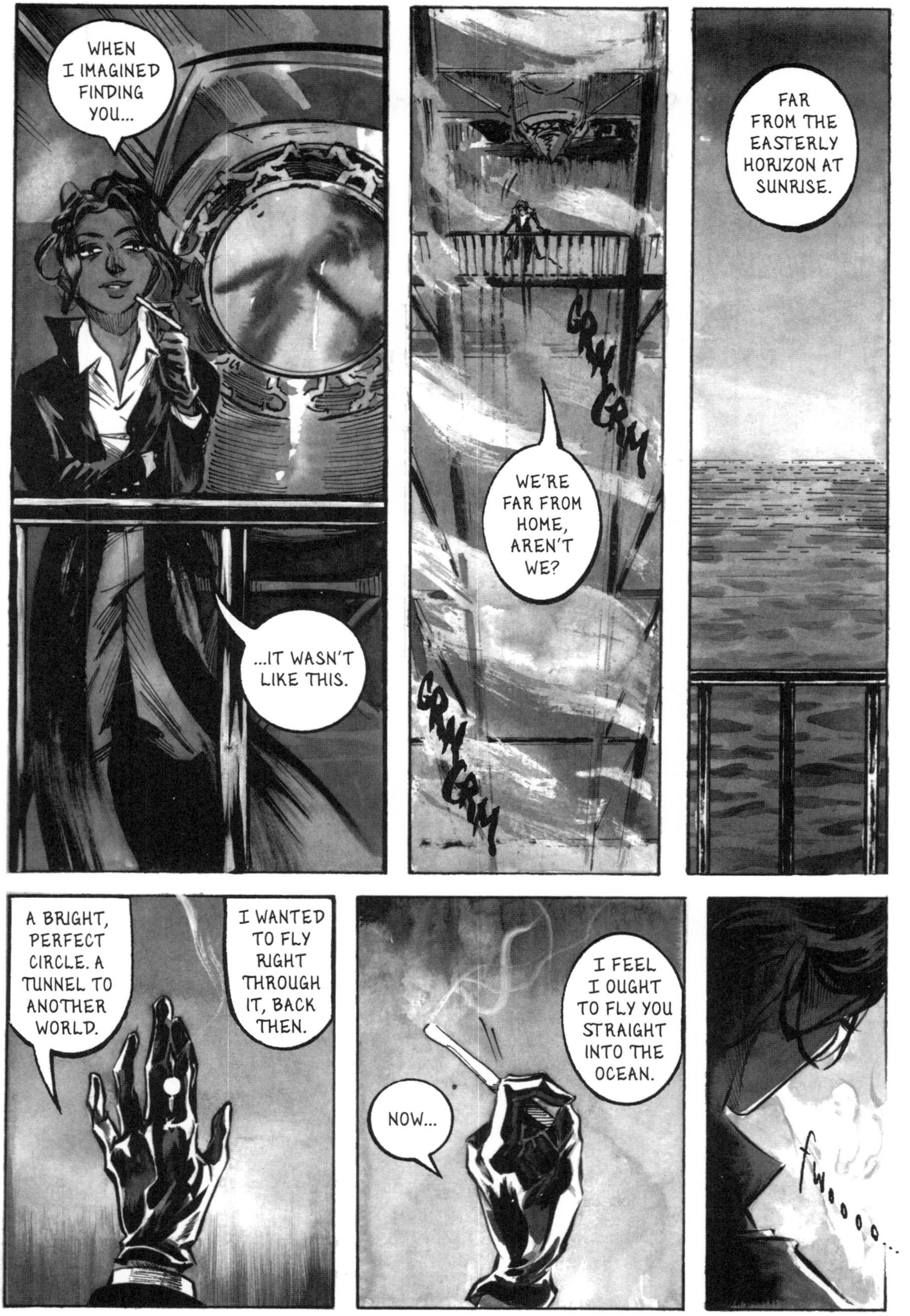
WHEN I IMAGINED FINDING YOU...
...IT WASN'T LIKE THIS.
GRM GRM
WE'RE FAR FROM HOME, AREN'T WE?
GRM GRM
FAR FROM THE EASTERLY HORIZON AT SUNRISE.
A BRIGHT, PERFECT CIRCLE. A TUNNEL TO ANOTHER WORLD.
I WANTED TO FLY RIGHT THROUGH IT, BACK THEN.
NOW...
I FEEL I OUGHT TO FLY YOU STRAIGHT INTO THE OCEAN.
fwoooo...

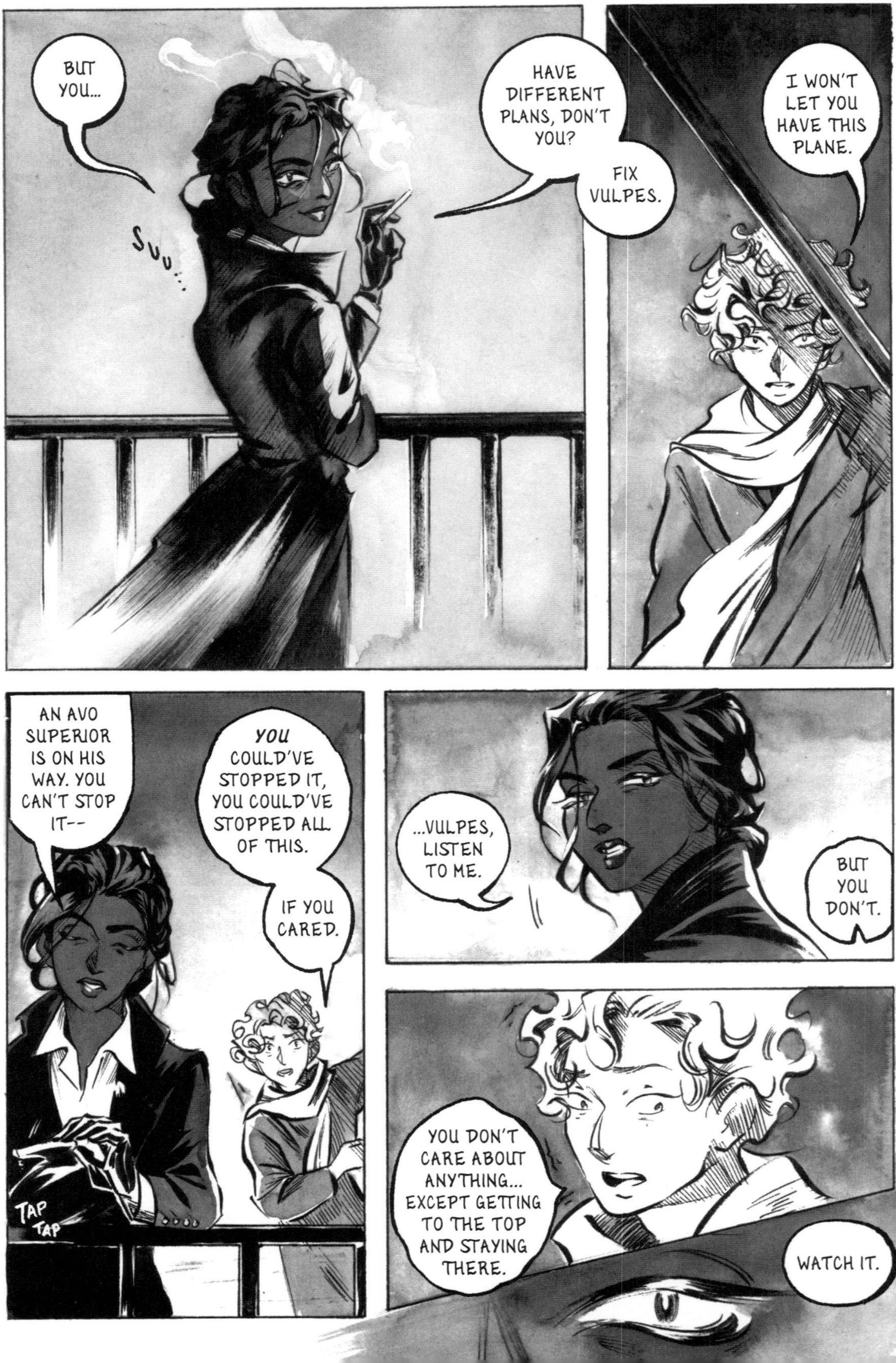
BUT YOU...
SUU...
HAVE DIFFERENT PLANS, DON'T YOU?
FIX VULPES.
I WON'T LET YOU HAVE THIS PLANE.
AN AVO SUPERIOR IS ON HIS WAY. YOU CAN'T STOP IT--
YOU COULD'VE STOPPED IT, YOU COULD'VE STOPPED ALL OF THIS.
IF YOU CARED.
TAP TAP
...VULPES, LISTEN TO ME.
BUT YOU DON'T.
YOU DON'T CARE ABOUT ANYTHING... EXCEPT GETTING TO THE TOP AND STAYING THERE.
WATCH IT.

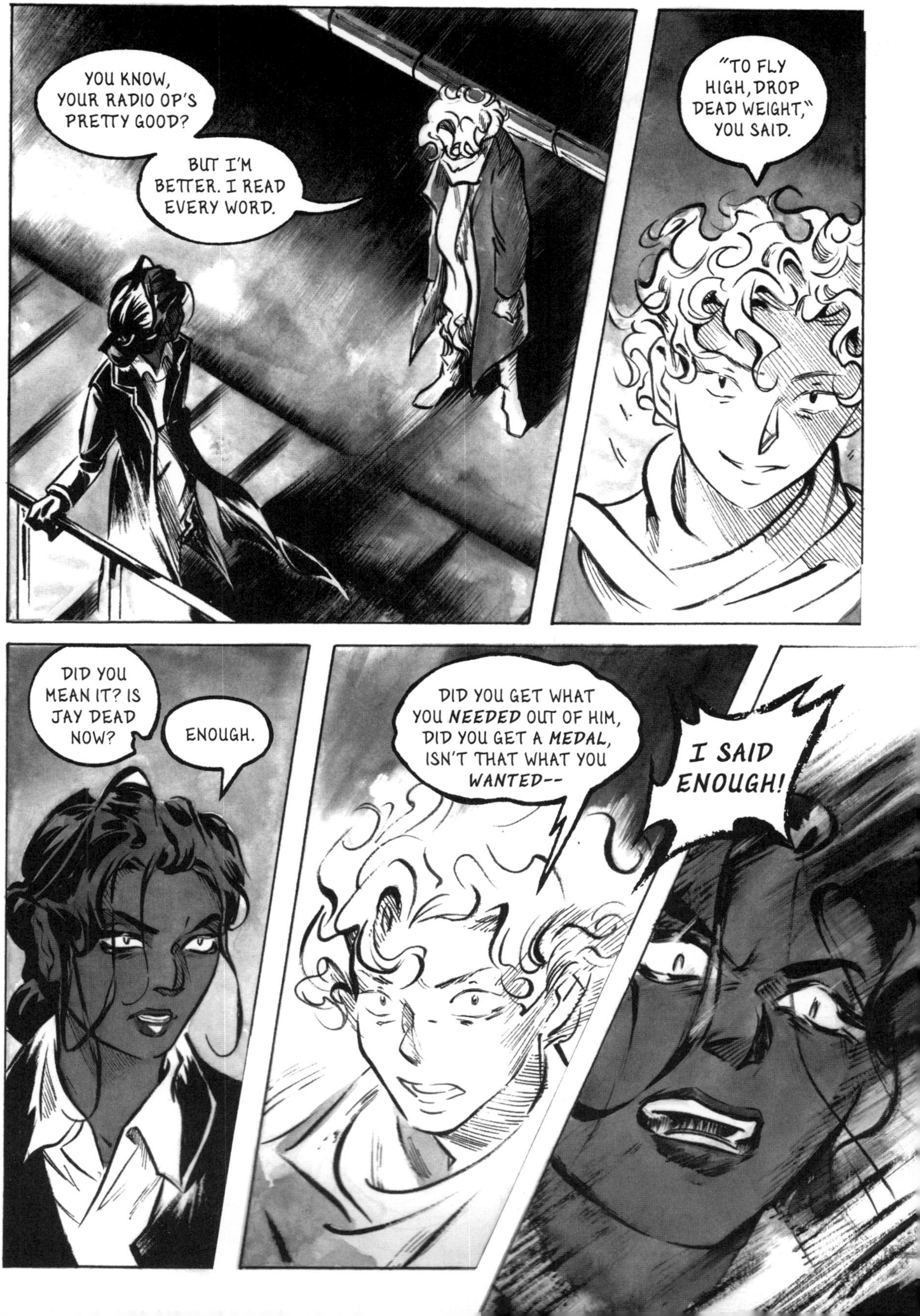
YOU KNOW, YOUR RADIO OP'S PRETTY GOOD?
BUT I'M BETTER. I READ EVERY WORD.
"TO FLY HIGH, DROP DEAD WEIGHT," YOU SAID.
DID YOU MEAN IT? IS JAY DEAD NOW?
ENOUGH.
DID YOU GET WHAT YOU *NEEDED* OUT OF HIM, DID YOU GET A *MEDAL*, ISN'T THAT WHAT YOU *WANTED*--
I SAID ENOUGH!

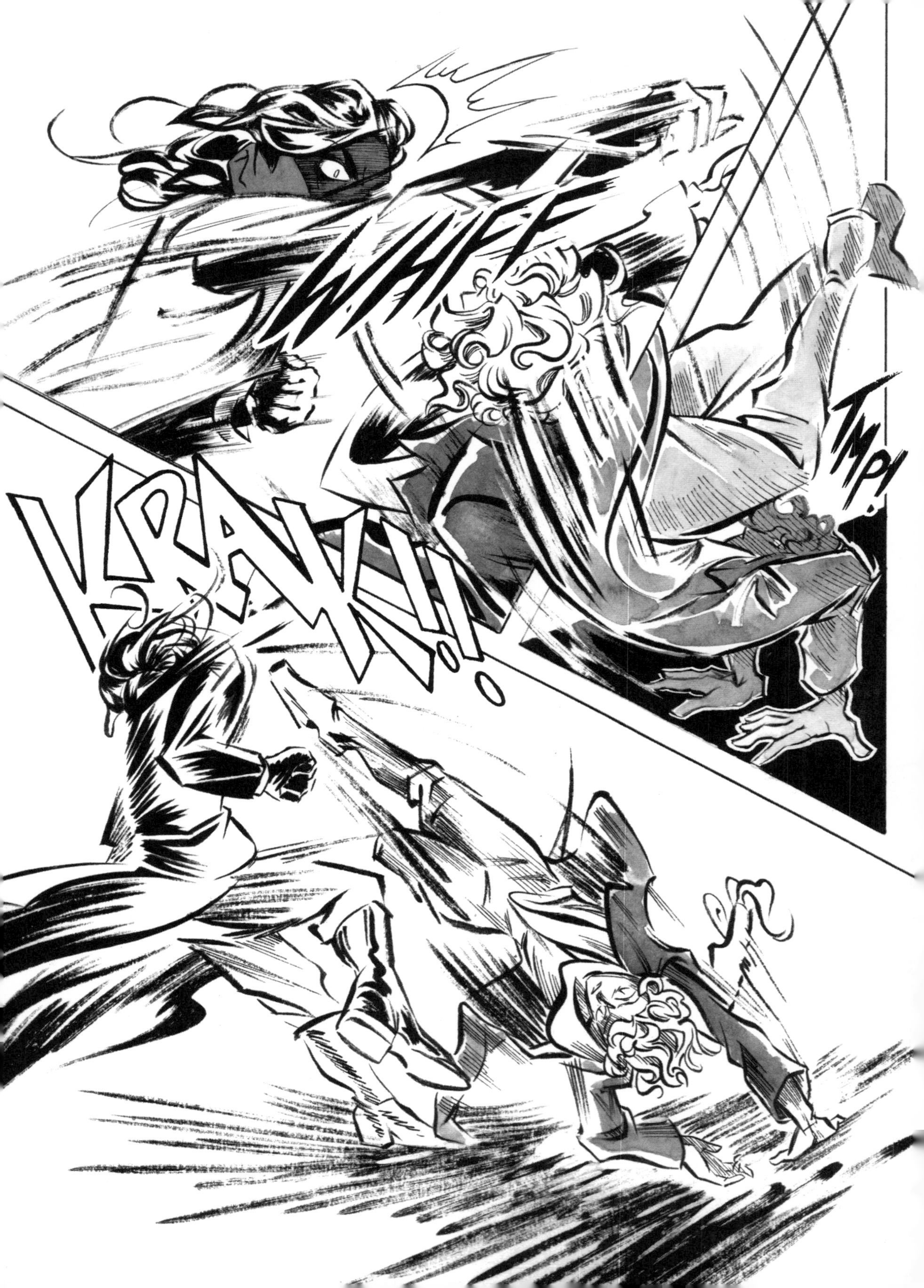
WHIFF
TMP!
KRAKK!!

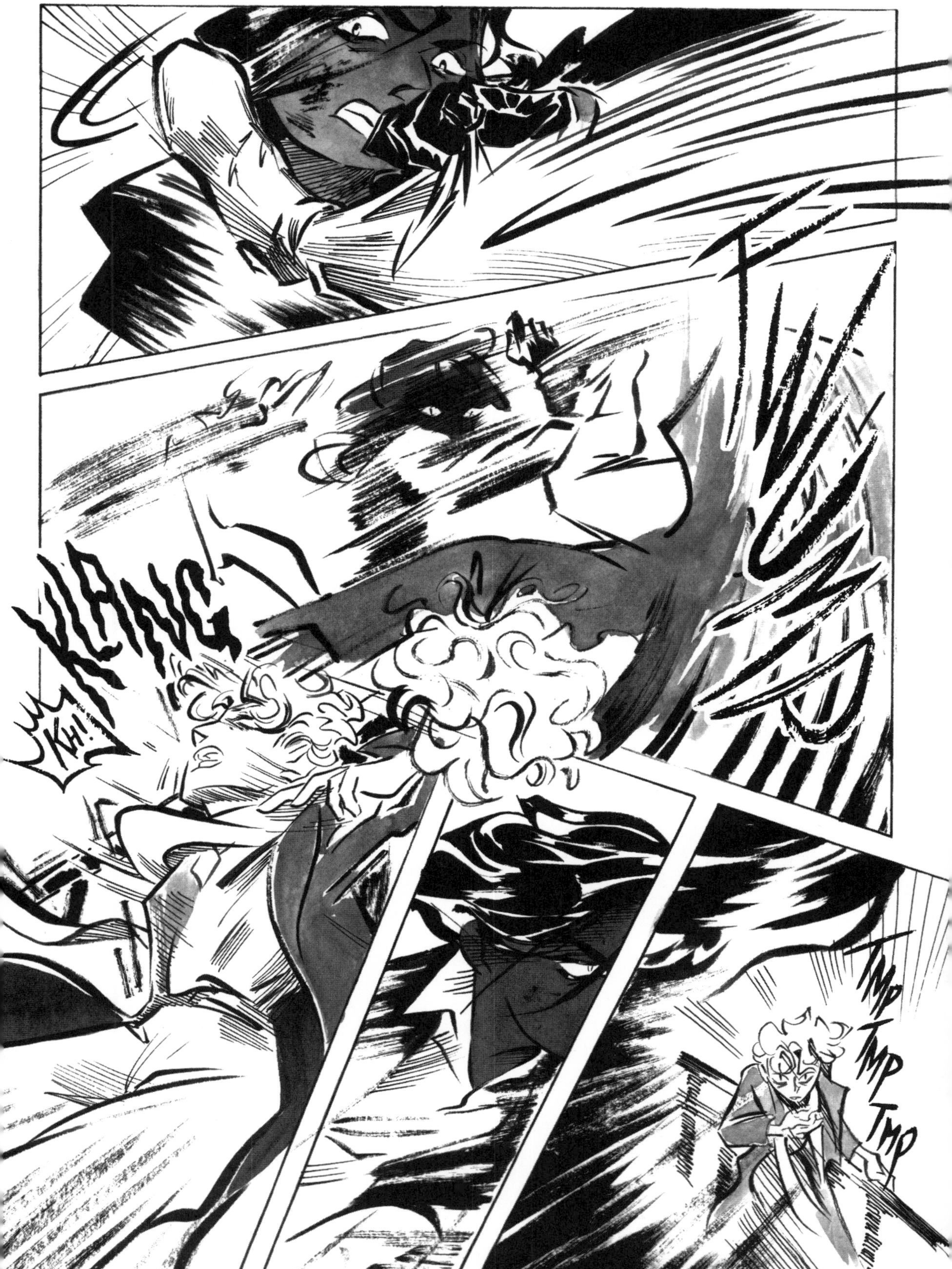
THUNK
KRANG!
KH!
TMP TMP TMP

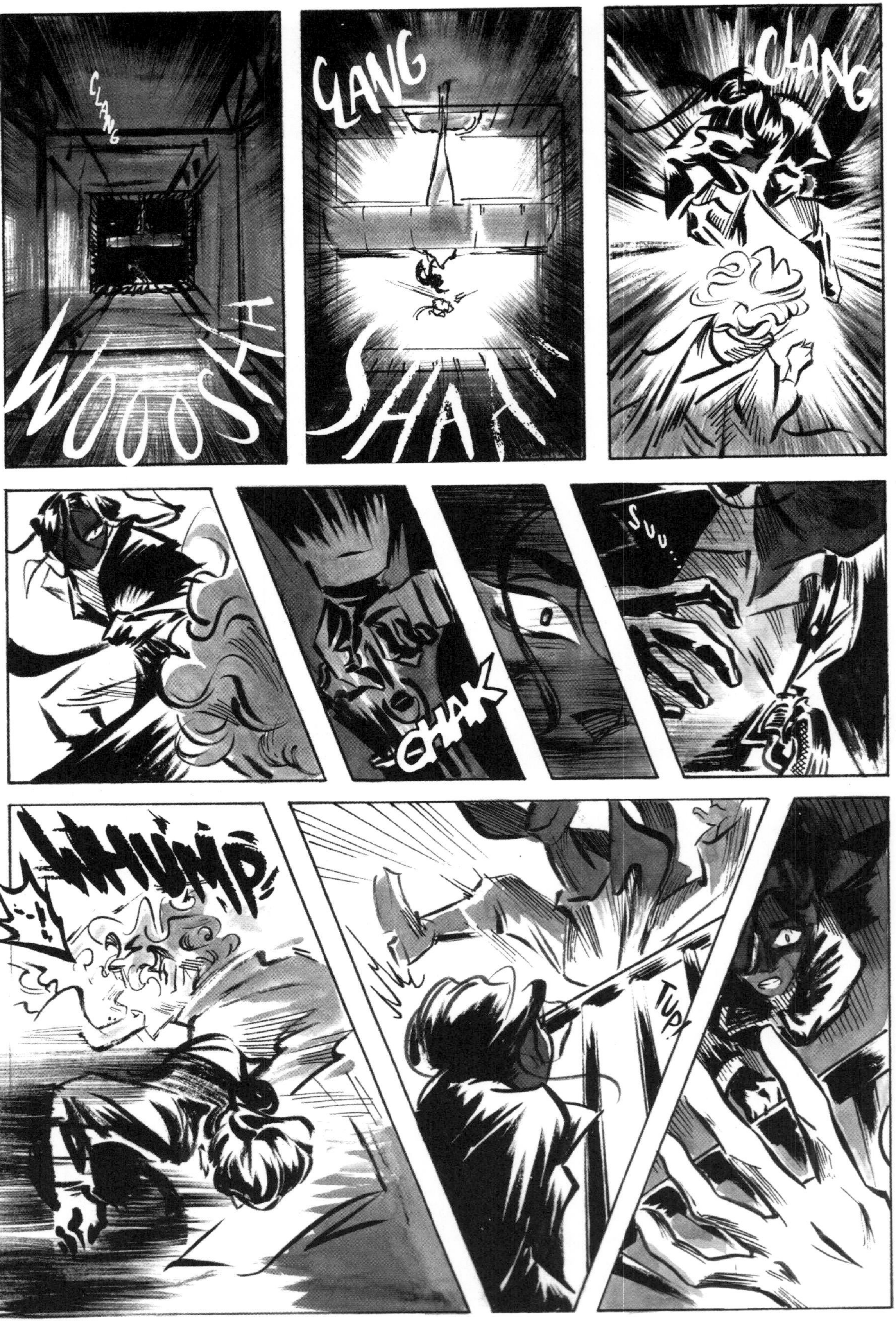
CLANG
WOOOSH
CLANG
SHAK
CLANG
CHAK
SUU...
WHUMP
!!
TUP

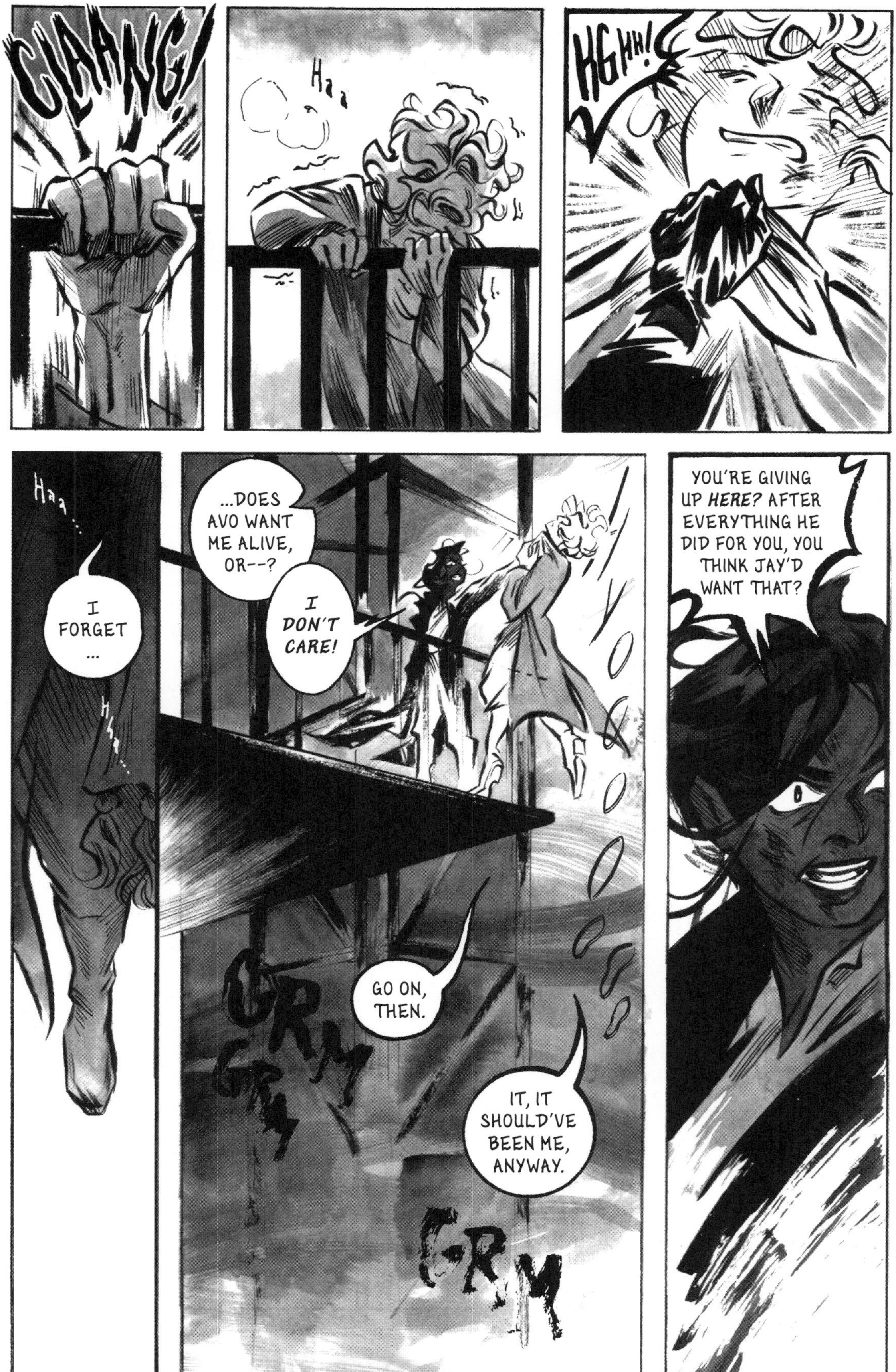
CLAANG!
Haa
KGHH!
Haa...
I FORGET ...
Haa...
...DOES AVO WANT ME ALIVE, OR--?
I DON'T CARE!
GO ON, THEN.
IT, IT SHOULD'VE BEEN ME, ANYWAY.
GRM
GRM
GRM
YOU'RE GIVING UP HERE? AFTER EVERYTHING HE DID FOR YOU, YOU THINK JAY'D WANT THAT?

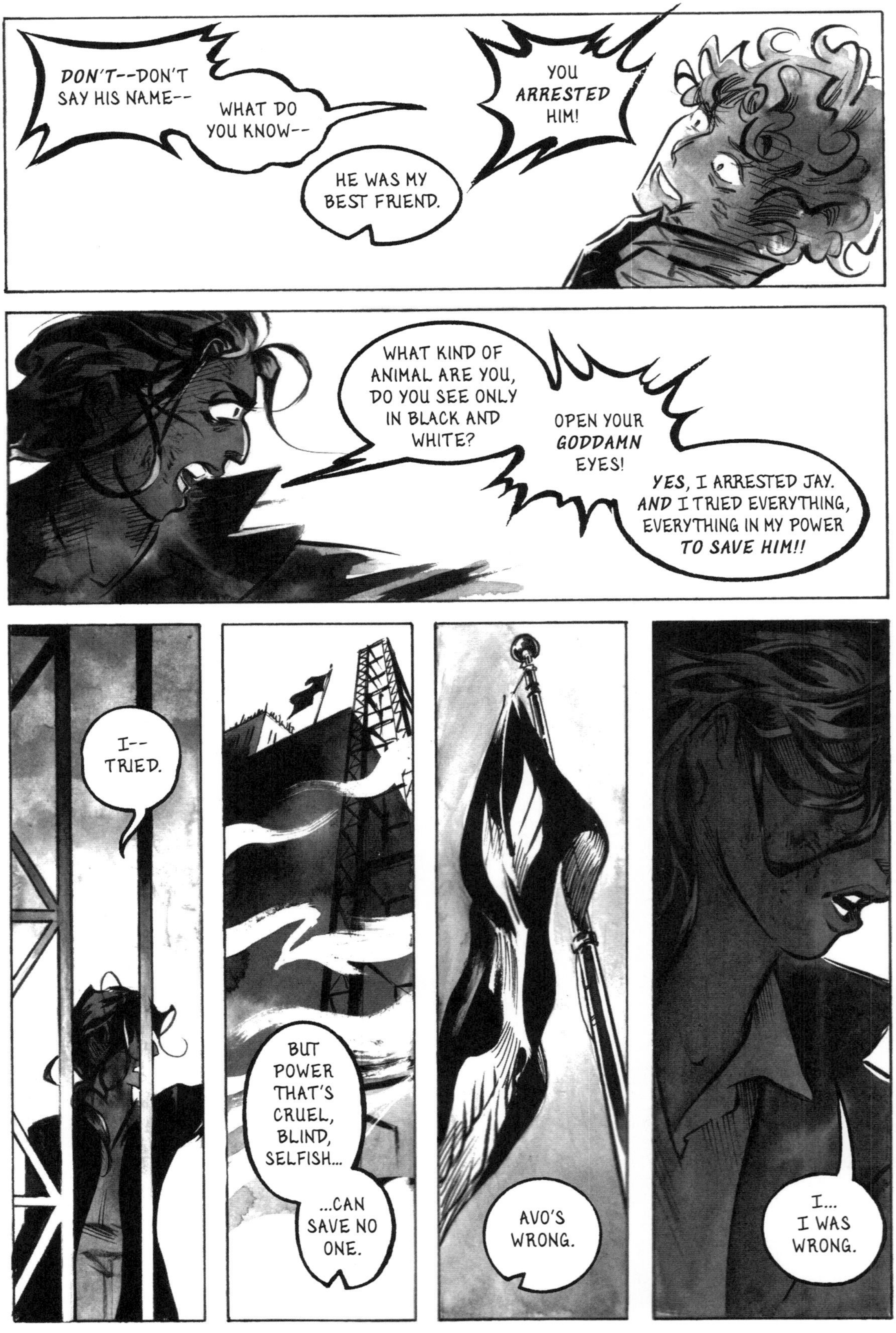
DON'T--DON'T SAY HIS NAME--
WHAT DO YOU KNOW--
HE WAS MY BEST FRIEND.
YOU ARRESTED HIM!
WHAT KIND OF ANIMAL ARE YOU, DO YOU SEE ONLY IN BLACK AND WHITE?
OPEN YOUR GODDAMN EYES!
YES, I ARRESTED JAY. AND I TRIED EVERYTHING, EVERYTHING IN MY POWER TO SAVE HIM!!
I-- TRIED.
BUT POWER THAT'S CRUEL, BLIND, SELFISH...
...CAN SAVE NO ONE.
AVO'S WRONG.
I... I WAS WRONG.

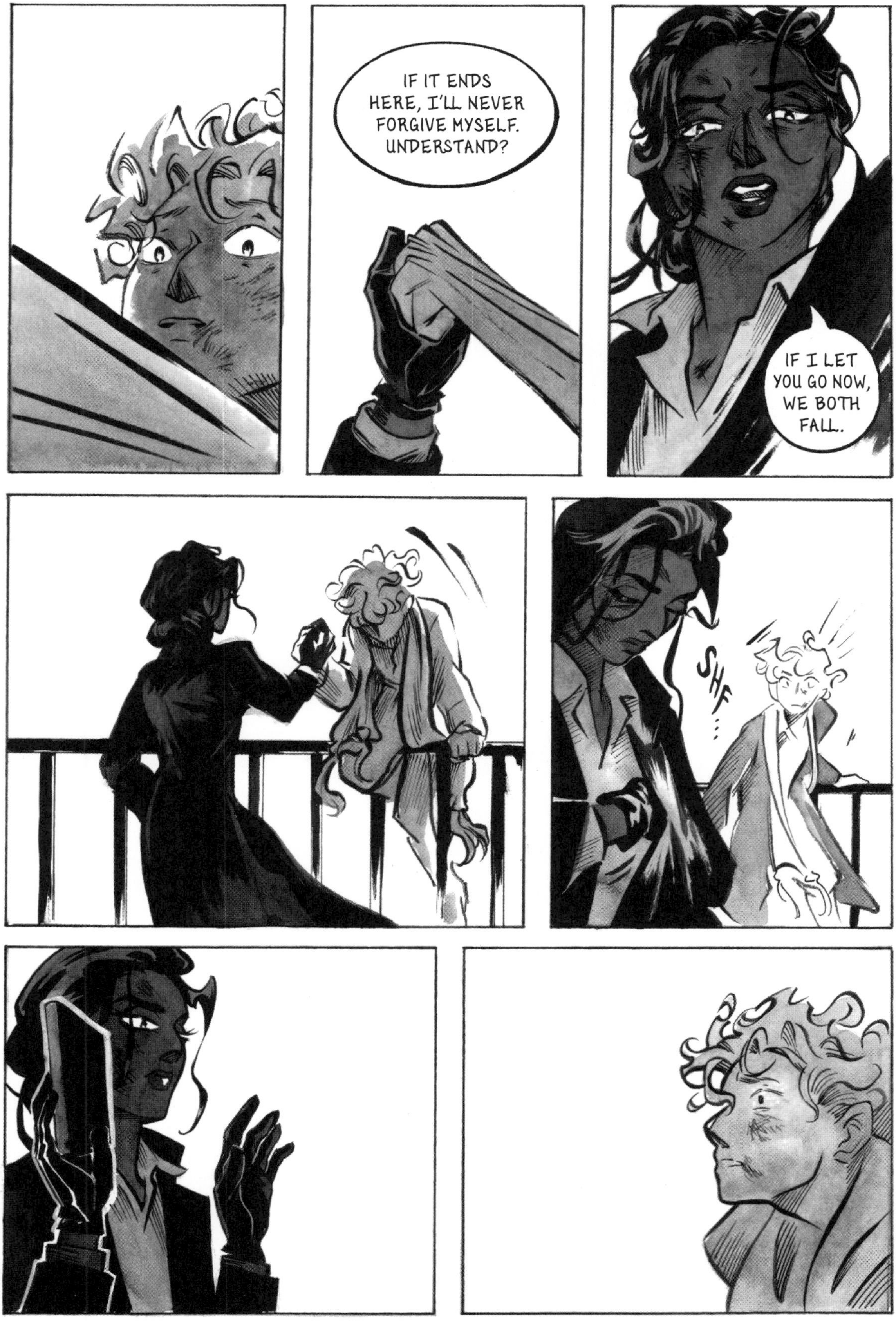
IF IT ENDS HERE, I'LL NEVER FORGIVE MYSELF. UNDERSTAND?
IF I LET YOU GO NOW, WE BOTH FALL.
SHF...

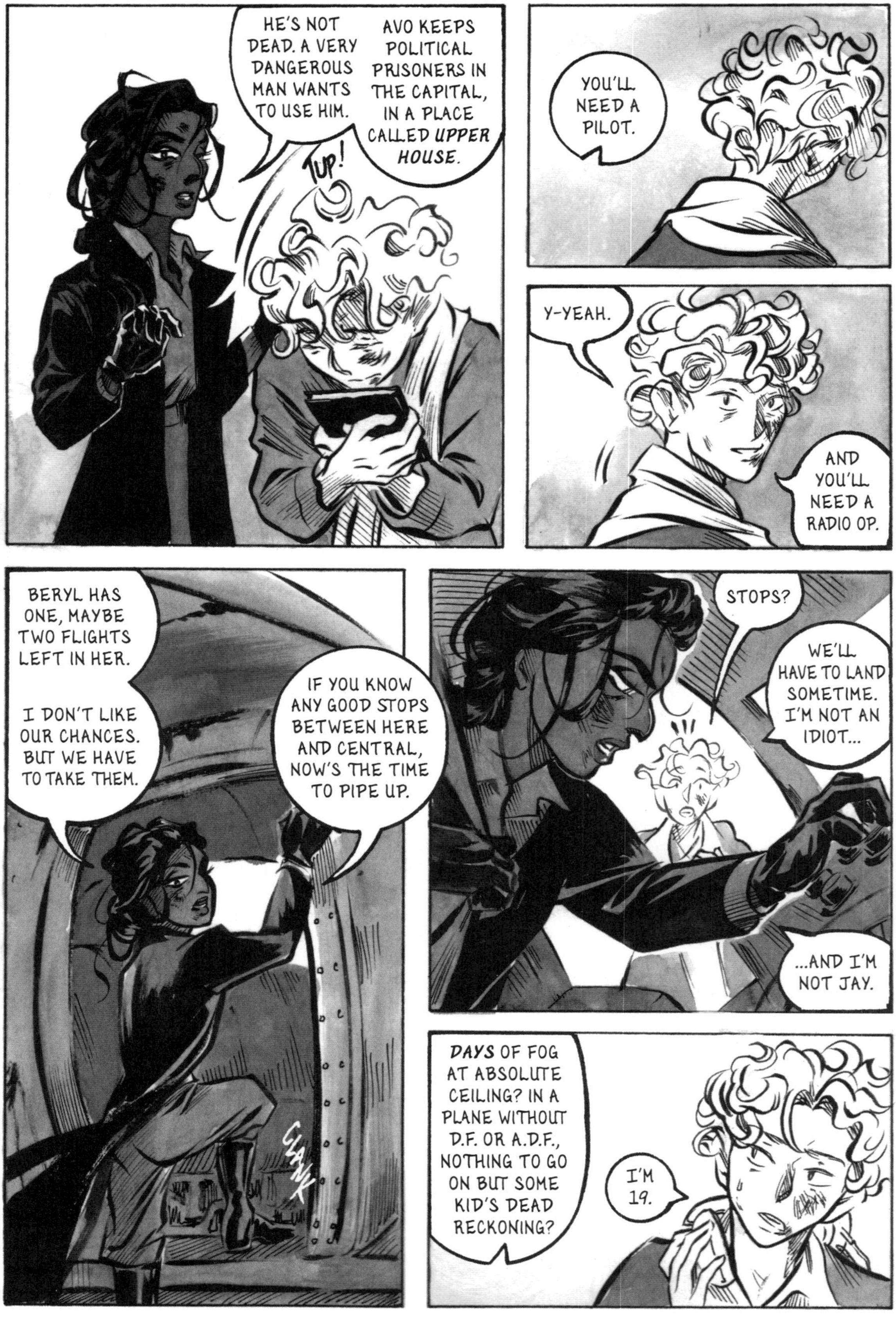
HE'S NOT DEAD. A VERY DANGEROUS MAN WANTS TO USE HIM.
AVO KEEPS POLITICAL PRISONERS IN THE CAPITAL, IN A PLACE CALLED *UPPER HOUSE*.
TUP!
YOU'LL NEED A PILOT.
Y-YEAH.
AND YOU'LL NEED A RADIO OP.
BERYL HAS ONE, MAYBE TWO FLIGHTS LEFT IN HER.
I DON'T LIKE OUR CHANCES. BUT WE HAVE TO TAKE THEM.
IF YOU KNOW ANY GOOD STOPS BETWEEN HERE AND CENTRAL, NOW'S THE TIME TO PIPE UP.
CLANK
STOPS?
WE'LL HAVE TO LAND SOMETIME. I'M NOT AN IDIOT...
...AND I'M NOT JAY.
DAYS OF FOG AT ABSOLUTE CEILING? IN A PLANE WITHOUT D.F. OR A.D.F., NOTHING TO GO ON BUT SOME KID'S DEAD RECKONING?
I'M 19.

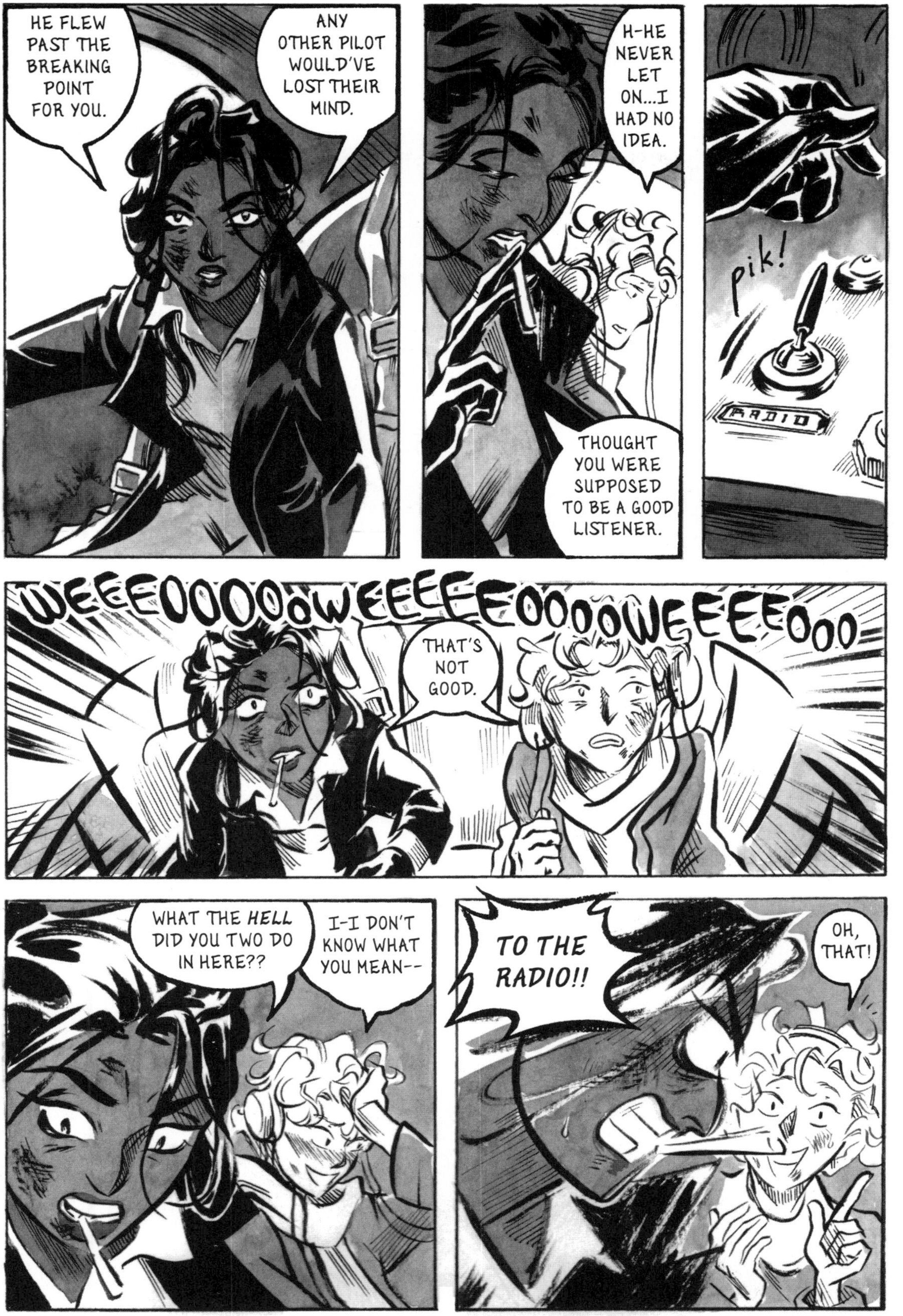
HE FLEW PAST THE BREAKING POINT FOR YOU.
ANY OTHER PILOT WOULD'VE LOST THEIR MIND.
H-HE NEVER LET ON...I HAD NO IDEA.
THOUGHT YOU WERE SUPPOSED TO BE A GOOD LISTENER.
pik!
RADIO
WEEEOOOOOWEEEEEOOOOWEEEEOOO
THAT'S NOT GOOD.
WHAT THE *HELL* DID YOU TWO DO IN HERE??
I-I DON'T KNOW WHAT YOU MEAN--
TO THE RADIO!!
OH, THAT!

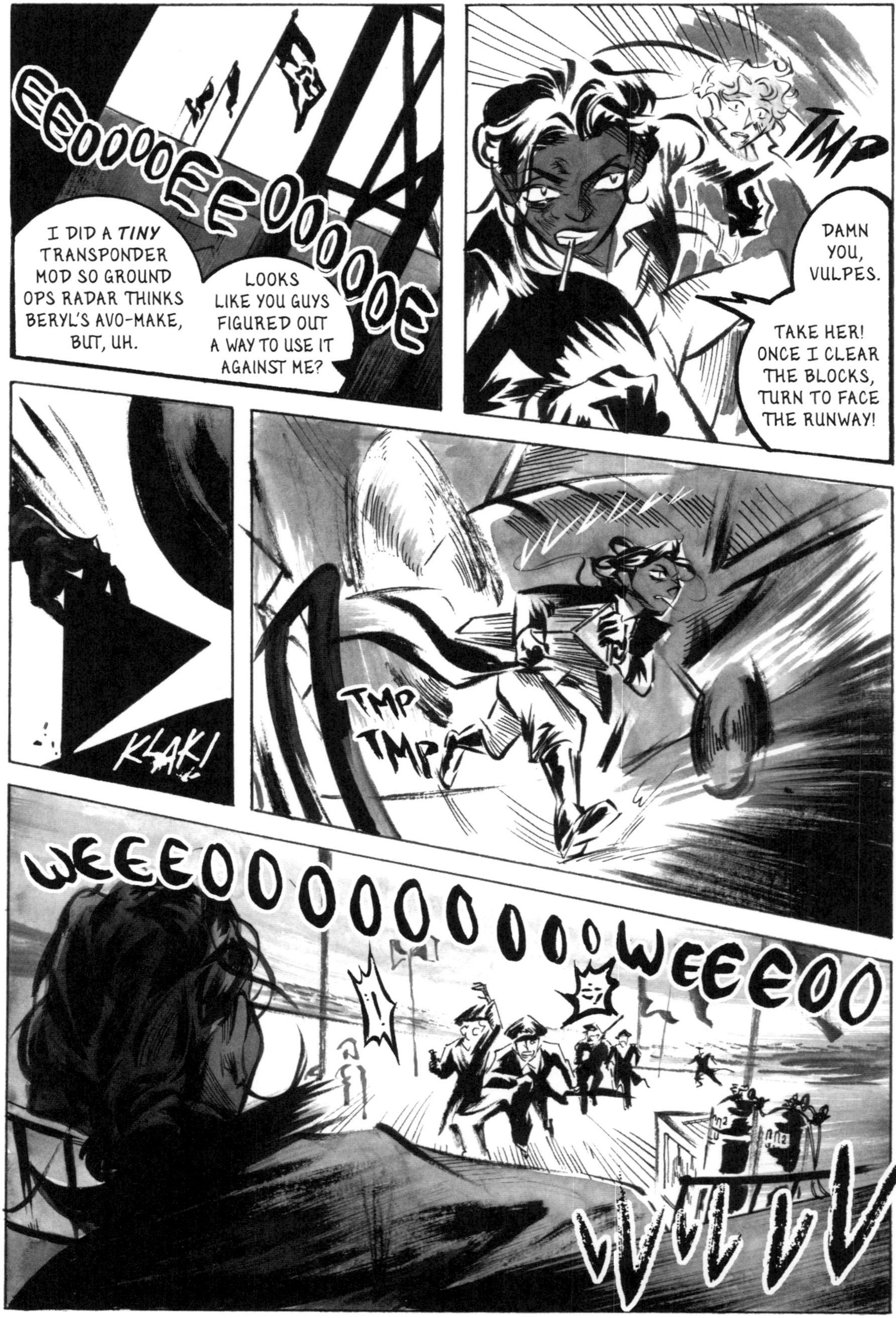
EEOOOOEEOOOOOOE
I DID A *TINY* TRANSPONDER MOD SO GROUND OPS RADAR THINKS BERYL'S AVO-MAKE, BUT, UH.
LOOKS LIKE YOU GUYS FIGURED OUT A WAY TO USE IT AGAINST ME?
TMP
DAMN YOU, VULPES.
TAKE HER! ONCE I CLEAR THE BLOCKS, TURN TO FACE THE RUNWAY!
KLAK!
TMP TMP
WEEEOOOOOOOOOOWEEEOO
!

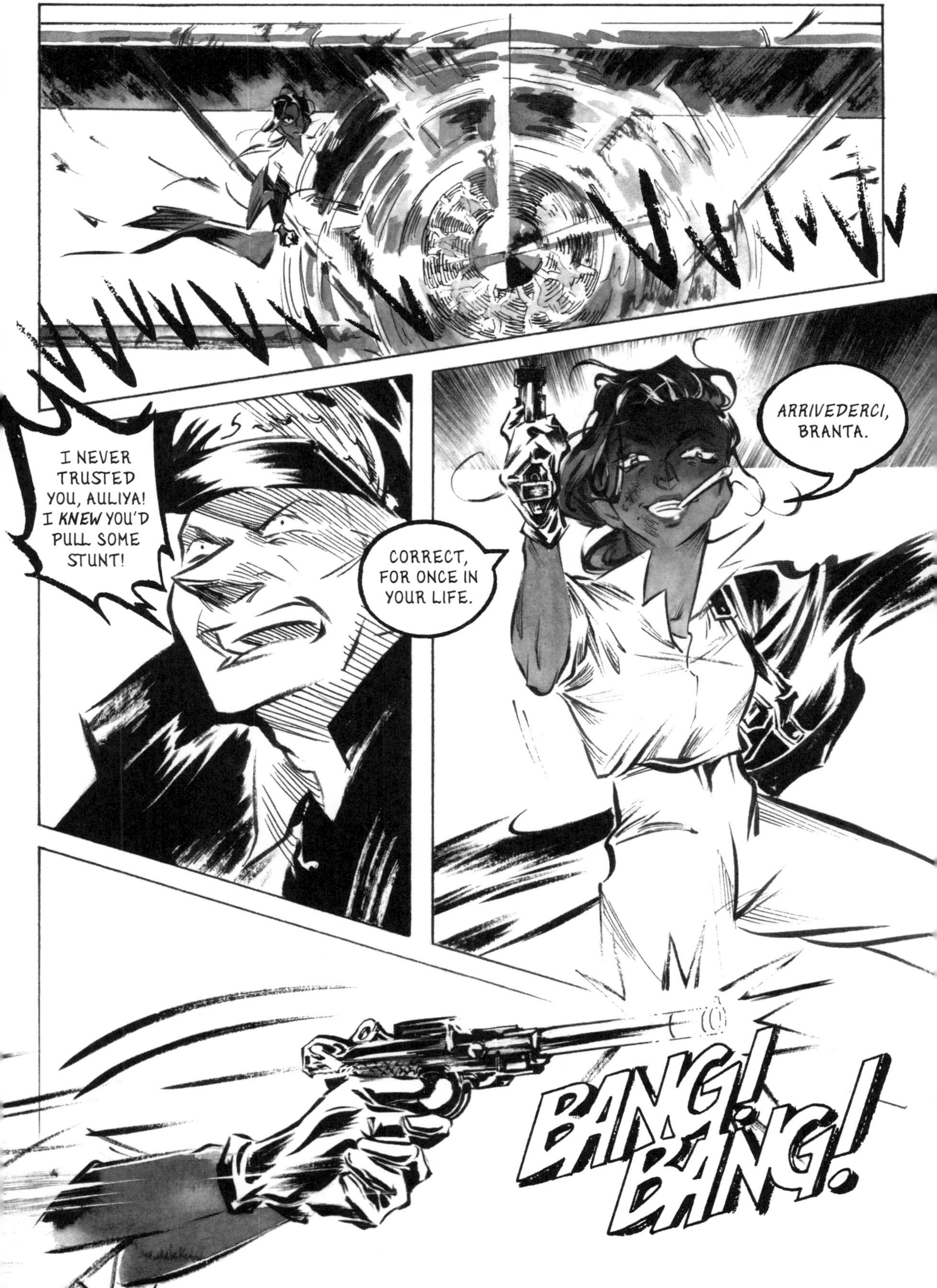
I NEVER TRUSTED YOU, AULIYA! I *KNEW* YOU'D PULL SOME STUNT!
CORRECT, FOR ONCE IN YOUR LIFE.
ARRIVEDERCI, BRANTA.
BANG! BANG!

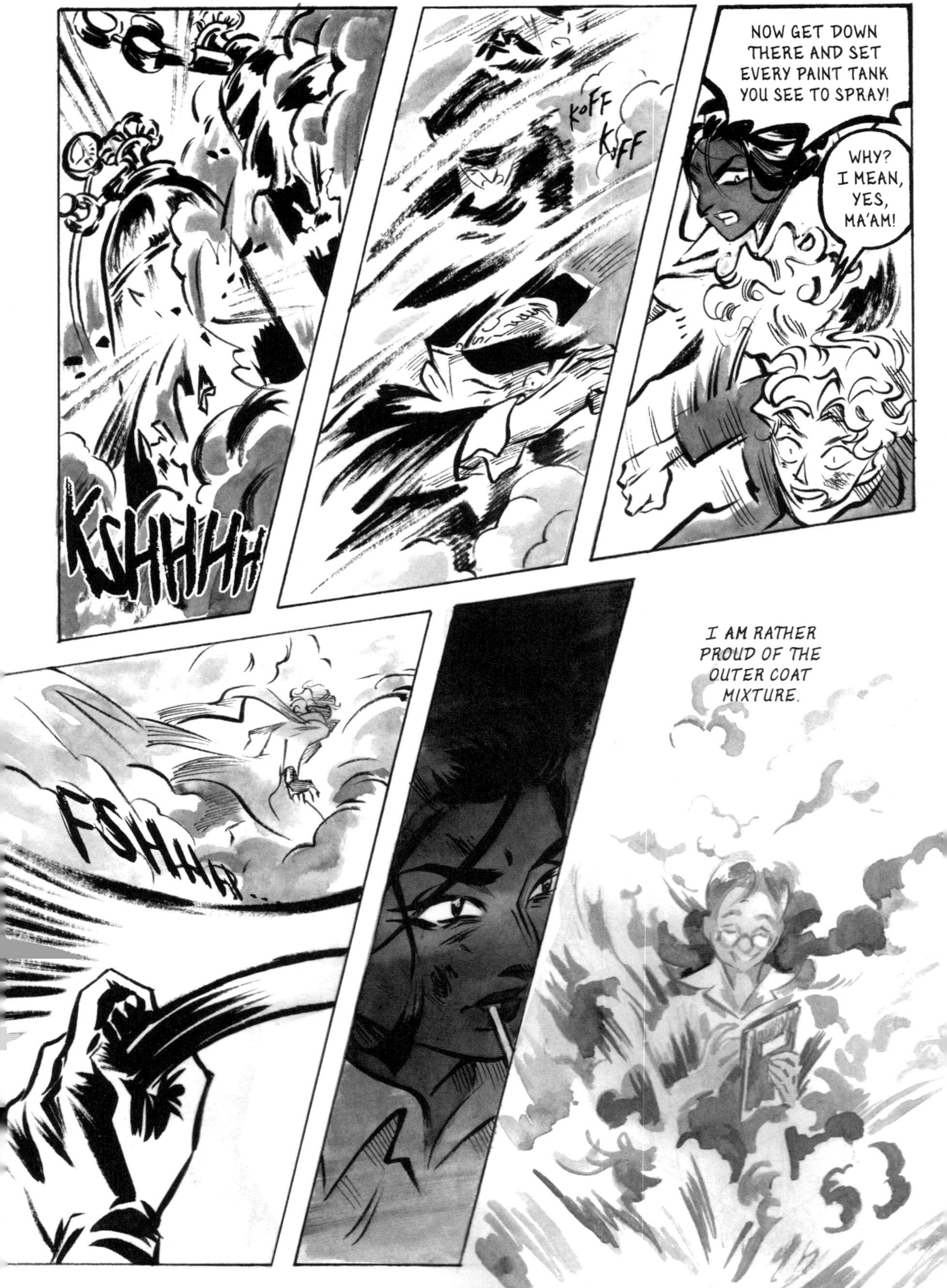
KSHHHH
KOFF
KOFF
NOW GET DOWN THERE AND SET EVERY PAINT TANK YOU SEE TO SPRAY!
WHY? I MEAN, YES, MA'AM!
FSHHHH...
I AM RATHER PROUD OF THE OUTER COAT MIXTURE.

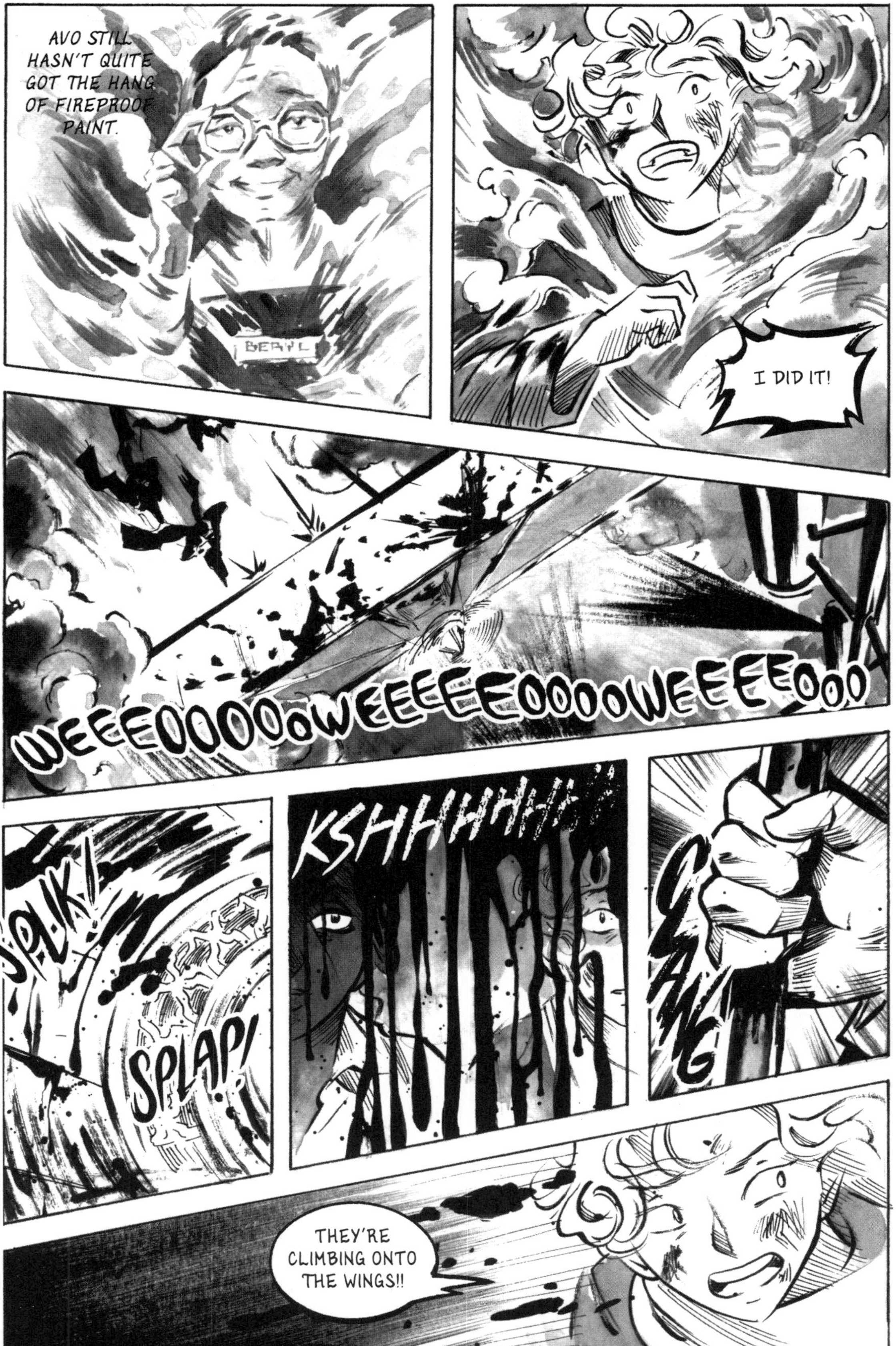
AVO STILL HASN'T QUITE GOT THE HANG OF FIREPROOF PAINT.
BERYL
I DID IT!
WEEEOOOOOoWEEEEEOOOOWEEEEOOO
SPLIK!
SPLAP!
KSHHHHHH!
CLANG
THEY'RE CLIMBING ONTO THE WINGS!!

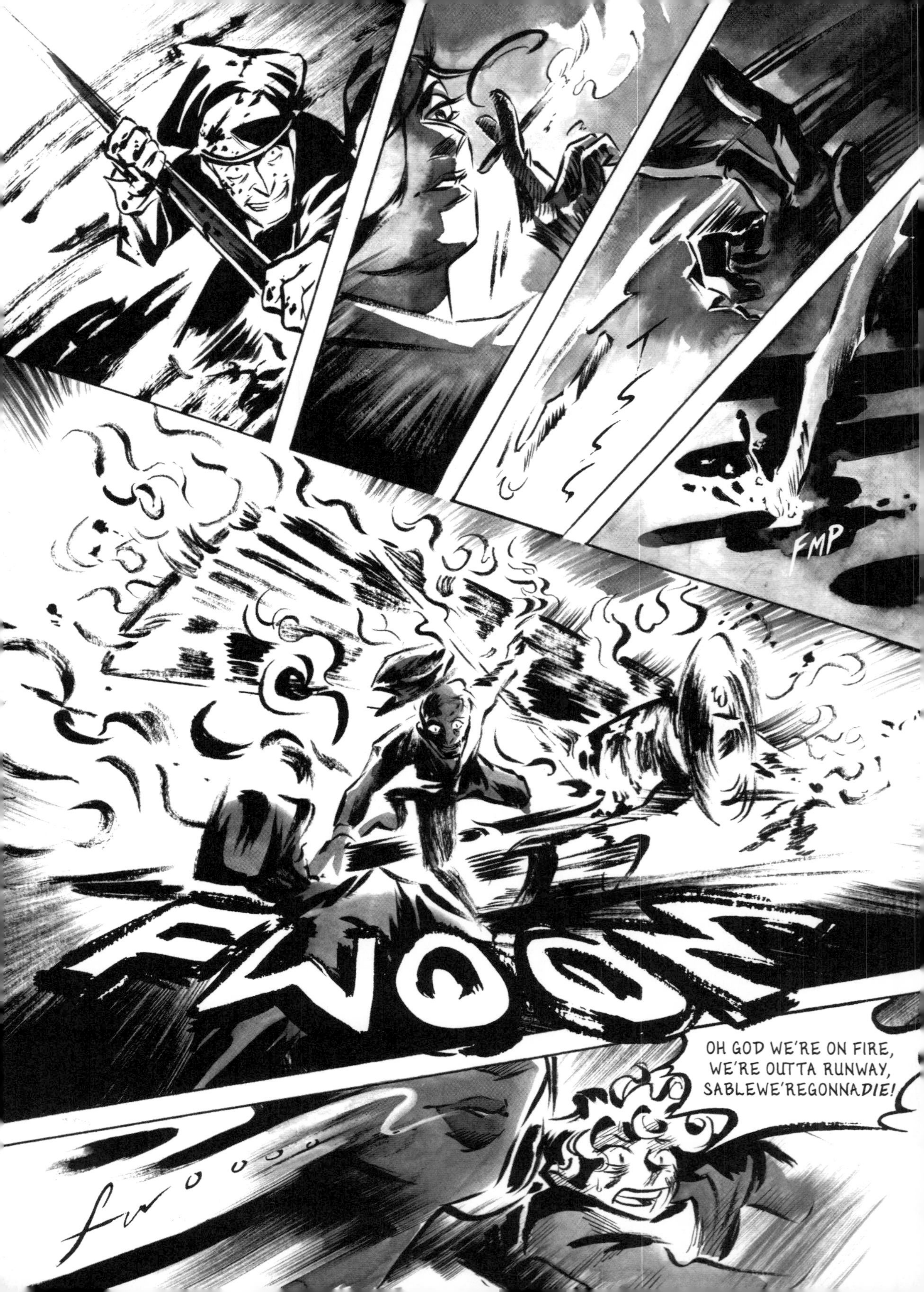
FMP
FWOOM
OH GOD WE'RE ON FIRE, WE'RE OUTTA RUNWAY, SABLEWE'REGONNADIE!
fwooo

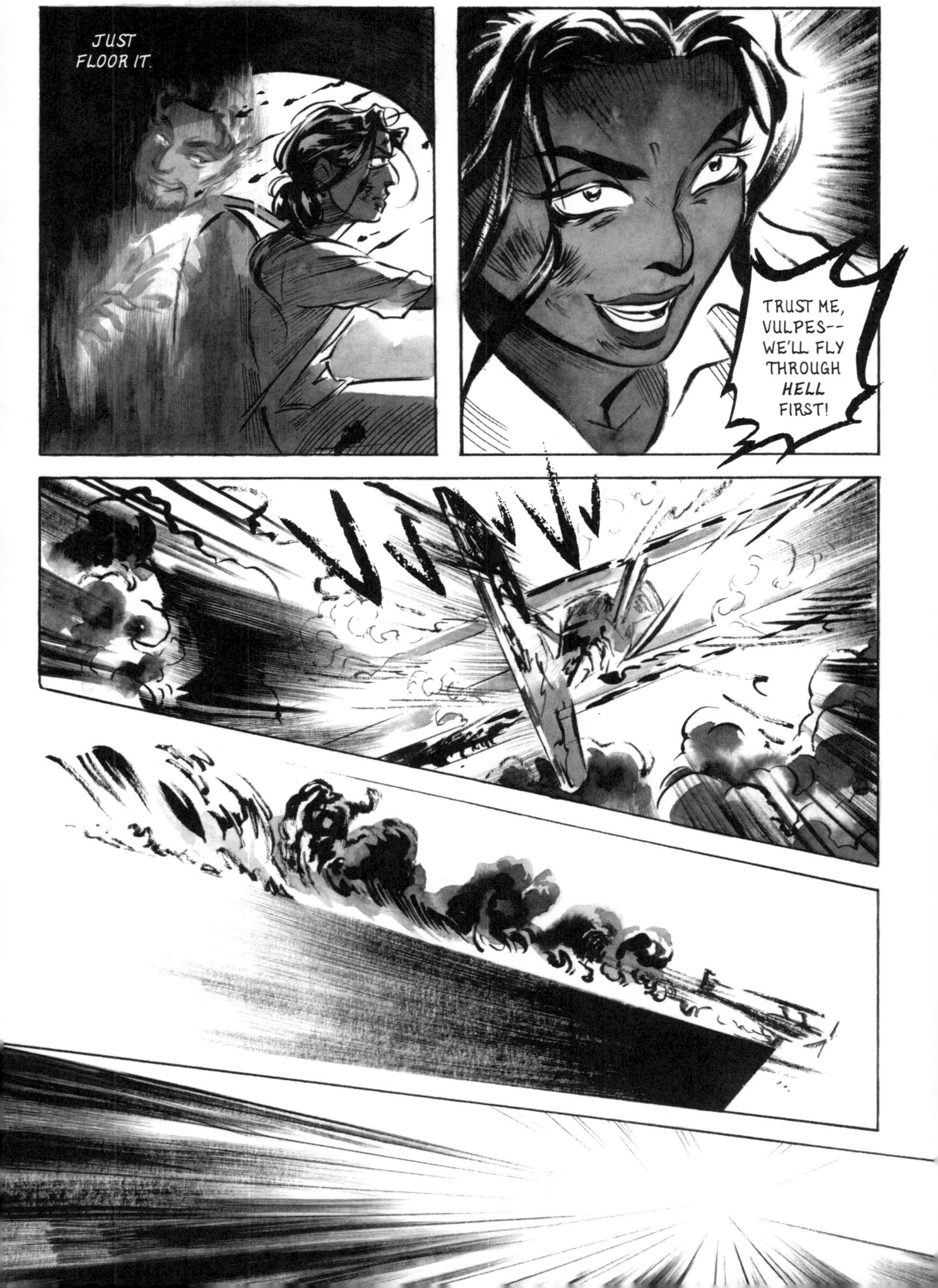
JUST FLOOR IT.
TRUST ME, VULPES-- WE'LL FLY THROUGH HELL FIRST!

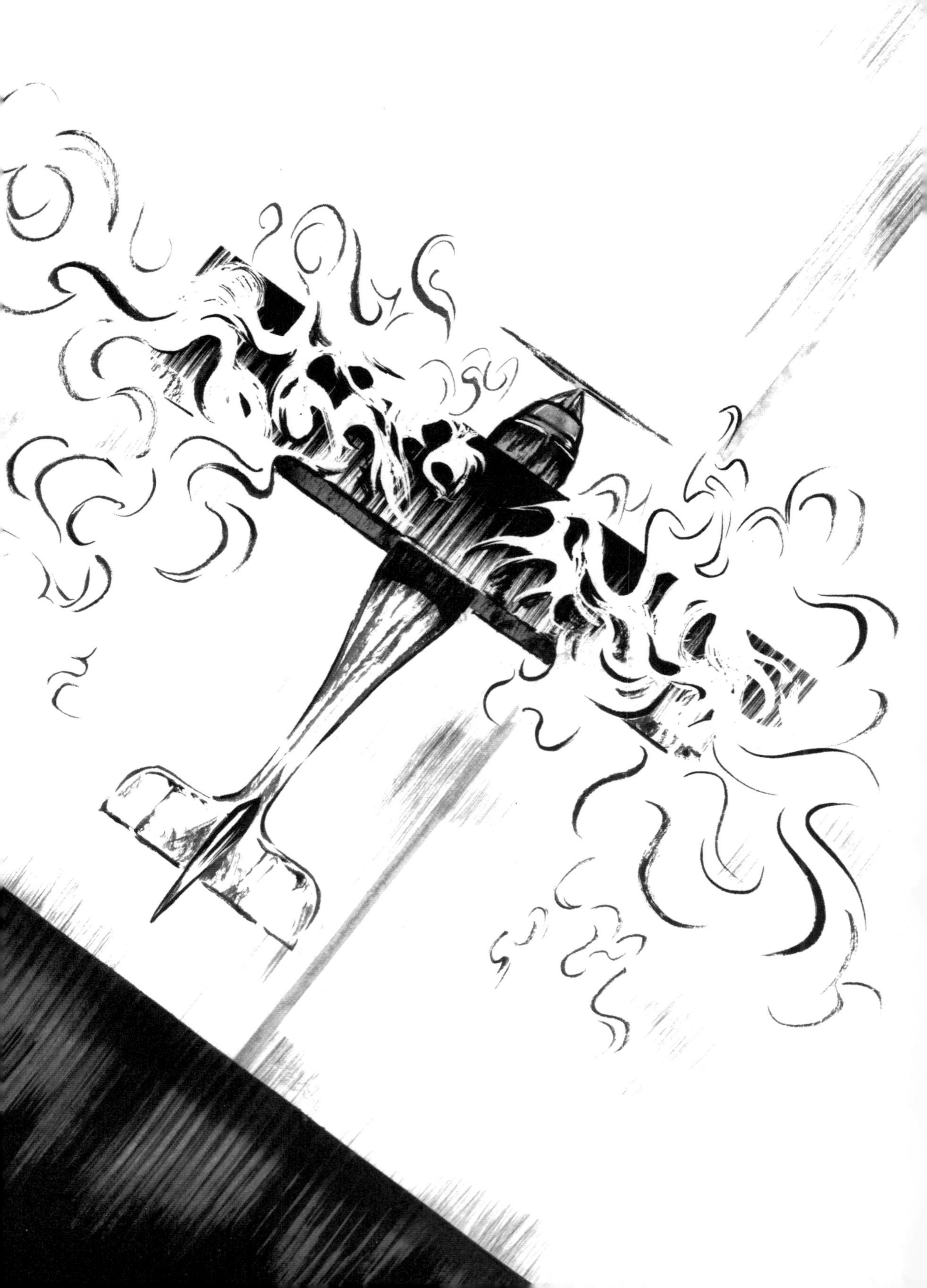

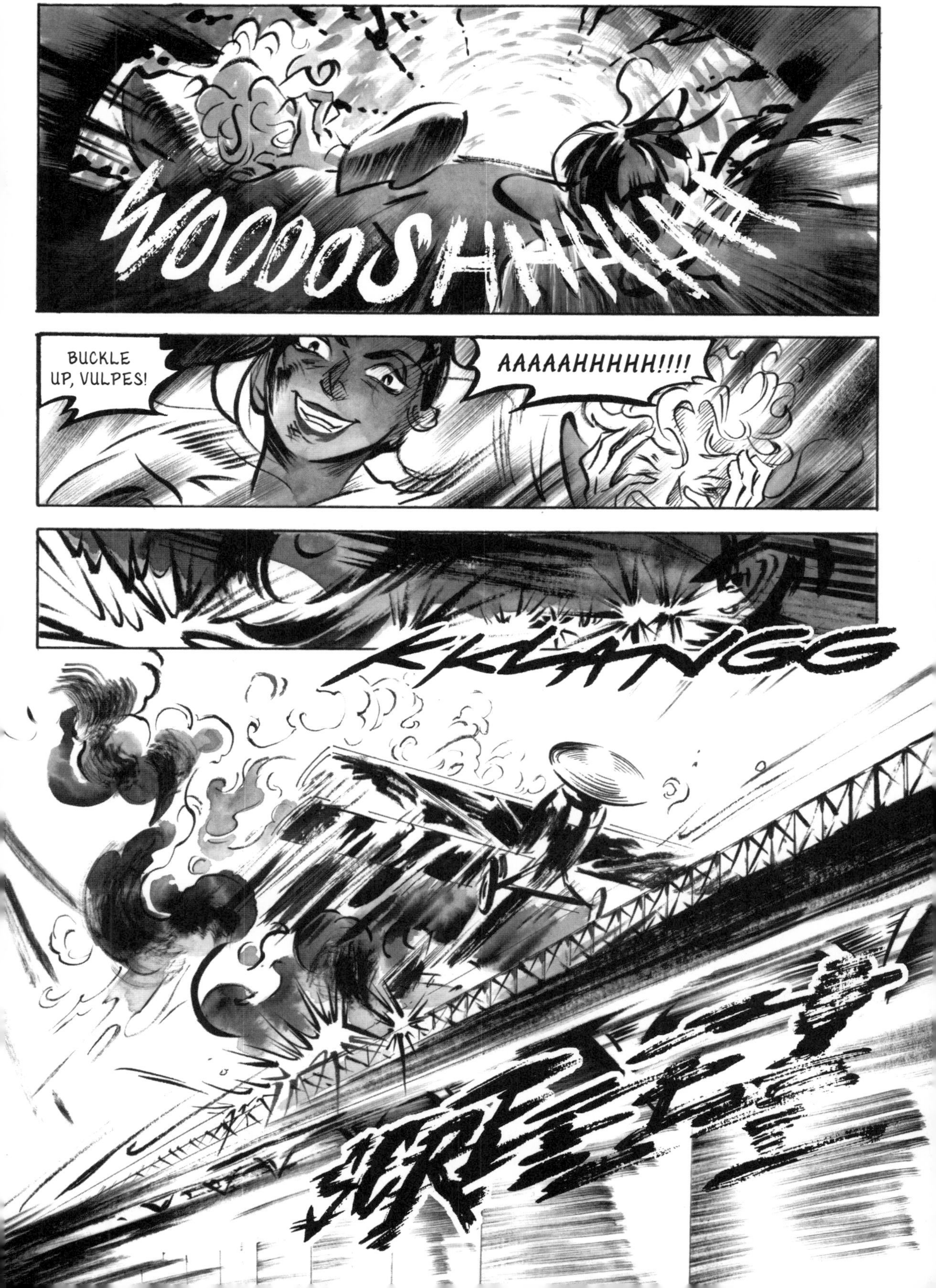
WOOOOSHHHH
BUCKLE UP, VULPES!
AAAAAHHHHH!!!!
KKLANGG
SCREE

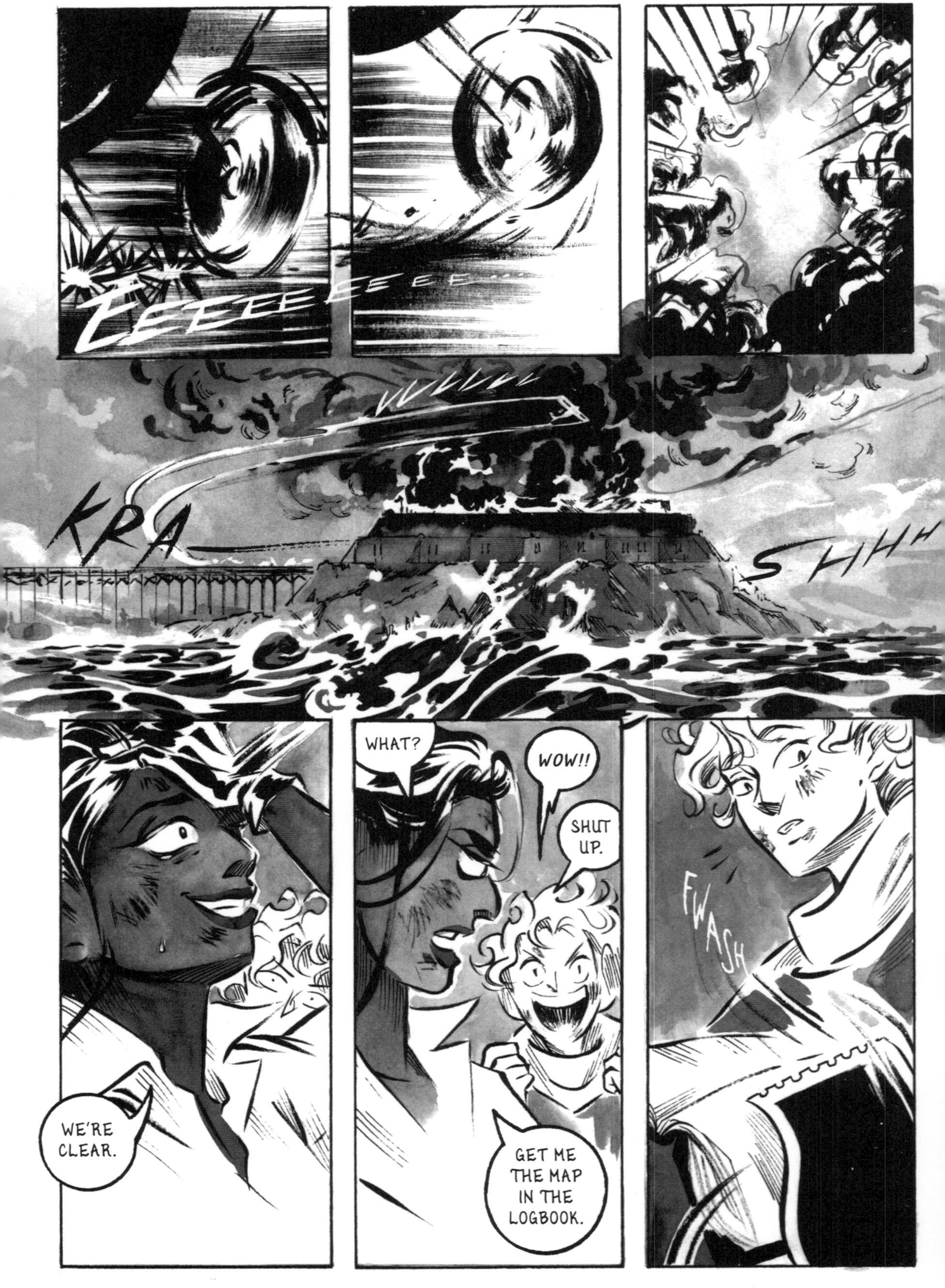
EEEEEEEEEEE...
VVVVVVV
KRA
SHHH
WE'RE CLEAR.
WHAT?
WOW!!
SHUT UP.
GET ME THE MAP IN THE LOGBOOK.
FWASH

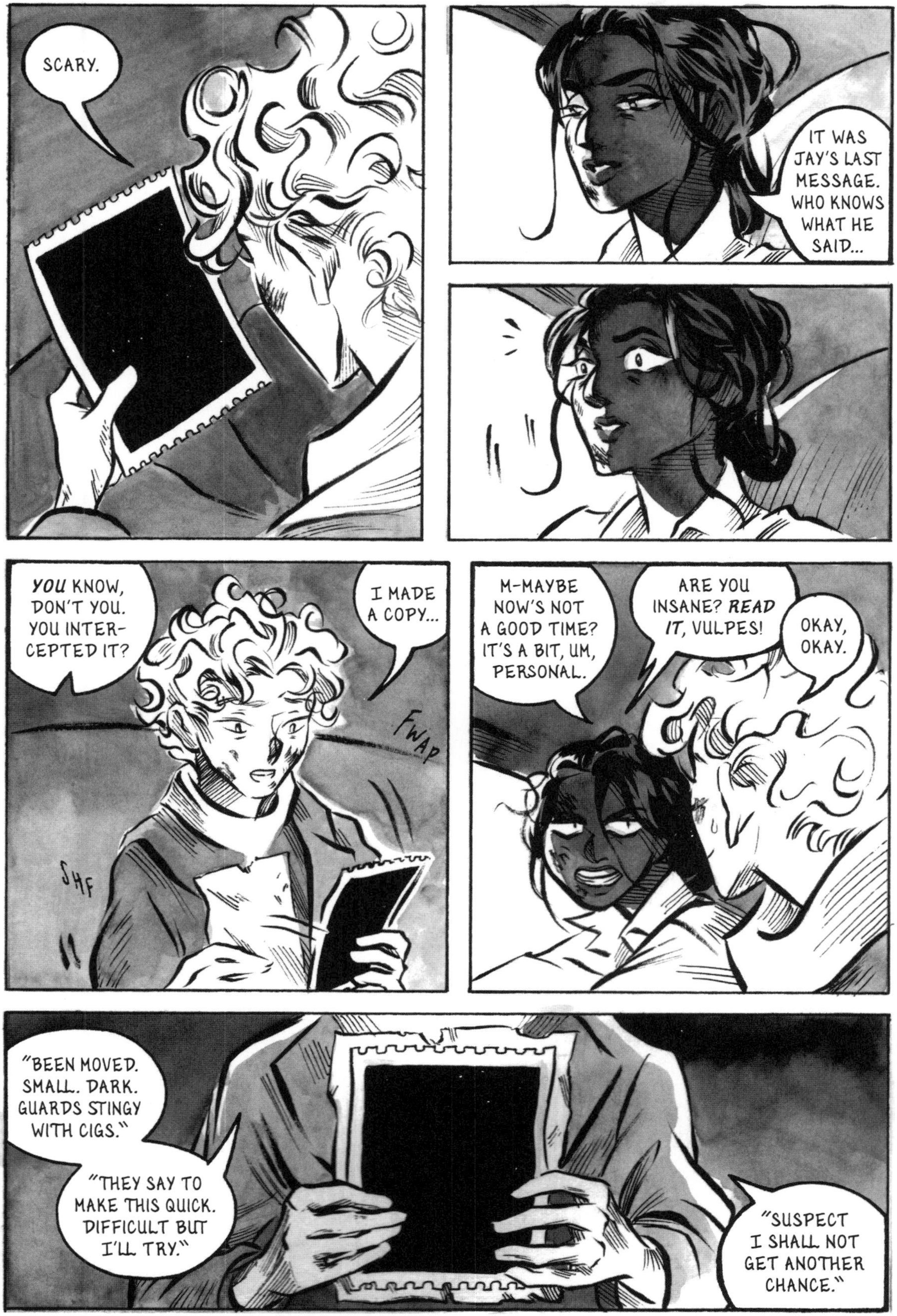
SCARY.
IT WAS JAY'S LAST MESSAGE. WHO KNOWS WHAT HE SAID...
YOU KNOW, DON'T YOU. YOU INTER-CEPTED IT?
I MADE A COPY...
FWAP
SHF
M-MAYBE NOW'S NOT A GOOD TIME? IT'S A BIT, UM, PERSONAL.
ARE YOU INSANE? READ IT, VULPES!
OKAY, OKAY.
"BEEN MOVED. SMALL. DARK. GUARDS STINGY WITH CIGS."
"THEY SAY TO MAKE THIS QUICK. DIFFICULT BUT I'LL TRY."
"SUSPECT I SHALL NOT GET ANOTHER CHANCE."

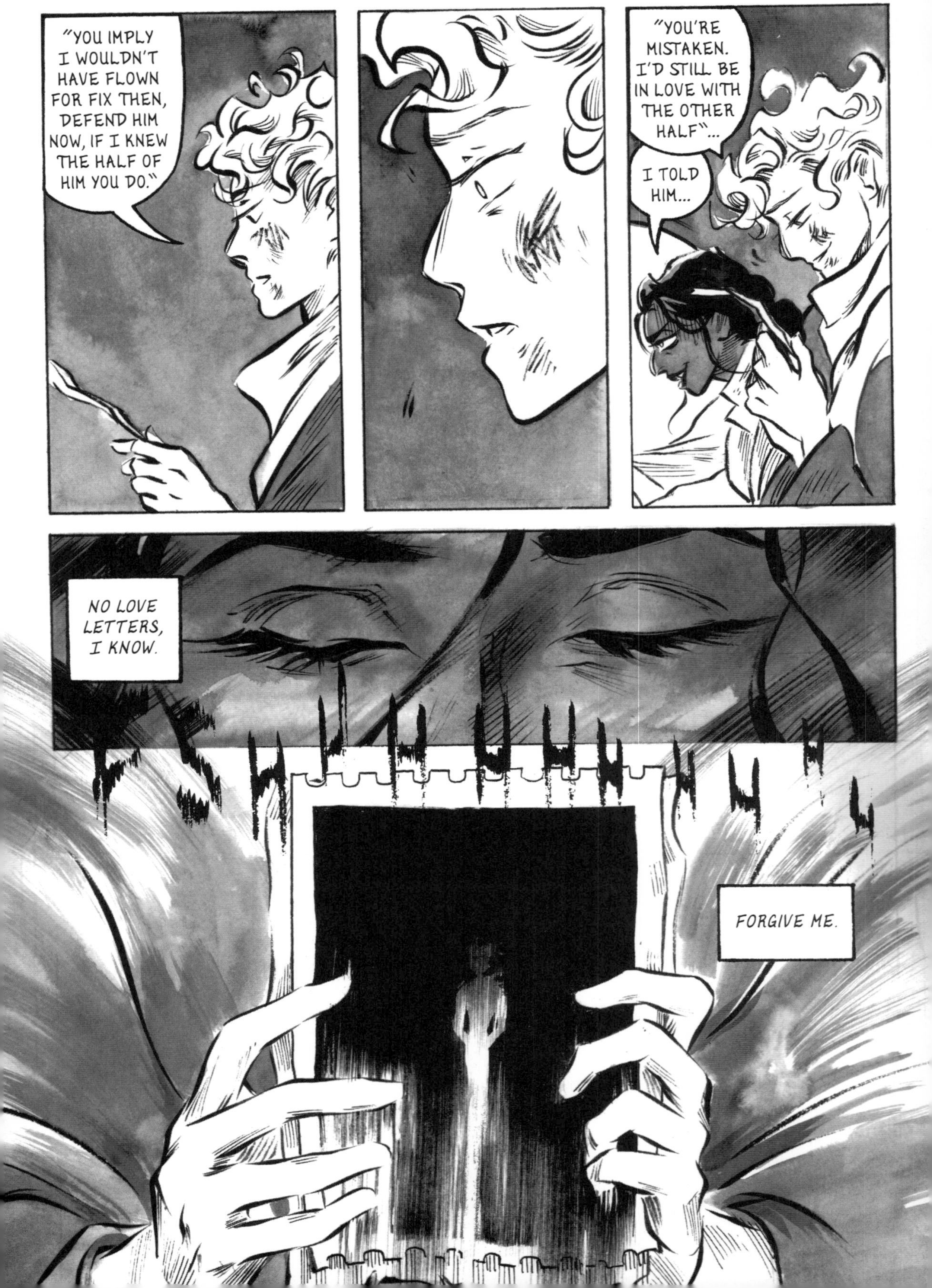
"YOU IMPLY I WOULDN'T HAVE FLOWN FOR FIX THEN, DEFEND HIM NOW, IF I KNEW THE HALF OF HIM YOU DO."
"YOU'RE MISTAKEN. I'D STILL BE IN LOVE WITH THE OTHER HALF"...
I TOLD HIM...
NO LOVE LETTERS, I KNOW.
FORGIVE ME.

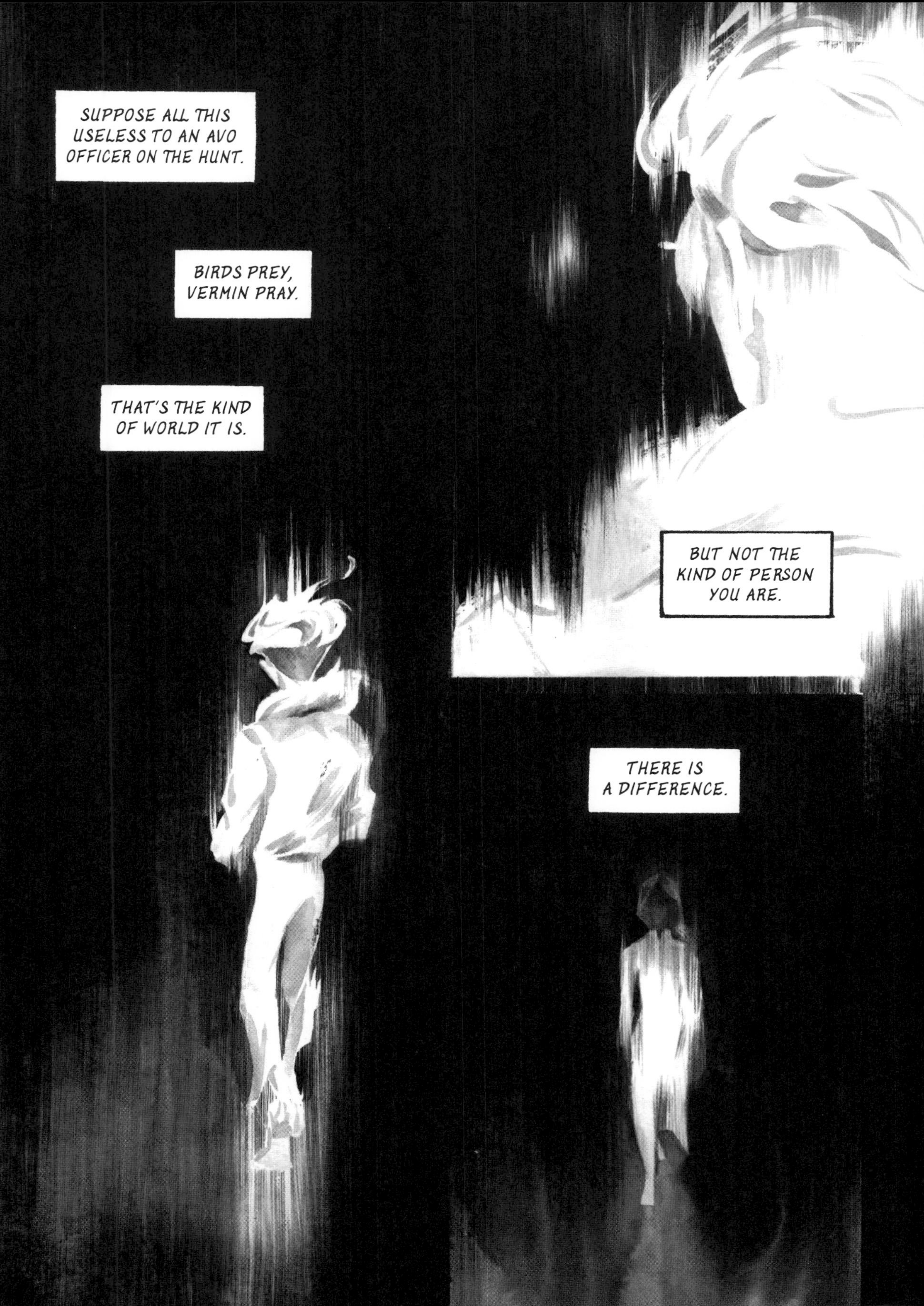
SUPPOSE ALL THIS USELESS TO AN AVO OFFICER ON THE HUNT.
BIRDS PREY, VERMIN PRAY.
THAT'S THE KIND OF WORLD IT IS.
BUT NOT THE KIND OF PERSON YOU ARE.
THERE IS A DIFFERENCE.

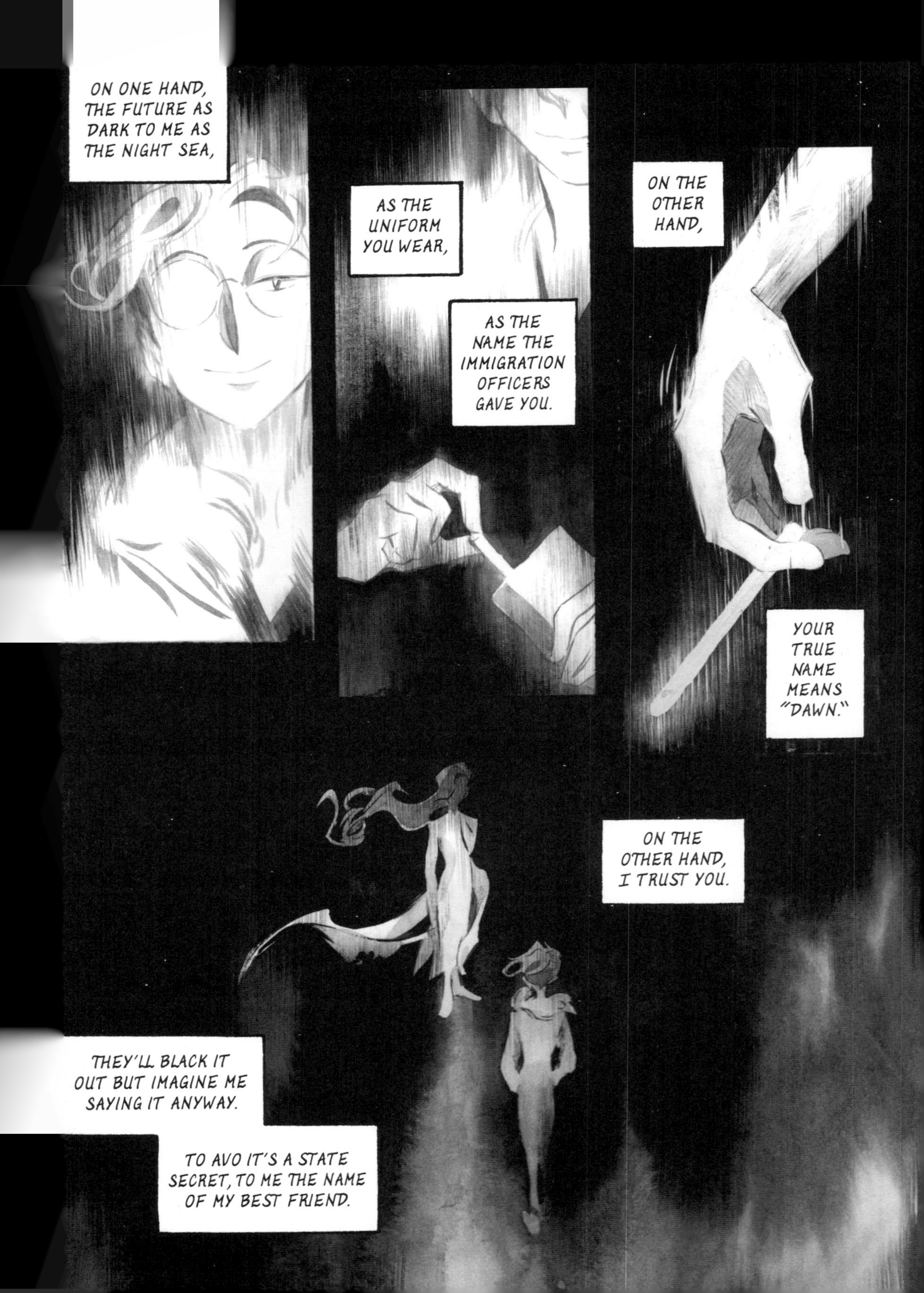
ON ONE HAND, THE FUTURE AS DARK TO ME AS THE NIGHT SEA,
AS THE UNIFORM YOU WEAR,
AS THE NAME THE IMMIGRATION OFFICERS GAVE YOU.
ON THE OTHER HAND,
YOUR TRUE NAME MEANS "DAWN."
ON THE OTHER HAND, I TRUST YOU.
THEY'LL BLACK IT OUT BUT IMAGINE ME SAYING IT ANYWAY.
TO AVO IT'S A STATE SECRET, TO ME THE NAME OF MY BEST FRIEND.

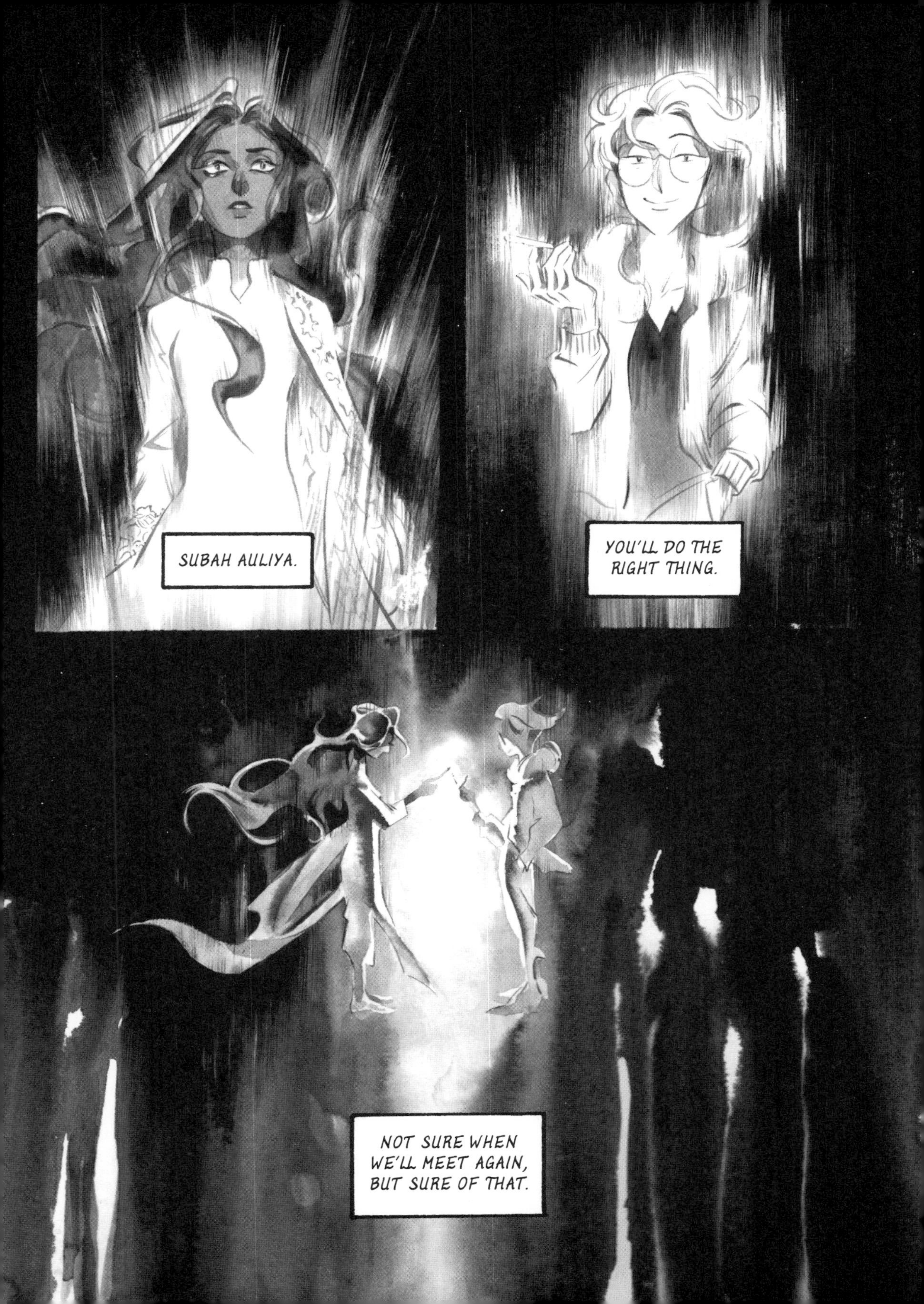
SUBAH AULIYA.
YOU'LL DO THE RIGHT THING.
NOT SURE WHEN WE'LL MEET AGAIN, BUT SURE OF THAT.

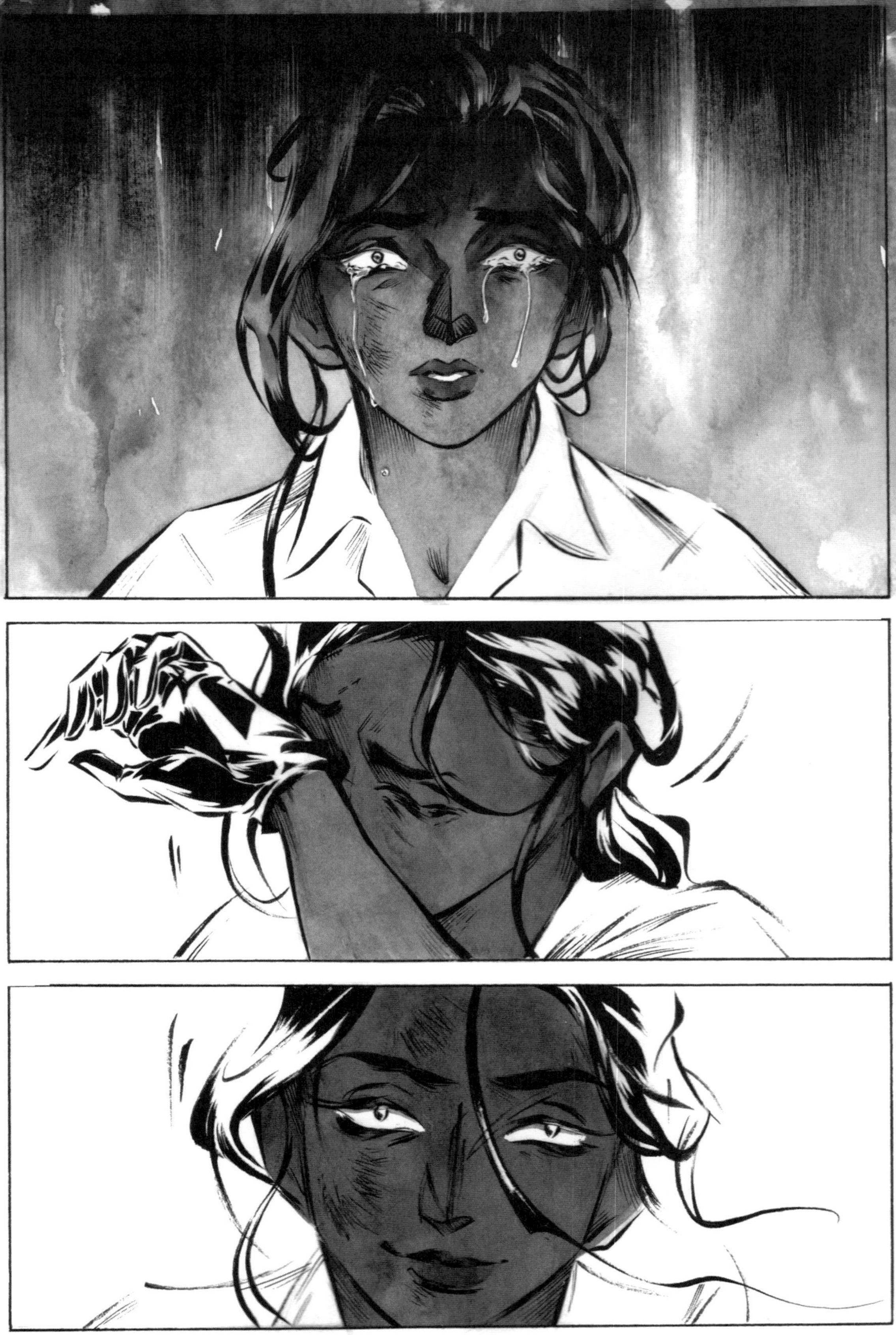

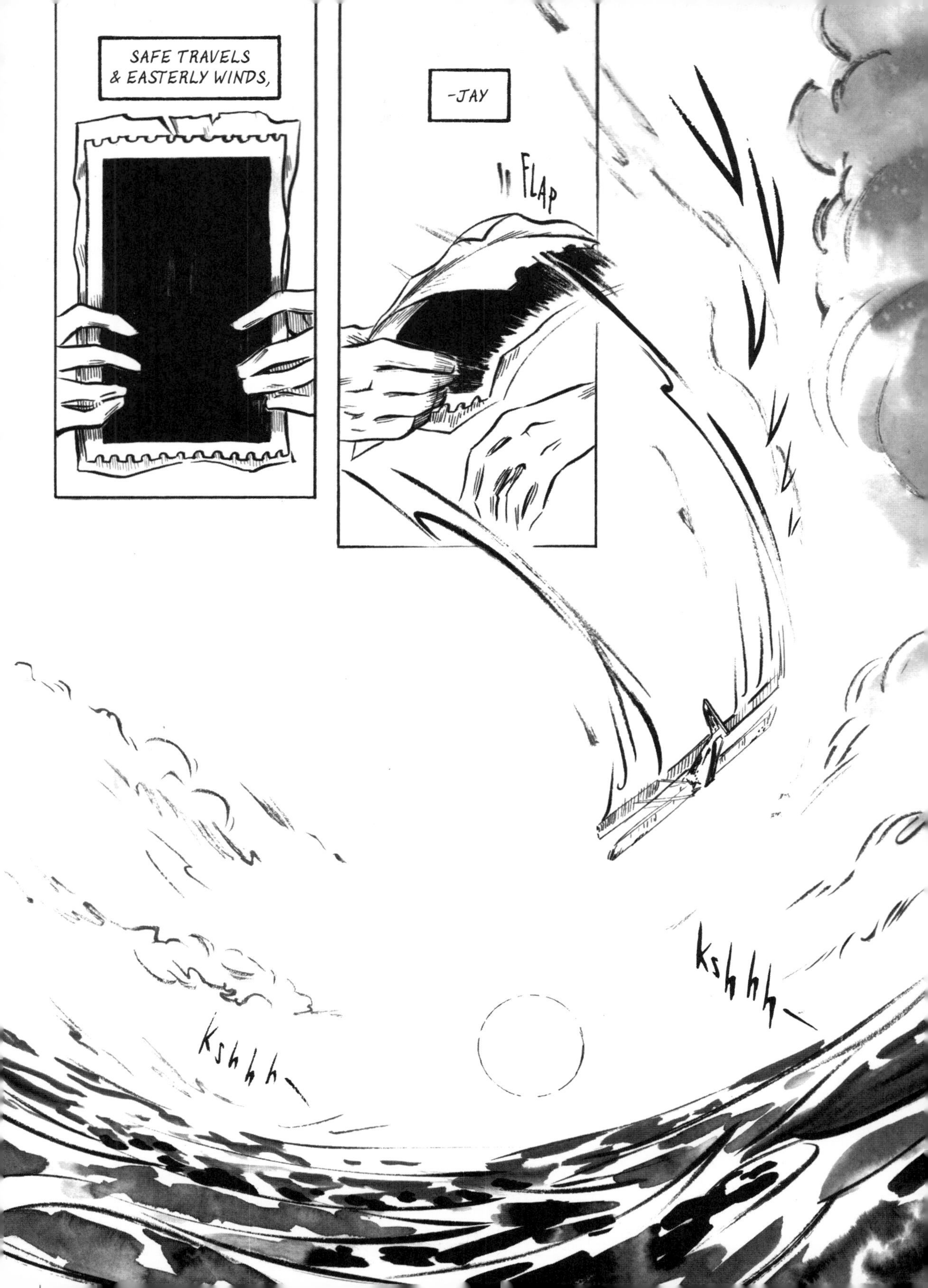
SAFE TRAVELS
& EASTERLY WINDS,
-JAY
FLAP
Kshhh-
Kshhh-

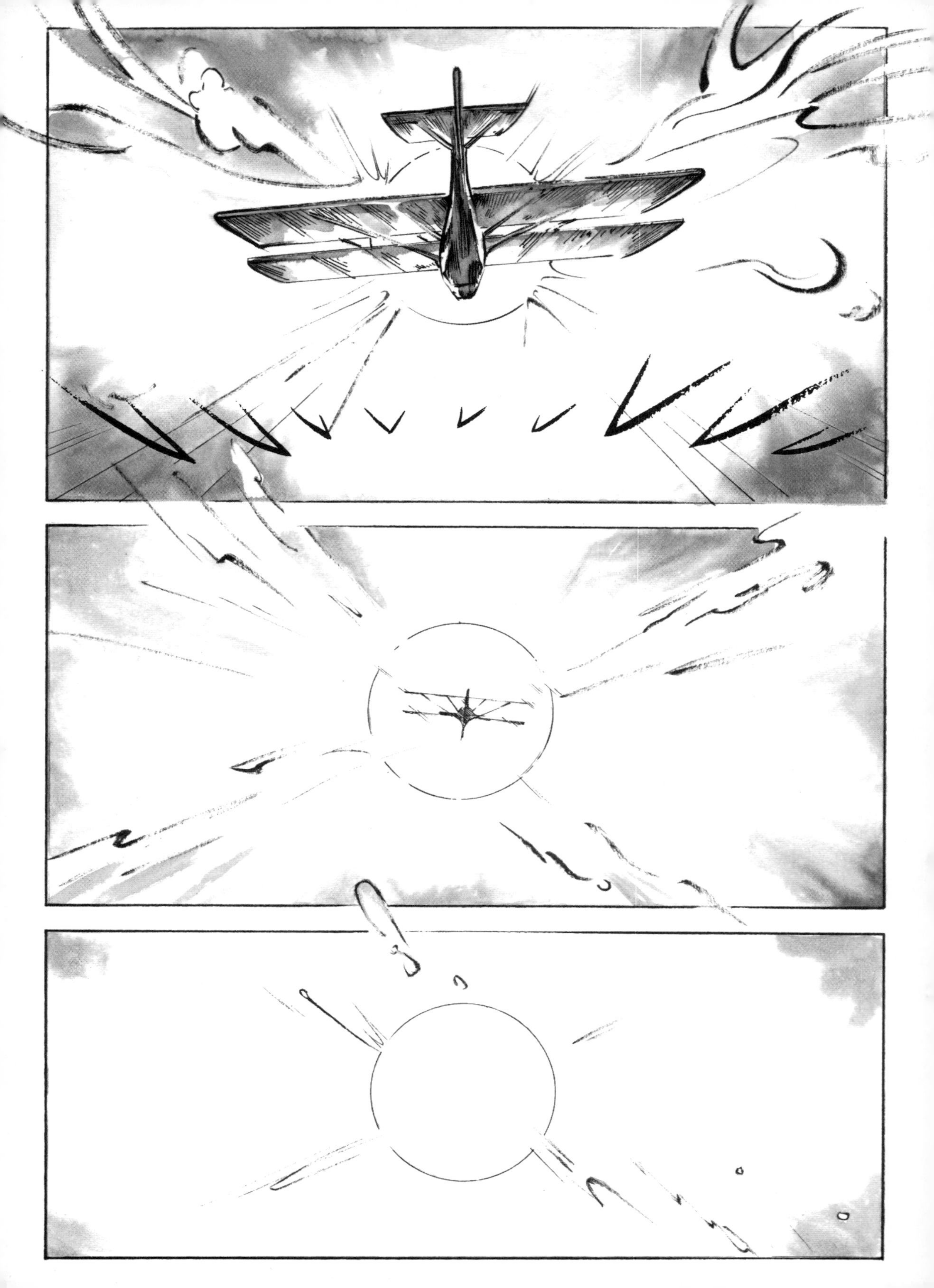

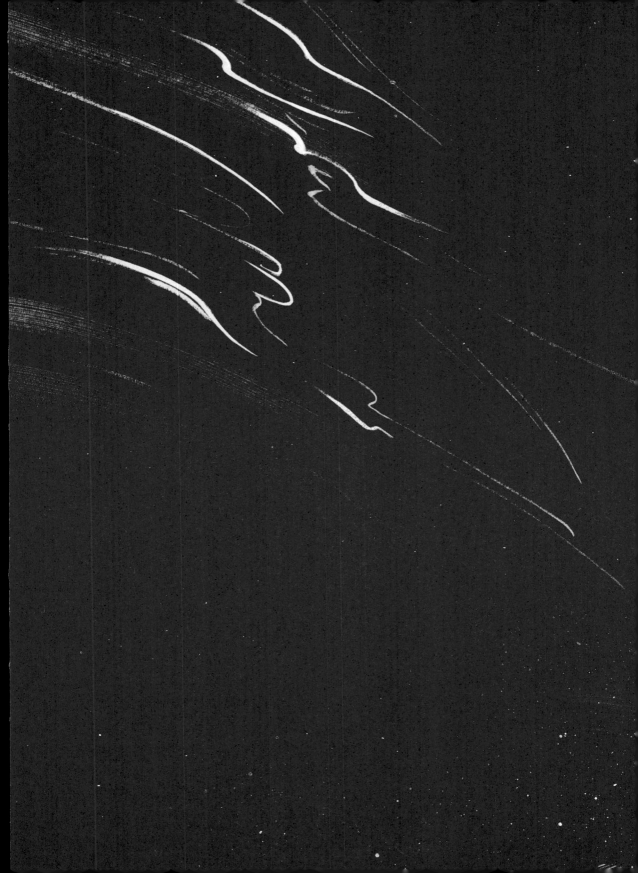

BOOK III
FEATHERWEIGHT

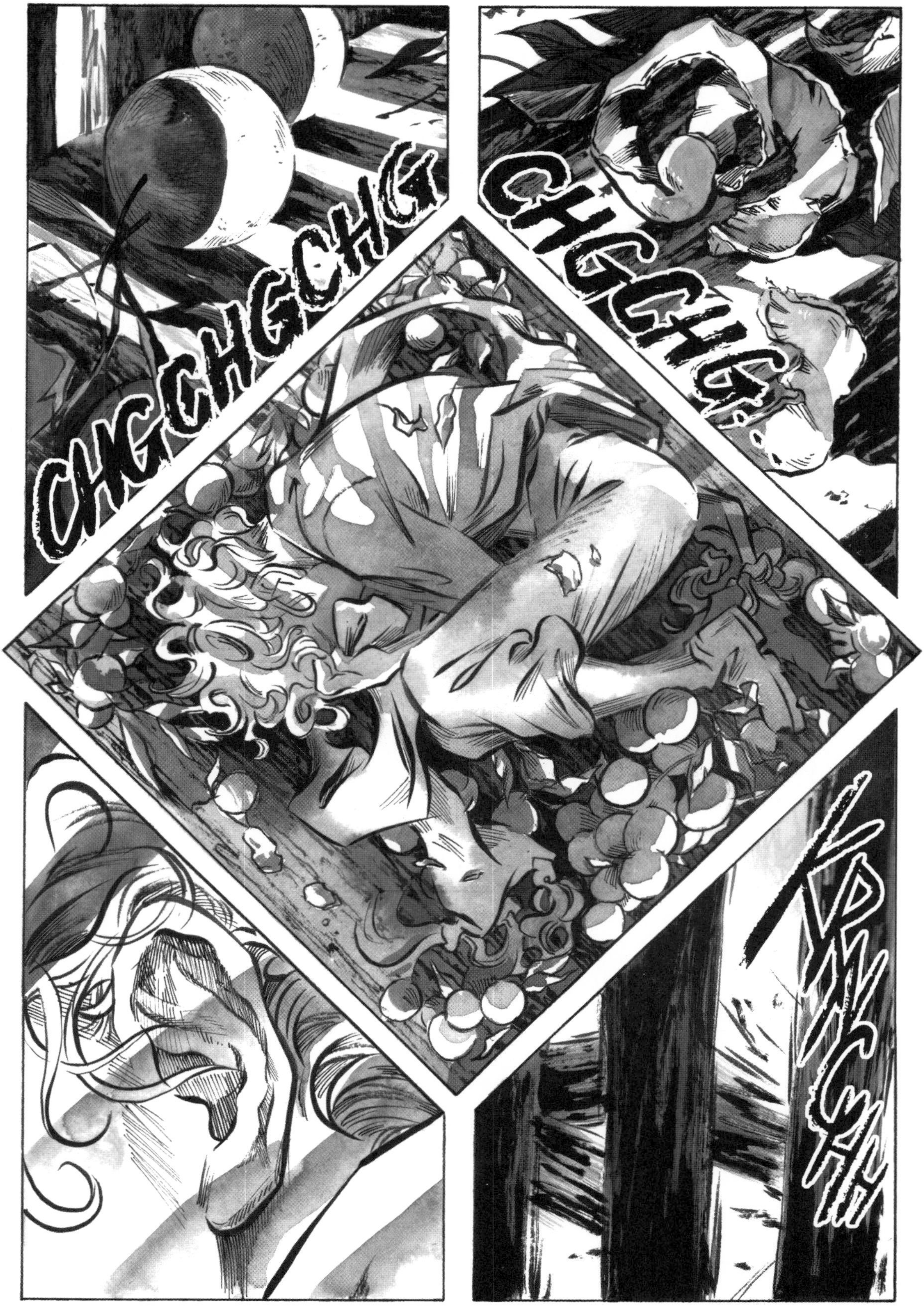
CHGCHGCHG
CHGCHG.

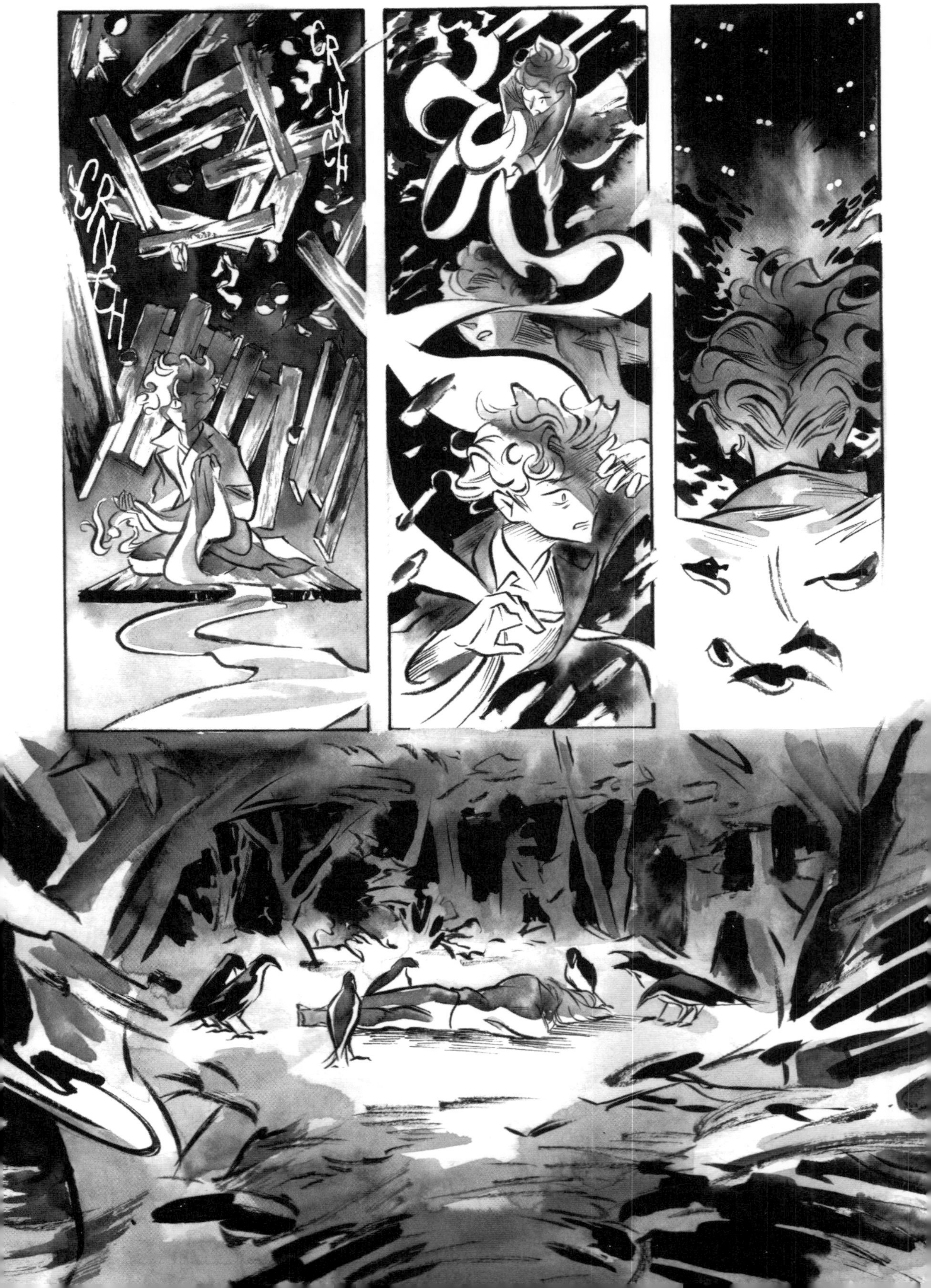
CRUNCH
CRUNCH

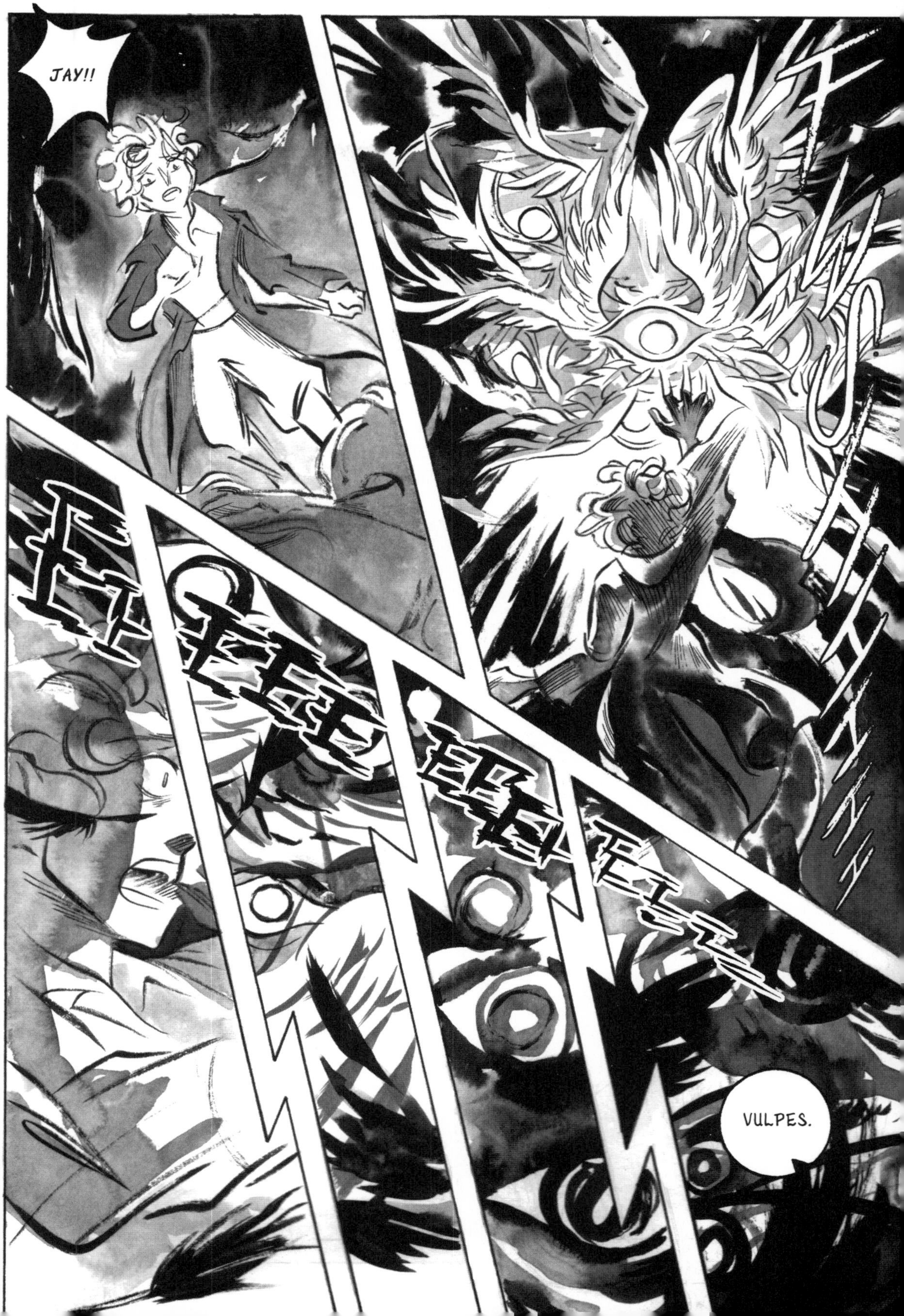
JAY!!
VULPES.

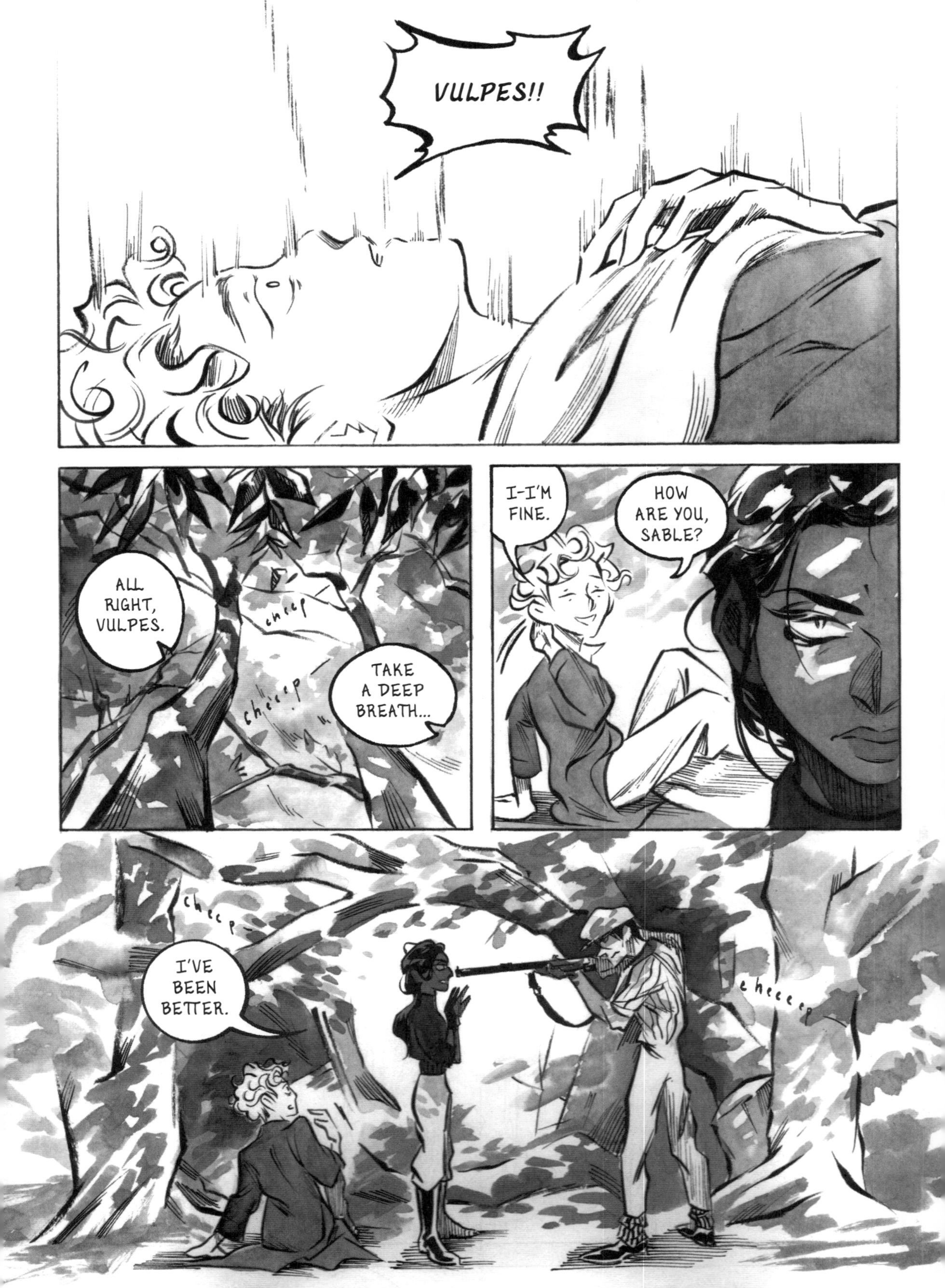
VULPES!!
ALL RIGHT, VULPES.
cheep
cheeep
TAKE A DEEP BREATH...
I-I'M FINE.
HOW ARE YOU, SABLE?
cheep-
I'VE BEEN BETTER.
cheeeeep

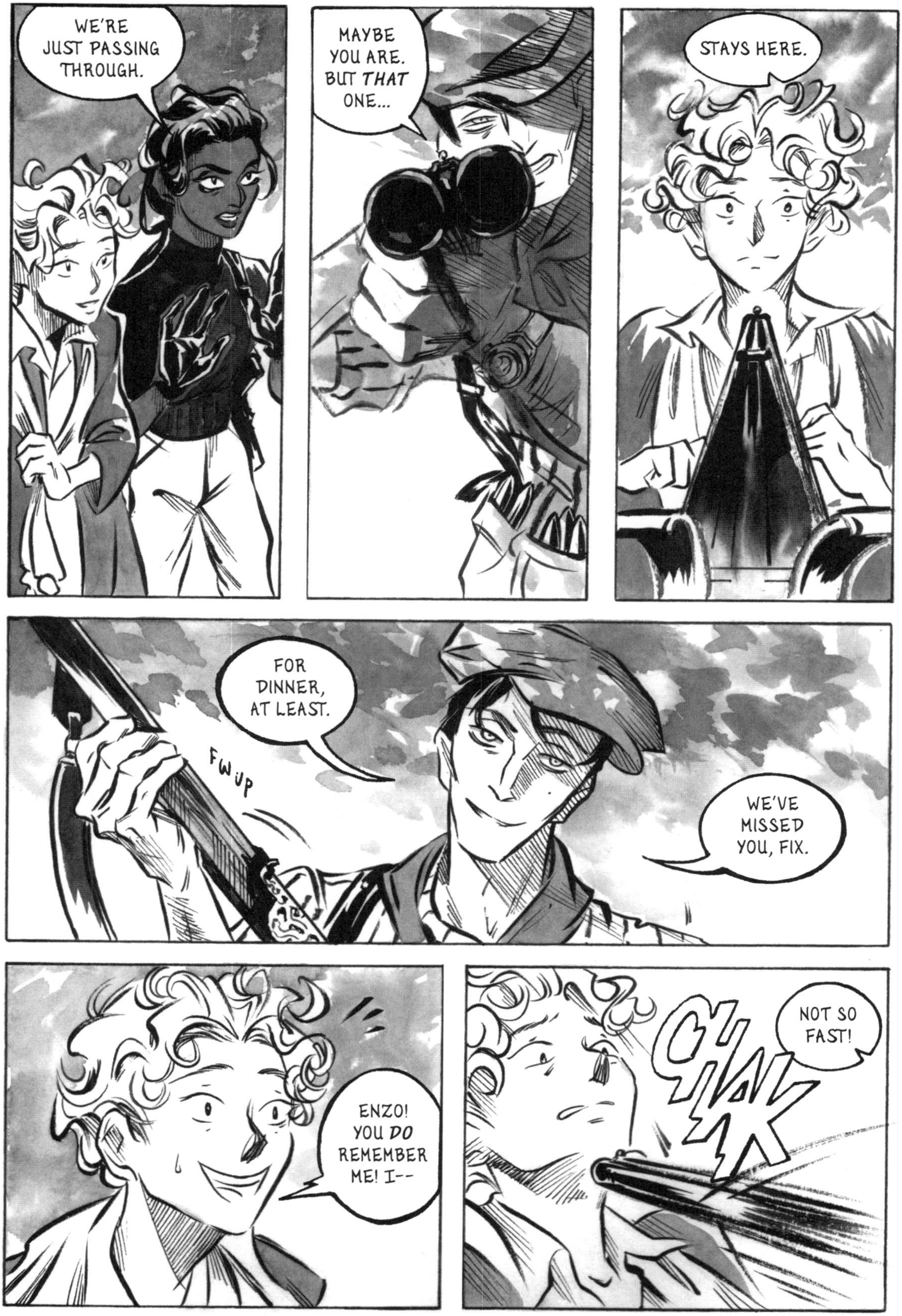
WE'RE JUST PASSING THROUGH.
MAYBE YOU ARE. BUT *THAT* ONE...
STAYS HERE.
FOR DINNER, AT LEAST.
FWUP
WE'VE MISSED YOU, FIX.
ENZO! YOU *DO* REMEMBER ME! I--
CHAK
NOT SO FAST!

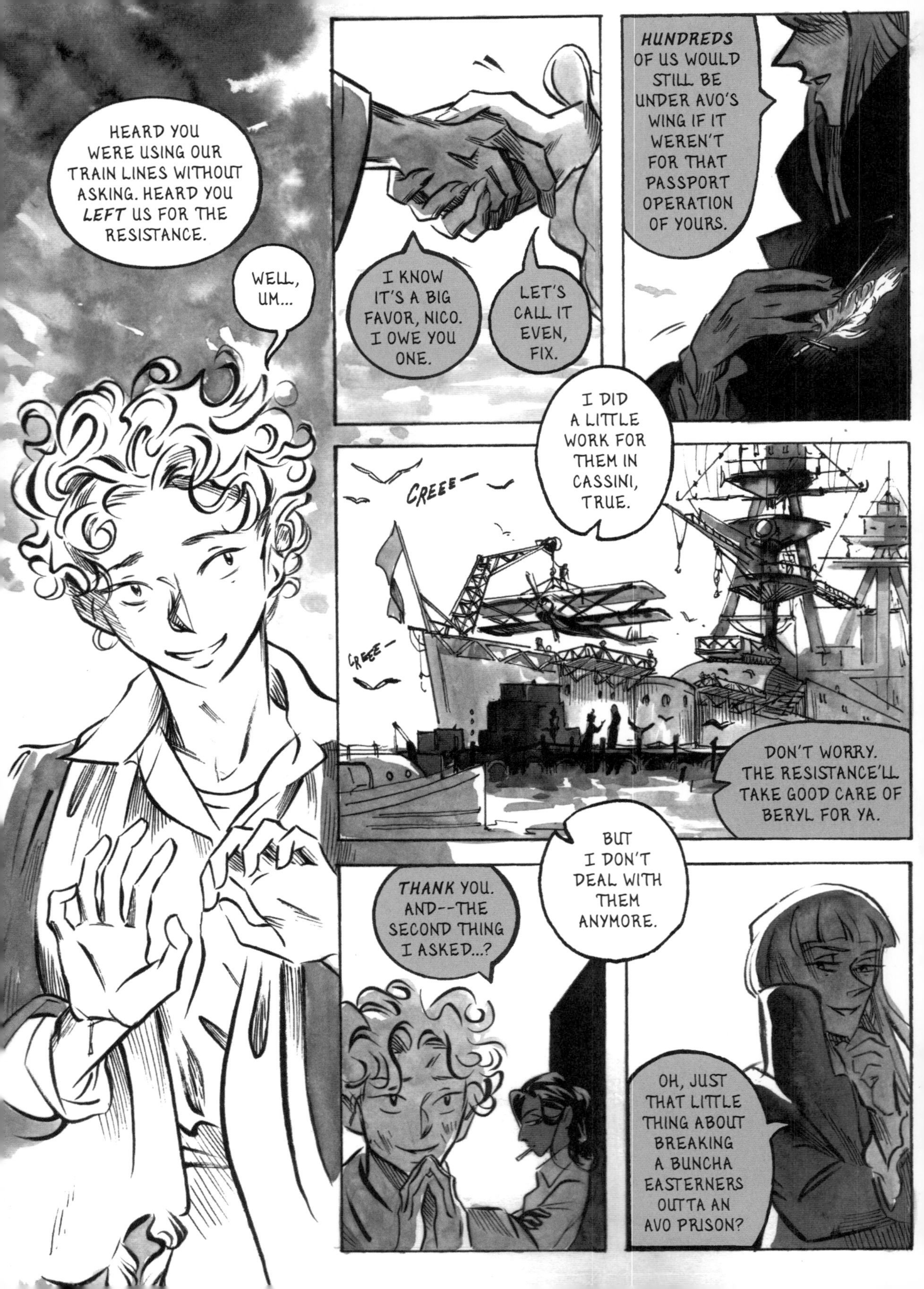

HEARD YOU WERE USING OUR TRAIN LINES WITHOUT ASKING. HEARD YOU *LEFT* US FOR THE RESISTANCE.
WELL, UM...
I KNOW IT'S A BIG FAVOR, NICO. I OWE YOU ONE.
LET'S CALL IT EVEN, FIX.
HUNDREDS OF US WOULD STILL BE UNDER AVO'S WING IF IT WEREN'T FOR THAT PASSPORT OPERATION OF YOURS.
I DID A LITTLE WORK FOR THEM IN CASSINI, TRUE.
CREEE—
CREEE—
DON'T WORRY. THE RESISTANCE'LL TAKE GOOD CARE OF BERYL FOR YA.
BUT I DON'T DEAL WITH THEM ANYMORE.
THANK YOU. AND--THE SECOND THING I ASKED...?
OH, JUST THAT LITTLE THING ABOUT BREAKING A BUNCHA EASTERNERS OUTTA AN AVO PRISON?

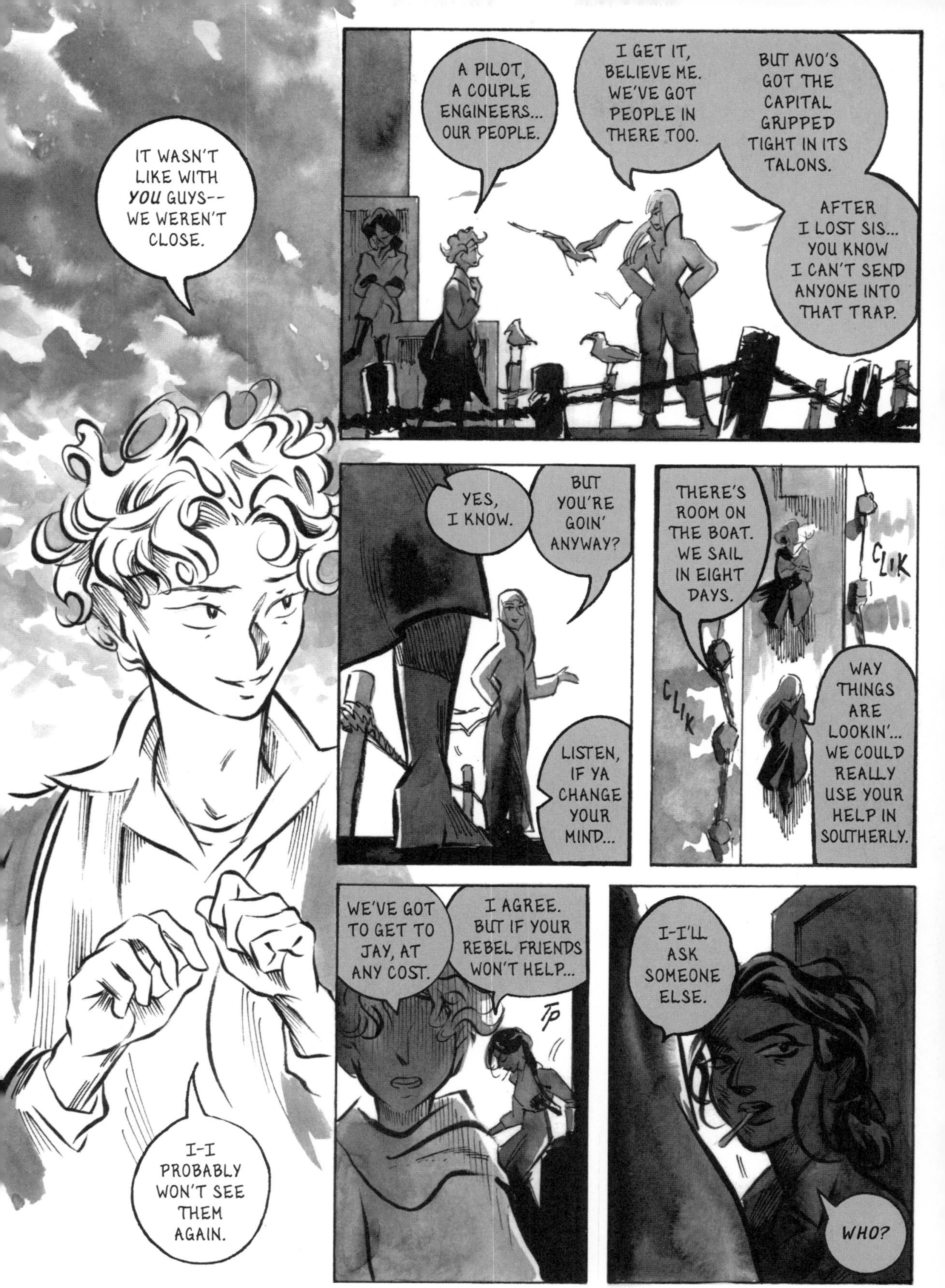

IT WASN'T LIKE WITH *YOU* GUYS-- WE WEREN'T CLOSE.
A PILOT, A COUPLE ENGINEERS... OUR PEOPLE.
I GET IT, BELIEVE ME. WE'VE GOT PEOPLE IN THERE TOO.
BUT AVO'S GOT THE CAPITAL GRIPPED TIGHT IN ITS TALONS.
AFTER I LOST SIS... YOU KNOW I CAN'T SEND ANYONE INTO THAT TRAP.
YES, I KNOW.
BUT YOU'RE GOIN' ANYWAY?
LISTEN, IF YA CHANGE YOUR MIND...
THERE'S ROOM ON THE BOAT. WE SAIL IN EIGHT DAYS.
CLIK
CLIK
WAY THINGS ARE LOOKIN'... WE COULD REALLY USE YOUR HELP IN SOUTHERLY.
I-I PROBABLY WON'T SEE THEM AGAIN.
WE'VE GOT TO GET TO JAY, AT ANY COST.
I AGREE. BUT IF YOUR REBEL FRIENDS WON'T HELP...
TP
I-I'LL ASK SOMEONE ELSE.
WHO?

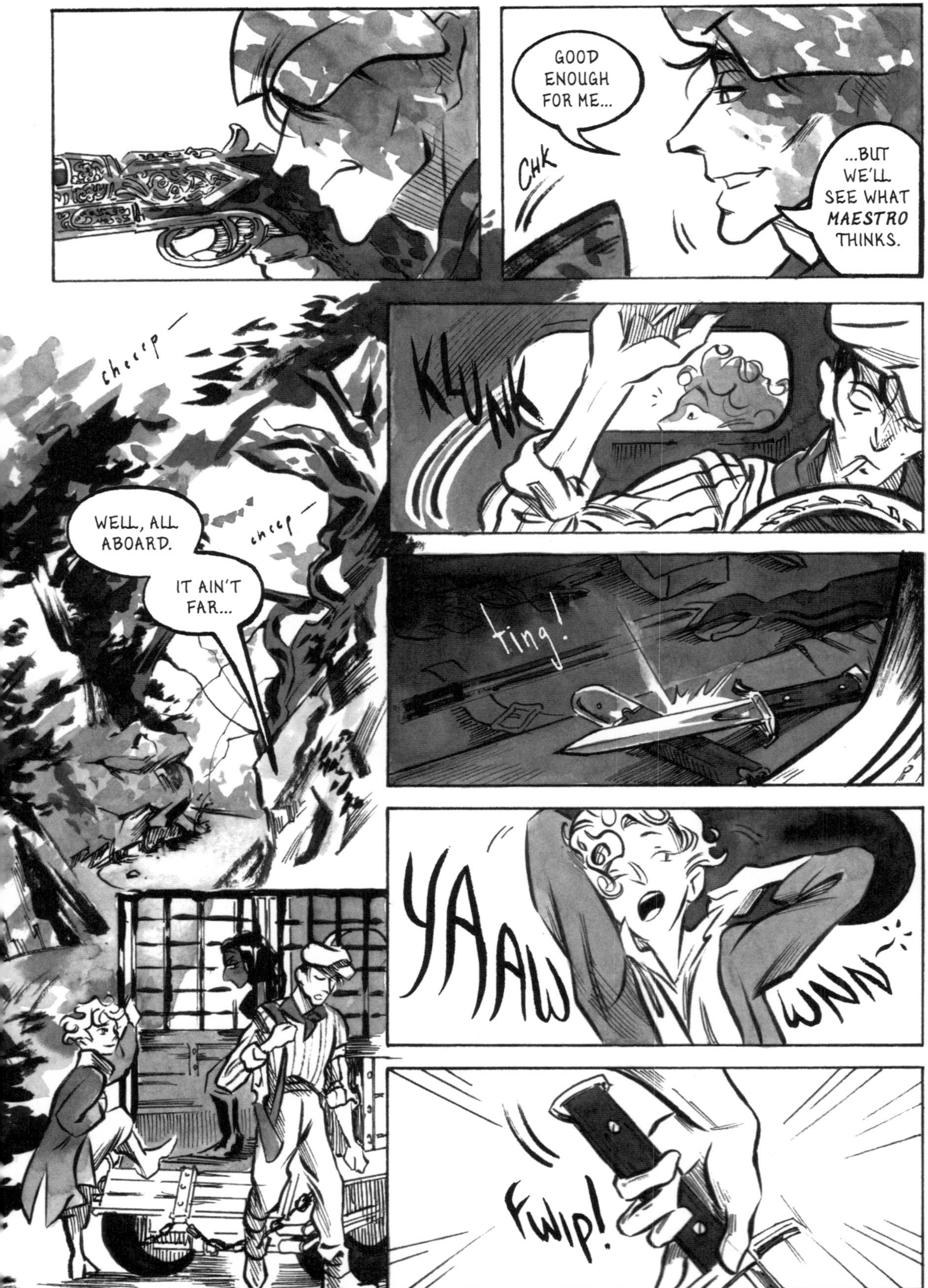
GOOD ENOUGH FOR ME...
CHK
...BUT WE'LL SEE WHAT MAESTRO THINKS.
cheep—
WELL, ALL ABOARD.
cheep—
IT AIN'T FAR...
KLUNK
ting!
YAAWWNN
fwip!

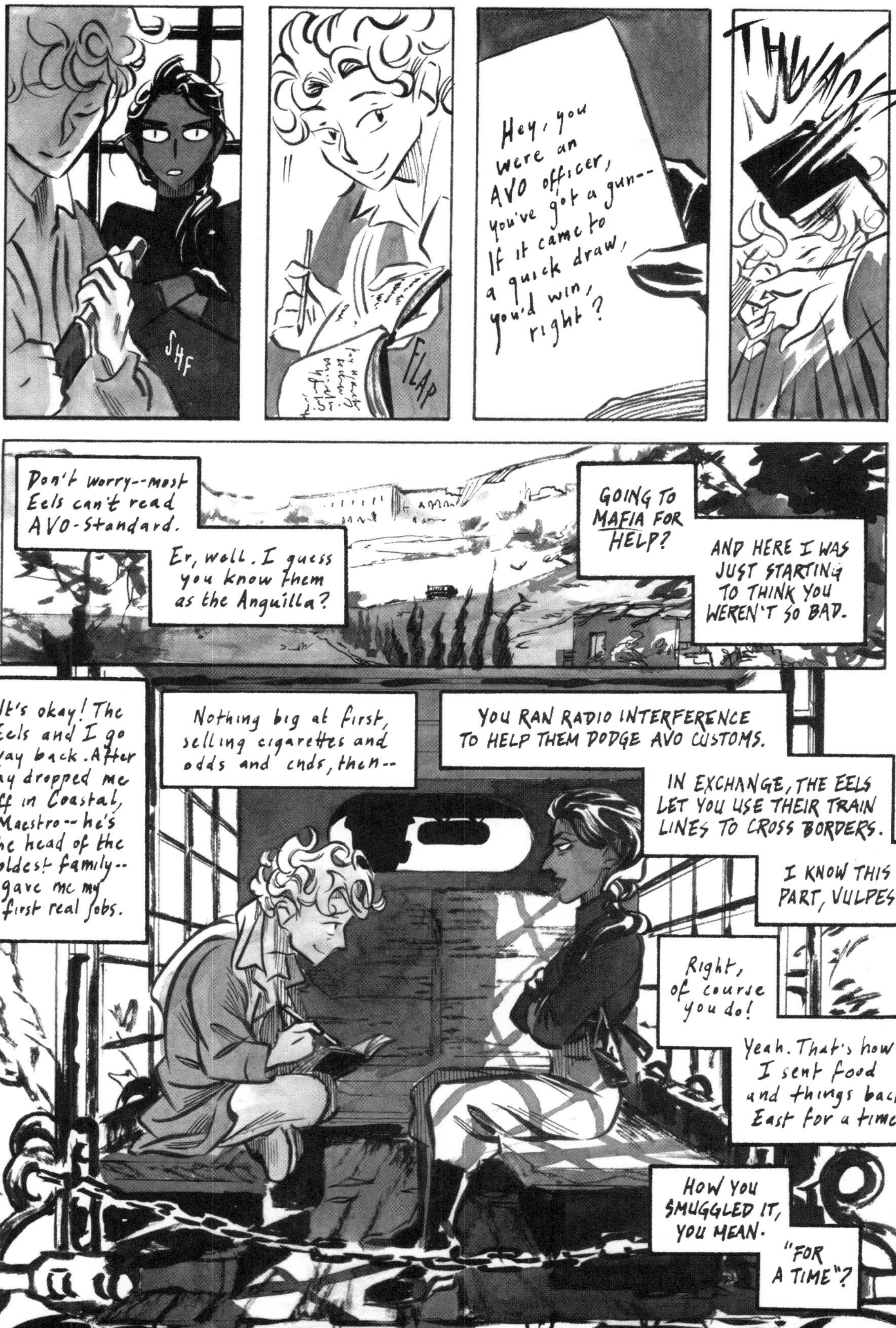
SHF
FLAP
Hey, you were an AVO officer, you've got a gun-- If it came to a quick draw, you'd win, right?
THWACK!
Don't worry--most Eels can't read AVO-Standard.
Er, well. I guess you know them as the Anguilla?
GOING TO MAFIA FOR HELP?
AND HERE I WAS JUST STARTING TO THINK YOU WEREN'T SO BAD.
It's okay! The Eels and I go way back. After Jay dropped me off in Coastal, Maestro--he's the head of the oldest family--gave me my first real jobs.
Nothing big at first, selling cigarettes and odds and ends, then--
YOU RAN RADIO INTERFERENCE TO HELP THEM DODGE AVO CUSTOMS.
IN EXCHANGE, THE EELS LET YOU USE THEIR TRAIN LINES TO CROSS BORDERS.
I KNOW THIS PART, VULPES.
Right, of course you do!
Yeah. That's how I sent food and things back East for a time.
HOW YOU SMUGGLED IT, YOU MEAN.
"FOR A TIME"?

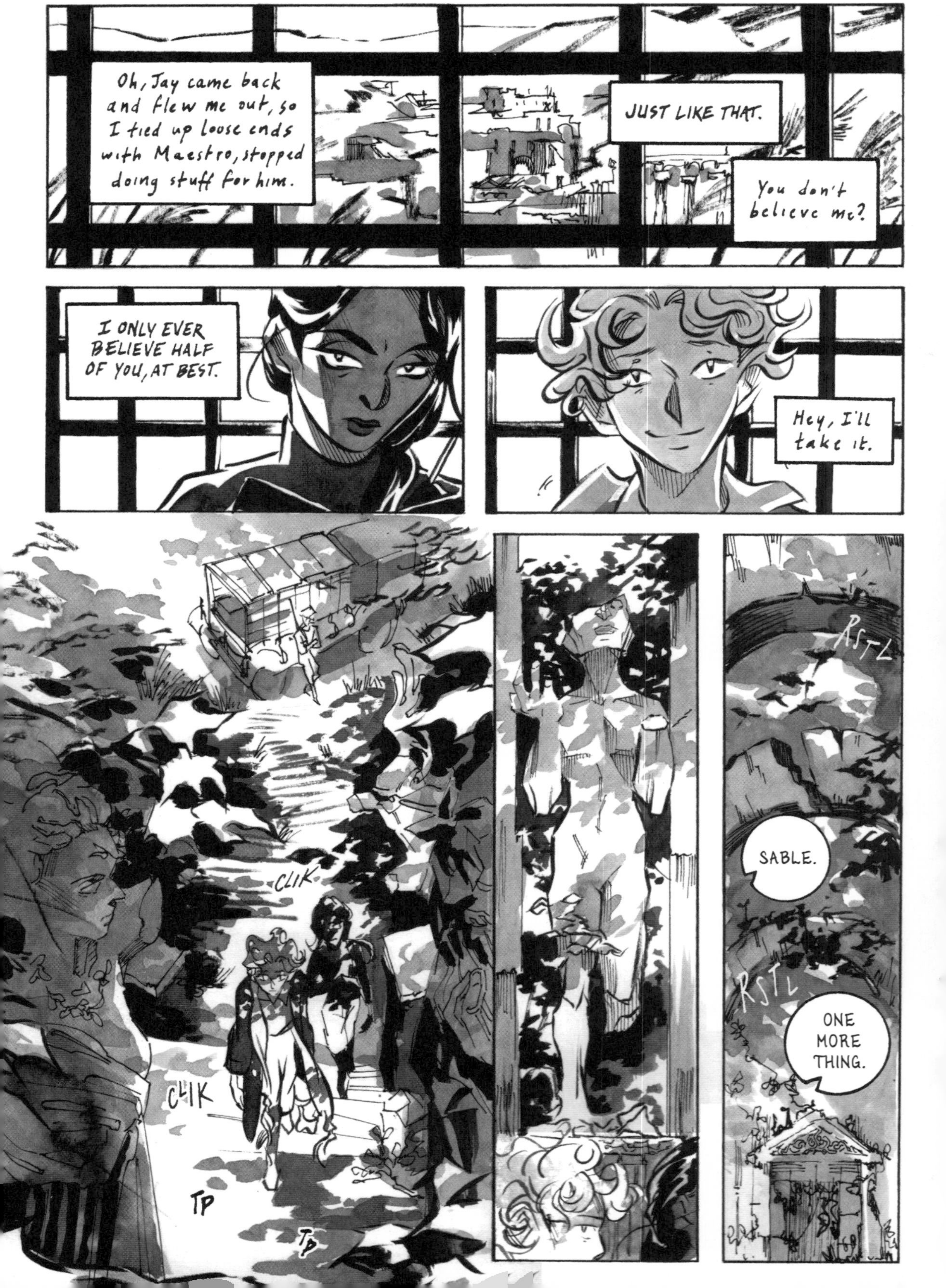
Oh, Jay came back and flew me out, so I tied up loose ends with Maestro, stopped doing stuff for him.
JUST LIKE THAT.
You don't believe me?
I ONLY EVER BELIEVE HALF OF YOU, AT BEST.
Hey, I'll take it.
CLIK
CLIK
TP
TP
RSTL
SABLE.
RSTL
ONE MORE THING.

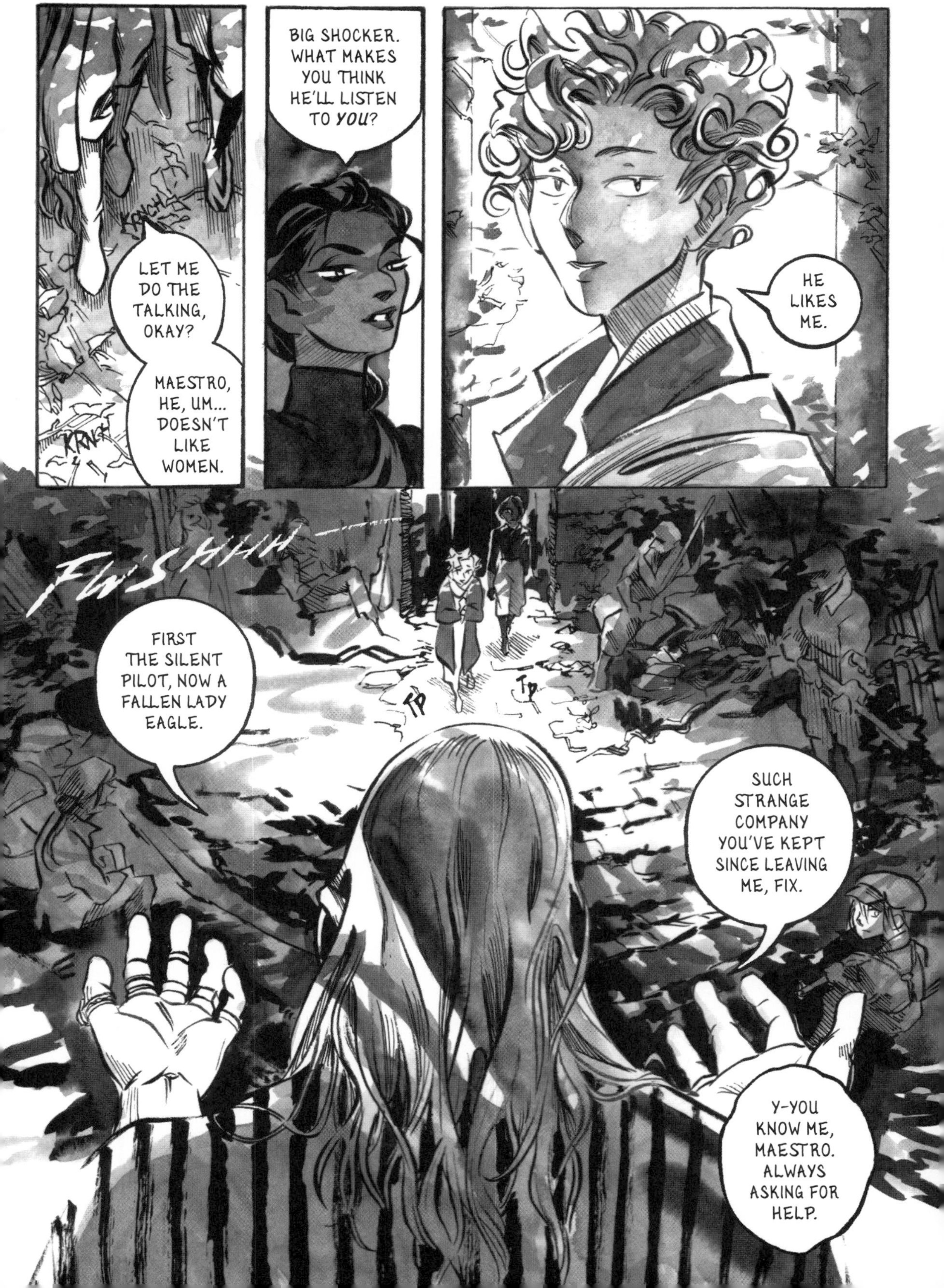
KRNCH
LET ME DO THE TALKING, OKAY?
MAESTRO, HE, UM... DOESN'T LIKE WOMEN.
KRNCH
BIG SHOCKER. WHAT MAKES YOU THINK HE'LL LISTEN TO *YOU*?
HE LIKES ME.
FWSHHH
FIRST THE SILENT PILOT, NOW A FALLEN LADY EAGLE.
TP
TP
SUCH STRANGE COMPANY YOU'VE KEPT SINCE LEAVING ME, FIX.
Y-YOU KNOW ME, MAESTRO. ALWAYS ASKING FOR HELP.

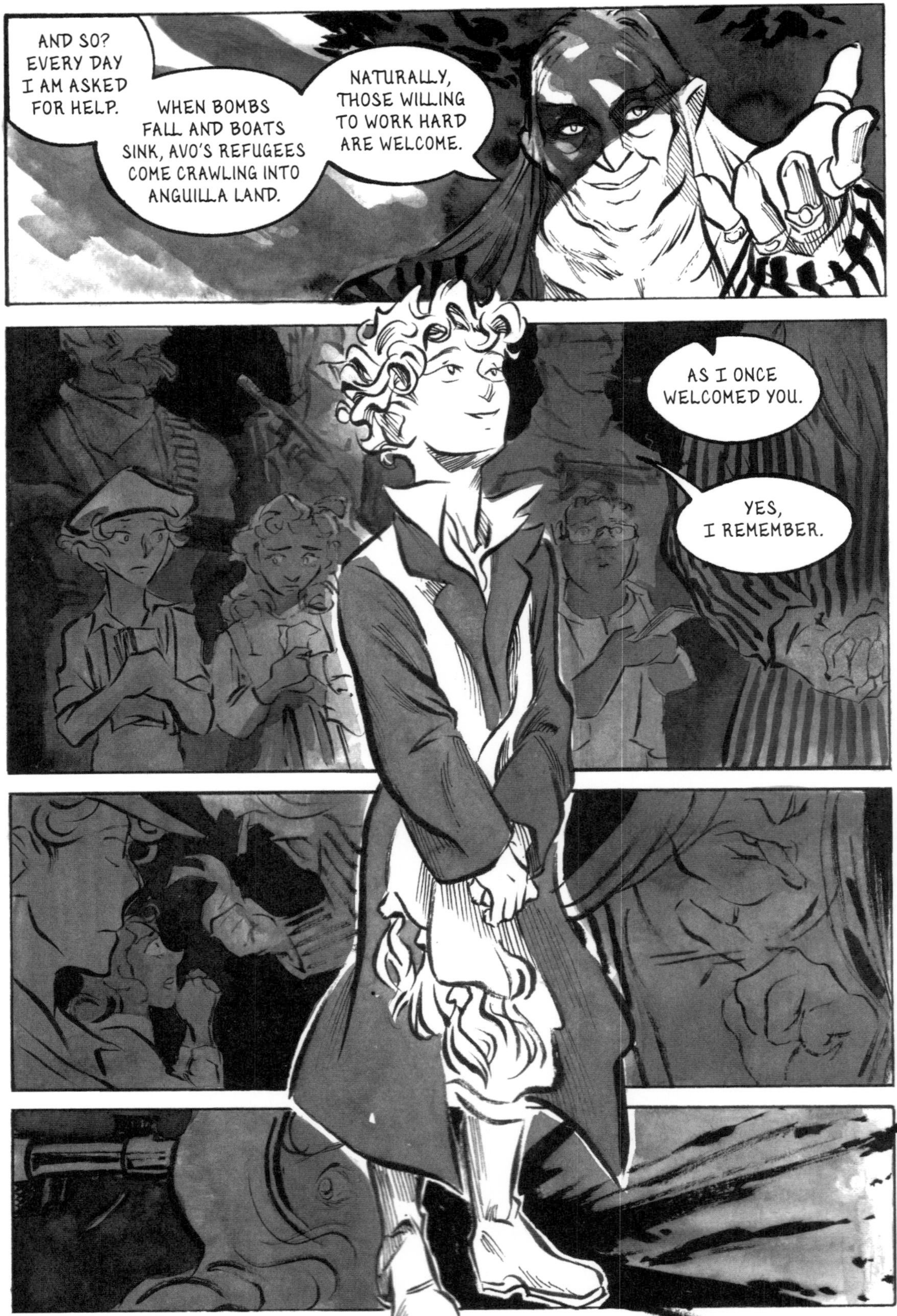
AND SO? EVERY DAY I AM ASKED FOR HELP.
WHEN BOMBS FALL AND BOATS SINK, AVO'S REFUGEES COME CRAWLING INTO ANGUILLA LAND.
NATURALLY, THOSE WILLING TO WORK HARD ARE WELCOME.
AS I ONCE WELCOMED YOU.
YES, I REMEMBER.

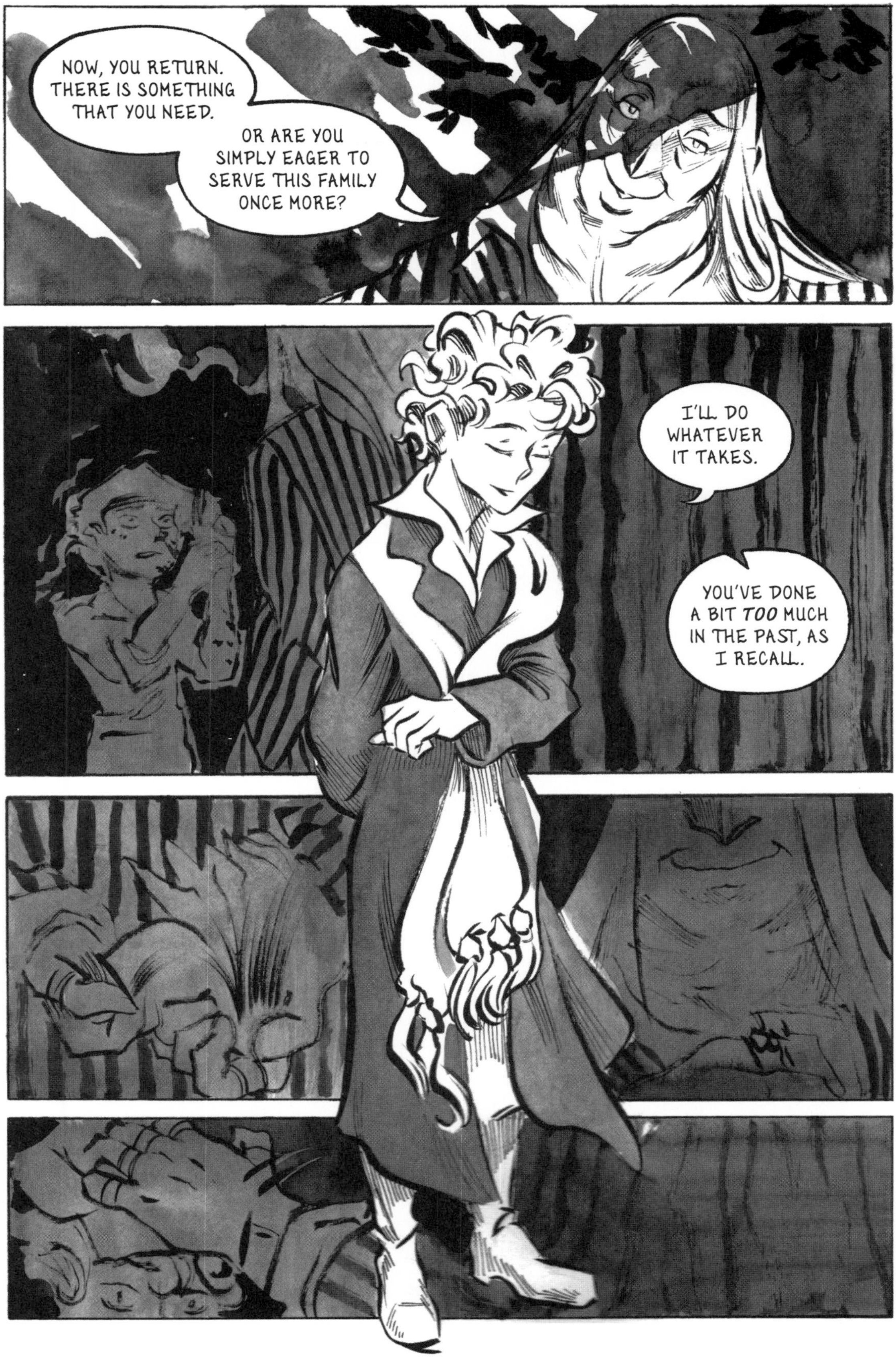
NOW, YOU RETURN. THERE IS SOMETHING THAT YOU NEED.
OR ARE YOU SIMPLY EAGER TO SERVE THIS FAMILY ONCE MORE?
I'LL DO WHATEVER IT TAKES.
YOU'VE DONE A BIT *TOO* MUCH IN THE PAST, AS I RECALL.

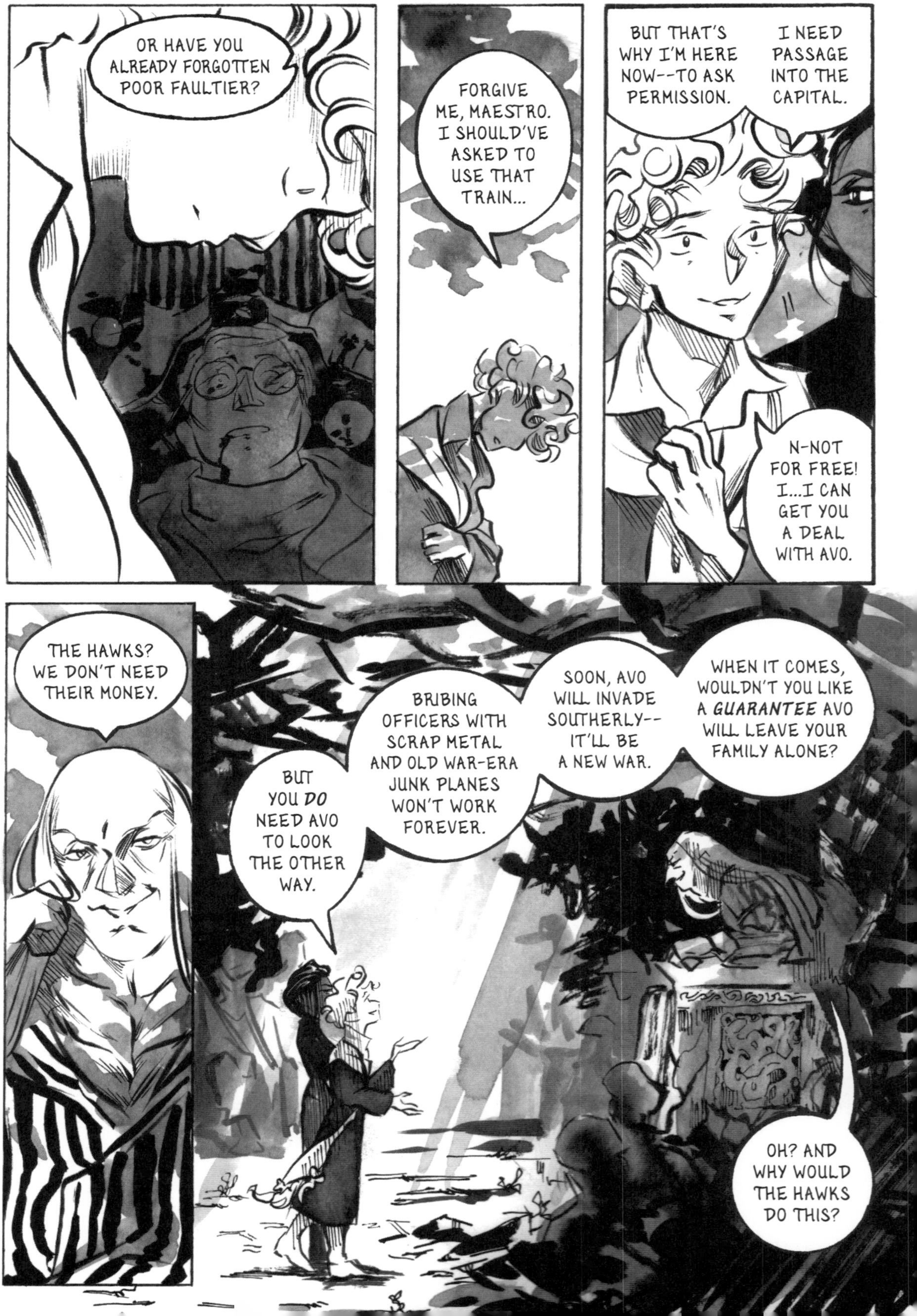
OR HAVE YOU ALREADY FORGOTTEN POOR FAULTIER?
FORGIVE ME, MAESTRO. I SHOULD'VE ASKED TO USE THAT TRAIN...
BUT THAT'S WHY I'M HERE NOW--TO ASK PERMISSION.
I NEED PASSAGE INTO THE CAPITAL.
N-NOT FOR FREE! I...I CAN GET YOU A DEAL WITH AVO.
THE HAWKS? WE DON'T NEED THEIR MONEY.
BUT YOU *DO* NEED AVO TO LOOK THE OTHER WAY.
BRIBING OFFICERS WITH SCRAP METAL AND OLD WAR-ERA JUNK PLANES WON'T WORK FOREVER.
SOON, AVO WILL INVADE SOUTHERLY-- IT'LL BE A NEW WAR.
WHEN IT COMES, WOULDN'T YOU LIKE A ***GUARANTEE*** AVO WILL LEAVE YOUR FAMILY ALONE?
OH? AND WHY WOULD THE HAWKS DO THIS?

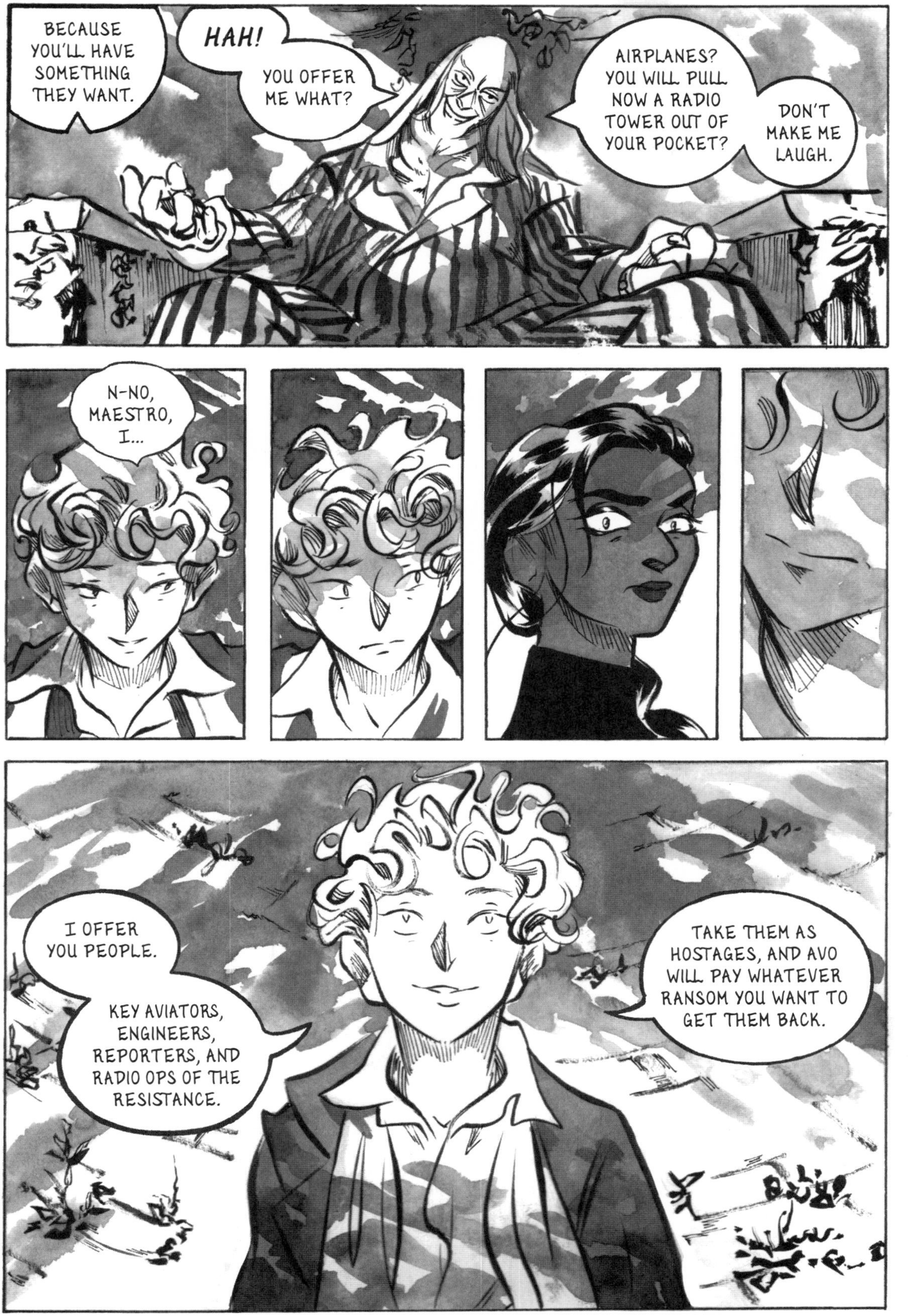
BECAUSE YOU'LL HAVE SOMETHING THEY WANT.
HAH!
YOU OFFER ME WHAT?
AIRPLANES? YOU WILL PULL NOW A RADIO TOWER OUT OF YOUR POCKET?
DON'T MAKE ME LAUGH.
N-NO, MAESTRO, I...
I OFFER YOU PEOPLE.
KEY AVIATORS, ENGINEERS, REPORTERS, AND RADIO OPS OF THE RESISTANCE.
TAKE THEM AS HOSTAGES, AND AVO WILL PAY WHATEVER RANSOM YOU WANT TO GET THEM BACK.

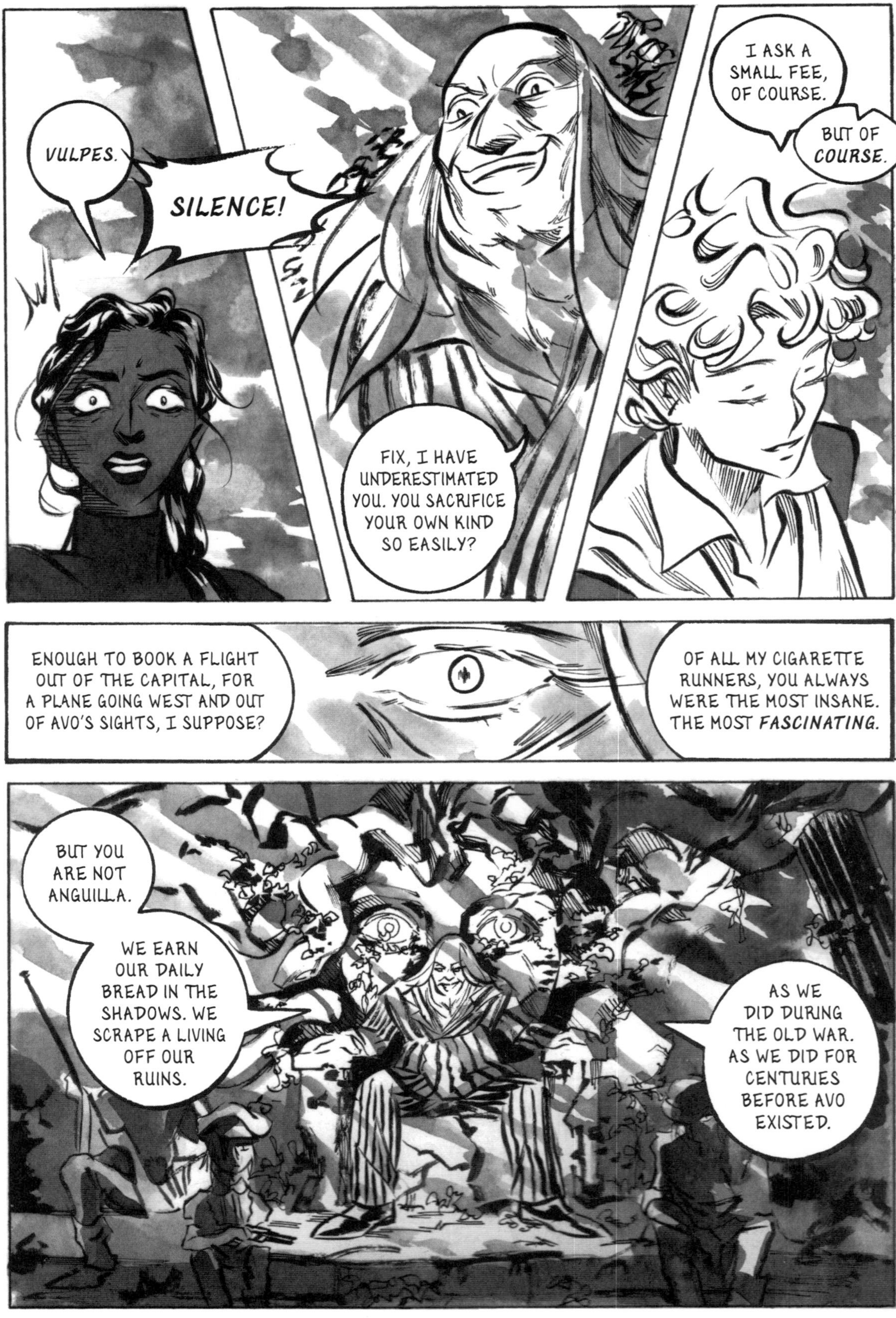
VULPES.
SILENCE!
FIX, I HAVE UNDERESTIMATED YOU. YOU SACRIFICE YOUR OWN KIND SO EASILY?
I ASK A SMALL FEE, OF COURSE.
BUT OF COURSE.
ENOUGH TO BOOK A FLIGHT OUT OF THE CAPITAL, FOR A PLANE GOING WEST AND OUT OF AVO'S SIGHTS, I SUPPOSE?
OF ALL MY CIGARETTE RUNNERS, YOU ALWAYS WERE THE MOST INSANE. THE MOST FASCINATING.
BUT YOU ARE NOT ANGUILLA.
WE EARN OUR DAILY BREAD IN THE SHADOWS. WE SCRAPE A LIVING OFF OUR RUINS.
AS WE DID DURING THE OLD WAR. AS WE DID FOR CENTURIES BEFORE AVO EXISTED.

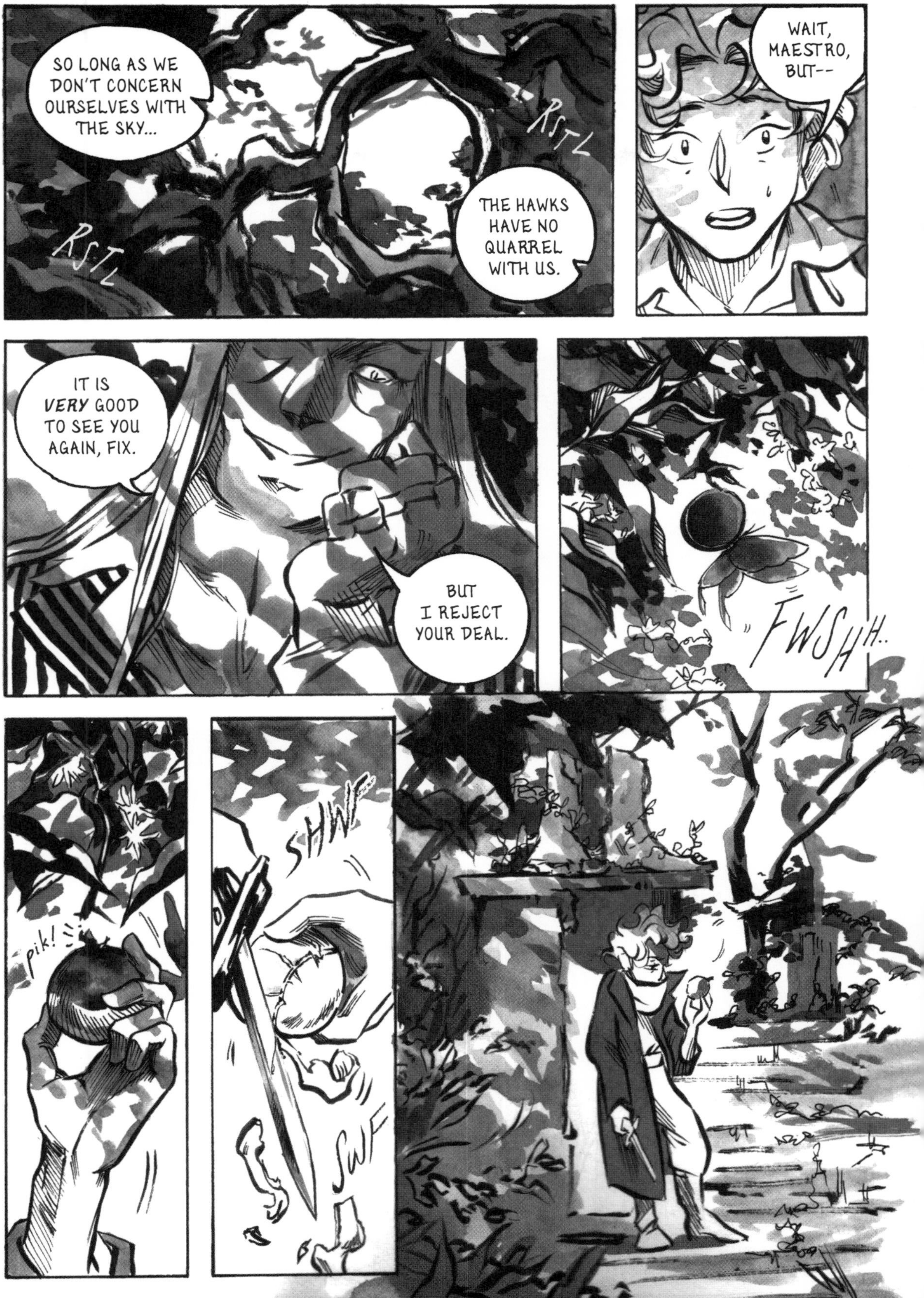
SO LONG AS WE DON'T CONCERN OURSELVES WITH THE SKY...
RSTL
RSTL
THE HAWKS HAVE NO QUARREL WITH US.
WAIT, MAESTRO, BUT--
IT IS **VERY** GOOD TO SEE YOU AGAIN, FIX.
BUT I REJECT YOUR DEAL.
FWSHH..
pik!
SHWF
SWF

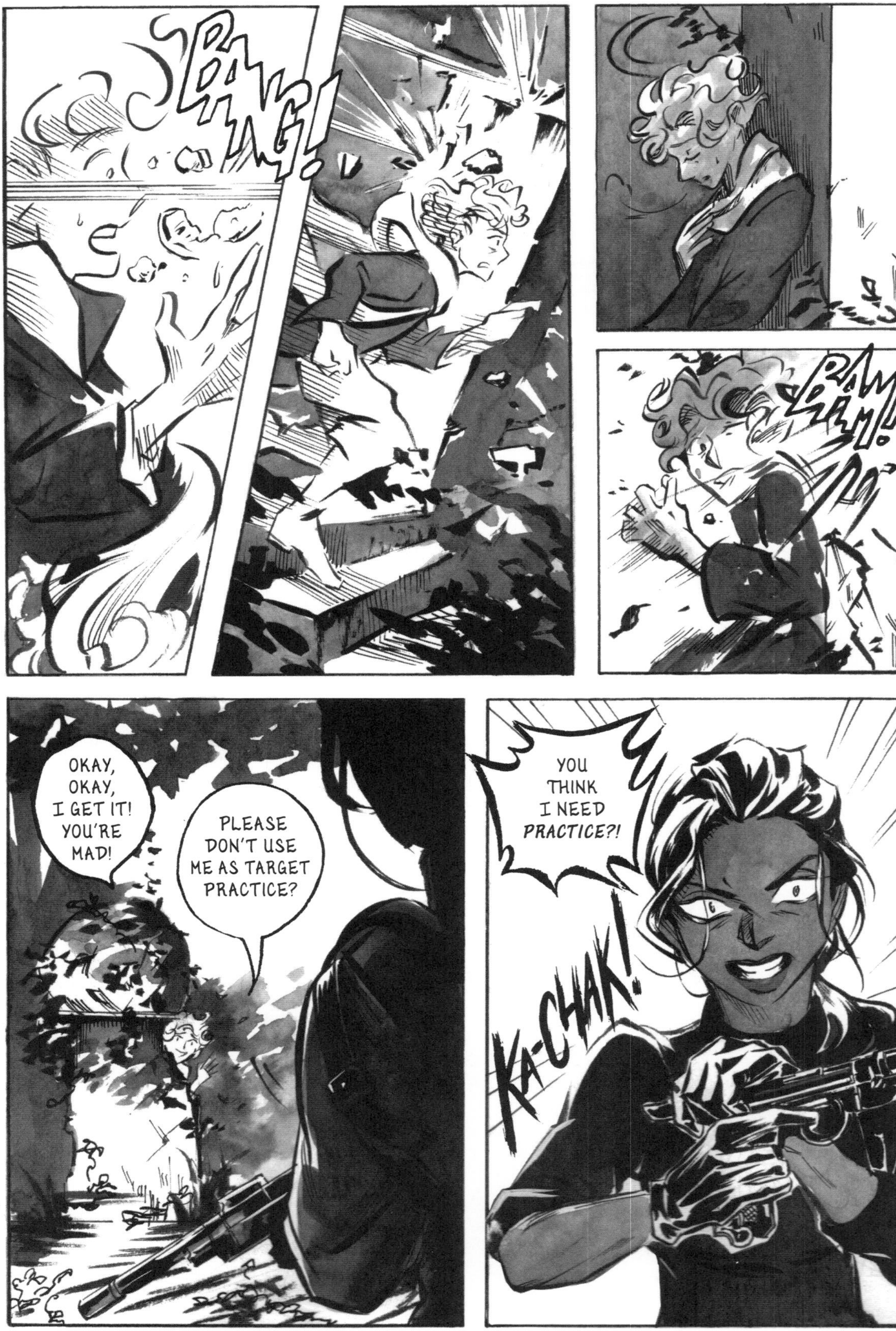
BANG!
BAM!
BAM!
OKAY, OKAY, I GET IT! YOU'RE MAD!
PLEASE DON'T USE ME AS TARGET PRACTICE?
YOU THINK I NEED *PRACTICE?!*
KA-CHAK!

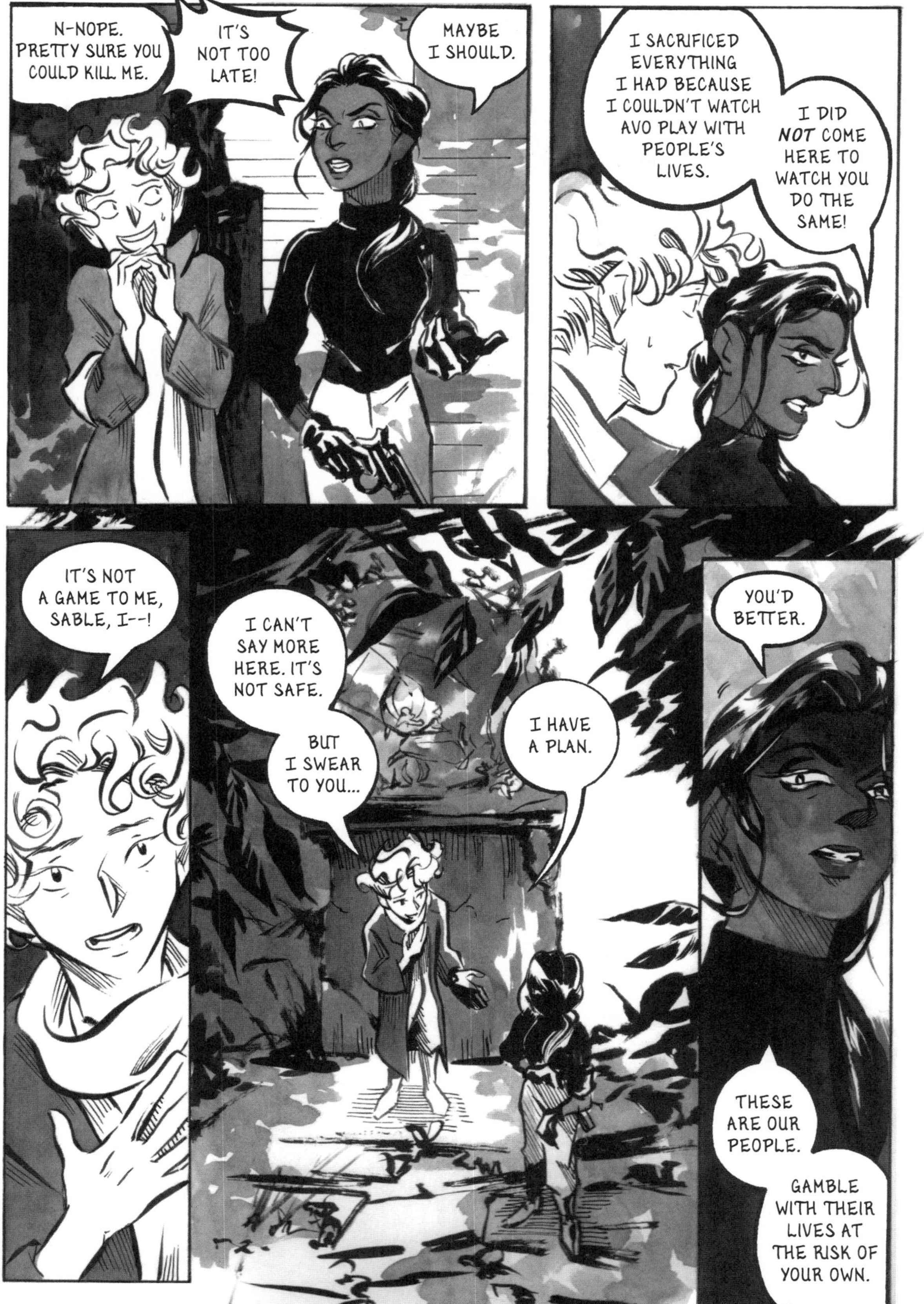
N-NOPE. PRETTY SURE YOU COULD KILL ME.
IT'S NOT TOO LATE!
MAYBE I SHOULD.
I SACRIFICED EVERYTHING I HAD BECAUSE I COULDN'T WATCH AVO PLAY WITH PEOPLE'S LIVES.
I DID *NOT* COME HERE TO WATCH YOU DO THE SAME!
IT'S NOT A GAME TO ME, SABLE, I--!
I CAN'T SAY MORE HERE. IT'S NOT SAFE.
BUT I SWEAR TO YOU...
I HAVE A PLAN.
YOU'D BETTER.
THESE ARE OUR PEOPLE.
GAMBLE WITH THEIR LIVES AT THE RISK OF YOUR OWN.

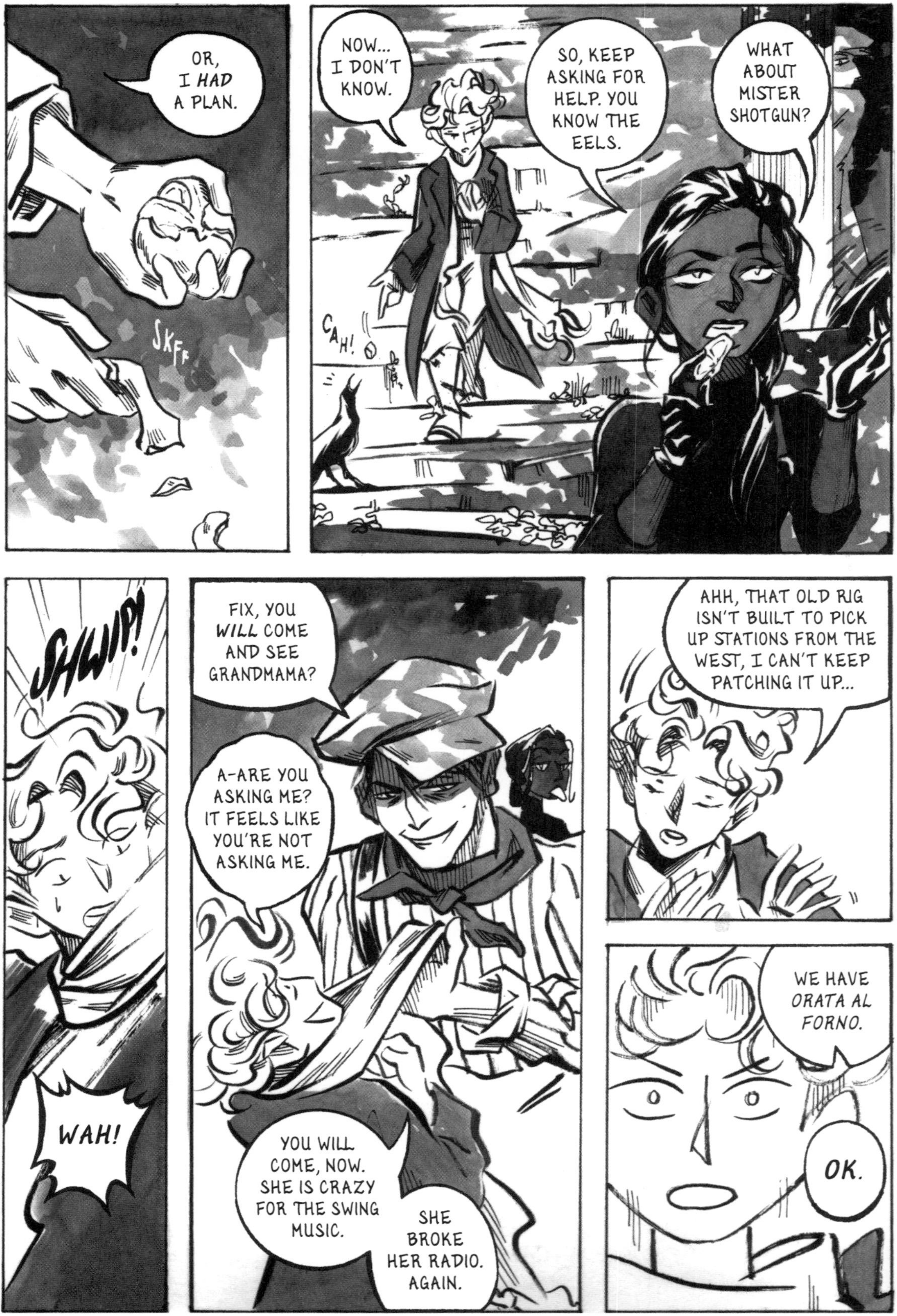
OR, I HAD A PLAN.
SKFF
NOW... I DON'T KNOW.
SO, KEEP ASKING FOR HELP. YOU KNOW THE EELS.
WHAT ABOUT MISTER SHOTGUN?
CAH!
SHWIP!
WAH!
FIX, YOU WILL COME AND SEE GRANDMAMA?
A-ARE YOU ASKING ME? IT FEELS LIKE YOU'RE NOT ASKING ME.
YOU WILL COME, NOW. SHE IS CRAZY FOR THE SWING MUSIC.
SHE BROKE HER RADIO. AGAIN.
AHH, THAT OLD RIG ISN'T BUILT TO PICK UP STATIONS FROM THE WEST, I CAN'T KEEP PATCHING IT UP...
WE HAVE ORATA AL FORNO.
OK.

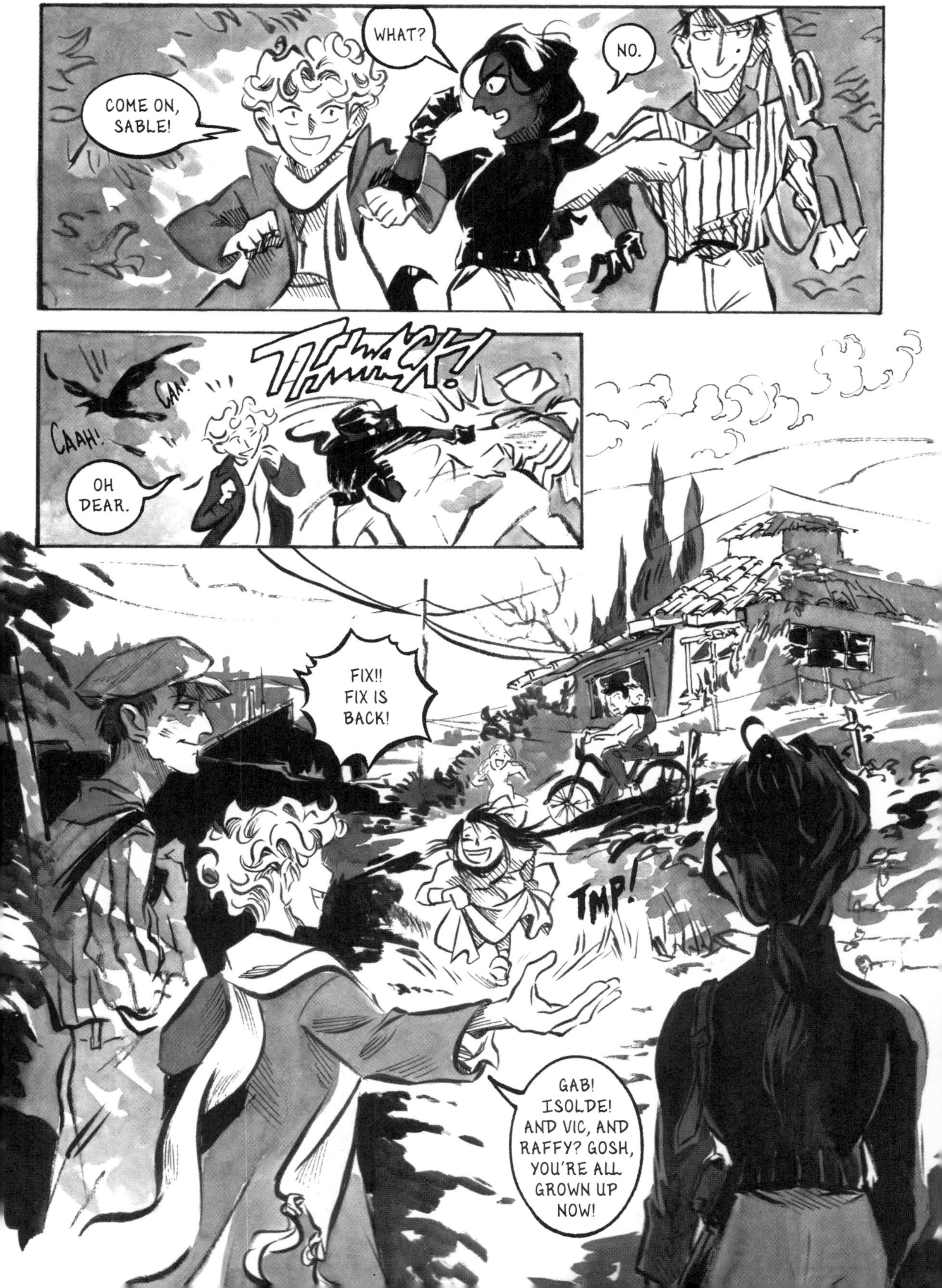
COME ON, SABLE!
WHAT?
NO.
THWACK!
CAAH!
CAAH!
OH DEAR.
FIX!! FIX IS BACK!
TMP!
GAB! ISOLDE! AND VIC, AND RAFFY? GOSH, YOU'RE ALL GROWN UP NOW!

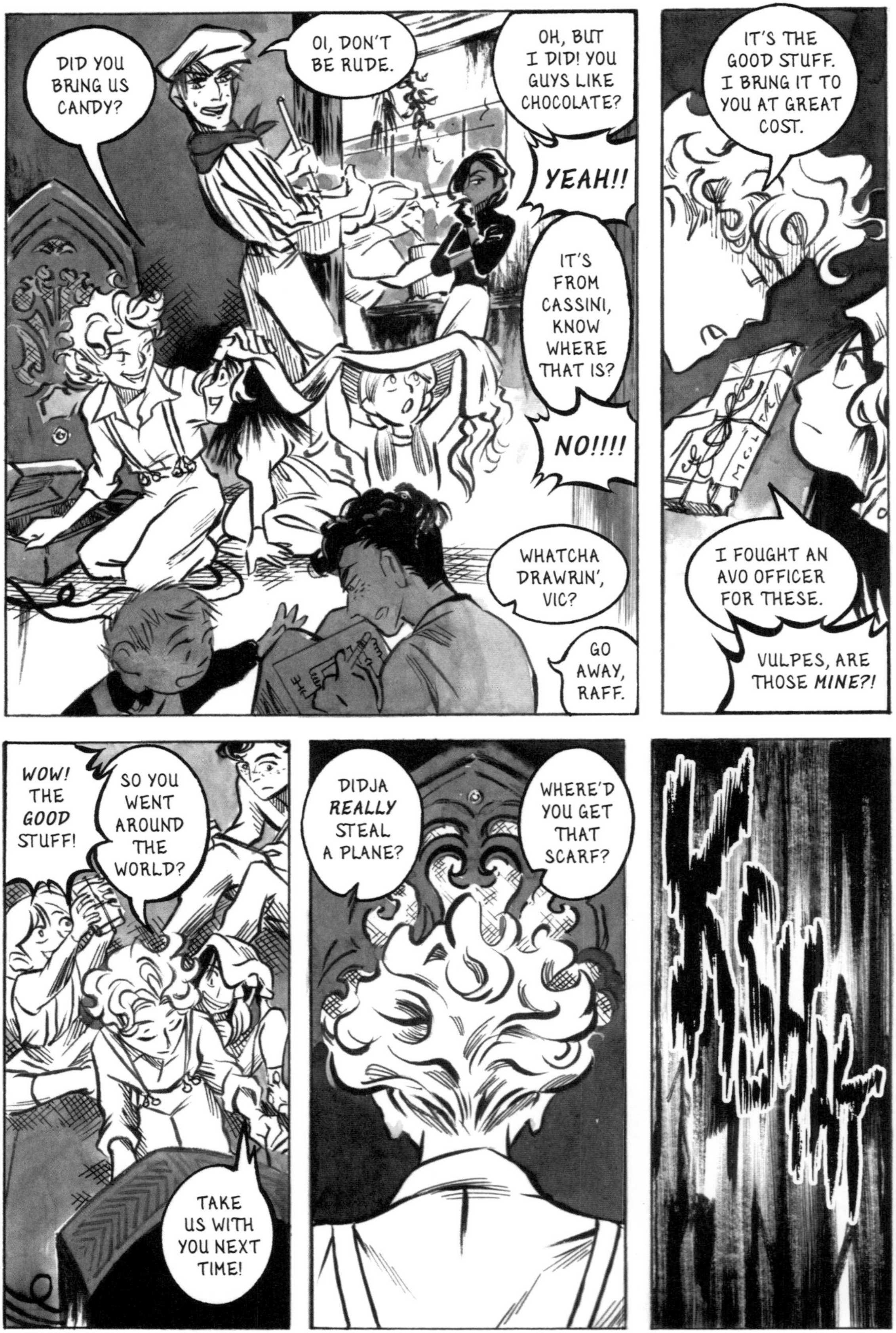
DID YOU BRING US CANDY?
OI, DON'T BE RUDE.
OH, BUT I DID! YOU GUYS LIKE CHOCOLATE?
YEAH!!
IT'S FROM CASSINI, KNOW WHERE THAT IS?
NO!!!!
WHATCHA DRAWRIN', VIC?
GO AWAY, RAFF.
IT'S THE GOOD STUFF. I BRING IT TO YOU AT GREAT COST.
I FOUGHT AN AVO OFFICER FOR THESE.
VULPES, ARE THOSE *MINE?!*
WOW! THE *GOOD* STUFF!
SO YOU WENT AROUND THE WORLD?
TAKE US WITH YOU NEXT TIME!
DIDJA ***REALLY*** STEAL A PLANE?
WHERE'D YOU GET THAT SCARF?

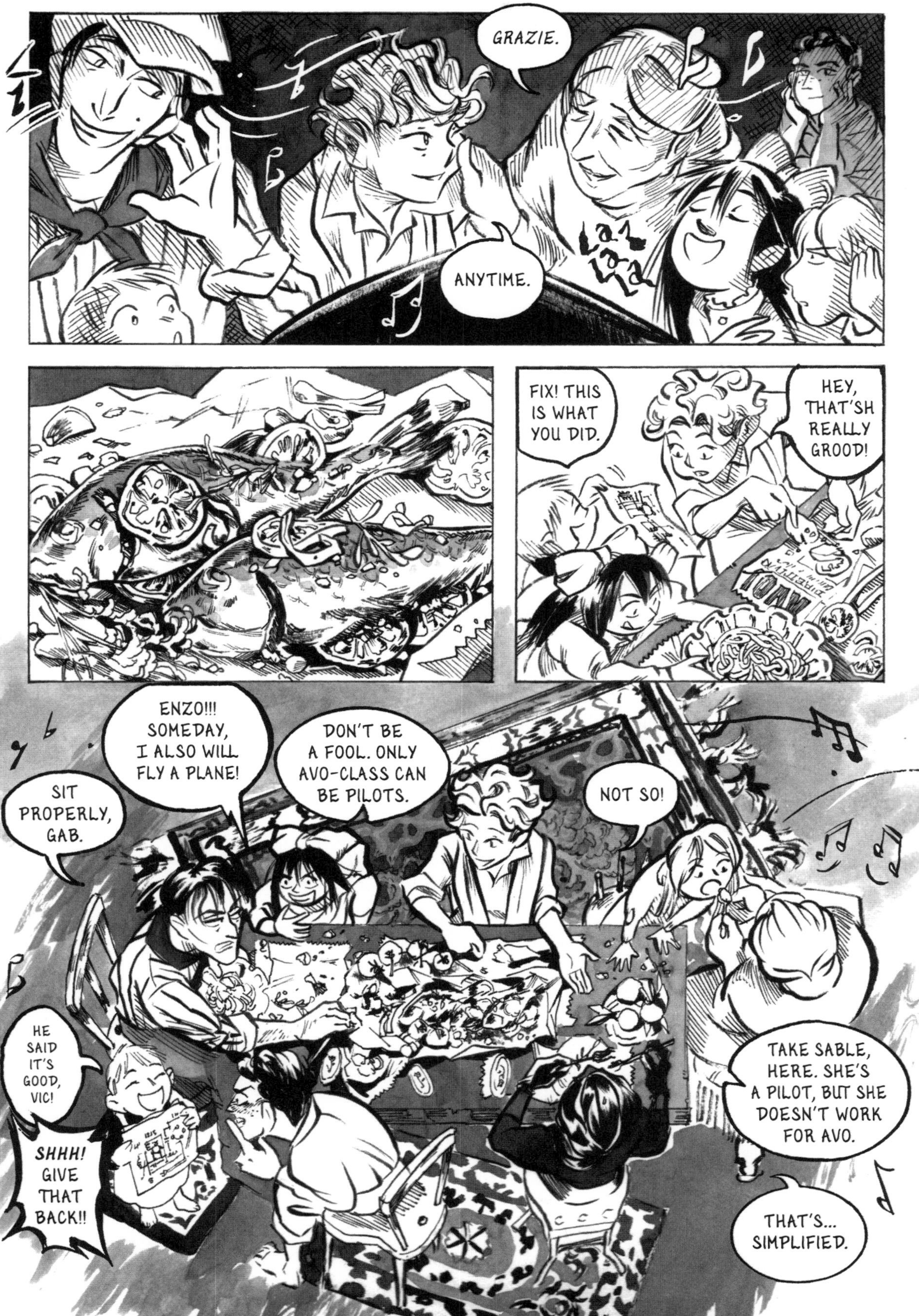
GRAZIE.
ANYTIME.
FIX! THIS IS WHAT YOU DID.
HEY, THAT'SH REALLY GROOD!
SIT PROPERLY, GAB.
ENZO!!! SOMEDAY, I ALSO WILL FLY A PLANE!
DON'T BE A FOOL. ONLY AVO-CLASS CAN BE PILOTS.
NOT SO!
TAKE SABLE, HERE. SHE'S A PILOT, BUT SHE DOESN'T WORK FOR AVO.
THAT'S... SIMPLIFIED.
HE SAID IT'S GOOD, VIC!
SHHH! GIVE THAT BACK!!

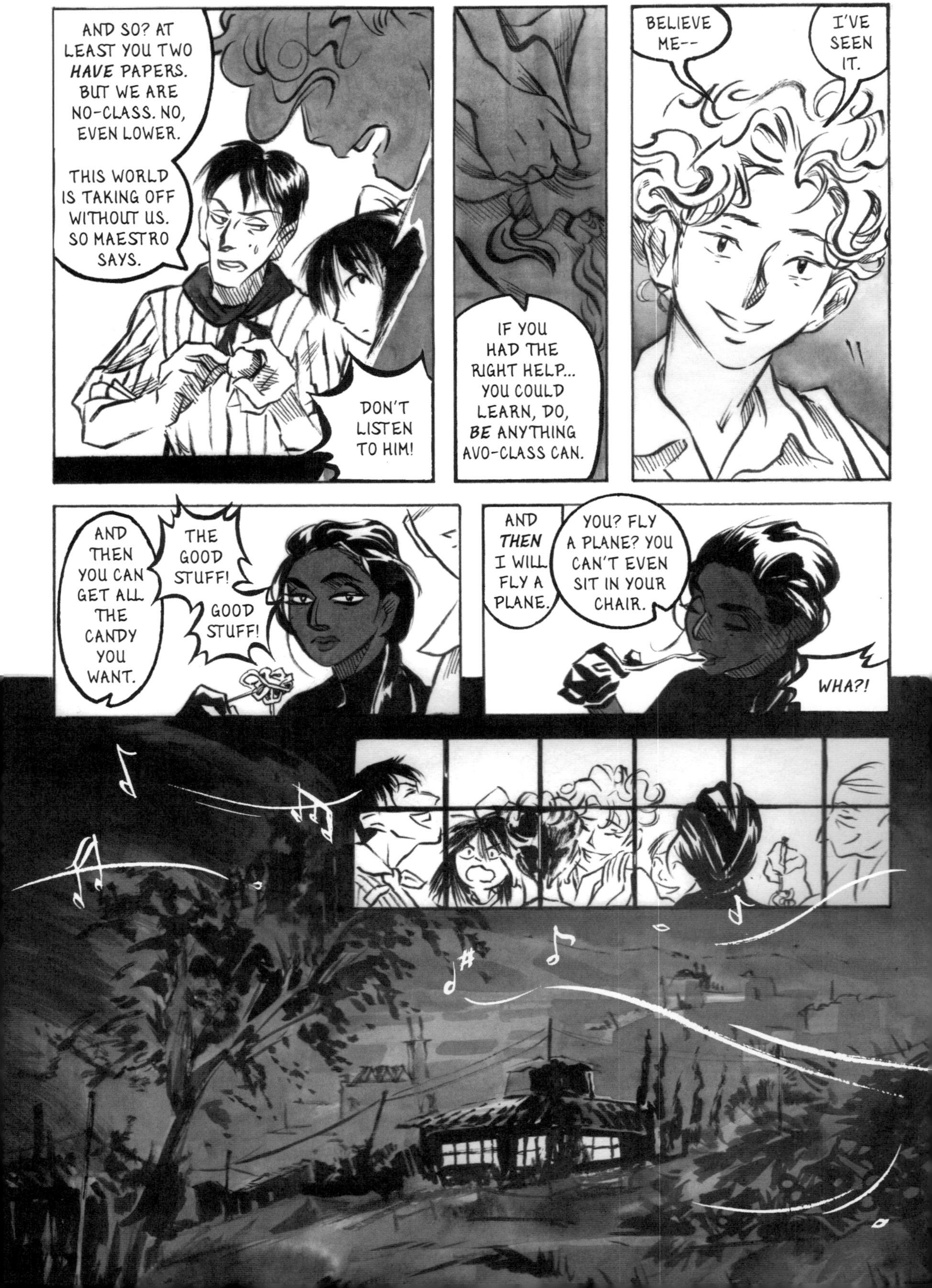
AND SO? AT LEAST YOU TWO HAVE PAPERS. BUT WE ARE NO-CLASS. NO, EVEN LOWER.
THIS WORLD IS TAKING OFF WITHOUT US. SO MAESTRO SAYS.
DON'T LISTEN TO HIM!
IF YOU HAD THE RIGHT HELP... YOU COULD LEARN, DO, BE ANYTHING AVO-CLASS CAN.
BELIEVE ME--
I'VE SEEN IT.
AND THEN YOU CAN GET ALL THE CANDY YOU WANT.
THE GOOD STUFF!
GOOD STUFF!
AND THEN I WILL FLY A PLANE.
YOU? FLY A PLANE? YOU CAN'T EVEN SIT IN YOUR CHAIR.
WHA?!

FOOM!

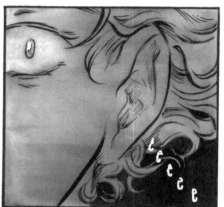

teeee

SABLE.

DO YOU HEAR THAT?

HM...?

SLEEP, VULPES... PROBABLY A STORM OFF THE COAST...

IT'S NOT COMING FROM THE SEA.

GET UP, GET ENZO.

NOW!

WHOOOSHHH

MAESTRO, I'M CERTAIN.

WARN THE OTHERS, PLEASE, HURRY!

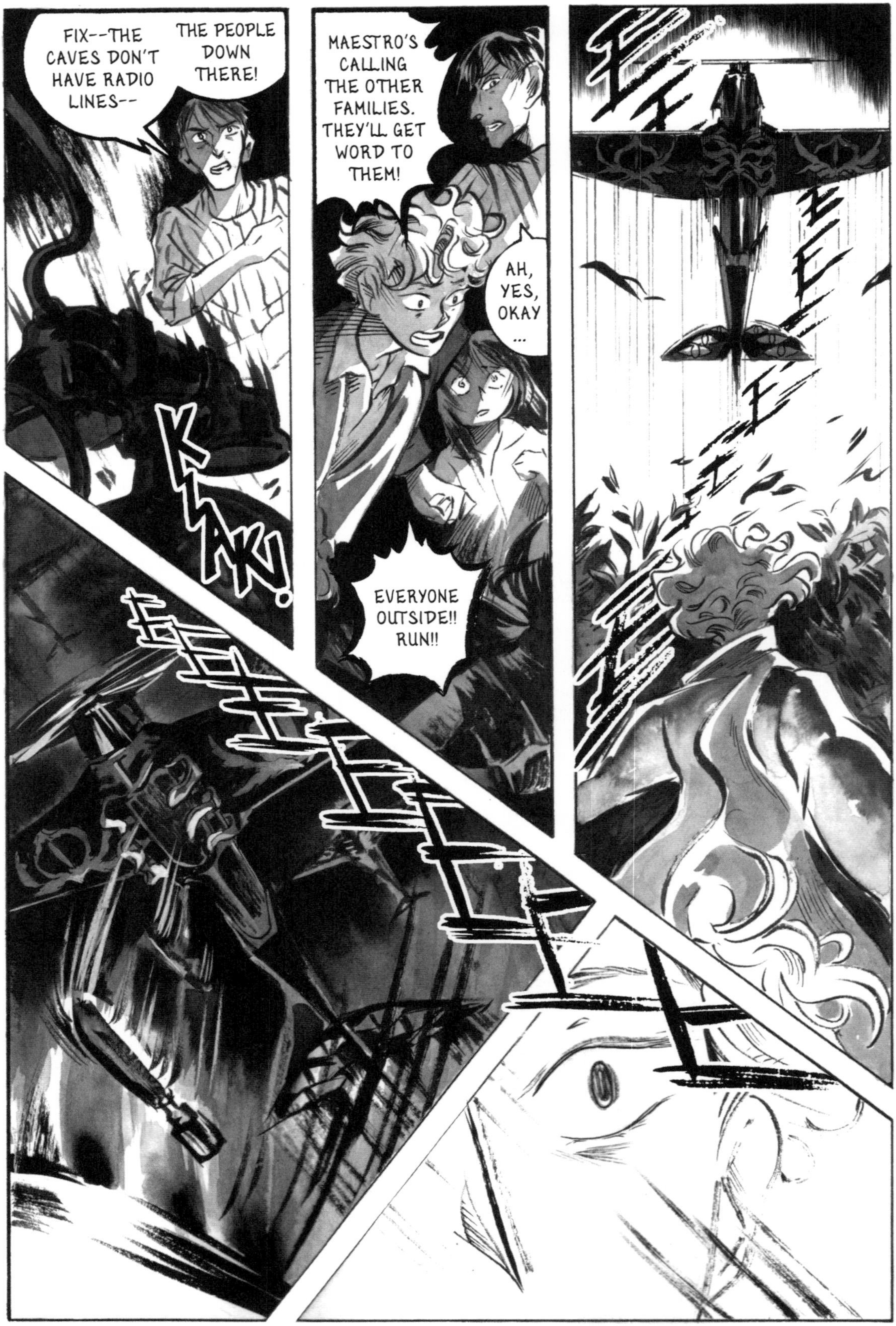
FIX--THE CAVES DON'T HAVE RADIO LINES--
THE PEOPLE DOWN THERE!
MAESTRO'S CALLING THE OTHER FAMILIES. THEY'LL GET WORD TO THEM!
AH, YES, OKAY ...
KLAK!
EVERYONE OUTSIDE!! RUN!!

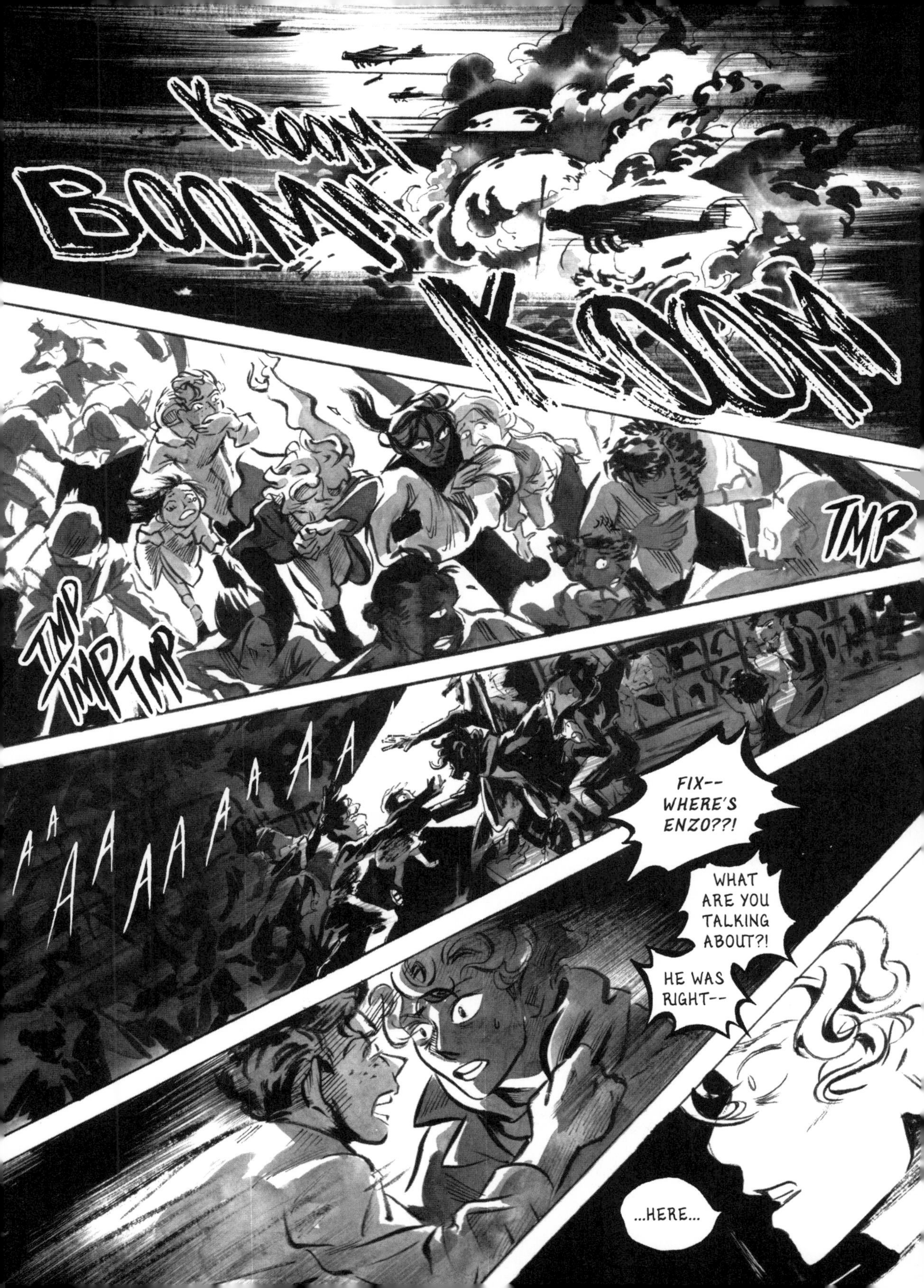
KROOM
BOOM!
KDOOM
TMP
TMP TMP TMP
AAAAAAAAAAAAAA
FIX-- WHERE'S ENZO??!
WHAT ARE YOU TALKING ABOUT?!
HE WAS RIGHT--
...HERE...

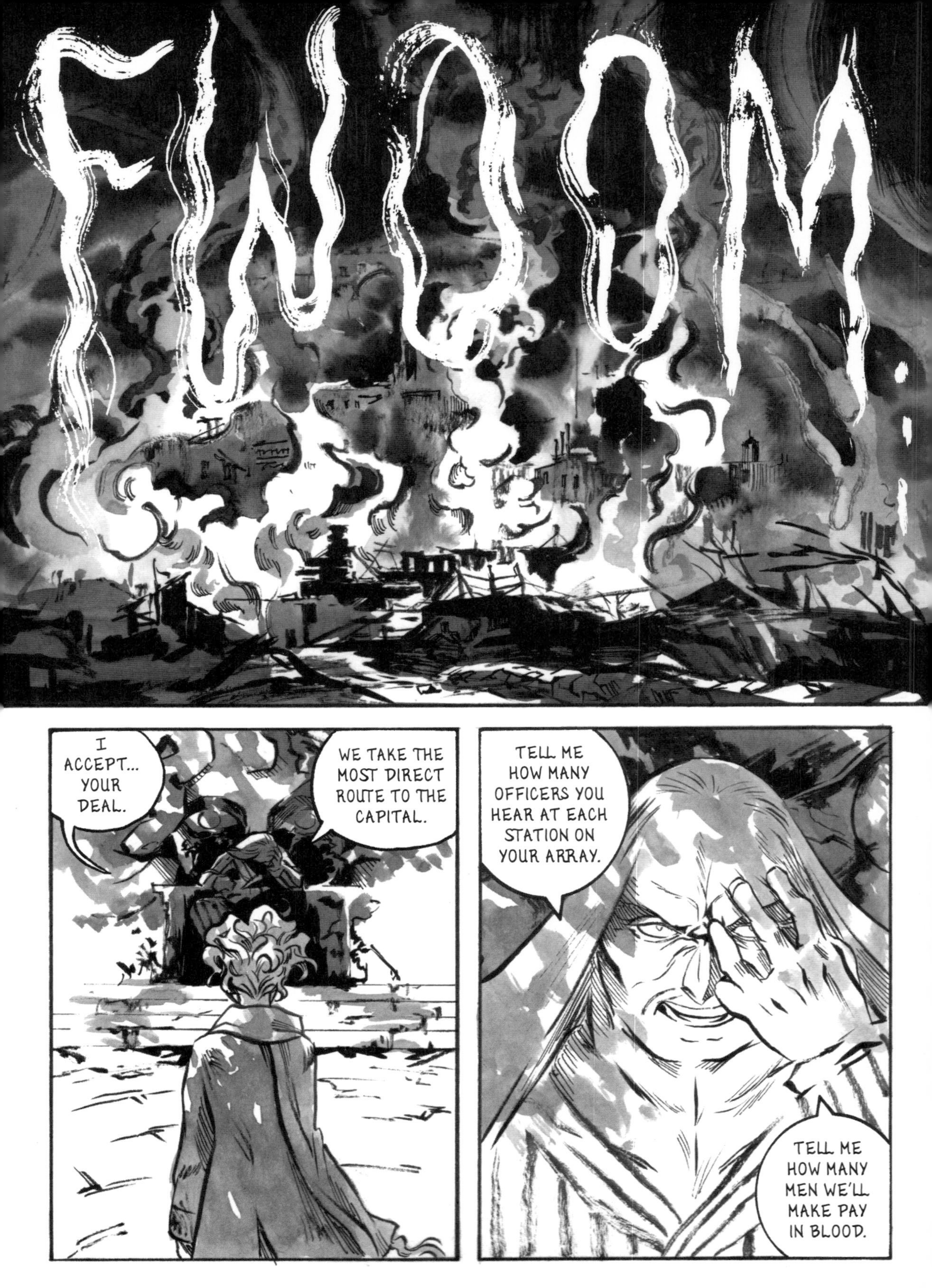
FWOOM
I ACCEPT... YOUR DEAL.
WE TAKE THE MOST DIRECT ROUTE TO THE CAPITAL.
TELL ME HOW MANY OFFICERS YOU HEAR AT EACH STATION ON YOUR ARRAY.
TELL ME HOW MANY MEN WE'LL MAKE PAY IN BLOOD.

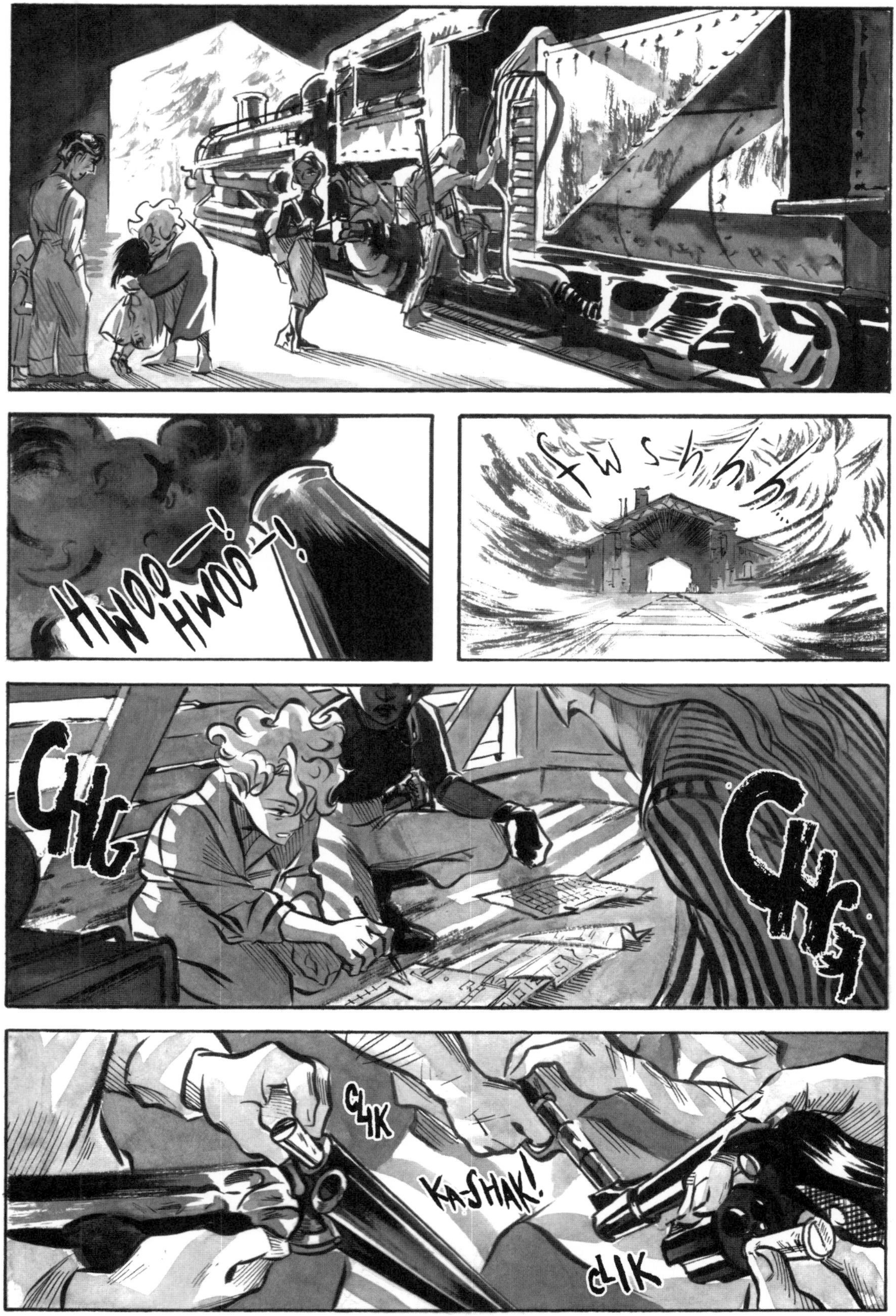
HWOO—!
HWOO—!
fwshhh...
CHG
CHG
CLIK
KA-SHAK!
CLIK

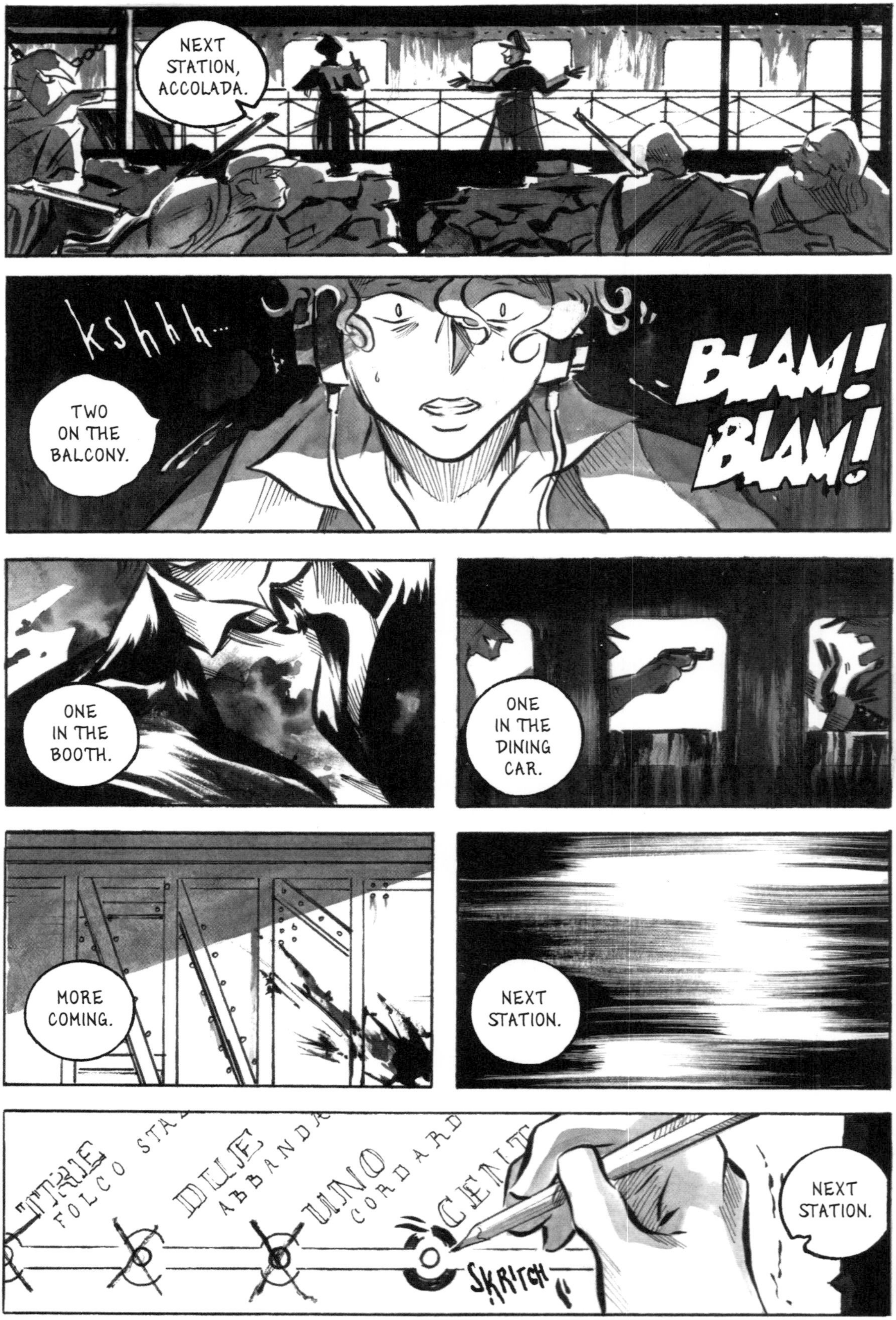
NEXT STATION, ACCOLADA.
kshhh...
TWO ON THE BALCONY.
BLAM! BLAM!
ONE IN THE BOOTH.
ONE IN THE DINING CAR.
MORE COMING.
NEXT STATION.
TRE
FOLCO STA
DUE
ABBANDA
UNO
CORDARD
CENT
SKRITCH
NEXT STATION.

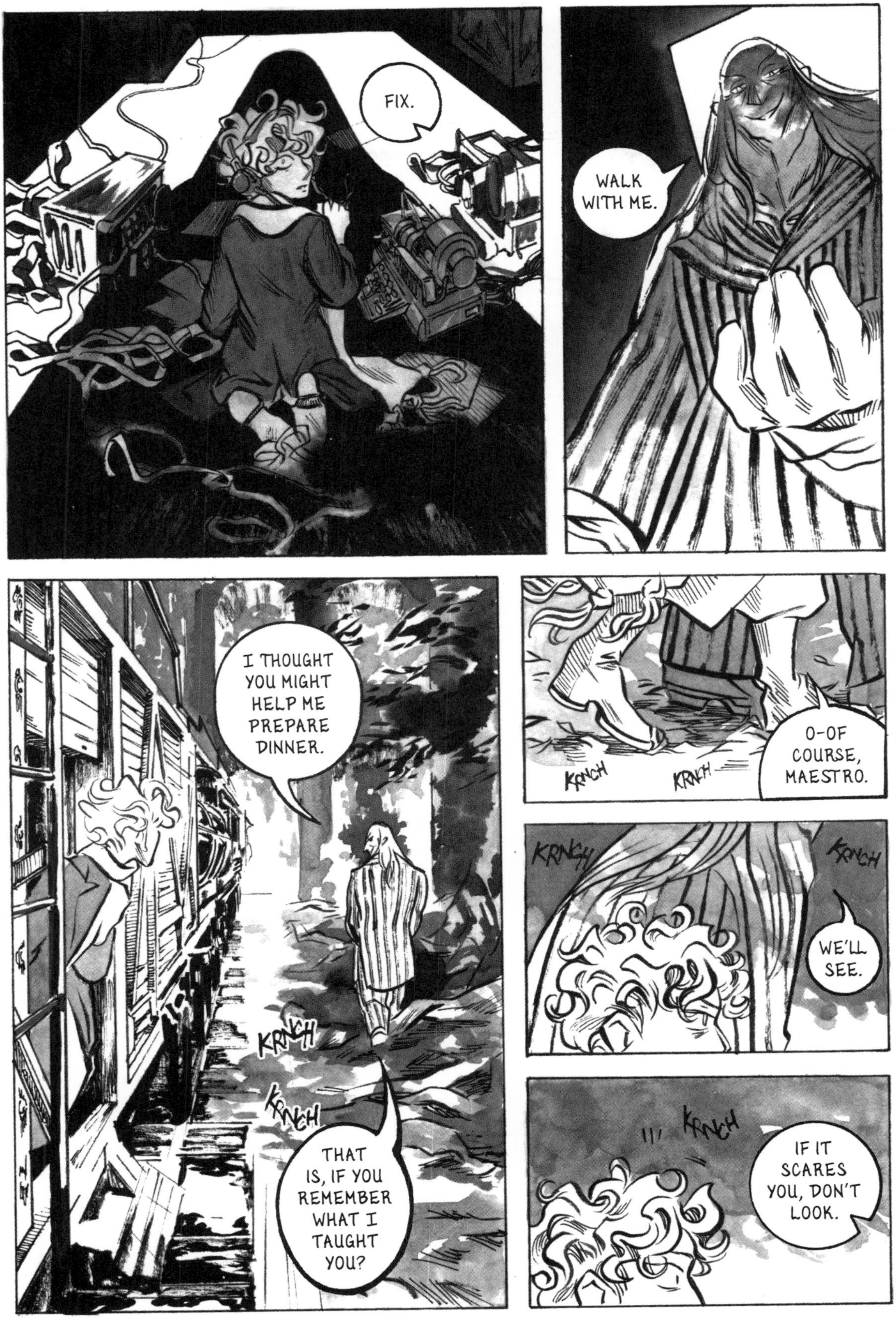
FIX.
WALK WITH ME.
I THOUGHT YOU MIGHT HELP ME PREPARE DINNER.
KRNCH
KRNCH
THAT IS, IF YOU REMEMBER WHAT I TAUGHT YOU?
KRNCH
KRNCH
O-OF COURSE, MAESTRO.
KRNCH
KRNCH
WE'LL SEE.
KRNCH
IF IT SCARES YOU, DON'T LOOK.

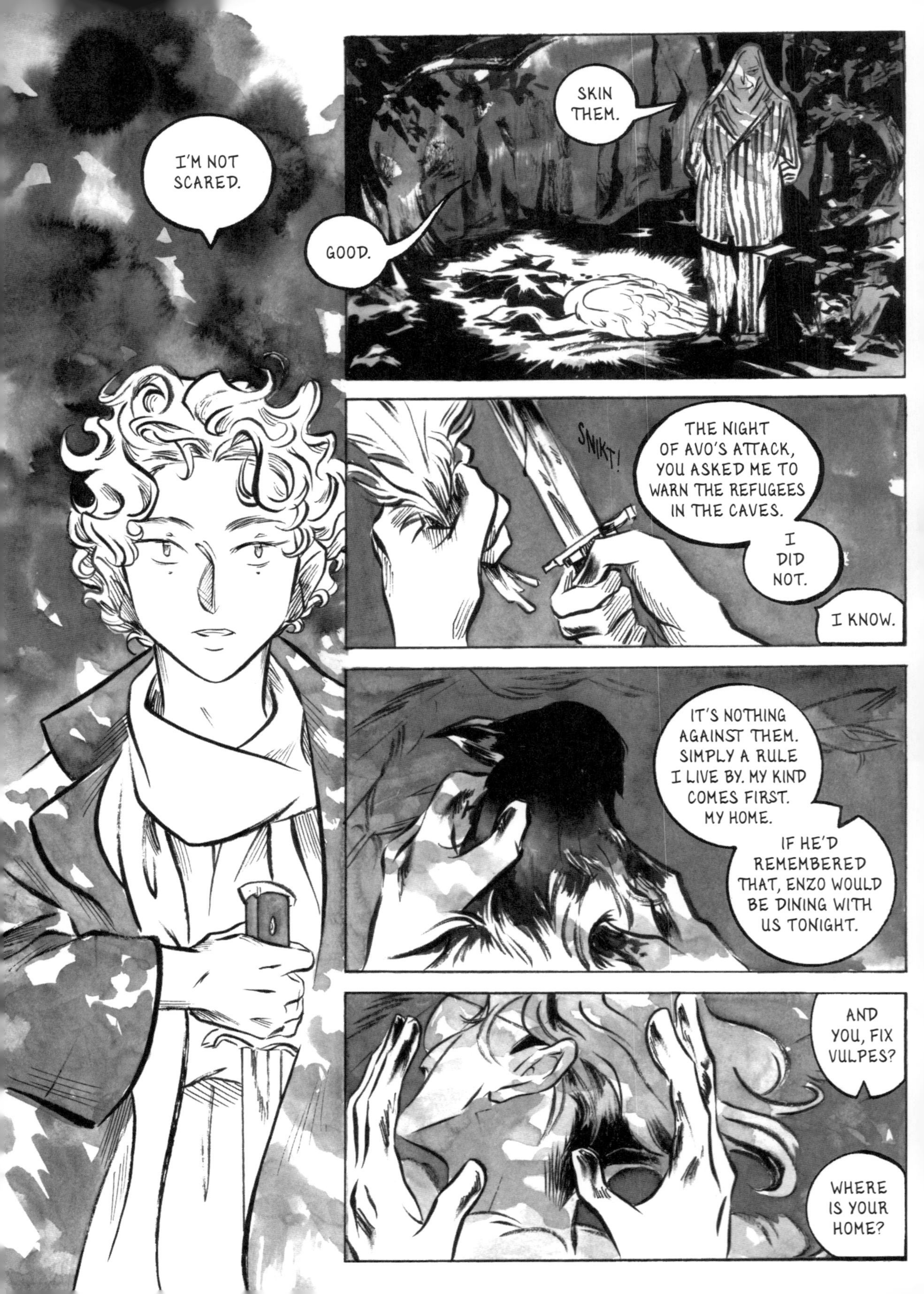
I'M NOT SCARED.
SKIN THEM.
GOOD.
SNIKT!
THE NIGHT OF AVO'S ATTACK, YOU ASKED ME TO WARN THE REFUGEES IN THE CAVES.
I DID NOT.
I KNOW.
IT'S NOTHING AGAINST THEM. SIMPLY A RULE I LIVE BY. MY KIND COMES FIRST. MY HOME.
IF HE'D REMEMBERED THAT, ENZO WOULD BE DINING WITH US TONIGHT.
AND YOU, FIX VULPES?
WHERE IS YOUR HOME?

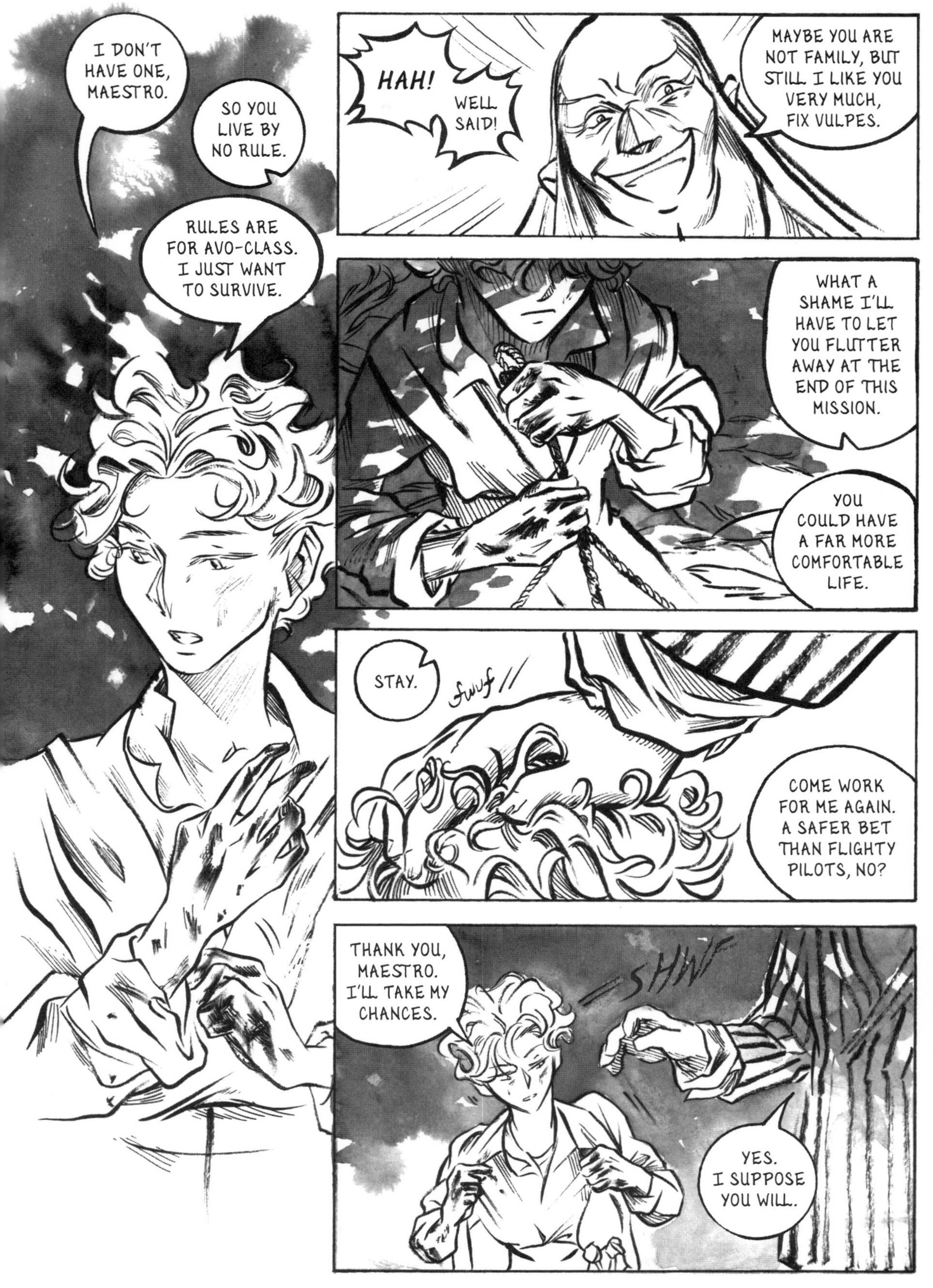
I DON'T HAVE ONE, MAESTRO.
SO YOU LIVE BY NO RULE.
RULES ARE FOR AVO-CLASS. I JUST WANT TO SURVIVE.
HAH!
WELL SAID!
MAYBE YOU ARE NOT FAMILY, BUT STILL I LIKE YOU VERY MUCH, FIX VULPES.
WHAT A SHAME I'LL HAVE TO LET YOU FLUTTER AWAY AT THE END OF THIS MISSION.
YOU COULD HAVE A FAR MORE COMFORTABLE LIFE.
STAY.
fwuf
COME WORK FOR ME AGAIN. A SAFER BET THAN FLIGHTY PILOTS, NO?
THANK YOU, MAESTRO. I'LL TAKE MY CHANCES.
SHWF
YES. I SUPPOSE YOU WILL.

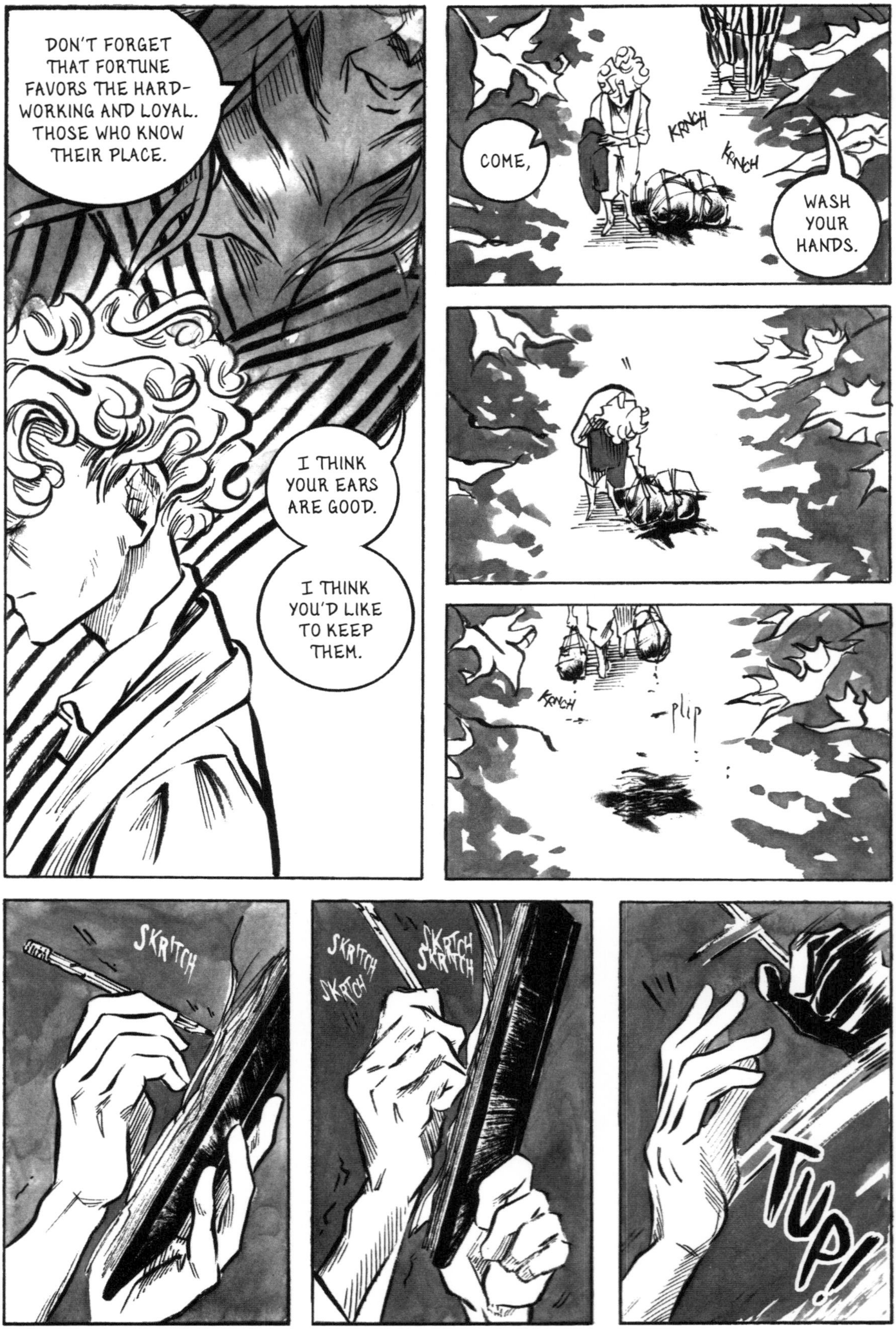
DON'T FORGET THAT FORTUNE FAVORS THE HARD-WORKING AND LOYAL. THOSE WHO KNOW THEIR PLACE.
I THINK YOUR EARS ARE GOOD.
I THINK YOU'D LIKE TO KEEP THEM.
COME,
KRNCH
KRNCH
WASH YOUR HANDS.
KRNCH
plip
SKRITCH
SKRITCH
SKRITCH
SKRITCH
SKRITCH
TUP!

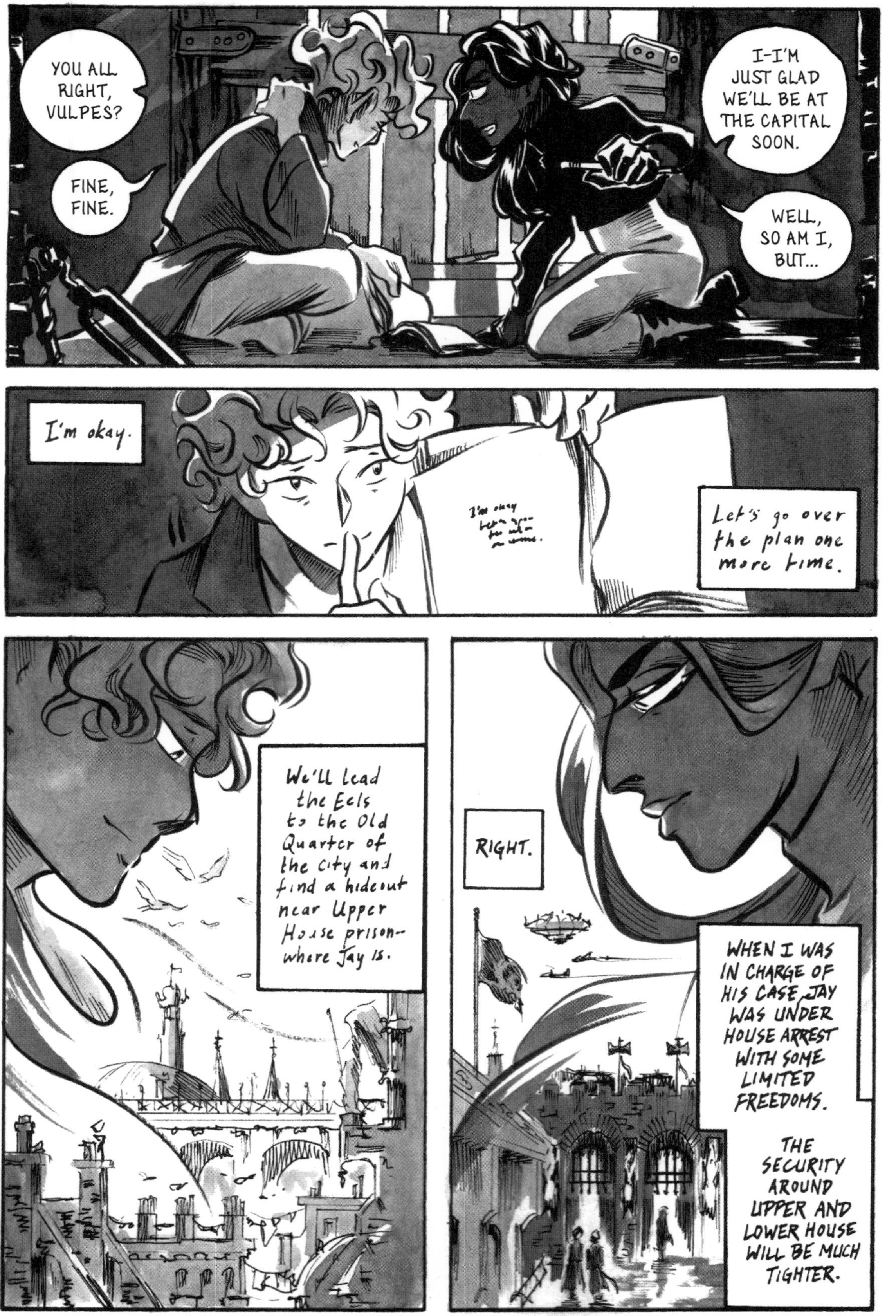
YOU ALL RIGHT, VULPES?
I-I'M JUST GLAD WE'LL BE AT THE CAPITAL SOON.
FINE, FINE.
WELL, SO AM I, BUT...
I'm okay.
Let's go over the plan one more time.
We'll lead the Eels to the Old Quarter of the city and find a hideout near Upper House prison--where Jay is.
RIGHT.
WHEN I WAS IN CHARGE OF HIS CASE JAY WAS UNDER HOUSE ARREST WITH SOME LIMITED FREEDOMS.
THE SECURITY AROUND UPPER AND LOWER HOUSE WILL BE MUCH TIGHTER.

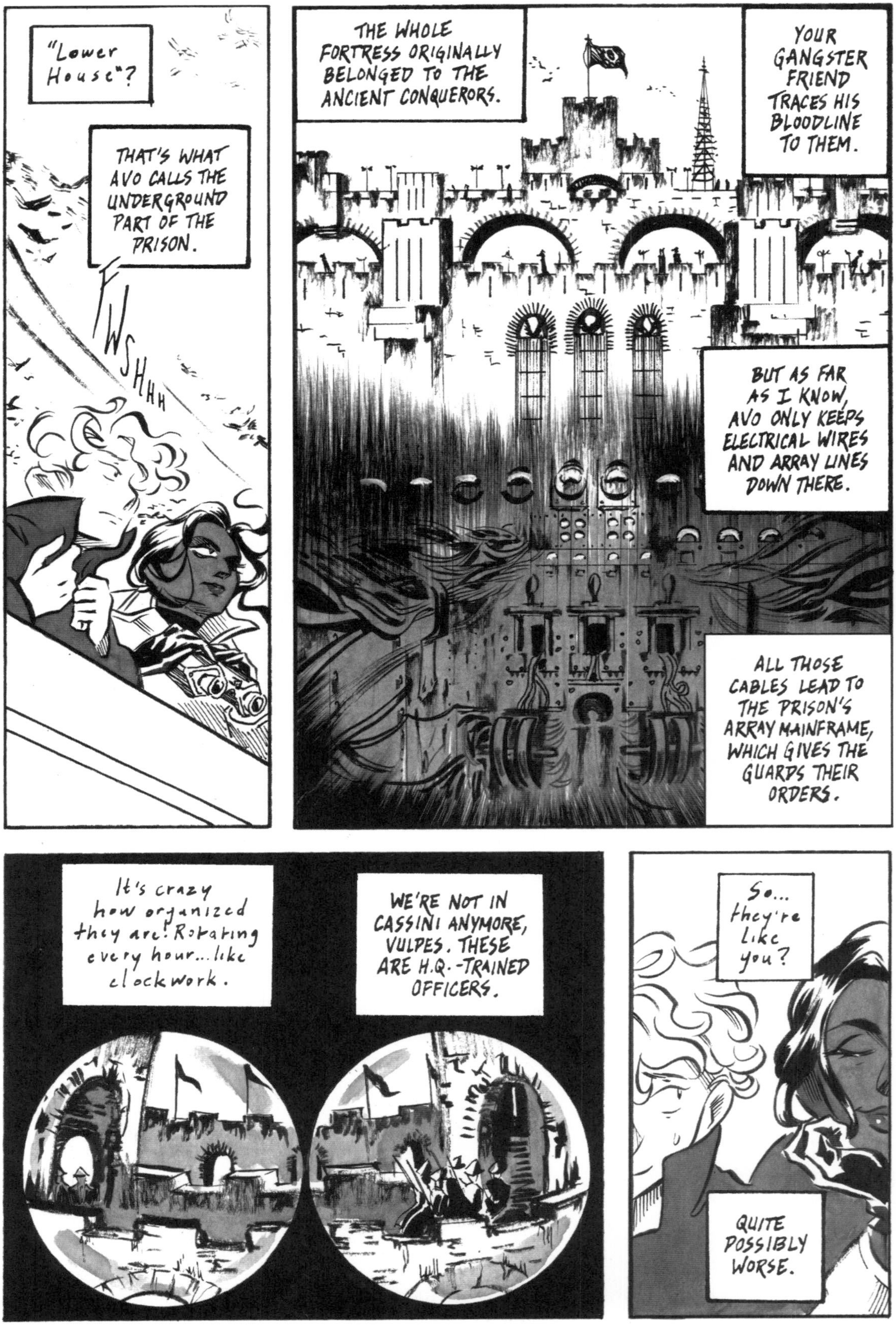
"Lower House"?
THAT'S WHAT AVO CALLS THE UNDERGROUND PART OF THE PRISON.
FWSHHHH
THE WHOLE FORTRESS ORIGINALLY BELONGED TO THE ANCIENT CONQUERORS.
YOUR GANGSTER FRIEND TRACES HIS BLOODLINE TO THEM.
BUT AS FAR AS I KNOW, AVO ONLY KEEPS ELECTRICAL WIRES AND ARRAY LINES DOWN THERE.
ALL THOSE CABLES LEAD TO THE PRISON'S ARRAY MAINFRAME, WHICH GIVES THE GUARDS THEIR ORDERS.
It's crazy how organized they are! Rotating every hour... like clockwork.
WE'RE NOT IN CASSINI ANYMORE, VULPES. THESE ARE H.Q.-TRAINED OFFICERS.
So... they're like you?
QUITE POSSIBLY WORSE.

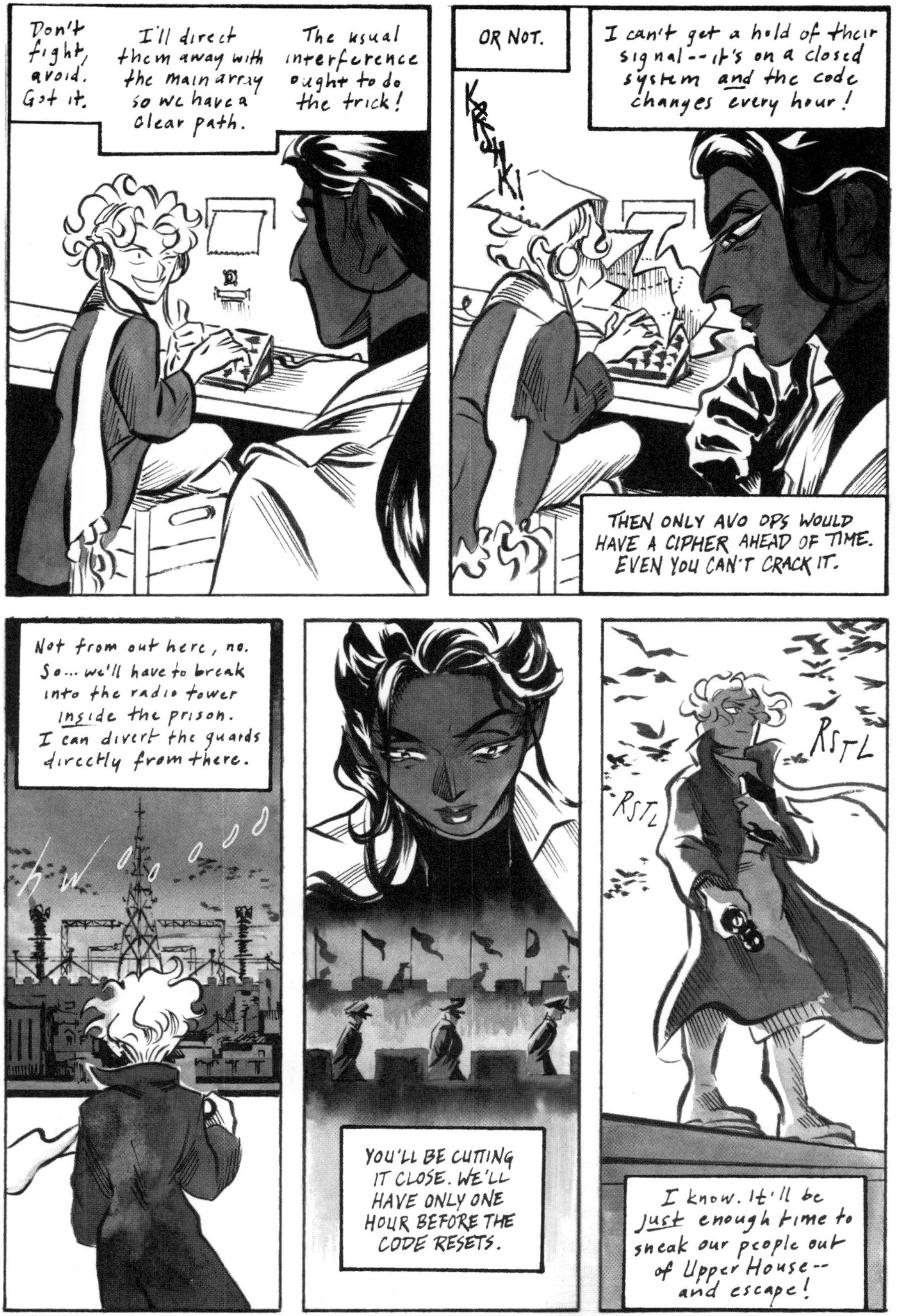
Don't fight, avoid. Got it.
I'll direct them away with the main array so we have a clear path.
The usual interference ought to do the trick!
OR NOT.
KRRSHKK!
I can't get a hold of their signal--it's on a closed system and the code changes every hour!
THEN ONLY AVO OPS WOULD HAVE A CIPHER AHEAD OF TIME. EVEN YOU CAN'T CRACK IT.
Not from out here, no. So... we'll have to break into the radio tower inside the prison. I can divert the guards directly from there.
hwooooo
YOU'LL BE CUTTING IT CLOSE. WE'LL HAVE ONLY ONE HOUR BEFORE THE CODE RESETS.
RSTL
RSTL
I know. It'll be just enough time to sneak our people out of Upper House--and escape!

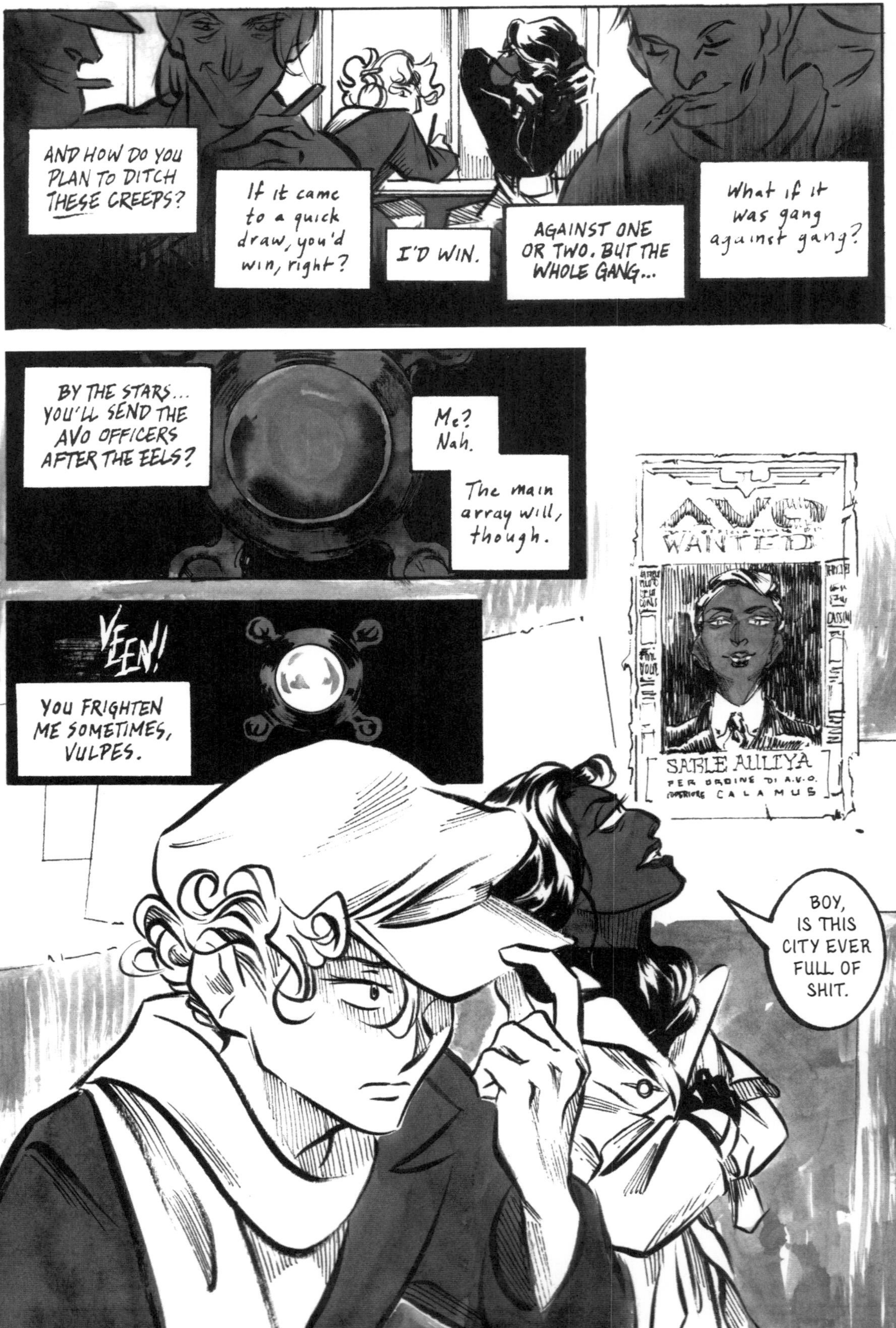
AND HOW DO YOU PLAN TO DITCH THESE CREEPS?
If it came to a quick draw, you'd win, right?
I'D WIN.
AGAINST ONE OR TWO. BUT THE WHOLE GANG...
What if it was gang against gang?
BY THE STARS... YOU'LL SEND THE AVO OFFICERS AFTER THE EELS?
Me? Nah.
The main array will, though.
VEEN!
YOU FRIGHTEN ME SOMETIMES, VULPES.
WANTED
SABLE AULIYA
PER ORDINE DI A.V.O.
CALAMUS
BOY, IS THIS CITY EVER FULL OF SHIT.

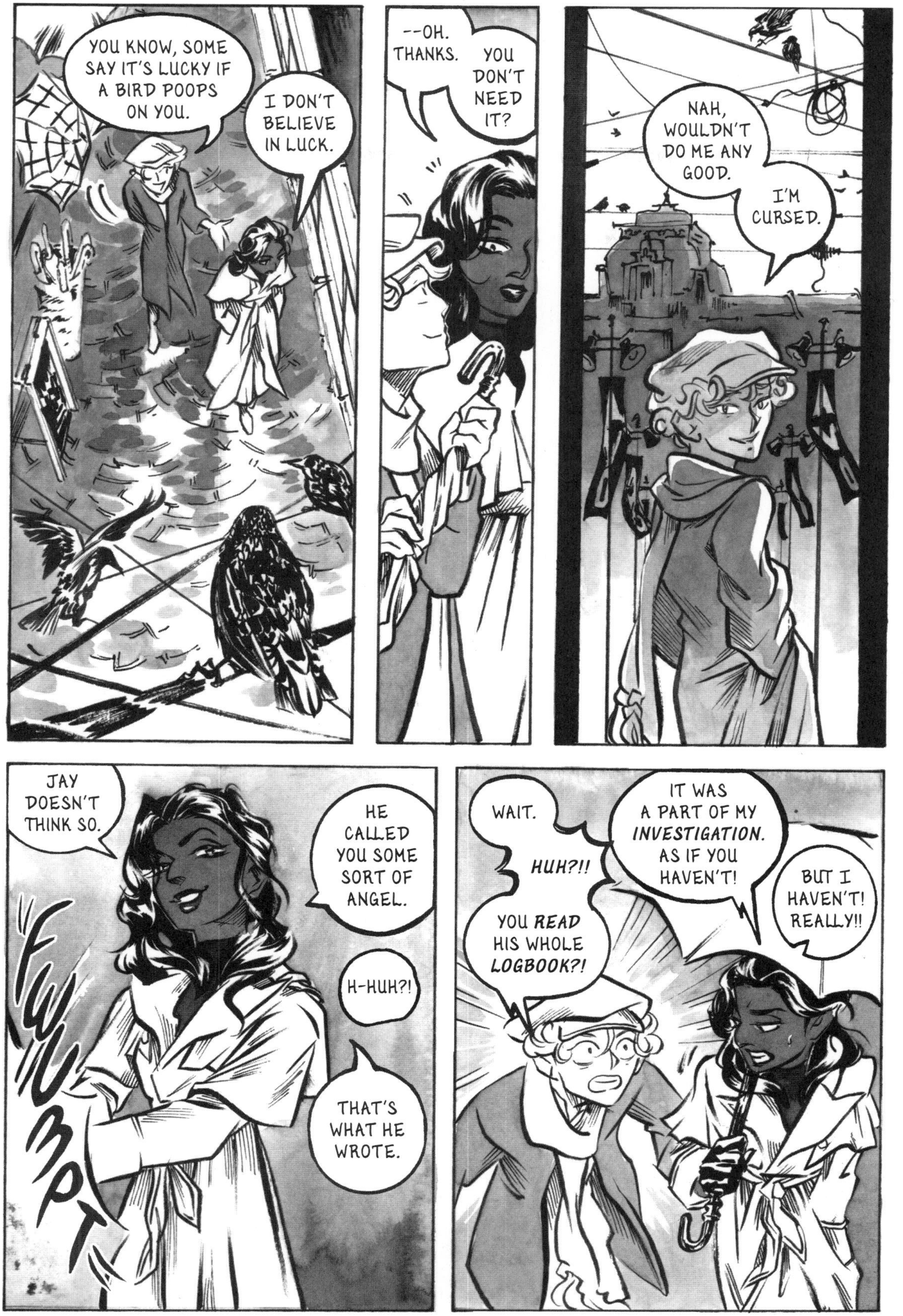
YOU KNOW, SOME SAY IT'S LUCKY IF A BIRD POOPS ON YOU.
I DON'T BELIEVE IN LUCK.
--OH. THANKS.
YOU DON'T NEED IT?
NAH, WOULDN'T DO ME ANY GOOD.
I'M CURSED.
JAY DOESN'T THINK SO.
HE CALLED YOU SOME SORT OF ANGEL.
H-HUH?!
THAT'S WHAT HE WROTE.
FWUMPT
WAIT.
HUH?!!
YOU READ HIS WHOLE LOGBOOK?!
IT WAS A PART OF MY INVESTIGATION. AS IF YOU HAVEN'T!
BUT I HAVEN'T! REALLY!!

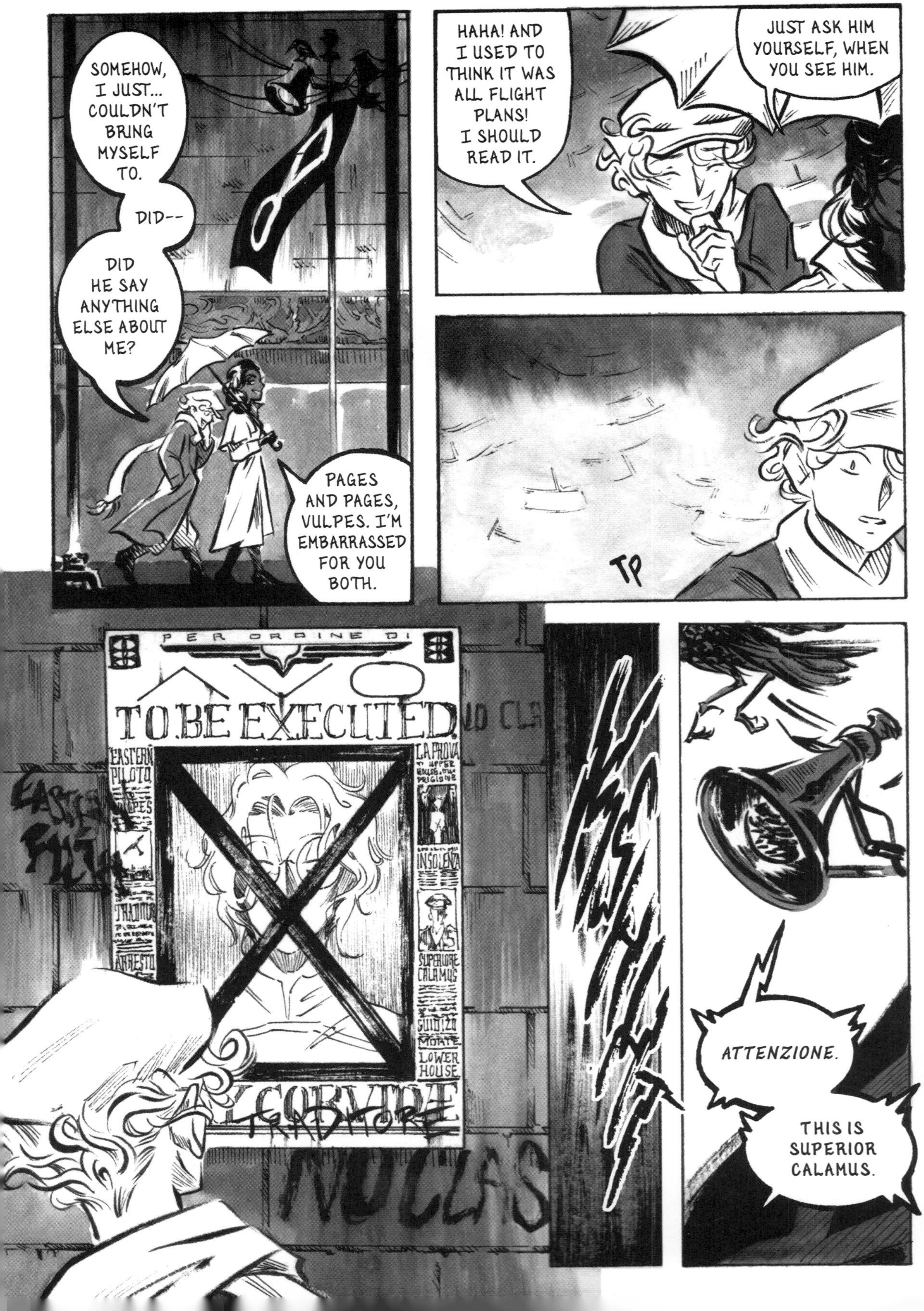
SOMEHOW, I JUST... COULDN'T BRING MYSELF TO.
DID--
DID HE SAY ANYTHING ELSE ABOUT ME?
PAGES AND PAGES, VULPES. I'M EMBARRASSED FOR YOU BOTH.
HAHA! AND I USED TO THINK IT WAS ALL FLIGHT PLANS! I SHOULD READ IT.
JUST ASK HIM YOURSELF, WHEN YOU SEE HIM.
TP
PER ORDINE DI
TO BE EXECUTED
EASTERN PILOTA
VULPES
TRADITORE
ARRESTO
LA PROVA
INSOLENZA
SUPERIORE CALAMUS
GIUDIZIO
MORTE
LOWER HOUSE
TRADITORE
ATTENZIONE.
THIS IS SUPERIOR CALAMUS.

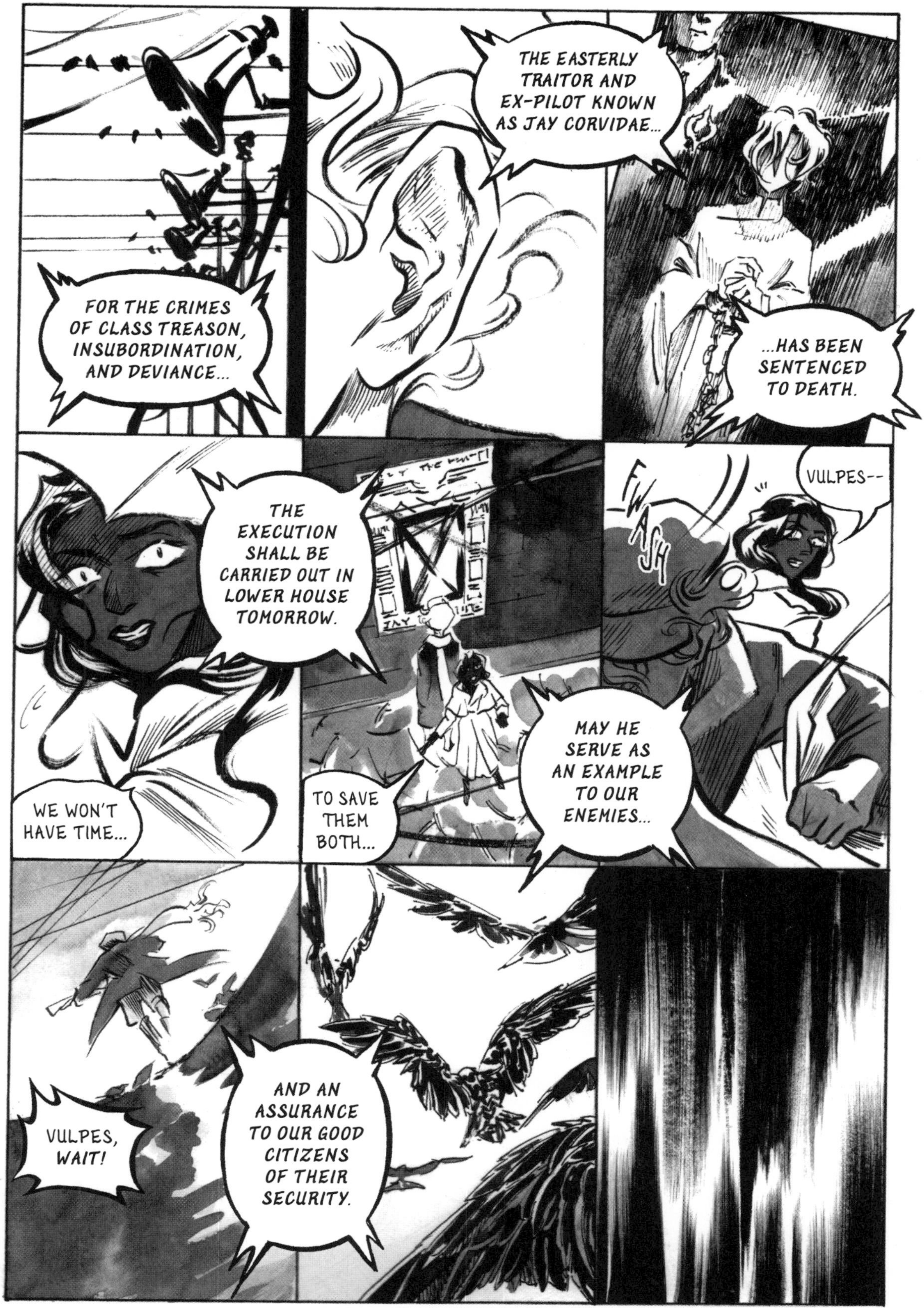
FOR THE CRIMES OF CLASS TREASON, INSUBORDINATION, AND DEVIANCE...
THE EASTERLY TRAITOR AND EX-PILOT KNOWN AS JAY CORVIDAE...
...HAS BEEN SENTENCED TO DEATH.
THE EXECUTION SHALL BE CARRIED OUT IN LOWER HOUSE TOMORROW.
WE WON'T HAVE TIME...
TO SAVE THEM BOTH...
MAY HE SERVE AS AN EXAMPLE TO OUR ENEMIES...
FWASH
VULPES--
VULPES, WAIT!
AND AN ASSURANCE TO OUR GOOD CITIZENS OF THEIR SECURITY.

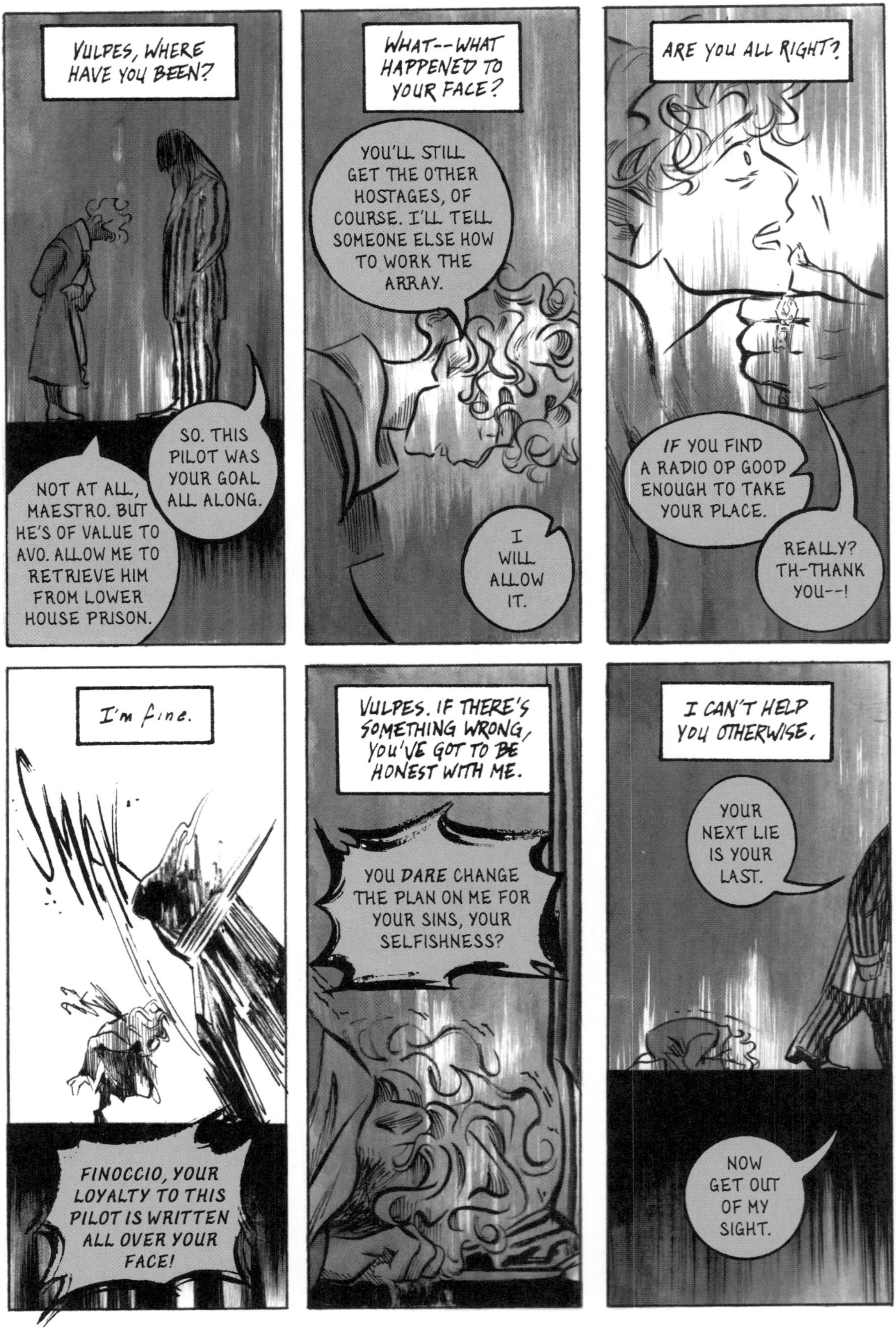
VULPES, WHERE HAVE YOU BEEN?
SO. THIS PILOT WAS YOUR GOAL ALL ALONG.
NOT AT ALL, MAESTRO. BUT HE'S OF VALUE TO AVO. ALLOW ME TO RETRIEVE HIM FROM LOWER HOUSE PRISON.
WHAT--WHAT HAPPENED TO YOUR FACE?
YOU'LL STILL GET THE OTHER HOSTAGES, OF COURSE. I'LL TELL SOMEONE ELSE HOW TO WORK THE ARRAY.
I WILL ALLOW IT.
ARE YOU ALL RIGHT?
IF YOU FIND A RADIO OP GOOD ENOUGH TO TAKE YOUR PLACE.
REALLY? TH-THANK YOU--!
I'm fine.
SMAK
FINOCCIO, YOUR LOYALTY TO THIS PILOT IS WRITTEN ALL OVER YOUR FACE!
VULPES. IF THERE'S SOMETHING WRONG, YOU'VE GOT TO BE HONEST WITH ME.
YOU DARE CHANGE THE PLAN ON ME FOR YOUR SINS, YOUR SELFISHNESS?
I CAN'T HELP YOU OTHERWISE.
YOUR NEXT LIE IS YOUR LAST.
NOW GET OUT OF MY SIGHT.

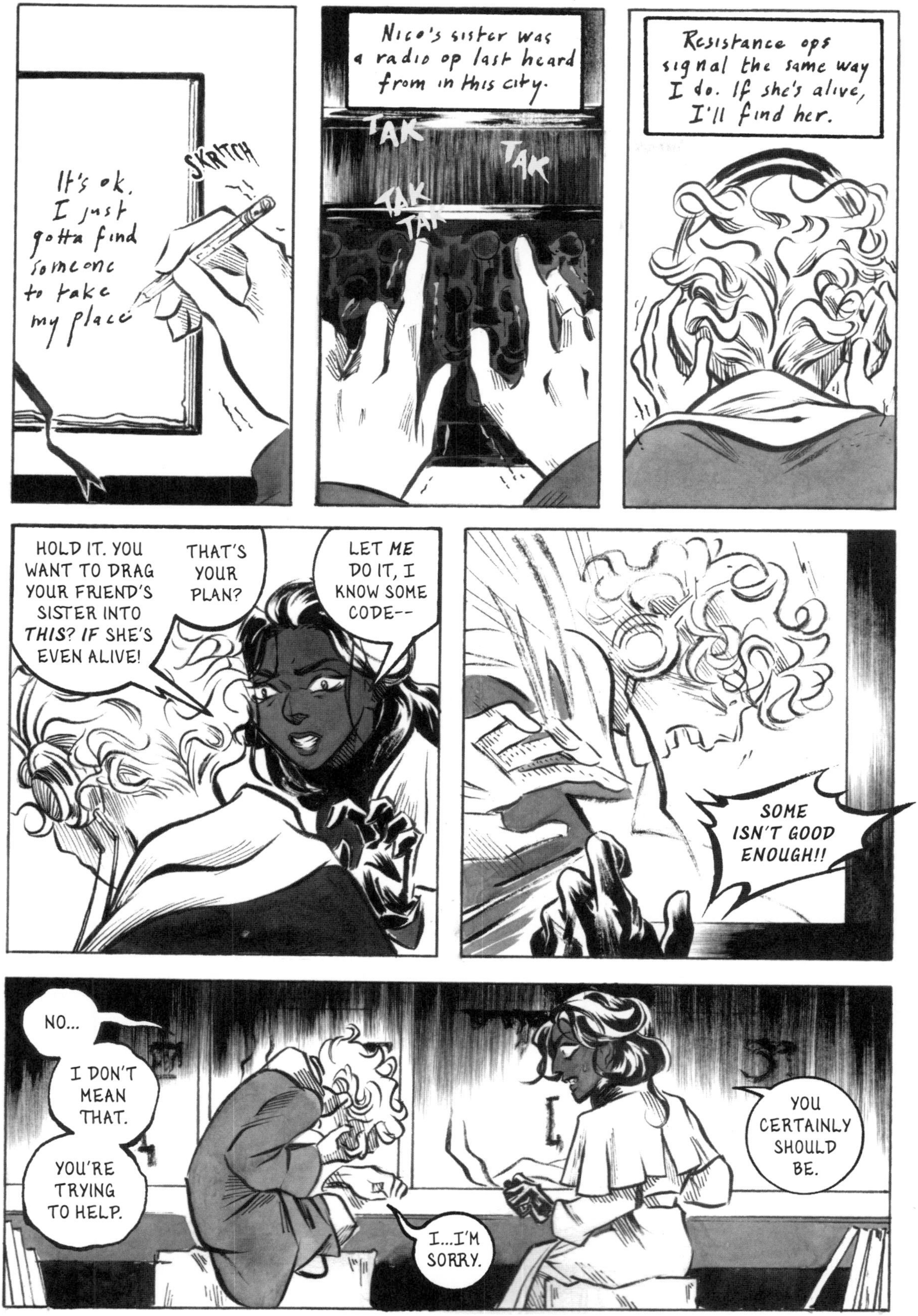
SKRITCH
It's ok. I just gotta find someone to take my place
Nico's sister was a radio op last heard from in this city.
TAK
TAK
TAK
TAK
Resistance ops signal the same way I do. If she's alive, I'll find her.
HOLD IT. YOU WANT TO DRAG YOUR FRIEND'S SISTER INTO THIS? IF SHE'S EVEN ALIVE!
THAT'S YOUR PLAN?
LET ME DO IT, I KNOW SOME CODE--
SOME ISN'T GOOD ENOUGH!!
NO...
I DON'T MEAN THAT.
YOU'RE TRYING TO HELP.
I...I'M SORRY.
YOU CERTAINLY SHOULD BE.

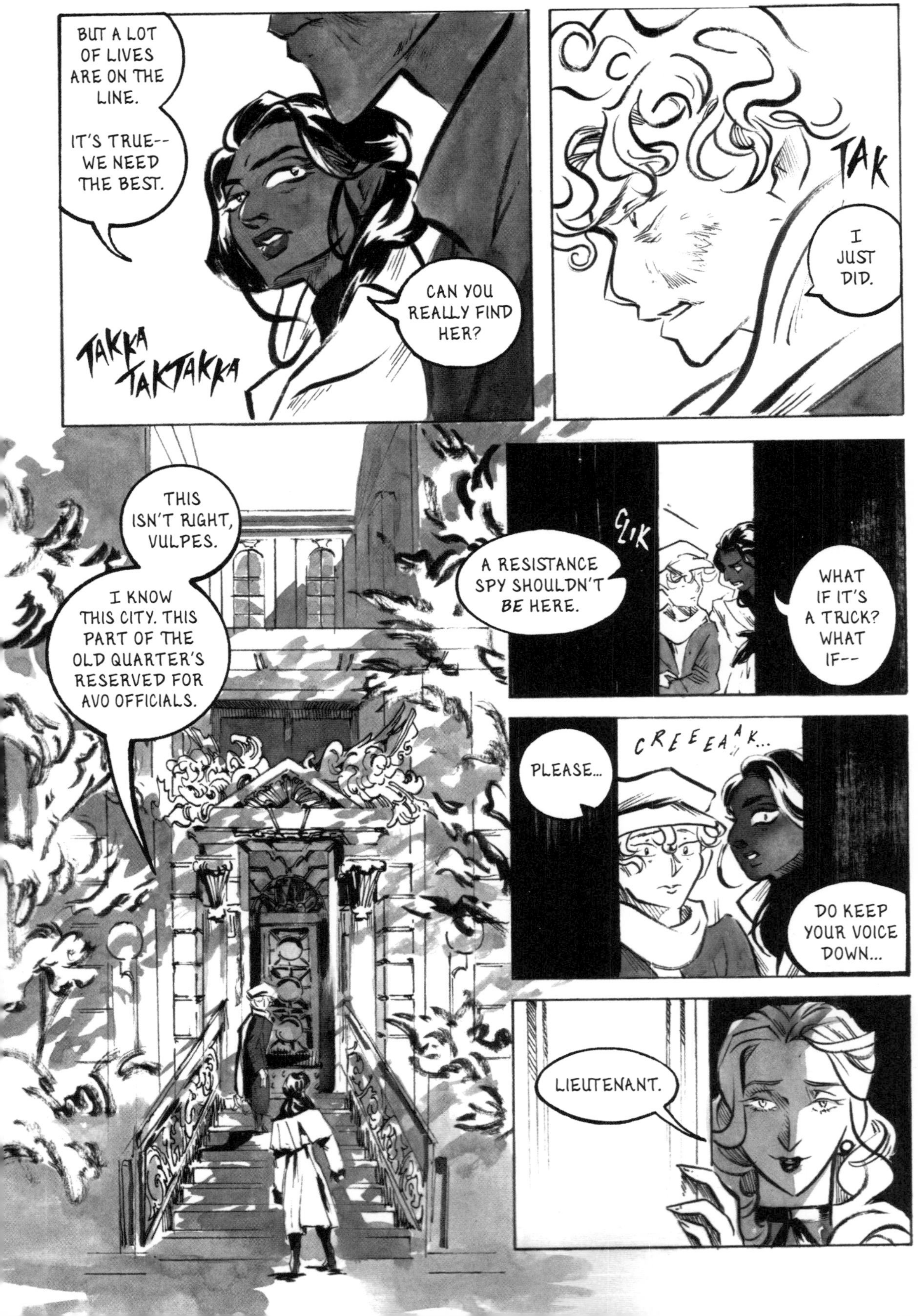
BUT A LOT OF LIVES ARE ON THE LINE.
IT'S TRUE-- WE NEED THE BEST.
TAKKA TAKTAKKA
CAN YOU REALLY FIND HER?
TAK
I JUST DID.
THIS ISN'T RIGHT, VULPES.
I KNOW THIS CITY. THIS PART OF THE OLD QUARTER'S RESERVED FOR AVO OFFICIALS.
CLIK
A RESISTANCE SPY SHOULDN'T BE HERE.
WHAT IF IT'S A TRICK? WHAT IF--
CREEEAAK...
PLEASE...
DO KEEP YOUR VOICE DOWN...
LIEUTENANT.

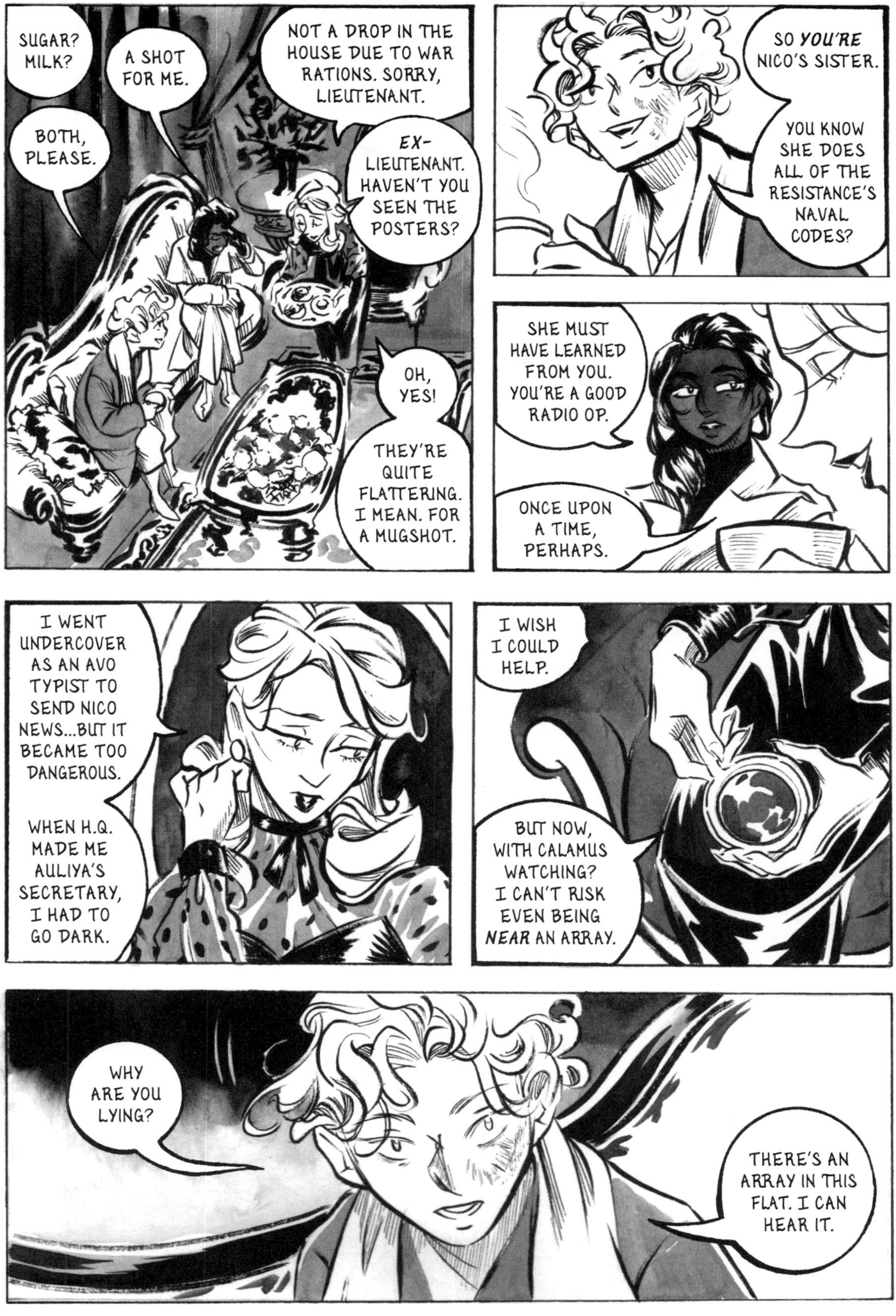
SUGAR? MILK?
BOTH, PLEASE.
A SHOT FOR ME.
NOT A DROP IN THE HOUSE DUE TO WAR RATIONS. SORRY, LIEUTENANT.
EX-LIEUTENANT. HAVEN'T YOU SEEN THE POSTERS?
OH, YES!
THEY'RE QUITE FLATTERING. I MEAN. FOR A MUGSHOT.
SO YOU'RE NICO'S SISTER.
YOU KNOW SHE DOES ALL OF THE RESISTANCE'S NAVAL CODES?
SHE MUST HAVE LEARNED FROM YOU. YOU'RE A GOOD RADIO OP.
ONCE UPON A TIME, PERHAPS.
I WENT UNDERCOVER AS AN AVO TYPIST TO SEND NICO NEWS...BUT IT BECAME TOO DANGEROUS.
WHEN H.Q. MADE ME AULIYA'S SECRETARY, I HAD TO GO DARK.
I WISH I COULD HELP.
BUT NOW, WITH CALAMUS WATCHING? I CAN'T RISK EVEN BEING NEAR AN ARRAY.
WHY ARE YOU LYING?
THERE'S AN ARRAY IN THIS FLAT. I CAN HEAR IT.

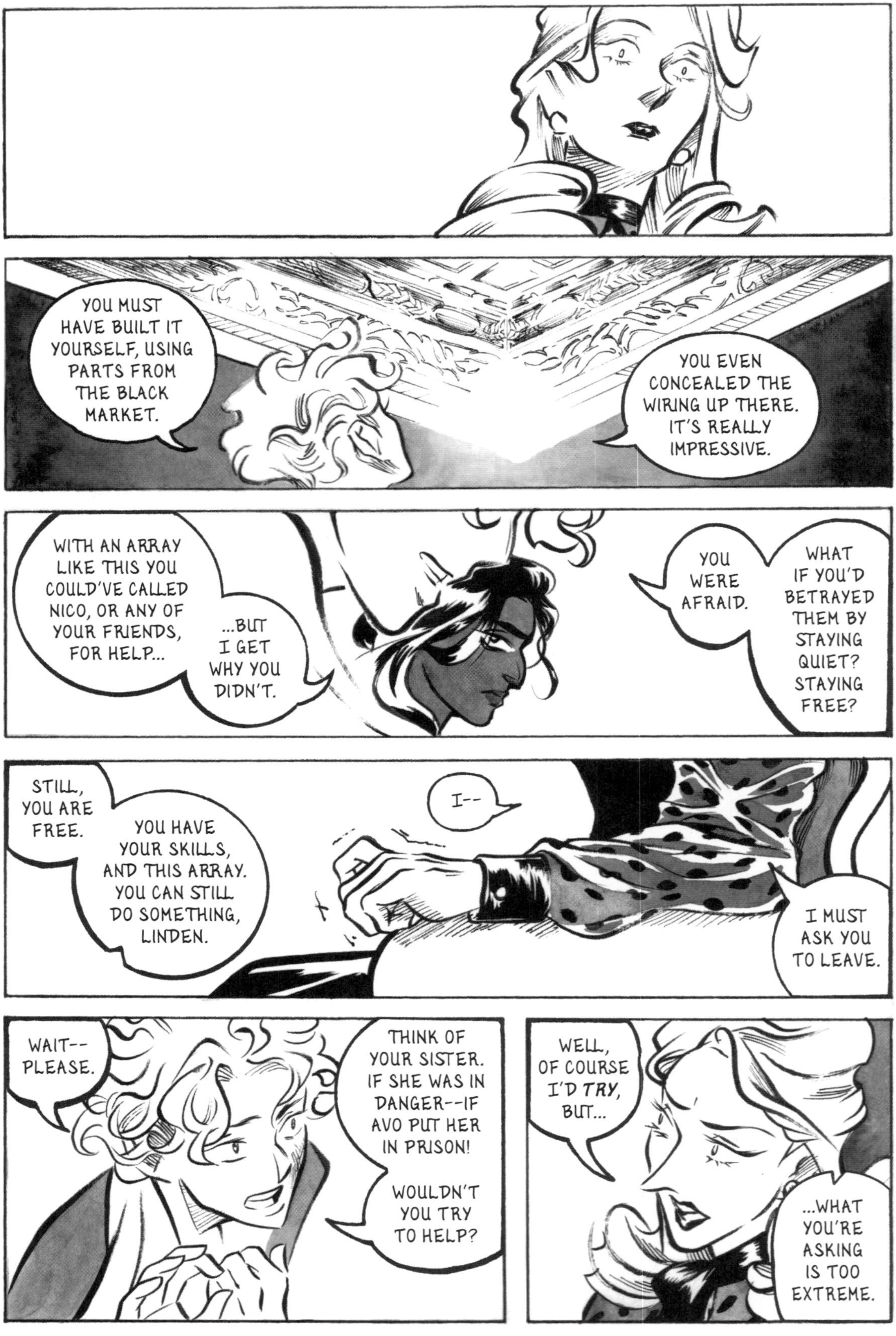
YOU MUST HAVE BUILT IT YOURSELF, USING PARTS FROM THE BLACK MARKET.
YOU EVEN CONCEALED THE WIRING UP THERE. IT'S REALLY IMPRESSIVE.
WITH AN ARRAY LIKE THIS YOU COULD'VE CALLED NICO, OR ANY OF YOUR FRIENDS, FOR HELP...
...BUT I GET WHY YOU DIDN'T.
YOU WERE AFRAID.
WHAT IF YOU'D BETRAYED THEM BY STAYING QUIET? STAYING FREE?
STILL, YOU ARE FREE.
YOU HAVE YOUR SKILLS, AND THIS ARRAY. YOU CAN STILL DO SOMETHING, LINDEN.
I--
I MUST ASK YOU TO LEAVE.
WAIT-- PLEASE.
THINK OF YOUR SISTER. IF SHE WAS IN DANGER--IF AVO PUT HER IN PRISON!
WOULDN'T YOU TRY TO HELP?
WELL, OF COURSE I'D *TRY*, BUT...
...WHAT YOU'RE ASKING IS TOO EXTREME.

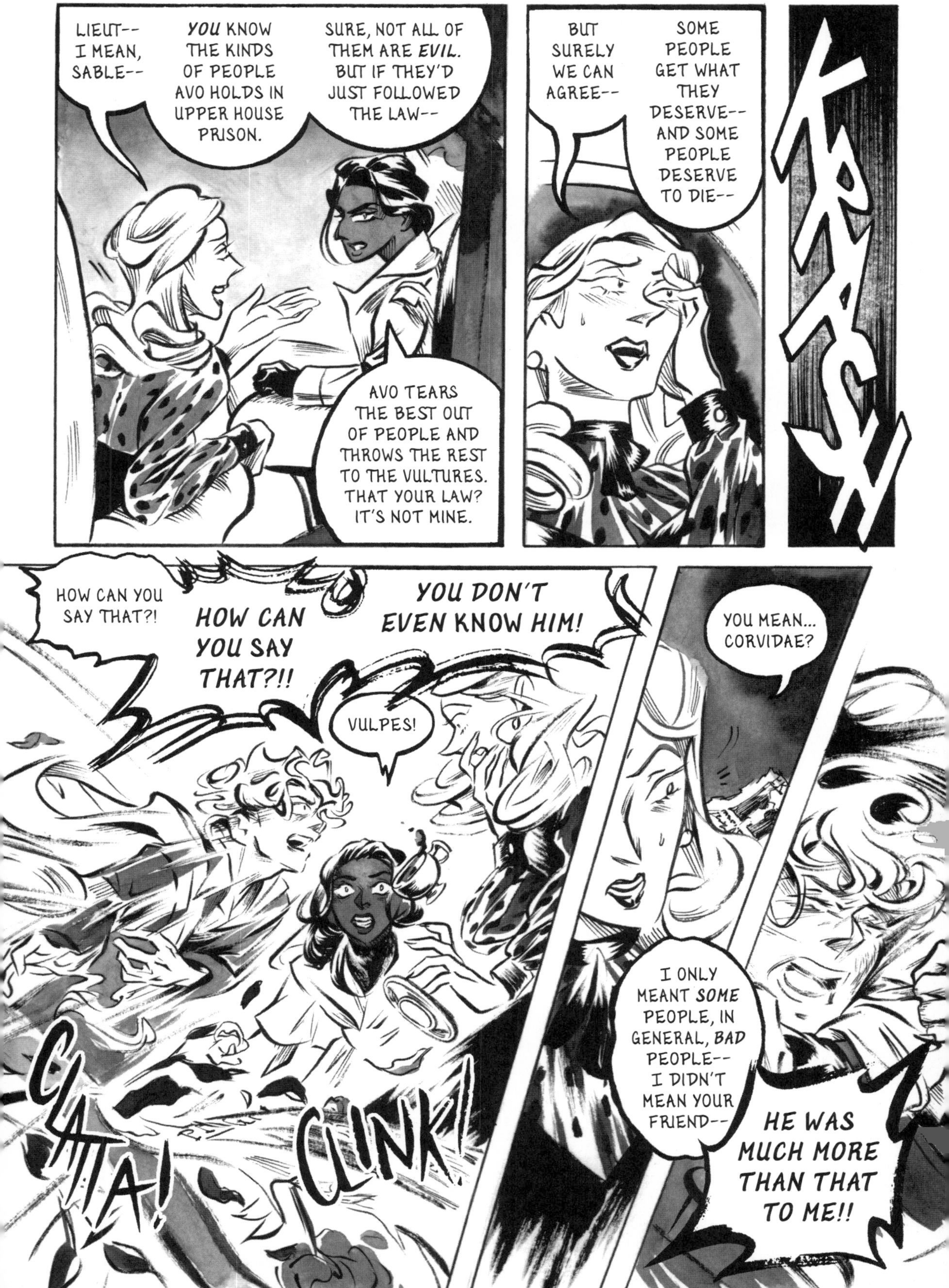
LIEUT-- I MEAN, SABLE--
YOU KNOW THE KINDS OF PEOPLE AVO HOLDS IN UPPER HOUSE PRISON.
SURE, NOT ALL OF THEM ARE *EVIL*. BUT IF THEY'D JUST FOLLOWED THE LAW--
AVO TEARS THE BEST OUT OF PEOPLE AND THROWS THE REST TO THE VULTURES. THAT YOUR LAW? IT'S NOT MINE.
BUT SURELY WE CAN AGREE--
SOME PEOPLE GET WHAT THEY DESERVE-- AND SOME PEOPLE DESERVE TO DIE--
KRACK
HOW CAN YOU SAY THAT?!
HOW CAN YOU SAY THAT?!!
YOU DON'T EVEN KNOW HIM!
VULPES!
YOU MEAN... CORVIDAE?
CLATTA!
CLINK!
I ONLY MEANT *SOME* PEOPLE, IN GENERAL, *BAD* PEOPLE-- I DIDN'T MEAN YOUR FRIEND--
HE WAS MUCH MORE THAN THAT TO ME!!

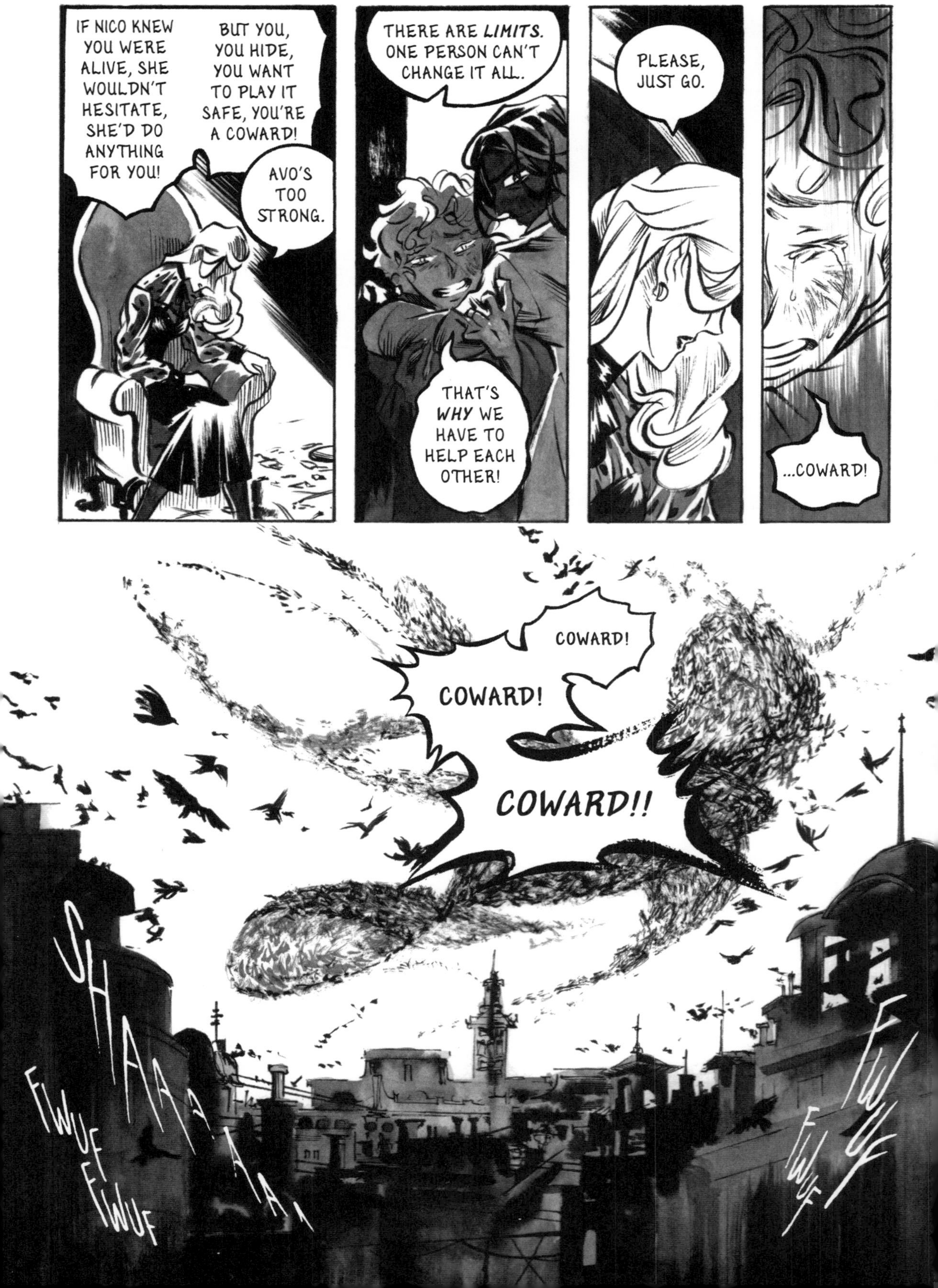
IF NICO KNEW YOU WERE ALIVE, SHE WOULDN'T HESITATE, SHE'D DO ANYTHING FOR YOU!
BUT YOU, YOU HIDE, YOU WANT TO PLAY IT SAFE, YOU'RE A COWARD!
AVO'S TOO STRONG.
THERE ARE *LIMITS*. ONE PERSON CAN'T CHANGE IT ALL.
THAT'S *WHY* WE HAVE TO HELP EACH OTHER!
PLEASE, JUST GO.
...COWARD!
COWARD!
COWARD!
COWARD!!
SHAAAAAA
FWUF FWUF
FWUF
FWUF

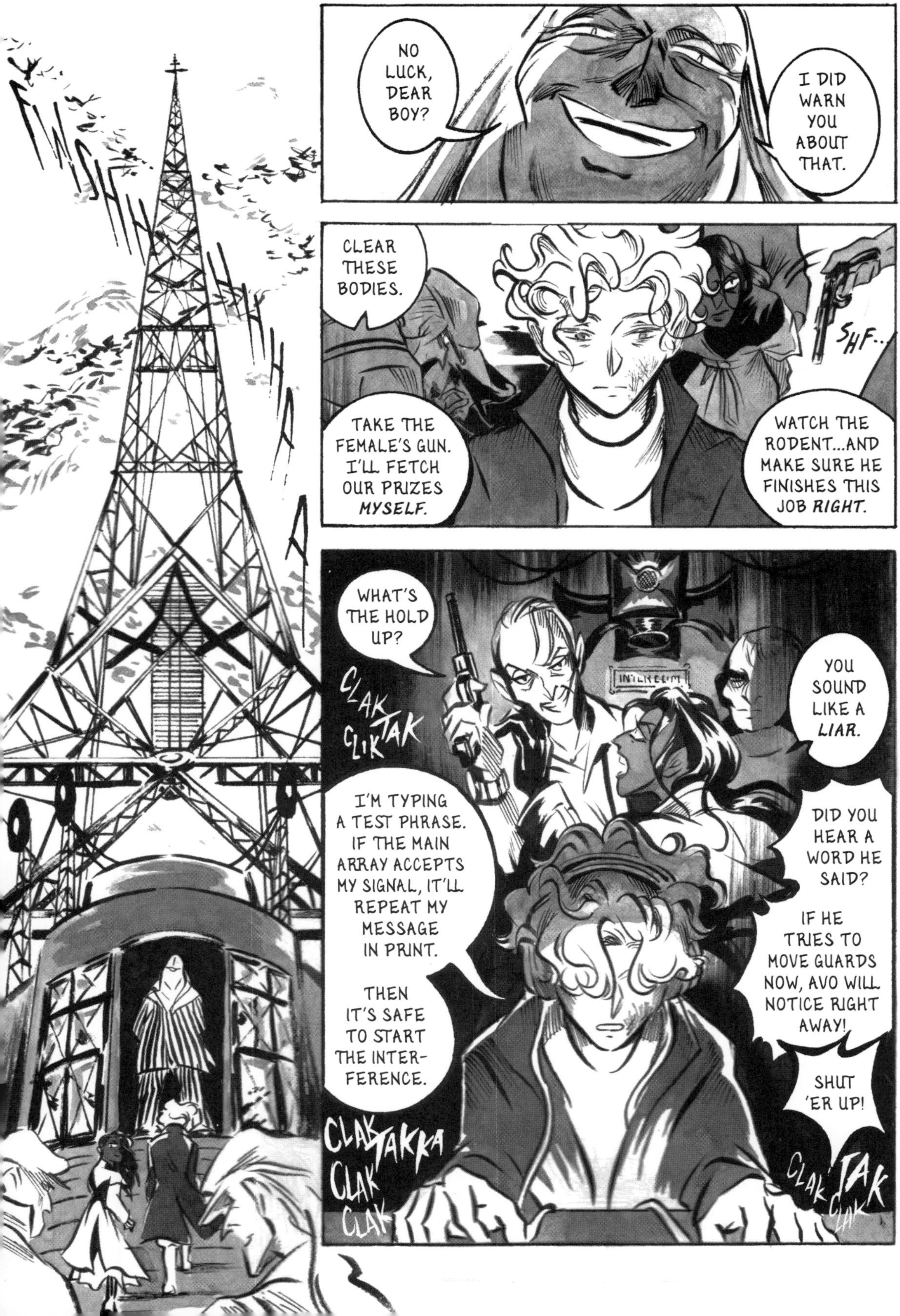

NO LUCK, DEAR BOY?
I DID WARN YOU ABOUT THAT.
CLEAR THESE BODIES.
SHF..
TAKE THE FEMALE'S GUN. I'LL FETCH OUR PRIZES *MYSELF*.
WATCH THE RODENT...AND MAKE SURE HE FINISHES THIS JOB *RIGHT*.
WHAT'S THE HOLD UP?
CLAK TAK CLIK TAK
YOU SOUND LIKE A *LIAR*.
I'M TYPING A TEST PHRASE. IF THE MAIN ARRAY ACCEPTS MY SIGNAL, IT'LL REPEAT MY MESSAGE IN PRINT.
THEN IT'S SAFE TO START THE INTER-FERENCE.
DID YOU HEAR A WORD HE SAID?
IF HE TRIES TO MOVE GUARDS NOW, AVO WILL NOTICE RIGHT AWAY!
SHUT 'ER UP!
CLAK TAKKA CLAK CLAK
CLAK TAK CLAK

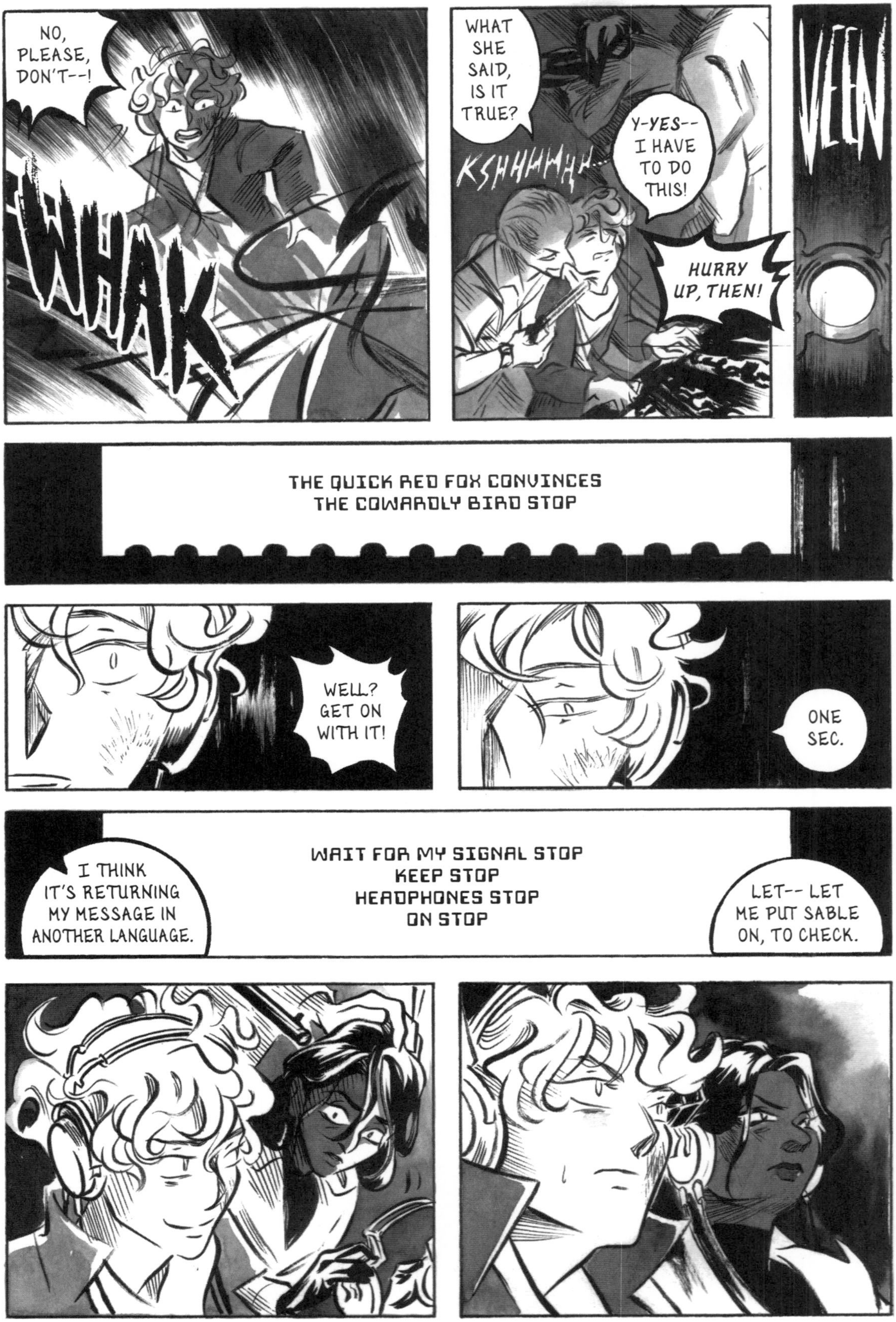
NO, PLEASE, DON'T--!
WHAK
WHAT SHE SAID, IS IT TRUE?
KSHHHHH...
Y-YES-- I HAVE TO DO THIS!
HURRY UP, THEN!
VEEN
THE QUICK RED FOX CONVINCES
THE COWARDLY BIRD STOP
WELL? GET ON WITH IT!
ONE SEC.
I THINK IT'S RETURNING MY MESSAGE IN ANOTHER LANGUAGE.
WAIT FOR MY SIGNAL STOP
KEEP STOP
HEADPHONES STOP
ON STOP
LET-- LET ME PUT SABLE ON, TO CHECK.

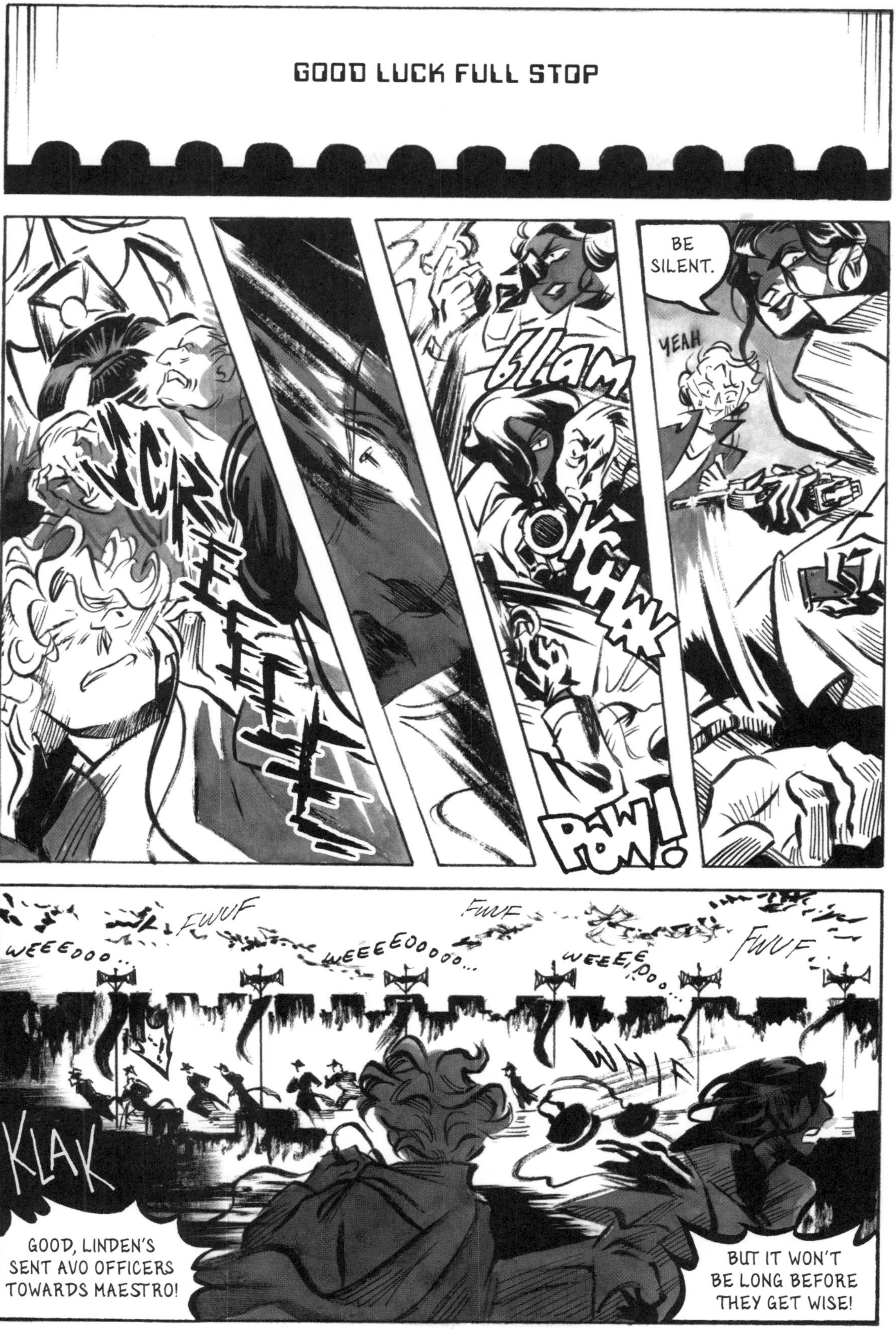
GOOD LUCK FULL STOP
BE SILENT.
YEAH
BLAM
POW POW!
FWUF
FWUF
FWUF
WEEEOOO...
WEEEEOOOOO...
WEEEEOOO...
KLAK
GOOD, LINDEN'S SENT AVO OFFICERS TOWARDS MAESTRO!
BUT IT WON'T BE LONG BEFORE THEY GET WISE!

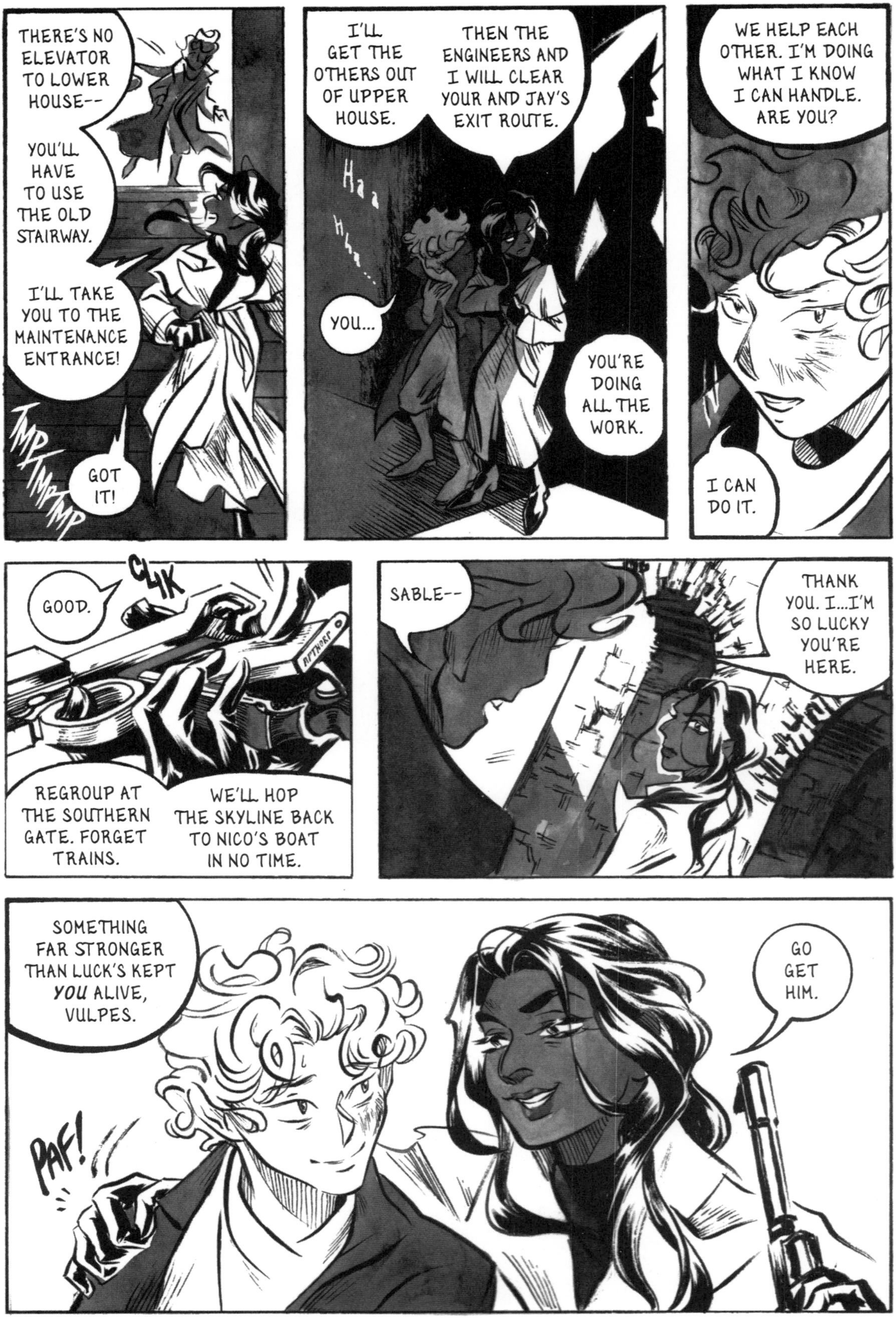
THERE'S NO ELEVATOR TO LOWER HOUSE--
YOU'LL HAVE TO USE THE OLD STAIRWAY.
I'LL TAKE YOU TO THE MAINTENANCE ENTRANCE!
TMPTMPTMP
GOT IT!
I'LL GET THE OTHERS OUT OF UPPER HOUSE.
THEN THE ENGINEERS AND I WILL CLEAR YOUR AND JAY'S EXIT ROUTE.
Haa Hha...
YOU...
YOU'RE DOING ALL THE WORK.
WE HELP EACH OTHER. I'M DOING WHAT I KNOW I CAN HANDLE. ARE YOU?
I CAN DO IT.
GOOD.
CLAK
REGROUP AT THE SOUTHERN GATE. FORGET TRAINS.
WE'LL HOP THE SKYLINE BACK TO NICO'S BOAT IN NO TIME.
SABLE--
THANK YOU. I...I'M SO LUCKY YOU'RE HERE.
SOMETHING FAR STRONGER THAN LUCK'S KEPT *YOU* ALIVE, VULPES.
GO GET HIM.
PAF!

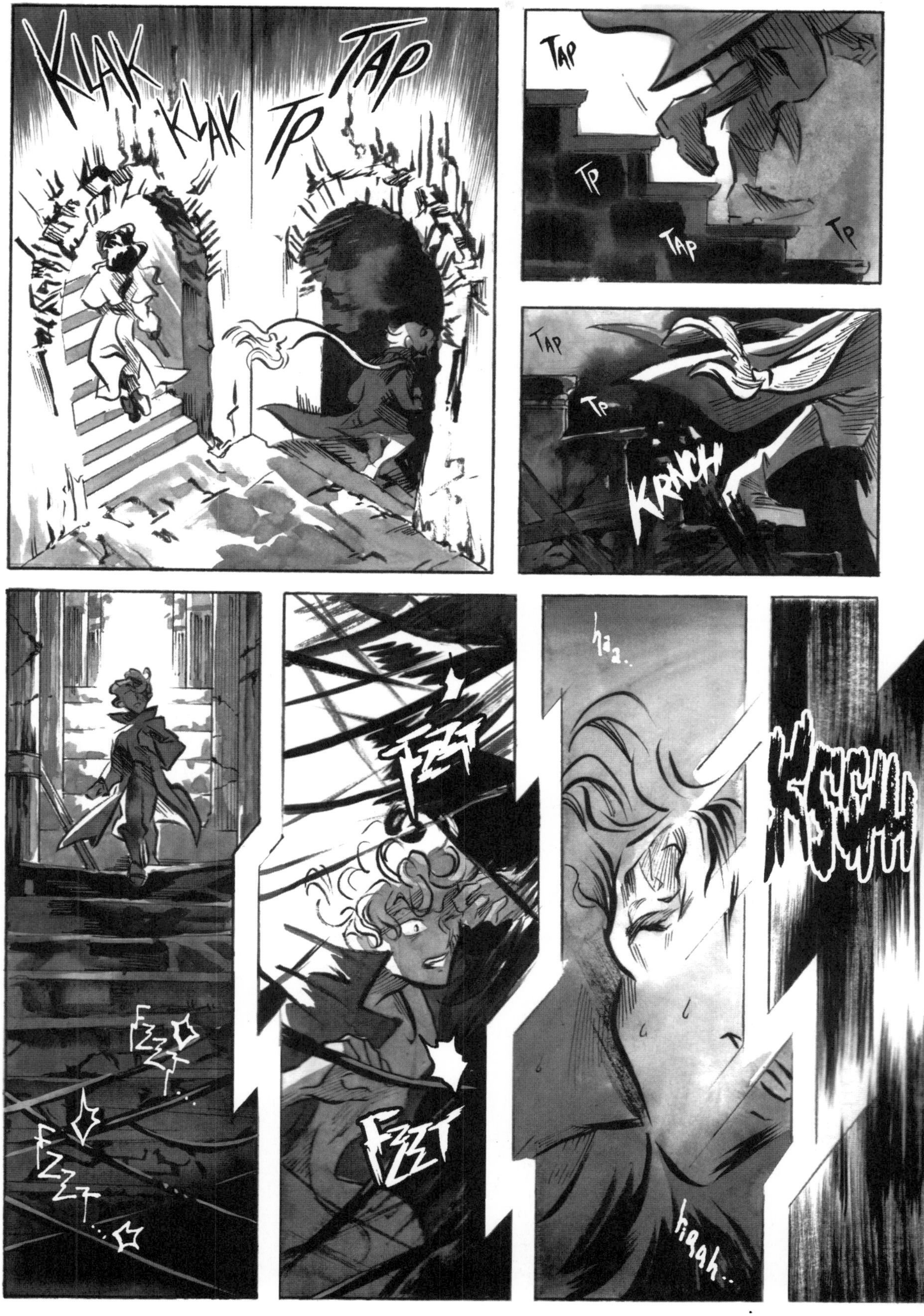
KLAK
KLAK
TAP
TP
TAP
TP
TAP
TP
TAP
TP
KRNCH
FZZZT...
FZZZT...
FZZT
FZZT
haa..

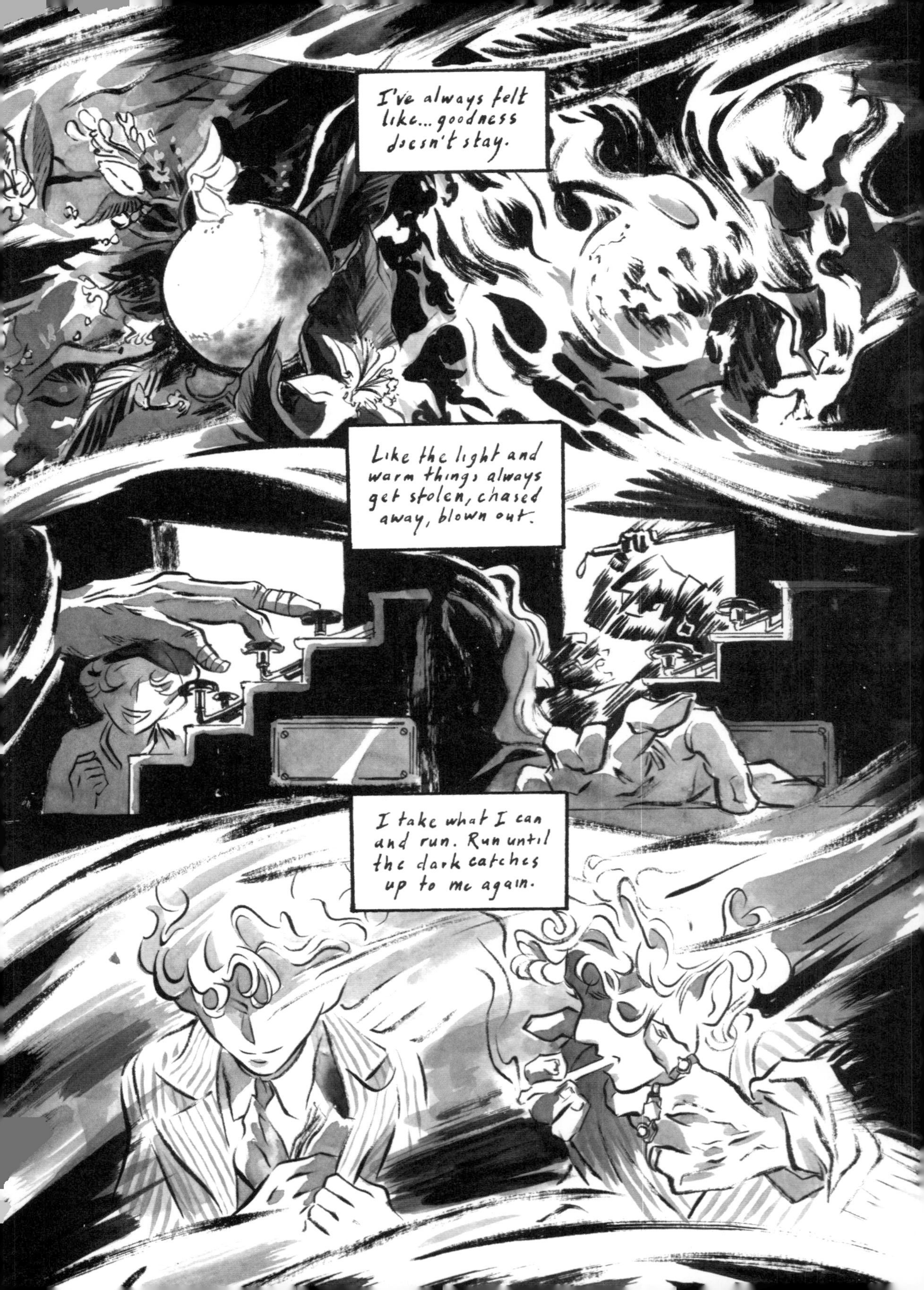
I've always felt like... goodness doesn't stay.
Like the light and warm things always get stolen, chased away, blown out.
I take what I can and run. Run until the dark catches up to me again.

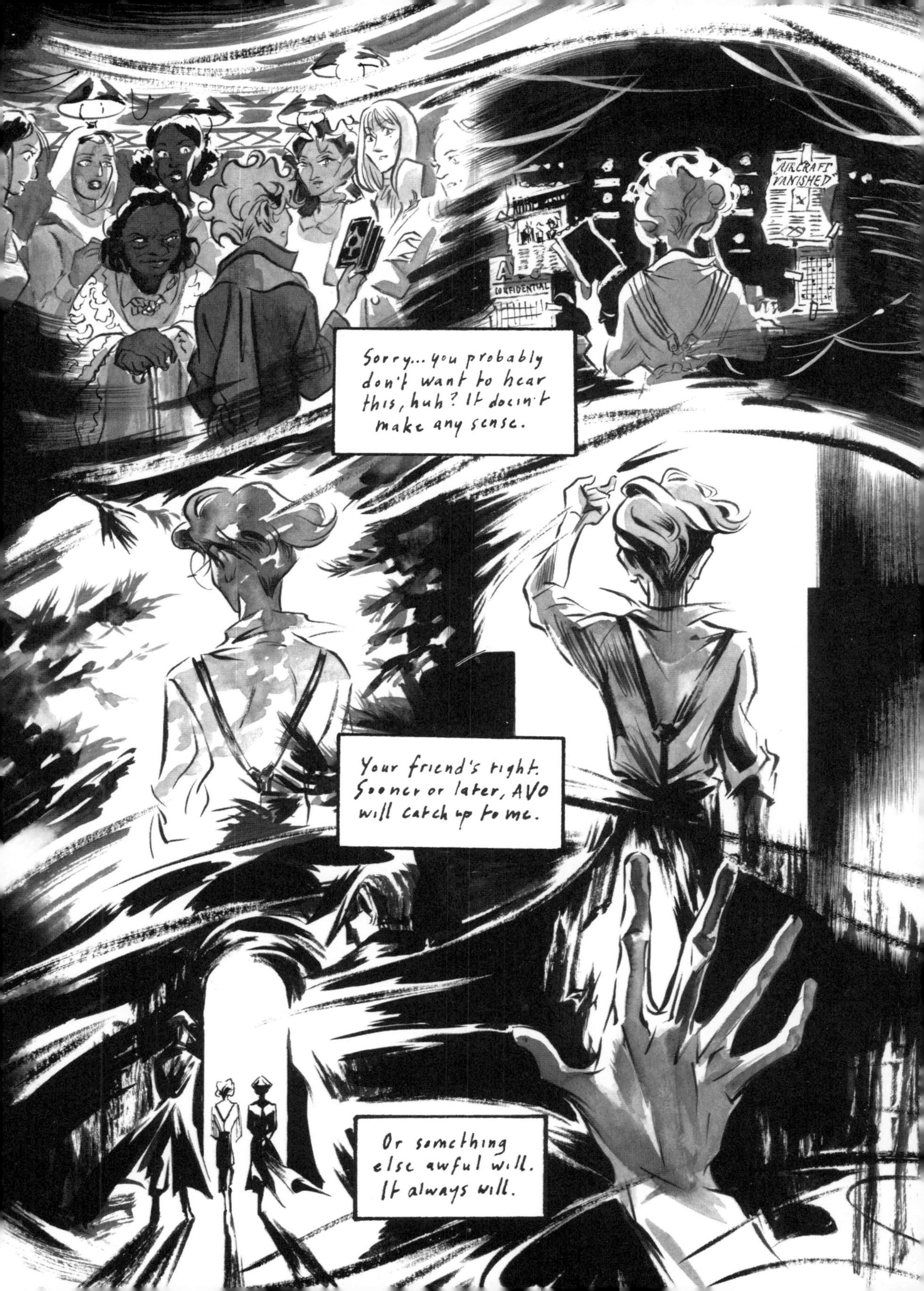
AIRCRAFT VANISHED
CONFIDENTIAL
Sorry... you probably don't want to hear this, huh? It doesn't make any sense.
Your friend's right. Sooner or later, AVO will catch up to me.
Or something else awful will. It always will.

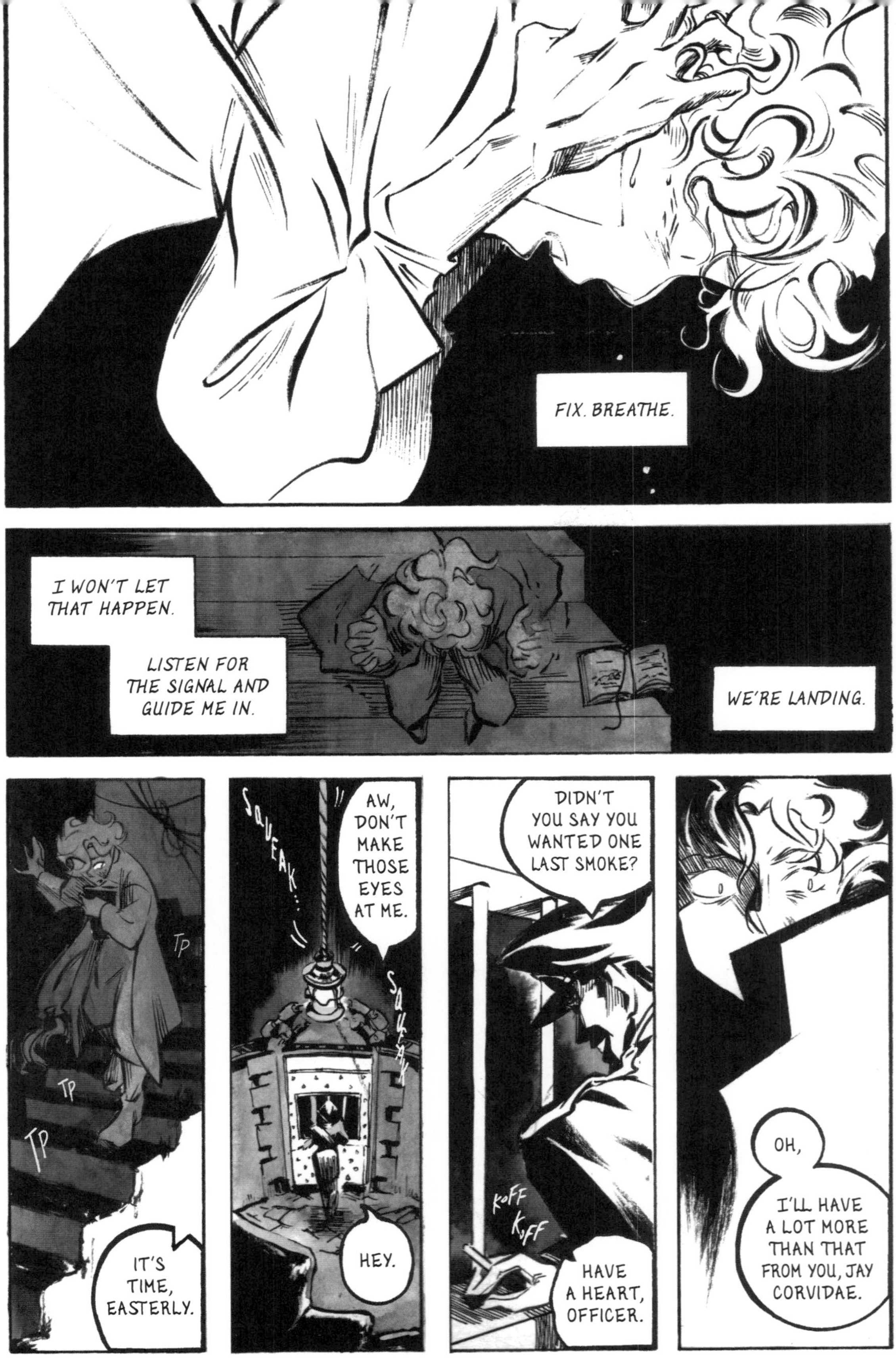
FIX. BREATHE.
I WON'T LET THAT HAPPEN.
LISTEN FOR THE SIGNAL AND GUIDE ME IN.
WE'RE LANDING.
TP
TP
TP
IT'S TIME, EASTERLY.
SQUEAK...
SQUEAK
AW, DON'T MAKE THOSE EYES AT ME.
HEY.
DIDN'T YOU SAY YOU WANTED ONE LAST SMOKE?
KOFF
KOFF
HAVE A HEART, OFFICER.
OH,
I'LL HAVE A LOT MORE THAN THAT FROM YOU, JAY CORVIDAE.

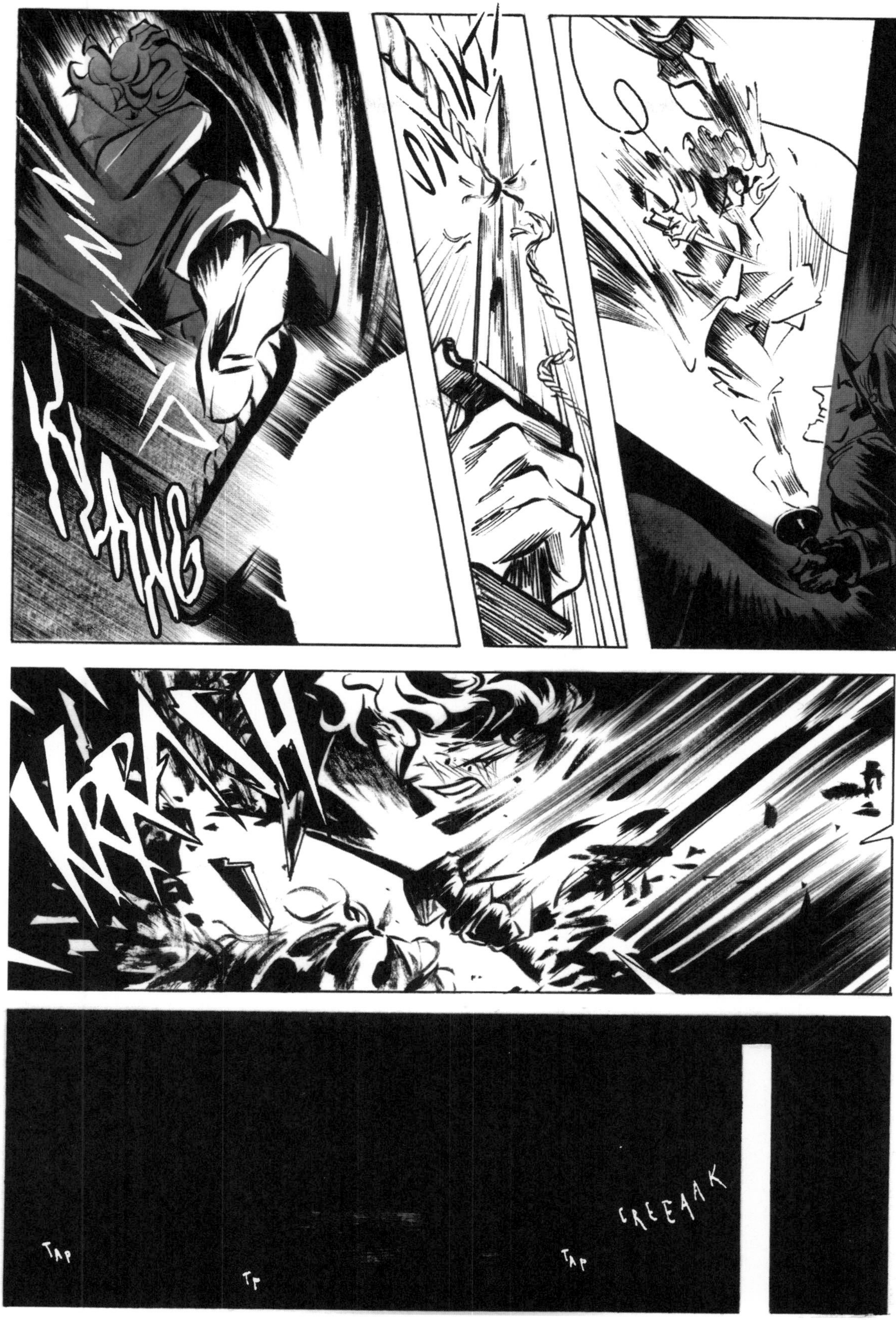
KLANG
SNIKT!
TAP
TP
TAP
CREEAAK

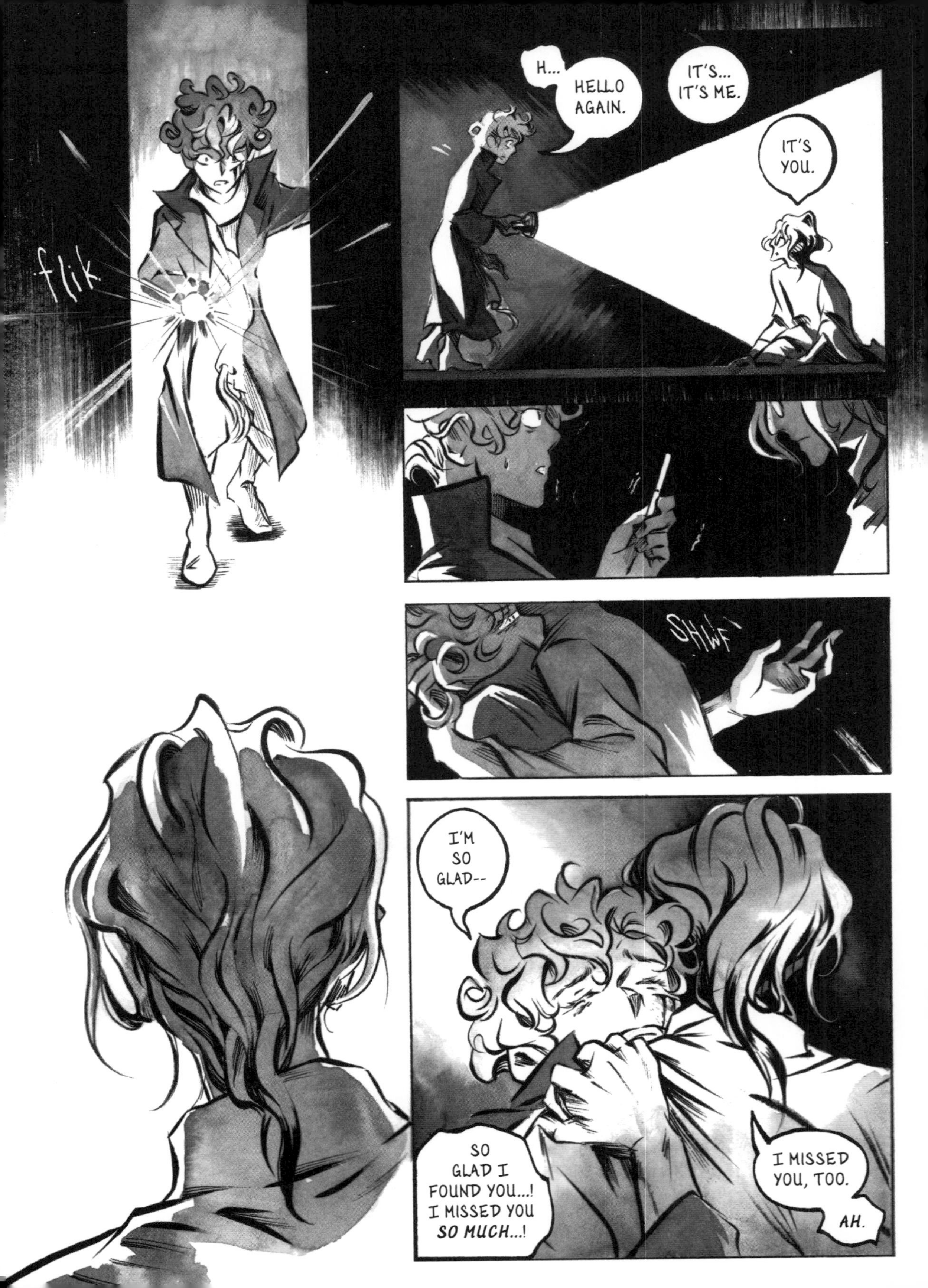
flik
H...
HELLO AGAIN.
IT'S... IT'S ME.
IT'S YOU.
SHWF
I'M SO GLAD--
SO GLAD I FOUND YOU...! I MISSED YOU *SO MUCH*...!
I MISSED YOU, TOO.
AH.

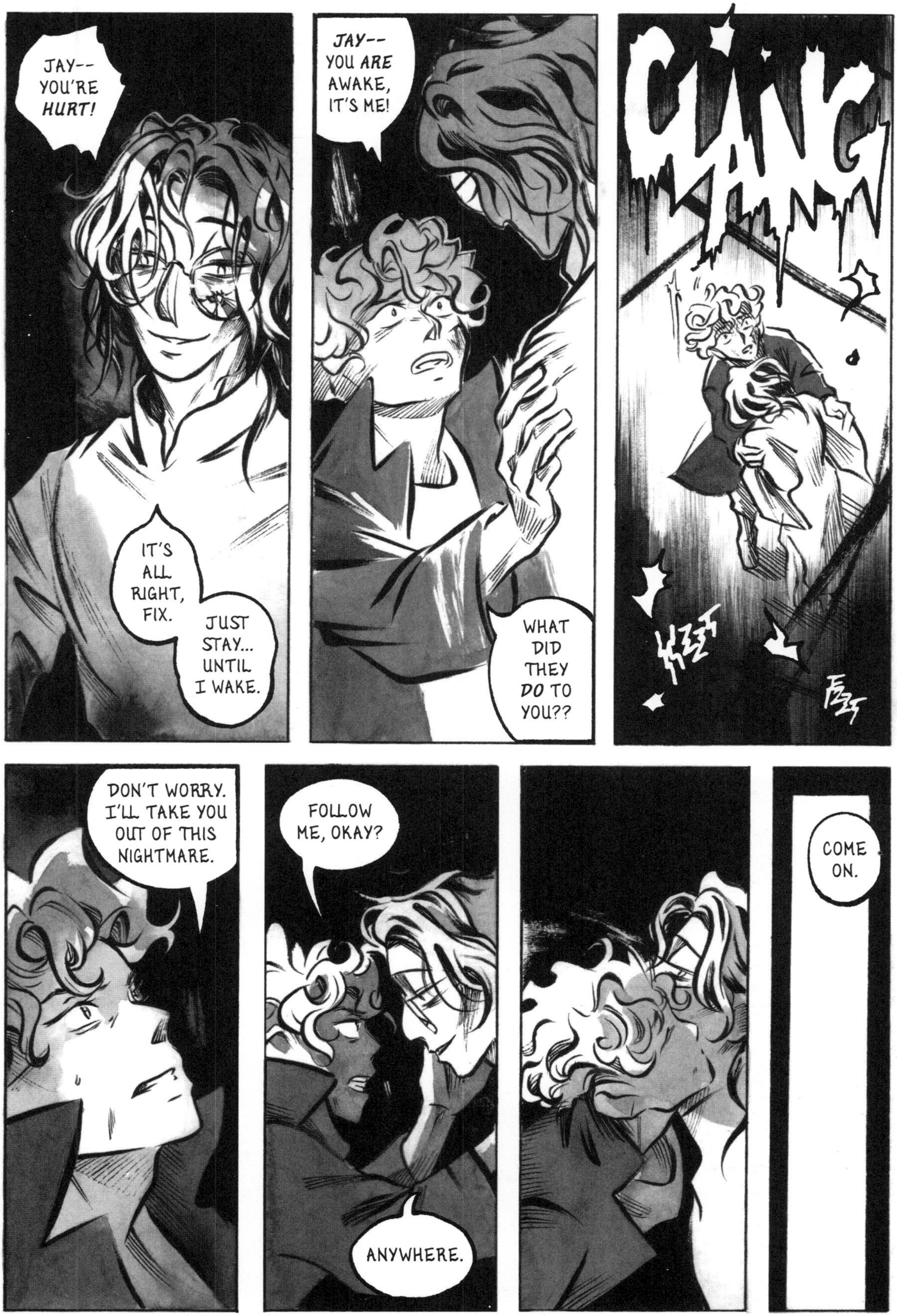
JAY-- YOU'RE HURT!
IT'S ALL RIGHT, FIX.
JUST STAY... UNTIL I WAKE.
JAY-- YOU ARE AWAKE, IT'S ME!
WHAT DID THEY DO TO YOU??
CLANG
DON'T WORRY. I'LL TAKE YOU OUT OF THIS NIGHTMARE.
FOLLOW ME, OKAY?
ANYWHERE.
COME ON.

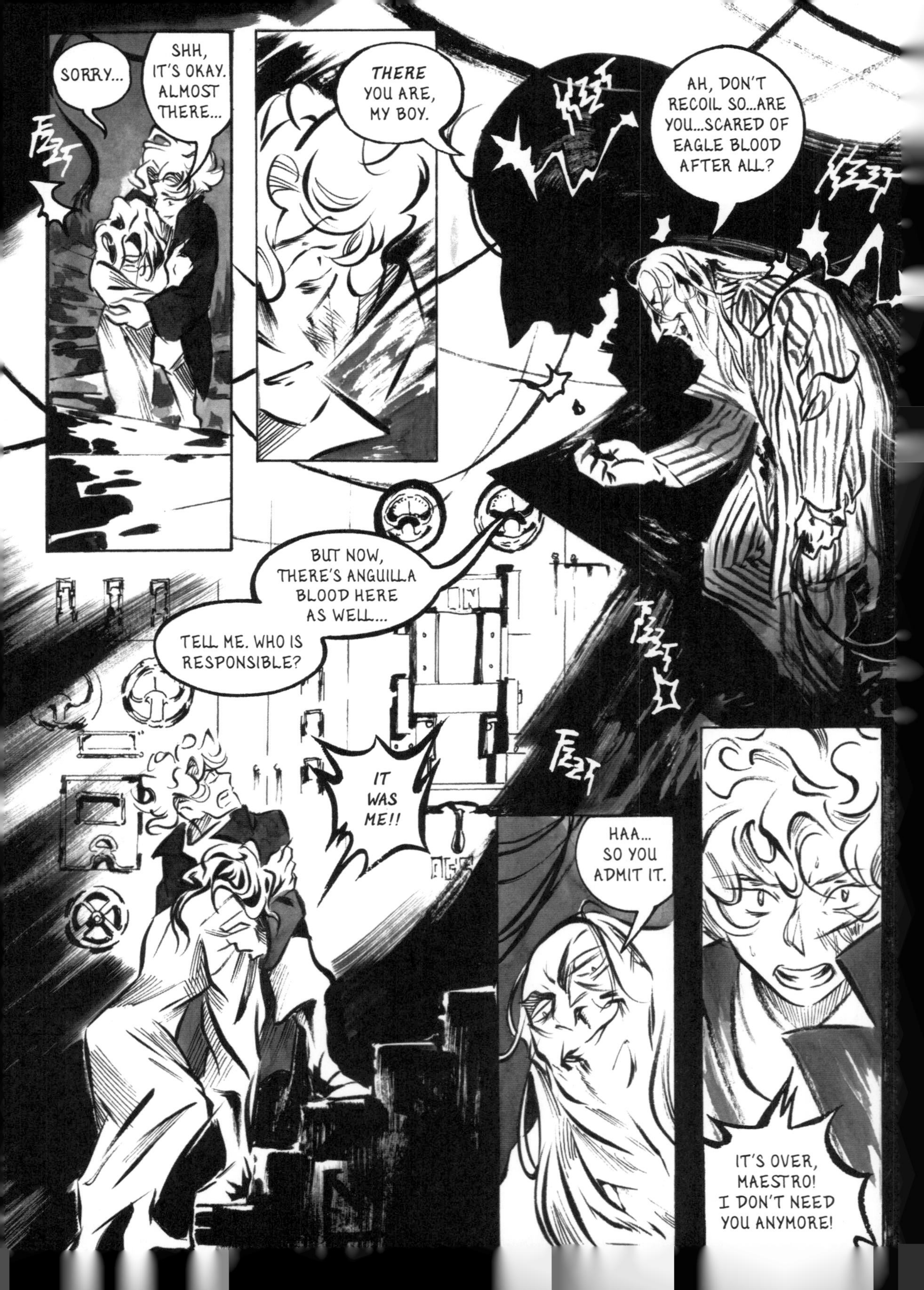
SORRY...
SHH, IT'S OKAY. ALMOST THERE...
FZZZT
THERE YOU ARE, MY BOY.
KZZZT
AH, DON'T RECOIL SO...ARE YOU...SCARED OF EAGLE BLOOD AFTER ALL?
KZZZT
BUT NOW, THERE'S ANGUILLA BLOOD HERE AS WELL....
TELL ME. WHO IS RESPONSIBLE?
FZZZT
IT WAS ME!!
FZZZT
HAA... SO YOU ADMIT IT.
IT'S OVER, MAESTRO! I DON'T NEED YOU ANYMORE!

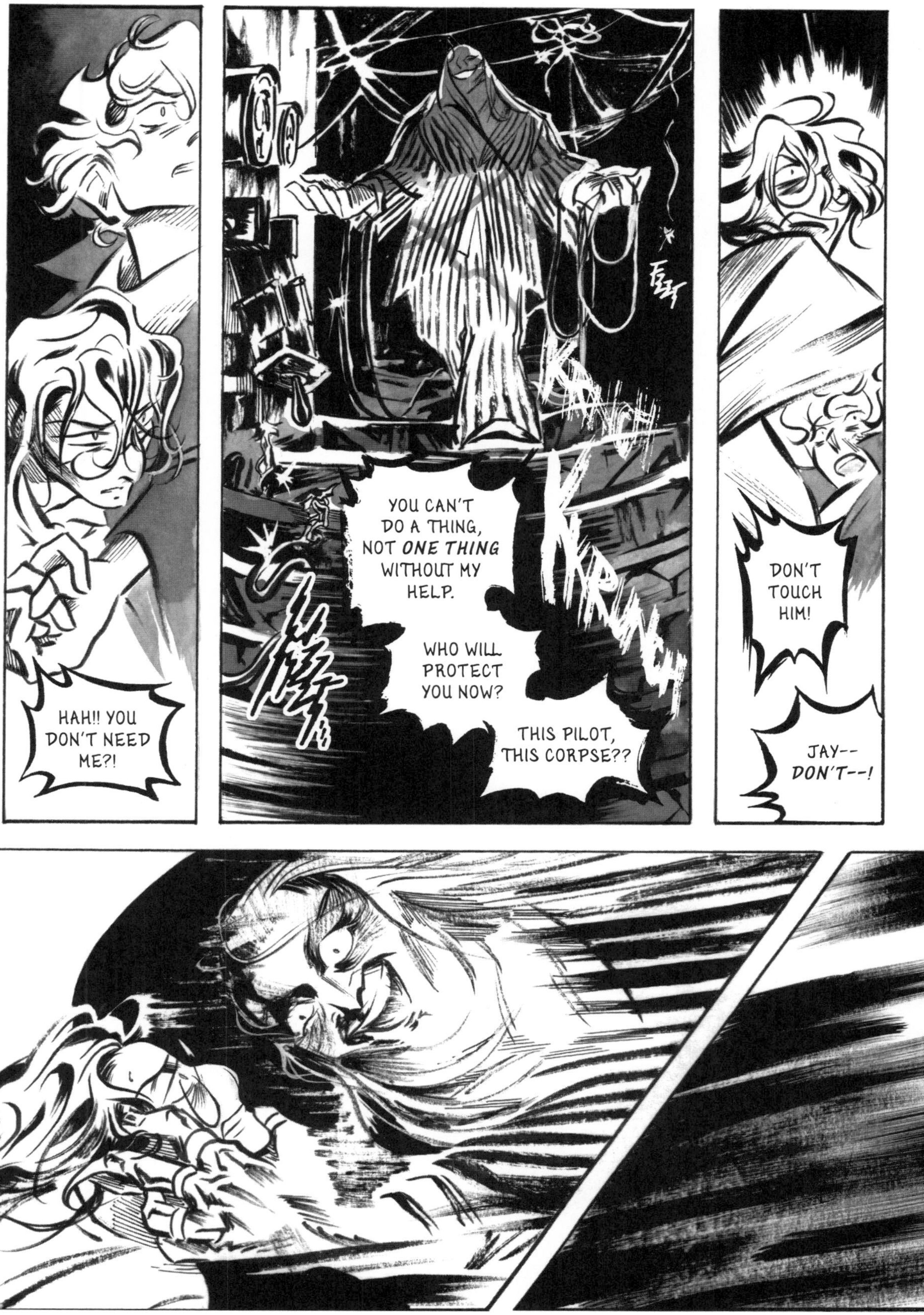
HAH!! YOU DON'T NEED ME?!
YOU CAN'T DO A THING, NOT *ONE THING* WITHOUT MY HELP.
WHO WILL PROTECT YOU NOW?
THIS PILOT, THIS CORPSE??
DON'T TOUCH HIM!
JAY-- *DON'T--!*

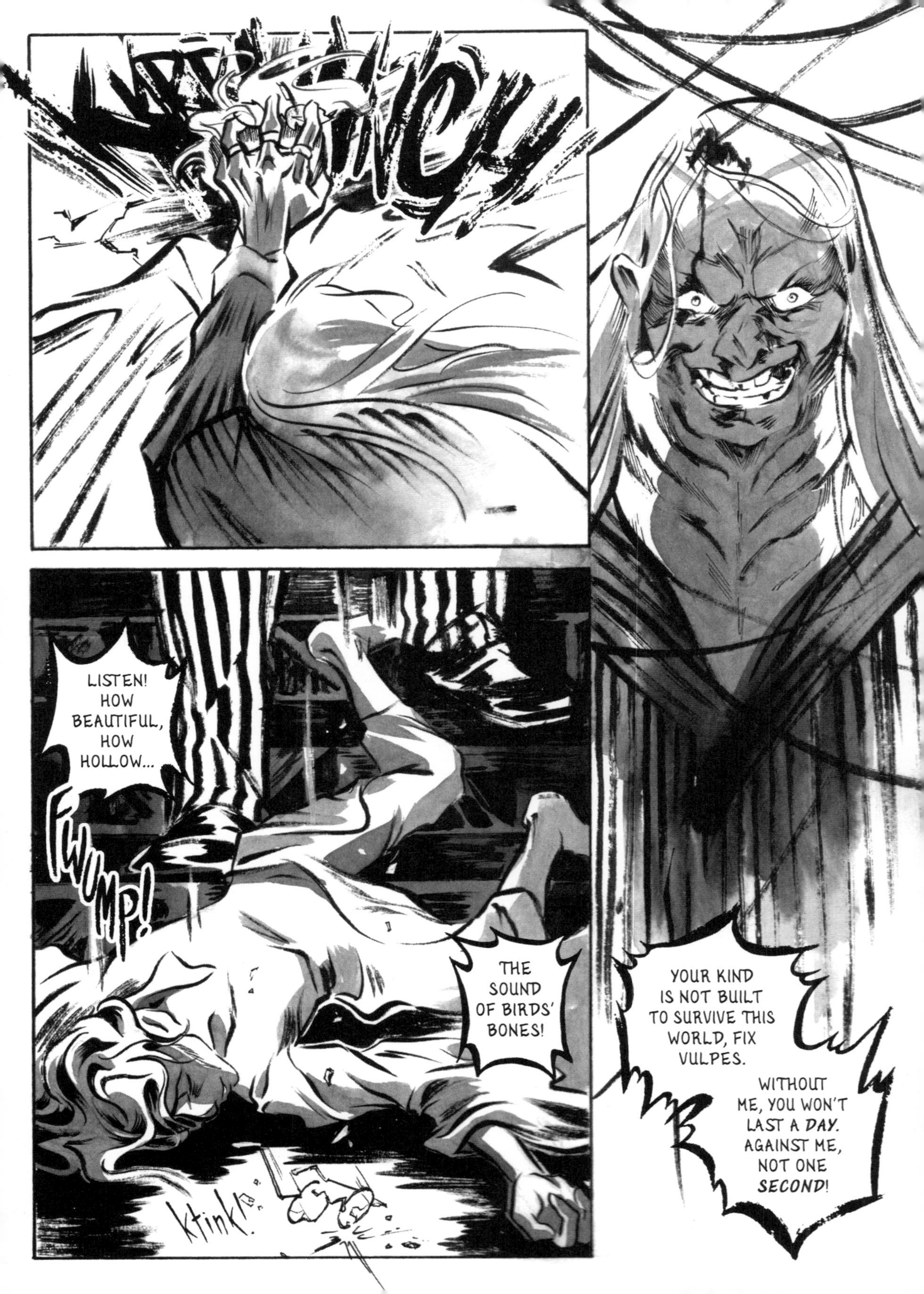
LISTEN! HOW BEAUTIFUL, HOW HOLLOW...
FWUMP!
THE SOUND OF BIRDS' BONES!
ktink!
YOUR KIND IS NOT BUILT TO SURVIVE THIS WORLD, FIX VULPES.
WITHOUT ME, YOU WON'T LAST A *DAY*. AGAINST ME, NOT ONE *SECOND*!

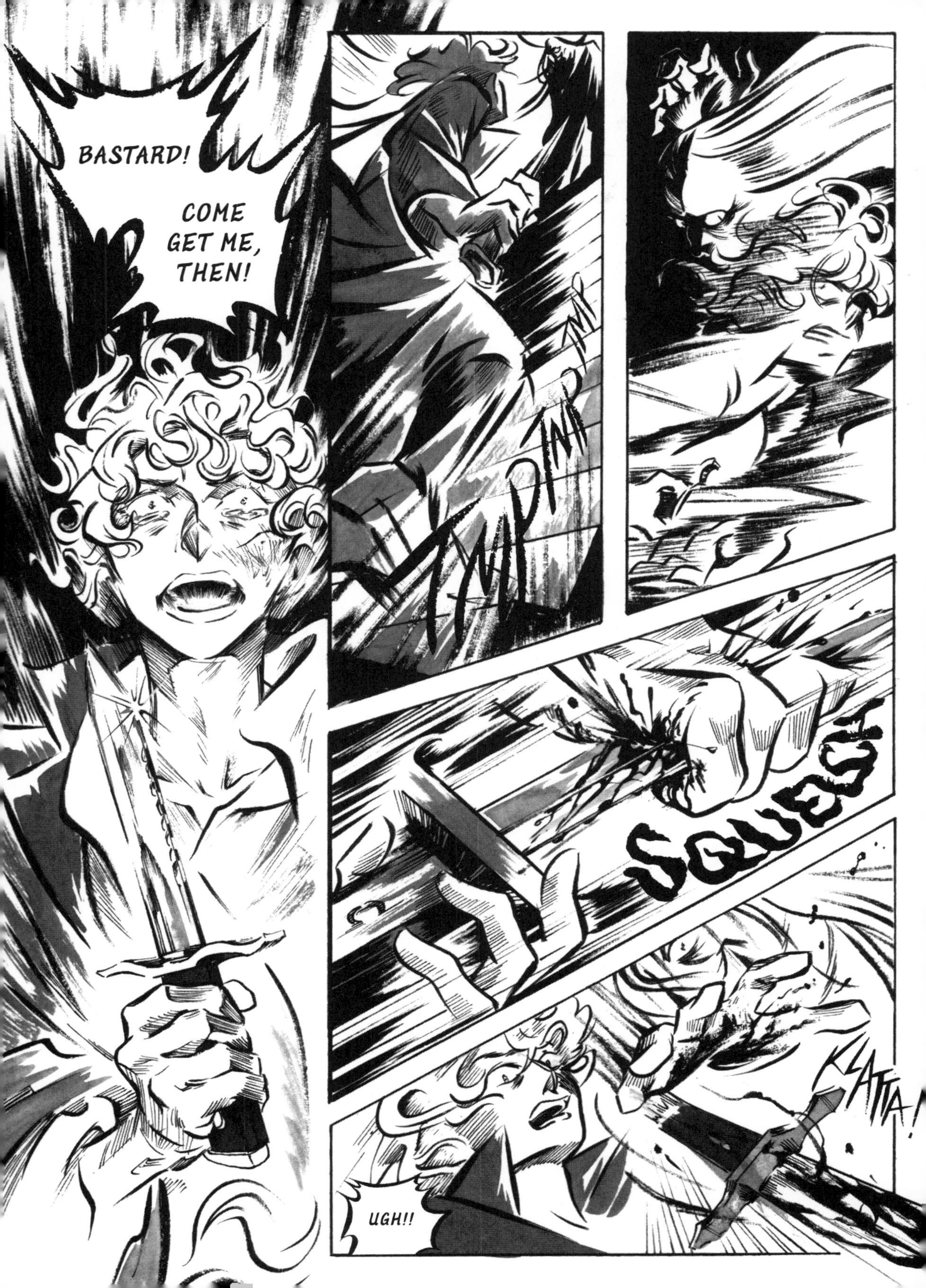
BASTARD!
COME GET ME, THEN!
THP THP
SQUEGT
KLATTA!
UGH!!

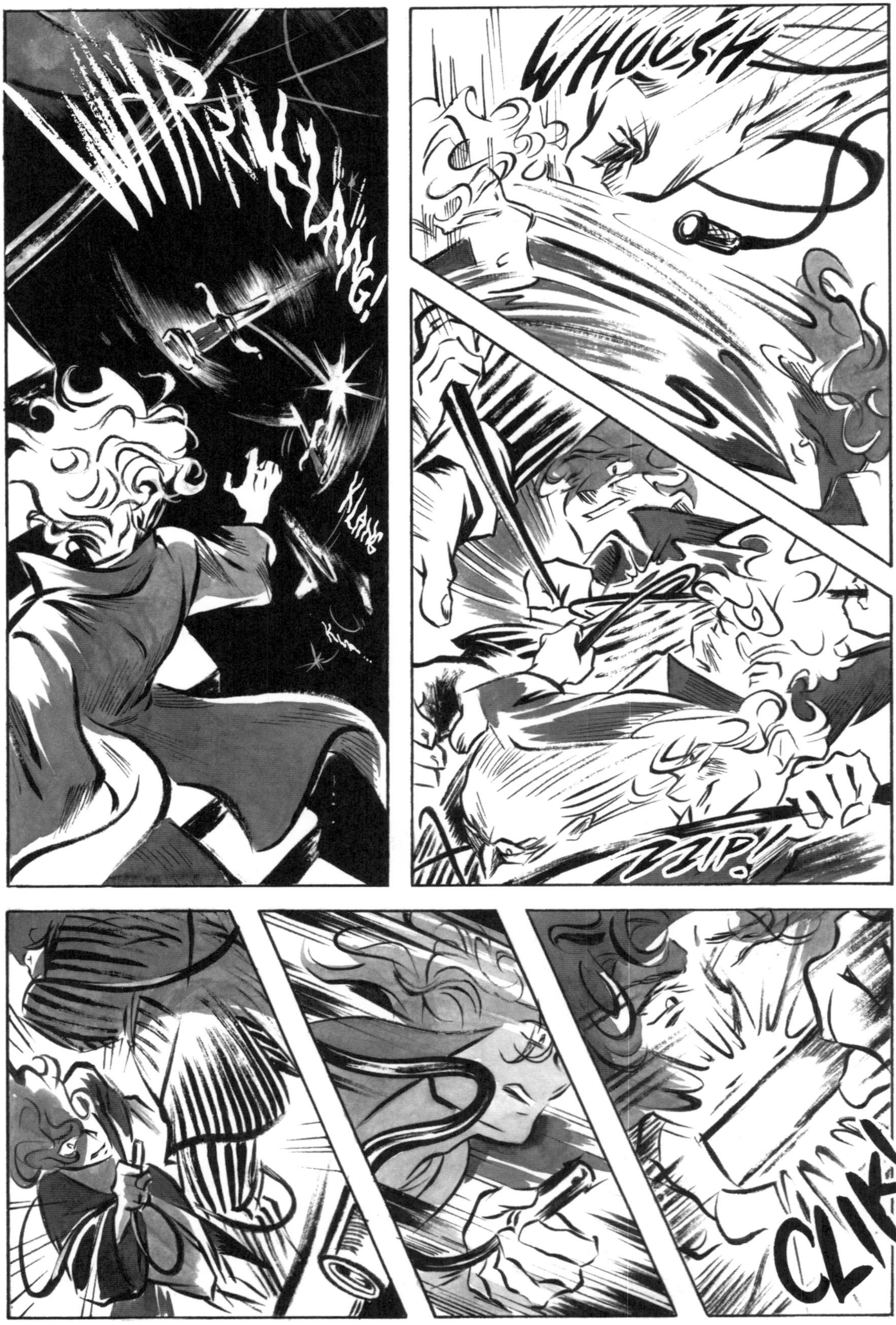
WIRKLANG!
KLANG
Klin...
WHOOSH
ZZIP!
CLIK!

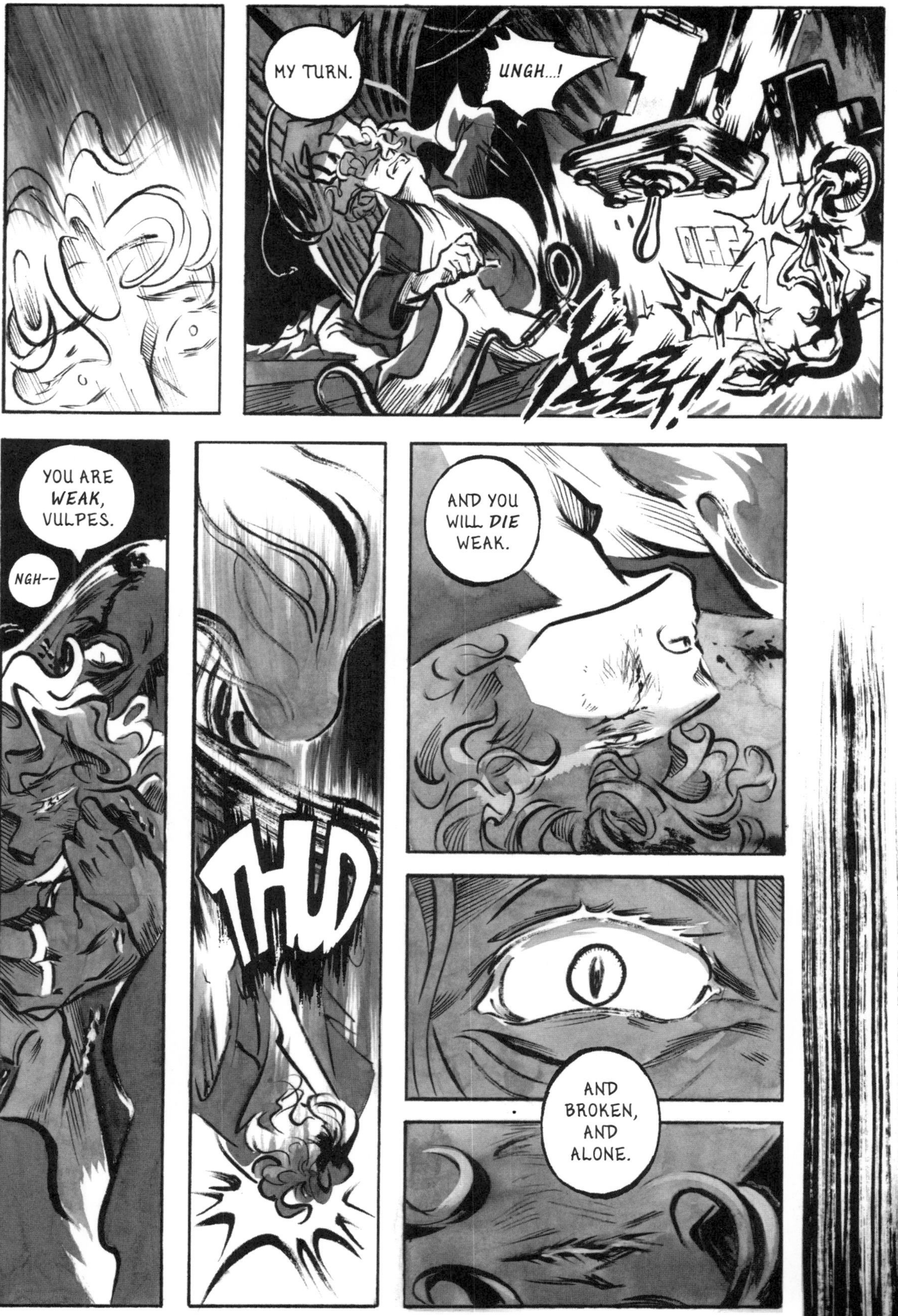
MY TURN.
UNGH...!
KRAKT!
YOU ARE WEAK, VULPES.
NGH--
THUD
AND YOU WILL DIE WEAK.
AND BROKEN, AND ALONE.

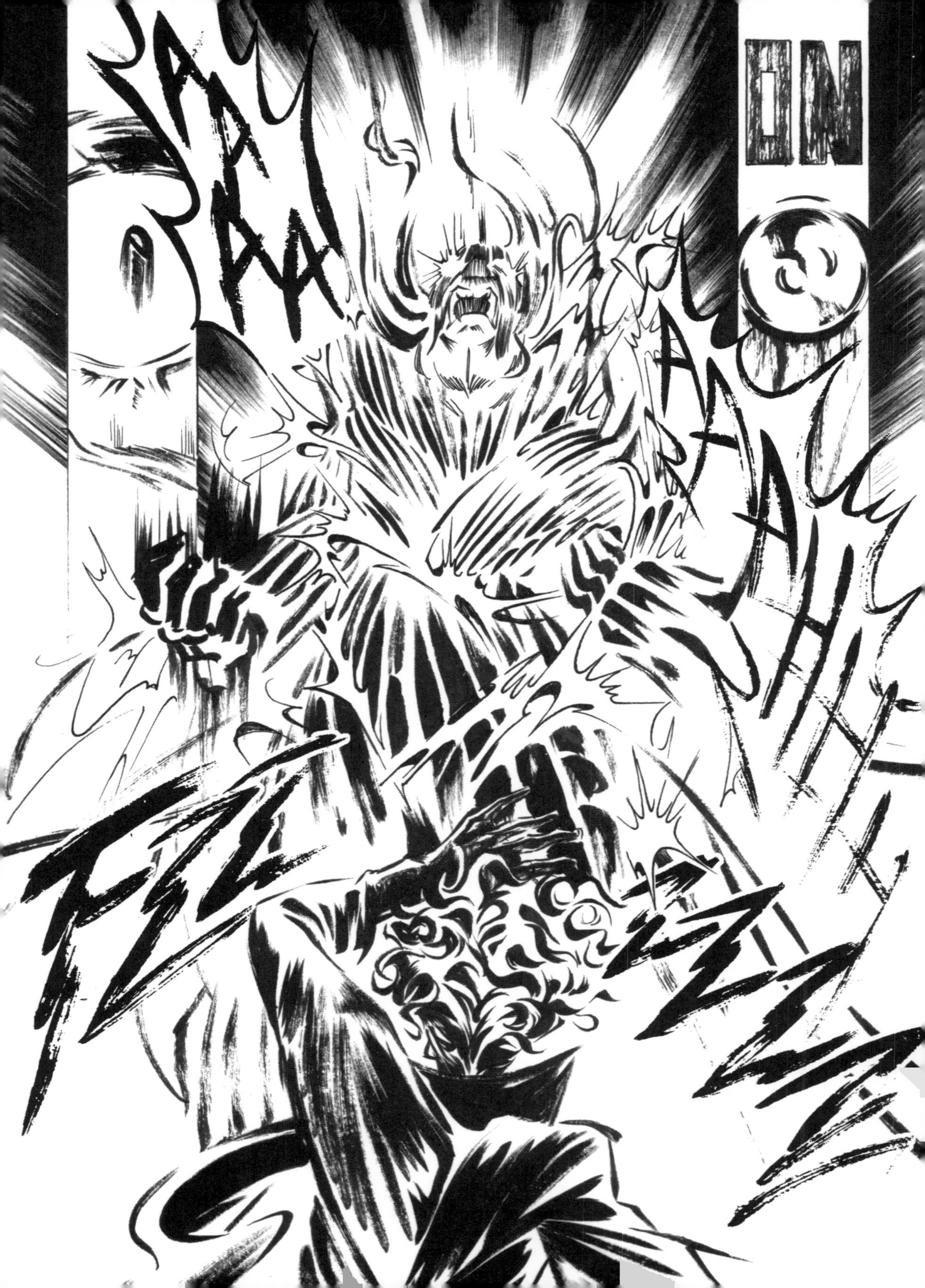

ON

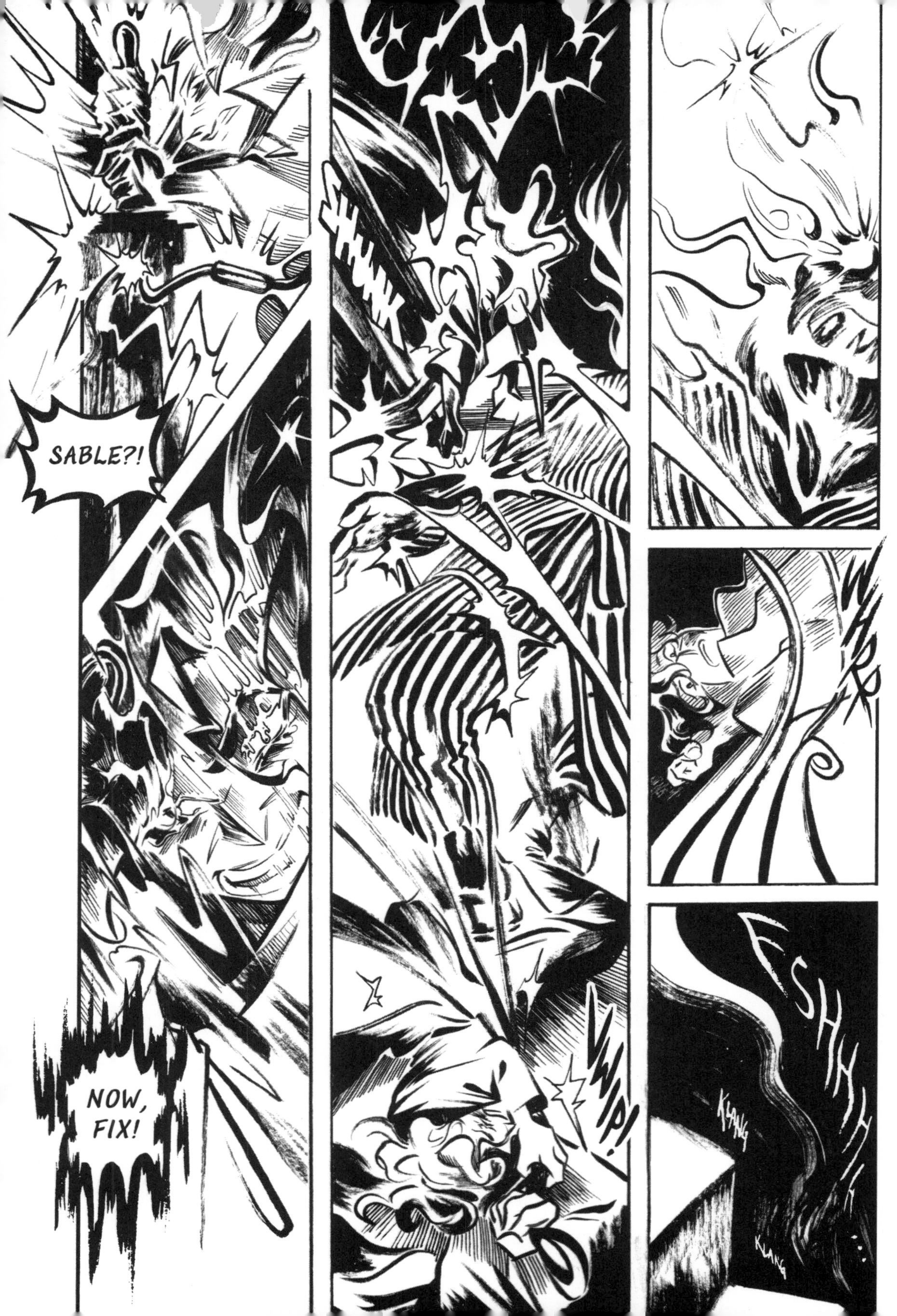
SABLE?!
NOW, FIX!
WHIP!
WHRR
FSHHHH...
KLANG
KLANG

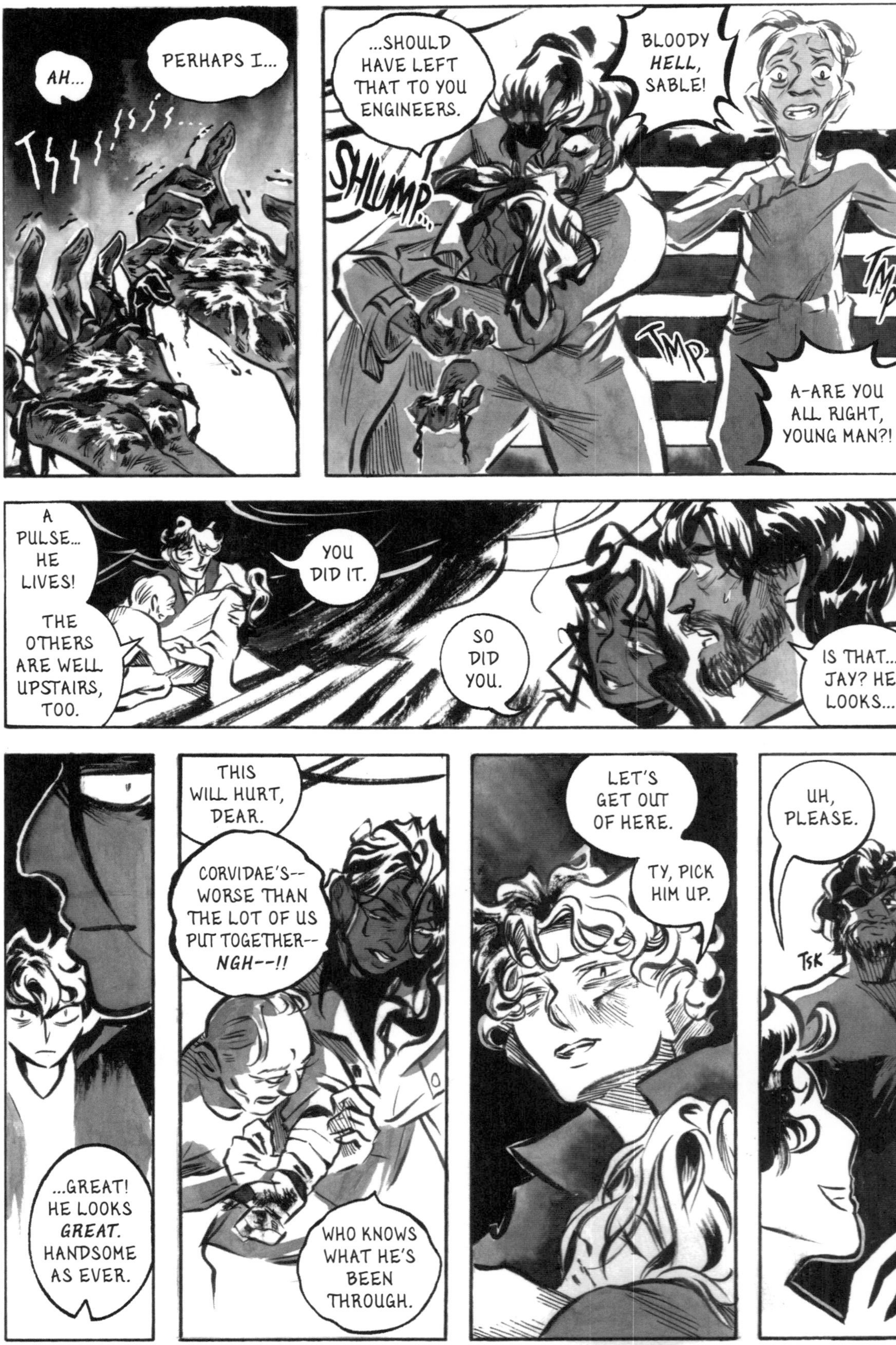
AH...
PERHAPS I...
TSSSSSSSS...
...SHOULD HAVE LEFT THAT TO YOU ENGINEERS.
SHLUMP...
BLOODY HELL, SABLE!
TMP
TMP
A-ARE YOU ALL RIGHT, YOUNG MAN?!
A PULSE... HE LIVES!
THE OTHERS ARE WELL UPSTAIRS, TOO.
YOU DID IT.
SO DID YOU.
IS THAT... JAY? HE LOOKS...
...GREAT! HE LOOKS GREAT. HANDSOME AS EVER.
THIS WILL HURT, DEAR.
CORVIDAE'S-- WORSE THAN THE LOT OF US PUT TOGETHER-- NGH--!!
WHO KNOWS WHAT HE'S BEEN THROUGH.
LET'S GET OUT OF HERE.
TY, PICK HIM UP.
UH, PLEASE.
TSK

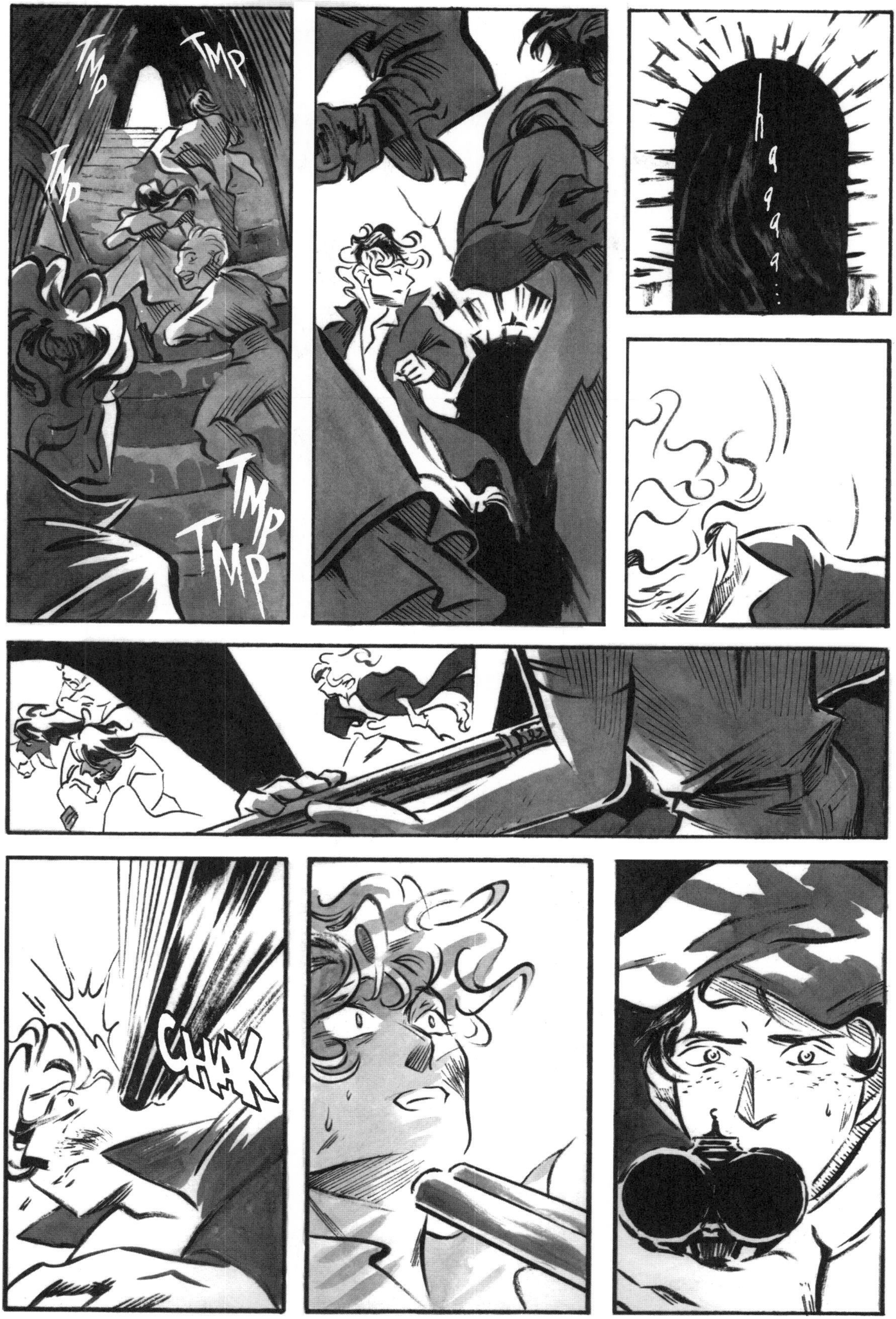
TMP
TMP
TMP
TMP
TMP
hqqqq...
CHAK

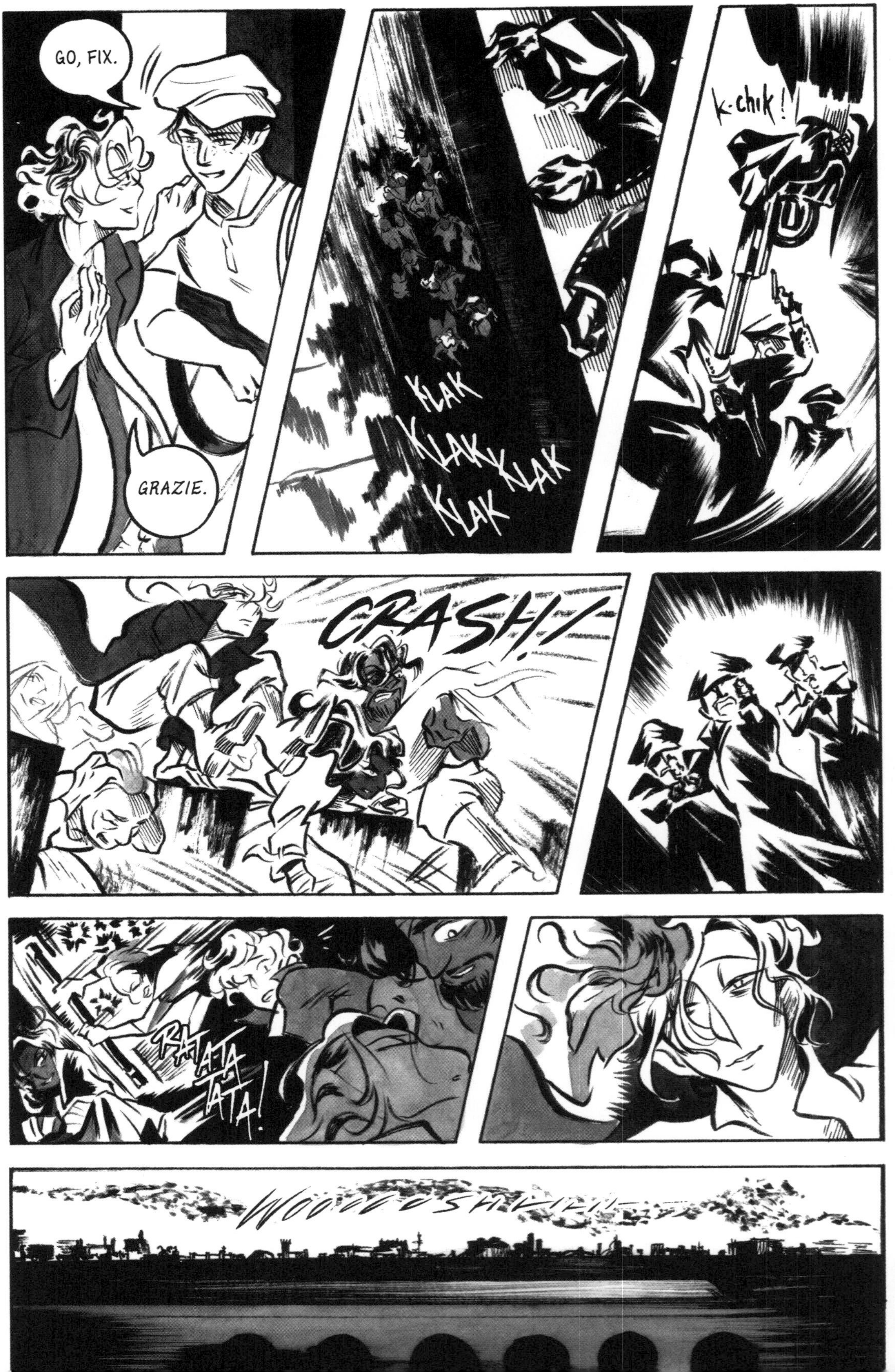
GO, FIX.
GRAZIE.
KLAK
KLAK KLAK
KLAK
k-chik!
CRASH!
RATATATATA!

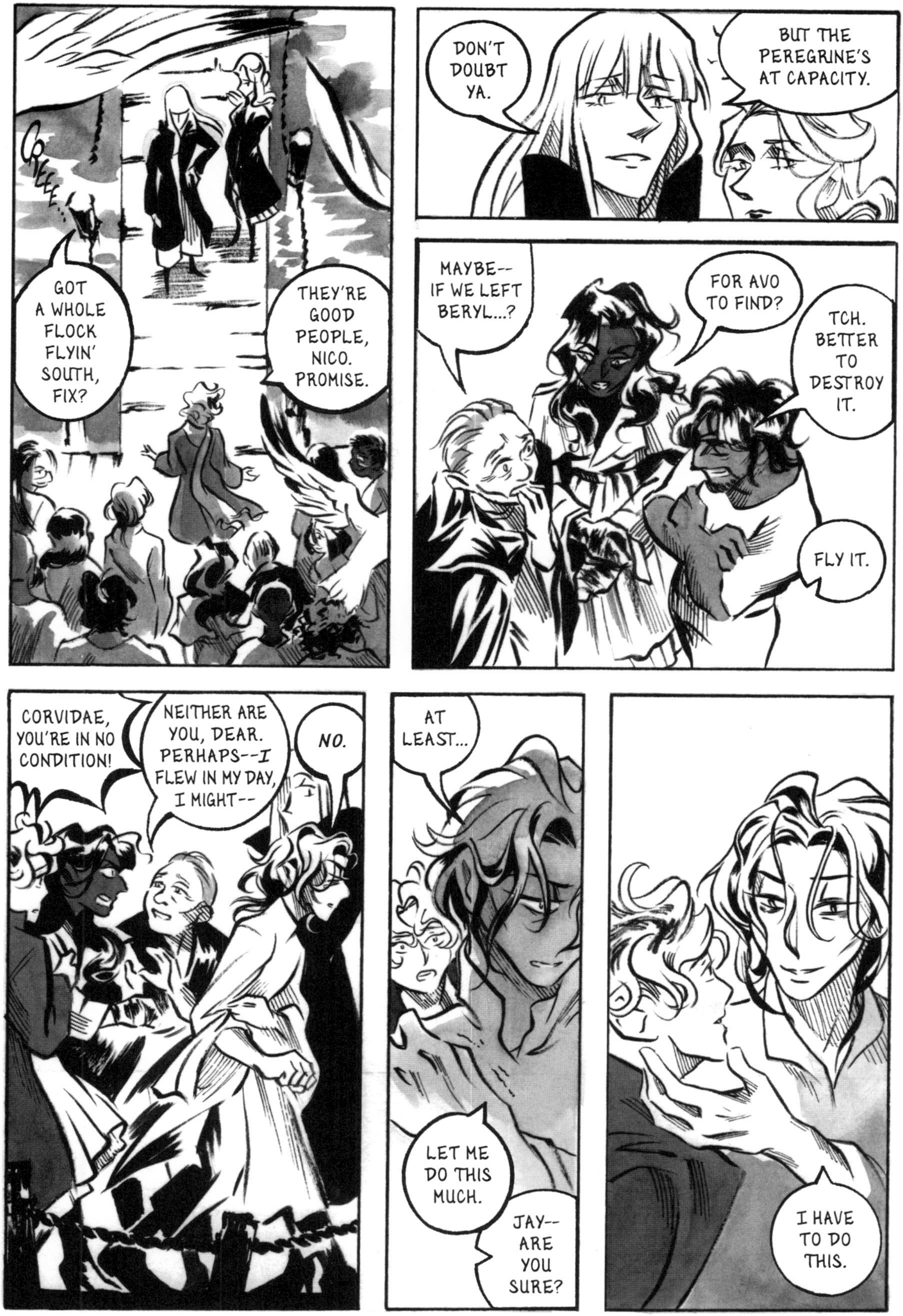
CREEEE...
GOT A WHOLE FLOCK FLYIN' SOUTH, FIX?
THEY'RE GOOD PEOPLE, NICO. PROMISE.
DON'T DOUBT YA.
BUT THE PEREGRINE'S AT CAPACITY.
MAYBE-- IF WE LEFT BERYL...?
FOR AVO TO FIND?
TCH. BETTER TO DESTROY IT.
FLY IT.
CORVIDAE, YOU'RE IN NO CONDITION!
NEITHER ARE YOU, DEAR. PERHAPS--*I* FLEW IN MY DAY, I MIGHT--
NO.
AT LEAST...
LET ME DO THIS MUCH.
JAY-- ARE YOU SURE?
I HAVE TO DO THIS.

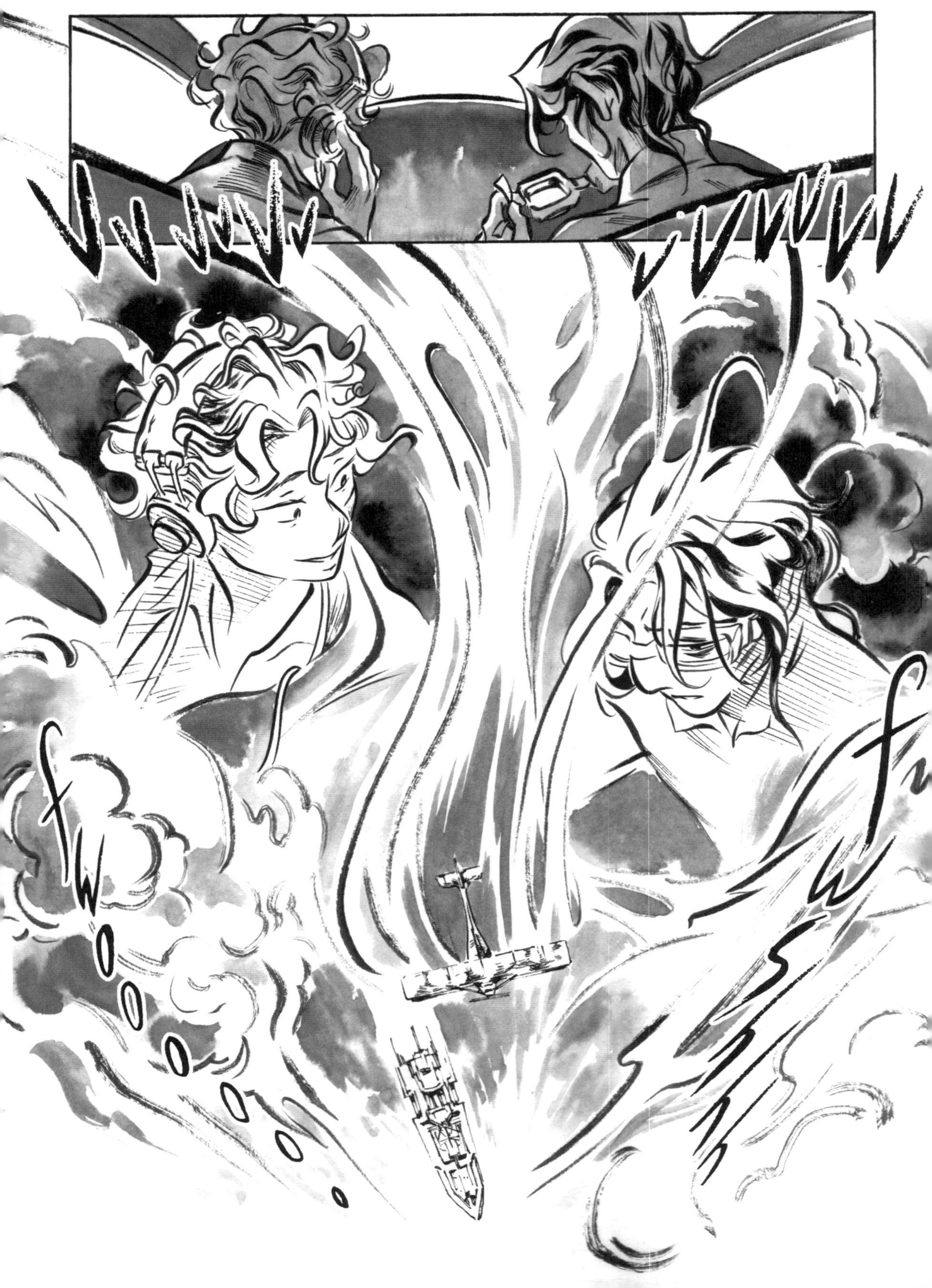
fwoooooo
fwsh

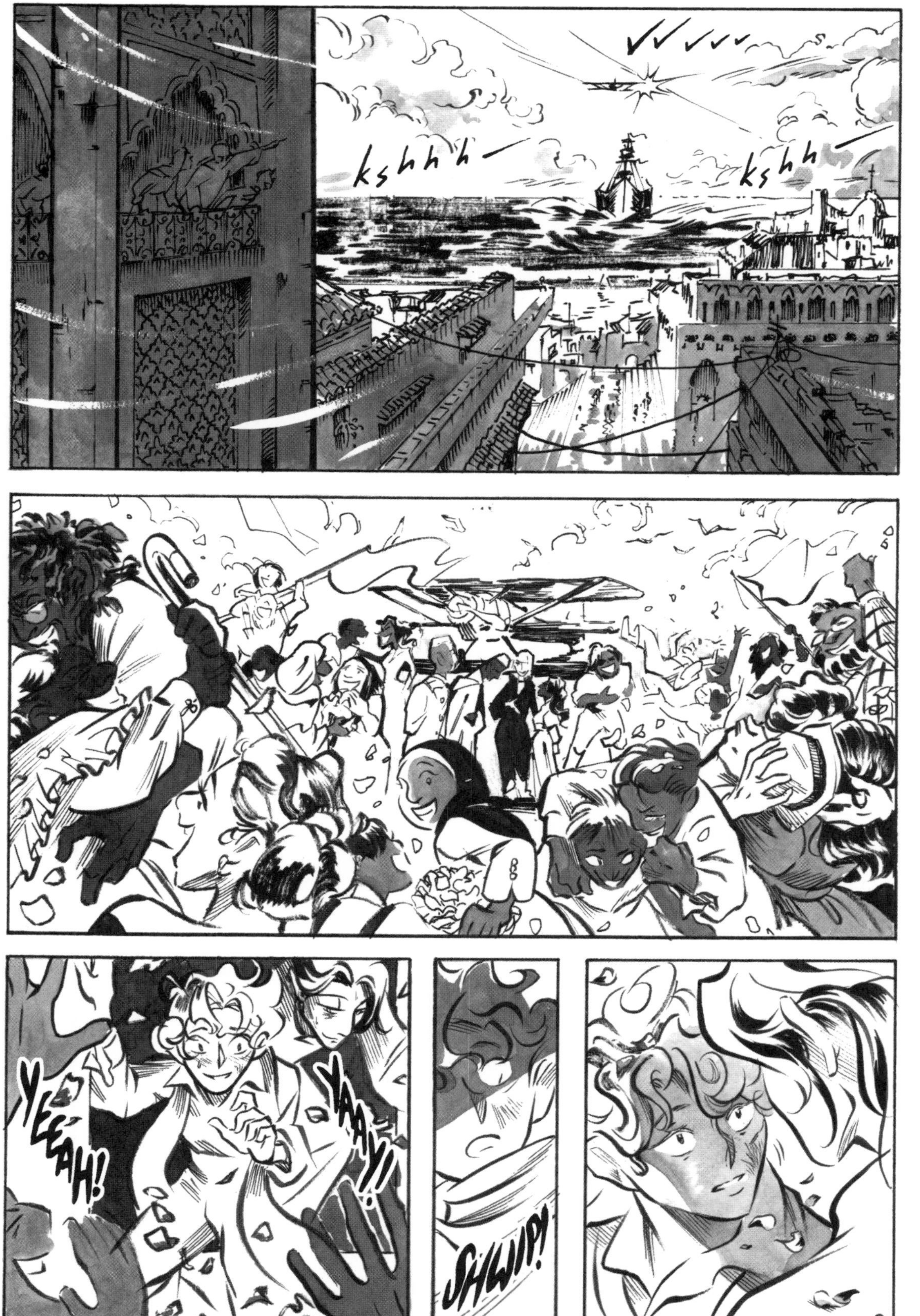

VVVVVV
kshhh—
kshhh—
YEEAH!
YAAAY!
SHWIP!

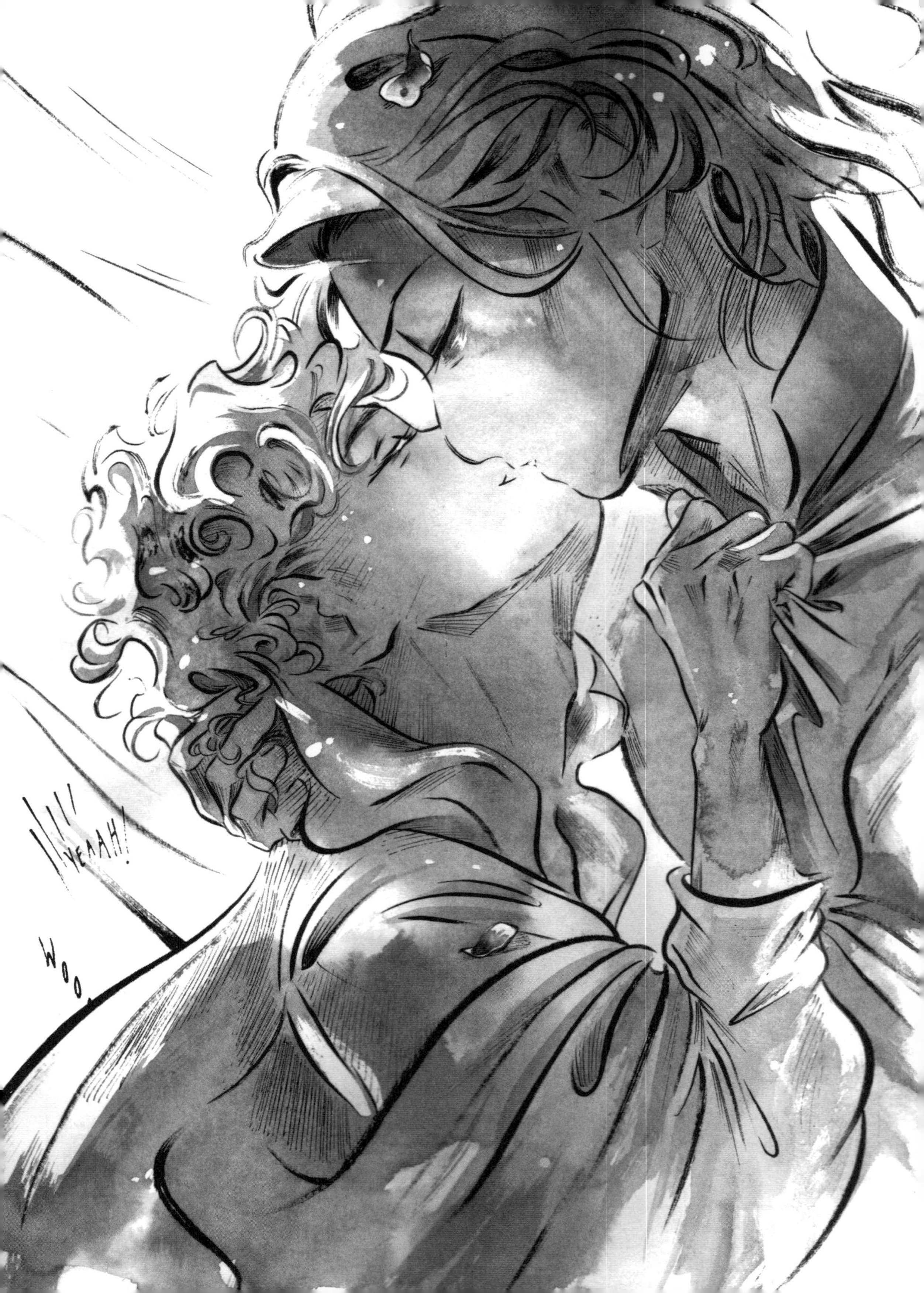
YEAAH!
Woo.

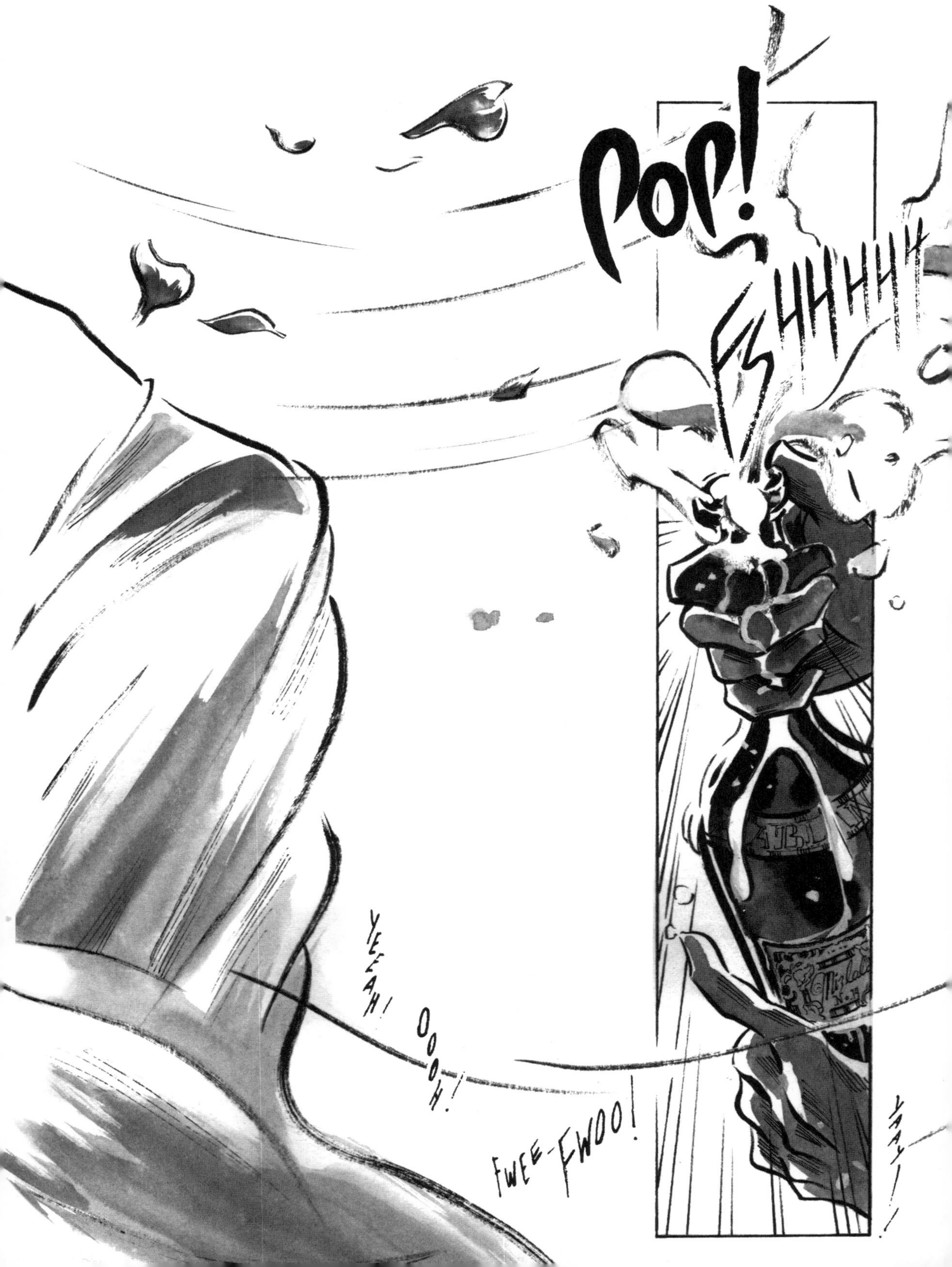
POP!
FSHHHHH
YEEAH! OOOOH!
FWEE-FWOO!
YAAY!!

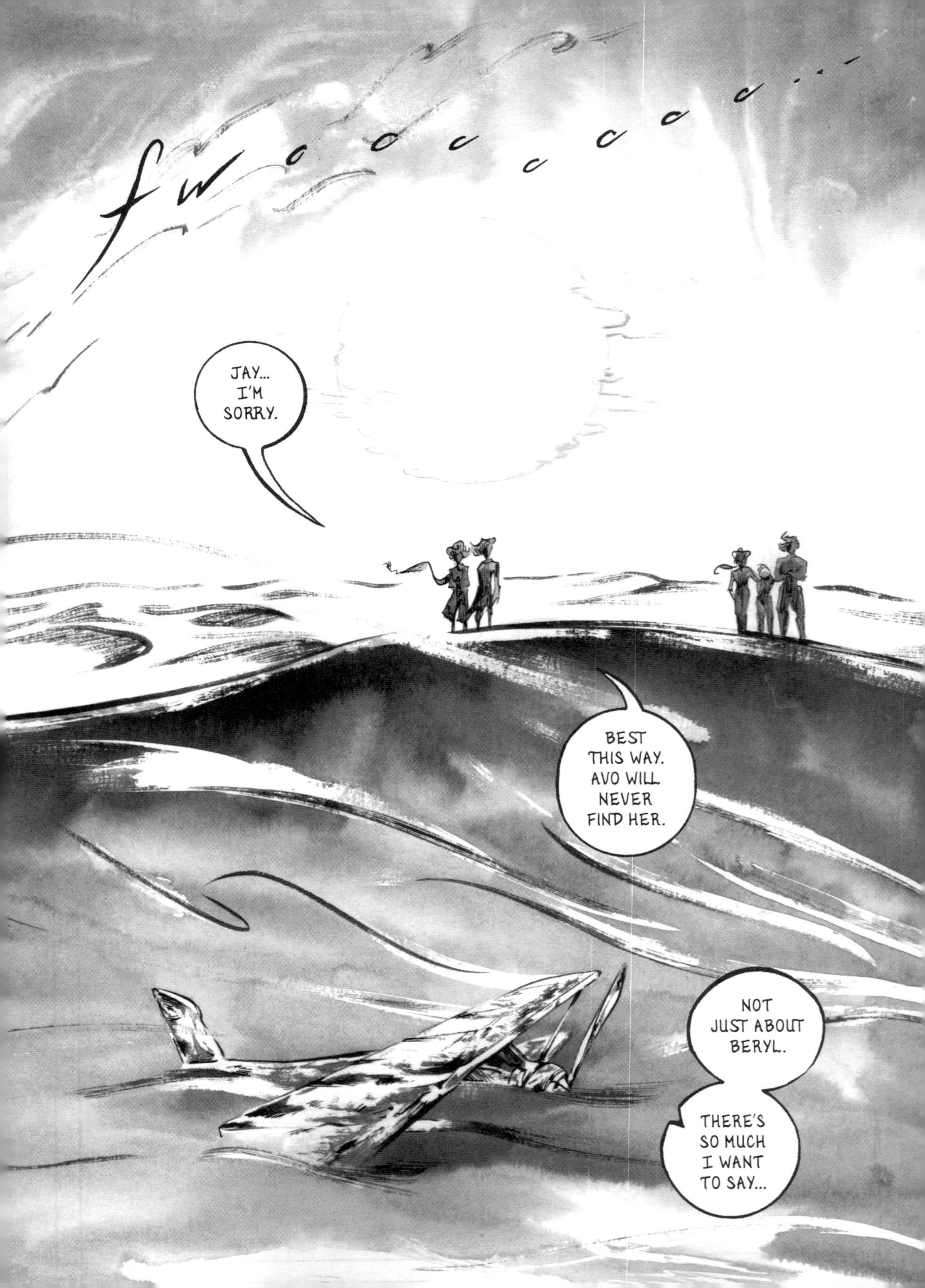
fwooooooo...
JAY... I'M SORRY.
BEST THIS WAY. AVO WILL NEVER FIND HER.
NOT JUST ABOUT BERYL.
THERE'S SO MUCH I WANT TO SAY...

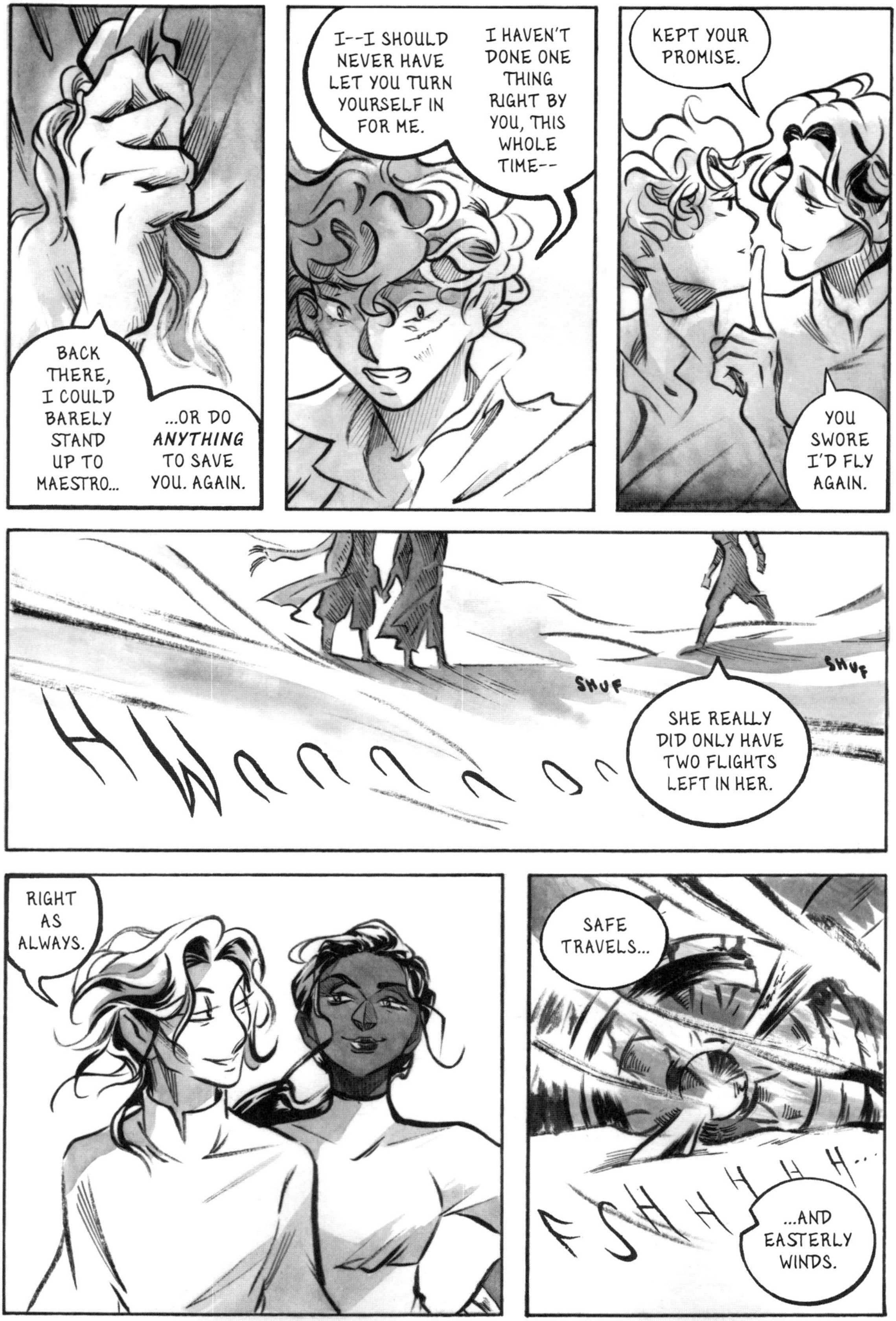
BACK THERE, I COULD BARELY STAND UP TO MAESTRO...
...OR DO ANYTHING TO SAVE YOU. AGAIN.
I--I SHOULD NEVER HAVE LET YOU TURN YOURSELF IN FOR ME.
I HAVEN'T DONE ONE THING RIGHT BY YOU, THIS WHOLE TIME--
KEPT YOUR PROMISE.
YOU SWORE I'D FLY AGAIN.
HWOOOOOOO
SHUF
SHUF
SHE REALLY DID ONLY HAVE TWO FLIGHTS LEFT IN HER.
RIGHT AS ALWAYS.
SAFE TRAVELS...
FSHHHHH...
...AND EASTERLY WINDS.

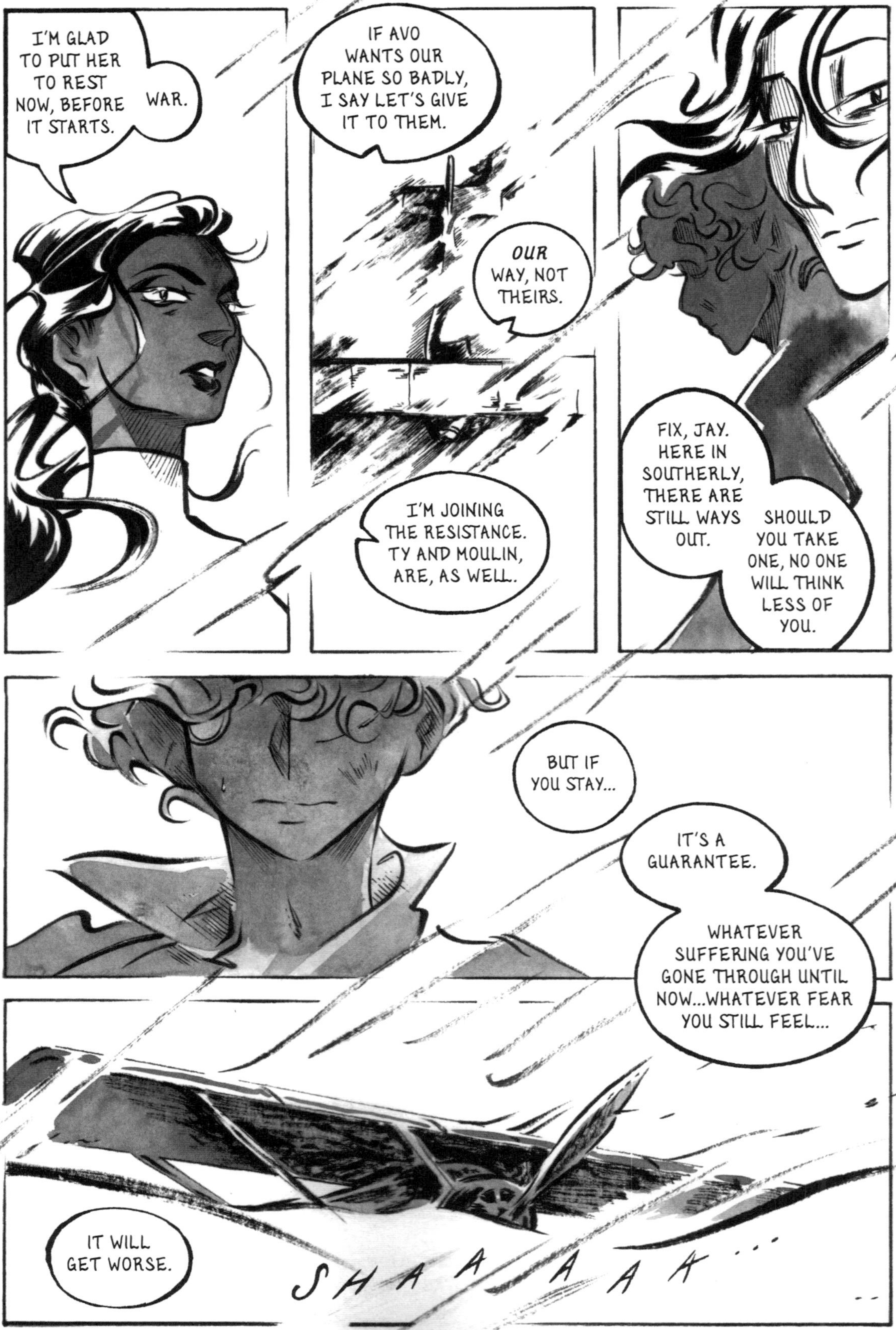
I'M GLAD TO PUT HER TO REST NOW, BEFORE IT STARTS.
WAR.
IF AVO WANTS OUR PLANE SO BADLY, I SAY LET'S GIVE IT TO THEM.
OUR WAY, NOT THEIRS.
I'M JOINING THE RESISTANCE. TY AND MOULIN, ARE, AS WELL.
FIX, JAY. HERE IN SOUTHERLY, THERE ARE STILL WAYS OUT.
SHOULD YOU TAKE ONE, NO ONE WILL THINK LESS OF YOU.
BUT IF YOU STAY...
IT'S A GUARANTEE.
WHATEVER SUFFERING YOU'VE GONE THROUGH UNTIL NOW...WHATEVER FEAR YOU STILL FEEL...
IT WILL GET WORSE.
SHAAAAA...

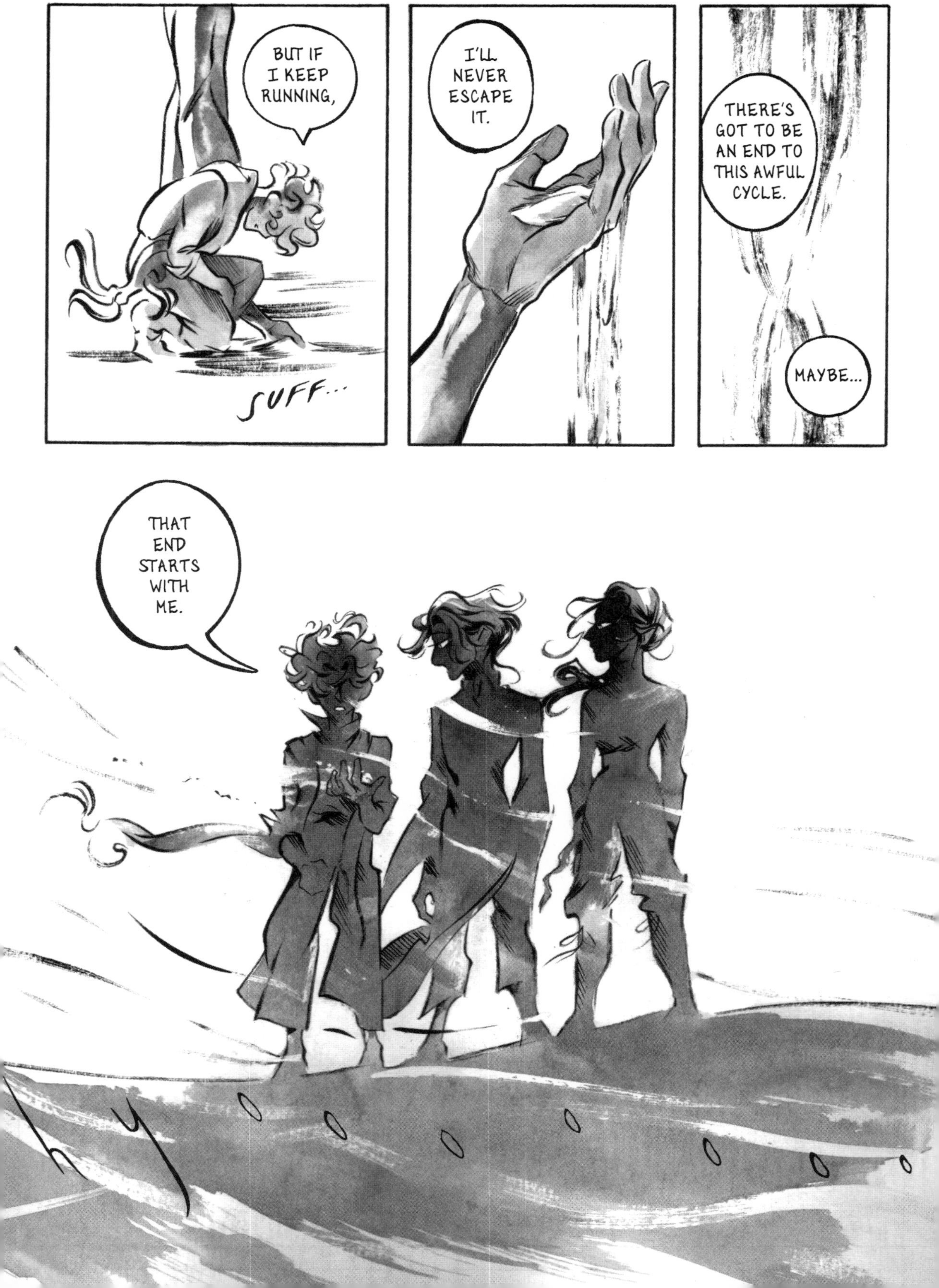
BUT IF I KEEP RUNNING,
SUFF...
I'LL NEVER ESCAPE IT.
THERE'S GOT TO BE AN END TO THIS AWFUL CYCLE.
MAYBE...
THAT END STARTS WITH ME.
hyoooooooo

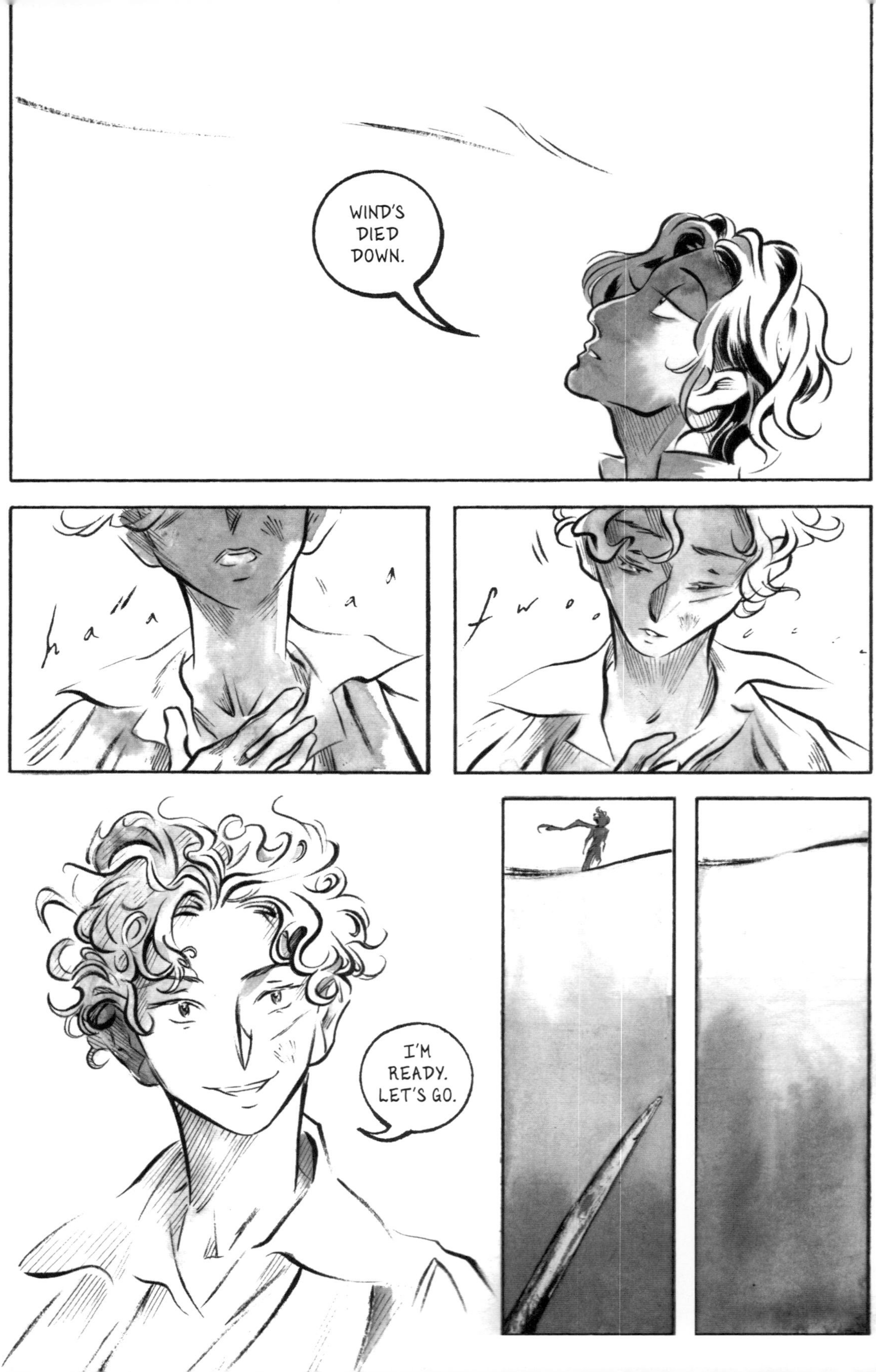
WIND'S DIED DOWN.
haaa
fwoo
I'M READY. LET'S GO.

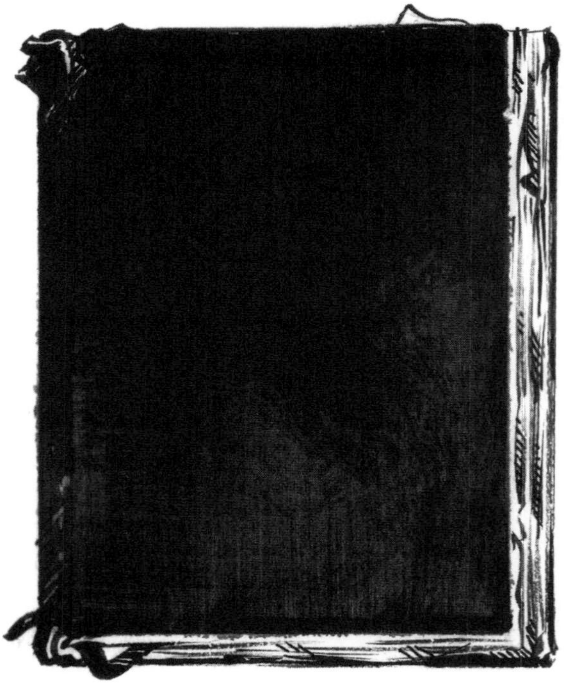

BOOK IV
20/20

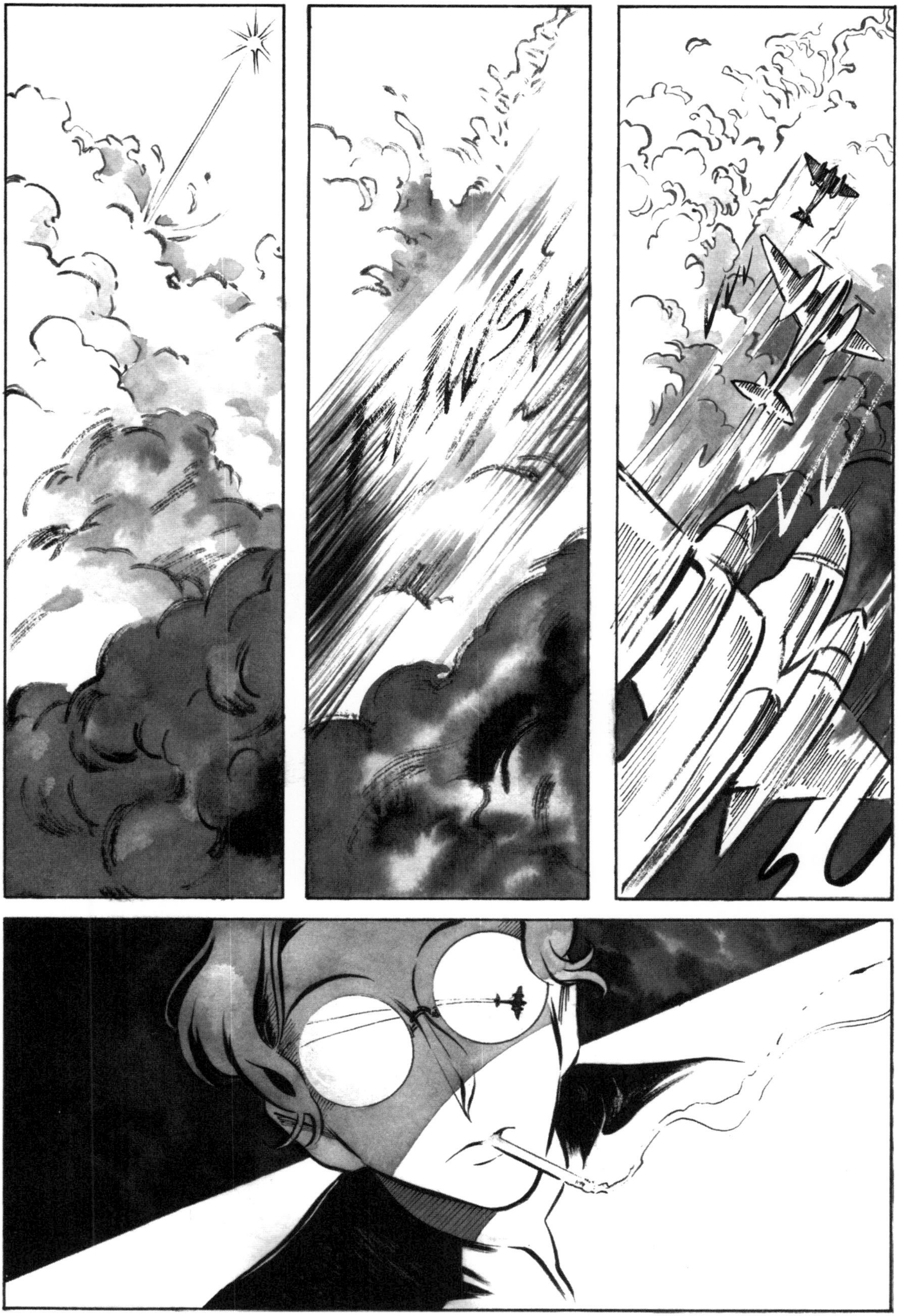

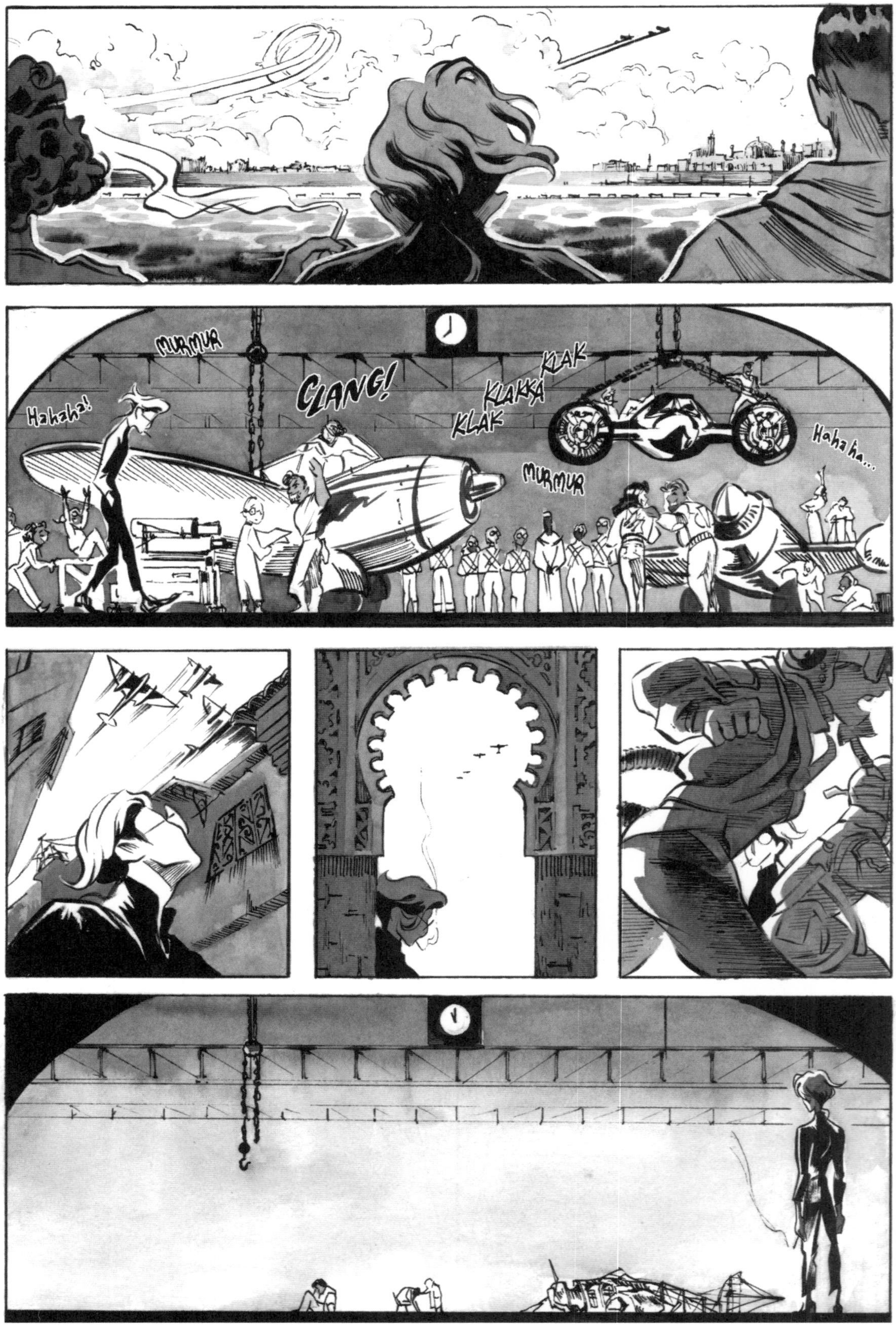
MURMUR
Hahaha!
CLANG!
KLAK
KLAKKA
KLAK
MURMUR
Haha ha...

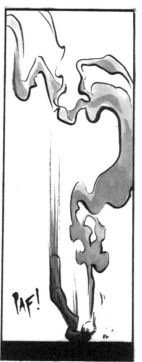

PAF!

KLAK

SKFF   SKUFF

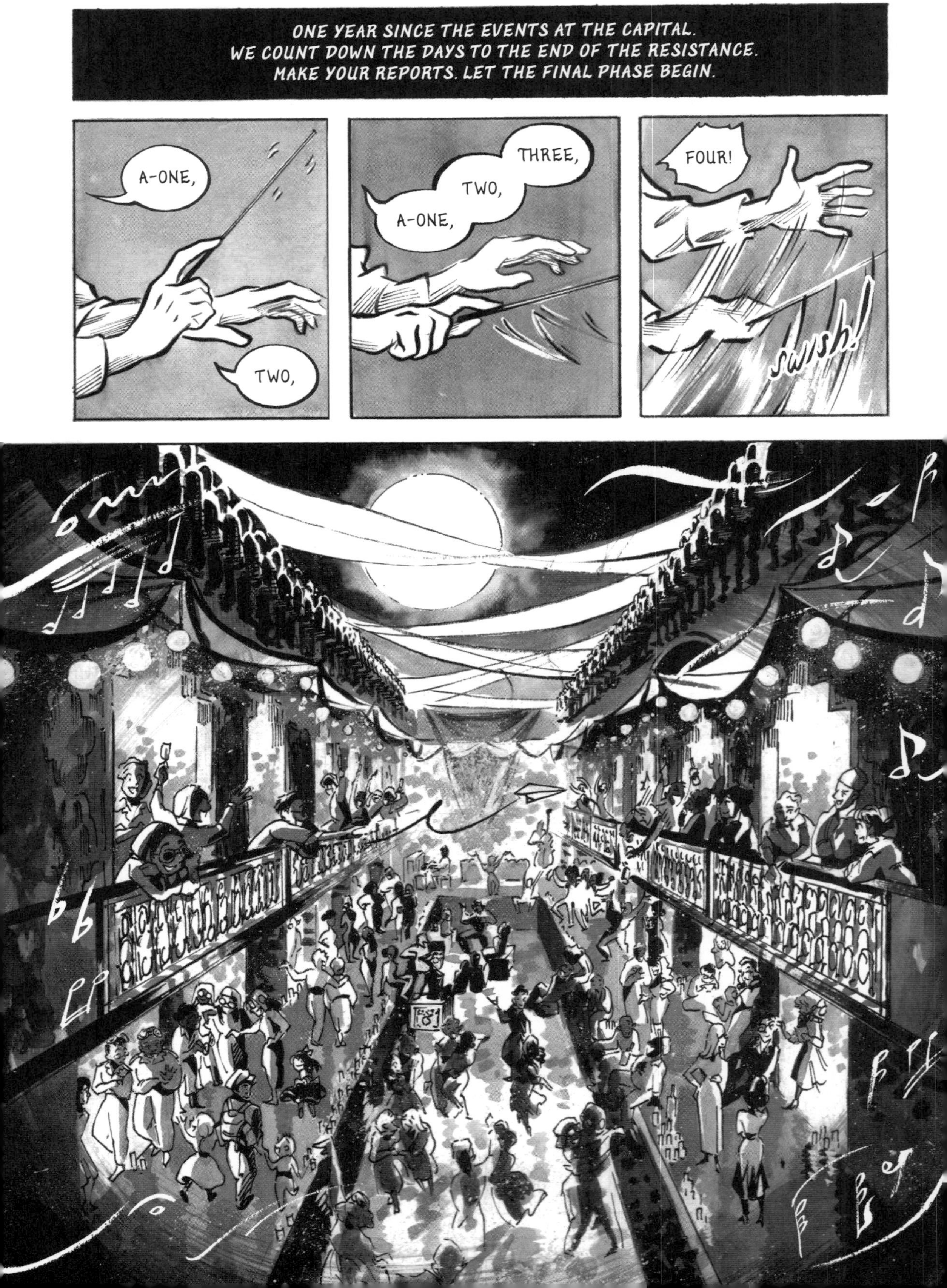
ONE YEAR SINCE THE EVENTS AT THE CAPITAL.
WE COUNT DOWN THE DAYS TO THE END OF THE RESISTANCE.
MAKE YOUR REPORTS. LET THE FINAL PHASE BEGIN.
A-ONE,
TWO,
A-ONE,
TWO,
THREE,
FOUR!
swish!

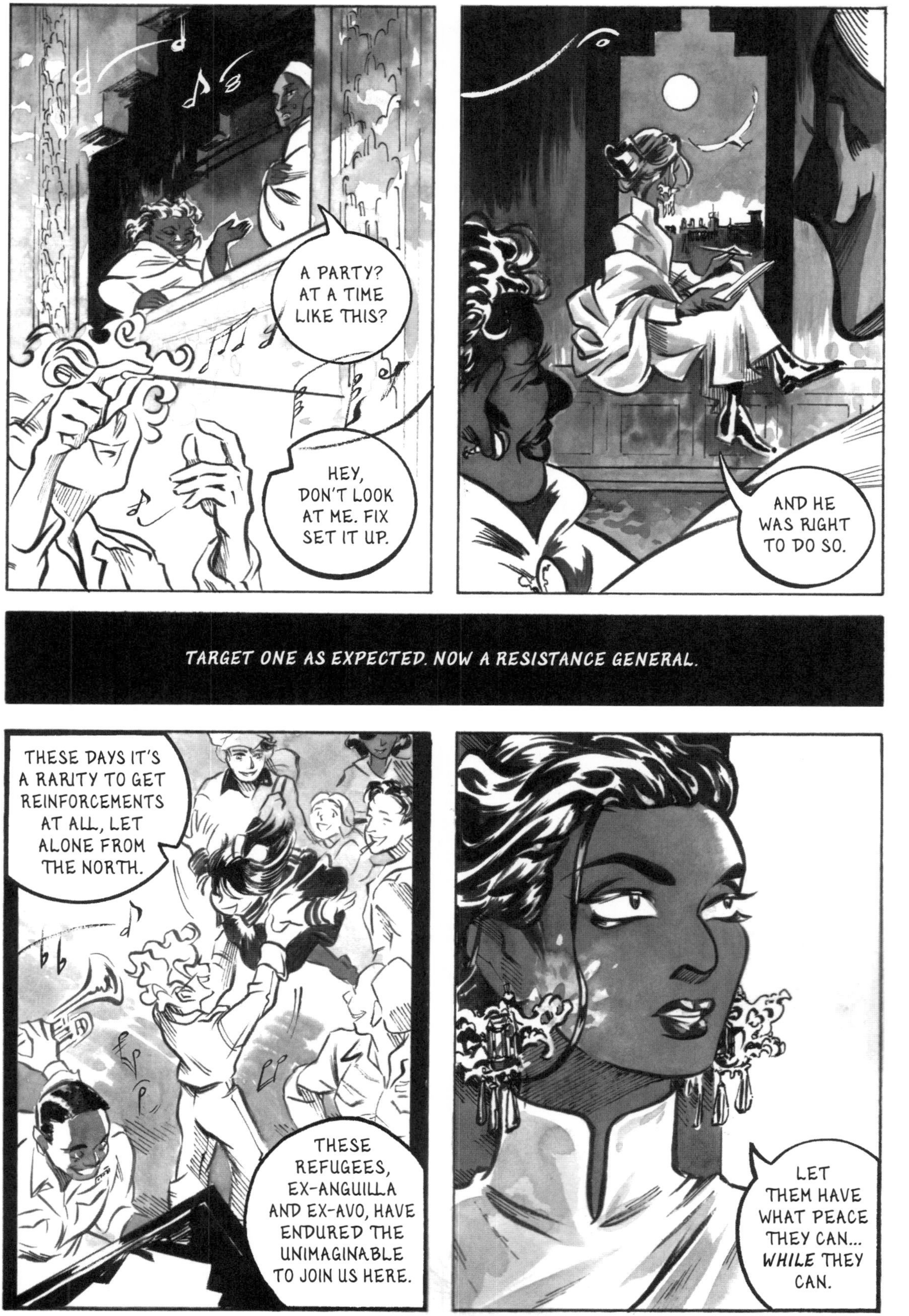
A PARTY? AT A TIME LIKE THIS?
HEY, DON'T LOOK AT ME. FIX SET IT UP.
AND HE WAS RIGHT TO DO SO.
TARGET ONE AS EXPECTED. NOW A RESISTANCE GENERAL.
THESE DAYS IT'S A RARITY TO GET REINFORCEMENTS AT ALL, LET ALONE FROM THE NORTH.
THESE REFUGEES, EX-ANGUILLA AND EX-AVO, HAVE ENDURED THE UNIMAGINABLE TO JOIN US HERE.
LET THEM HAVE WHAT PEACE THEY CAN... *WHILE* THEY CAN.

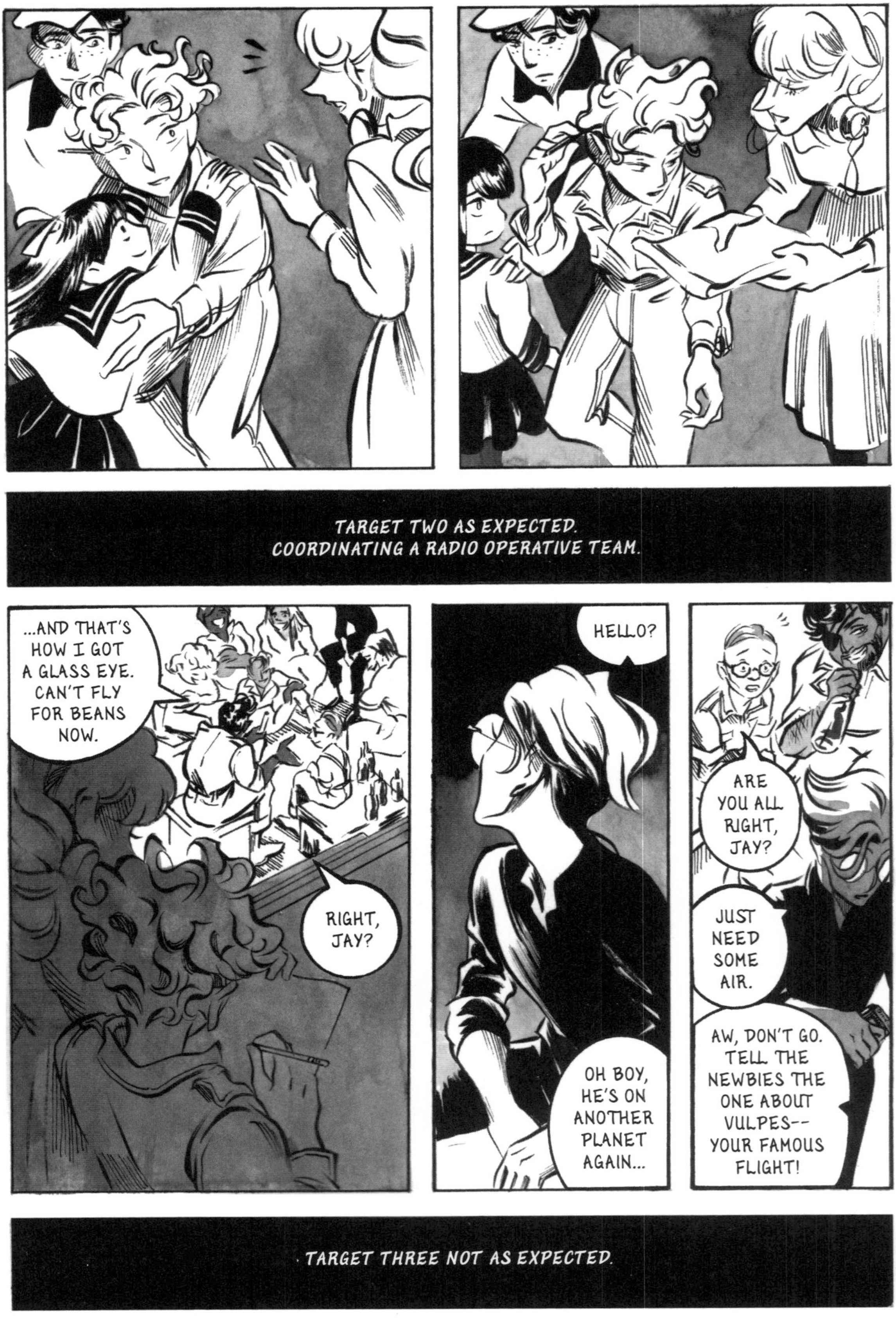
TARGET TWO AS EXPECTED.
COORDINATING A RADIO OPERATIVE TEAM.
...AND THAT'S HOW I GOT A GLASS EYE. CAN'T FLY FOR BEANS NOW.
RIGHT, JAY?
HELLO?
OH BOY, HE'S ON ANOTHER PLANET AGAIN...
ARE YOU ALL RIGHT, JAY?
JUST NEED SOME AIR.
AW, DON'T GO. TELL THE NEWBIES THE ONE ABOUT VULPES-- YOUR FAMOUS FLIGHT!
TARGET THREE NOT AS EXPECTED.

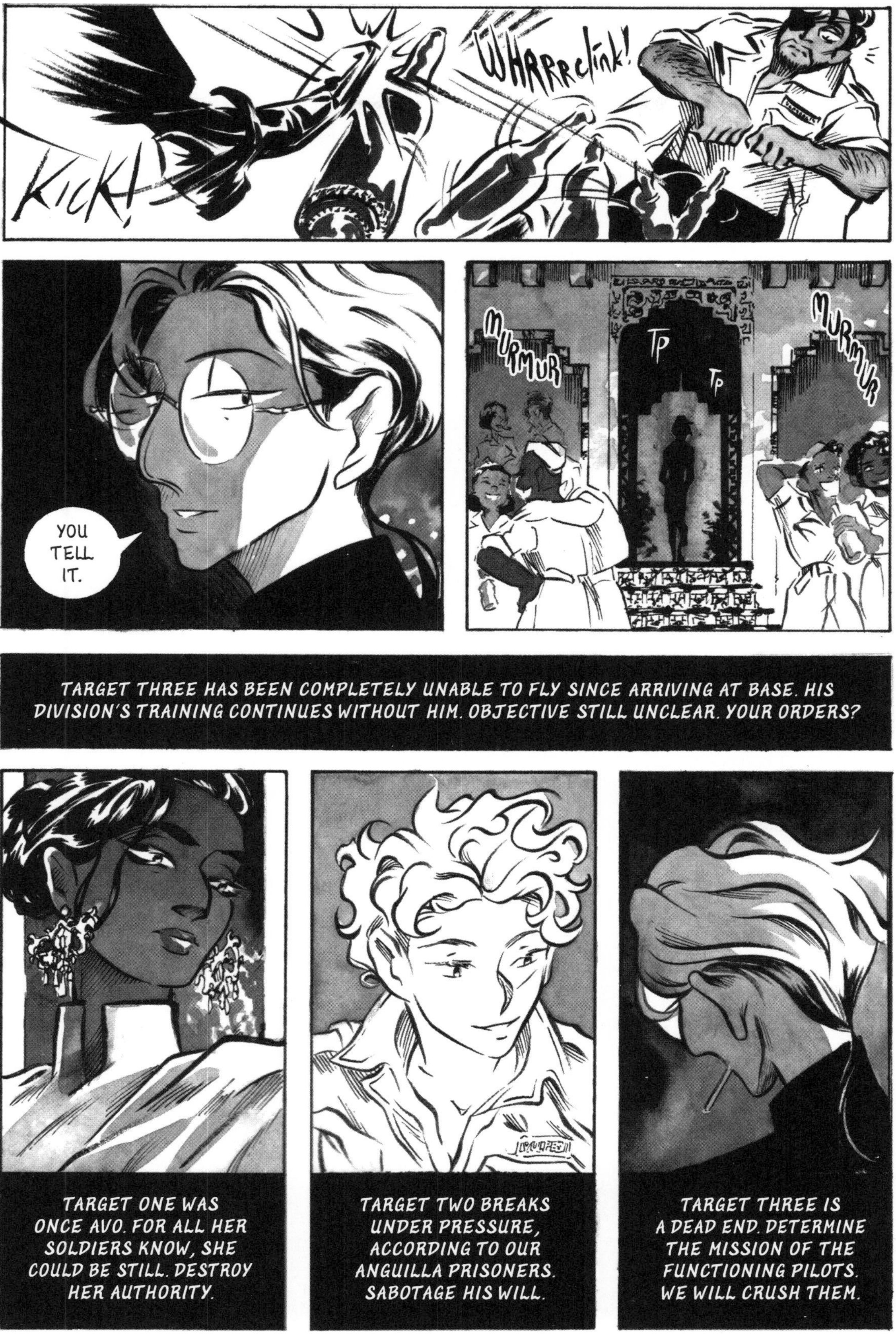
KICK!
WHRRRclink!
YOU TELL IT.
MURMUR
TP
TP
MURMUR
TARGET THREE HAS BEEN COMPLETELY UNABLE TO FLY SINCE ARRIVING AT BASE. HIS DIVISION'S TRAINING CONTINUES WITHOUT HIM. OBJECTIVE STILL UNCLEAR. YOUR ORDERS?
TARGET ONE WAS ONCE AVO. FOR ALL HER SOLDIERS KNOW, SHE COULD BE STILL. DESTROY HER AUTHORITY.
TARGET TWO BREAKS UNDER PRESSURE, ACCORDING TO OUR ANGUILLA PRISONERS. SABOTAGE HIS WILL.
TARGET THREE IS A DEAD END. DETERMINE THE MISSION OF THE FUNCTIONING PILOTS. WE WILL CRUSH THEM.

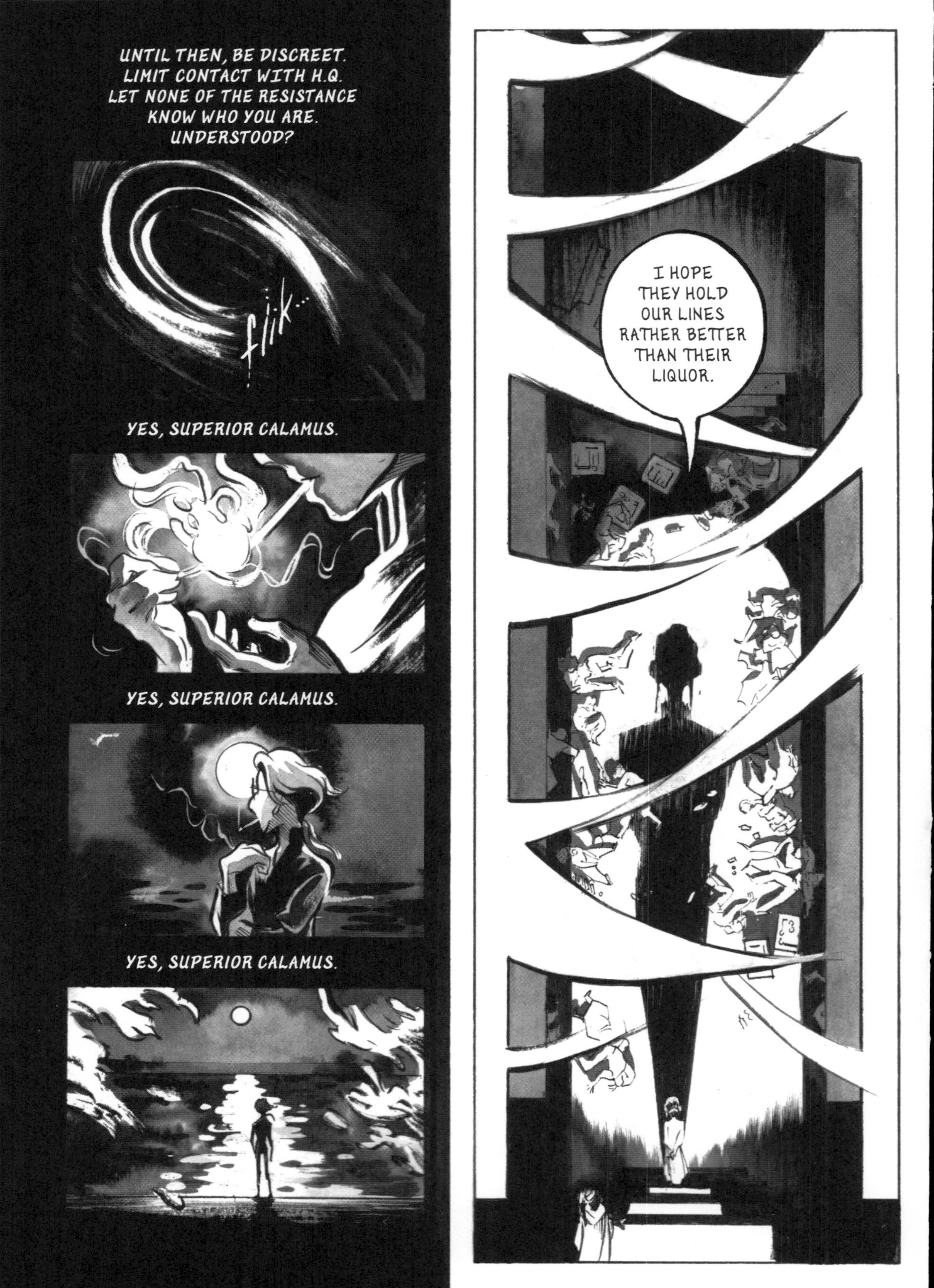
UNTIL THEN, BE DISCREET. LIMIT CONTACT WITH H.Q. LET NONE OF THE RESISTANCE KNOW WHO YOU ARE. UNDERSTOOD?
fliik...
YES, SUPERIOR CALAMUS.
YES, SUPERIOR CALAMUS.
YES, SUPERIOR CALAMUS.
I HOPE THEY HOLD OUR LINES RATHER BETTER THAN THEIR LIQUOR.

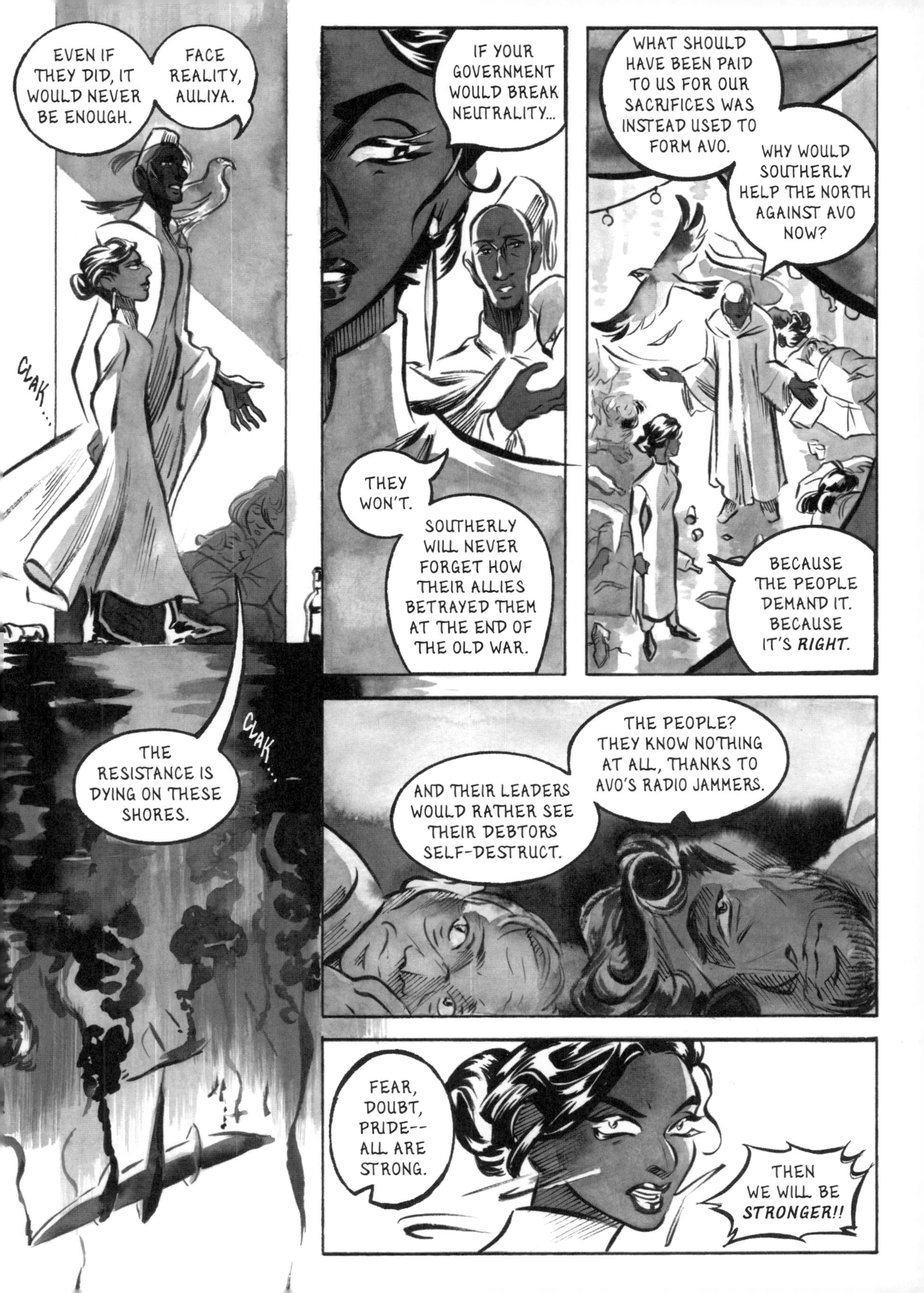
EVEN IF THEY DID, IT WOULD NEVER BE ENOUGH.
FACE REALITY, AULIYA.
CLAK...
THE RESISTANCE IS DYING ON THESE SHORES.
CLAK...
IF YOUR GOVERNMENT WOULD BREAK NEUTRALITY...
THEY WON'T.
SOUTHERLY WILL NEVER FORGET HOW THEIR ALLIES BETRAYED THEM AT THE END OF THE OLD WAR.
WHAT SHOULD HAVE BEEN PAID TO US FOR OUR SACRIFICES WAS INSTEAD USED TO FORM AVO.
WHY WOULD SOUTHERLY HELP THE NORTH AGAINST AVO NOW?
BECAUSE THE PEOPLE DEMAND IT. BECAUSE IT'S *RIGHT*.
THE PEOPLE? THEY KNOW NOTHING AT ALL, THANKS TO AVO'S RADIO JAMMERS.
AND THEIR LEADERS WOULD RATHER SEE THEIR DEBTORS SELF-DESTRUCT.
FEAR, DOUBT, PRIDE-- ALL ARE STRONG.
THEN WE WILL BE *STRONGER!!*

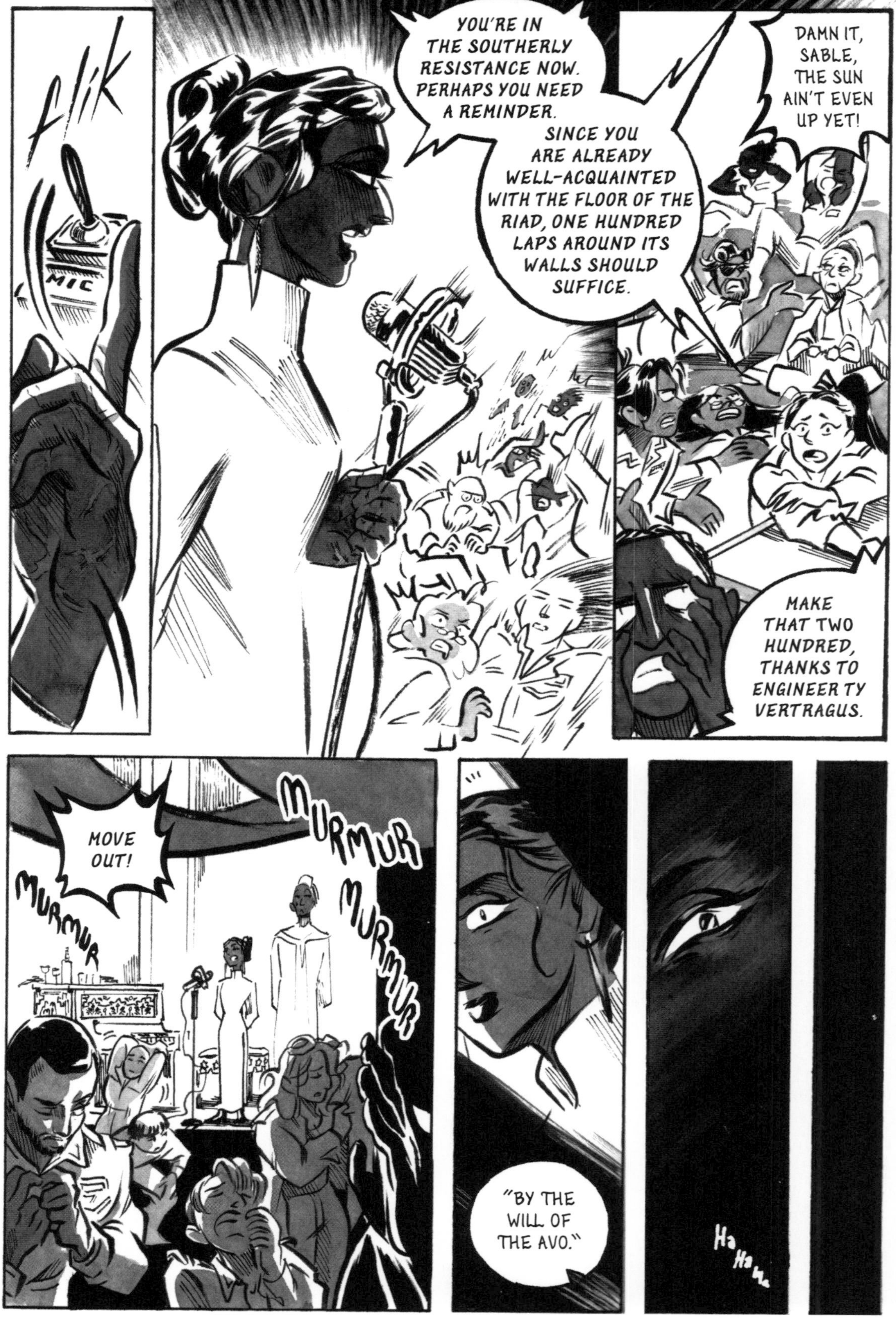
FLIK
MIC
YOU'RE IN THE SOUTHERLY RESISTANCE NOW. PERHAPS YOU NEED A REMINDER.
SINCE YOU ARE ALREADY WELL-ACQUAINTED WITH THE FLOOR OF THE RIAD, ONE HUNDRED LAPS AROUND ITS WALLS SHOULD SUFFICE.
DAMN IT, SABLE, THE SUN AIN'T EVEN UP YET!
MAKE THAT TWO HUNDRED, THANKS TO ENGINEER TY VERTRAGUS.
MOVE OUT!
MURMUR
MURMUR
MURMUR
MURMUR
"BY THE WILL OF THE AVO."
Ha Ha Ha

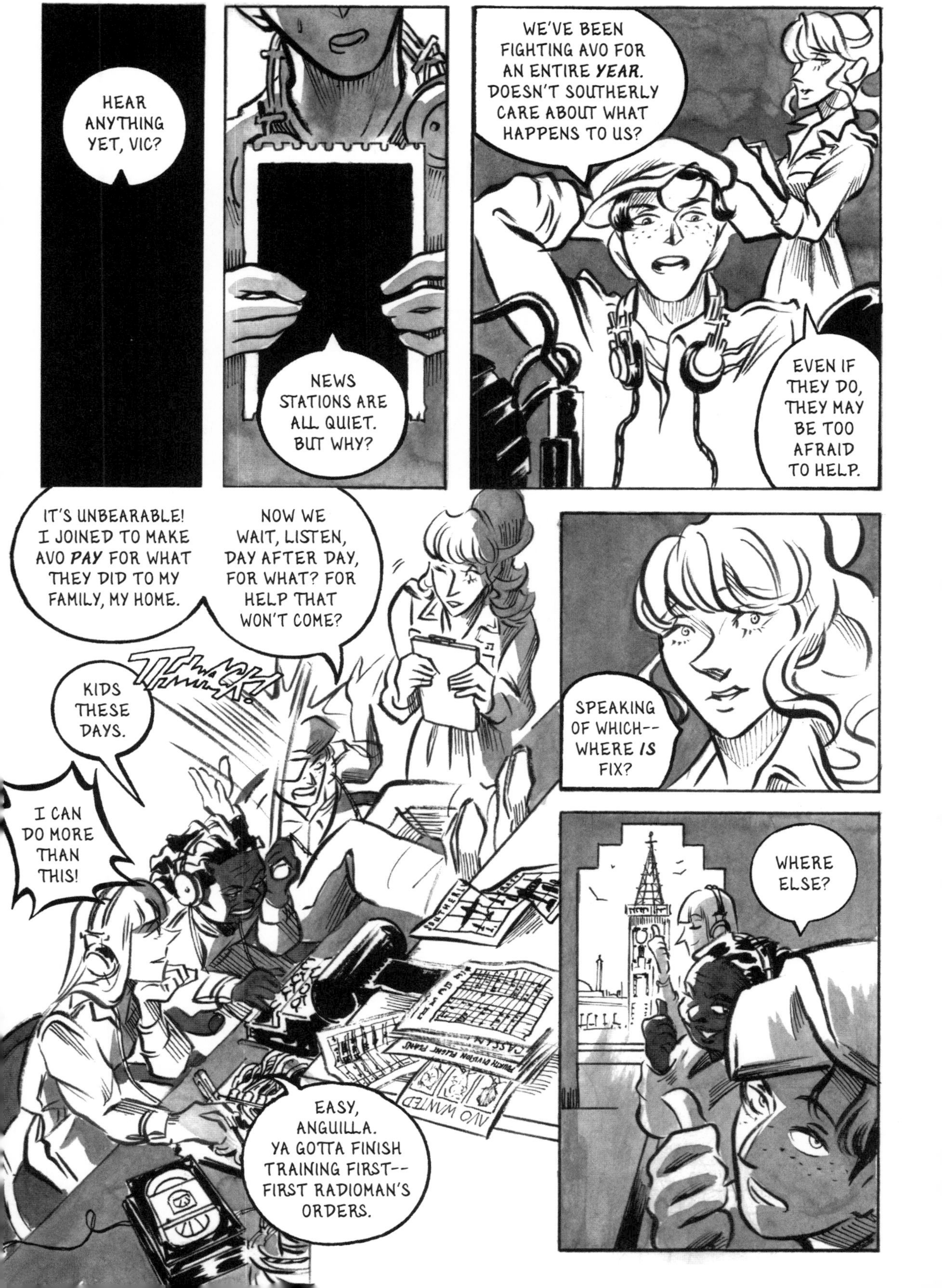
HEAR ANYTHING YET, VIC?
NEWS STATIONS ARE ALL QUIET. BUT WHY?
WE'VE BEEN FIGHTING AVO FOR AN ENTIRE YEAR. DOESN'T SOUTHERLY CARE ABOUT WHAT HAPPENS TO US?
EVEN IF THEY DO, THEY MAY BE TOO AFRAID TO HELP.
IT'S UNBEARABLE! I JOINED TO MAKE AVO PAY FOR WHAT THEY DID TO MY FAMILY, MY HOME.
NOW WE WAIT, LISTEN, DAY AFTER DAY, FOR WHAT? FOR HELP THAT WON'T COME?
THWACK!
KIDS THESE DAYS.
I CAN DO MORE THAN THIS!
EASY, ANGUILLA. YA GOTTA FINISH TRAINING FIRST-- FIRST RADIOMAN'S ORDERS.
AVO WANTED
SPEAKING OF WHICH-- WHERE IS FIX?
WHERE ELSE?

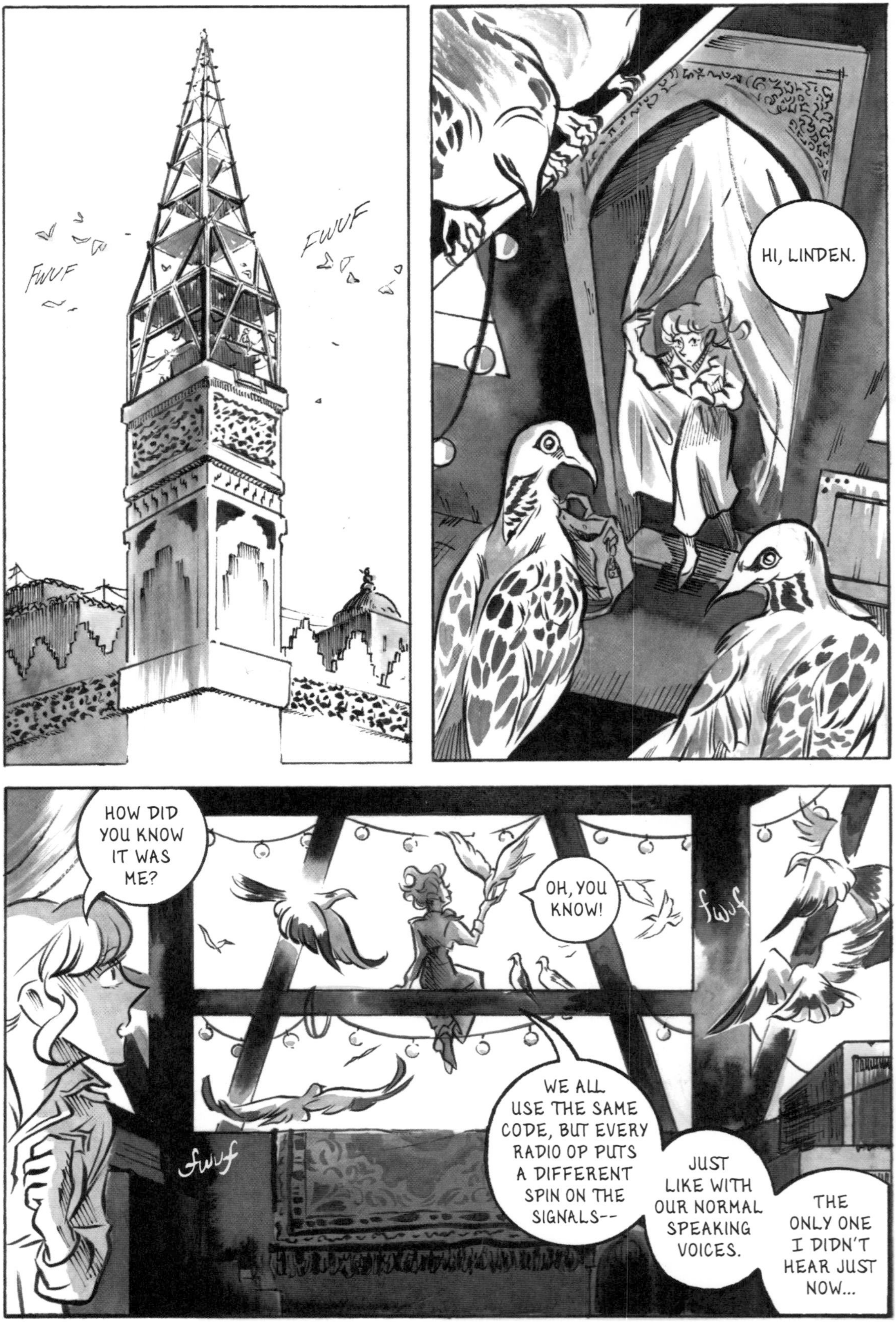
FWUF
FWUF
HI, LINDEN.
HOW DID YOU KNOW IT WAS ME?
OH, YOU KNOW!
fwuf
fwuf
WE ALL USE THE SAME CODE, BUT EVERY RADIO OP PUTS A DIFFERENT SPIN ON THE SIGNALS--
JUST LIKE WITH OUR NORMAL SPEAKING VOICES.
THE ONLY ONE I DIDN'T HEAR JUST NOW...

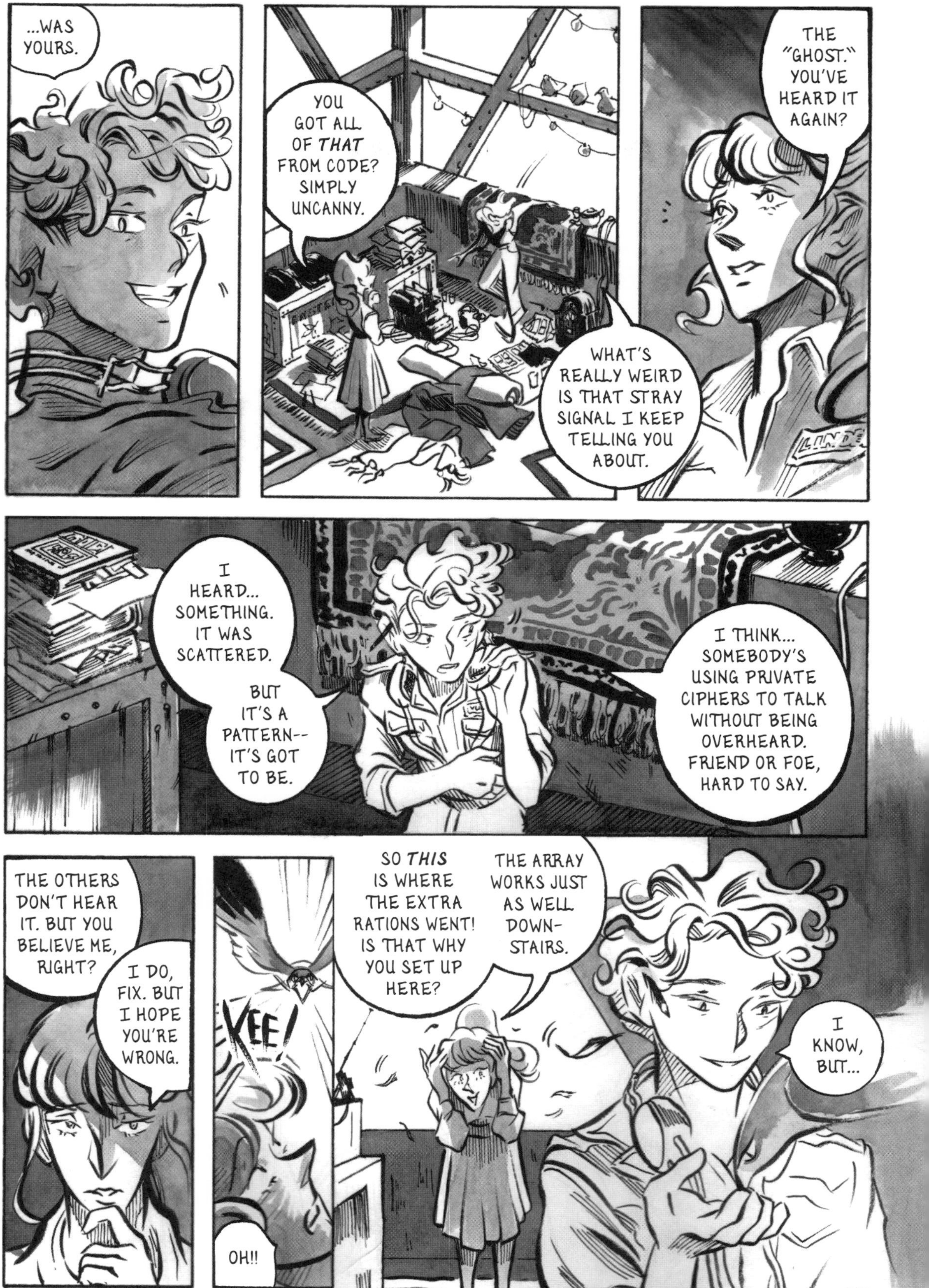
...WAS YOURS.
YOU GOT ALL OF *THAT* FROM CODE? SIMPLY UNCANNY.
WHAT'S REALLY WEIRD IS THAT STRAY SIGNAL I KEEP TELLING YOU ABOUT.
THE "GHOST." YOU'VE HEARD IT AGAIN?
I HEARD... SOMETHING. IT WAS SCATTERED.
BUT IT'S A PATTERN-- IT'S GOT TO BE.
I THINK... SOMEBODY'S USING PRIVATE CIPHERS TO TALK WITHOUT BEING OVERHEARD. FRIEND OR FOE, HARD TO SAY.
THE OTHERS DON'T HEAR IT. BUT YOU BELIEVE ME, RIGHT?
I DO, FIX. BUT I HOPE YOU'RE WRONG.
KEE!
OH!!
SO *THIS* IS WHERE THE EXTRA RATIONS WENT! IS THAT WHY YOU SET UP HERE?
THE ARRAY WORKS JUST AS WELL DOWN-STAIRS.
I KNOW, BUT...

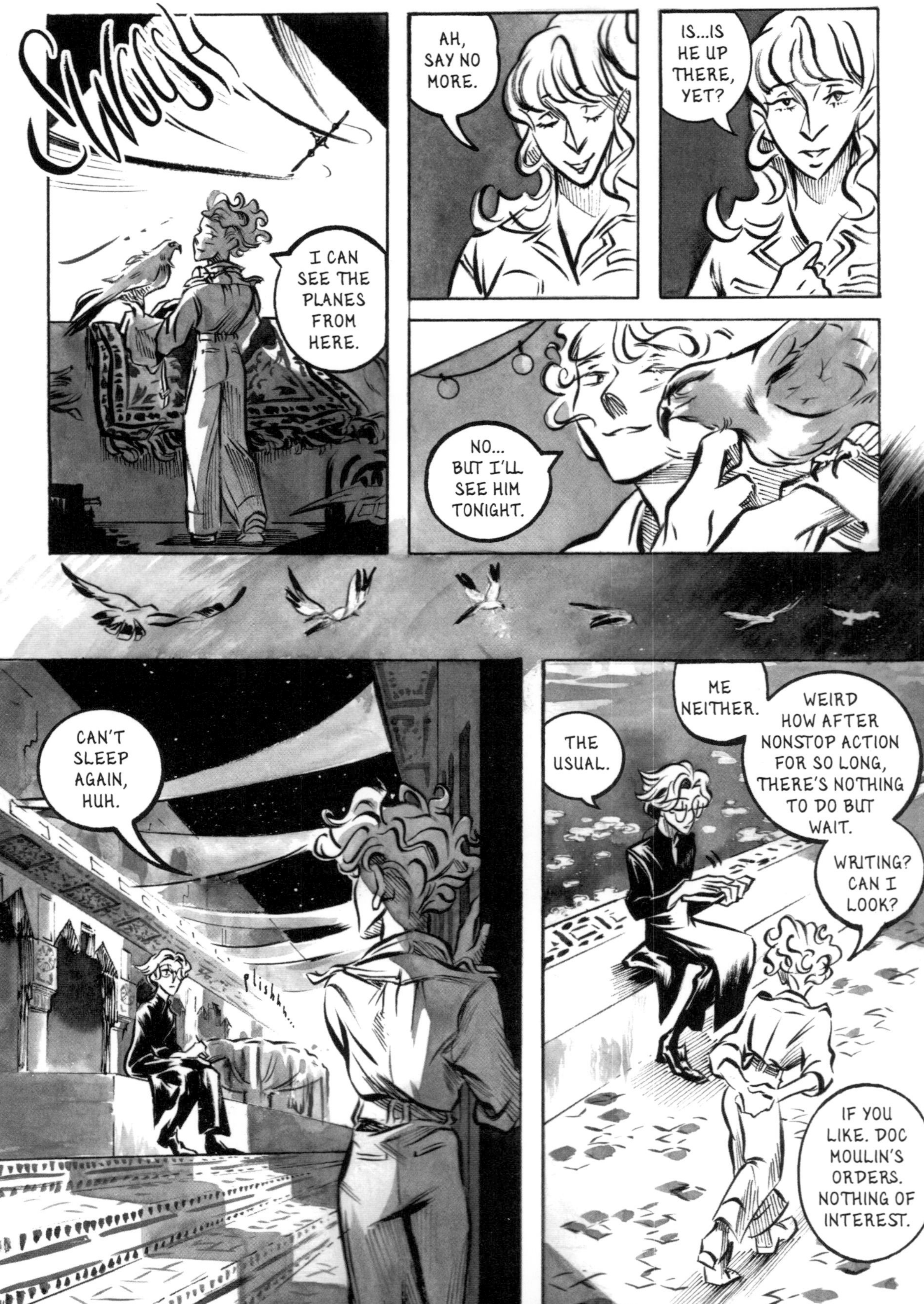
SWOOSH
I CAN SEE THE PLANES FROM HERE.
AH, SAY NO MORE.
IS...IS HE UP THERE, YET?
NO... BUT I'LL SEE HIM TONIGHT.
CAN'T SLEEP AGAIN, HUH.
plishhh...
THE USUAL.
ME NEITHER.
WEIRD HOW AFTER NONSTOP ACTION FOR SO LONG, THERE'S NOTHING TO DO BUT WAIT.
WRITING? CAN I LOOK?
IF YOU LIKE. DOC MOULIN'S ORDERS. NOTHING OF INTEREST.

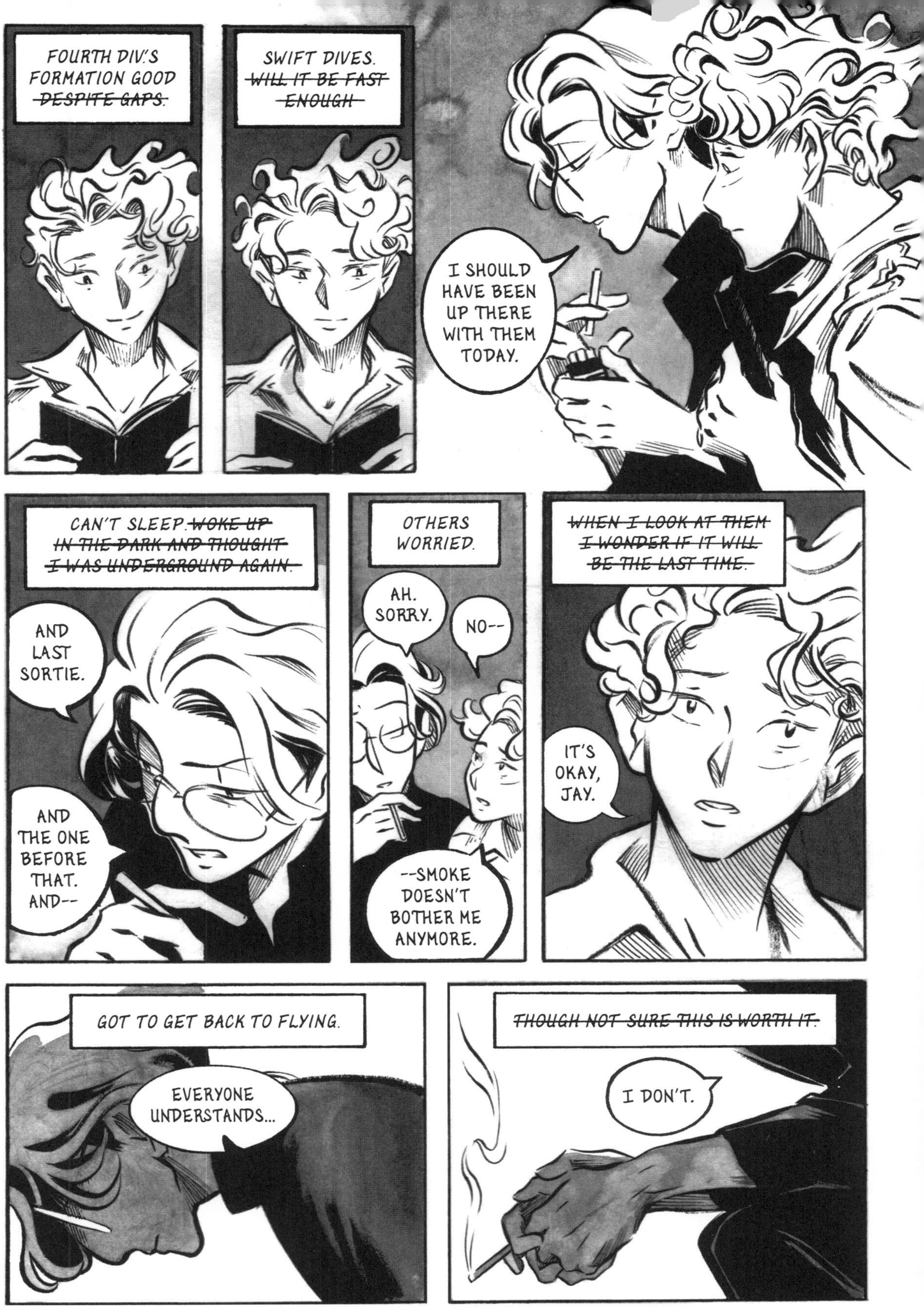
FOURTH DIV.'S FORMATION GOOD ~~DESPITE GAPS~~.
SWIFT DIVES. ~~WILL IT BE FAST ENOUGH~~
I SHOULD HAVE BEEN UP THERE WITH THEM TODAY.
CAN'T SLEEP. ~~WOKE UP IN THE DARK AND THOUGHT I WAS UNDERGROUND AGAIN.~~
AND LAST SORTIE.
AND THE ONE BEFORE THAT. AND--
OTHERS WORRIED.
AH. SORRY.
NO--
--SMOKE DOESN'T BOTHER ME ANYMORE.
~~WHEN I LOOK AT THEM I WONDER IF IT WILL BE THE LAST TIME.~~
IT'S OKAY, JAY.
GOT TO GET BACK TO FLYING.
EVERYONE UNDERSTANDS...
~~THOUGH NOT SURE THIS IS WORTH IT.~~
I DON'T.

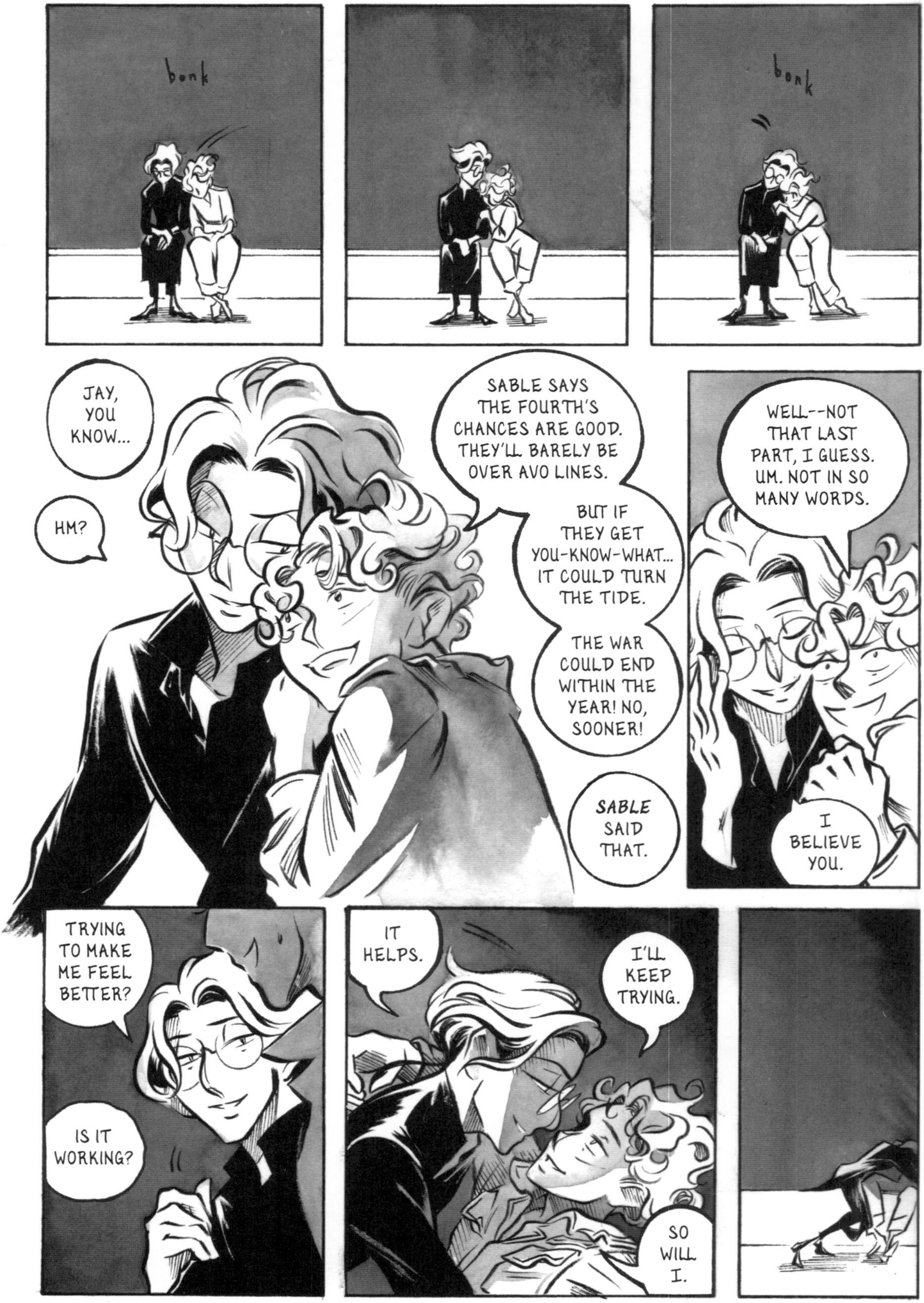
bonk
bonk
JAY, YOU KNOW...
HM?
SABLE SAYS THE FOURTH'S CHANCES ARE GOOD. THEY'LL BARELY BE OVER AVO LINES.
BUT IF THEY GET YOU-KNOW-WHAT... IT COULD TURN THE TIDE.
THE WAR COULD END WITHIN THE YEAR! NO, SOONER!
SABLE SAID THAT.
WELL--NOT THAT LAST PART, I GUESS. UM. NOT IN SO MANY WORDS.
I BELIEVE YOU.
TRYING TO MAKE ME FEEL BETTER?
IS IT WORKING?
IT HELPS.
I'LL KEEP TRYING.
SO WILL I.

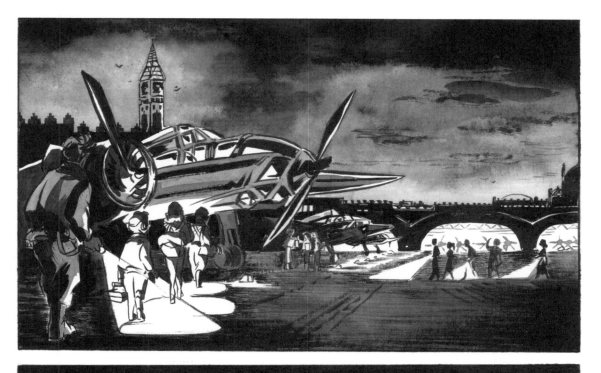

H.Q. HAS RECEIVED THE FOURTH DIVISION'S FLIGHT PATH. DO WE HAVE THEIR MISSION?

YES, SUPERIOR. FOURTH DIVISION IS FLYING OVER COASTAL TO PHOTOGRAPH AND ASSESS OUR FORCES.

A ROUTINE SURVEY...OR SO THEY WOULD HAVE US BELIEVE.

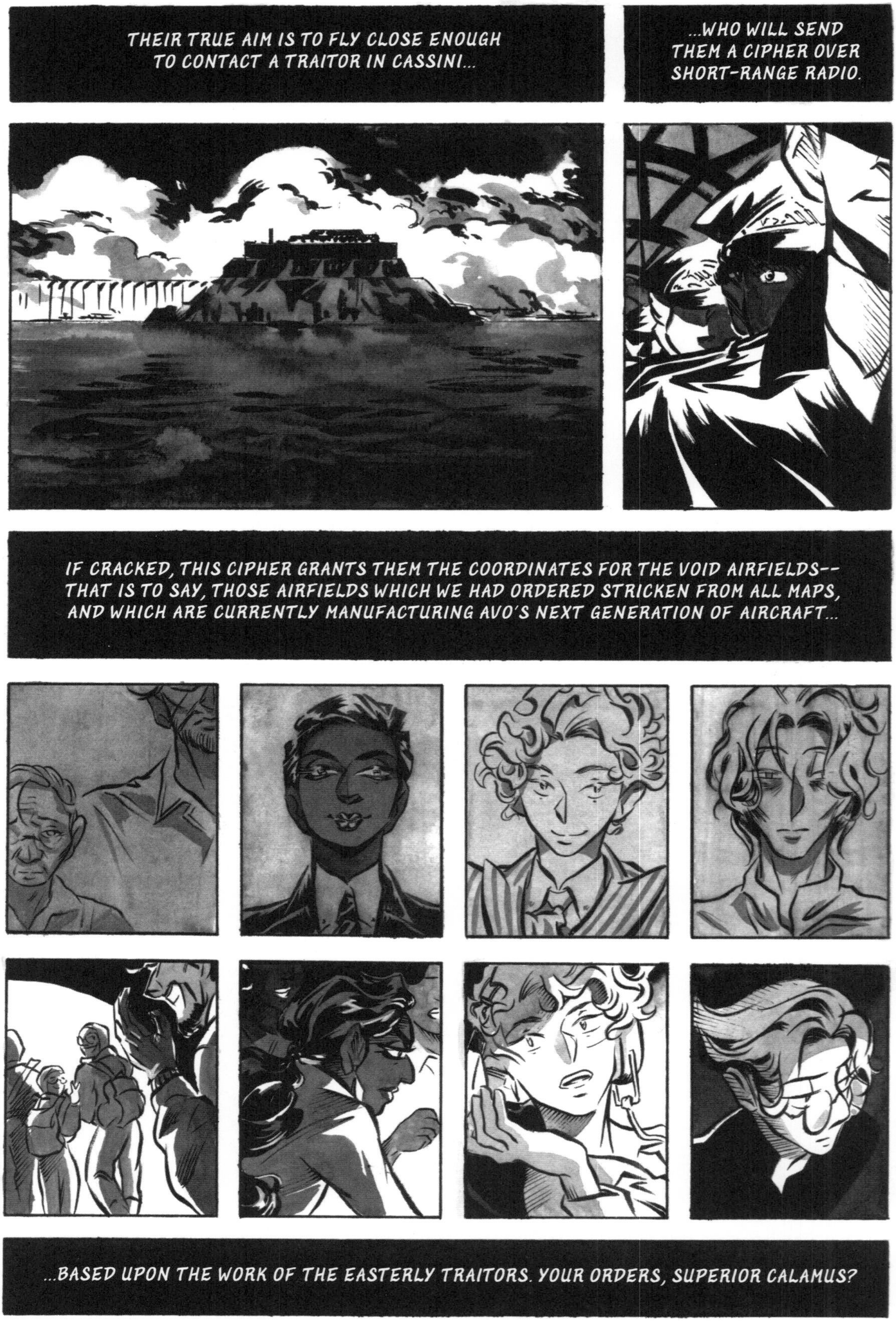
THEIR TRUE AIM IS TO FLY CLOSE ENOUGH TO CONTACT A TRAITOR IN CASSINI...
...WHO WILL SEND THEM A CIPHER OVER SHORT-RANGE RADIO.
IF CRACKED, THIS CIPHER GRANTS THEM THE COORDINATES FOR THE VOID AIRFIELDS-- THAT IS TO SAY, THOSE AIRFIELDS WHICH WE HAD ORDERED STRICKEN FROM ALL MAPS, AND WHICH ARE CURRENTLY MANUFACTURING AVO'S NEXT GENERATION OF AIRCRAFT...
...BASED UPON THE WORK OF THE EASTERLY TRAITORS. YOUR ORDERS, SUPERIOR CALAMUS?

DROWN THEM ALL.

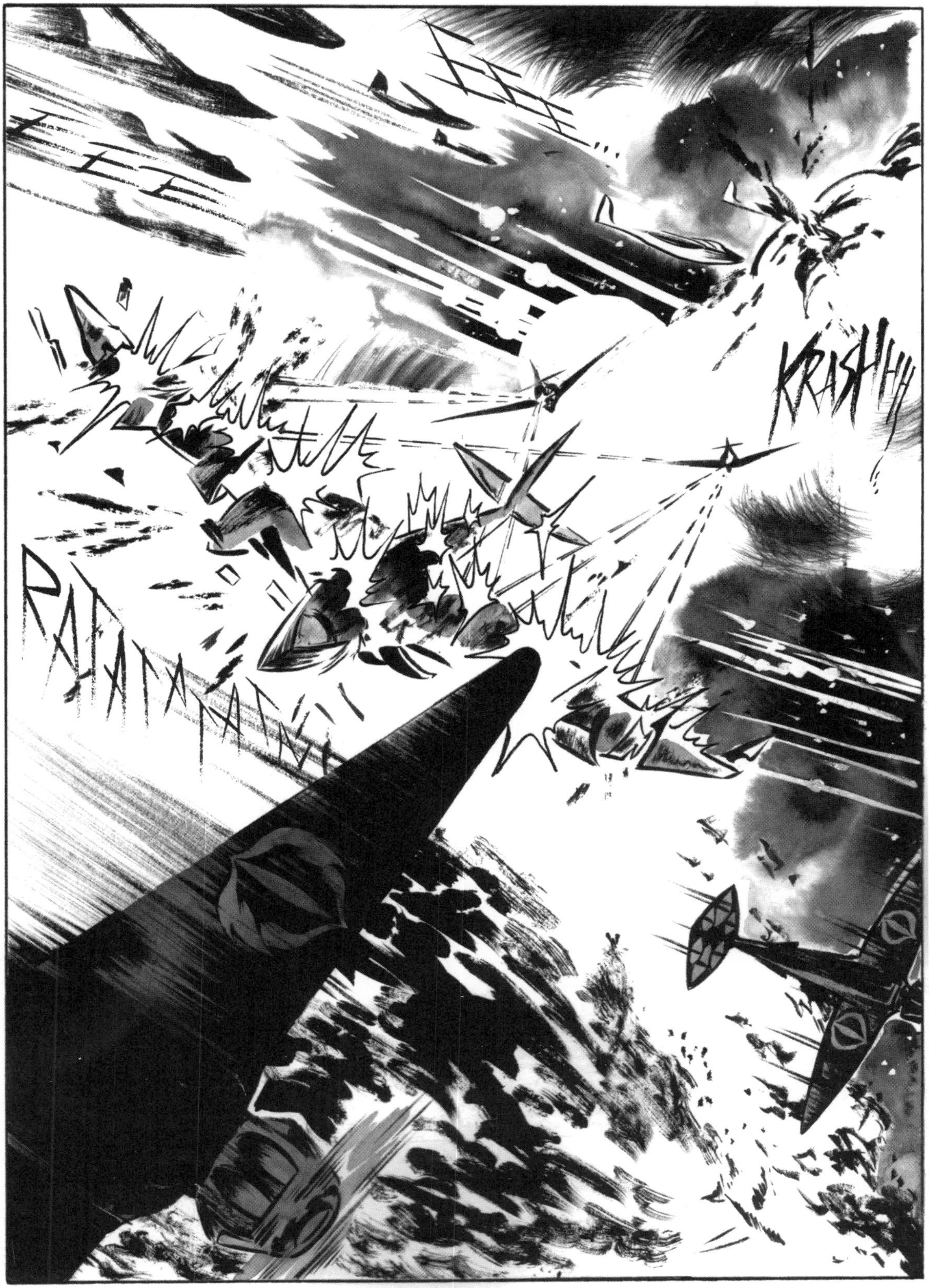
KRASHHH
RATATATATAT!!

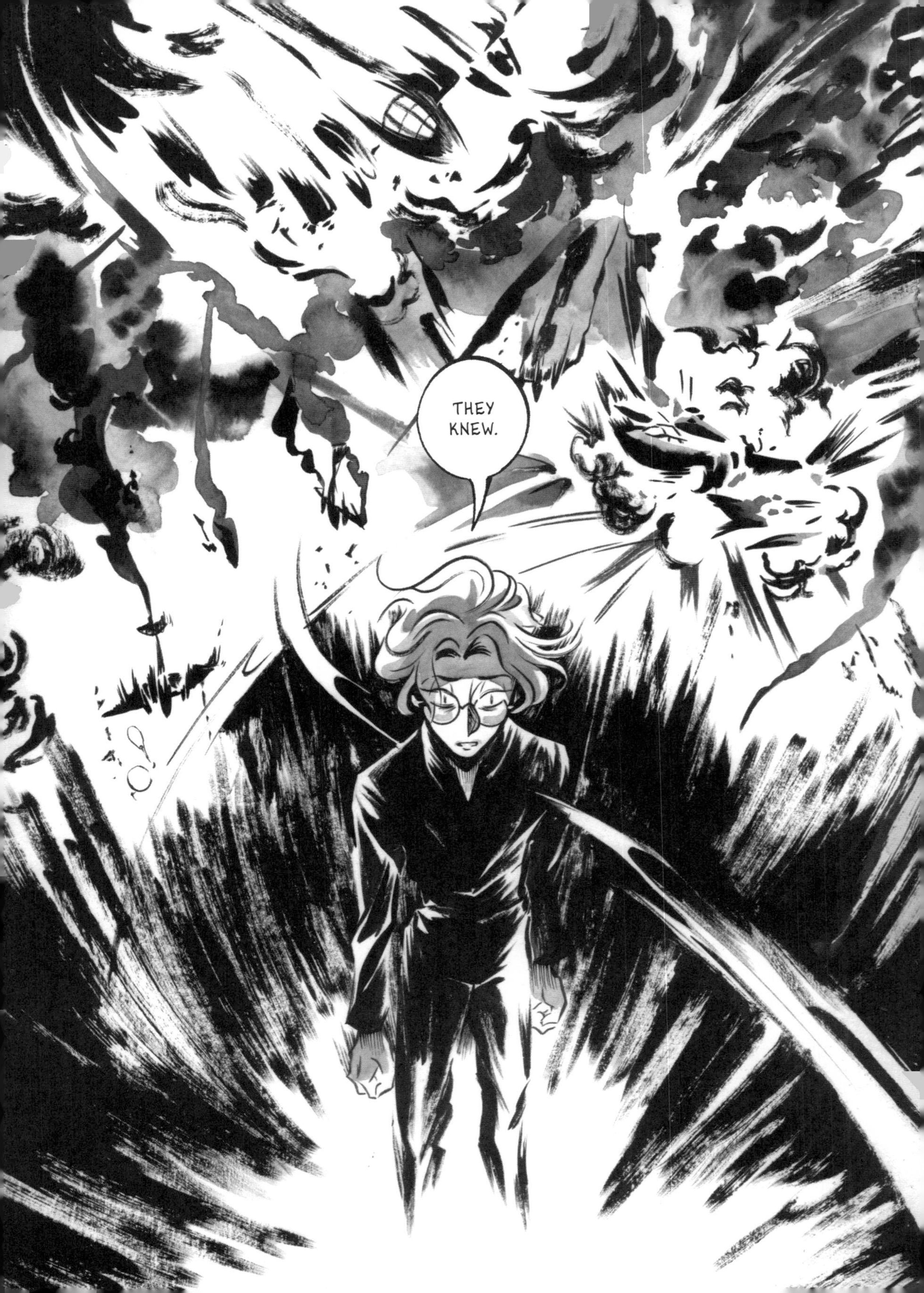
THEY KNEW.

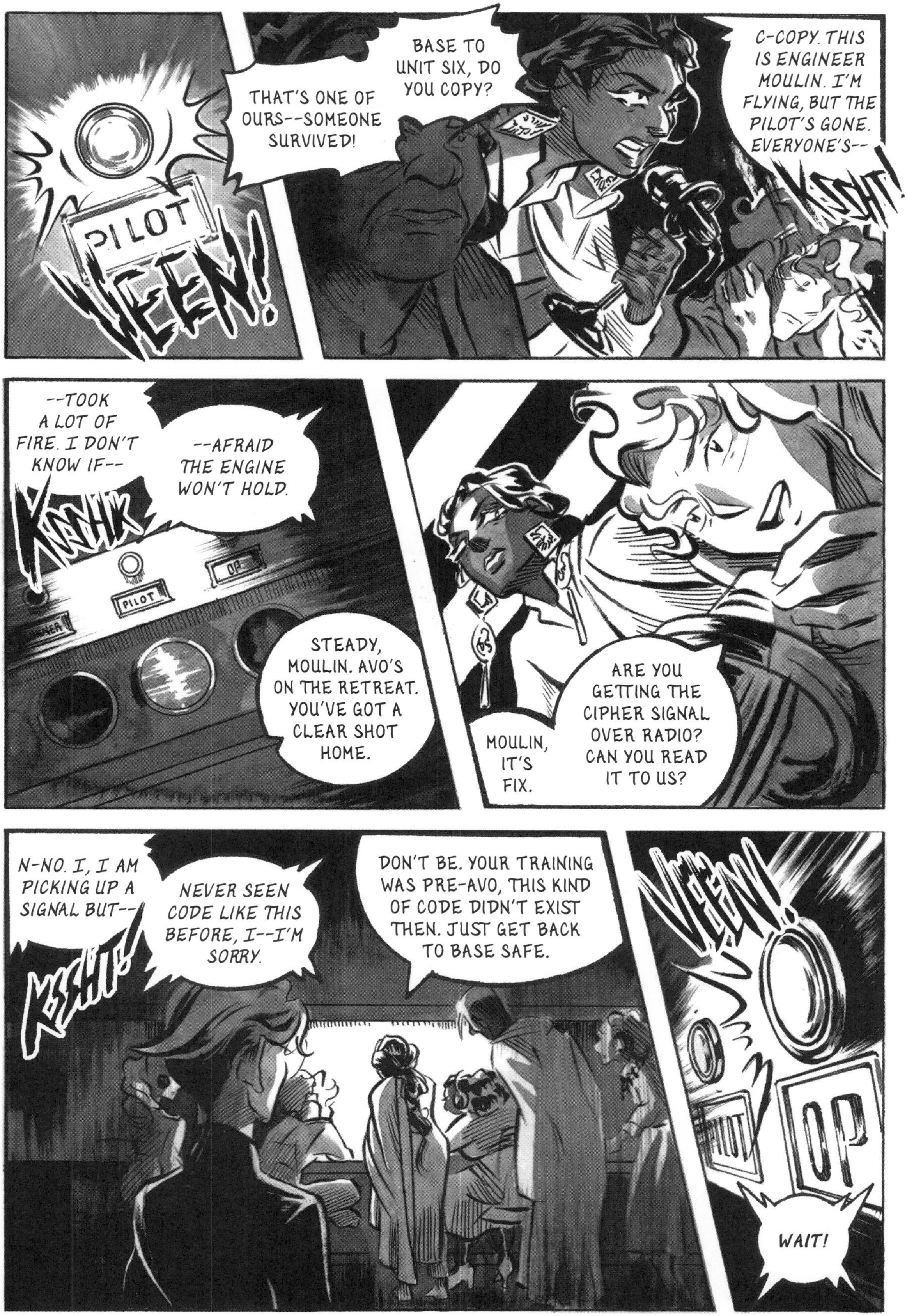
PILOT
VEEN!
THAT'S ONE OF OURS--SOMEONE SURVIVED!
BASE TO UNIT SIX, DO YOU COPY?
C-COPY. THIS IS ENGINEER MOULIN. I'M FLYING, BUT THE PILOT'S GONE. EVERYONE'S--
KSSHT!
--TOOK A LOT OF FIRE. I DON'T KNOW IF--
KSSHK
--AFRAID THE ENGINE WON'T HOLD.
OP
PILOT
STEADY, MOULIN. AVO'S ON THE RETREAT. YOU'VE GOT A CLEAR SHOT HOME.
MOULIN, IT'S FIX.
ARE YOU GETTING THE CIPHER SIGNAL OVER RADIO? CAN YOU READ IT TO US?
N-NO. I, I AM PICKING UP A SIGNAL BUT--
KSSHT!
NEVER SEEN CODE LIKE THIS BEFORE, I--I'M SORRY.
DON'T BE. YOUR TRAINING WAS PRE-AVO, THIS KIND OF CODE DIDN'T EXIST THEN. JUST GET BACK TO BASE SAFE.
VEEN!
PILOT
OP
WAIT!

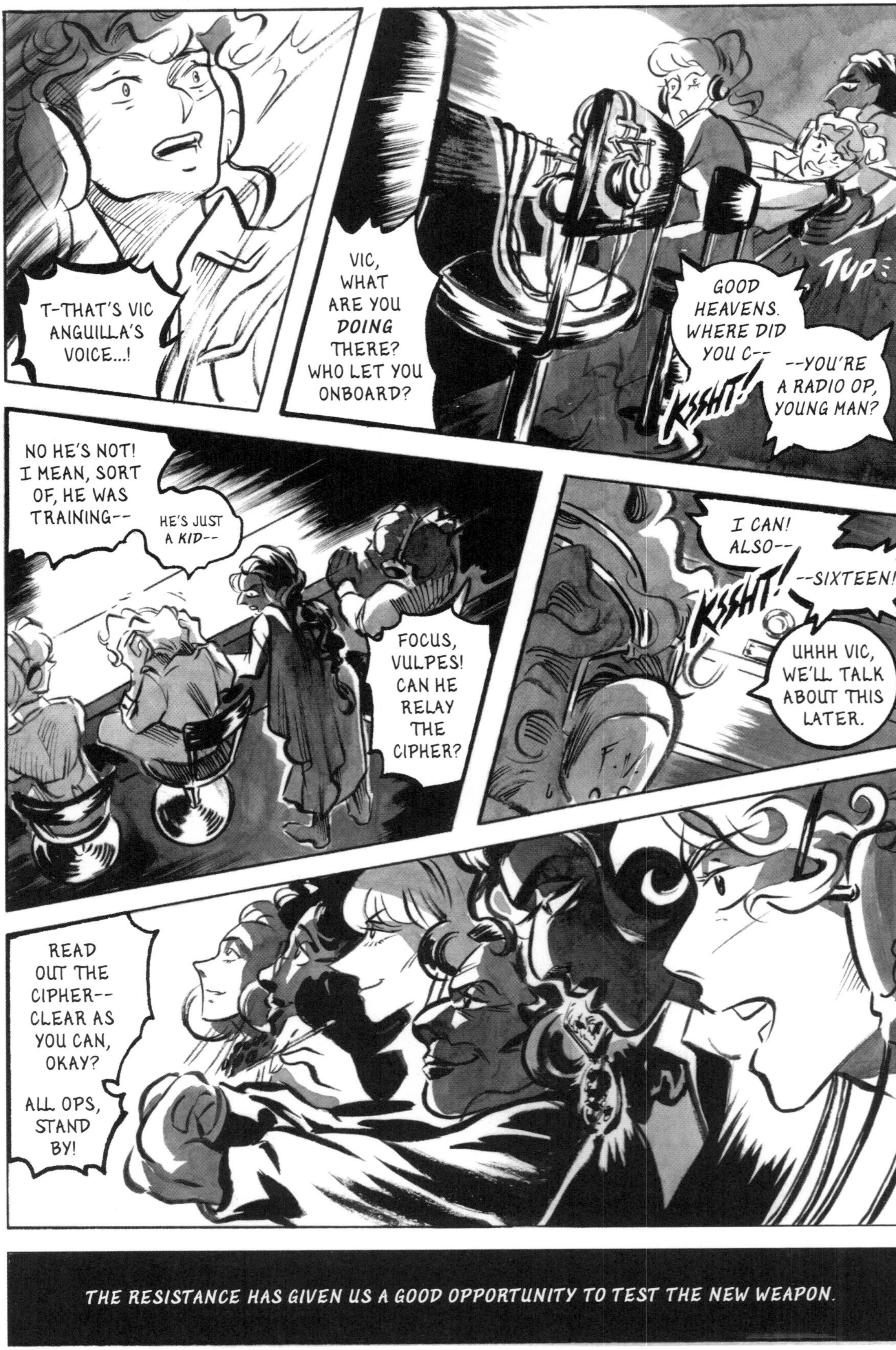
T-THAT'S VIC ANGUILLA'S VOICE...!
VIC, WHAT ARE YOU *DOING* THERE? WHO LET YOU ONBOARD?
TUP
GOOD HEAVENS. WHERE DID YOU C--
KSSHT!
--YOU'RE A RADIO OP, YOUNG MAN?
NO HE'S NOT! I MEAN, SORT OF, HE WAS TRAINING--
HE'S JUST A *KID*--
FOCUS, VULPES! CAN HE RELAY THE CIPHER?
I CAN! ALSO--
KSSHT!
--SIXTEEN!
UHHH VIC, WE'LL TALK ABOUT THIS LATER.
READ OUT THE CIPHER--CLEAR AS YOU CAN, OKAY?
ALL OPS, STAND BY!
THE RESISTANCE HAS GIVEN US A GOOD OPPORTUNITY TO TEST THE NEW WEAPON.

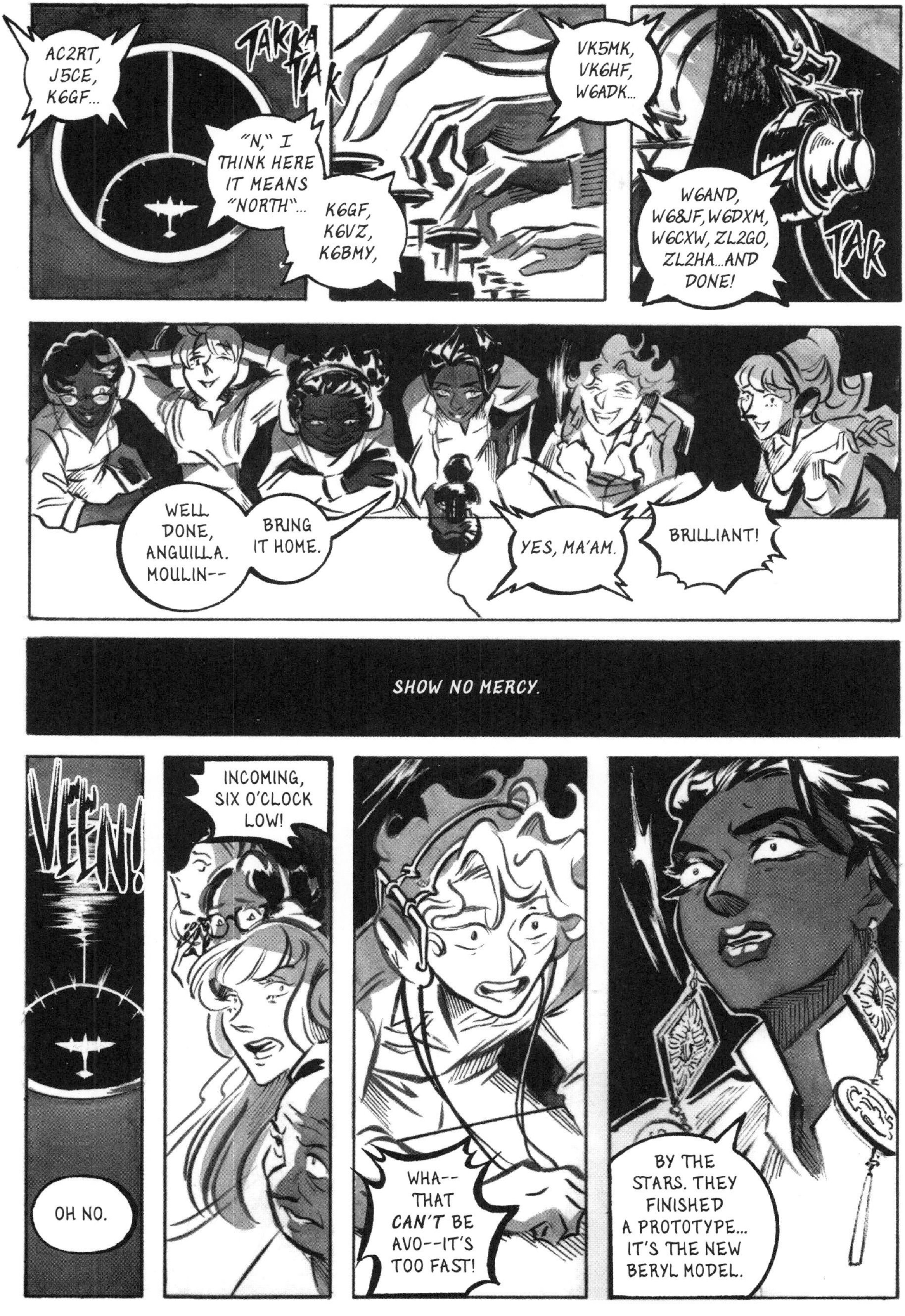
AC2RT, J5CE, K6GF...
TAKKA TAK
"N," I THINK HERE IT MEANS "NORTH"...
K6GF, K6VZ, K6BMY,
VK5MK, VK6HF, W6ADK...
W6AND, W6&JF, W6DXM, W6CXW, ZL2GO, ZL2HA...AND DONE!
TAK
WELL DONE, ANGUILLA. MOULIN--
BRING IT HOME.
YES, MA'AM.
BRILLIANT!
SHOW NO MERCY.
VEEN!
OH NO.
INCOMING, SIX O'CLOCK LOW!
WHA-- THAT *CAN'T* BE AVO--IT'S TOO FAST!
BY THE STARS. THEY FINISHED A PROTOTYPE... IT'S THE NEW BERYL MODEL.

A HUNDRED METERS-- CLOSING IN!

KSSHH

ARE WE-- ARE WE GONNA MAKE IT, SIR?

TOO FAST.

MOULIN! EVASIVE ACTION!

I CAN'T, NOT--

KSSHK

THE ENGINE DAMAGE, I DON'T--

--NO CHANCE, MISTER?

--I'M SORRY.

KSSHKK

TWENTY METERS.

I'M SO SORRY.

OH, GOD.

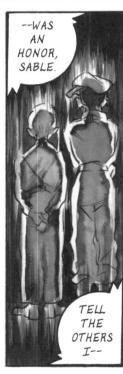

--WAS AN HONOR, SABLE.

TELL THE OTHERS I--

FIX--

HELP--!

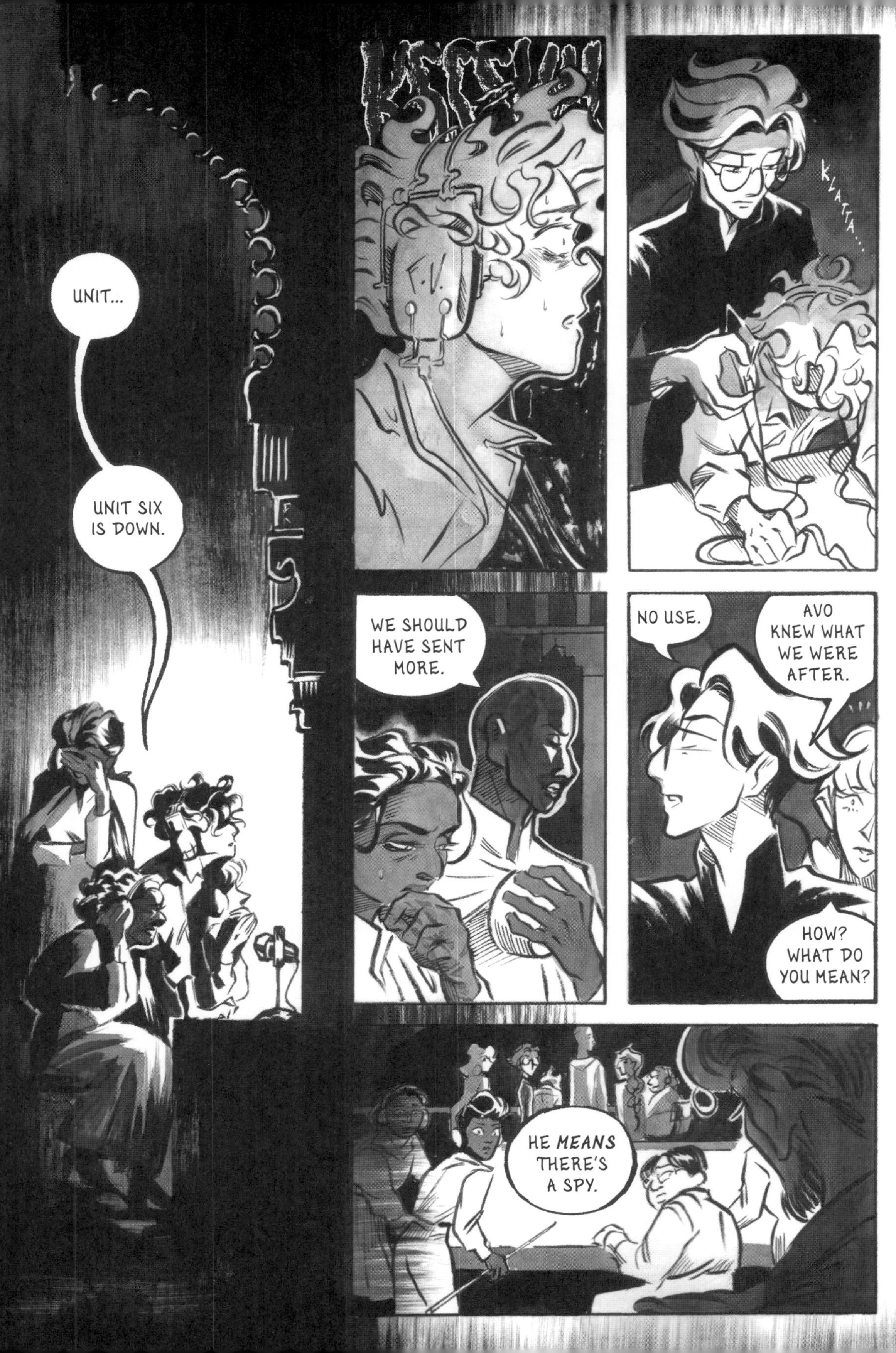
UNIT...
UNIT SIX IS DOWN.
KLATTA...
WE SHOULD HAVE SENT MORE.
NO USE.
AVO KNEW WHAT WE WERE AFTER.
HOW? WHAT DO YOU MEAN?
HE *MEANS* THERE'S A SPY.

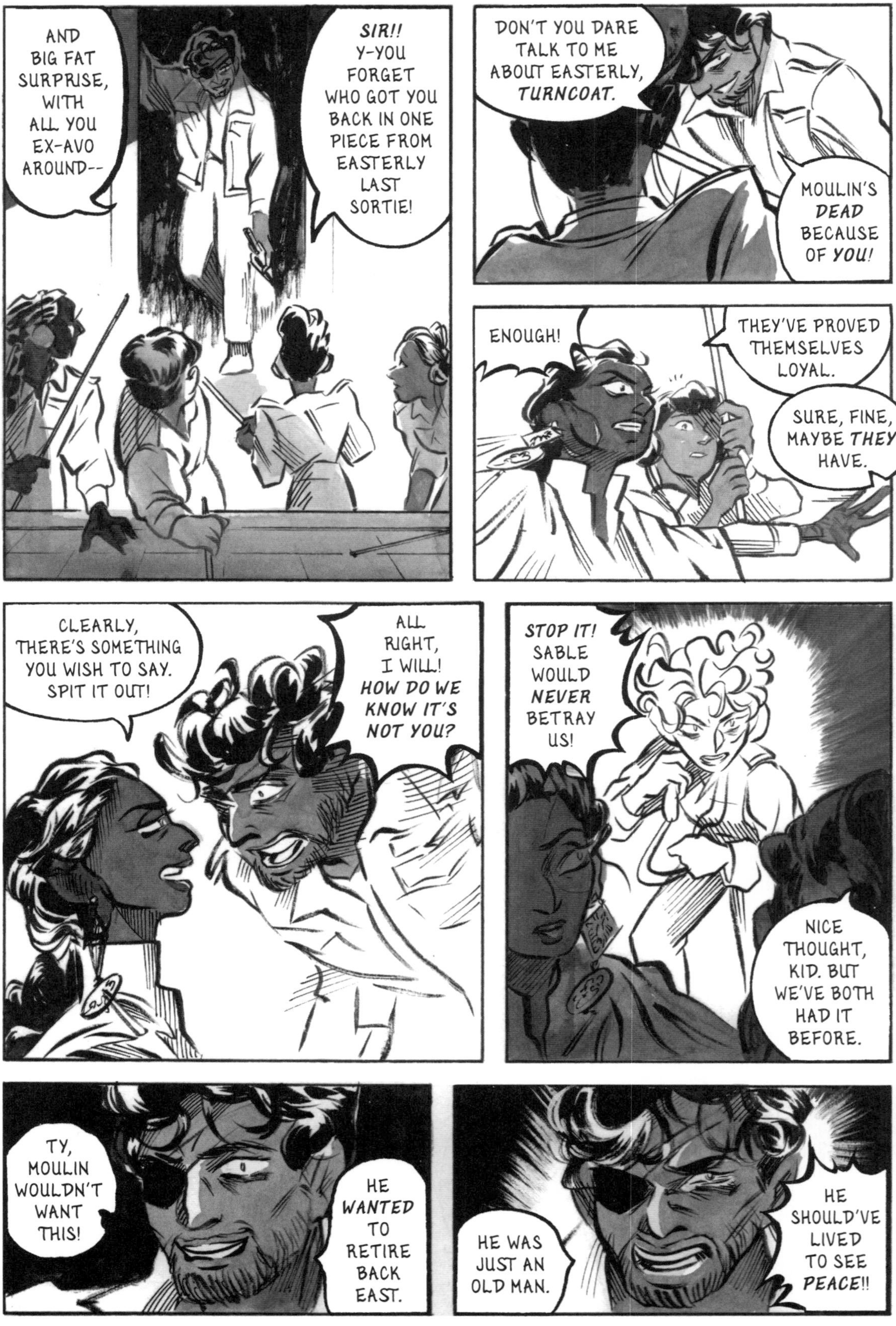
AND BIG FAT SURPRISE, WITH ALL YOU EX-AVO AROUND--
SIR!! Y-YOU FORGET WHO GOT YOU BACK IN ONE PIECE FROM EASTERLY LAST SORTIE!
DON'T YOU DARE TALK TO ME ABOUT EASTERLY, TURNCOAT.
MOULIN'S DEAD BECAUSE OF YOU!
ENOUGH!
THEY'VE PROVED THEMSELVES LOYAL.
SURE, FINE, MAYBE THEY HAVE.
CLEARLY, THERE'S SOMETHING YOU WISH TO SAY. SPIT IT OUT!
ALL RIGHT, I WILL! HOW DO WE KNOW IT'S NOT YOU?
STOP IT! SABLE WOULD NEVER BETRAY US!
NICE THOUGHT, KID. BUT WE'VE BOTH HAD IT BEFORE.
TY, MOULIN WOULDN'T WANT THIS!
HE WANTED TO RETIRE BACK EAST.
HE WAS JUST AN OLD MAN.
HE SHOULD'VE LIVED TO SEE PEACE!!

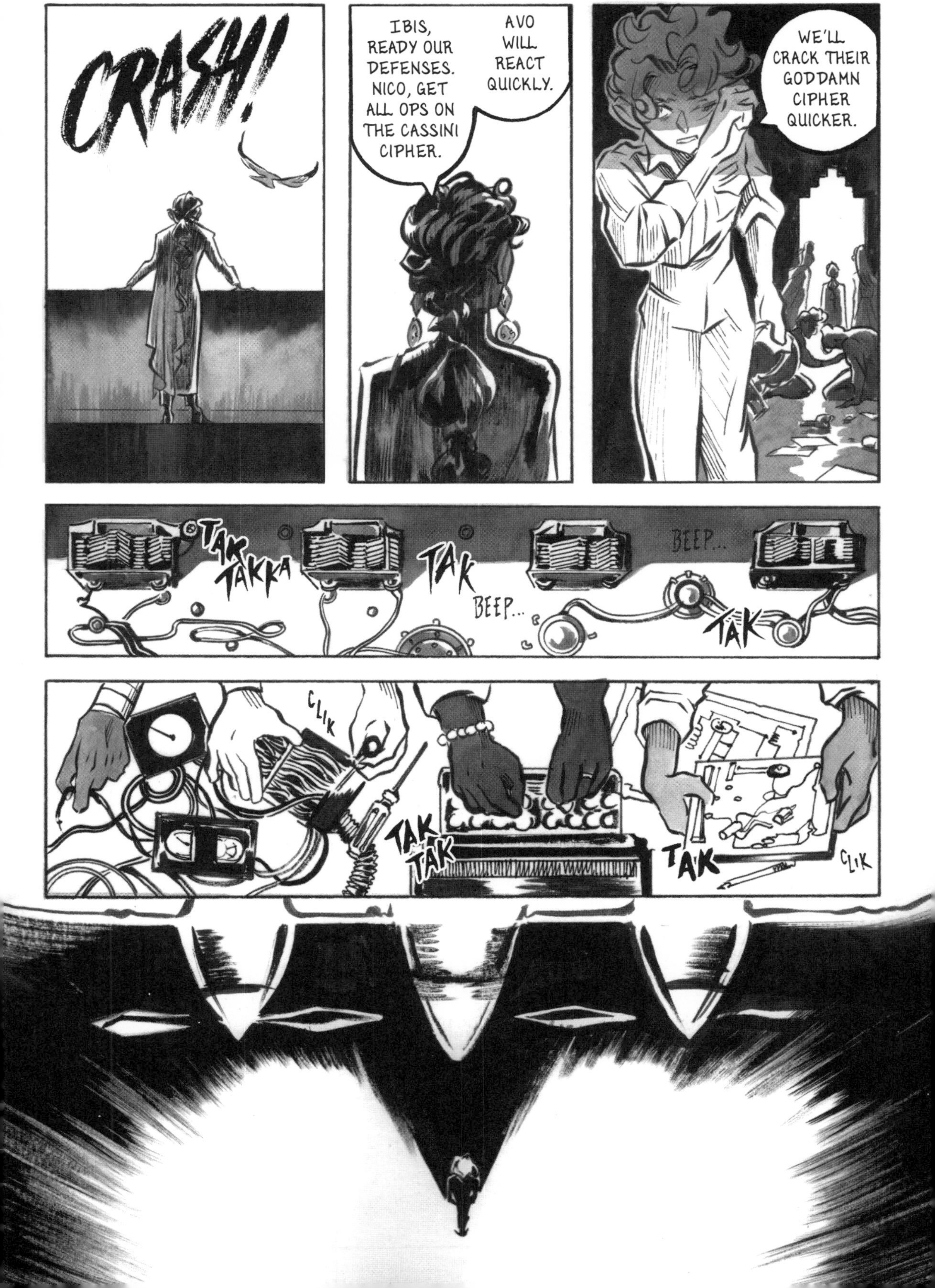
CRASH!
IBIS, READY OUR DEFENSES. NICO, GET ALL OPS ON THE CASSINI CIPHER.
AVO WILL REACT QUICKLY.
WE'LL CRACK THEIR GODDAMN CIPHER QUICKER.
TAK TAKKA
TAK
BEEP...
BEEP...
TAK
CLIK
TAK TAK
TAK
CLIK

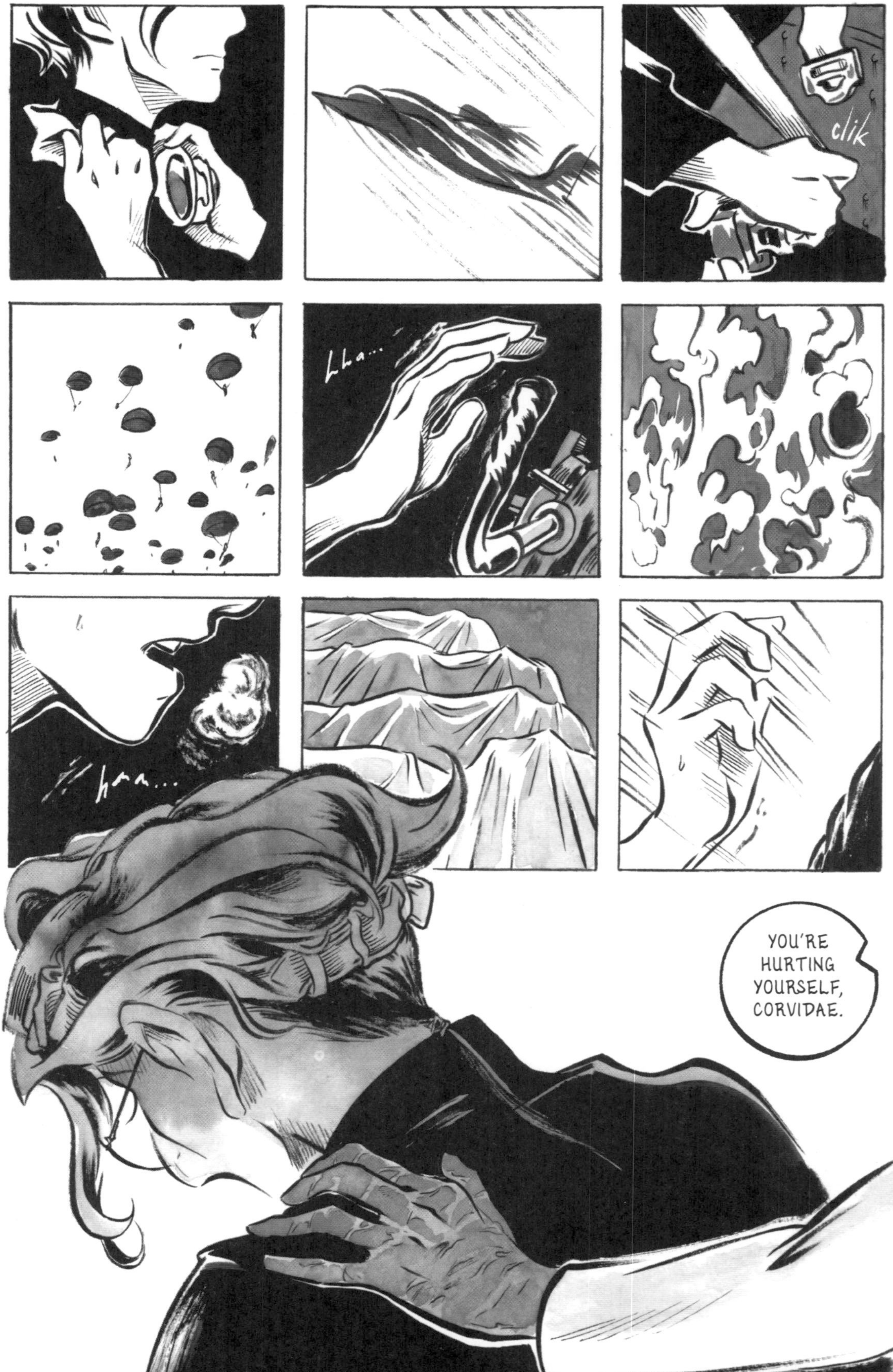

clik
hha...
hhaa...
YOU'RE HURTING YOURSELF, CORVIDAE.

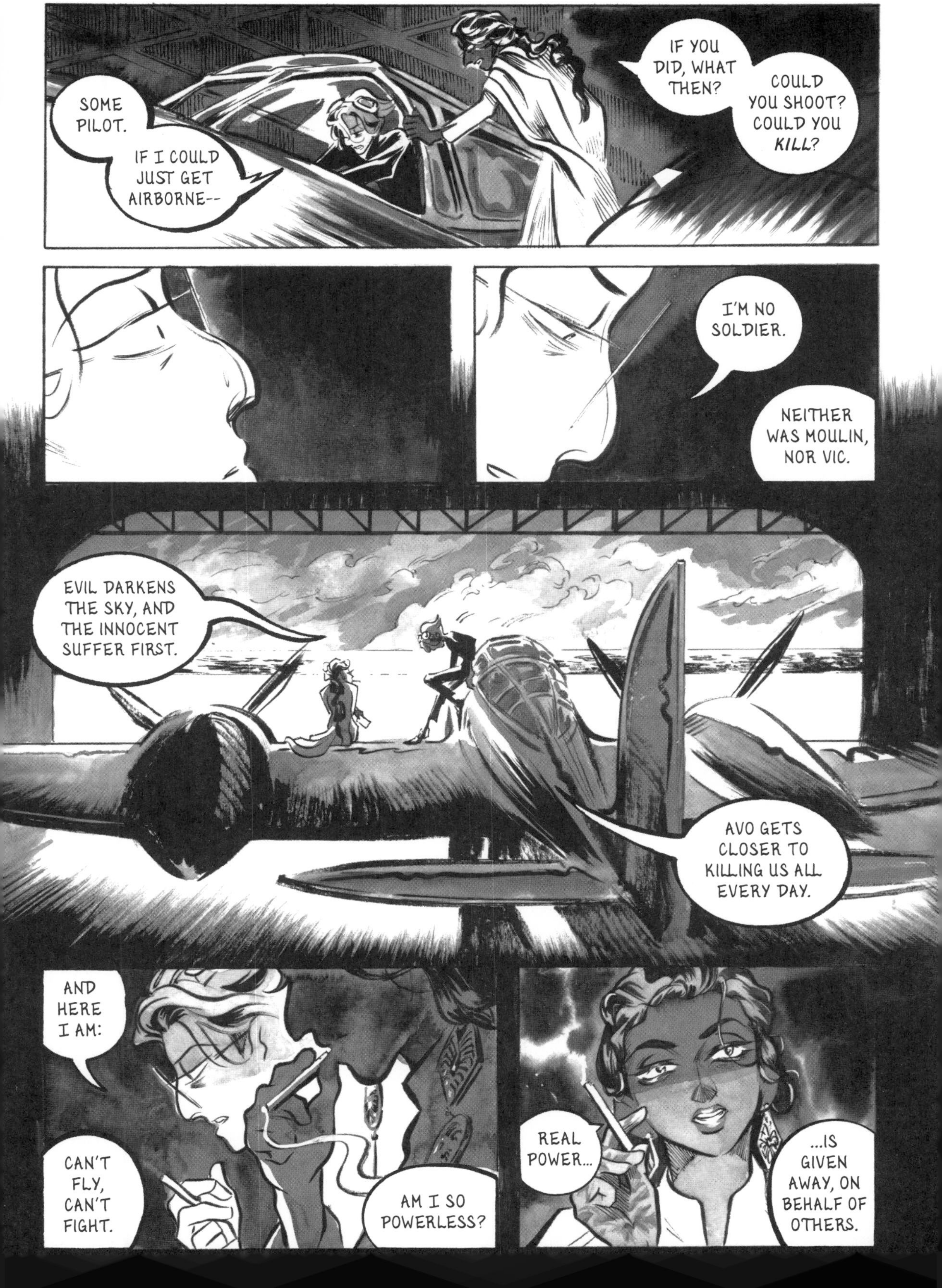
SOME PILOT.
IF I COULD JUST GET AIRBORNE--
IF YOU DID, WHAT THEN?
COULD YOU SHOOT? COULD YOU KILL?
I'M NO SOLDIER.
NEITHER WAS MOULIN, NOR VIC.
EVIL DARKENS THE SKY, AND THE INNOCENT SUFFER FIRST.
AVO GETS CLOSER TO KILLING US ALL EVERY DAY.
AND HERE I AM:
CAN'T FLY, CAN'T FIGHT.
AM I SO POWERLESS?
REAL POWER...
...IS GIVEN AWAY, ON BEHALF OF OTHERS.

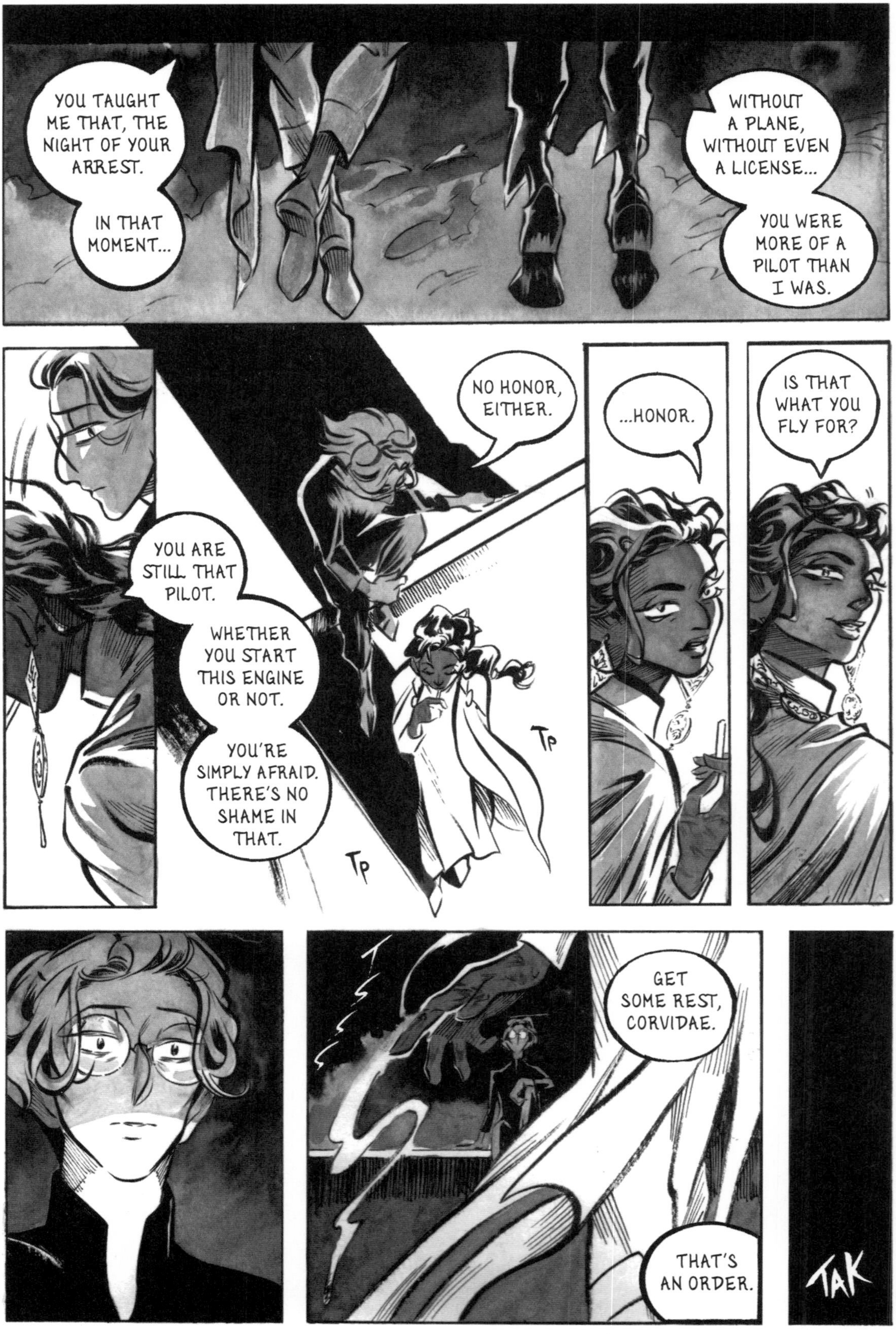
YOU TAUGHT ME THAT, THE NIGHT OF YOUR ARREST.
IN THAT MOMENT...
WITHOUT A PLANE, WITHOUT EVEN A LICENSE...
YOU WERE MORE OF A PILOT THAN I WAS.
NO HONOR, EITHER.
YOU ARE STILL THAT PILOT.
WHETHER YOU START THIS ENGINE OR NOT.
YOU'RE SIMPLY AFRAID. THERE'S NO SHAME IN THAT.
TP
TP
...HONOR.
IS THAT WHAT YOU FLY FOR?
GET SOME REST, CORVIDAE.
THAT'S AN ORDER.
TAK

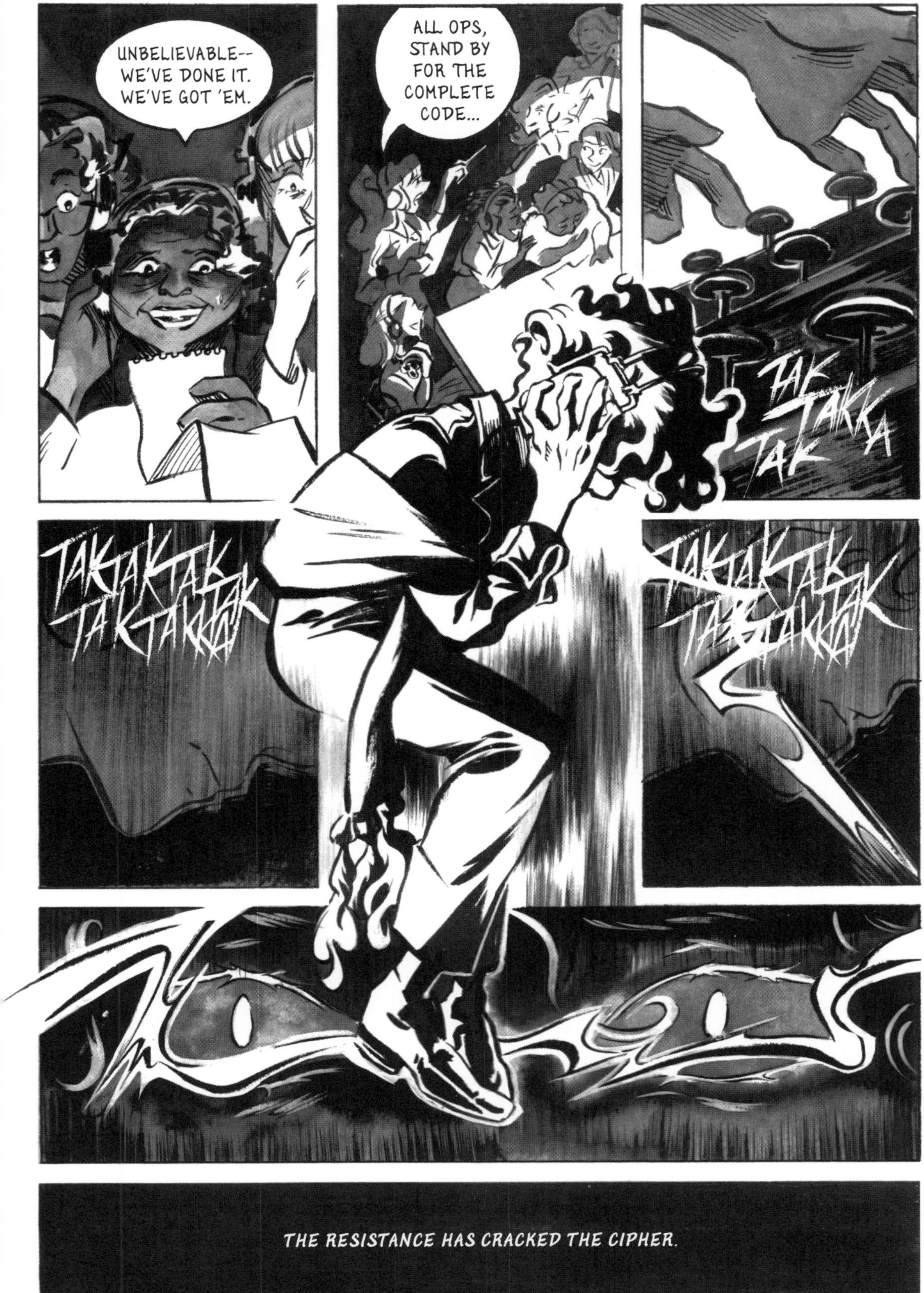
UNBELIEVABLE-- WE'VE DONE IT. WE'VE GOT 'EM.
ALL OPS, STAND BY FOR THE COMPLETE CODE...
TAK TAKKA TAK
TAKTAKTAK TAKTAKKATAK
TAKTAKTAK TAKTAKKATAK
THE RESISTANCE HAS CRACKED THE CIPHER.

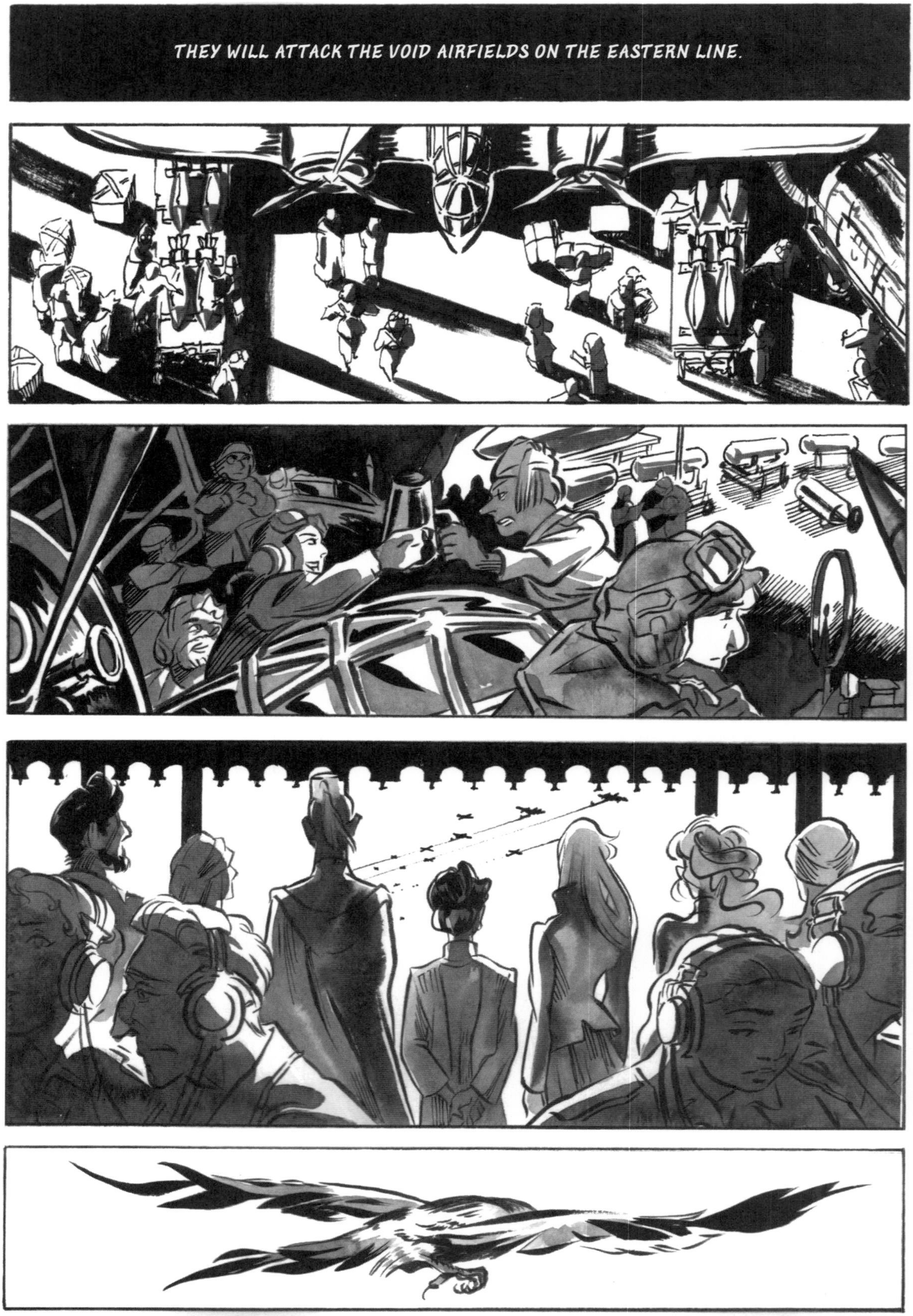
THEY WILL ATTACK THE VOID AIRFIELDS ON THE EASTERN LINE.

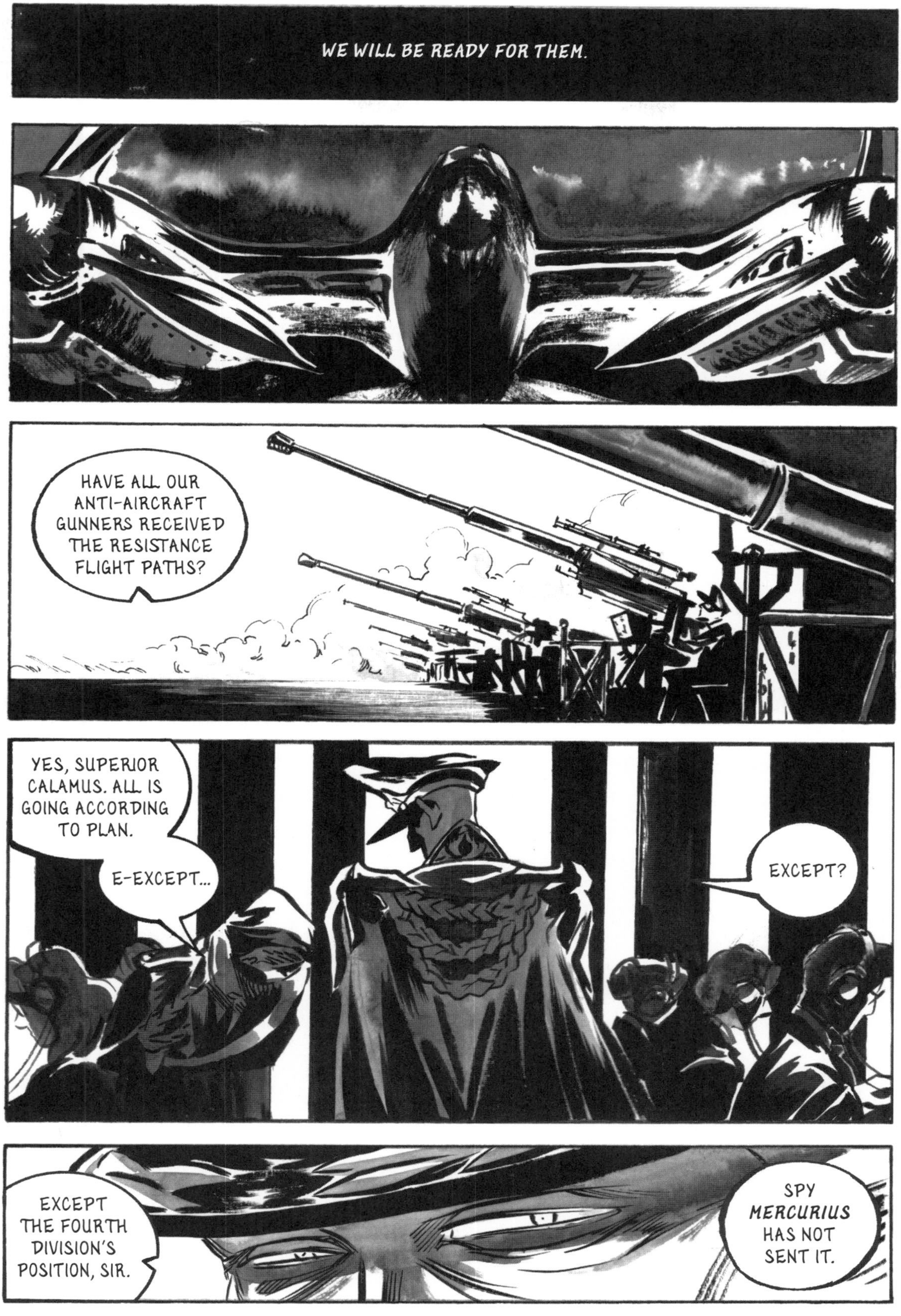
WE WILL BE READY FOR THEM.
HAVE ALL OUR ANTI-AIRCRAFT GUNNERS RECEIVED THE RESISTANCE FLIGHT PATHS?
YES, SUPERIOR CALAMUS. ALL IS GOING ACCORDING TO PLAN.
E-EXCEPT...
EXCEPT?
EXCEPT THE FOURTH DIVISION'S POSITION, SIR.
SPY MERCURIUS HAS NOT SENT IT.

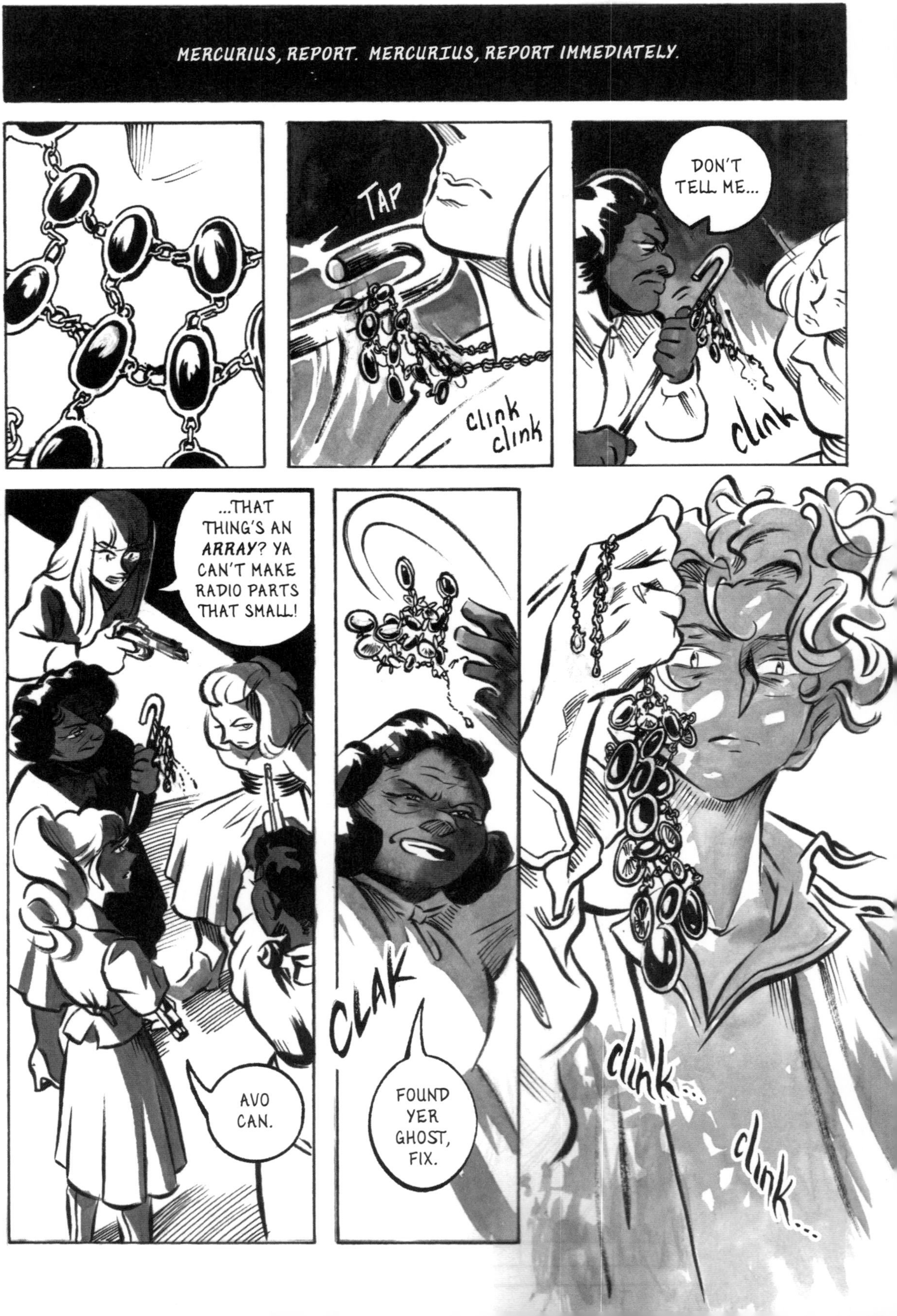
MERCURIUS, REPORT. MERCURIUS, REPORT IMMEDIATELY.
TAP
clink clink
DON'T TELL ME...
clink
...THAT THING'S AN ARRAY? YA CAN'T MAKE RADIO PARTS THAT SMALL!
AVO CAN.
CLAK
FOUND YER GHOST, FIX.
clink...
clink...

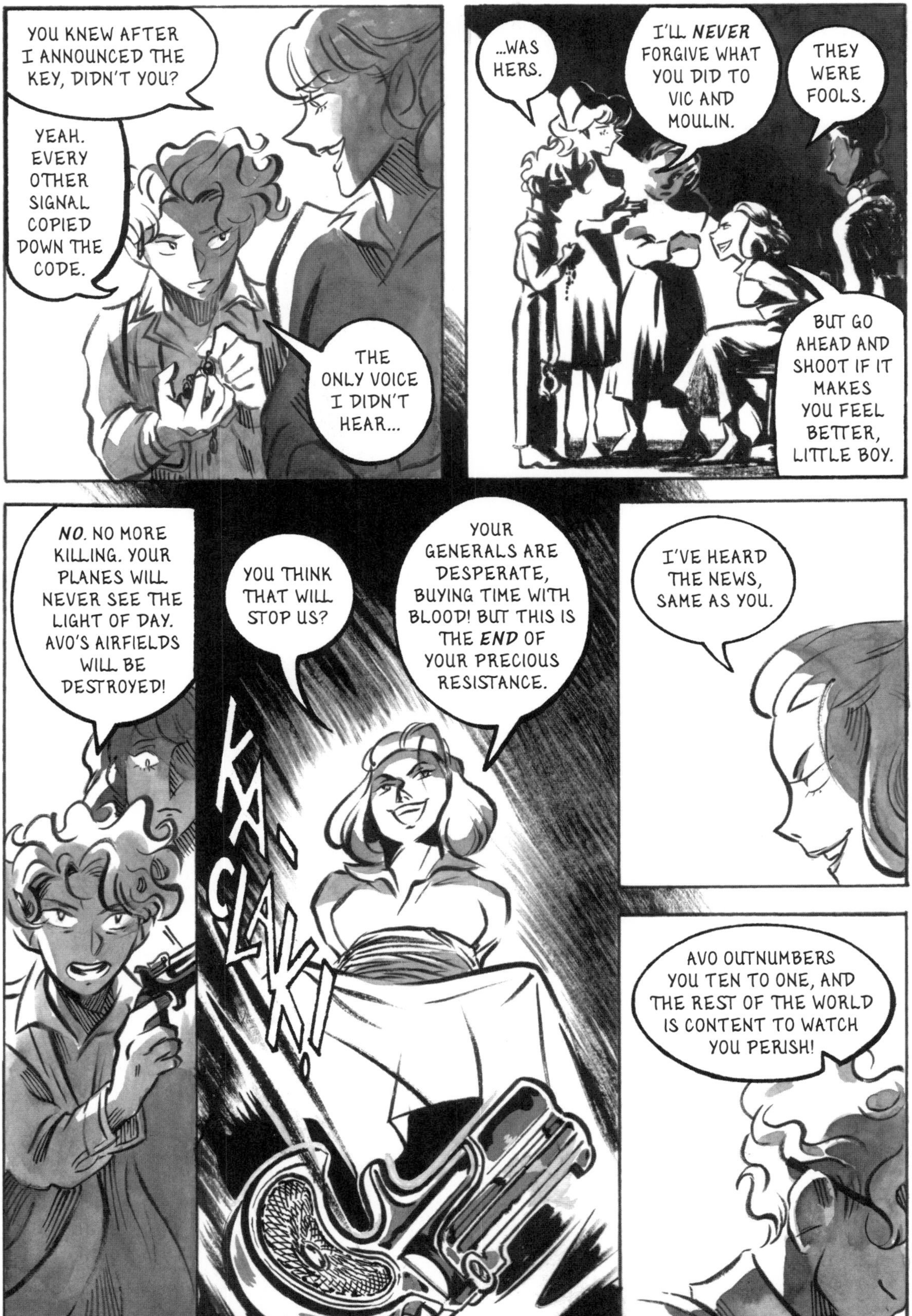
YOU KNEW AFTER I ANNOUNCED THE KEY, DIDN'T YOU?
YEAH. EVERY OTHER SIGNAL COPIED DOWN THE CODE.
THE ONLY VOICE I DIDN'T HEAR...
...WAS HERS.
I'LL NEVER FORGIVE WHAT YOU DID TO VIC AND MOULIN.
THEY WERE FOOLS.
BUT GO AHEAD AND SHOOT IF IT MAKES YOU FEEL BETTER, LITTLE BOY.
NO. NO MORE KILLING. YOUR PLANES WILL NEVER SEE THE LIGHT OF DAY. AVO'S AIRFIELDS WILL BE DESTROYED!
YOU THINK THAT WILL STOP US?
YOUR GENERALS ARE DESPERATE, BUYING TIME WITH BLOOD! BUT THIS IS THE END OF YOUR PRECIOUS RESISTANCE.
KA-CLAK!
I'VE HEARD THE NEWS, SAME AS YOU.
AVO OUTNUMBERS YOU TEN TO ONE, AND THE REST OF THE WORLD IS CONTENT TO WATCH YOU PERISH!

I HEARD DIFFERENTLY.

MERCURIUS

MINERVA

WE'VE LOST MERCURIUS, SUPERIOR!

WHERE IS THIS RESISTANCE AIRPOWER *COMING* FROM?

BY THE STARS-- T-THEY'RE *NOT* RESISTANCE AT ALL!

CONTRADICT ME AGAIN AND I'LL SEE YOU *HANG*--

SIR-- PLEASE-- SEE FOR YOURSELF--

GOT VISUAL ON ENEMY GULLS IDENTIFIED ORIGIN...

IT'S THE SOUTHERLY AIR FORCE!!

GET ME SPY *MINERVA!*

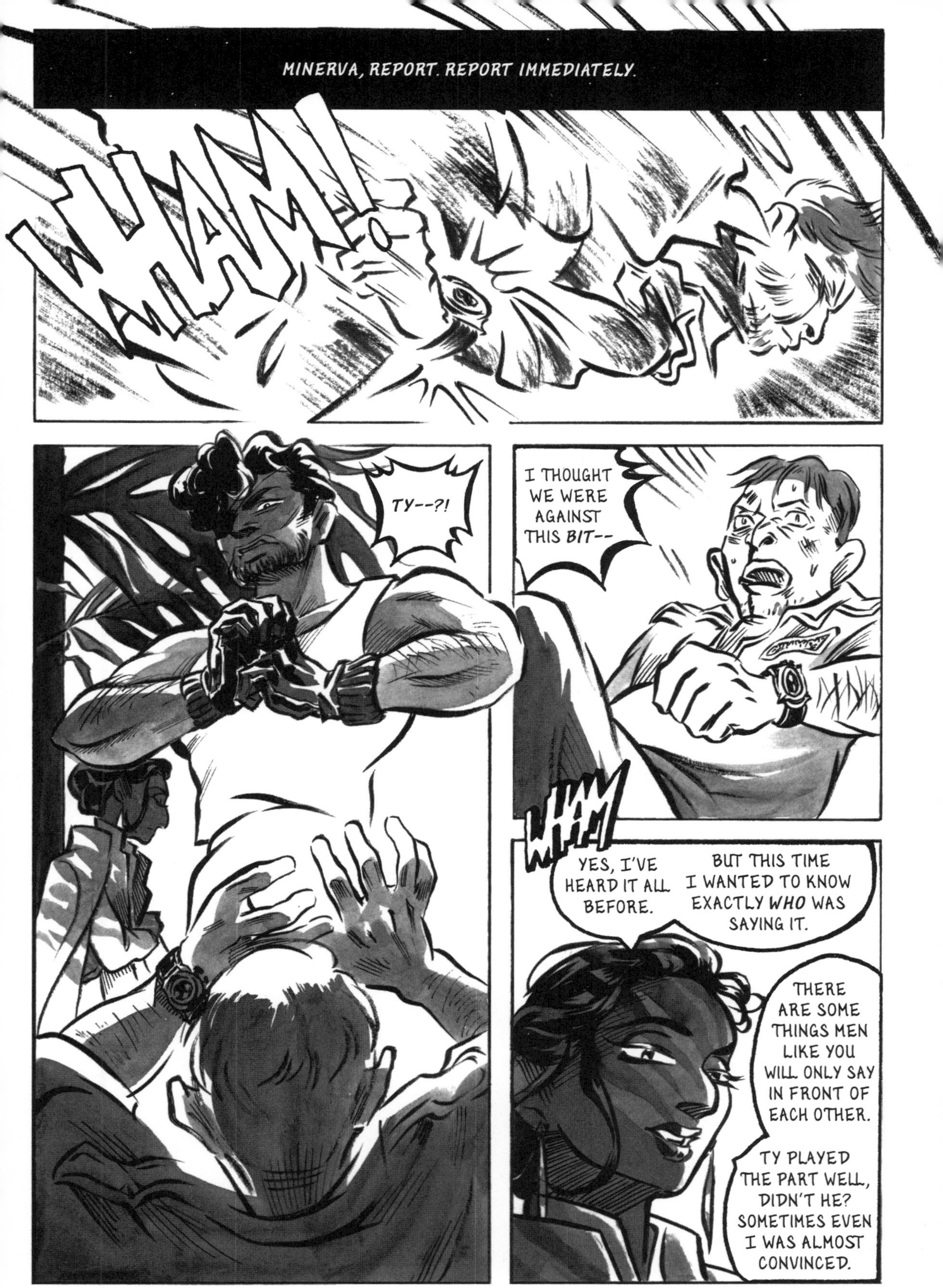
MINERVA, REPORT. REPORT IMMEDIATELY.
WHAM!
TY--?!
I THOUGHT WE WERE AGAINST THIS BIT--
WHAM
YES, I'VE HEARD IT ALL BEFORE.
BUT THIS TIME I WANTED TO KNOW EXACTLY WHO WAS SAYING IT.
THERE ARE SOME THINGS MEN LIKE YOU WILL ONLY SAY IN FRONT OF EACH OTHER.
TY PLAYED THE PART WELL, DIDN'T HE? SOMETIMES EVEN I WAS ALMOST CONVINCED.

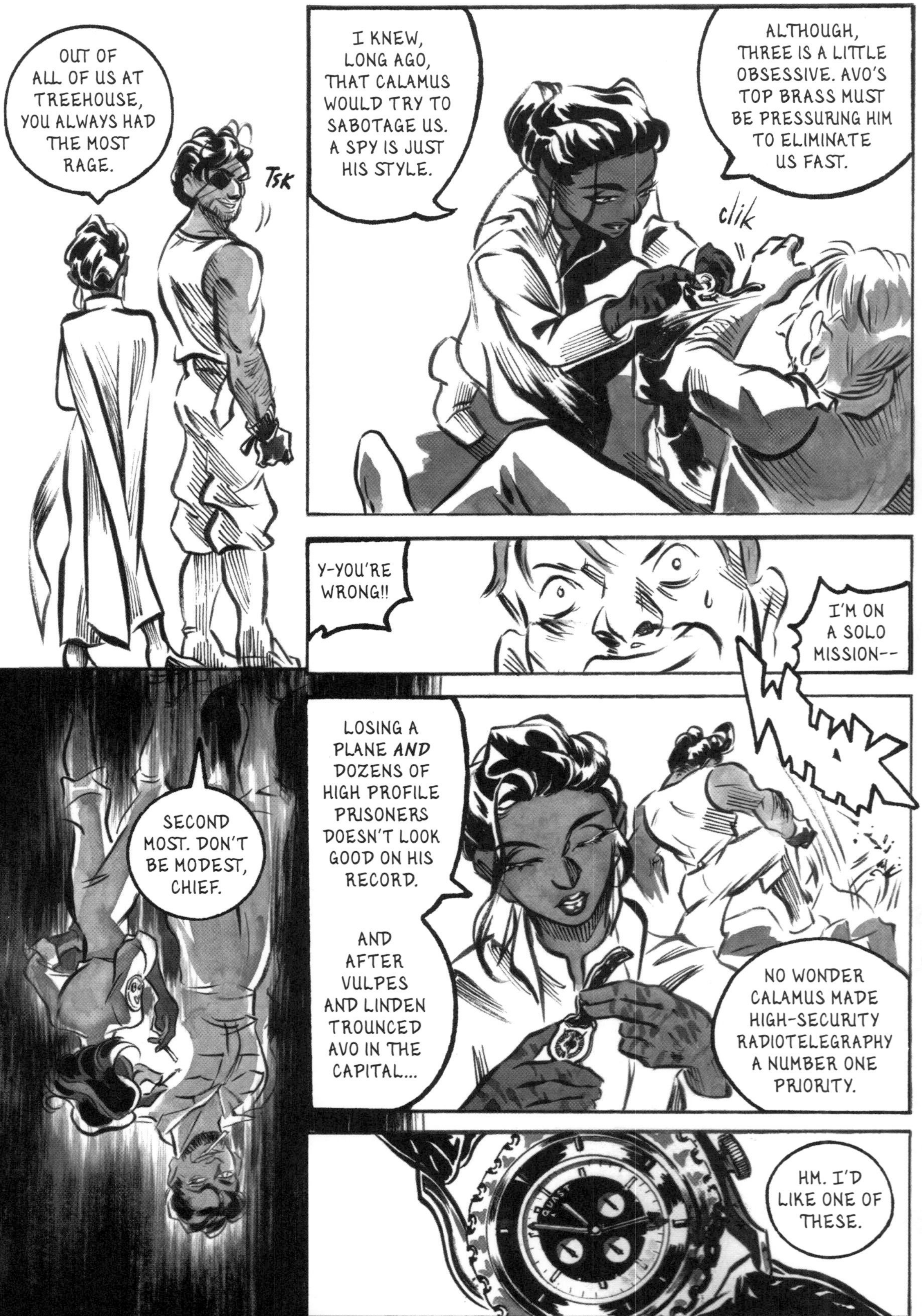
OUT OF ALL OF US AT TREEHOUSE, YOU ALWAYS HAD THE MOST RAGE.
TSK
SECOND MOST. DON'T BE MODEST, CHIEF.
I KNEW, LONG AGO, THAT CALAMUS WOULD TRY TO SABOTAGE US. A SPY IS JUST HIS STYLE.
ALTHOUGH, THREE IS A LITTLE OBSESSIVE. AVO'S TOP BRASS MUST BE PRESSURING HIM TO ELIMINATE US FAST.
clik
Y-YOU'RE WRONG!!
I'M ON A SOLO MISSION--
WHAK
LOSING A PLANE *AND* DOZENS OF HIGH PROFILE PRISONERS DOESN'T LOOK GOOD ON HIS RECORD.
AND AFTER VULPES AND LINDEN TROUNCED AVO IN THE CAPITAL...
NO WONDER CALAMUS MADE HIGH-SECURITY RADIOTELEGRAPHY A NUMBER ONE PRIORITY.
HM. I'D LIKE ONE OF THESE.

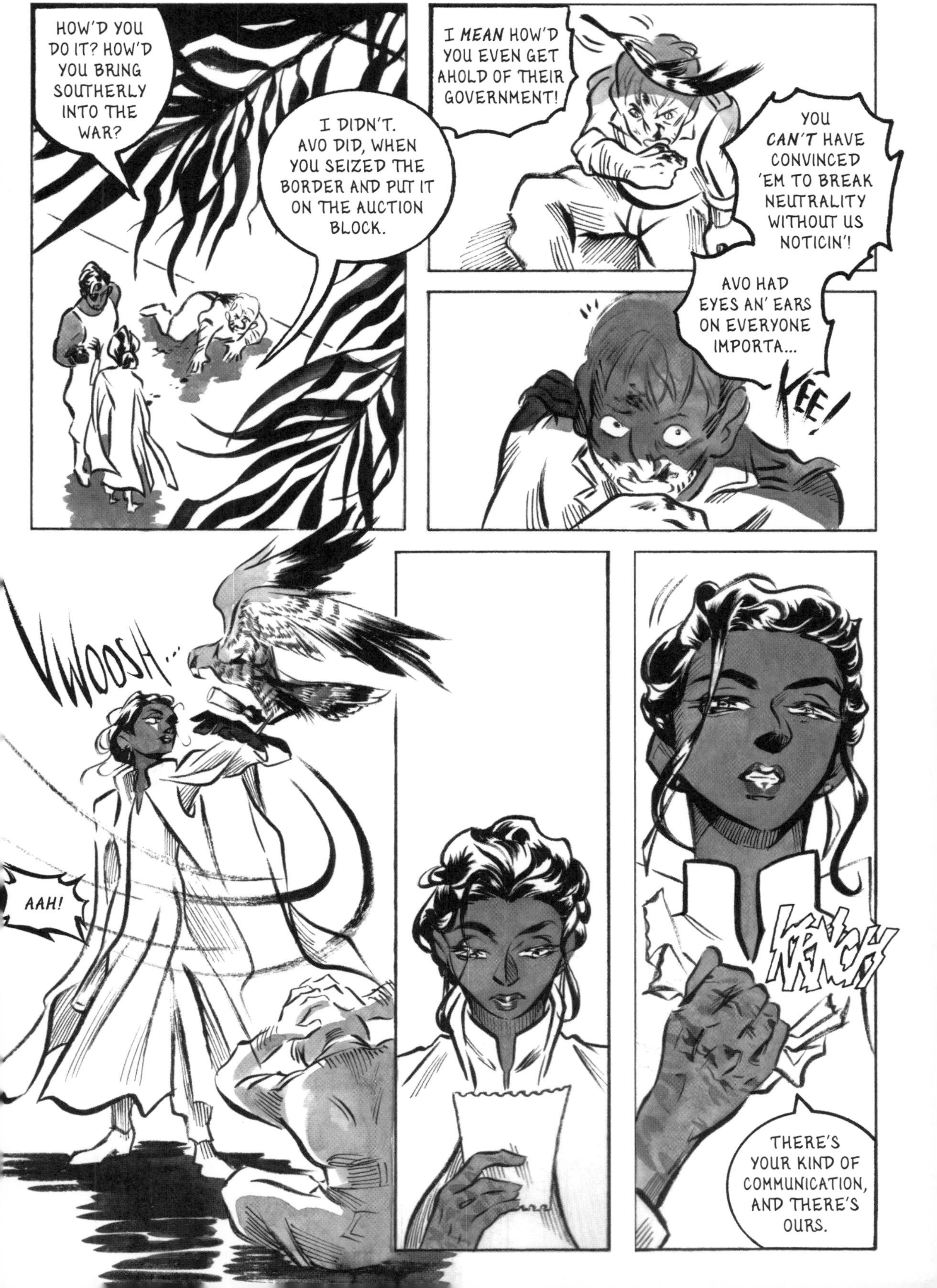
HOW'D YOU DO IT? HOW'D YOU BRING SOUTHERLY INTO THE WAR?
I DIDN'T. AVO DID, WHEN YOU SEIZED THE BORDER AND PUT IT ON THE AUCTION BLOCK.
I MEAN HOW'D YOU EVEN GET AHOLD OF THEIR GOVERNMENT!
YOU CAN'T HAVE CONVINCED 'EM TO BREAK NEUTRALITY WITHOUT US NOTICIN'!
AVO HAD EYES AN' EARS ON EVERYONE IMPORTA...
KEE!
VWOOSH...
AAH!
KRNCH
THERE'S YOUR KIND OF COMMUNICATION, AND THERE'S OURS.

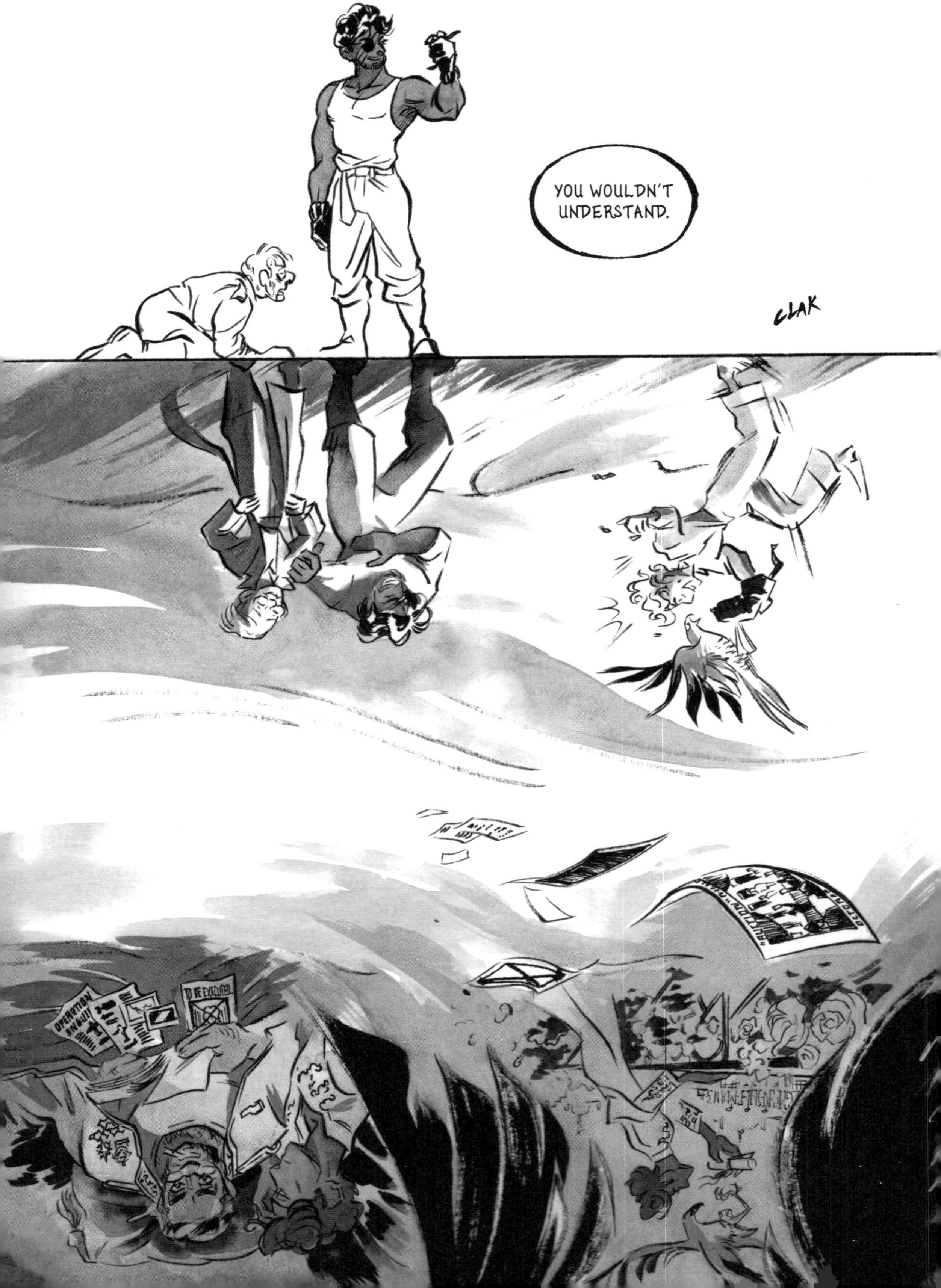

YOU WOULDN'T UNDERSTAND.
CLAK

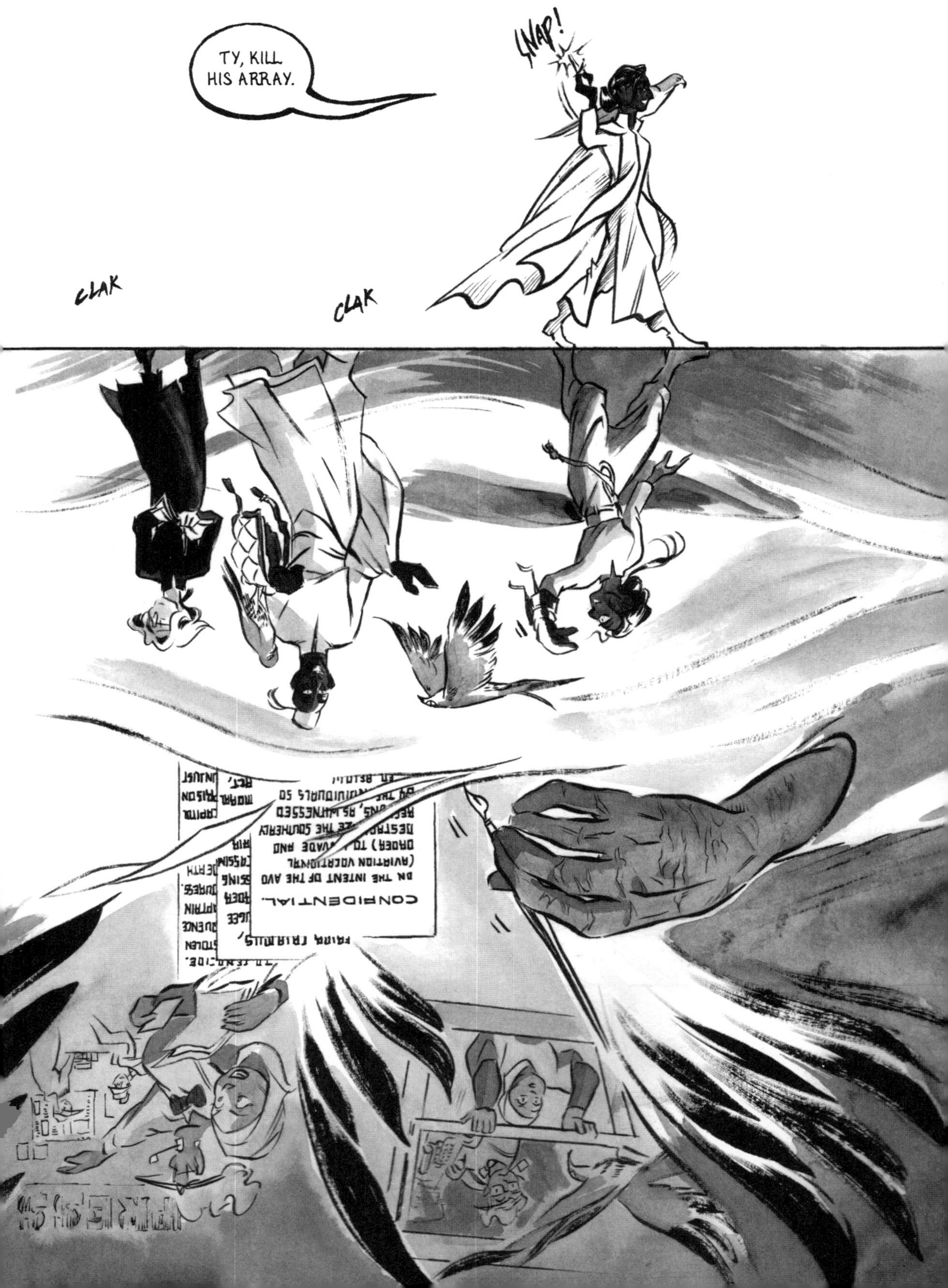
TY, KILL HIS ARRAY.
SNAP!
CLAK
CLAK

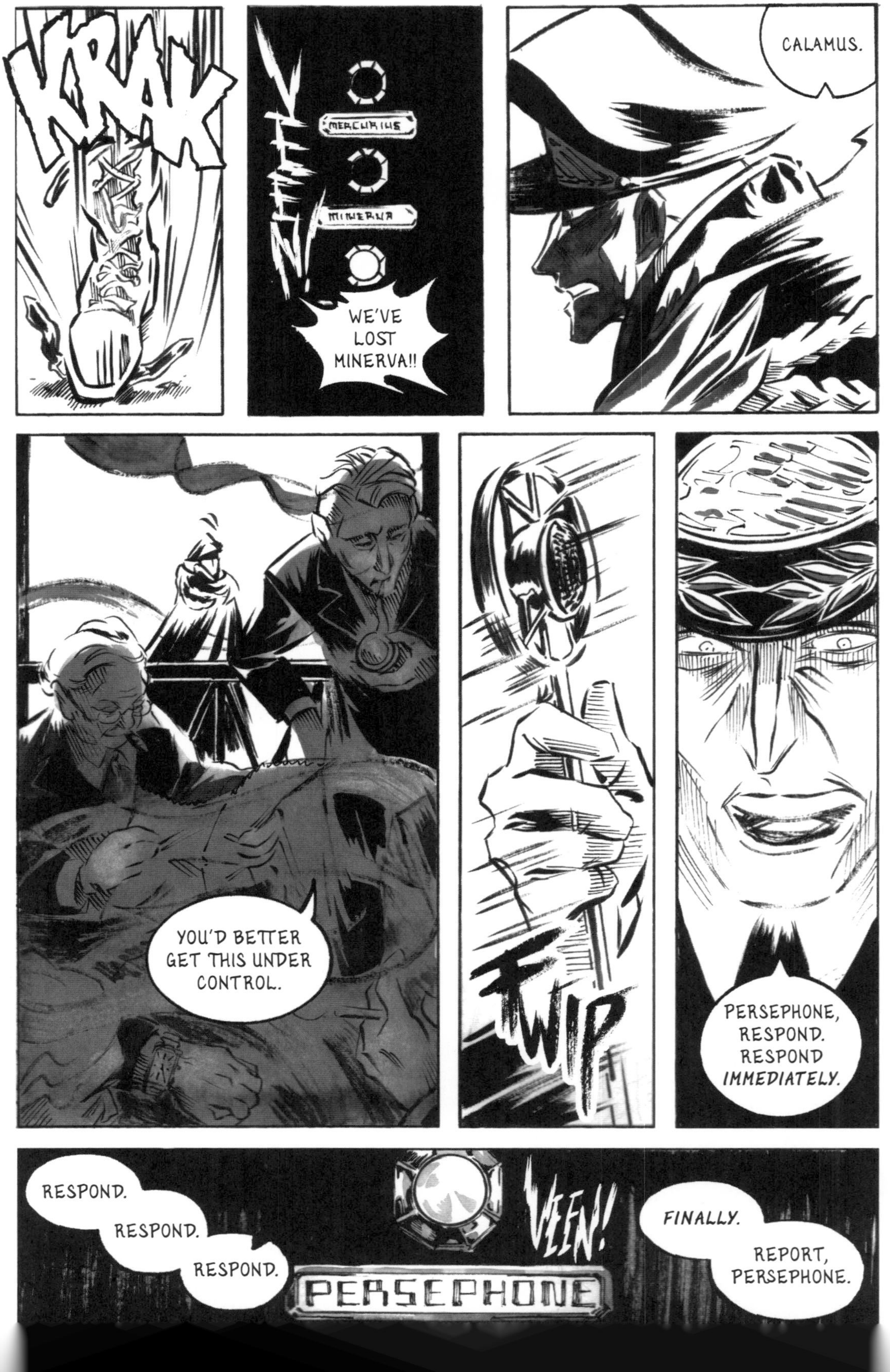
KRAK
MERCURIUS
MINERVA
WE'VE LOST MINERVA!!
CALAMUS.
YOU'D BETTER GET THIS UNDER CONTROL.
FWIP
PERSEPHONE, RESPOND. RESPOND *IMMEDIATELY.*
RESPOND.
RESPOND.
RESPOND.
PERSEPHONE
VEEN!
FINALLY.
REPORT, PERSEPHONE.

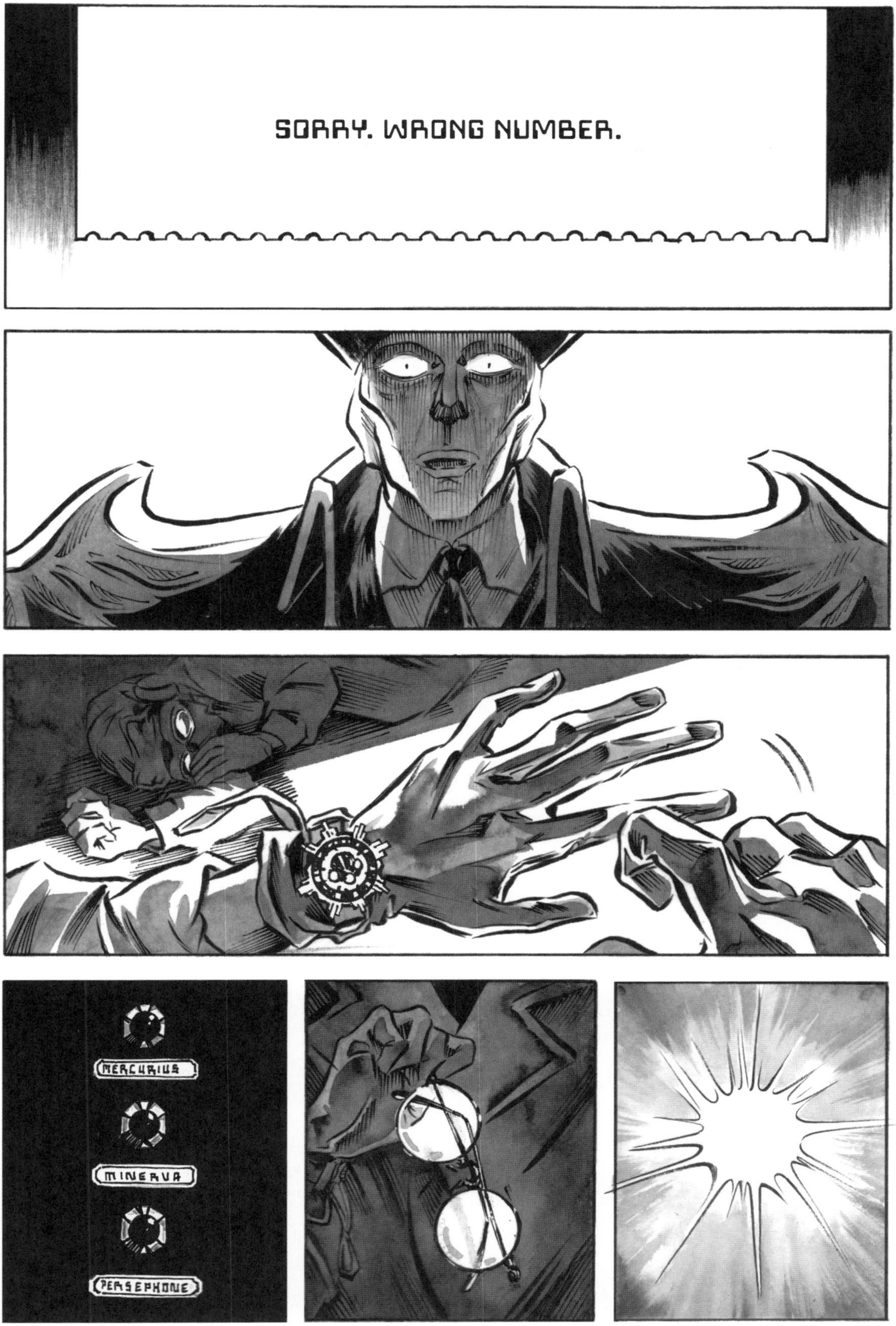

SORRY. WRONG NUMBER.

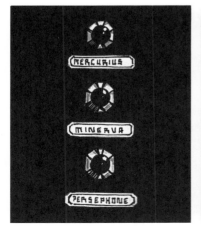

MERCURIUS

MINERVA

PERSEPHONE

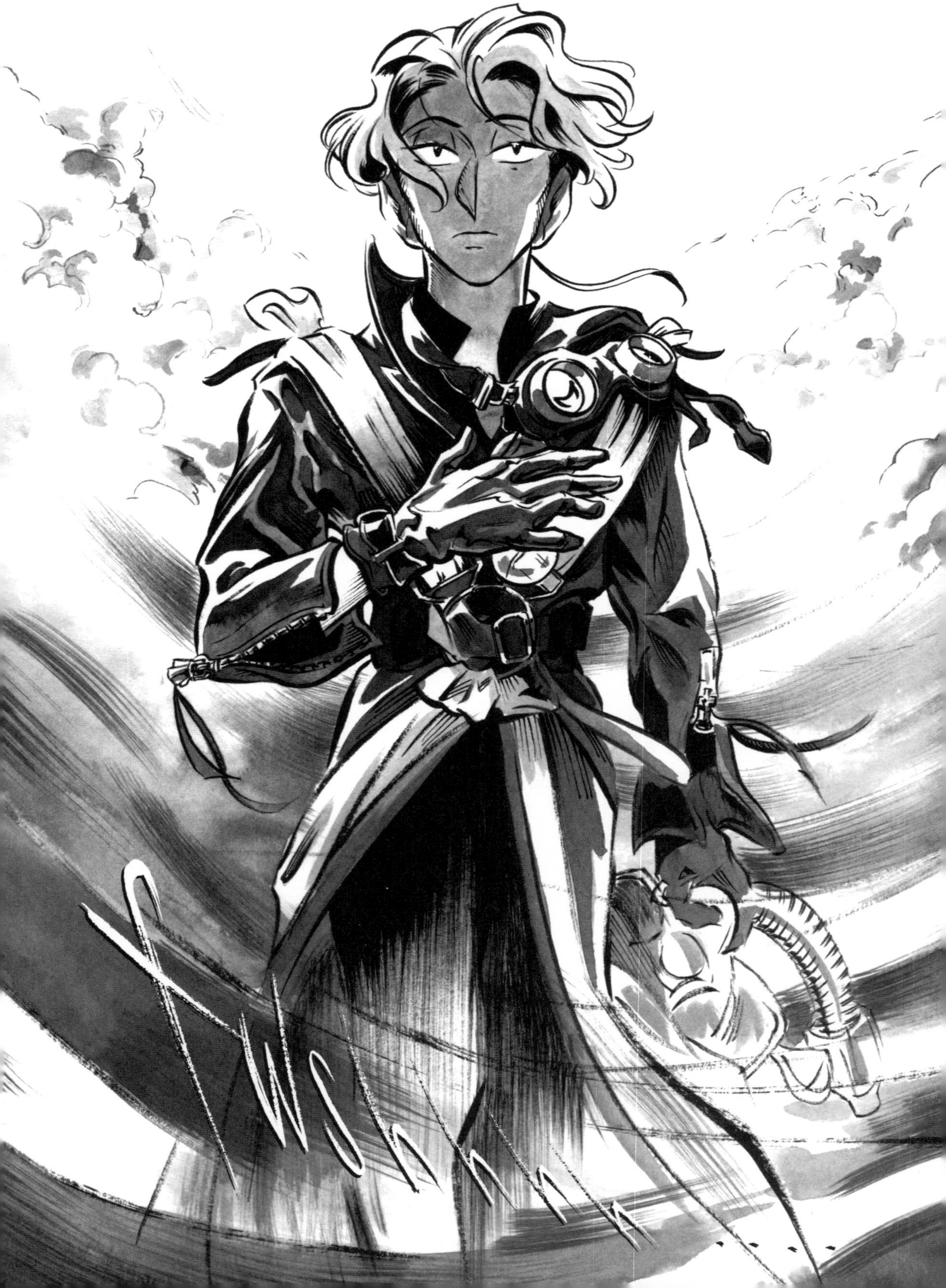

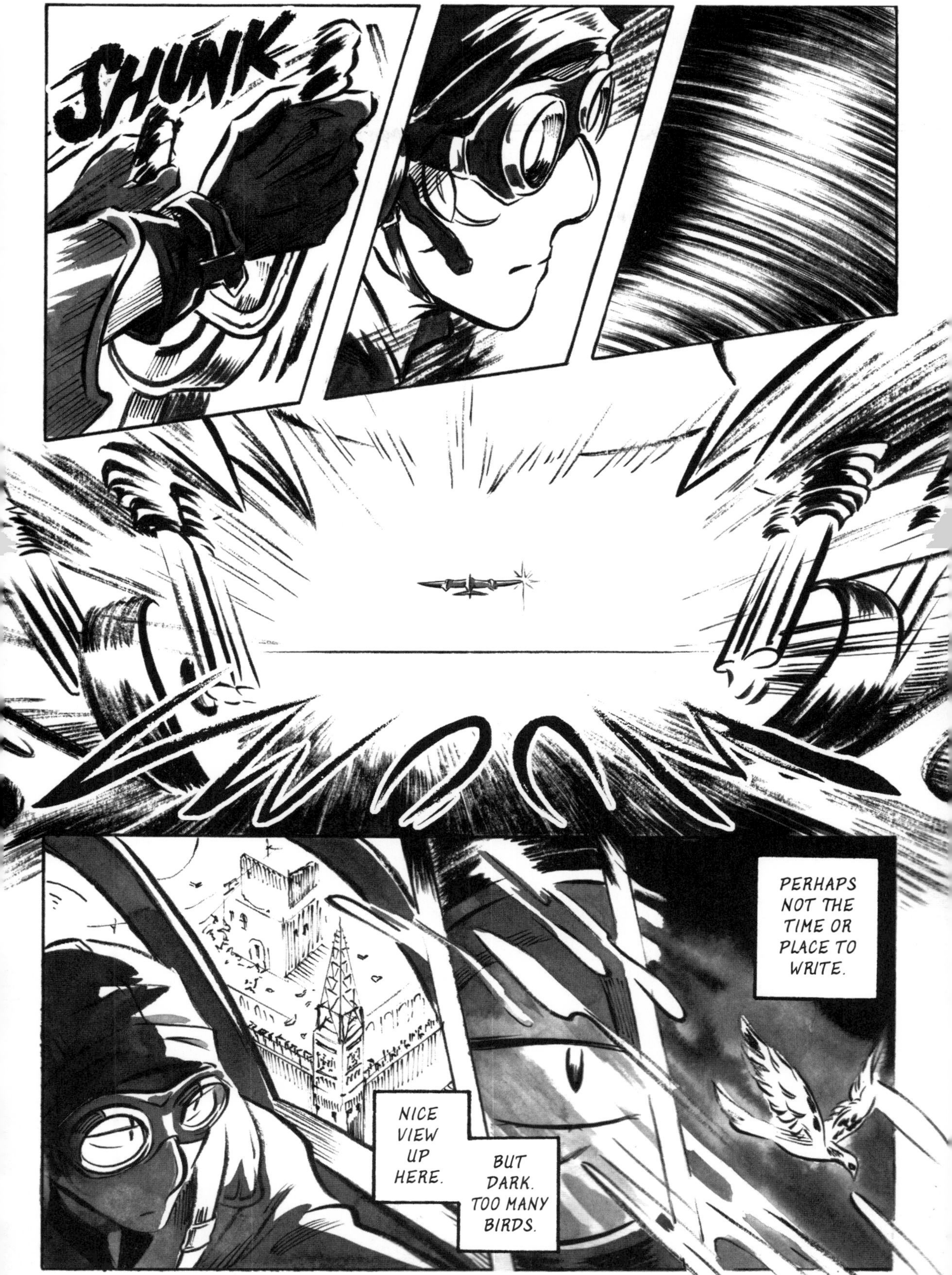
SHUNK
PERHAPS NOT THE TIME OR PLACE TO WRITE.
NICE VIEW UP HERE.
BUT DARK. TOO MANY BIRDS.

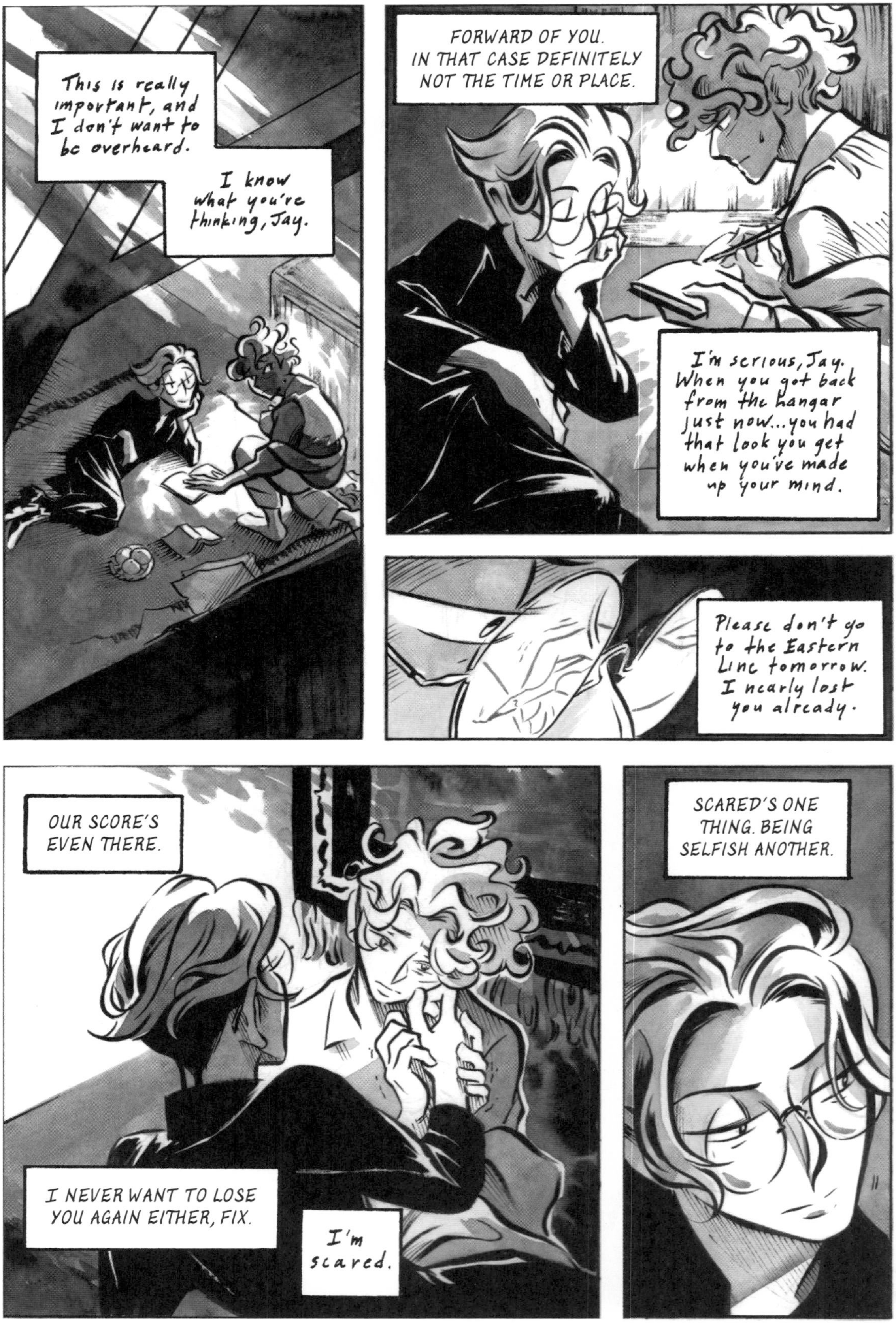
This is really important, and I don't want to be overheard.
I know what you're thinking, Jay.
FORWARD OF YOU. IN THAT CASE DEFINITELY NOT THE TIME OR PLACE.
I'm serious, Jay. When you got back from the hangar just now...you had that look you get when you've made up your mind.
Please don't go to the Eastern Line tomorrow. I nearly lost you already.
OUR SCORE'S EVEN THERE.
I NEVER WANT TO LOSE YOU AGAIN EITHER, FIX.
I'm scared.
SCARED'S ONE THING. BEING SELFISH ANOTHER.

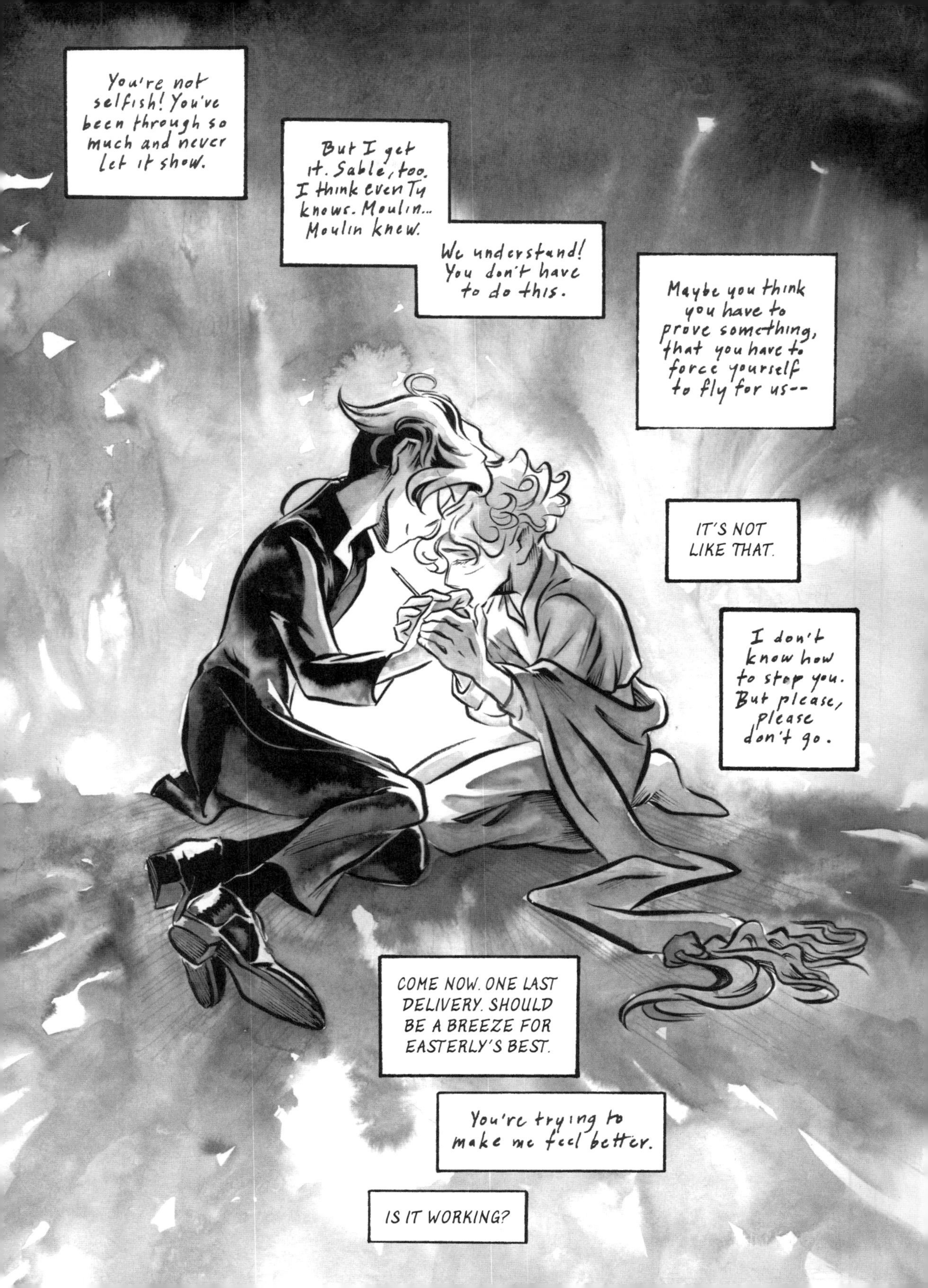
You're not selfish! You've been through so much and never let it show.
But I get it. Sable, too. I think even Ty knows. Moulin... Moulin knew.
We understand! You don't have to do this.
Maybe you think you have to prove something, that you have to force yourself to fly for us--
IT'S NOT LIKE THAT.
I don't know how to stop you. But please, please don't go.
COME NOW. ONE LAST DELIVERY. SHOULD BE A BREEZE FOR EASTERLY'S BEST.
You're trying to make me feel better.
IS IT WORKING?

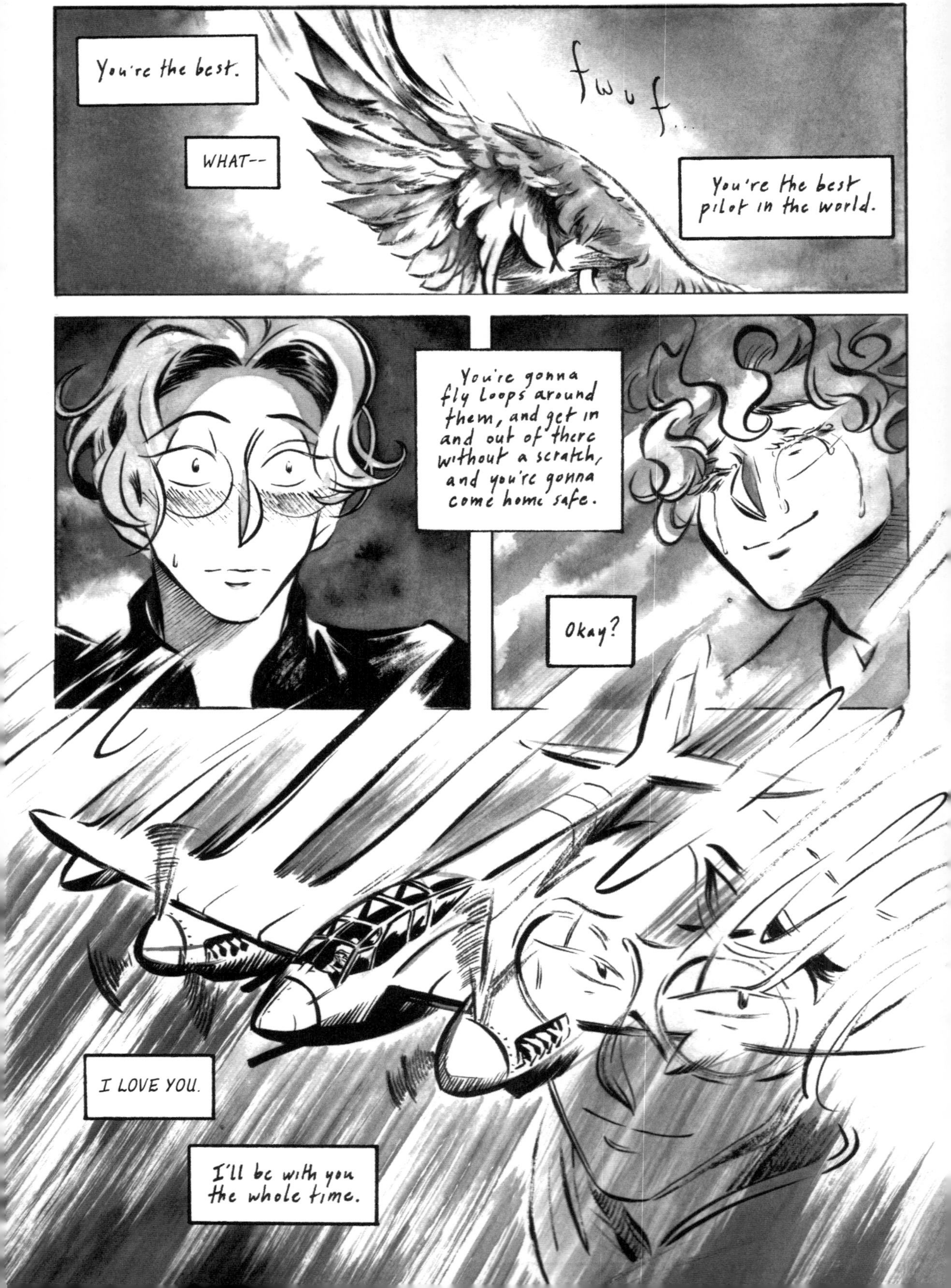
You're the best.
WHAT--
fwuf...
You're the best pilot in the world.
You're gonna fly loops around them, and get in and out of there without a scratch, and you're gonna come home safe.
Okay?
I LOVE YOU.
I'll be with you the whole time.

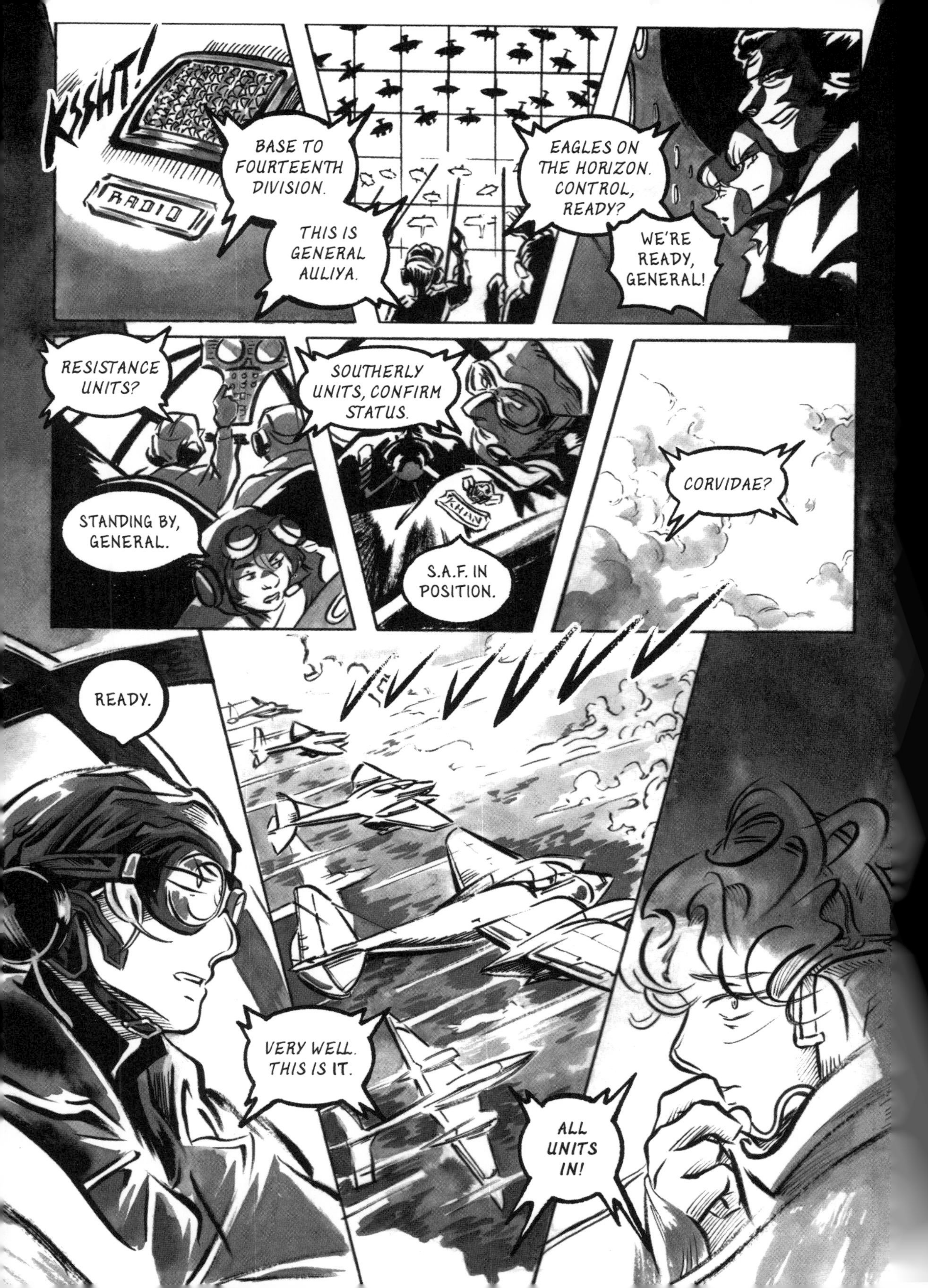
KSSHT!
RADIO
BASE TO FOURTEENTH DIVISION.
THIS IS GENERAL AULIYA.
EAGLES ON THE HORIZON. CONTROL, READY?
WE'RE READY, GENERAL!
RESISTANCE UNITS?
STANDING BY, GENERAL.
SOUTHERLY UNITS, CONFIRM STATUS.
S.A.F. IN POSITION.
CORVIDAE?
READY.
VERY WELL. THIS IS IT.
ALL UNITS IN!

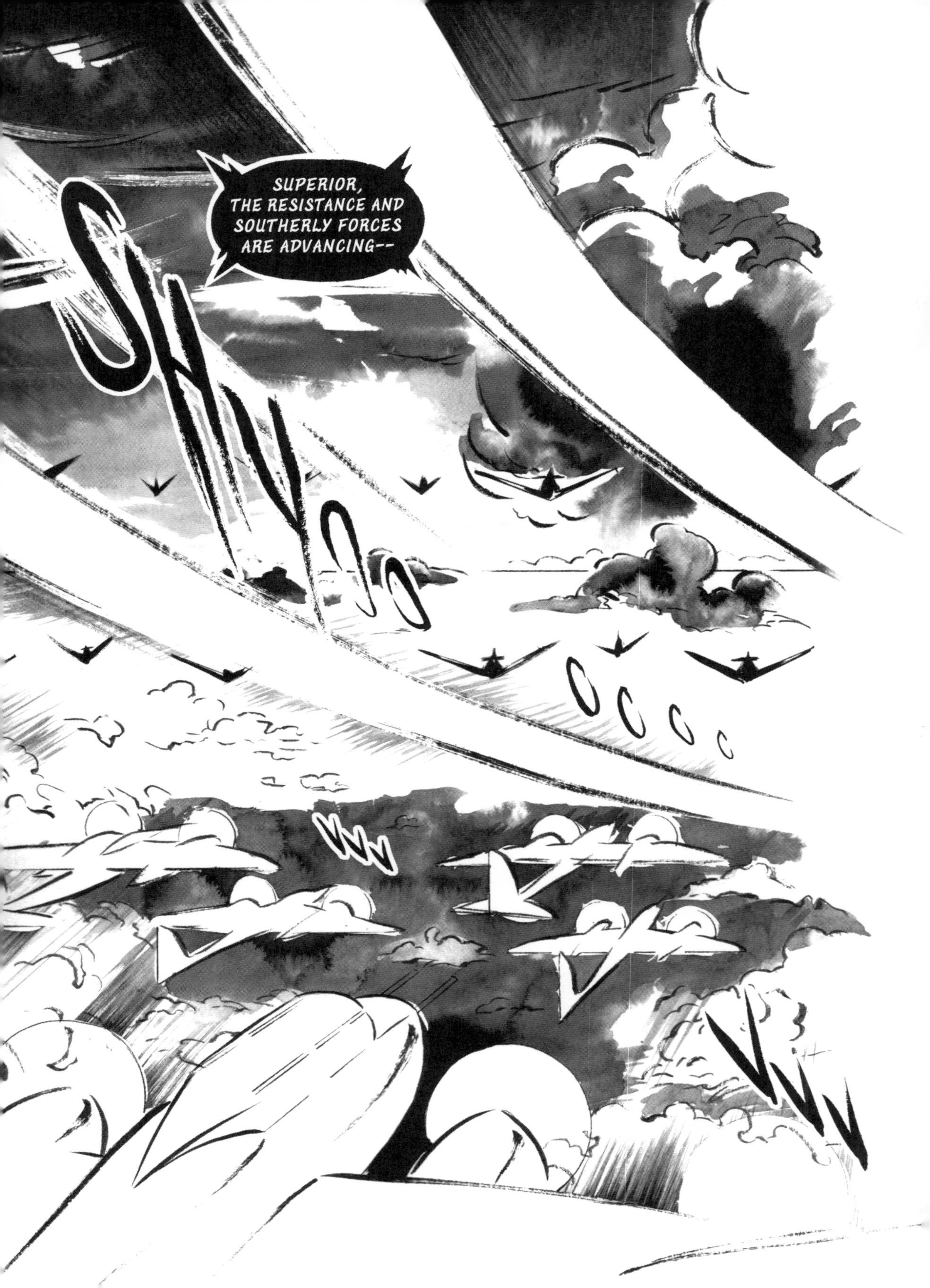
SUPERIOR, THE RESISTANCE AND SOUTHERLY FORCES ARE ADVANCING--

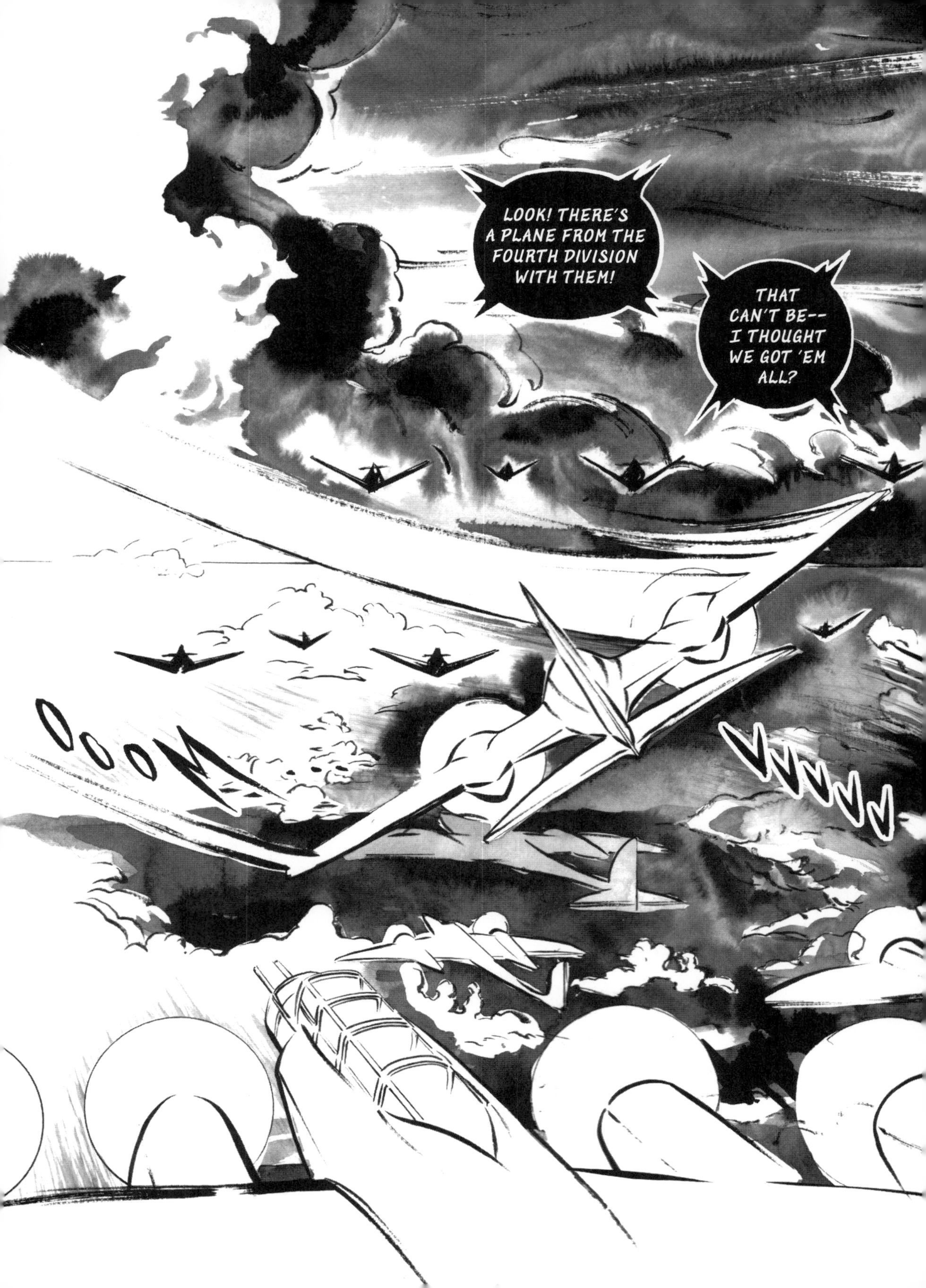

LOOK! THERE'S A PLANE FROM THE FOURTH DIVISION WITH THEM!
THAT CAN'T BE-- I THOUGHT WE GOT 'EM ALL?
OooM
VVVVVV

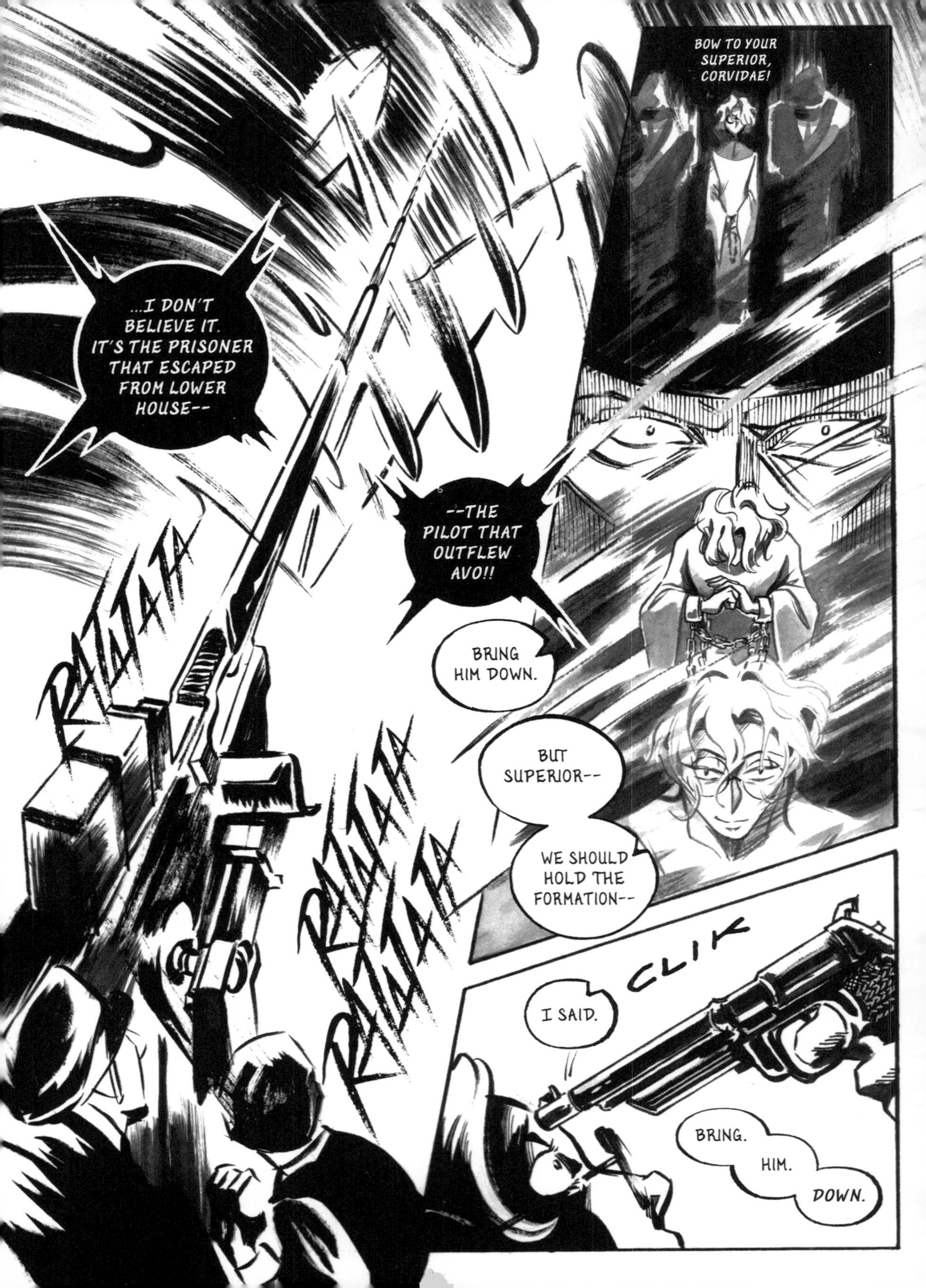
BOW TO YOUR SUPERIOR, CORVIDAE!
...I DON'T BELIEVE IT. IT'S THE PRISONER THAT ESCAPED FROM LOWER HOUSE--
--THE PILOT THAT OUTFLEW AVO!!
RATATATA
BRING HIM DOWN.
BUT SUPERIOR--
WE SHOULD HOLD THE FORMATION--
RATATATA
RATATATA
CLIK
I SAID.
BRING.
HIM.
DOWN.

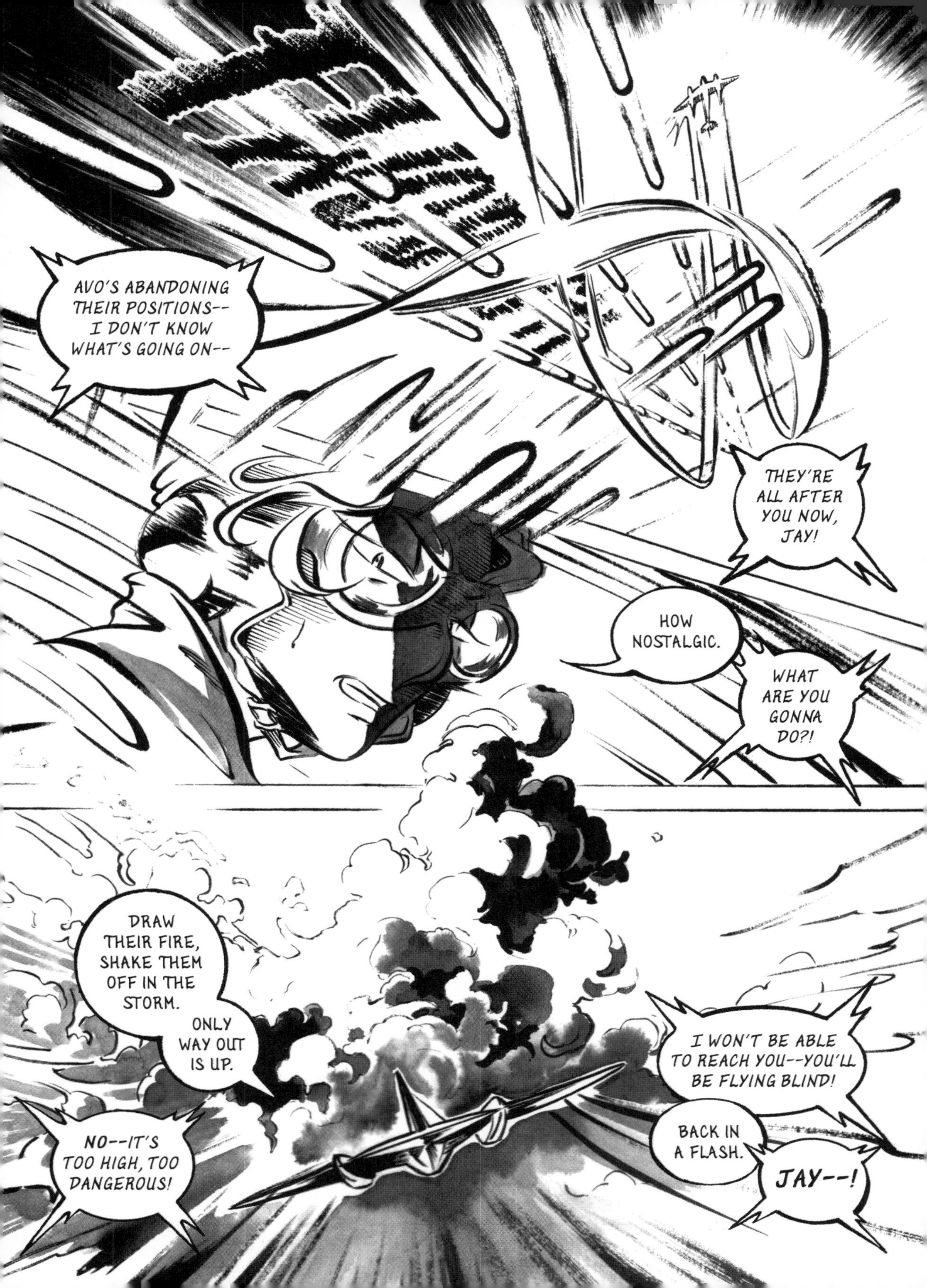
AVO'S ABANDONING THEIR POSITIONS-- I DON'T KNOW WHAT'S GOING ON--
THEY'RE ALL AFTER YOU NOW, JAY!
HOW NOSTALGIC.
WHAT ARE YOU GONNA DO?!
DRAW THEIR FIRE, SHAKE THEM OFF IN THE STORM.
ONLY WAY OUT IS UP.
NO--IT'S TOO HIGH, TOO DANGEROUS!
I WON'T BE ABLE TO REACH YOU--YOU'LL BE FLYING BLIND!
BACK IN A FLASH.
JAY--!

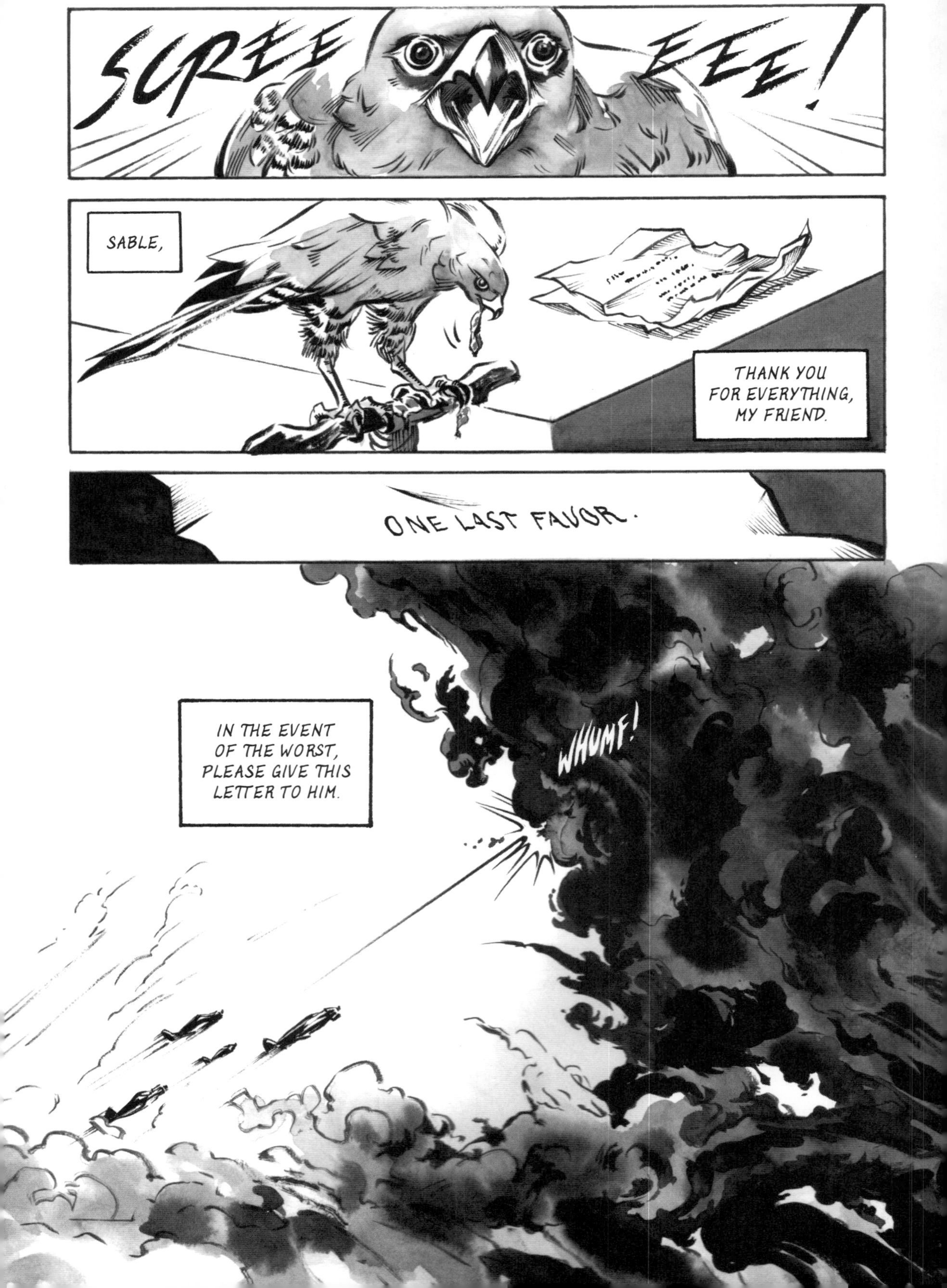
SCREEEEE!
SABLE,
THANK YOU FOR EVERYTHING, MY FRIEND.
ONE LAST FAVOR.
IN THE EVENT OF THE WORST, PLEASE GIVE THIS LETTER TO HIM.
WHUMF!

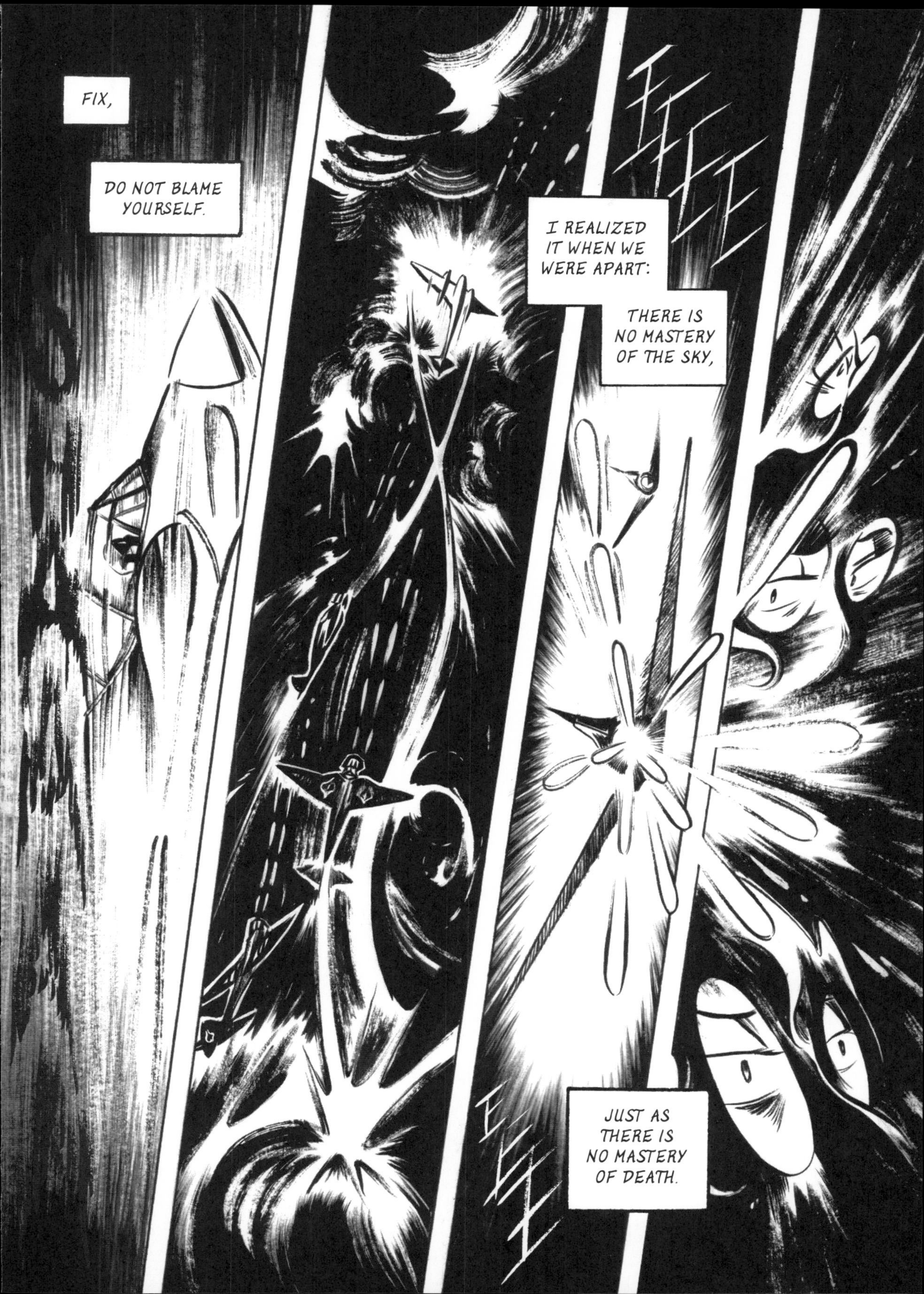
FIX,
DO NOT BLAME YOURSELF.
I REALIZED IT WHEN WE WERE APART:
THERE IS NO MASTERY OF THE SKY,
JUST AS THERE IS NO MASTERY OF DEATH.

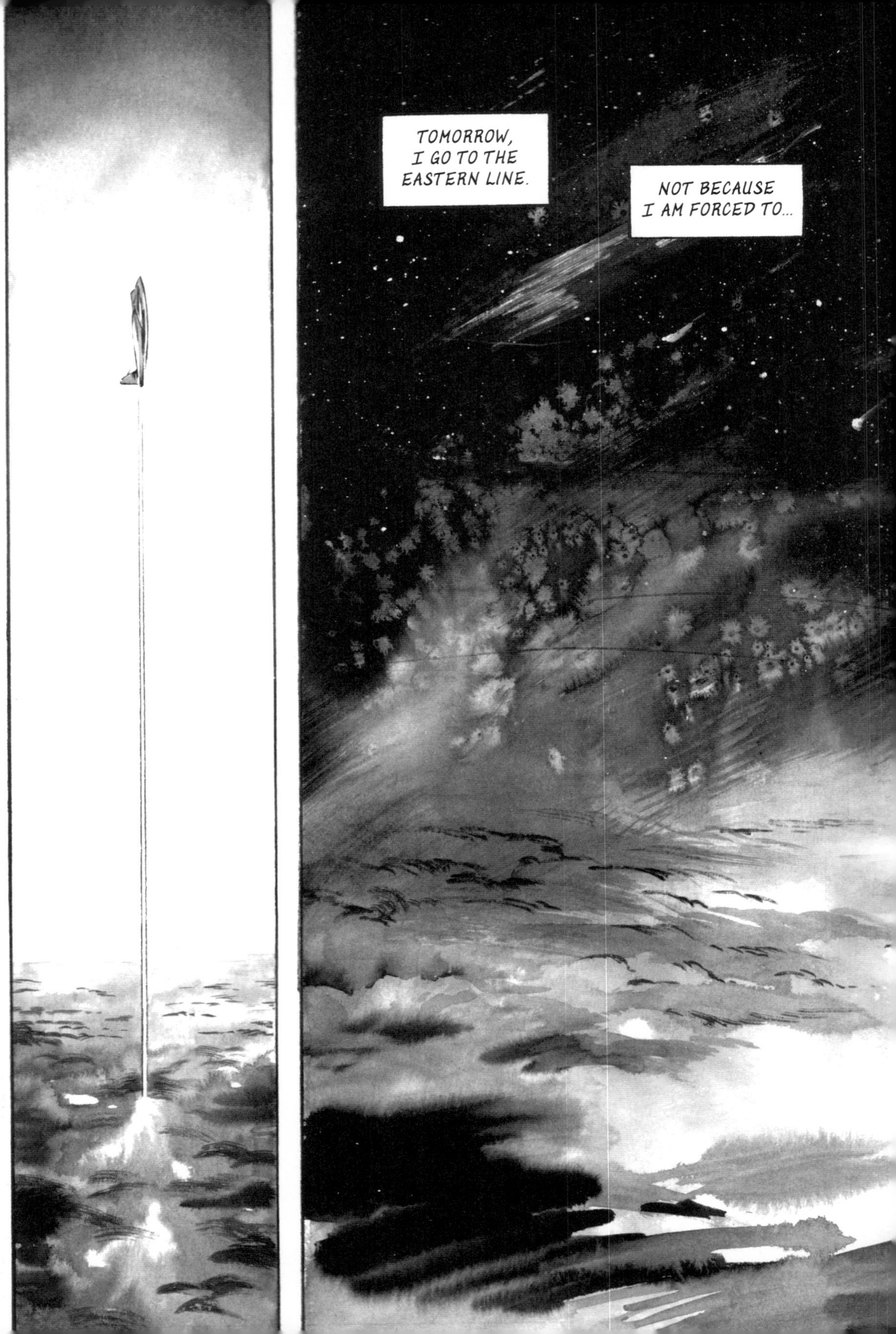
TOMORROW, I GO TO THE EASTERN LINE.
NOT BECAUSE I AM FORCED TO...

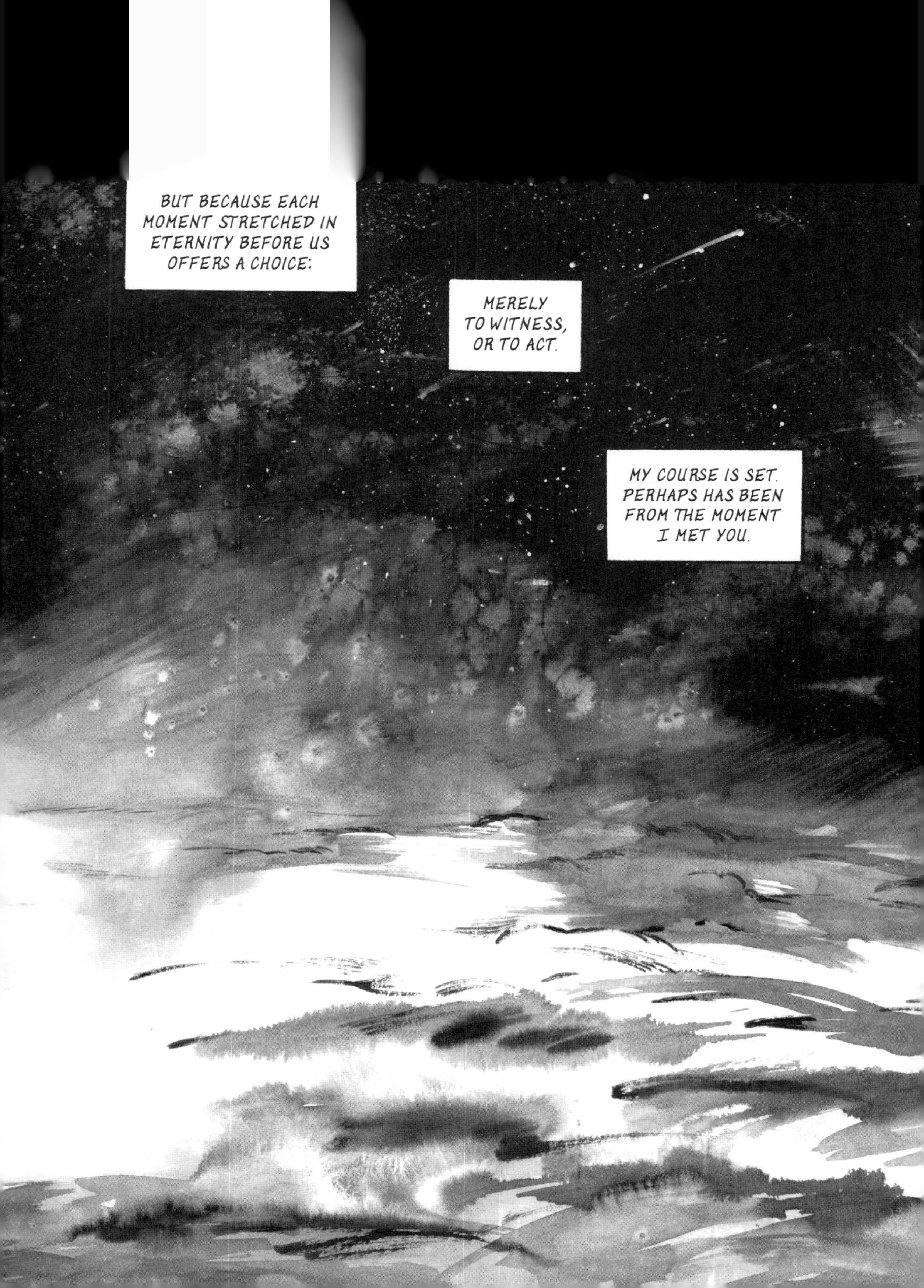
BUT BECAUSE EACH MOMENT STRETCHED IN ETERNITY BEFORE US OFFERS A CHOICE:
MERELY TO WITNESS, OR TO ACT.
MY COURSE IS SET. PERHAPS HAS BEEN FROM THE MOMENT I MET YOU.

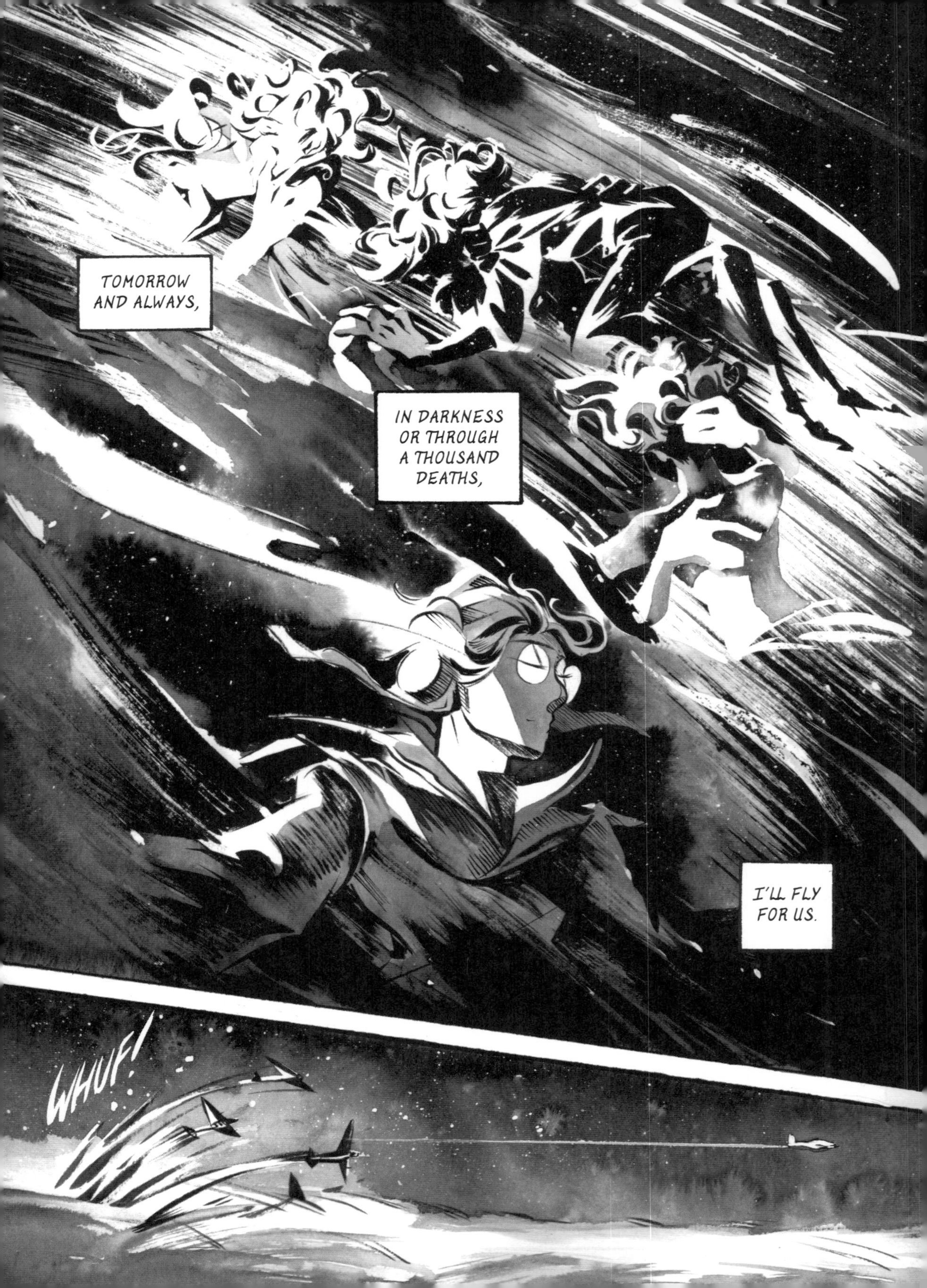
TOMORROW AND ALWAYS,
IN DARKNESS OR THROUGH A THOUSAND DEATHS,
I'LL FLY FOR US.
WHUF!

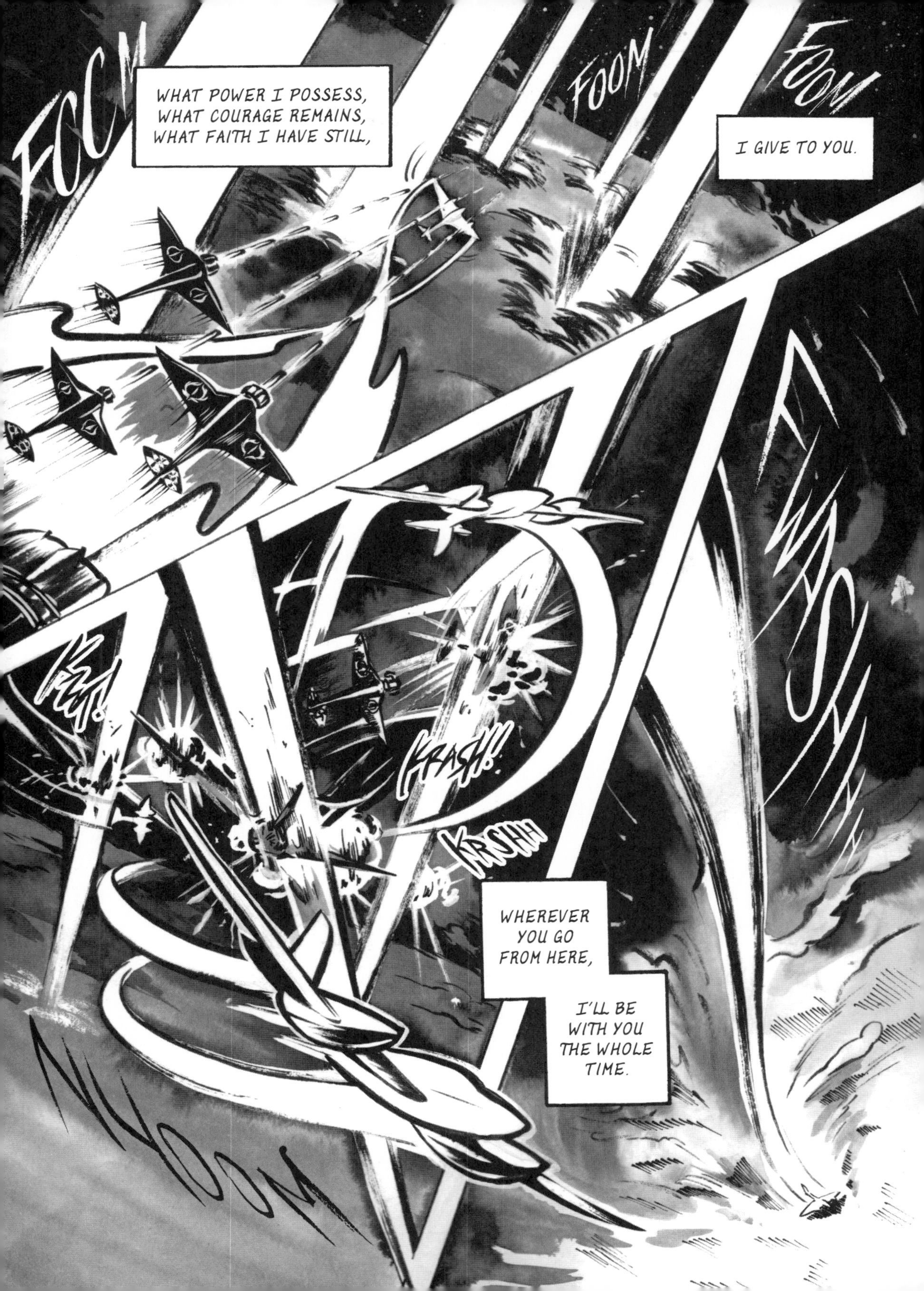
FOOM
WHAT POWER I POSSESS, WHAT COURAGE REMAINS, WHAT FAITH I HAVE STILL,
FOOM
FOOM
I GIVE TO YOU.
FWASH
KRASH!
WHEREVER YOU GO FROM HERE,
I'LL BE WITH YOU THE WHOLE TIME.

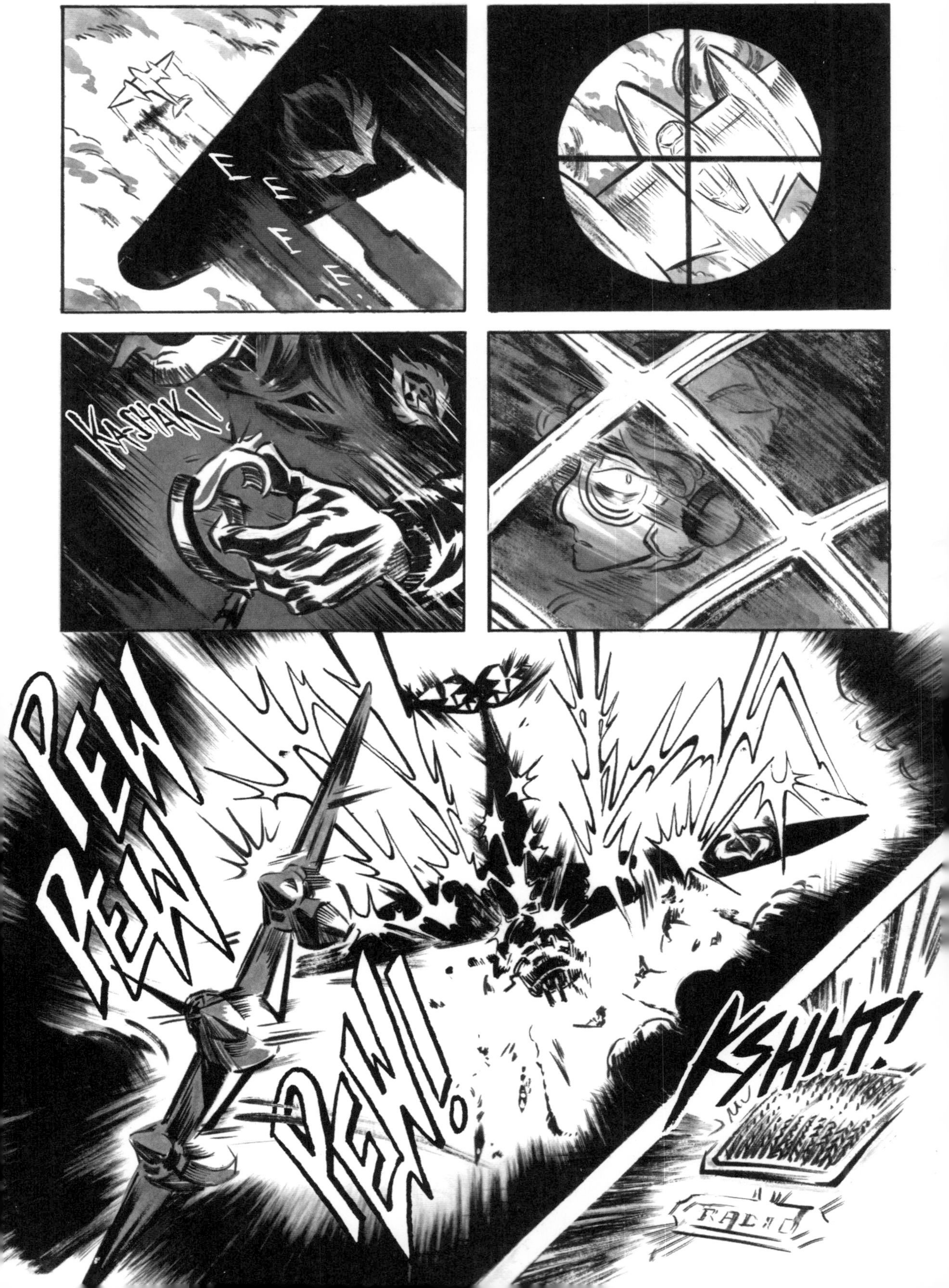

KASHAK!
BEW BEW
BEW!
KSHHT!
RADIO

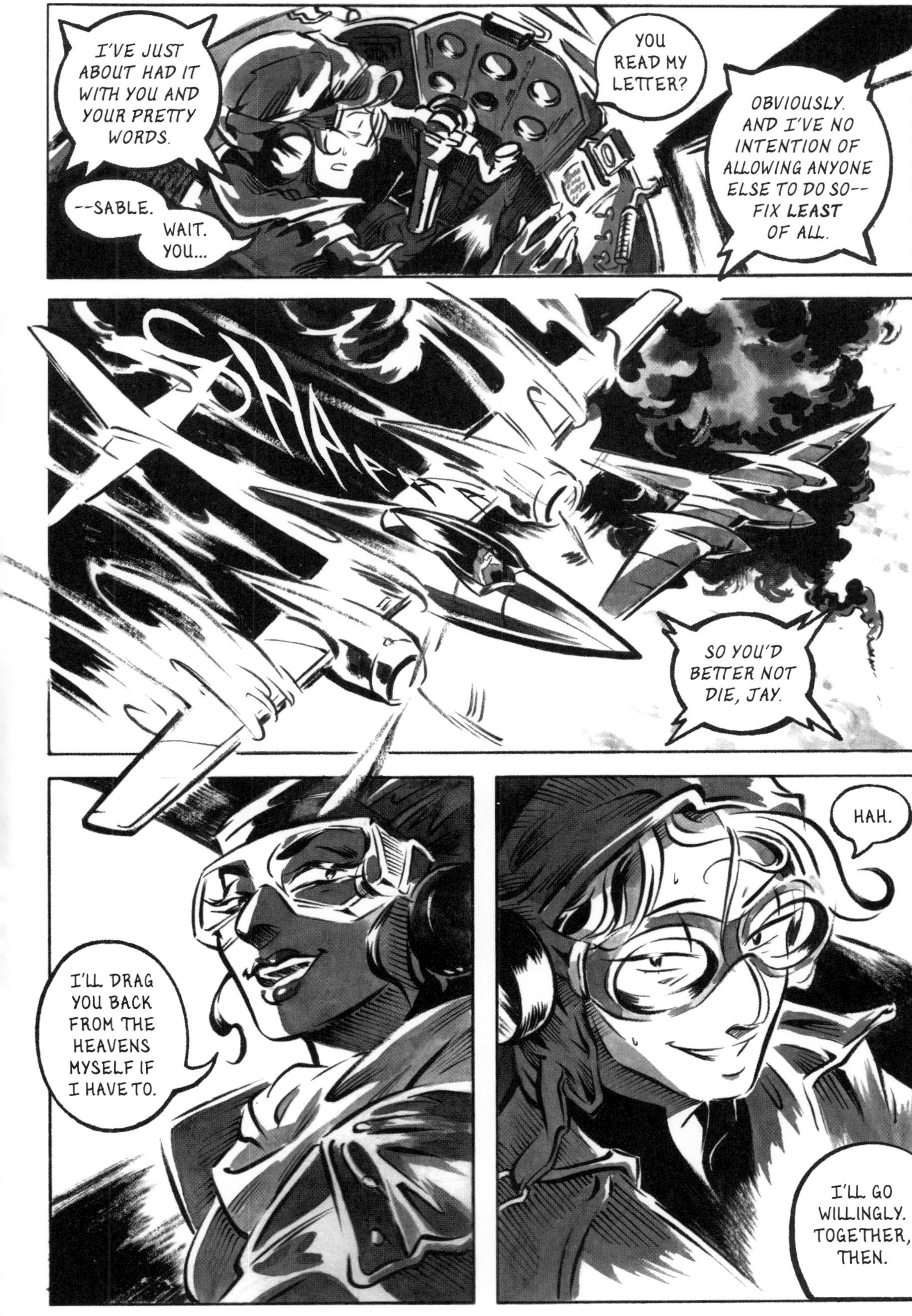
I'VE JUST ABOUT HAD IT WITH YOU AND YOUR PRETTY WORDS.
YOU READ MY LETTER?
OBVIOUSLY. AND I'VE NO INTENTION OF ALLOWING ANYONE ELSE TO DO SO-- FIX LEAST OF ALL.
--SABLE.
WAIT. YOU...
SO YOU'D BETTER NOT DIE, JAY.
I'LL DRAG YOU BACK FROM THE HEAVENS MYSELF IF I HAVE TO.
HAH.
I'LL GO WILLINGLY. TOGETHER, THEN.

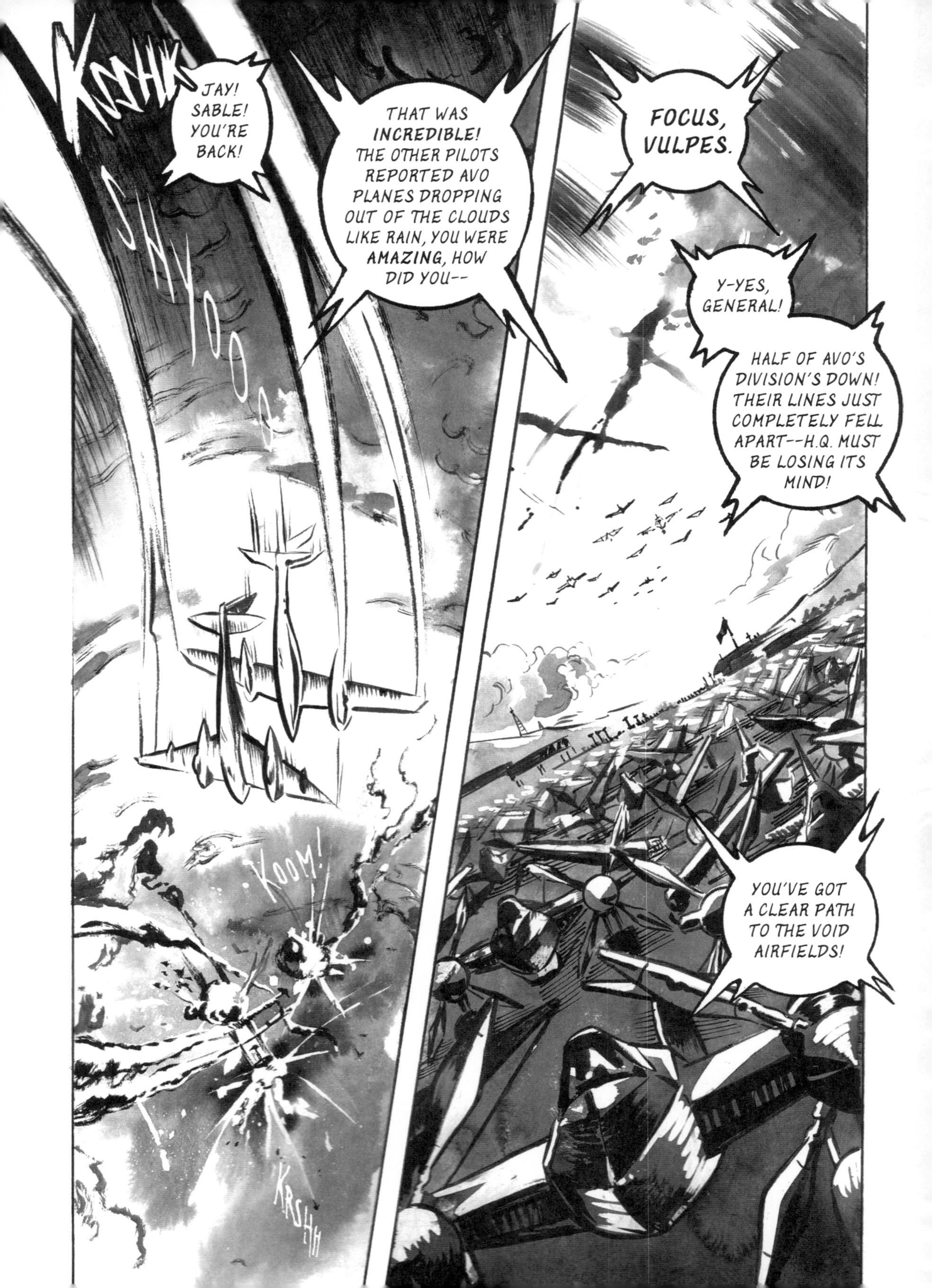
KSSHK
JAY! SABLE! YOU'RE BACK!
SHYOOOO
THAT WAS INCREDIBLE! THE OTHER PILOTS REPORTED AVO PLANES DROPPING OUT OF THE CLOUDS LIKE RAIN, YOU WERE AMAZING, HOW DID YOU--
FOCUS, VULPES.
Y-YES, GENERAL!
HALF OF AVO'S DIVISION'S DOWN! THEIR LINES JUST COMPLETELY FELL APART--H.Q. MUST BE LOSING ITS MIND!
KOOM!
YOU'VE GOT A CLEAR PATH TO THE VOID AIRFIELDS!
KRSHH

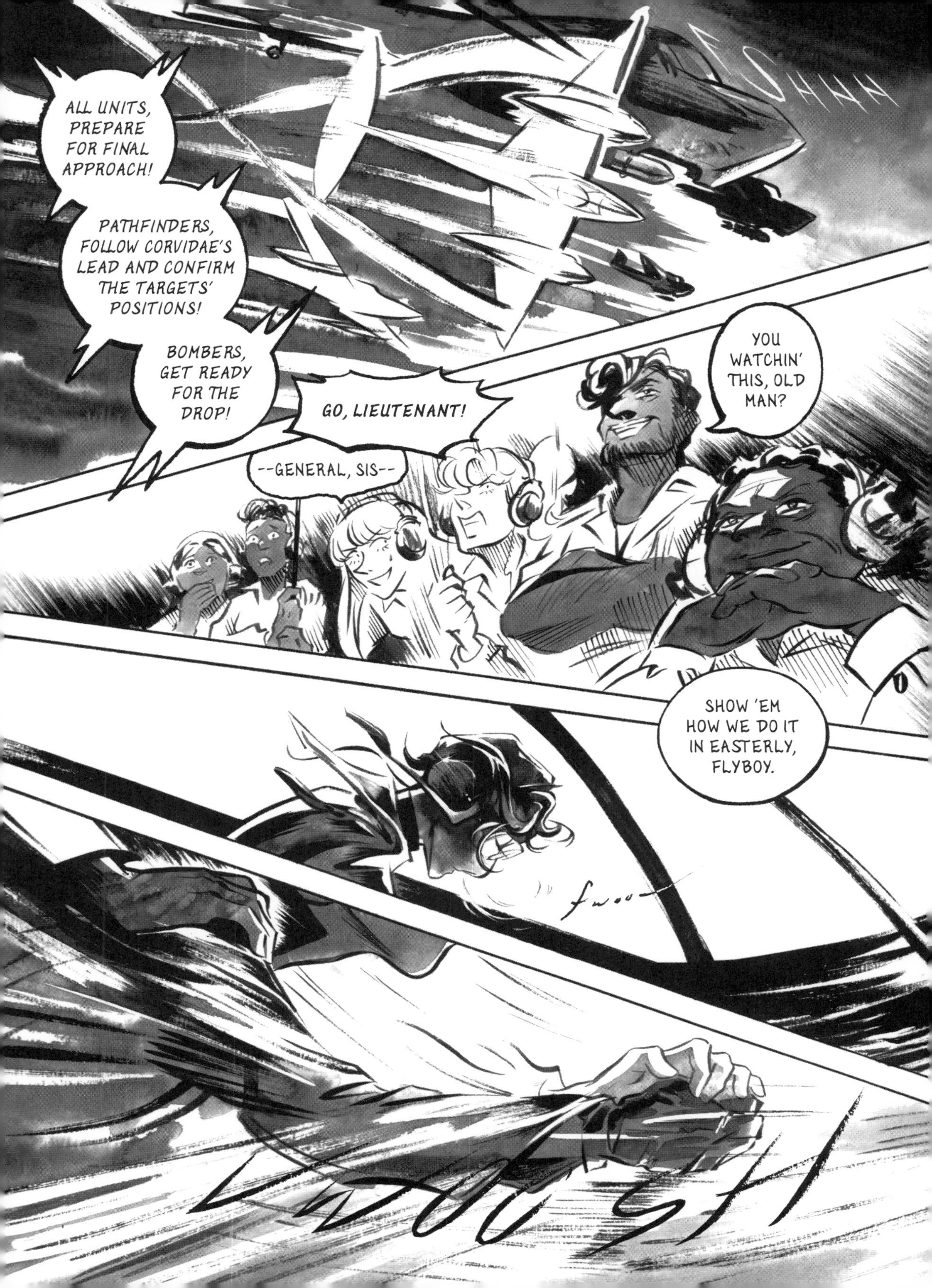
FSHHH
ALL UNITS, PREPARE FOR FINAL APPROACH!
PATHFINDERS, FOLLOW CORVIDAE'S LEAD AND CONFIRM THE TARGETS' POSITIONS!
BOMBERS, GET READY FOR THE DROP!
GO, LIEUTENANT!
--GENERAL, SIS--
YOU WATCHIN' THIS, OLD MAN?
SHOW 'EM HOW WE DO IT IN EASTERLY, FLYBOY.
fwoo
WHOOSH!

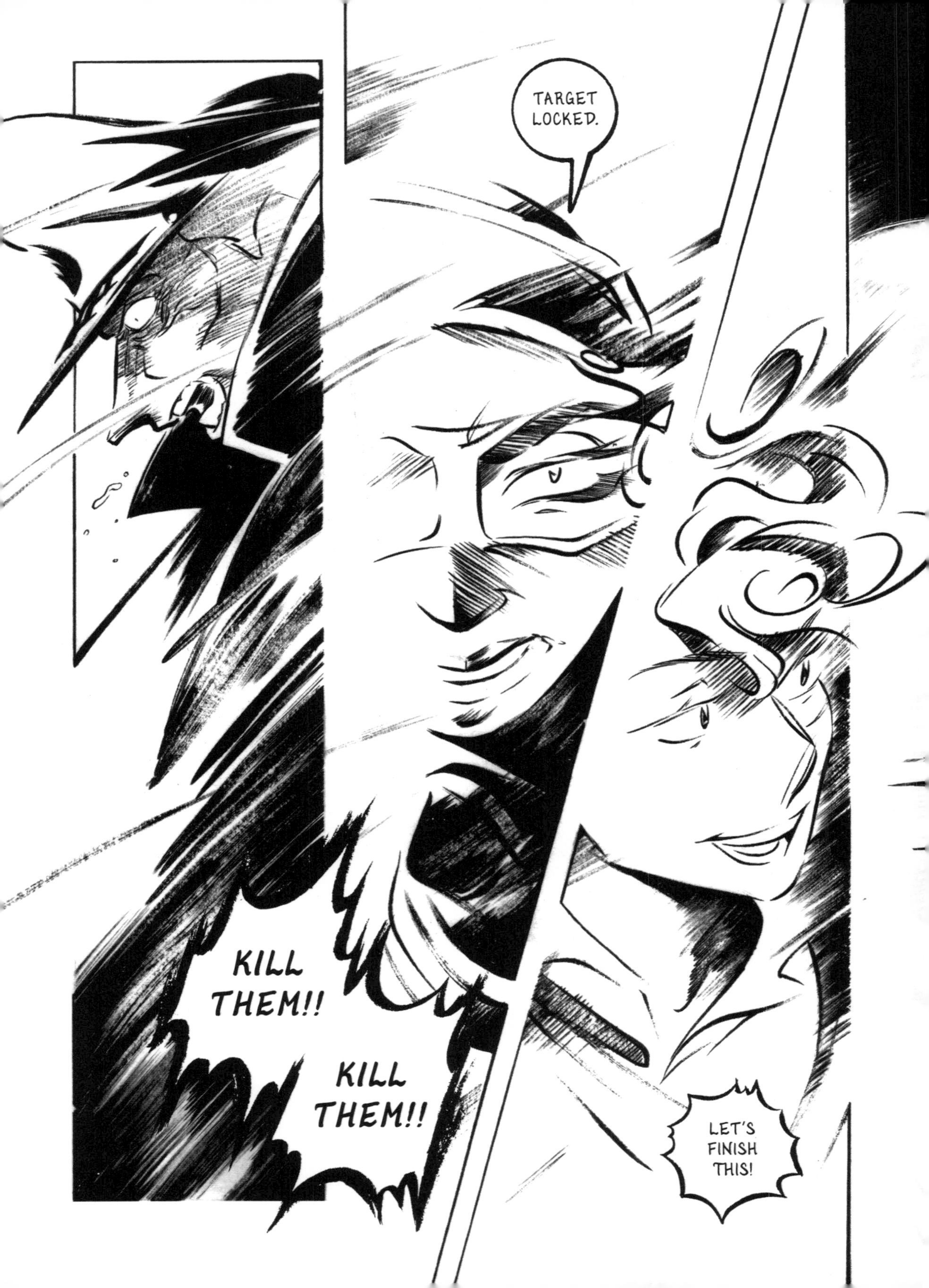
TARGET LOCKED.
KILL THEM!!
KILL THEM!!
LET'S FINISH THIS!

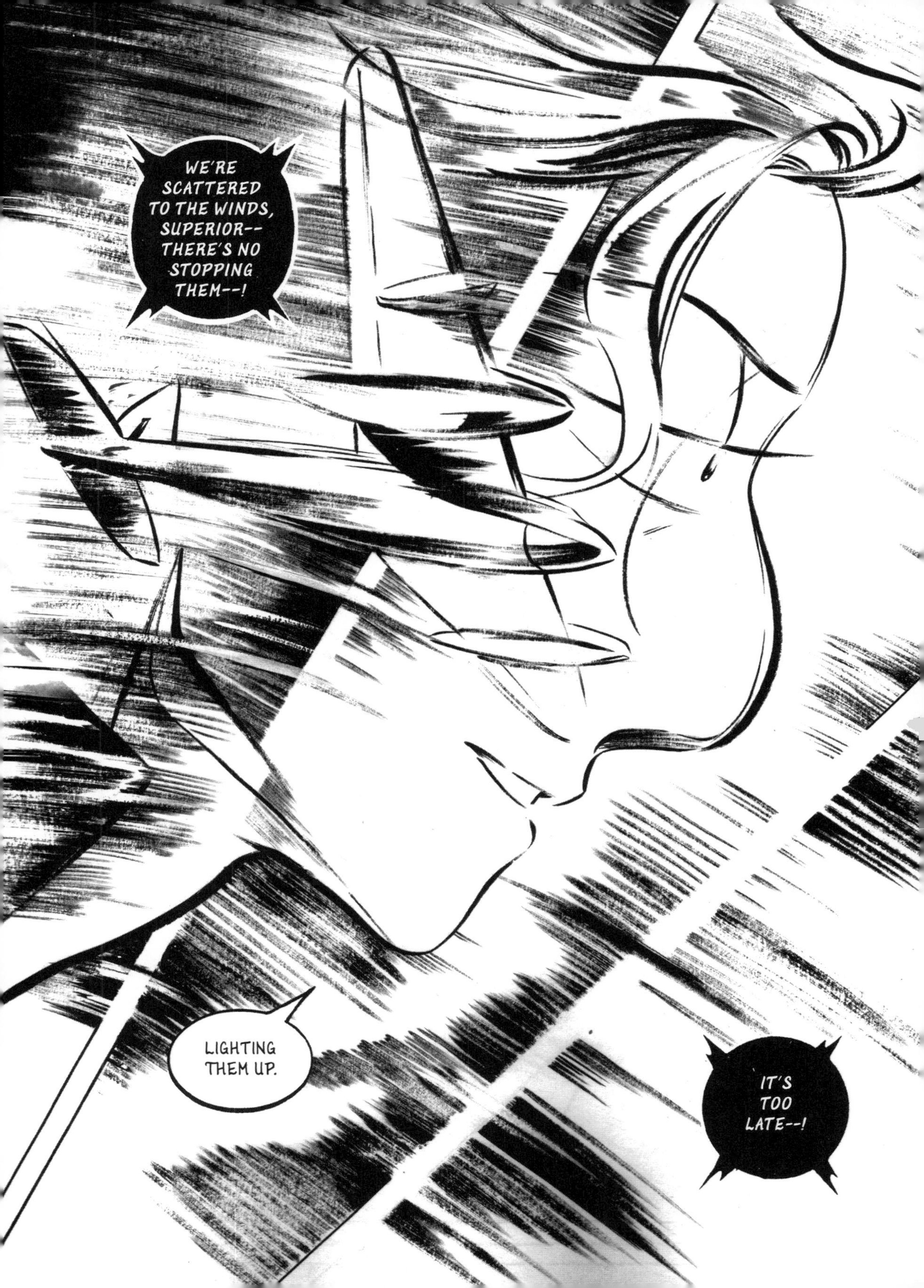
WE'RE SCATTERED TO THE WINDS, SUPERIOR-- THERE'S NO STOPPING THEM--!
LIGHTING THEM UP.
IT'S TOO LATE--!

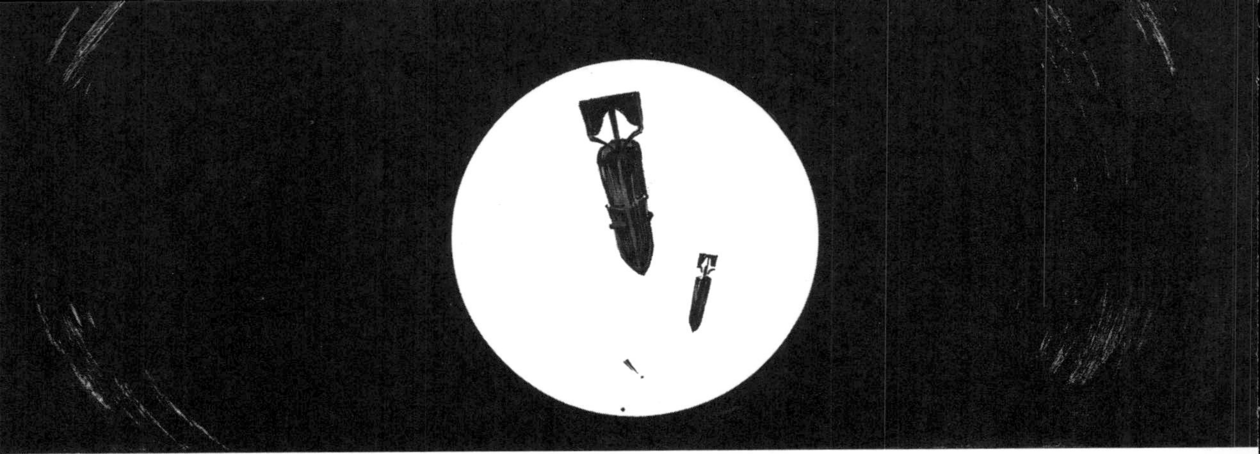

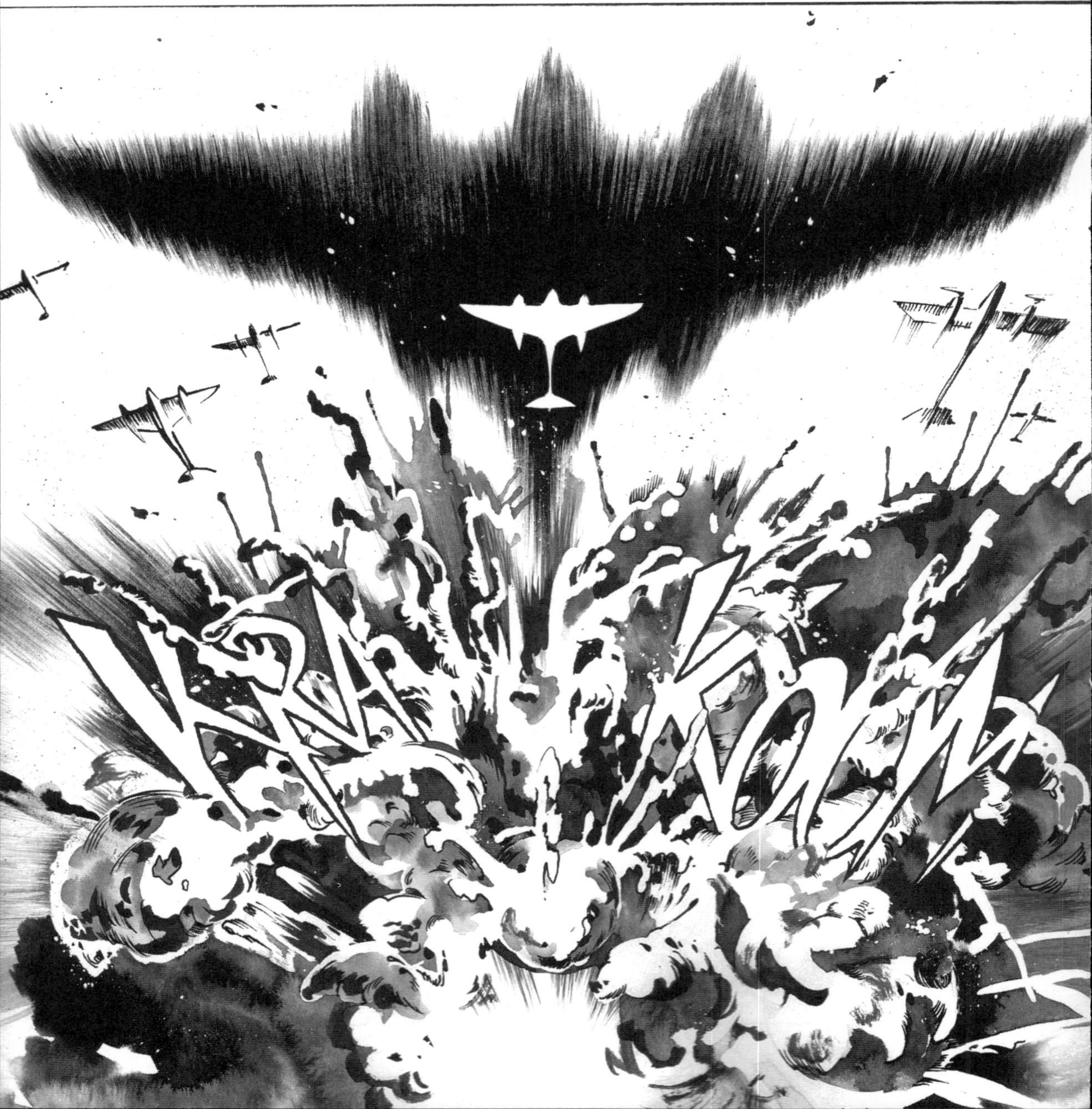
KRAKOOM

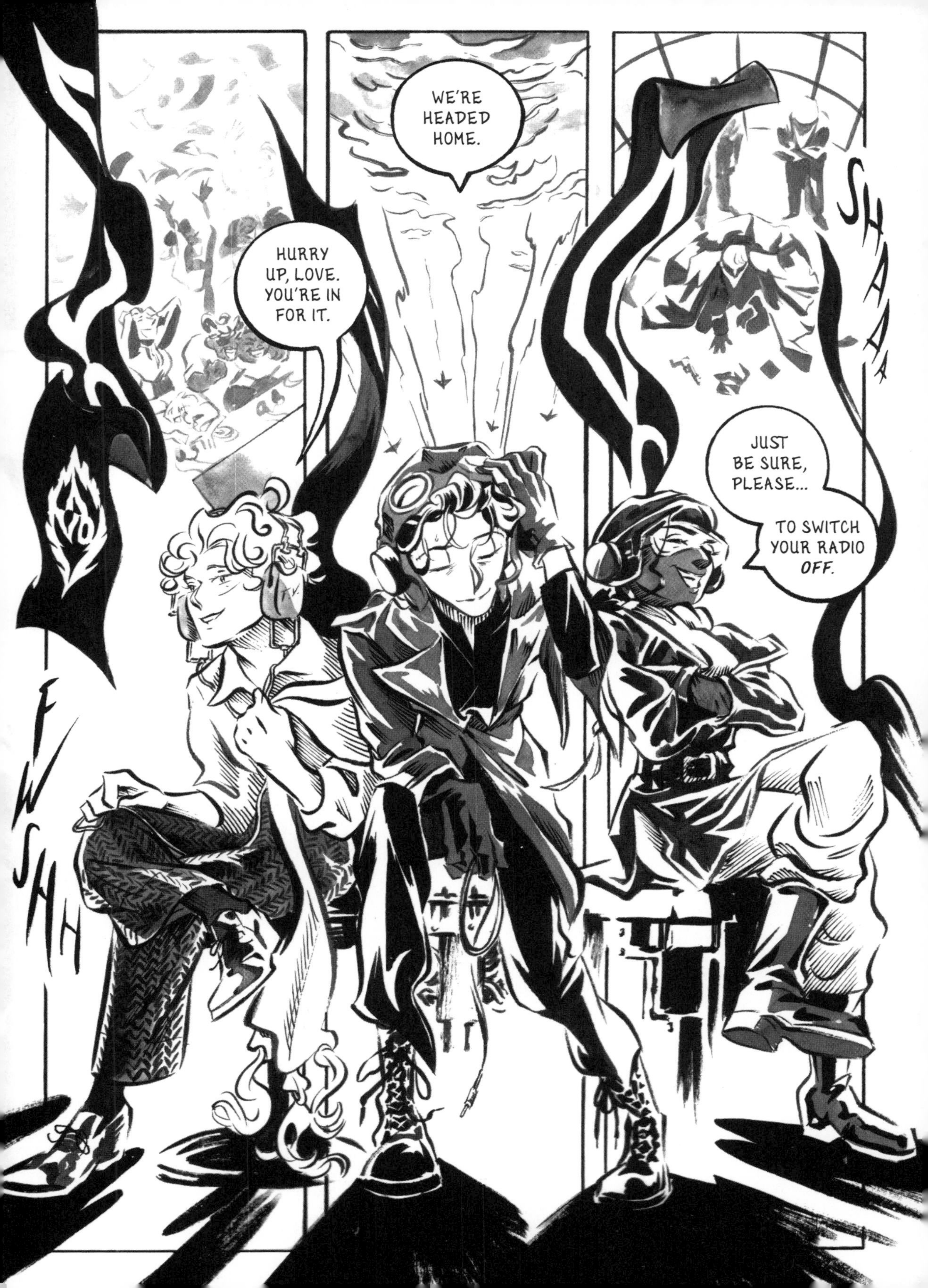
HURRY UP, LOVE. YOU'RE IN FOR IT.
WE'RE HEADED HOME.
SHAAA
JUST BE SURE, PLEASE...
TO SWITCH YOUR RADIO *OFF*.
FWSHH

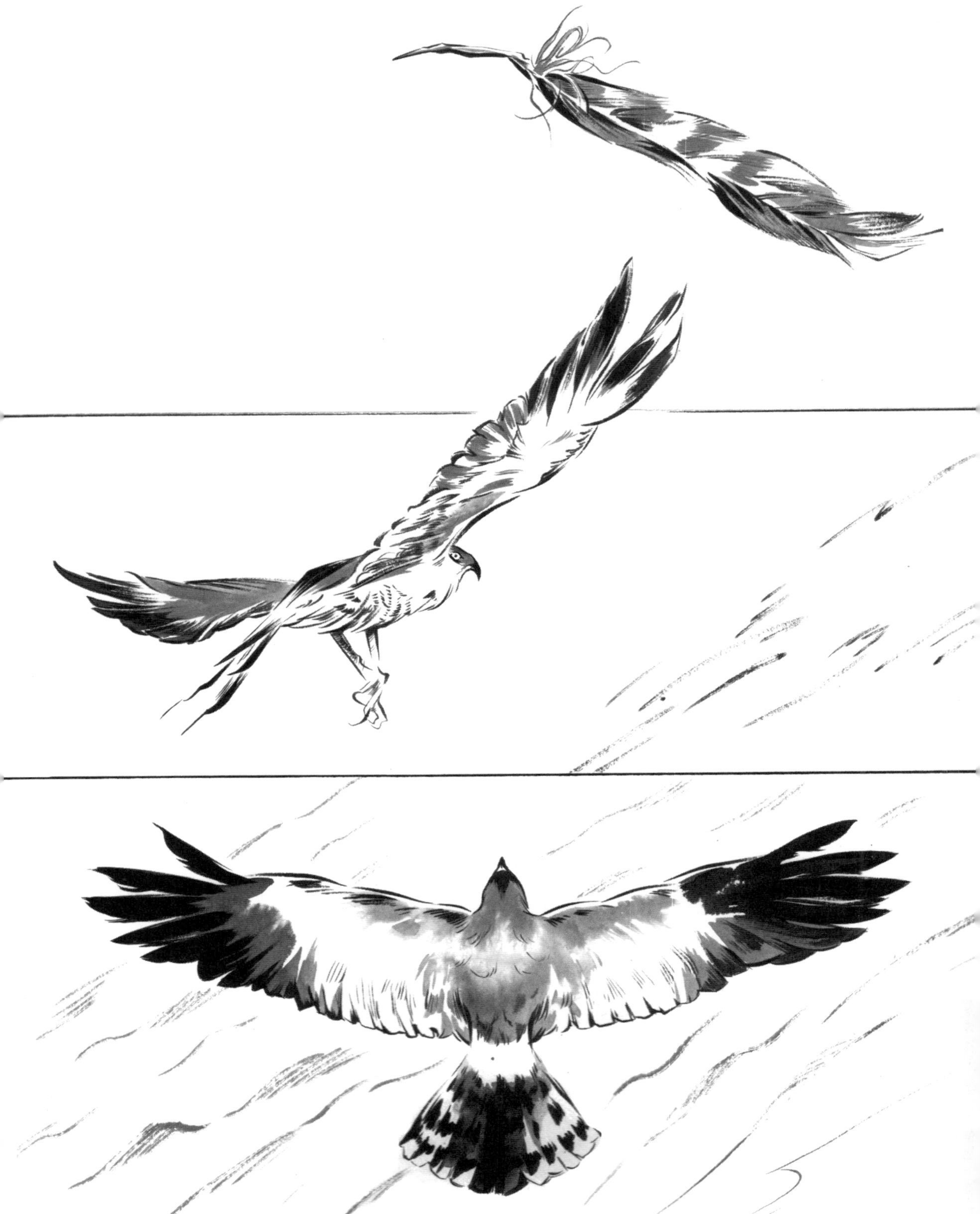

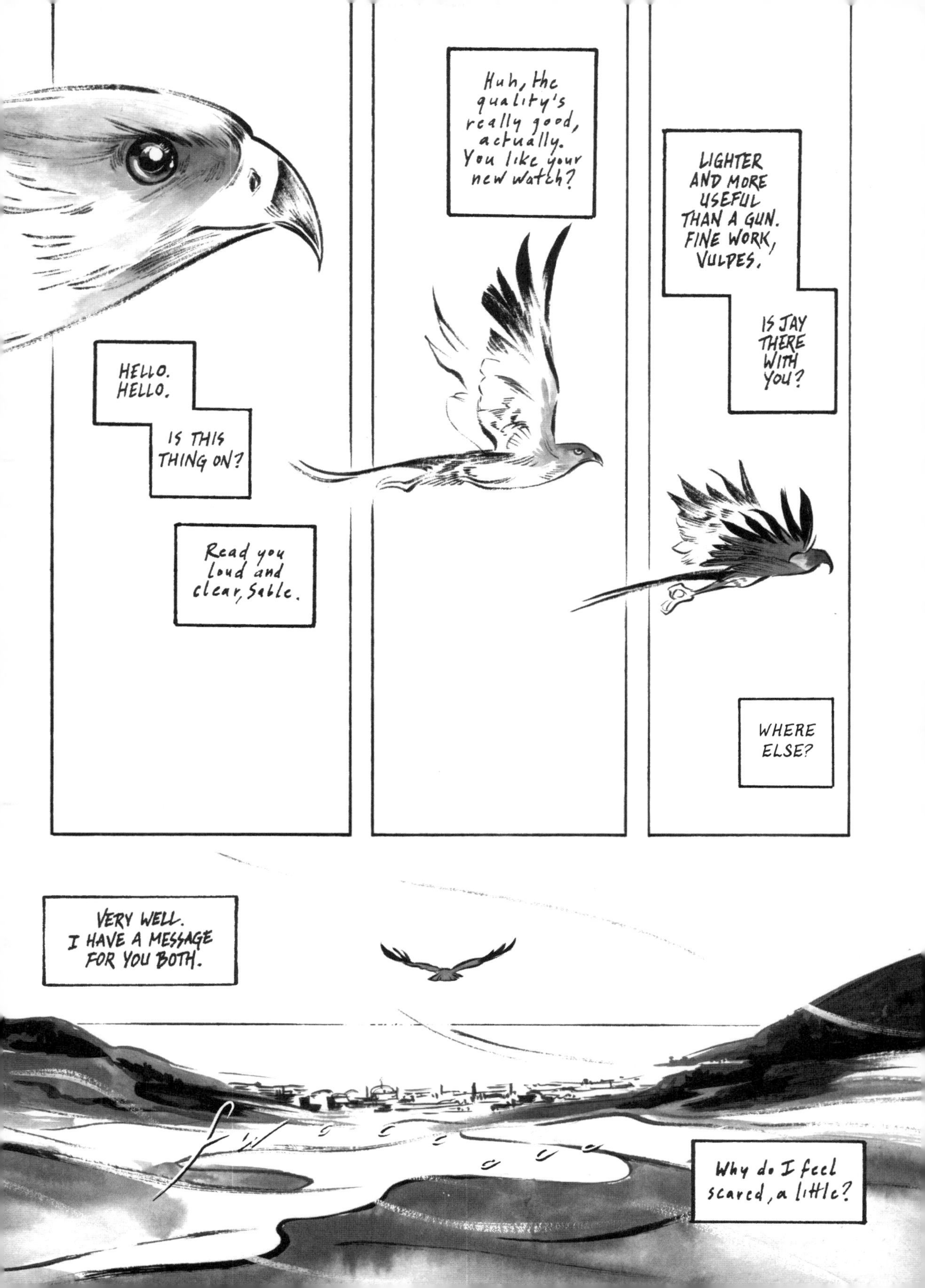
HELLO.
HELLO.
IS THIS THING ON?
Read you loud and clear, Sable.
Huh, the quality's really good, actually. You like your new watch?
LIGHTER AND MORE USEFUL THAN A GUN. FINE WORK, VULPES.
IS JAY THERE WITH YOU?
WHERE ELSE?
VERY WELL. I HAVE A MESSAGE FOR YOU BOTH.
Fwoooosh
Why do I feel scared, a little?

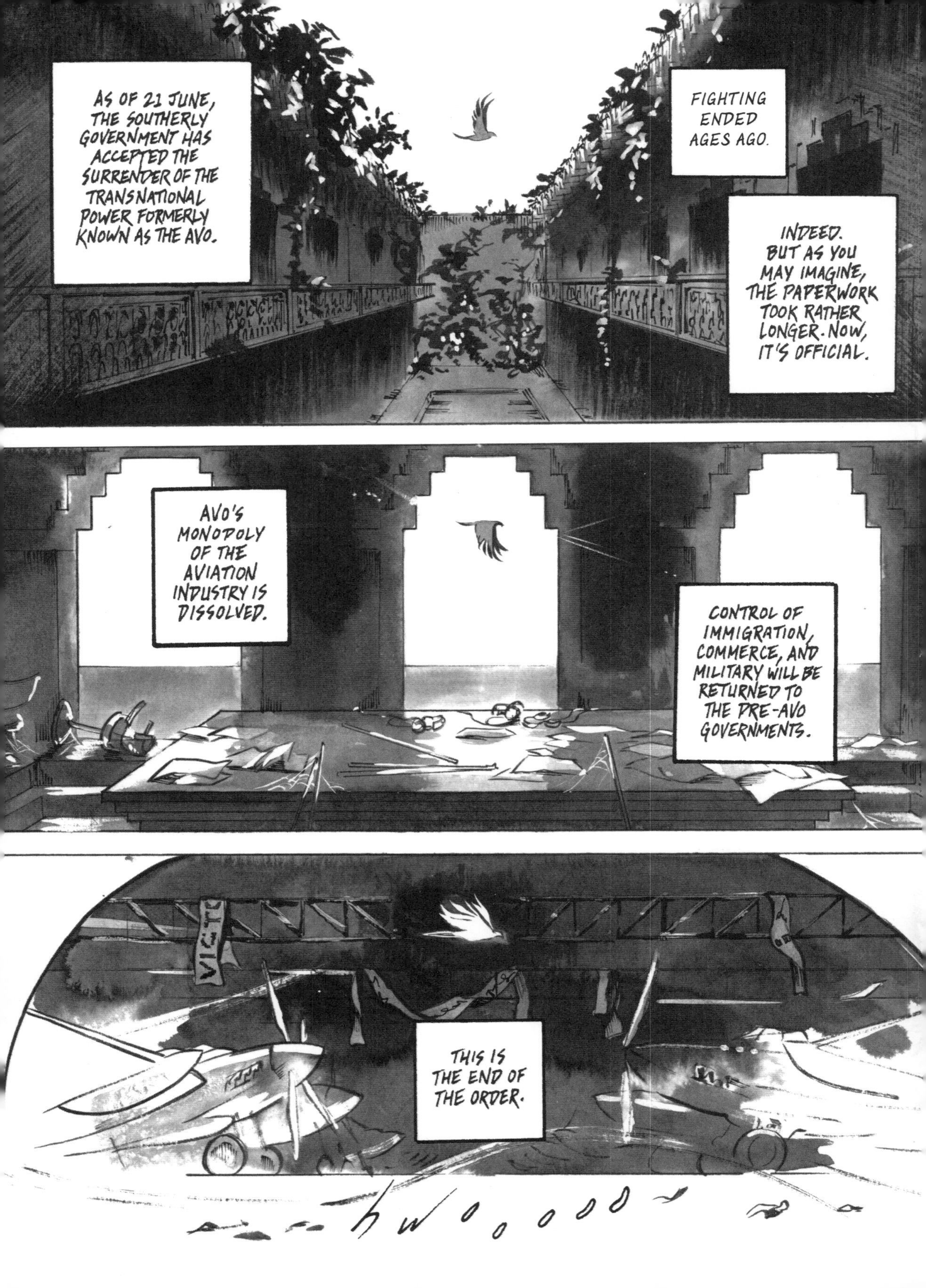
AS OF 21 JUNE, THE SOUTHERLY GOVERNMENT HAS ACCEPTED THE SURRENDER OF THE TRANSNATIONAL POWER FORMERLY KNOWN AS THE AVO.
FIGHTING ENDED AGES AGO.
INDEED. BUT AS YOU MAY IMAGINE, THE PAPERWORK TOOK RATHER LONGER. NOW, IT'S OFFICIAL.
AVO'S MONOPOLY OF THE AVIATION INDUSTRY IS DISSOLVED.
CONTROL OF IMMIGRATION, COMMERCE, AND MILITARY WILL BE RETURNED TO THE PRE-AVO GOVERNMENTS.
THIS IS THE END OF THE ORDER.
hwoooooo

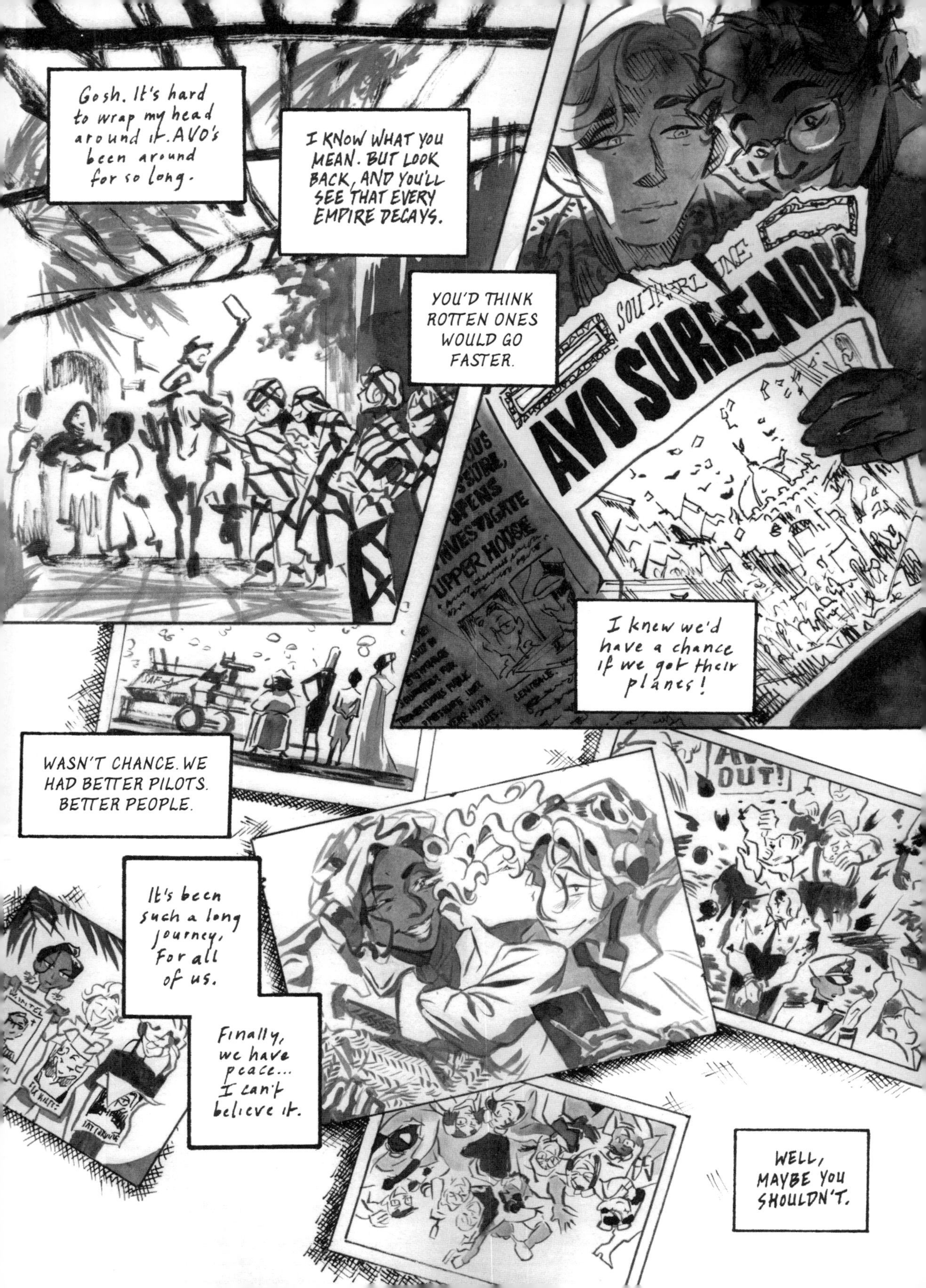
Gosh. It's hard to wrap my head around it. AVO's been around for so long.
I KNOW WHAT YOU MEAN. BUT LOOK BACK, AND YOU'LL SEE THAT EVERY EMPIRE DECAYS.
YOU'D THINK ROTTEN ONES WOULD GO FASTER.
AVO SURRENDE
UPPER HOUSE
I knew we'd have a chance if we got their planes!
WASN'T CHANCE. WE HAD BETTER PILOTS. BETTER PEOPLE.
OUT!
It's been such a long journey, for all of us.
Finally, we have peace... I can't believe it.
WELL, MAYBE YOU SHOULDN'T.

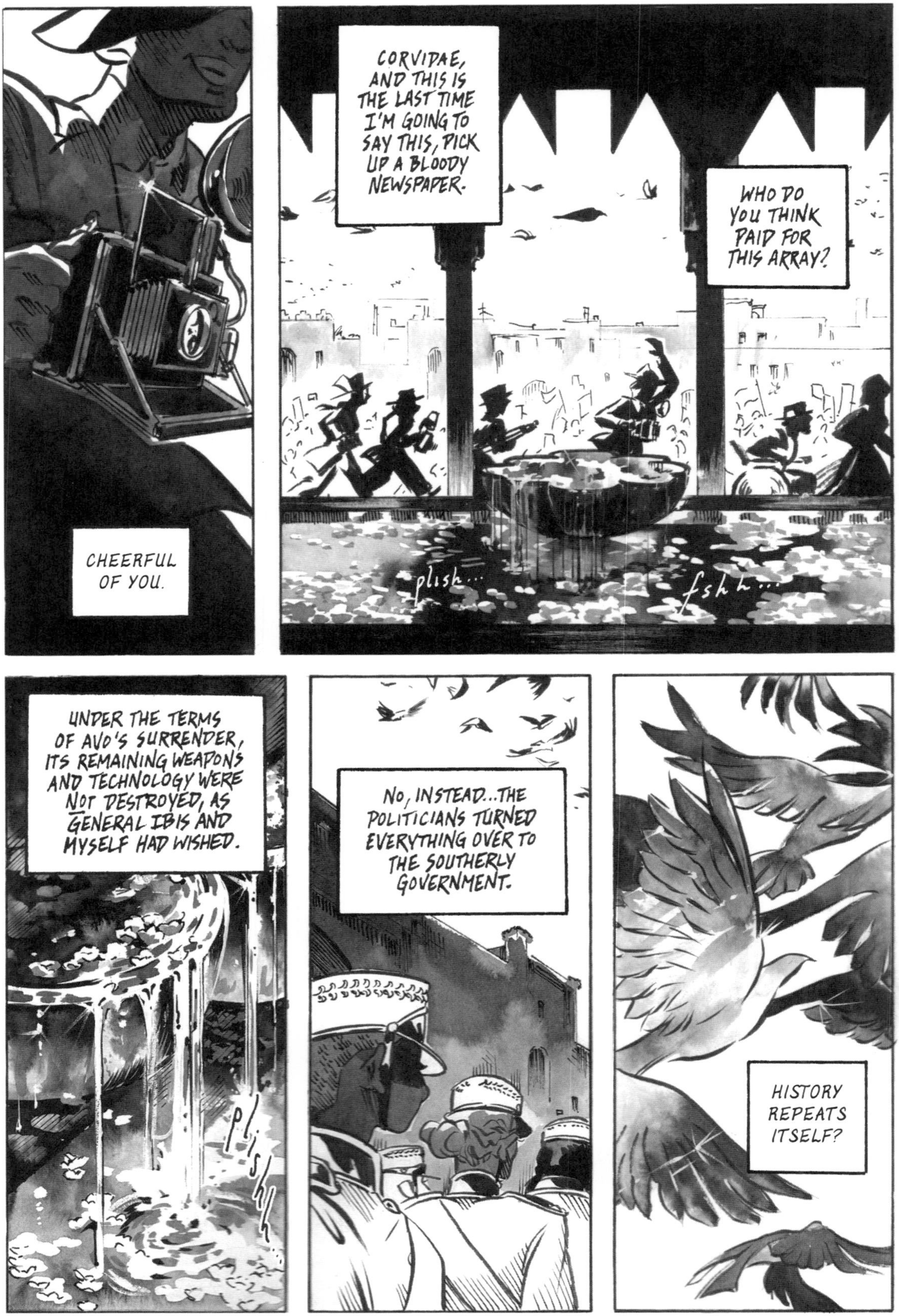
CHEERFUL OF YOU.
CORVIDAE, AND THIS IS THE LAST TIME I'M GOING TO SAY THIS, PICK UP A BLOODY NEWSPAPER.
WHO DO YOU THINK PAID FOR THIS ARRAY?
plish...
fshh...
UNDER THE TERMS OF AVO'S SURRENDER, ITS REMAINING WEAPONS AND TECHNOLOGY WERE NOT DESTROYED, AS GENERAL IBIS AND MYSELF HAD WISHED.
plishh...
NO, INSTEAD...THE POLITICIANS TURNED EVERYTHING OVER TO THE SOUTHERLY GOVERNMENT.
HISTORY REPEATS ITSELF?

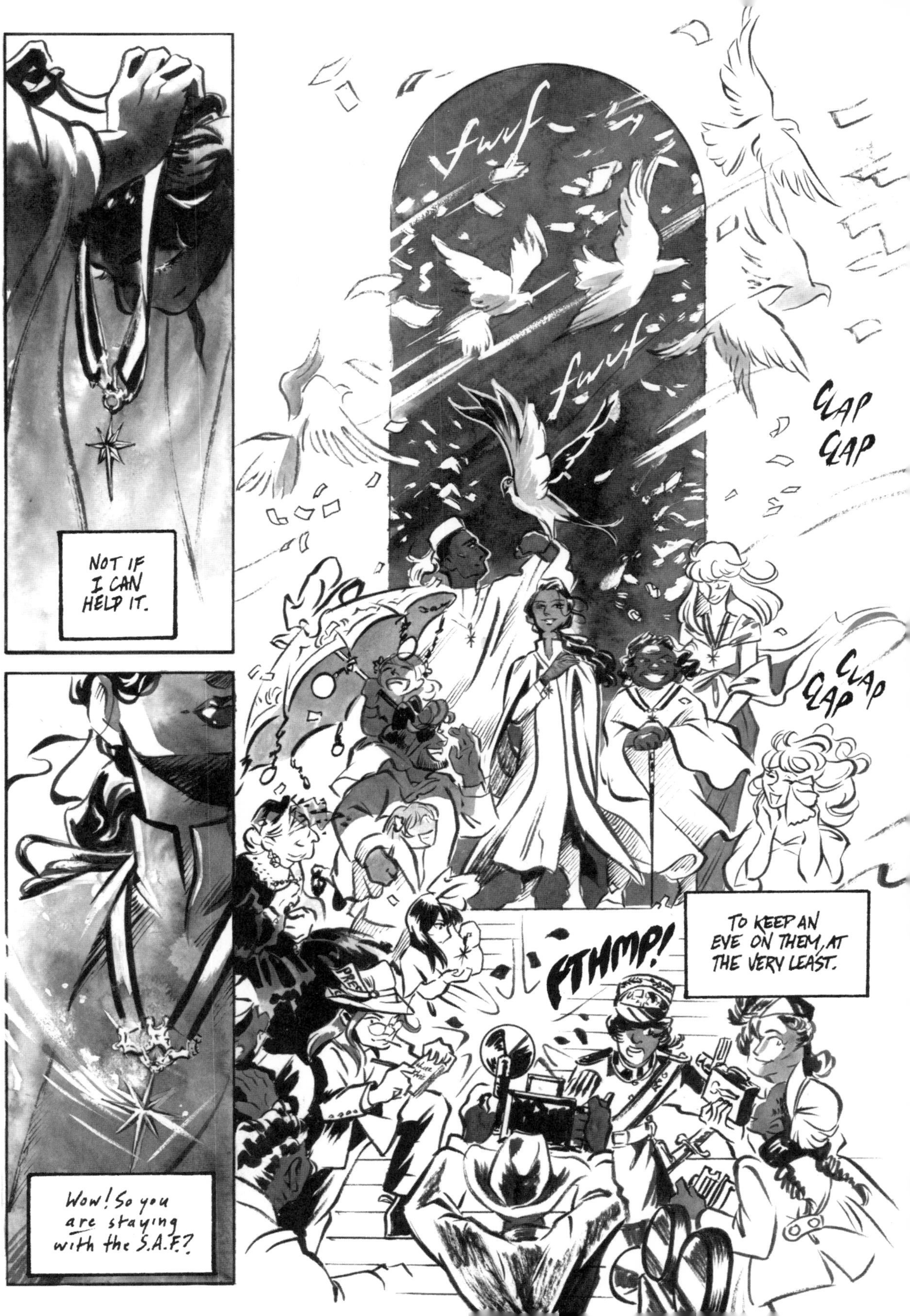
NOT IF I CAN HELP IT.
Wow! So you are staying with the S.A.F.?
fwif
fwif
CLAP CLAP
CLAP CLAP
FTHMP!
TO KEEP AN EYE ON THEM, AT THE VERY LEAST.

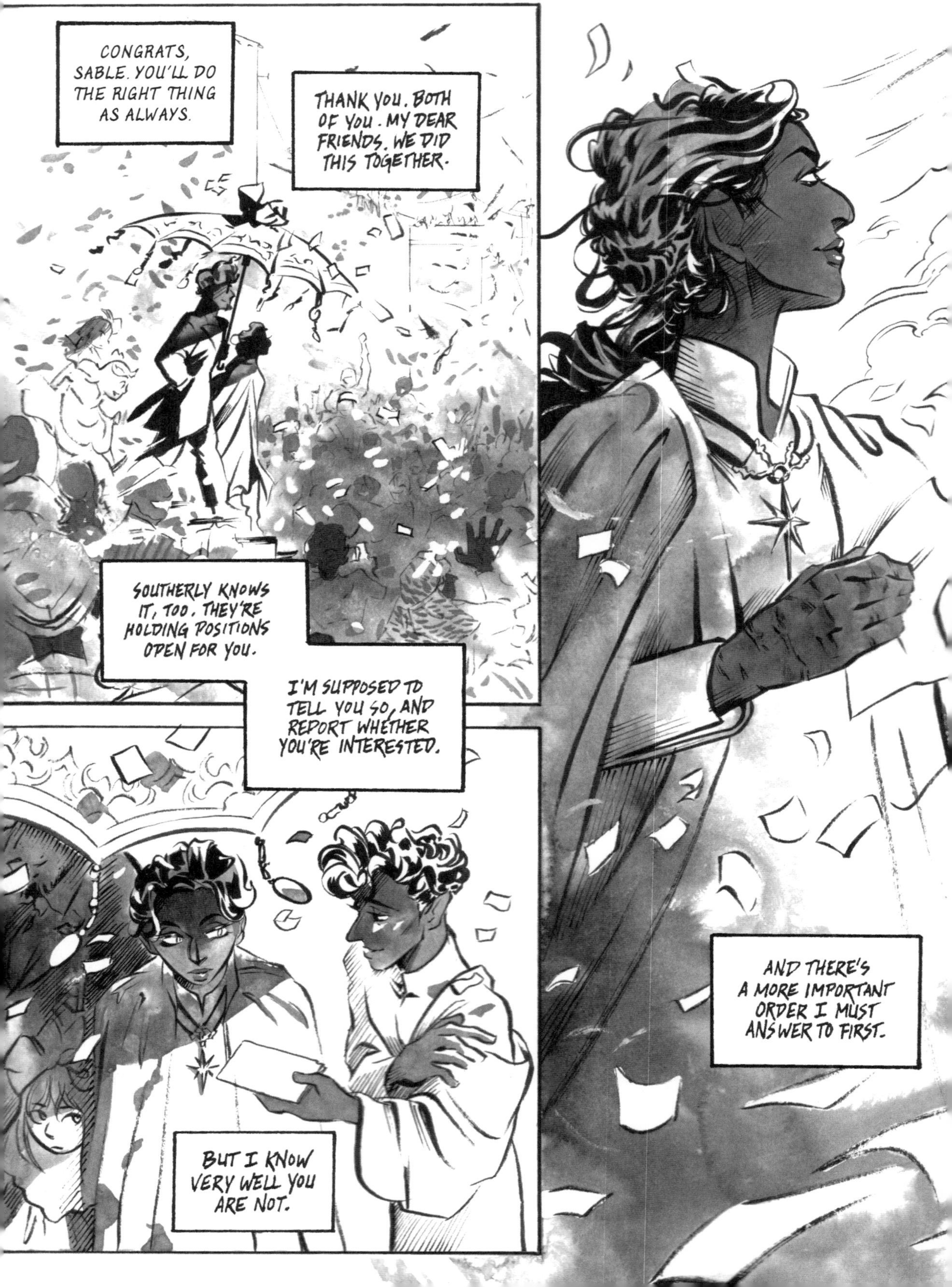
CONGRATS, SABLE. YOU'LL DO THE RIGHT THING AS ALWAYS.
THANK YOU. BOTH OF YOU. MY DEAR FRIENDS. WE DID THIS TOGETHER.
SOUTHERLY KNOWS IT, TOO. THEY'RE HOLDING POSITIONS OPEN FOR YOU.
I'M SUPPOSED TO TELL YOU SO, AND REPORT WHETHER YOU'RE INTERESTED.
BUT I KNOW VERY WELL YOU ARE NOT.
AND THERE'S A MORE IMPORTANT ORDER I MUST ANSWER TO FIRST.

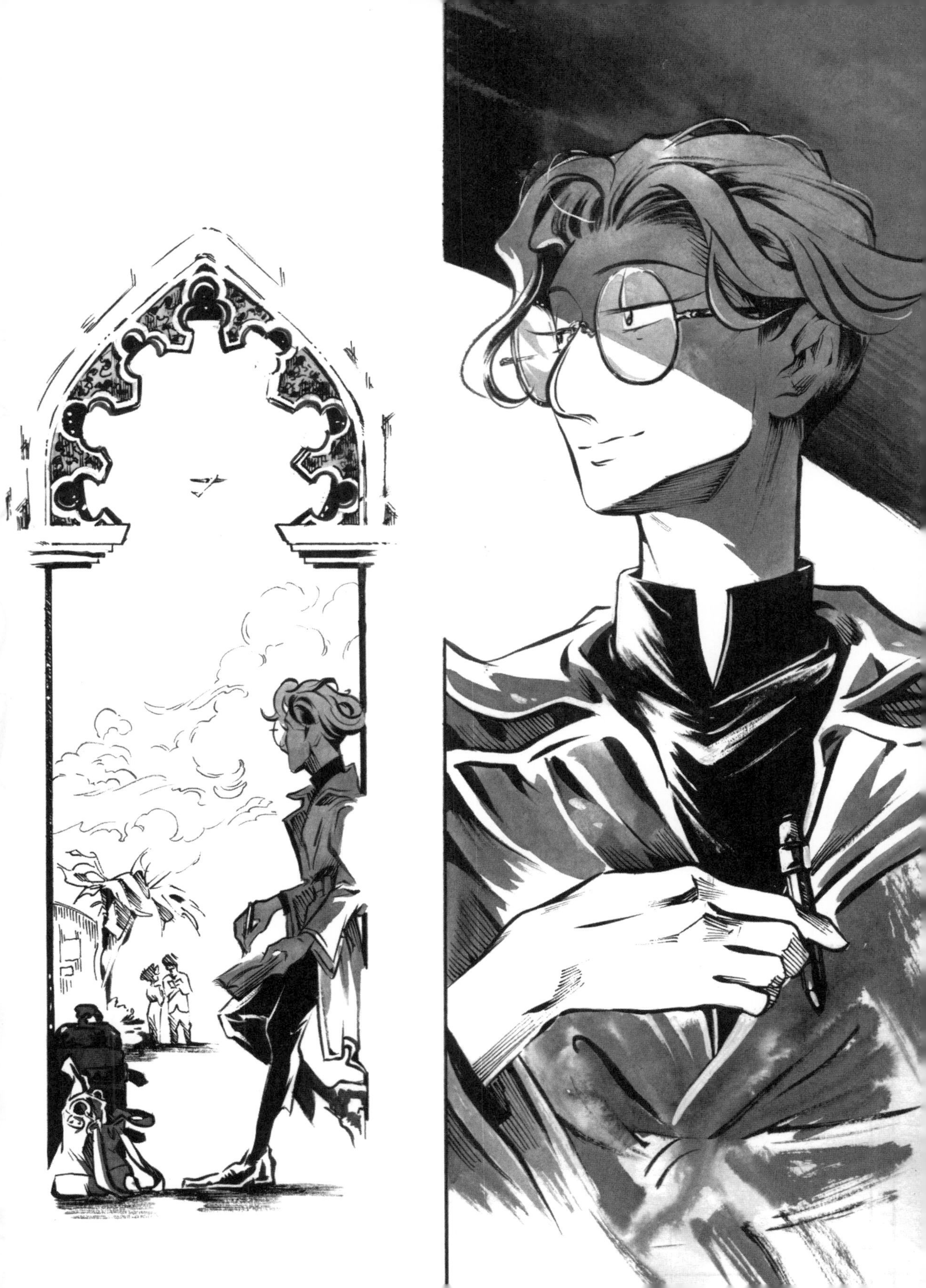

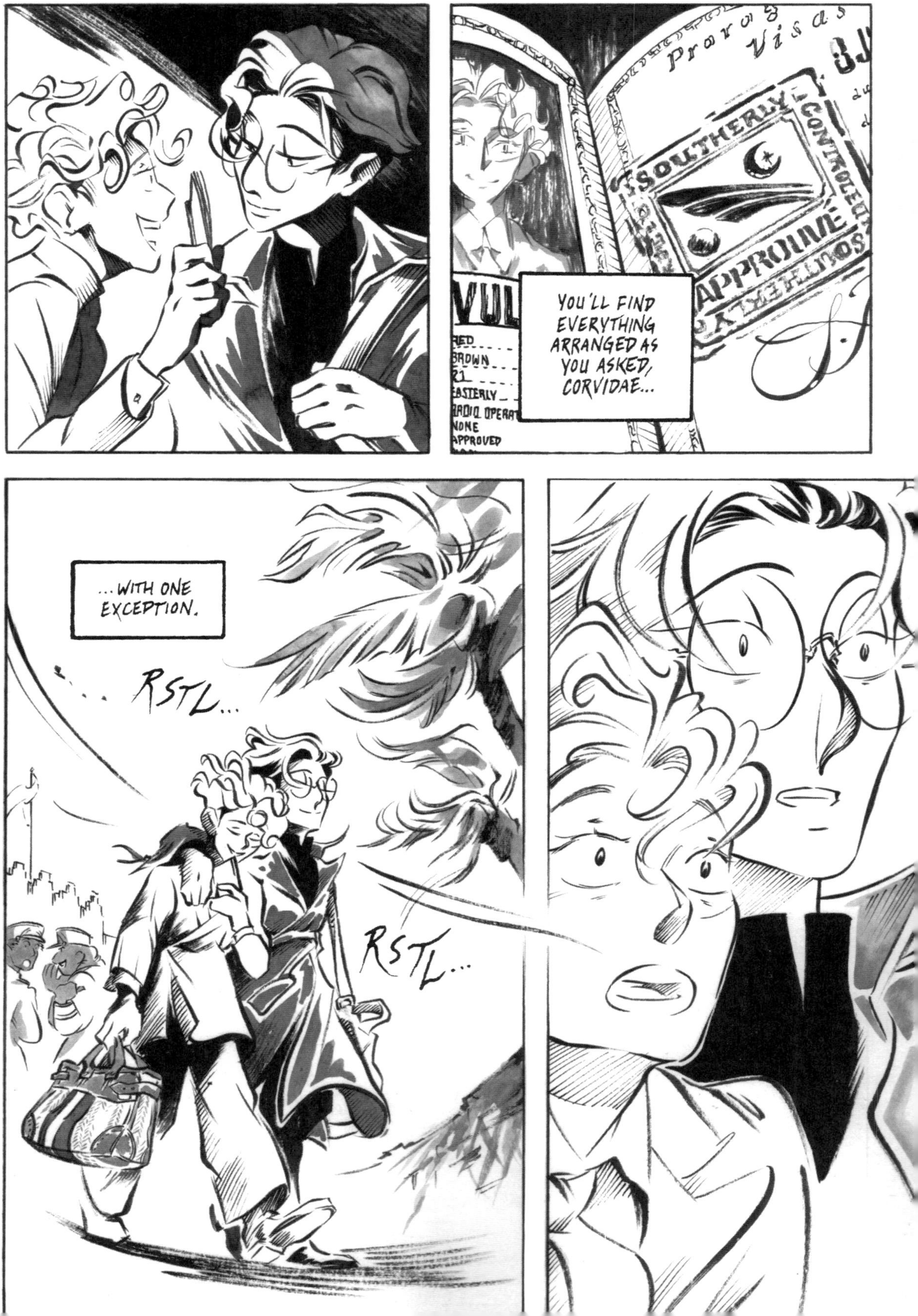

Provog
Visas
SOUTHERLY
CONTROLLED
APPROVED
VUL
RED
BROWN
EASTERLY
RADIO OPERAT
NONE
APPROVED
YOU'LL FIND EVERYTHING ARRANGED AS YOU ASKED, CORVIDAE...
...WITH ONE EXCEPTION.
...RSTL...
RSTL...

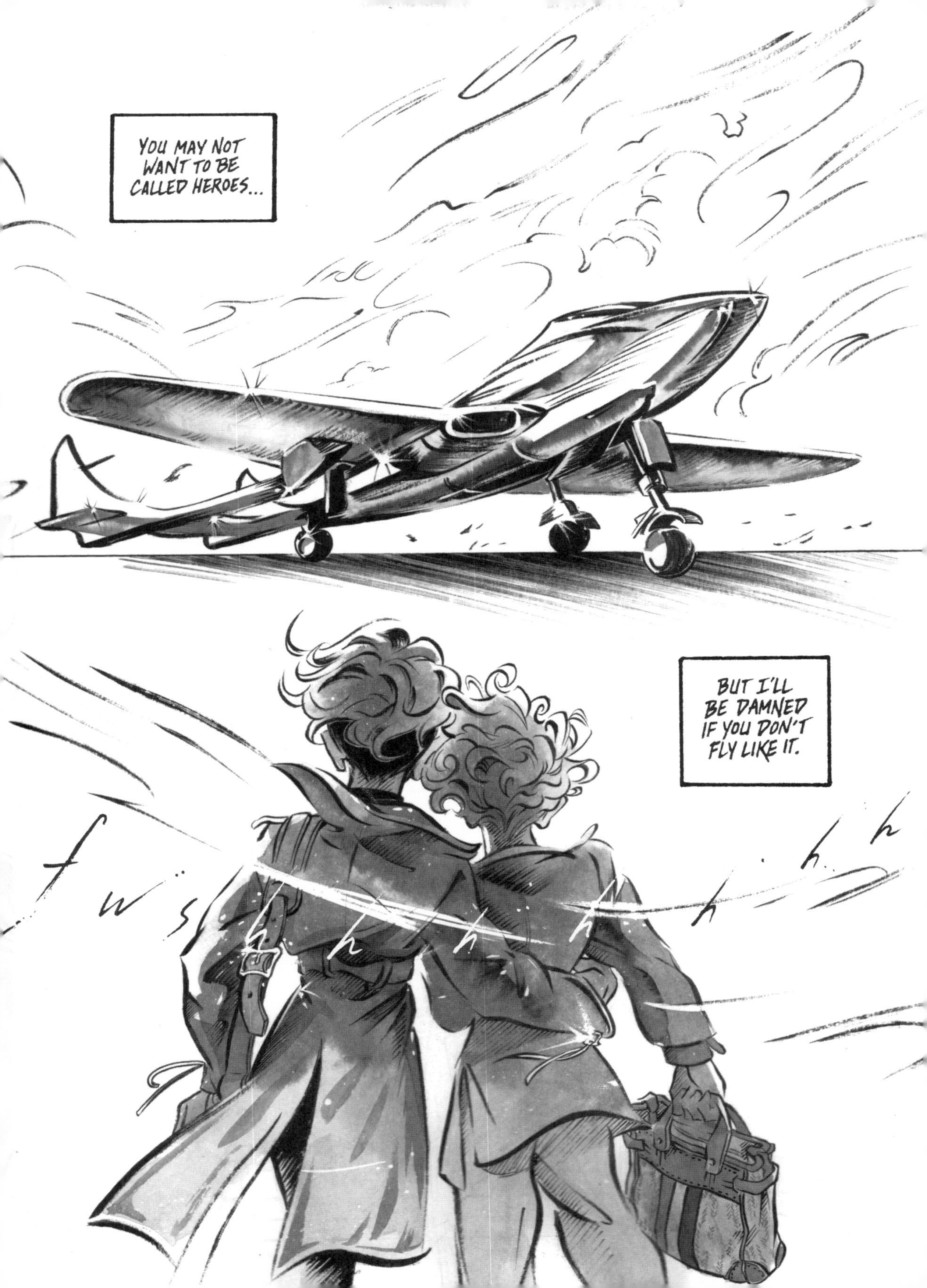
YOU MAY NOT WANT TO BE CALLED HEROES...
BUT I'LL BE DAMNED IF YOU DON'T FLY LIKE IT.

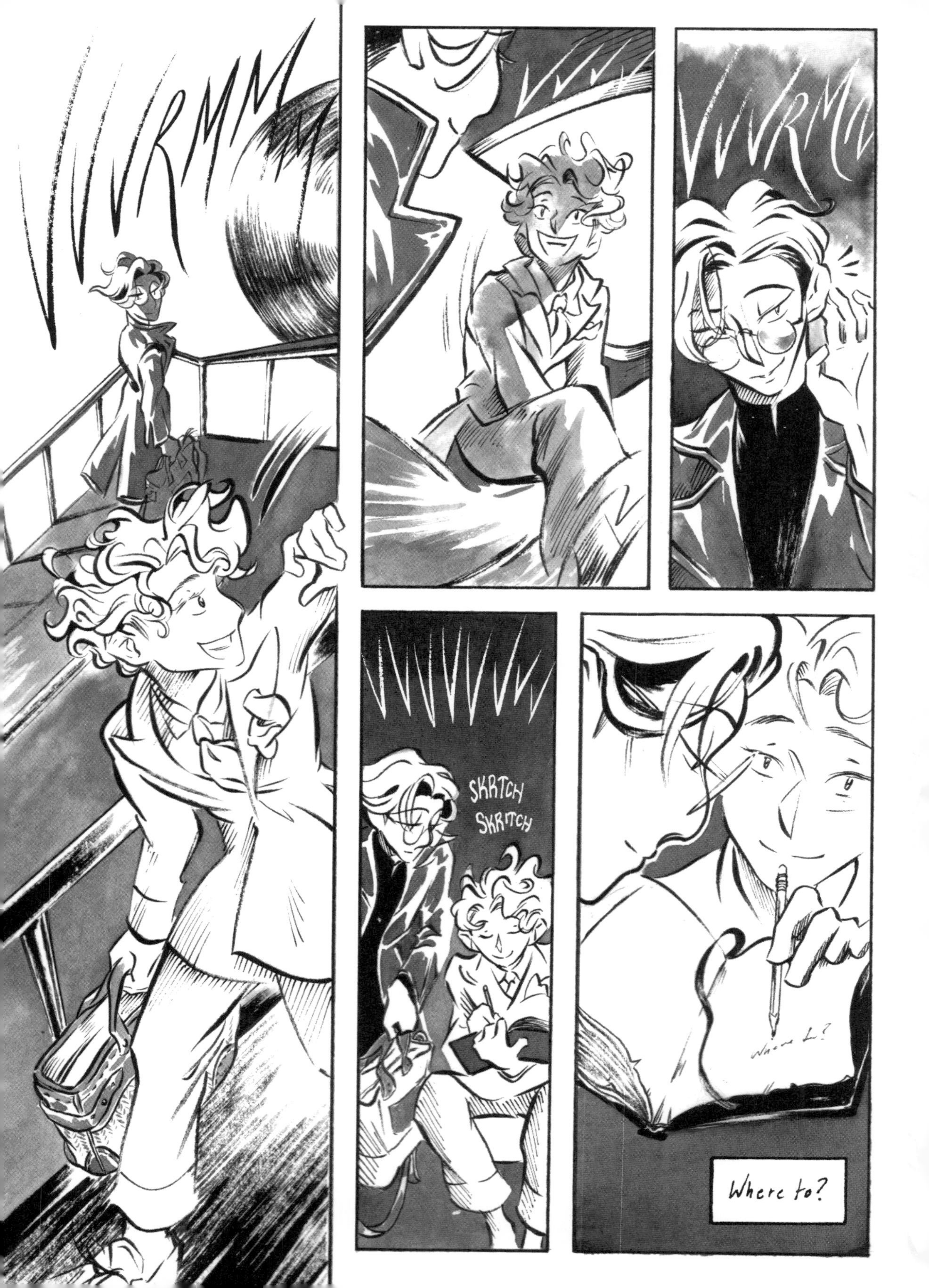
SKRTCH
SKRITCH
Where to?

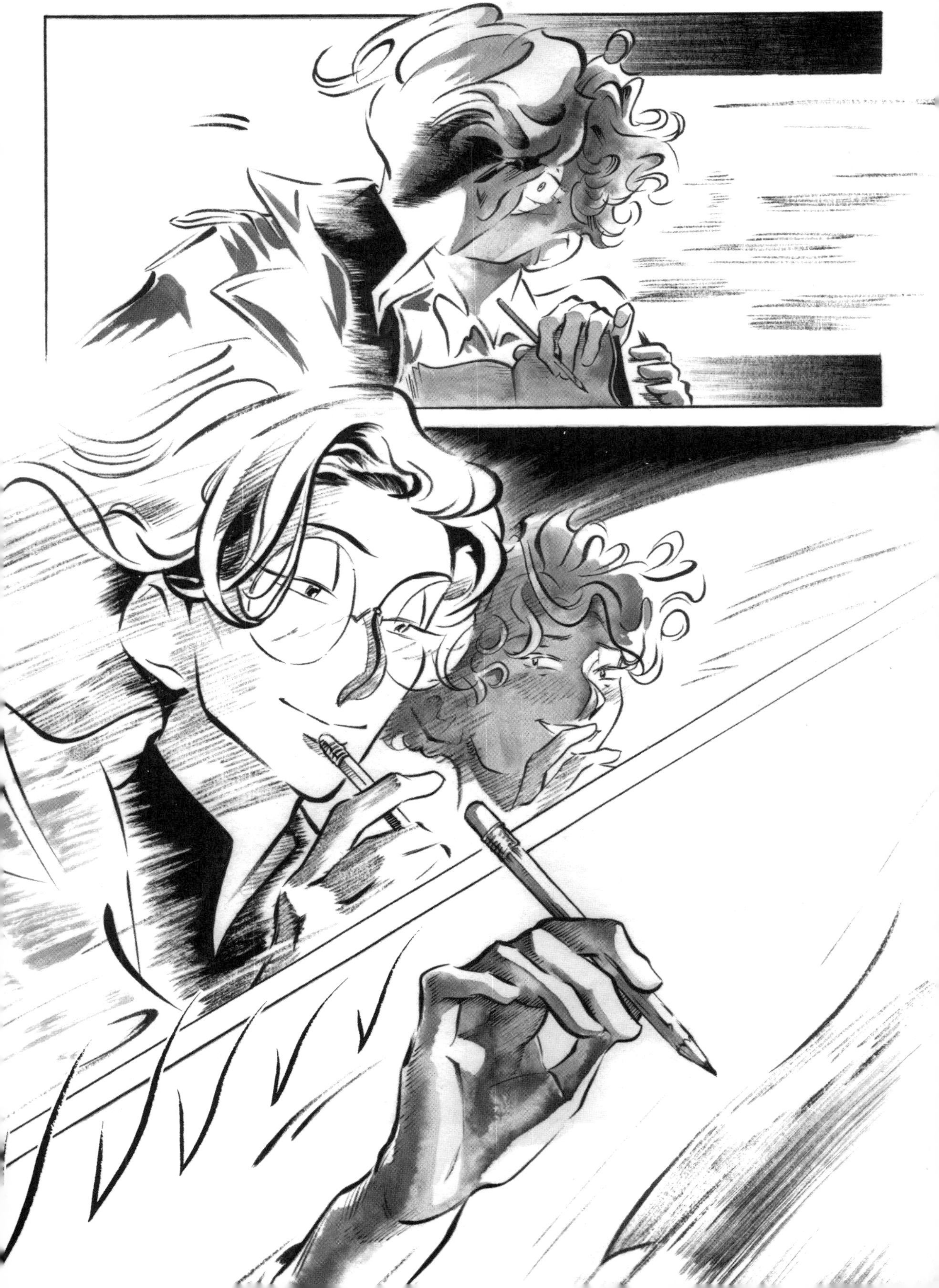

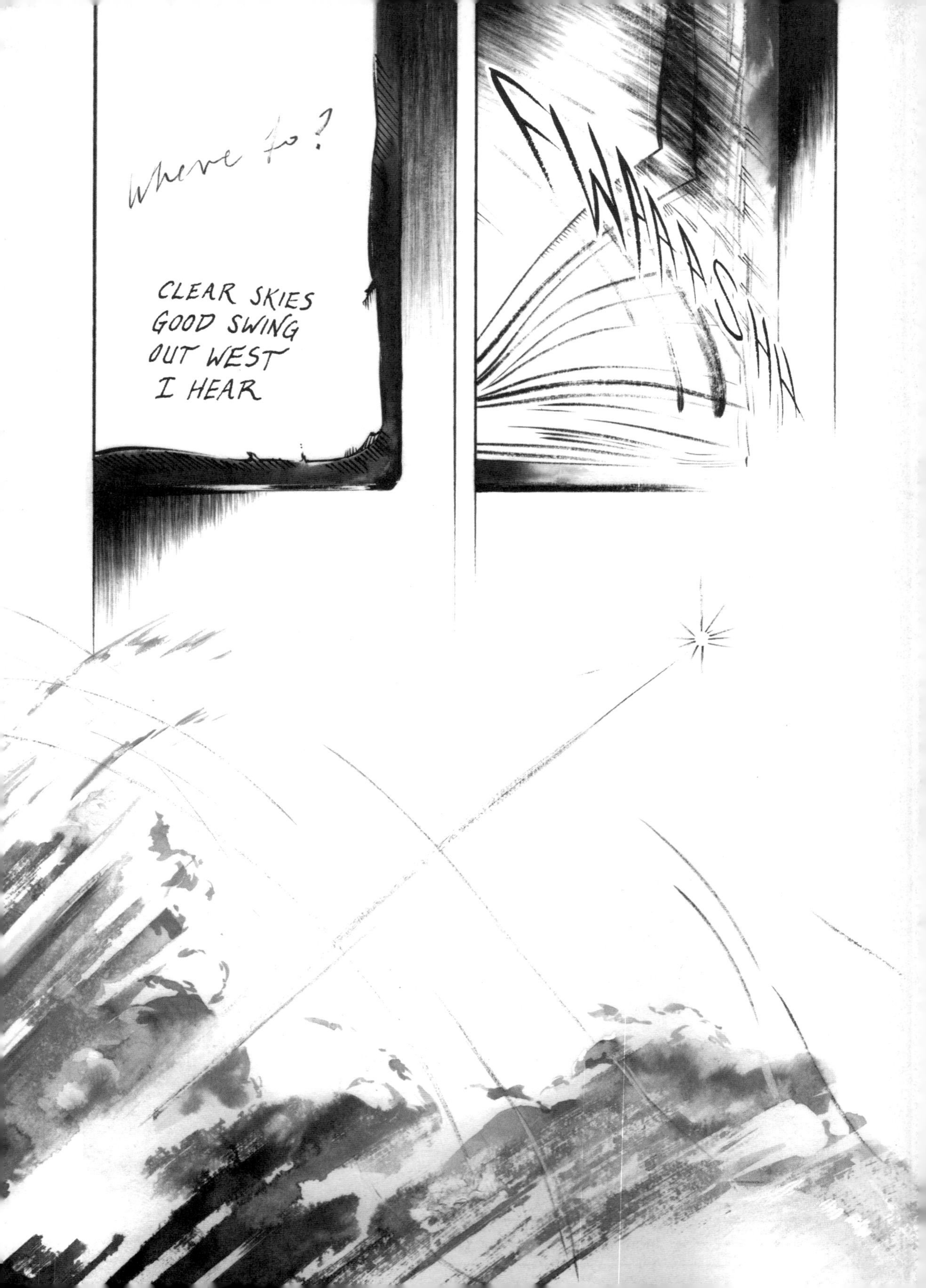
where to?
CLEAR SKIES GOOD SWING OUT WEST I HEAR
CHWAAASHHH

A.C. ESGUERRA is a comics author and illustrator who works primarily in traditional ink and watercolor. Previous clients include BOOM! Studios and Northwest Press for art, and Baum-kuchen Studio for writing. In 2016, they received a PRISM Comics Queer Press Grant Award for the novella version of this book. They were born in Manila, Philippines and now live in Los Angeles, California with their partner and dog.

Eighty Days is their debut graphic novel.